Secure
Electronic Commerce
Building the Infrastructure
for Digital Signatures
and Encryption

Second Edition

Warwick Ford
Michael S. Baun

ISBN 0-13-027276-0

90000

9 780130 272768

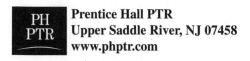

Prentice Hall PTR
Upper Saddle River, NJ 07458
www.phptr.com

PH
PTR

Library of Congress Cataloging-in-Publication Data

Ford, Warwick.
    Secure electronic commerce: building the infrastructure for digital signatures and encryption / Warwick Ford, Michael S. Baum.--2nd ed.
        p. cm.
    Includes bibliographical references and index.
    ISBN 0-13-027276-0 (pbk.)
    1. Computer security. 2. Computer networks--Security measures. 3. Business communication--Security measures.   I. Baum, Michael S.   II. Title.

    QA 76.9.A25 F655 2000
    658.8'4--dc21

                                                            00-052842

Editorial/Production Supervision: *Precision Graphics*
Interior Compositor: *Precision Graphics*
Acquisitions Editor: *Mary Franz*
Editorial Assistant: *Noreen Regina*
Marketing Manager: *Dan DePasquale*
Buyer: *Maura Zaldivar*
Cover Design Director: *Jerry Votta*
Cover Design: *Talar Agasyan*
Project Coordinator: *Anne Trowbridge*

©2001 Prentice Hall PTR
Prentice-Hall, Inc.
Upper Saddle River, New Jersey 07458

Prentice Hall books are widely used by corporations and government agencies for training, marketing, and resale.
The publisher offers discounts on this book when ordered in bulk quantities.
For more information, contact:
Corporate Sales Department
Prentice Hall PTR
One Lake Street
Upper Saddle River, NJ 07548
Phone: 800-382-3419; Fax: 201-236-7141; E-mail: corpsales@prenhall.com

Printed in the United States of America
10   9   8   7   6   5   4   3   2

ISBN 0-13-027276-0 (pbk.)

Prentice-Hall International (UK) Limited, *London*
Prentice-Hall of Australia Pty. Limited, *Sydney*
Prentice-Hall Canada Inc., *Toronto*
Prentice-Hall Hispanoamericana, S. A., *Mexico*
Prentice-Hall of India Private Limited, *New Delhi*
Prentice-Hall of Japan, Inc., *Tokyo*
Pearson Education Asia Pte. Ltd.
Editora Prentice-Hall do Brasil, Ltda., *Rio de Janeiro*

Contents

Forewords

From Spence Abraham, U.S. Senate

We live in exciting times now, with apparently limitless improvements and evolution in the high technology sector. There is a need for continued education and re-examination of the systems, security, and even the very business models used by organizations. From smart cards to biometrics to cryptography, creative solutions will be required to weather the changes at hand. The use of public-key cryptography can be an important arrow in the security quiver of both businesses and consumers alike.

In recent years, the U.S. Congress has begun to recognize the truly revolutionary changes for which the Internet and the multitude of associated technologies are responsible. To its credit, this same Congress has worked hard to foster and promote the continued growth of the technological sector by avoiding traditional regulatory mechanisms and removing legal impediments to electronic commerce.

The recent passage of S. 761, the Electronic Signatures and Global and National Commerce (E-Sign) law is intended to further enhance public access and confidence in secure methods for electronic commerce. Congress worked with the private sector, federal agencies and extensively with states to assure a consistent legal baseline nationally for e-signatures and records. The new rules for state and federal laws in this area are well summarized by the National Governors' Association, in their September 28 paper "What Governors Need to Know," where they say the federal Act "is a framework for the use and retention of records and signatures" which "recognizes that electronic signatures and electronic records are as legally effective, valid and enforceable as manual signatures and paper writings; and, recognizes that laws should be neutral as to the specific technologies and means used to create such records and signatures."

As *Secure Electronic Commerce* clearly articulates, it is necessary for businesses, consumers, and governments to use discretion to choose the types and amount of security they determine is needed for their applications. More now than ever, business has a responsibility to understand the trade offs, costs, benefits and risks involved in choosing information security technology. That necessary due diligence begins in Chapter 1 of this book.

SPENCE ABRAHAM
U.S. SENATE

Senator Abraham of Michigan was the architect of the federal E-Sign law that con-firmed the validity of electronic signatures in electronic commerce. He also sponsored the Government Paperwork Elimination Act, which opened the door for the use of electronic signatures with federal governmental agencies.

From Rhonda MacLean, Bank of America

The 1994 emergence of the Web browser, more than any other application, helped to create the Internet revolution. Simple, intuitive, and interactive, Web browsing has been compared to the printing press in its impact on society, the economy, and politics. This revolution in the way information is presented, distributed, accessed, and used has driven the U.S. economy through an unprecedented period of growth. Dubbed the *new economy*, this revolution has now taken root throughout the world. Its impact is still growing and shows little sign of abating. Rather, it seems to be deepening as more *old economy* businesses adopt the new principles and technology in delivering their goods and services. This information revolution has spread faster than any previous technology.

Numerous magazines, television programs, books, and other media have documented and hyped the new economy. These sources highlight how the ready availability of information and unprecedented access to it change the way people interact and conduct business. The Internet's open standards for information presentation, transport, and exchange, have greatly facilitated the launching of new economy applications for millions of users. For the past two or three years it has seemed that any business idea could be made, remade, and continuously enhanced through the Internet. Electronic activities such as electronic banking and electronic sales have become e-banking and e-sales, right up to e-names like eBay, the Internet auction site. Innovative e-commerce continues to expand in new and different ways.

Unfortunately, the new economy is not all wonder and delight. The e-world enables more than new business ideas. Crime too has gone electronic. The Internet's use of protocols and services designed for open

information exchange with relatively little security provides ample opportunity for exploitation. There are many scams and schemes intended to separate
money from victims. E-crime and cracking (criminal hacking) have led to
numerous highly publicized e-break-ins. Inadequately secured e-commerce
retailing sites have reportedly lost thousands of customers' credit card numbers. A major bank in England inadvertently made thousands of customers'
account information available on the Internet. These breaches erode customer
confidence and undermine business relationships. Such events demonstrate a
wide and growing need for the valuable information and ideas presented in
this book.

The promise of the new economy also requires high availability of services. Information and commerce transactions are designed to be available
worldwide 24 hours a day, every day of the year. Several high profile
e-commerce businesses have been taken off-line through malicious attacks
known as *denial of service* attacks. Those who have experienced these attacks
have incurred significant business losses and much inconvenience.

Surveys and polls show that roughly 80% of Internet users are concerned about privacy and the security of their credit card or other purchasing
information. Most have experienced some level of difficulty trying to purchase goods and services electronically. Many people place greater trust in
human contact and purchases made from brick-and-mortar businesses.

Identity theft and misrepresentation are becoming increasingly worri-
some. The ability to truly know with whom you are doing business is essential, thus authentication services are fundamental to achieving secure
e-commerce. Protecting privacy and safeguarding information entrusted to
others are also essential.

For the promise of the Internet revolution to succeed, both real and perceived security architecture must improve significantly. Without consistent,
fundamental improvements in security, the full power of the Internet and
e-commerce may never be realized. The Internet must become trustworthy as
a medium for business and financial exchange. Enterprises need the guidance
and understanding of experts like the authors of this book to make
e-commerce successful, possibly even exceeding the prophecies of the new
economy. By applying security principles and technologies, e-commerce can
gain customer acceptance.

Financial institutions have historically appreciated the fact that security
and trust are core competencies and make every effort to ensure information
and transactions are adequately protected. Bank of America is committed to
making banking work for its customers in ways it never has before. One way

of doing this is to ensure that banking is convenient, easy to use, and secure. We are focused on implementing privacy and security as few have seen it before. The principles and technology described in this book will be seen throughout our efforts.

For example, internationally, Bank of America and many other financial institutions are implementing security mechanisms such as digital certificates through a contractual framework incorporated as Identrus. Identrus will provide interoperable public-key infrastructure to verify the validity of digital certificates and the authenticity of digital signatures. This system aims to foster secure, authentic e-commerce applications throughout the international business arena on any scale from thousands to millions of dollars.

To fully realize the power of the new economy through e-commerce, security is essential. There are too few security experts; too many ways to build insecure applications, and too many commercial products are inadequately configured out-of-the-box. Consider products that have been evaluated and approved by security testing laboratories, such as the Financial Services Roundtable's *BITS* Laboratory. Also consider joining industry groups focused on sharing information around security vulnerabilities, issues, and problems—such as the Financial Services Information Sharing and Analysis Center (FSISAC), where information can be shared anonymously between trusted members.

This book will help you enormously in understanding the environment in which e-commerce must operate. In addition, the information presented will help you choose the right security direction for your business, to meet your specific business's security needs. All of the fundamental elements of e-commerce and Internet security are eloquently addressed in these pages. Make good use of this comprehensive guide and refer to it often.

Good luck!

RHONDA MACLEAN
SENIOR VICE PRESIDENT—DIVISION MANAGER,
INFORMATION PROTECTION
BANK OF AMERICA

From Mark Hogan, General Motors Corporation

No company is more impacted by the Internet revolution than GM—the largest manufacturing company in the world, in the one business for over 80 years. Now the Internet is changing virtually everything we do. A vehicle is roughly 5,000 different parts coming together to develop a flawless article. The Internet is changing our manufacturing model, because rather than having long pipelines of work-in-progress inventory and long pipelines of finished-good inventory at the dealerships we are rapidly shortening both. Plants that used to handle 5,000 parts are now handling a fraction of those parts. Our factories get smaller, and the quality and efficiency of the plant goes up. The size of the individual dealers gets smaller and more efficient, and we spend a lot more time in personal contact with our customers using the Web.

We see the customization model emerging in the marketplace. What Michael Dell did with computers we will soon be doing with cars; that is, building to order what the customer orders online. The customer gets the right vehicle at the right price at the right place, in his or her own time frame. Furthermore, the iterative design opportunities that the Internet offers mean that we can design vehicles in real time and be much more precise in hitting the mark in terms of what our target customers want.

E-GM was created last year as an umbrella unit to oversee most of GM's online efforts. Our BuyPower Web site and alliances with other sites, including AOL, have been enormously successful in drawing customers to showrooms. In 12 months of operation, the volume of sales leads forwarded to dealers has tripled.

However, *e-commerce* is the key to our future, in terms of reversing or at least halting the erosion of market share that U.S. automobile manufacturers are experiencing in the face of foreign competitors. We have many initiatives under way on both the supply and distribution sides of the business. Internet-based business-to-business e-commerce represents an enormous opportunity for cost reduction and process streamlining.

For e-commerce to become mainstream, however, we still face one impediment. Users of these new technologies need to become comfortable in understanding and applying the new business risk models that the new technologies bring to bear. In that regard, this book fills a critical need. It is refreshing to be able to find, in one place, a complete and lucid explanation of all of the issues surrounding risk management in e-commerce, including not only comprehensive descriptions of the security technologies but also an up-to-date analysis of the legislative and regulatory issues that impact the risk management decisions of enterprises seeking to exploit them.

MARK HOGAN, GROUP VICE PRESIDENT, E-GM
GENERAL MOTORS CORPORATION

From Hank Vigil, Microsoft

For those seeking the benefits of electronic commerce, the Internet presents enormous promise. Unfortunately, it has one major shortcoming in comparison with all previous methods of transacting business-it is totally public. Without the use of specialized security technologies and supporting infrastructure, transaction contents can be read by, modified by, or concocted by anyone who is sufficiently tenacious. Failure to meet the security challenge would severely undermine the commercial exploitation potential of the Internet, owing to low user confidence and high costs of repeatedly reacting to security attacks.

Microsoft's mission for Internet security includes four aspects: (1) providing the most robust technology to meet customer security needs as they interact on the Internet; (2) working with standards bodies to ensure adoption of the best technology to meet customer needs and ensure interoperability; (3) proliferating security standards in Microsoft technologies and delivering them in our operating systems and World Wide Web browsers and servers; and, (4) building security into our existing applications.

In particular, Microsoft has developed a cross-platform security framework for electronic commerce and online communications called the Microsoft Internet Security Framework. This open and interoperable framework of technologies supports Internet security standards and several new technologies, many of which are explained in this book. These technologies include World Wide Web authentication and encryption, public-key certificate services, a digital wallet, and the Secure Electronic Transaction (SET) protocol for credit card transactions.

The security problems to be dealt with on the Internet are wide-ranging. For example, one of the greatest risks users face today is the possibility of unknowingly downloading altered or malicious software to their computers. To help mitigate this risk, Microsoft has developed the Authenticode system, which provides Web users with confidence in the authenticity of software downloaded over the Internet. Authenticode lets users know who published the software and whether it has been tampered with since it was published. The result is a user who can make more informed decisions about accepting or rejecting downloaded software.

Solving the security problems will allow us to make such concepts as the *Internet storefront* a reality. Internet storefronts must be based on integrated, industrial-strength solutions that address all parts of the merchandising value chain, including storefront management, order purchasing, financial transactions, distribution, and fulfillment, in a consistent, easy, flexible, extensible, and reliable way. Creation and operation of online stores must be easy, allowing merchants to focus on merchandising. The Microsoft Merchant product family addresses this market need, using the Microsoft Internet Security Framework as the basis of its security.

While the incorporation of appropriate security features into software products is essential for the realization of secure electronic commerce, it is far from the full story. Other necessary factors include: (1) base information security technologies, such as encryption and digital signatures; (2) agreed-upon standards for security architecture, protocols, and methods; (3) security infrastructure service providers, such as certification authorities; (4) accepted business and legal practices; and, (5) legislation, regulation, and legal guidelines. On its own, none of these subjects is simple.

If one considers the combination of all of these factors, taking into account all the interactions, the result can be amazingly complex. This is what makes this book so important. *Secure Electronic Commerce* represents a unique and invaluable contribution to the advancement of electronic commerce. Warwick Ford and Michael Baum explain, in a highly readable style, the essential aspects of the full breadth of the field.

The emergence of Internet-based electronic commerce is an exciting phenomenon, and Microsoft is proud to be a part of it. However, the full potential for massive, rapid expansion of Internet-based commerce can only be realized if there is sufficient understanding of all the security aspects of the field on the part of those using, providing, and administering the services and products involved. This book makes a major contribution to us all achieving such an understanding. Read, learn, and enjoy.

HANK VIGIL
VP, CONSUMER STRATEGY AND PARTNERSHIPS
MICROSOFT CORPORATION

Hank Vigil's Foreword was written in 1997 for the First Edition

Preface

Our entry into the twenty-first century has been accompanied by the emergence of electronic commerce (e-commerce) as both an enabler and a component of business reengineering. E-commerce offers great rewards for all who embrace it. However, it also brings considerable risks for the unwary. While new technologies, with their complexities and explosive adoption rates, can be largely blamed for creating these new risks, new technologies also represent a large part of the solution, in managing and mitigating these risks. The latter technologies include, in particular, digital signatures and public-key cryptography. However, achieving *secure electronic commerce* requires much more than the mere application of such core technologies. It also depends upon interdependent technological, business, and legal infrastructures that are needed to enable the use of these core technologies on a large scale. Our goal in this book is to describe the ingredients and recipe for making e-commerce secure, with emphasis on the role, practical deployment, and use of these infrastructures.

Why have an engineer and a lawyer teamed up to write this book? The answer is that secure e-commerce can only be achieved through a delicate interweaving of technological safeguards and legal controls. The most critical issues cannot be understood by studying either the technological or legal aspects in isolation. Therefore, an effective treatise on this subject must draw on both technological and legal expertise.

This book is targeted at a broad audience, including business professionals, information technologists, and lawyers—anyone who is concerned about the security of e-commerce. Readers are not expected to have substantive technological or legal backgrounds. To make this book valuable to businesspersons, consumers, bankers, product developers, service providers, legal counsel, policymakers, and students alike, we include introductory material to virtually all topics, with a view to bringing all readers up to a base knowledge threshold before addressing the more complex issues.

Since the first edition was published, there has been enormous progress in the field of secure e-commerce. While the core technologies have not changed materially, there have been significant advances in software tools and packaging, standards, legislation globally, and experience in applying the technologies described in the first edition to real-world e-commerce. In the standards arena, for example, we have seen the completion and widespread adoption of the S/MIME secure messaging specifications, IPsec virtual private network specifications, and IETF PKIX specifications for public-key infrastructure. Notable legislative activities have included diverse national and state digital signature laws, and the U.S. Federal E-Sign Act. There has also been solid progress on the assessment and accreditation of secure e-commerce infrastructure components, such as certification authorities. These advances have occurred in conjunction with a massive increase in e-commerce deployment generally, in particular, the rapid emergence of business-to-business Internet commerce. Consequently, in this edition we have focused more on those aspects of the field that are proving most important in today's marketplace and that require rigorous analysis to ensure successful deployment.

We have written this book with an international audience in mind. However, the reader will observe, especially in our coverage of practices and legal issues, a predominance of coverage from the U.S. perspective. In general, we believe the problems faced globally are much the same as those faced in the United States, so we anticipate that our coverage of problems and progress in the United States will map meaningfully to developments in other nations. If we sometimes fall short in this respect, we apologize to our international colleagues.

One organization we need to recognize for making this book possible is VeriSign, Inc., the employer of both authors. The company provided significant moral support and graciously tolerated our being distracted from our regular duties on many occasions. Opinions expressed herein are, however, those of the authors and are not necessarily those of VeriSign or any other entity.

We also need to acknowledge the contributions of several individuals. First and foremost, we must recognize the work of Eric Pearson, who played a major role in assembling and reviewing legal-related material.

The following people helped us greatly by critically reviewing the manuscript, or parts thereof:

JOSEPH ALHADEFF	KAYE CALDWELL
RICH ANKNEY	ERIC CAPRIOLI
LEE BARRETT	KEVIN COLEMAN
DAVID BILLITER	BRUCE CRABTREE
BARCLAY BLAIR	WALTER EFFROSS
JIM BRANDT	GILLIAN ELCOCK
PAT CAIN	DAVID FILLINGHAM

TERRY FORD	SAM PHILLIPS
TWYLA FURGER	STEPHANIE PLASSE
JOHN GREGORY	TIM POLK
PETER GREGORY	MICHAEL POWER
RICH GUIDA	RON RIVEST
PHILLIP HALLAM-BAKER	RON ROSS
PAUL HEATH	GREG ROWLEY
MACK HICKS	MARK RUSSELL
JEREMY HILTON	BRUCE SCHNEIER
CRIS HOLLIER	STRATTON SCLAVOS
RUSS HOUSLEY	MARK SILVERN
JEFF KALWERISKY	RENAUD SORIEUL
HOYT KESTERSON	GARY STONEBURNER
MARCUS LEECH	RIAD TALLIM
JUDAH LEVINE	ROBERT TEMPLE
DAVID W. MAHER	PAUL VAN OORSCHOT
REBECCA MATTHIAS	IAN WATERS
CHARLES MERRILL	PETER WILLIAMS
MICHAEL MYERS	STEPHEN WU
STEVE ORLOWSKI	

We also want to thank Sharon Boeyen, X.509 Editor, for her review of the X.509-related material, and West Publishing Co. for their contribution of their online research resources.

Finally, we want to thank our respective spouses, Nola and Vera, for their amazing tolerance, understanding, and encouragement throughout the project.

WARWICK FORD, CAMBRIDGE, MASSACHUSETTS, U.S.A., *and*

MICHAEL S. BAUM, LOS ALTOS, CALIFORNIA, U.S.A.

Introduction

*E*lectronic *commerce* (e-commerce) is rapidly and massively changing our business and personal lives—our jobs, our purchasing experiences, our fortunes, our business strategies, and our expectations for the times ahead. It is causing upheavals in the way that businesses, large and small, must strive to become or continue to be successful. It is changing the ways in which businesses and consumers interact with their product and service suppliers. It is creating opportunities for whole new breeds of business ventures. It is causing governments to rethink aspects of their traditional regulatory roles. It has an impact on virtually all businesses, professionals, consumers, entrepreneurs, investors, and governments. It is global in scope, with the ability to leap national boundaries in ways never seen before.

The term *electronic commerce* defies precise definition. Most fundamentally, e-commerce represents the realization of digital, as opposed to paper-based, commercial transactions between businesses, between a business and its consumers, or between a government and its citizens or constituent businesses. E-commerce is the practical result, in the business and government spheres, of the exploding availability, performance-curve advancement, and real-world adoption of technologies relating to the IC chip, personal computer, Internet-age communications, and advanced application software solutions. These technological advances reinforce and are reinforced by the emergence of a new, global, geopolitical-economic community.

1.1   The Upside

The opportunities that e-commerce presents to the business world include

- *Productivity advances:* E-commerce adoption represents one of the few remaining avenues for the productivity advances needed to satisfy shareholder value
  expectations, attract new investment capital, and overcome competitive
  onslaughts. In today's supercompetitive world, e-commerce frequently represents an essential avenue for corporate survival and success.
- *Expanded and better-focused markets:* E-commerce can expand market reach
  dramatically. For example, a small local firm can now easily market its wares on
  a national or even global scale. At the same time, new information-gathering and
  storage technologies allow market segments and individual leads to be more
  precisely targeted and more accurately qualified than in the past.
- *Cost reduction:* Costs of performing traditional business tasks—such as external
  and internal communications, inventory control, accounting, customer relations
  management, and procurement—can be slashed.
- *Quality gains:* Reductions in transaction times and error rates, resulting from the
  elimination of manual steps such as telephone operator and telesales representative transaction entry, can allow inventories to be trimmed, processes to be
  streamlined, and both customer and employee satisfaction to increase.
- *Improved customer appeal:* E-commerce empowers the customer by putting
  information and control of transactions in the customer's hands. Customers get
  better access to comparative shopping and new computer-based customization
  offerings such as the ability to specify a unique configuration of an otherwise
  mass-market product. Self-service customer support can be offered. These
  factors, coupled with an increasing range of services, faster response times, and
  fewer transaction errors, can improve customer satisfaction and increase customer retention levels.
- *Improved employee satisfaction:* As overall job satisfaction increases through the
  shift away from repetitive task execution and toward the knowledge-worker
  model, improved employee communication processes and hands-on access to
  benefits systems provide new opportunities to increase retention rates of most-
  valued employees.

- *New partnerships based on better information sharing:* Improved means for the controlled sharing of information with partners open up the opportunity for new forms of strategic business relationships.
- *New business opportunities:* The Internet world has spawned a set of entirely new business opportunities, such as online commodity marketplaces, online auction houses, online brokerages, and Internet trust institutions.

1.2 The Downside

While the potential benefits of e-commerce are multifaceted and vast, there is also a possible downside. The electronic systems and infrastructures that support e-commerce are susceptible to abuse, misuse, and diverse failures. Tremendous damage can occur to all e-commerce participants. The damage may result from human error, system failure, criminal intent, or mischief.

Risks to a business engaged in e-commerce include

- *Direct financial loss resulting from fraud:* An external attacker or a fraudulent insider might, for example, order goods but charge payment to someone else's or a nonexistent account, transfer funds between accounts without authorization, or destroy or hide financial records that might reveal illegal conduct.
- *Exposure of the "crown jewels":* Proprietary information, such as intellectual property or marketing or competitive pricing information, that is crucial to a business's success might be unwittingly exposed to competitors or others.
- *Damage to relations with customers or business partners:* Relationships might be severely damaged due to disclosure of confidential information, disputed transactions that are not easily resolved because of the absence of convincing records, or excessive unavailability or unreliability of information or services.
- *Unforeseen costs:* Legal, public relations, or business resumption costs might be incurred in recovering from a security compromise, whether caused by external intrusions, employee dishonesty, inadequate controls, human error, or electronic system failures. Also, final settlement of major business transactions might be delayed pending lengthy resolution of disputes, if convincing records are not at hand.

- *Public relations damage:* Damage to corporate image or credibility might result from outsiders' masquerading as corporate spokespersons, manipulation of corporate Web site content, spreading of malicious rumors (such as in the investment community), or bad press resulting from newsworthy security penetrations.
- *Uptake failure due to lack of confidence:* Security concerns, whether founded or unfounded, can easily diminish the uptake of e-commerce generally, resulting in loss of business opportunity and lack of realization of the benefits identified in section 1.1.

Consumers also face risks, despite consumer protection regulation. The consumer who entrusts his or her money to electronic systems that are attacked or fail can unquestionably suffer loss. Ultimately, all of the business risks noted earlier can hurt consumers, in the form of direct costs, hidden costs passed on by businesses, or inconvenience factors.[1]

There have been many well-documented reports of attacks on, or failures of, computer networks and e-commerce services, including alteration of content on commercial or government Web sites, falsification of news bulletins, penetration of a major bank's cash management system, and systematic "sniffing" of passwords on a scale of millions.

It is not easy to assemble reliable statistics on the likelihood that such attacks will affect a given business, nor on the real costs of such attacks. An organization that suffers a security-related attack or failure must consider carefully whether or not to publicize it. The publicity may be so damaging, in terms of loss of customer confidence or competitive advantage, that it is easier, and possibly more profitable, to absorb quietly the resulting damages.

Notwithstanding the reluctance to disclose details of security compromises or related losses, it is clear to anyone following the popular press that security risks for e-commerce are real and can have a massive impact on businesses. Prudent users of e-commerce systems cannot ignore security concerns on the grounds that a successful attack is statistically unlikely to occur. Rather, all users must take protective steps, including appropriate countermeasures and recovery strategies, to avert or marginalize the damage caused by such attacks.

The perception of the role of security in e-commerce has changed in recent years. Whereas security was once widely considered as an optional, discretionary add-on feature, it is now painfully evident that security is an essential ingredient of any e-commerce solution. Therefore, security is now recognized as not just a safeguard of e-commerce but more an *enabler* of it. Furthermore, artful businesses can leverage their risk management strengths into positive success factors, driving competitive advantage and creating strategic barriers to entry.

1.3   E-Commerce Compared with Paper-Based Commerce

The need for commerce to be secure is not new. Traditional commercial transaction systems have always shared the needs for predictability, confidentiality, and resistance to fraud. So why is e-commerce different?

Much has been learned about the nature of computer-based information since it became a subject of renewed concern in the mid- to late 1980s. For example, great intellectual energy has been spent in trying to define a precise legal and business equivalency between paper-based and computer-based data. Most of these efforts have failed.[2]

It is now apparent that there are fundamental, practical, and legal differences between traditional paper-based commerce and computer-based commerce. Signed paper documents have inherent security attributes that are absent in computer-based records. These attributes include the semipermanence of ink embedded in paper fibers, the uniqueness of any particular printing process (such as for letterhead), watermarks, the biometrics of signatures (where characteristics such as pressure, shape, and pen direction are unique to the signer), the availability of time stamps (such as a postmark), and the obviousness of modifications, interlineations, and deletions.

Computer-based messages and records do not inherently enjoy such security attributes, if any at all. Computer-based messages are simply strings of binary digits or *bits*— zeros and ones—that represent information, such as words and numbers, in a coded form. The difference between a zero and a one depends on where the message happens to currently reside. For example, when residing in a computer memory, the difference amounts to a fraction of a volt variation at some point within an electronic circuit. Without the application of specialized external security mechanisms, computer-based records can be modified freely and without detection. That is, certain supplemental control mechanisms, including both physical and electronic protections, must be applied to achieve a level of trustworthiness comparable to that which inherently exists on paper.

Furthermore, paper-based and computer-based documents may not perform equal or exactly analogous functions in business and law. Negotiable documents of title exemplify differences between these media because of their need for originality and uniqueness. The negotiation of a paper document of title serves legally to transfer the goods or property that the document represents. The recipient of that document can have confidence that the transfer will be legally recognized, in part because proof of transfer is evidenced by a unique, original, paper document.

In contrast, computer-based records are not inherently unique. Indeed, one benefit of digital data is that one can make any number of identical copies with a simple keystroke, with each copy being indistinguishable from the original. Unfortunately, this characteristic counters the use of such records for providing robust legal proof in the same way as traditional paper-based documents. Thus, the inherent differences between paper documents and computer-based records demand different methods and procedures for achieving negotiability and other similar legal functions. Whereas a single paper document is adequate to negotiate a transfer of title, it may take a series of cryptographically secured computer-based messages, in conjunction with logical and physical controls, to accomplish the same task with a computerized title registry.

In reality, there are few straightforward, one-to-one, legal analogs for paper-based transactions in the e-commerce world. Rather, it is necessary to find relative *functional* analogs while taking into account the unique qualities of digital media.

1.4 Making E-Commerce Secure

The risks inherent in e-commerce can be mitigated by the use of appropriate security countermeasures in conjunction with the establishment of necessary business and legal frameworks. Some of the security safeguards required are comparatively obvious—for example, restricting access to systems that store sensitive information or performing background checks on personnel trusted to perform critical tasks—and we shall not spend time on them in this book. Rather, we focus on special security countermeasures and the supporting technical and legal infrastructure needed because of the unique characteristics of the e-commerce environment. Apart from the fundamental issues identified in section 1.3, environmental factors include

- *Open communications infrastructure:* E-commerce is largely conducted on open, interconnected, unregulated, and largely unpoliced or unpoliceable networks (such as the Internet), as compared with the closed, point-to-point channels (such as leased circuits between major trading partners) typically used in earlier business communications systems.

- *Global reach:* Businesses now demand to trade globally, with at least a comparable degree of confidence as in the insular, controlled digital communities of the past. Because trading partners can reside halfway around the world, there is a great incentive to avoid legal disputes that might end up in a foreign court. This is particularly important when one considers that cyberspace may have no clear jurisdictional boundaries and that messages can pass through a potentially uncontrollable number of jurisdictions. E-commerce may become the most regulated activity in history, with every jurisdiction through which a message passes claiming at least some authority.[3] By utilizing good security methods, parties can provide and secure the best possible probative evidence of their transactions and avoid such a legal quagmire.

- *Real-time trading:* In comparison to the batched, EDI-style,[4] delayed transactions of the past, real-time trading has both negative and positive implications. On the negative side, real-time trading diminishes the opportunity for parties to meaningfully investigate one another and erodes other safety factors inherent in delayed transactions. On the positive side, an opportunity is introduced for real-time authentication of the transacting parties and the excuse that "the check is in the mail" can less easily be used to gain an unintended free trial period before making final payment.

- *Political influences:* Information security has become a major political issue, involving industrial/economic, national security, and law enforcement communities. The interests of the latter two communities often diverge from those of the business community. Information security issues also raise questions about fundamental constitutional rights.

Secure e-commerce means the reliable execution of business transactions over untrustworthy underlying communications and storage systems, in which transactions may be exposed to unknown parties. Furthermore, business information needs to be secured between users who may never meet each other personally. Satisfaction of these requirements depends heavily on widespread deployment of information security solutions, including authentication, confidentiality, access control, and integrity.

Most significantly, secure e-commerce depends upon the use of cryptographic-based technologies, such as digital signatures and encryption, especially when valuable or private information is involved or when the potential for repudiation of transactions is considered a material risk.

Cryptographic-based technologies are not new. However, until the emergence of e-commerce, their use was essentially limited to the national security arena and a limited set of banking applications. E-commerce has raised many new questions and issues regarding the deployment of cryptographic and related information security technologies on a large—ideally global—scale. In particular, scalability and non-repudiation requirements have led to the widespread application of *public-key cryptography*, which satisfies these needs well. This, in turn, has created demand for *certification authorities* and other *public-key infrastructure* (PKI) functions.

The widespread deployment of digital signatures and other cryptographic technologies also raises many issues relating to legal and business practices and controls. The roles and responsibilities of the parties involved, the legal effect of the information transferred, and the efficacy of computer-based commercial practices in general all present issues pertinent to secure e-commerce.

This book covers the breadth of these issues, within the context of the following definition of secure e-commerce: *Secure e-commerce is e-commerce that uses security procedures and techniques, including cryptography and digital signatures, commensurate with anticipated risks.*

1.5 Book Road Map

This book is structured with the following chapters:

- *Chapter 2—The Internet:* For the uninitiated, this chapter introduces various fundamental concepts and terminology relating to computer networking and, in particular, the Internet. The primary Internet applications and main roles in the Internet community are introduced. E-commerce transactions and their use of the Internet are discussed, together with some examples.
- *Chapter 3—Business and Legal Principles:* This chapter explains the general business and legal concepts that relate to this field and proposes business-legal models that may be considered to underlie e-commerce. Particular attention is

given to the enforceability and provability of digital commerce transactions. Efforts to address uncertainties in the current legal context of e-commerce are discussed.

- *Chapter 4—Information Security Technologies:* Primarily for the benefit of the reader without a background in information security, this chapter presents an overview of information security principles and explains the main technological concepts and terms used later in the book. Topics covered include cryptography, digital signatures, cryptographic key management, and authentication techniques.
- *Chapter 5—Internet Security:* This chapter addresses how to take advantage of the Internet's capabilities without exposing oneself to unacceptable risks. Coverage includes technology such as firewalls, virtual private networks, Internet mail security, and World Wide Web security.
- *Chapter 6—Certificates:* This chapter describes the role of public-key certificates and the entities that issue such certificates. Standard certificate formats are described, and general procedures for key and certificate management, including certificate revocation, are outlined.
- *Chapter 7—Public-Key Infrastructure:* This chapter discusses several issues associated with building public-key infrastructures (PKIs) capable of supporting very large user populations. Topics addressed include ways to structure relationships between multiple certification authorities, ways to associate different certification policies and practices with different certification paths, and certificate management protocols used in interfacing application products to a supporting PKI.
- *Chapter 8—Legislation, Regulation, and Guidelines:* This chapter discusses recent efforts to reduce legal uncertainties—including U.S. and other national laws, international conventions, guidelines, and model agreements and provisions—that affect computer-based commerce generally or digital signatures and PKI in particular.
- *Chapter 9—Non-repudiation:* This chapter discusses the concept of non-repudiation, including several of the finer points of the non-repudiation problem. It describes procedures and protocols for supporting non-repudiation characteristics. The role of trusted third-party services, including time-stamping and notary services, is also described.
- *Chapter 10—Certification Policy and Practices:* This chapter provides guidance on the development of certificate policies and certification practice statements to support secure e-commerce infrastructures. Topics addressed include responsibili-

ties of the parties concerned, legal safeguards, operational procedures, personnel controls, audits, and general security measures.

• *Chapter 11—Public-Key Infrastructure Assessment and Accreditation:* This chapter describes requirements and processes for ensuring that certification authorities meet requisite criteria for trustworthiness and interoperation.

Ancillary information is provided in the appendixes.

Notes

1. Traditionally, "consumers" are often defined as those who purchase goods or services for personal, family, or household purposes, and thus many consumer protection rules are intended to protect the consumer as the *buyer.* Paradoxically, e-commerce may render such rules ineffective for many related transactions. For example, eBay <http://www.ebay.com> and other e-auction sites service a disproportionate number of individual "consumers" as sellers rather than buyers. And yet, each eBay Web page states that the "seller assumes all responsibility for listing this item."

2. Nevertheless, some people continue to postulate such equivalents in the hope of one day discovering the elusive link.

3. This point was noted by Christopher Millard, a U.K. computer law expert.

4. Electronic data interchange—this term is generally associated with the pre-Internet form of business-to-business e-commerce.

The Internet

O ur journey into the realms of secure e-commerce will lead us head on into many complex topics on both the technological and legal fronts. For the benefit of readers unfamiliar with the fields concerned, chapters 2 and 3 introduce some basic concepts and terminology. In this chapter we outline the methods and principles underlying information communications on the public Internet or private networks that use Internet-based technologies. These technologies provide the critical foundation to e-commerce, since it is the Internet, with its ubiquity and low deployment and usage costs, that has made most e-commerce applications feasible and successful. We first introduce the concepts and vocabulary of general computer networking. We then discuss the major Internet applications and the roles of various participants in the Internet community. We address the ways that the Internet is used for e-commerce purposes and present some example Internet e-commerce scenarios. We shall use and build on these examples throughout the book. This chapter does not address Internet security in any depth—that is left until chapter 5. The Internet-savvy reader may wish to skip this chapter entirely.

2.1 Computer Networking

Distributed Applications

While many computer applications, including typical word processors and spreadsheets, reside on a single personal computer (PC), *distributed applications,* such as electronic mail (e-mail), inherently involve more than one computer that might be separated geo-graphically. *Computer networks* provide the means for transferring data between systems in support of distributed applications.

In this book, we generally use the term *system* to denote any device, embracing both its hardware and software, that forms part of a distributed application and consequently participates in a computer network. Examples are network-connected desktop PCs, mainframe or server computers in corporate data centers, personal data assistants (PDAs), automated teller machines, retail cash terminals, online point-of-sale devices, set-top boxes, and digital pagers and mobile phones. Indeed, the forms that a system may take are becoming increasingly diverse as innovation continually spurs the growth of new types of distributed applications.

Client-server applications are a class of distributed applications that involve two types of systems: a *client,* which is used directly by an end user, and a *server,* which provides or gives access to shared or centralized resources or services. Examples of servers are database servers, mail servers, business application servers, and directory servers. A server generally runs in unattended mode, typically around the clock, servicing incoming requests from multiple clients.

Computer Networks

The technologies used to implement computer networks are beyond the scope of this book.[1] For our purposes, the necessary understanding of network technologies extends little beyond recognizing that a computer network conveys *data items* from one system to another. A data item is a *representation* of a piece of information, usually obtained by encoding that information (or the words or numbers constituting that information) as a string of bits.

One computer-networking concept that the reader will encounter in this book is that of network protocols. A *protocol* is a set of rules understood by the hardware or software of systems that intercommunicate. These rules govern precisely how information is repre-sented for transfer purposes and how the communication activity is managed. For example, communication protocols include rules for attaching control bits to transmitted data items to help ensure that all of the transmitted data stream arrives without any part being lost or modified due to a noisy communications environment.

Computer networks have multiple *layers* of protocol, which operate independently of each other. Each layer solves a piece of the communications puzzle and, conceptually, provides a communications service to a higher layer while making use of a more basic communications service provided by a lower layer. Typical layers (progressing from lower to higher layers) are

- *Link layer or subnetwork layer:* Protocol to support the transfer of a string of data bits, called a *packet,* between two pieces of equipment that are directly connected using a particular subnetwork technology. Examples of such subnetwork technologies are Ethernet *local area network* (LAN) technology, which is typically used to interconnect equipment on one site, and frame-relay *wide area network* (WAN) technology, which is used to interconnect different sites via a public network service provider.
- *Network layer:* Protocol to support the delivery of a packet between systems connected via a path that may traverse multiple interconnected subnetworks, potentially of different technologies. For example, two systems at different locations may each be connected to a LAN, with the two LANs interconnected via a WAN. Networking products called *routers* or *gateways* provide for interconnecting different subnetworks, for example, a LAN to a WAN (see figure 2.1).

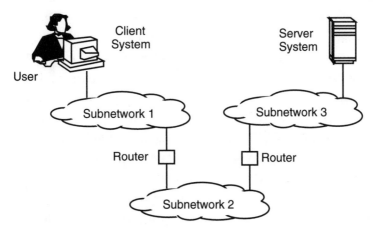

Figure 2.1 Typical Network Path

- *Transport layer:* Protocol to ensure that multiple data packets for an application that are conveyed using the network layer are delivered to that application in the correct order and that no packets are lost.
- *Application layer:* Protocol that generates and interprets the contents of the streams of data delivered by the transport layer, in support of a particular distributed application. For example, the application protocol for a financial transaction application typically governs how request and acknowledgment messages constituting a transaction can be distinguished from each other and how each message is represented as a string of bits. The application layer is the topmost layer of a complete *protocol stack.*

Because the layers are independent of each other, multiple higher-layer protocols can use a lower-layer protocol, or different lower-layer protocol alternatives can be made available for use by a higher-layer protocol. For example, many different application protocols can operate over the same transport protocol. While designers of application protocols must understand the basic functions provided by the transport layer, they need not know the inner workings of the transport protocol, nor need they know of the existence or characteristics of layers that are even lower, such as the network layer.

The Internet

While *Internet* denotes a technology family, it also denotes a massive, operational computer network or, more accurately, a network of networks.[2] The foundations of the Internet go back to 1969, when the U.S. Department of Defense supported the establishment of connections between computers at a few universities to create a model for a nationwide redundant network that would allow the armed forces and government personnel to maintain communications after an enemy attack.[3] The project expanded through the 1970s, with the Department of Defense Advanced Research Projects Agency (then ARPA, later DARPA) funding the continuing development of packet-switching network facilities for interconnecting computers in U.S. universities and government research institutions. The network, or collection of interconnected networks, initially constituted the ARPANET WAN (also called the *backbone* network), which provided connectivity to LANs on various sites throughout the country. The configuration has grown rapidly over the ensuing years, quickly becoming global in scope and expanding from a tool of research and development communities to a set of resources available for commercial exploitation. The

Internet today provides a rich and expanding set of services that is essential to all sectors of the economy and society.

The main technological achievement in building the Internet has been the development of a suite of public-domain network protocols suitable for interconnecting the products of all computer vendors. Two protocols, in particular, form the core of Internet interconnectivity: the transport-layer protocol, called *Transmission Control Protocol* (TCP), and the network-layer protocol, called *Internet Protocol* (IP).[4]

As the Internet has evolved, many different distributed applications and associated application-layer protocols have been designed and deployed. These include

- *World Wide Web* (WWW, or simply *the Web*): An information-browsing application that allows a user to locate and access information stored on a remote server and to follow references from one server to related information stored on another server. Browsed information can include text, graphics, color images, sound clips, and video recordings.
- *Electronic messaging:* An application to support the store-and-forward transfer of a message from an originating system to one or more destination systems. This application supports personal electronic mail (e-mail), as well as the communications needs of other applications called *mail-enabled applications.*
- *Network news:* An electronic bulletin board application that supports, in particular, the family of discussion groups known as *Usenet.* The application allows a user to join one or more discussion groups (*newsgroups*), to monitor and read new items posted in these discussion groups, and to post original notes to the groups.
- *File transfer:* An application that allows users to log in to a remote system, identify themselves, list file directories on the remote system, and copy files to or from the remote system. The application uses the File Transfer Protocol (FTP).
- *Directory access:* An application that allows a user to search, retrieve, and modify data stored in a directory. The protocol used is the Lightweight Directory Access Protocol (LDAP).[5]
- *Remote login:* A simple remote terminal application that allows a user at one site to establish a connection to a remote login server, passing keystrokes and responses between them. The protocol used is called TELNET.

Of these applications, the two most important to e-commerce are the World Wide Web and electronic messaging; these are discussed further in section 2.2.

Intranets, Extranets, and Virtual Private Networks

An *intranet* is a network constructed using Internet-based communications and application technologies that serves only the internal purposes of an enterprise. For example, a typical corporate intranet allows the employees of a corporation to communicate with one another and to access internal corporate resources.

An *extranet* is a network operated by or on behalf of an enterprise to support communication between the enterprise and a community of external users. An extranet uses the communications capabilities of the public Internet but denies access to all users except recognized members of the community. An example of an extranet is a configuration that allows the customers, affiliated organizations, or business partners of the operating enterprise to access that enterprise's resources via extranet-accessible Web servers. Extranets are generally associated with a particular Internet application (usually the Web).

A *virtual private network* (VPN) is a network that has similar security characteristics to a private network built using dedicated communications links, but which instead uses paths on the public Internet for the underlying data transfer. A VPN is implemented by creating secure *tunnels* at the network protocol (IP) layer and is generally application independent. A VPN may link remote sites of an enterprise to one another, in which case the tunnel is created between VPN gateway systems on the various sites. Alternatively, a VPN may link remote, mobile users to a home network access point, in which case the tunnel is created between a VPN client software module on the remote user's PC and a VPN gateway system on the home network.[6]

2.2 Internet Applications

The two Internet applications of most relevance to e-commerce are the Web and electronic messaging.

The World Wide Web

The Web[7] is a sophisticated information-browsing application, which has become so popular that, to many people, it is synonymous with *Internet*. The application works by presenting a user with a view of what is called a *hypermedia* document. A hypermedia document comprises multimedia (text, graphic, image, sound, and video) information, which may also have embedded references (called *links*) to other hypermedia documents stored on the same server or on any other system accessible via the Web.

Each hypermedia document, sometimes called a *page,* has a unique identifier called a *Uniform Resource Identifier.*[8] While a Uniform Resource Identifier can, in principle, take different forms, the most commonly used form is called a *Uniform Resource Locator* (URL). A URL identifies the application-layer protocol required to access a document, the server on which the target document is held, and the particular document on that server. (Note the use of URLs in the notes in this book as pointers to further information on referenced documents.[9]) A *Web site* is a collection of related pages created and maintained by a person or organization.

A Web user has client software, typically the familiar *Web browser,* which enables the retrieval and local display or rendering of content from a Web server. A document can be requested by the user's supplying that document's Uniform Resource Identifier or by the user's calling up a reference to that document, typically via a mouse-click on a *hypertext* reference in a previously displayed page. The client is in communication with only one server at a time. However, through creative use of referencing facilities, the user is able to easily retrieve related documents in succession from multiple, different Web servers. Thereby, the user can *navigate the Web.*

In the e-commerce arena, the Web has proven an ideal application for

- Vendors to disseminate details of their goods and services
- Buyers to browse the marketplace; consider product features, availability, and price; and select a vendor
- Buyers and vendors to execute sales agreements online
- Vendors to provide postsale customer services
- Providers of online services, such as Internet-based home banking or online brokerages, to host their services

The Web application is supported by various application protocols, including, in particular, the *Hypertext Transport Protocol* (HTTP), which is the primary application-layer protocol used by a Web client to access a Web server. The contents and formatting of hypermedia documents accessed via the Web are commonly defined using the *Hypertext Markup Language* (HTML). The newer and more powerful *Extensible Markup Language* (XML) enables a content provider to create custom markup languages that are tailored for special application purposes and that can be automatically interpreted by modern Web browsers.[10]

In addition to delivering passive content to a browser, Web sites can download executable code in the form of JavaScript or VBScript scripts, Java applets, or ActiveX controls for execution by the client.[11] While these software download mechanisms add much power to the Web experience, they also raise various security concerns that we shall address later.

Electronic Messaging

Electronic messaging allows a user on one system (the *originator*) to send a message to one or more users on other systems (*recipients*). Because a recipient is not necessarily using his or her computer at the time a message is sent, the message is temporarily held in a recipient's *mailbox,* a data repository on a mail server. The recipient's e-mail software, acting as a network client, periodically or on command communicates with the mail server to check its mailbox and retrieve any new messages.[12] It is possible for messages to traverse several mail servers en route from originator to recipient, hence the term *store-and-forward* messaging.

Several different electronic messaging technologies provide the same basic functions but use different application-layer protocols. The Internet mail transfer protocol[13] and message format[14] are the nuclei of the Internet's standard electronic messaging protocol set. Proprietary electronic messaging applications and protocols, which are available from various computer or software vendors, are used locally within private networks. Electronic messaging systems of different technologies can usually be interconnected via *mail gateways* that can relay messages between the different environments.

While message contents are most commonly textual, they can be multimedia in nature, also including graphics, images, sound clips, and files from an ever-increasing set of desktop applications such as word processors and spreadsheets. Multimedia messages are based on the specifications known as *Multipurpose Internet Mail Extensions* (MIME).[15] MIME provides for the combining and nesting of message components[16] of many different types. For example, the MIME content type *text/plain* is used for unstructured text, *image/gif* is used for image data encoded in Graphics Interchange Format (GIF), and *multipart/alternative* is used for conveying multiple different representations (such as text and image representations) of one piece of information.[17]

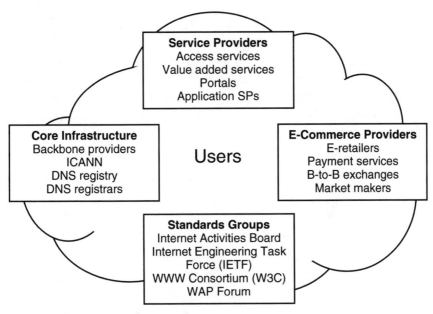

Figure 2.2 The Internet Community

2.3 The Internet Community

The public Internet is not inherently a centrally administered infrastructure. One view of the Internet is that it is an *extraterritorial entity* that is neither controlled nor controllable by any government or organization, but instead operates exclusively on a basis of mutual cooperation.[18] The operation of the Internet has been described as *controlled chaos.* The chaos is held at bay by a combination of agreements, guidelines, policies, and practices. The system operates on a largely collaborative basis—all members of the Internet community cooperate to keep the Internet functioning. Figure 2.2 shows some of the more important roles in the Internet community.

Service Providers

In general, users access the Internet via Internet service providers (ISPs). ISPs range in size from tiny, sole-proprietor, basement operations to major corporations such as America Online, Inc. The service offerings, technological capabilities, and market strategies of ISPs vary tremendously. The services provided can generally be classified as follows:

- *Access services:* These services give users connectivity to an Internet backbone, that is, one of the major WANs that tie the Internet together. Access services are provided either by the backbone operator or by a local reseller of service off a backbone. For users who operate servers that are to be accessible from the Internet, direct, full-time connections are required. A user who only operates client systems may need only a part-time, dial-up access service. Any business classed as an ISP offers, at a minimum, access services to its customers.
- *Value-added services:* These services include e-mail, Web site hosting, and application support. The service provider may provide extensive user support services and may also offer ancillary services such as Web page design. Most ISPs offer value-added services, often packaged with their access services.

The provision of services by an ISP to an Internet user is governed by a service provider agreement. Such agreements are discussed in appendix A.

Other types of service providers in the Internet environment, distinct from ISPs, include

- *Portals:* Portals provide packaged Web content and online services to their customers. While the larger ISPs, such as America Online, include their own portal functionality, other service providers, such as Yahoo!, serve as independent portals and obtain their revenue primarily from advertising and commissions on sales of merchandise and third-party services accessed via the portal. Portals may target one or more specific market segments.
- *Application service providers* (ASPs): Application service providers outsource applications, such as enterprise resource planning (ERP) applications,[19] for their customers, who are typically small to medium businesses.

Internet Standards

The Internet community depends heavily on a set of well-specified and widely adopted technical and procedural standards. The body responsible for coordinating Internet design, engineering, and management is the Internet Activities Board (IAB).[20] The IAB's subsidiary task force, called the Internet Engineering Task Force (IETF), is responsible for developing Internet standards specifications. Final decisions on Internet standardization are made by the IAB and are based on recommendations from the Internet Engineering Steering Group (IESG), the leadership body of the IETF. Participants of the IETF are individual technical contributors, rather than formal organizational representatives. The IETF meets three times annually. At these large conventions, many IETF working groups meet to work on the development of Internet standards and guidelines. However, the standards development process is conducted primarily via open e-mail exchanges through public mail distribution lists. The process depends greatly on a spirit of cooperation among participants.

Specifications that are destined to become Internet standards evolve through a set of maturity levels known as the *standards track*.[21] The standards track has three recognized maturity levels, as follows:

- *Proposed standard:* A specification entering the standards track. It must be generally stable, have resolved known design choices, be believed to be well understood, have received significant community review, and appear to enjoy enough community interest to be considered valuable. A specification must remain at the proposed standard level for at least six months.
- *Draft standard:* A specification from which at least two independent and interoperable implementations have been developed and for which adequate operational experience has been obtained. It must be well understood and known to be quite stable, both in its semantics and as a basis for developing an implementation. A standard must remain at the draft standard level for at least four months.
- *Standard:* A specification characterized by a high degree of technical maturity and by a generally held belief that the specified protocol or service provides significant benefit to the Internet community.

Anyone can readily track the development of Internet standards directly; furthermore, anyone can easily contribute to the process via e-mail.[22]

All standards track specifications are published in the Internet Request for Comments (RFC) document series. Despite the somewhat misleading title, this is a series of stable documents that includes, in addition to Internet standards track specifications, various documents issued for general information and documents intended to stimulate comment and discussion. Internet RFCs can be obtained online from the IETF Web site.[23]

Another important series of Internet publications is the Internet-Drafts series. These are working documents prepared by the IETF, its working groups, or other groups or individuals working on Internet technical topics. Internet-Drafts are valid for a maximum of six months and may be updated, replaced, or made obsolete by other documents at any time. As with RFCs, Internet-Drafts are available online.[24]

Apart from the IETF, another organization that contributes heavily to the development of standards for the Web application space is the World Wide Web Consortium (W3C). Specifications such as HTML and XML are largely the result of W3C's efforts, and W3C has also led the development of mechanisms to support personal privacy on the Web.[25] The reader can learn much about ongoing developments in these fields by following the work of this group.[26]

IETF standards sometimes reference standards from other international standards organizations, such as ISO/IEC and the ITU, but these standards are not generally available online for free. Copies may be purchased from the publishing organization.[27]

Internet Name Assignment

One somewhat thorny problem faced by the Internet community has long been the assignment of names to networks or organizations (called Internet *domains*).[28] Domain names form part of an Internet-wide naming tree. Each domain name needs to be registered, along with a corresponding IP address, in the Domain Name System (DNS).[29] Not surprisingly, ownership of domain names can be fiercely competitive, and disputed name claims are not necessarily easy to resolve.

In the Internet's early period, many coordination functions were handled by the U.S. government—or its contractors and volunteers—on an ad hoc basis. This informal structure represented the spirit and culture of the research community in which the Internet developed. In particular, from 1993 to 1999, Network Solutions, Inc., was the only provider of domain name registration services in the .com, .net, and .org top-level domains pursuant to a cooperative agreement with the United States government. There are also over 250 other top-level domains. These include the country code domains, whereby each nation has a two-letter top level domain, for example, *.ca* for Canada and *.fr* for France.

However, the growing international importance of the Internet necessitated the creation of a technical management and policy development body that would be independent of the U.S. government, more formalized in structure, and more fully reflective of the diversity of the Internet community.

In 1997, the Clinton administration published an executive order calling for privatization of the Internet Domain Name System (DNS) and in June 1998 began an open and consultative policy development process that led to the publication of a document commonly known as the *White Paper.*[30] The White Paper stated the desire of the U.S. government that a private, nonprofit corporation be formed to assume responsibility for the Domain Name and IP addressing systems and certain related functions and called for proposals to be submitted to accomplish this goal.[31]

Consequently, in late 1998, a nonprofit, private-sector corporation called the Internet Corporation for Assigned Names and Numbers (ICANN) was formed to serve as the global consensus entity to which the U.S. government would transfer the responsibility for coordinating Internet naming.[32] The cooperative agreement with Network Solutions was amended to reflect a commitment to develop a protocol and associated software supporting a *shared registration system* that would permit multiple registrars to provide registration services within .com, .net, and .org.

ICANN has subsequently assumed responsibility for the stable operation of the Internet in four key areas, including the Domain Name System and the allocation of the IP address space. There are now multiple registrars for domain names in the .com, .net, and .org top-level domains. Any organization can apply to become such a registrar, subject to ICANN accreditation.[33] VeriSign, Inc. (which acquired Network Solutions) operates the DNS Registry for these top-level domains on behalf of the community.

Domain name disputes are handled under a uniform dispute resolution policy. ICANN summarizes this policy as follows:

> In general, this policy provides that registrars receiving complaints concerning the impact of domain names they have registered on trademarks or service marks will take no action until they receive instructions from the domain-name holder or an order of a court, arbitrator, or other neutral decision maker deciding the parties' dispute. There is an exception in the policy, however, for disputes involving domain names that are shown to have been registered in abusive attempts to profit from another's trademark (i.e., cybersquatting and cyberpiracy). In these cases of abusive registration, the complaining party can invoke a special administrative procedure to resolve the dispute. Under this procedure, the dispute will be decided by neutral persons selected from panels established for that purpose. The procedure will be handled in

large part online, is designed to take less than 45 days, and is expected to cost about $1,000 in fees to be paid to the entities providing the neutral persons. Parties to such disputes will also be able to go to court to resolve their dispute or to contest the outcome of the procedure.

Securing the Internet

The maintenance of Internet security has traditionally been considered a community responsibility. One long-standing publication giving guidance on how the Internet community should work together to achieve a secure environment is RFC 1281, *Guidelines for the Secure Operation of the Internet.*[34] This document addresses the respective responsibilities of users, service providers, and product vendors as follows:

- Users are individually responsible for understanding and respecting the security policies of the systems (computers and networks) that they are using. Users are individually accountable for their own behavior.
- Users have a responsibility to employ available security mechanisms and procedures for protecting their own data. They also have a responsibility for assisting in the protection of the systems they use.
- Computer and network service providers are responsible for maintaining the security of the systems they operate. They are further responsible for notifying users of their security policies and any changes to these policies.
- Vendors and system developers are responsible for providing systems that are sound and that embody adequate security controls.
- Users, service providers, and hardware and software vendors are responsible for cooperating to provide security.
- Technical improvements in Internet security protocols should be sought on a continuing basis. At the same time, personnel developing new protocols, hardware, or software for the Internet are expected to include security considerations as part of the design and development process.

In recent years, securing the Internet has become a community priority. The IETF has built up a strong Security Area, which develops security-related technical standards and which also has an oversight role in ensuring that all Internet standards address security issues adequately. Many technological solutions have been developed, and many of the supporting specifications are progressing through the Internet standards track. The main developments relevant to e-commerce are discussed in chapter 5.

Another important community function has proven to be the coordination of security incident reporting. Leadership in this area has been assumed by the CERT Coordination Center, part of the Software Engineering Institute, a federally funded research and development center at Carnegie Mellon University. The CERT Coordination Center was established by DARPA in 1988 in the wake of the Morris worm incident, which crippled approximately 10% of all computers connected to the Internet. The center

- coordinates the efforts of teams when responding to large-scale incidents;
- trains incident-response professionals; and
- researches the causes of security vulnerabilities, the prevention of vulnerabilities, and system security improvements.[35]

Mobile Wireless Internet Access

Wireless e-commerce and other applications that involve access to Internet resources from mobile devices, such as digital phones, two-way pagers, or wireless-enabled PDAs, are changing the face of the Internet from the PC-centric model of the past. Given the accelerating adoption of these mobile wireless devices, there is enormous appeal in using them for such purposes as instant messaging, stock trading, auction bidding, and home banking.

From the communications technology perspective, wireless Internet access is not particularly challenging: Wireless data transfer fits seamlessly into the lower levels of the Internet's protocol stack design. However, wireless access does raise new application requirements and has introduced some new players into the service provision food chain. Perhaps the most significant difference relates to the user interface: small screen, no mouse, and highly limited keyboard capabilities (if any). This means that content for a mobile wireless client generally has to be designed specially and delivered differently from that for a wired PC client.[36]

Many scenarios of wireless access to the Internet introduce the need for a wireless gateway function, as illustrated in figure 2.3. The gateway performs protocol translation, which may include content translation, between the wireless world and the wired Internet world.

From the community perspective, new participants potentially include the wireless network carrier and the wireless gateway operator (frequently one entity performs both roles).

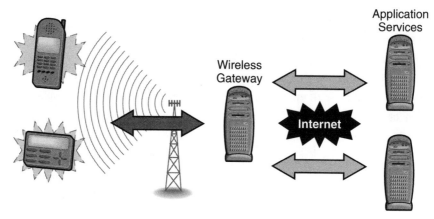

Figure 2.3   Wireless Access to the Internet

One industry organization that is contributing substantially to the orderly integration of Internet and wireless technologies is the Wireless Application Protocol (WAP) Forum.[37] This consortium of digital mobile telephone vendors, carriers, and other relevant entities is developing specifications for standard protocols to support the extension of Internet (especially Web) functions to digital mobile phone handsets. The first WAP phones became available in 1999, and new functionality continues to be added progressively.

The wireless environment also introduces some security risks not inherent in the wired world. In chapter 5, we discuss the security features inherent in WAP.

2.4   Internet Commerce

Business-to-Consumer E-Commerce

The first stages of commercialization of the Internet focused primarily on services for the consumer. Several different consumer models have been successfully implemented, including:

- *Consumer marketing:* A vendor disseminates information such as catalogs, product specifications, order forms, and customer service information to consumers via the Internet (but the order is not consummated electronically).

- *Internet retailing:* A vendor offers and sells its products or services directly to consumers via its Web site.
- *Consumer portal:* A portal service provider aims to attract repetitively a large consumer community to its site and sell to this community its own products and services and those of other vendors through appropriate joint marketing arrangements.
- *Online auction:* Consumers are offered the ability to competitively price-bid for products or services offered by diverse businesses or individuals. (In fact, this model can sometimes be categorized as *consumer-to-consumer* e-commerce.)[38]
- *Content aggregation/distribution:* Content from multiple sources is made available to Web sites for redistribution to or referral-access by the clients of those Web sites, under appropriate revenue-sharing arrangements.[39]

One of the more challenging aspects of consumer e-commerce—in fact, any form of e-commerce—is the payment process. There are many different methods of executing a consumer payment transaction on the Internet. The security and risk management characteristics of all such payment methods are particularly important because of the serious risk of fraud. For example, fraud can result from online theft of personal payment data, such as credit card numbers, or by an online attacker charging payment to someone else or a nonexistent account. Additionally, identity theft resulting from such disclosures must be considered. Subsequent chapters in this book address in depth the mitigation of such concerns.

Business-to-Business E-Commerce

Many business models have emerged for business-to-business e-commerce. The models vary in such respects as how buyers and sellers are brought together, how business partners secure the requisite trust in each another, how business terms (including price) are communicated and negotiated, how transactions are executed and enforced, and what roles are played by intermediaries or trusted third parties.

The models include

- *Buy-side procurement:* This model focuses on empowering the buyer to gain access to multiple suppliers. This model is supported by procurement software products, which are frequently packaged into enterprise resource planning (ERP) software suites.

- *Vertical communities:* Communities of buyers are brought into contact with a community of sellers within the context of a business-to-business exchange supporting a particular industry vertical sector. Services provided in such communities vary but might include such functions as dissemination of vendor product and service information and buyer procurement requirements, negotiation of terms, order placement, and transaction clearinghouse operations. Such communities have been established for many verticals, including health care, insurance, life sciences, electronic components, chemicals, and construction.
- *Market makers:* Electronic marketplaces are established to support competitive bidding to buy or sell commodities, products, or services. Exchanges of this type exist for such industries as energy, metals, and transportation.

Organizations that operate services to facilitate business-to-business Internet commerce using such models are commonly known as business-to-business exchanges or business-to-business portals. Such organizations typically raise revenue through subscriptions or per-transaction charges.

EDI on the Internet

Business-to-business e-commerce is not a particularly new concept, having existed in the form of Electronic Data Interchange (EDI) since the 1980s.[40] EDI has traditionally meant the computer-to-computer exchange of business transactions, including purchase orders, invoices, and payment advices within large industrial communities, such as the automotive industry,[41] or for government purposes, such as defense procurements. Pre-Internet EDI typically employed dedicated communications lines, dial-up links, and mainframe terminal emulation.

Pre-Internet EDI generally relied on the use of value-added network (VAN) service providers. VANs typically provided services to map proprietary message formats and database constructs to and from standard formats and to translate from one EDI format to another. Some also provided data communications services and assisted their clients in areas such as software configuration, enhanced acknowledgments, security, auditing, transaction tracing, and recovery of lost data. The commercialization of the Internet has made certain roles of the EDI VAN obsolete by eliminating interconnectivity barriers. However, some of the roles remain and have been assumed by business-to-business exchanges or VANs that have adapted to operate in the Internet environment.

Standardized EDI message formats were developed primarily under the auspices of two organizations:

- The American National Standards Institute (ANSI) Accredited Standards Committee (ASC) X12[42]
- The United Nations Economic Commission for Europe, which developed the EDIFACT (EDI for Administration, Commerce, and Transport) standards[43]

One approach to migrating EDI to the Internet environment has been to transport EDI traffic via Internet-based electronic messaging. Leveraging the MIME framework for accommodating specialized messaging traffic, the IETF defined a set of MIME content types for conveying EDI traffic.[44] These MIME content types can be used to transfer EDI messages between an EDI user and a VAN or among EDI users. MIME content types have been defined for conveying ANSI X12 standard interchanges, EDIFACT standard interchanges, and EDI messages of any other unspecified format.[45]

With the emergence of XML as a powerful tool for designing and implementing structured business transactions, XML-based EDI transaction formats are being progressively introduced as alternatives to the original X12 and EDIFACT formats. It is unclear to what extent and in what time frame the XML formats will replace the original formats. Large corporate users that have the original formats substantially deployed see little advantage in moving to XML formats, which, incidentally, have the disadvantage of being larger than the original formats and requiring more bandwidth and storage. However, XML-based EDI is expected to extend EDI capabilities to the many smaller users who could not previously afford them.

Open Internet Commerce

Pre-Internet EDI transactions typically required weeks of preparation between the transacting parties. This preparation included negotiating technical and administrative protocols and executing legal agreements.[46] The parties' electronic trade relationships generally entailed long-term, high-volume trading between familiar, if not primary, business partners; indeed, only this type of relationship could typically justify the high start-up costs of using EDI.

The Internet, however, facilitates one-time or short-term periodic relationships between transacting parties. The Web makes it easy to find buyers and sellers for goods and services and, increasingly, to provide efficient means for transacting business between them. E-mail can provide an excellent means of quickly negotiating business agreements and of communicating electronic counterparts of paper documents. In addition, new application protocols have emerged for purposes such as Internet-based electronic payments.[47]

This new e-commerce environment—sometimes known as *open* e-commerce—is characterized by Internet-based, ubiquitous commerce without prenegotiated, customized, bilateral or multilateral agreements. New approaches to contract negotiation suitable for this environment are still evolving. The dynamics and benefits of secure, open e-commerce are discussed further in chapter 3.

2.5   Example Transaction Scenarios

To assist in developing an understanding of Internet-based e-commerce, we present some example scenarios. These examples provide a foundation for later illustrations of technical and legal principles.

Scenario 1: Internet Procurement—Vera and Danielle

Vera, owner of Vera's Manufacturing, needs a new lathe. Instead of going to the local machine tool store, where the selection is mediocre and the prices somewhat uncompetitive, she decides to buy her lathe over the Internet. She does this using the Web as follows:

- On her Web browser, Vera initiates a search for lathes across diverse commercial sites.
- The search returns a list of Web sites with details and prices from competing vendors. After comparing these items, including checking the prices of comparable lathes being offered on an online public auction, Vera decides on a model offered by Danielle's Machine Makers. She then investigates the vendor electronically,[48] fills out the electronic order form, and transmits the order online to Danielle's.
- Danielle's Machine Makers checks that the order is indeed from Vera's Manufacturing[49] and confirms the order by returning an electronic invoice.

- Vera pays for the lathe using an online process supported by her browser, for example:

(a) sending her credit card account number to Danielle's (in encrypted form, to ensure its confidentiality);

(b) using an online payment mechanism, such as electronic cash or electronic check;[50] or

(c) sending a payment order message to instruct Vera's bank to credit Danielle's bank account and to pass remittance information (similar to the information contained on a check stub) to the vendor.

- Danielle's Machine Makers delivers the lathe to Vera's Manufacturing through conventional distribution channels and delivers the necessary software to operate the lathe directly via the Internet.

Scenario 2: Business-to-Business Trading—Danielle and Sharon

Danielle's Machine Makers is a medium-sized business based in Canada. Danielle's, whose largest resource requirement lies in high-grade steel, has a long-established trading arrangement with the leading multinational steel supplier, Sharon's Steelcorp, headquartered in the United States. These two corporations execute many transactions weekly.

Sharon's Steelcorp, with a view to reducing costs of trading with its many business customers, has decided to use e-mail-based e-commerce to support transactions with some of its more highly valued customers. As a result, Danielle's Machine Makers and Sharon's Steelcorp now perform most of their information exchanges via the public Internet.

However, ordinary e-mail presents too many risks, so the system used by Danielle's and Sharon's needs to incorporate the following safeguards:

- The originator of every message must be securely authenticated. For example, when anyone at Sharon's receives a message purportedly from anyone at Danielle's, the recipient can be certain of exactly who in Danielle's sent the message and can also be certain that Danielle's, the corporation, recognizes that person as an employee.

- All messages between the two organizations must be confidentiality-protected so that outsiders cannot learn what is being communicated between the two corporations.

Scenario 3: Internet Retailing—Nola and the Consumer

Nola is an entrepreneurial small-business owner who, from her home's basement, operates a large Internet shopping center, Nola's Electronic Market. Nola seeks out suppliers of quality products who are prepared to do business wholly electronically. She sells the products through a Web site that maximizes use of the latest technological gimmicks to attract customers. Due to effective marketing of her Web site on the Internet and through traditional media, Nola's endeavor is an amazing success. Her tiny overhead, high volume, and low margins make her a challenging competitor.

Buying a product from Nola involves a process similar to that followed by Vera in buying her lathe. Nola herself uses the Web and e-mail exclusively for all negotiations with and orders from her suppliers, who may be located anywhere in the world. Clearly, Nola faces some substantial risks because she has to deal with many customers and suppliers with whom she has no prior business relationship.

In the real world, the procedures used and their sequence may vary considerably from these example scenarios, depending upon the particular application, implementation, and prevailing business practices. Nevertheless, these scenarios will prove useful in illustrating the significance to e-commerce of security mechanisms, legal ground rules, and business controls.

2.6 Summary

A computer network provides the means for transferring data between systems that participate in distributed applications such as client-server applications. Computer networking depends upon network protocols, which are agreed-upon communication rules. Protocols are built in layers, such as the network layer, transport layer, and application layer.

The term *Internet* signifies both the global public computer network and a family of protocols that is used in that public network and in private networks. The Internet protocol suite is built upon the TCP transport-layer protocol and the IP network-layer protocol.

There are many Internet applications and associated application-layer protocols. Two key applications for e-commerce are the World Wide Web and electronic messaging. The Web is an advanced information-browsing client-server application that supports the delivery of hypermedia documents to users running client software called browsers. Hypermedia documents can contain multimedia information and can include hypertext references to other documents stored on the same or different servers. Electronic messaging allows a message originator to send a message (for example, personal e-mail) to one or more recipients via store-and-forward procedures through multiple intermediate server or gateway systems. The Multipurpose Internet Mail Extensions (MIME) specifications support the transfer of structured, multimedia messages.

The public Internet operates on a collaborative basis, with all members of the community cooperating to keep the network functioning. The Internet community includes users, Internet service providers, and certain infrastructural bodies such as the Internet Activities Board (IAB) and ICANN. The IAB is responsible for Internet standards and other aspects of Internet design, engineering, and management. ICANN is responsible for the stable operation of the Internet Domain Name System (DNS) and the allocation of the IP address space.

Internet e-commerce solutions can generally be classified as either business-to-consumer or business-to-business. Business-to-consumer e-commerce models include consumer marketing, Internet retailing, consumer portals, online auctions, and content aggregation/distribution. Business-to-business models include buy-side procurement, vertical communities, and market makers.

Pre-Internet business-to-business e-commerce was manifested predominantly as Electronic Data Interchange (EDI) transactions, usually via the services of an EDI value-added network (VAN) service provider. The Internet can be used to convey EDI traffic, but many of the roles of the traditional EDI VAN are now obsolete. In contrast to pre-Internet EDI, the Internet has opened up unbounded opportunities for *open e-commerce,* in which businesses can quickly locate new trading partners, negotiate business agreements, and transfer electronic equivalents of paper documents online.

In this chapter, we also introduced Vera's Manufacturing, Danielle's Machine Makers, Sharon's Steelcorp, and Nola's Electronic Market as example businesses that depend on the use of secure e-commerce. We shall build upon and use these examples throughout the remainder of the book.

Notes

1. For an introduction to computer networking for the uninitiated, we recommend A. S. Tanenbaum, *Computer Networks,* 3rd ed. (Upper Saddle River, NJ: Prentice Hall PTR, 1996) <http://www.phptr.com/ptrbooks/ptr_0133499456.html> or D. E. Comer and R. E. Droms, *Computer Networks and Internets,* 2nd ed. (Upper Saddle River, NJ: Prentice Hall PTR, 1999) <http://www.phptr.com/ptrbooks/esm_0130836176.html>.

2. Comer and Droms, *Computer Networks and Internets;* D. P. Dern, *Internet Business Handbook* (Upper Saddle River, NJ: Prentice Hall PTR, 2000) <http://www.phptr.com/ptrbooks/ptr_0131856200.html>; E. Hoffman and L. Jackson, *FYI on Introducing the Internet—A Short Bibliography of Introductory Internetworking Readings for the Network Novice,* Request for Comments (RFC) 1463 (Internet Activities Board, 1993) <ftp://ftp.isi.edu/in-notes/rfc1463.txt>.

3. See M. S. Baum et al.,"Survivability of the Defense Data Network," *Signal* 40, no. 9 (May 1986): 148–158.

4. Consequently, the Internet protocols are often referred to as the TCP/IP protocol suite.

5. M. Wahl, T. Howes, and S. Kille, *Lightweight Directory Access Protocol (v3),* RFC 2251, (Internet Activities Board, 1997) <ftp://ftp.isi.edu/in-notes/rfc2251.txt>; T. Howes, M. C. Smith, G. S. Wood, and T. A. Howes, *Understanding and Deploying LDAP Directory Services* (Indianapolis: Macmillan Technical, 1999) <http://www.mcp.com>.

6. For a general tutorial on VPN technologies, see N. Doraswamy and D. Harkins, *IPSec: The New Security Standard for the Internet, Intranets, and Virtual Private Networks* (Upper Saddle River, NJ: Prentice Hall PTR, 1999) <http://vig.prenhall.com/acadbookpage?ISBN=0130118982>.

7. T. Berners-Lee, M. Fischetti, and M. Dertouzos, *Weaving the Web: The Original Design and Ultimate Destiny of the World Wide Web by Its Inventor* (San Francisco: Harper, 1999).

8. T. Berners-Lee, *Universal Resource Identifiers in WWW,* RFC 1630 (Internet Activities Board, 1993) <ftp://ftp.isi.edu/in-notes/rfc1630.txt>.

9. In this book, URLs are enclosed in angle brackets, e.g., <http://www.prenhall.com>. Readers are cautioned that URLs become obsolete sporadically; therefore, despite our care in selecting appropriate URLs, some may become obsolete by the time you read this book.

10. For a detailed overview of XML, see R. Anderson et al., *Professional XML* (Birmingham, U.K.: Wrox Press, 2000) <http://www.wrox.com>.

11. G. McComb, M. Bower, M. Robinson, *Web Programming Languages Source-book* (New York: John Wiley, 1997) <http://www.wiley.com>.

12. J. Meyers and M. Rose, *Post Office Protocol—Version 3,* RFC 1725 (Internet Activities Board, 1994) <ftp://ftp.isi.edu/in-notes/rfc1725.txt>.

13. J. B. Postel, *Simple Mail Transfer Protocol,* RFC 821 (Internet Activities Board, 1982) <ftp://ftp.isi.edu/in-notes/rfc821.txt>.

14. D. H. Crocker, *Standard for the Format of ARPA Internet Text Messages,* RFC 822 (Internet Activities Board, 1982) <ftp://ftp.isi.edu/in-notes/rfc822.txt>.

15. N. Freed and N. Borenstein, *Multipurpose Internet Mail Extensions (MIME) Part One: Format of Internet Message Bodies,* RFC 2045 (Internet Activities Board, 1996) <ftp://ftp.isi.edu/in-notes/rfc2045.txt>.

16. These message components are called *body parts.* Do not be alarmed if you encounter this term in MIME specifications!

17. For comprehensive tutorial coverage of the Internet electronic messaging protocols, see M. T. Rose and D. Strom, *Internet Messaging: From the Desktop to the Enterprise* (Upper Saddle River, NJ: Prentice Hall PTR, 1998) <http://www.phptr.com/ptrbooks/ptr_01397861040.html>.

18. However, nothing has prevented governments from trying. Indeed, the Internet is sometimes described as the most regulated network because each jurisdiction claims to exercise at least some control over it—often in a mutually exclusive manner.

19. The term *ERP* denotes a broad range of business applications including, for example, accounting, inventory, logistics, procurement, strategic planning, and human resources management.

20. V. Cerf, *The Internet Activities Board,* RFC 1160 (Internet Activities Board, 1990) <ftp://ftp.isi.edu/in-notes/rfc1160.txt>.

21. L. Chapin, *The Internet Standards Process,* RFC 1310 (Internet Activities Board, 1992) <ftp://ftp.isi.edu/in-notes/rfc1310.txt>.

22. For more information on the Internet standardization process and how to participate in it, refer to <http://www.ietf.org>.

23. To obtain online copies of Internet RFCs, see <http://www.ietf.org/rfc.html>.

24. To obtain online copies of Internet-Drafts, see the IETF Web site at <http://www.ietf.org>. The list of current Internet-Drafts can be accessed at <http://www.ietf.org/ietf/1id-abstracts.txt>. The list of Internet-Draft mirror directories can be accessed at <http://www.ietf.org/shadow.html>.

25. See discussion of Platform for Privacy Preferences (P3P) in chapter 5.

26. For information on the World Wide Web Consortium, see the W3C Web site at <http://www.w3.org>.

27. For information on obtaining copies of ISO/IEC standards, access the ISO Web site at <http://www.iso.ch>. For information on obtaining copies of ITU Recommendations, access the ITU Web site at <http://www.itu.ch>.

28. For example, the name "prenhall" as used in "www.prenhall.com" is assigned to Prentice Hall.

29. P. Albitz and C. Liu, *DNS and Bind* (Sebastopol, CA: O'Reilly & Associates, 1998) <http://www.oreilly.com/catalog/dns3>.

30. The White Paper, titled "Management of Internet Names and Addresses," is available at: <http://www.ntia.doc.gov/ntiahome/domainname/domainhome.htm#3>.

31. Information regarding the U.S. government's efforts to privatize the management of the Domain Name System and increase competition in domain name registration services is available at <http://www.ntia.doc.gov>.

32. For information on ICANN, see <http://www.icann.org>.

33. See ICANN's Statement of Registrar Accreditation Policy at <http://www.icann.org/policy_statement.html>.

34. R. Pethia, S. Crocker, and B. Fraser, *Guidelines for the Secure Operation of the Internet,* RFC 1281 (Internet Activities Board, 1991) <ftp://ftp.isi.edu/in-notes/rfc1281.txt>.

35. Extensive security-related resources are available at the CERT Coordination Center Web site, <http://www.cert.org>.

36. Also, the bandwidth and processing resource constraints in the wireless environment present some challenges in the use of technologies that traditionally aid security, including cryptographic techniques. This subject is discussed further in chapter 5.

37. For information on the WAP Forum, see <http://www.wapforum.org>.

38. An example of such an auction site is that operated by eBay, Inc., <http://www.ebay.com>.

39. An example is the Travelocity travel booking service, <http://www.traveloc-ity.com>, which is rebranded and resold through other sites, such as Yahoo!, <http://www.yahoo.com/>.

40. A.J. Marcella, Jr., and S. Chan, *EDI Security, Control, and Audit* (Boston: Artech House, 1993) <http://www.ncsa.com/catalog/is127.html>. The original EDI standards were initially developed in the late 1970s under the auspices of the Transportation Data Coordinating Committee (TDCC).

41. The Automobile Industry Action Group (AIAG), <http//:www.aiag.org>, pio-neered the deployment of EDI in the automobile industry.

42. For information on X12 standards, refer to <http://www.disa.org>.

43. United Nations Economic Commission (UN/EC), *Electronic Data Interchange for Administration, Commerce and Transport-Application Level Syntax Rules* (ISO 9735) (UN/EC, 1991) <http://www.unece.org/cefact>.

44. D. Crocker, *MIME Encapsulation of EDI Objects,* RFC 1767 (Internet Activi-ties Board, 1995) <ftp://ftp.isi.edu/in-notes/rfc1767.txt>.

45. For further information on using the Internet for EDI, see W. Houser, J. Griffin, and C. Hage, *EDI Meets the Internet: Frequently Asked Questions about Elec-tronic Data Interchange (EDI) on the Internet,* RFC 1865 (Internet Activities Board, 1996) <ftp://ftp.isi.edu/in-notes/rfc1865.txt>.

46. See *Forms of Agreement* in appendix A.

47. See section 5.8.

48. An electronic investigation can take many forms, including inquiring into an Internet *Better Business Bureau,* checking the vendor's use of and compliance to various business practice *seal programs,* consulting various industry-specific e-mail lists for user recommendations, and using credit reporting or company profile services.

49. In chapter 4 we introduce the concept of a *digital signature,* an ideal mecha-nism for facilitating such checks.

50. Using a credit card payment mechanism may give Vera certain advantages, including favorable dispute resolution options.

Business and Legal Principles

Any commercial transaction involves the parties' communicating the information that forms an agreement. This information must include identification of the parties, the essential terms and conditions, and the respective assent of the parties to those terms and conditions. Unless the parties can rely on the authenticity of such communications, the parties cannot be confident that they have created an enforceable agreement. In conducting traditional (paper-based) commerce, transacting parties have developed legally recognized practices, such as the use of writings, signatures, and seals, which typically provide ample assurances of authenticity.

In an e-commerce transaction, one or more of the essential elements of the bargain (identity, terms, and assent) are communicated electronically. As with traditional commerce, there is a compelling need for assurances of authenticity. *Secure* e-commerce implicates the technologies and business practices that provide assurances of authenticity and other relevant attributes of security. Rule-making bodies globally are fashioning rules to promote e-commerce reliability and, in so doing, are grappling with the role and required use of information security mechanisms.

This chapter presents foundational material upon which following chapters will draw. For the benefit of readers without a legal background, this chapter first explains the basics of contract and evidence law and their applicability to the creation and enforcement of binding commitments in e-commerce. It will be seen how the current state of the law presents some uncertainties in relation to the formation and enforcement of digital transactions. The chapter then discusses recent efforts to reduce remaining legal uncertainties.

The chapter concludes by discussing the operation of e-commerce within the purview of two business-legal models that illustrate the risk and uncertainty that digital transactions can present.

3.1 The Electronic Commerce Transaction

In most respects, e-commerce transactions are conceptually identical to traditional, paper-based counterparts. Vendors present their products or services for sale to prospective buyers at certain prices and on certain terms and conditions. In an auction scenario, vendors present their products or services for sale and permit prospective buyers to propose prices, or buyers indicate a desire to purchase a product or service and permit prospective vendors to submit bids.[1] Buyers consider their options, negotiate (where possible) the prices and terms, place orders, and make payment. Then vendors deliver the ordered products to the buyers. Although the sequence of these events and the mechanisms through which they are transacted vary, in principle these activities are fundamental to both traditional and e-commerce methods.

Nevertheless, because of the ways in which it differs from traditional commerce, e-commerce raises some new and interesting technical and legal challenges, including these:

- Satisfying traditional legal requirements for reduction of agreements to signed writings
- Applying legal rules of evidence to computer-based information
- Interpreting, adapting, and complying with many other existing legal standards in the context of electronic transactions

One of the most significant legal issues in e-commerce is how to create electronic contracts for the sale of goods and services that will be at least as *enforceable* as their traditional paper-based analogs.[2] In every business environment, whether transactions are executed in person or remotely over distance, there are accepted customs and understandings that, in conjunction with applicable legal rules, determine with relative certainty the parties' rights and responsibilities. These practices often include controls, such as

- Signatures, to evidence agreements

- Time- and date-stamping, to provide proof of dispatch, submission, delivery, receipt, or acceptance
- In some cases, witnesses, notaries, or other *trusted third parties,* to acknowledge and authenticate transactions

These traditional controls help create legal certainty in business transactions. While sometimes founded upon complex legal theories, these controls are familiar to the business community. Legal rules established in the pre-electronic world mean that transactions employing these controls are more likely to be enforceable.

Although e-commerce is expanding rapidly, the development of a corresponding legal and control infrastructure has lagged behind.[3] Viable electronic analogs to traditional contracting are necessary to support e-commerce. It is important to prevent discrimination against e-commerce transactions and to make such transactions at least as efficient, secure, and legally binding as traditional transactions, without necessarily requiring users to negotiate customized terms and conditions. These e-commerce controls must be understood in terms of both requirements and corresponding effect.

3.2 Creating a Binding Commitment

At the heart of an e-commerce transaction is the intention—indeed, the critical need—to form a legally binding agreement between the transacting parties. In this chapter, we introduce the legal principles of contract and evidence and examine their relevance to e-commerce transactions.[4]

Functional Equivalence

The first question concerning the law of electronic contracts is what legal rules govern their formation, interpretation, and enforcement. For the most part, parties to e-commerce transactions have worked within the system of traditional contract law, promoting incremental adjustments to stretch and bend existing legal principles to fit new business practices. Most of the numerous legislative initiatives promoted in jurisdictions worldwide fall into this incremental category. This trend is likely to continue, with certain exceptions, for two reasons: first, technology most often outpaces the law—legal regimes are by nature primarily reactive—and second, e-commerce has enough in common with traditional business that the basic principles of contract and evidence law, with proper guidance, can usually be molded to accommodate digital transactions and govern them efficiently and appropriately.

However, there are important differences between electronic and traditional commerce. For example, electronic transactions diminish the necessity of relying on paper records to document a transaction. Electronic transactions also diminish the role of human participation (and corresponding availability of witnesses to testify as to certain details) in such transactions. Nevertheless, these variances do not overcome the underlying functional equivalence[5] between the major goals of each type of transaction: both involve parties coming together to buy or sell goods or services, both involve payment and delivery, and both involve the intent of parties to create an enforceable agreement. These functional similarities justify the prevailing approach of modest, incremental adjustments to traditional principles in order to accommodate many aspects of e-commerce while simultaneously addressing with more aggressive legal treatment certain isolated technical and business processes that can vary considerably from traditional methods.[6]

Sources of Law

The law that governs the validity and enforceability of a contract depends on the choice-of-law rules of the jurisdiction in which an agreement's formation is formally disputed.[7] Generally, in contract disputes, unless it can be shown that the parties agreed otherwise, choice-of-law rules[8] mandate that the law of the place where the contract was "formed" governs.[9] Due to the inherent uncertainty in many e-commerce transactions regarding exactly "where" an agreement may have been entered into (that is, what physical jurisdiction can competently claim to own the "cyberspace" in which the agreement was struck), it is highly advisable for parties in an e-commerce transaction to agree explicitly on the following items in the contract:

- A governing law (e.g., "the laws of the State of California, U.S.A., without reference to its choice of law provisions"[10])
- A forum for resolution of any dispute that arises (for example, the courts of a certain specified jurisdiction or an agreed-upon alternative dispute resolution mechanism)

The fundamental law of Anglo-American jurisdictions is the *common law*, the collection of legal principles developed by the respective English, U.S., and other common-law courts in reaction to cases presented before them.[11] Superimposed on the common law are statutes enacted by legislatures, both at the state and national level. An important example of such a model statute in the United States is the *Uniform Commercial Code* (UCC).[12] Other relevant model statutes, such as the United Nations (UN) Model Law on Electronic Commerce,[13] the Uniform Electronic Transactions Act (UETA),[14] and the Uniform Computer Information Transactions Act (UCITA),[15] once adopted by a jurisdiction, would also supplement or take precedence over the common law in certain respects. Regulations promulgated by governmental agencies and authorized by statute often are meant to implement statutory law.[16]

In non-Anglo-American jurisdictions, statutory codes, as opposed to court-made law, often serve as the set of fundamental rules and background law. These jurisdictions are generally referred to as following the "civil law" model.

In both common and civil law systems, statutes and other legal rules assign legal significance to both the *course of dealing* between parties over time and to the generally accepted and followed practices of the trade (*usage of trade*).[17] Moreover, with certain exceptions, the parties themselves have the autonomy to agree on principles to govern their own relationship, which may differ from statute and common law. This approach ought to be undertaken and emphasized particularly where the law would otherwise be ambiguous or uncertain.[18] Accordingly, where parties to e-commerce deal frequently with the same trading partners, they will often enter into *trading partner agreements* (TPAs), which establish ground rules for current and future dealings between themselves.[19] When parties deal with infrequent or one-time business partners (including consumers), as is becoming increasingly common over the Web, they should also formalize the important aspects of their legal relationship. Nevertheless, the practical limitation on negotiation in such instances urges the enactment of legislation or the establishment and recognition of systemwide rules or trade practices.[20] The set of laws and rules governing a transaction may be summarized generally as follows, and any inconsistency between them will, with certain exceptions,[21] be resolved in favor of the higher set of:

- Pertinent laws and regulations, such as the UCC and other legislative and administrative enactments
- The civil code of the jurisdiction or the common law, as applicable

- Provisions of the agreement between the parties[22]
- Course of dealing between the parties[23]
- Accepted trade practices in the applicable field of commerce[24]

The international business and legal community is striving to resolve a range of e-commerce issues by

- Promulgating model laws and rules such as the UN Model Law on Electronic Commerce and the draft UN Model Law on Electronic Signatures internationally, the Directive on a Community Framework for Electronic Signatures in Europe (the EU Directive),[25] and the UETA and UCITA, both promulgated by the National Conference of Commissioners on Uniform State Laws (NCCUSL) and the Federal E-Sign Law in the United States[26]
- Advancing legislation and regulation in individual jurisdictions based (in whole or in part) on these model laws and rules

In this chapter, we focus primarily on the U.S. legal regime. While U.S. legal principles may not necessarily apply elsewhere, the basic concepts of law discussed are typical of most Western legal systems, both common and civil, and the e-commerce issues addressed generally apply to U.S. and non-U.S. regimes alike.

3.3   Validity and Enforceability of Agreements

An agreement between parties is legally *valid* if it satisfies the requirements of applicable law regarding its formation; that is, primarily, the parties intended by their actions to create a contract. This intention is evidenced by compliance with the three classic cornerstones of a contract:

- an *offer* of specific terms,
- *acceptance* of the offer, and
- adequate *consideration* (payment) for the performance of the agreement.

Notwithstanding the actual validity of an agreement, a party may be unable to *enforce* a contract unless certain other requirements (where applicable) have been satisfied, such as the statute of frauds, which is described later in this chapter.[27]

Offer and Acceptance

The bargaining process must generate two essential items in order to produce a valid contract: (1) *mutual assent* as an expression of the parties' intent to contract and (2) sufficiently *definite terms*.[28] In arriving at such mutual assent and definite terms, the parties employ the mechanics of offer and acceptance. In most circumstances, the contract process is initiated by an offer. An offer is "a manifestation of assent to enter into a bargain made by the offeror to the offeree, conditional upon a manifestation of assent in the form of some action (promise or performance) by the offeree." Offers contain conditional promises that must be accepted by a return promise (such as to sell or to purchase) or a unilateral act.[29] The existence of a conditional promise is what separates an offer from an advertisement, price quotation, or from providing information as part of preliminary negotiations. In example scenario 1 (in section 2.5) involving Vera's purchase of a lathe from Danielle's Machine Makers, Vera would be the offeree, Danielle's Machine Makers would be the offeror, and Danielle's listing of product information and prices and solicitation of orders would constitute the offer. An acceptance is "the action (promise or performance) by the offeree that creates a contract." Vera's completion and transmission of the online order form would constitute such acceptance.

Notice that in Vera's case there is demonstrable human involvement in the assent to the agreement, particularly with respect to her acceptance. In contrast, doubts about legal validity might arise in connection with the issue of *assent* (the process of offer and acceptance) in the example of a retailer's computerized inventory system that automatically places an order for a specific item when data compiled from point-of-sale terminals indicate that inventory is low.

Jurisdictions adopting UETA could resolve uncertainty in such cases involving automated transactions without direct human intervention, because section 14 of UETA on automated transactions expressly provides that the interaction of electronic agents, or of an electronic agent of one party and an individual representing the other party, can result in a valid contract. Similarly, UCITA provides that a "contract may be formed by the interaction of electronic agents" and that a "person that uses an electronic agent . . . is bound by the operations of the electronic agent, even if no individual was aware of or reviewed the agent's operations. . . . "[30] Pending the adoption of any of these (or similar) statutory provisions, courts can simply impute assent in certain cases from the original human involvement in the programming of systems. Also, trading partner agreements may be executed that satisfy assent requirements. Such questions implicate the laws of "agency" and the issue of whether a person's computer can be that person's "agent," having legal authority to act on that person's behalf.[31]

In an electronic transaction without the interposition of human interaction, both the offeree and the offeror must assent to the agreement contemporaneously. In all transactions, electronic and otherwise, the timing and legal effectiveness of the offers, acceptances, and any revocations thereof affect the formation of a valid contract. Where both parties are in each other's presence, the timing of the offer and acceptance and the existence of any revocations are less in doubt. Section 64 of *The Restatement (Second) of Contracts* provides that "[a]cceptance given by telephone or other medium of substantially instantaneous two-way communication is governed by the principles applicable to acceptances where the parties are in the presence of each other." To qualify for this treatment, a medium of communication must be capable of "prompt, reliable verification that a message has been received, and that it has been received intact and without communication errors."[32] The purpose of such techniques is the verification that the receiving party has had legally sufficient notice that an offer or acceptance has been made. Various e-commerce systems certainly can satisfy this requirement, but delayed or store-and-forward communications such as e-mail may not.

A rule such as that set forth in section 64 of *The Restatement (Second) of Contracts* addresses problems with the so-called *mailbox rule*—the legal principle typically applied in cases where parties do not use a substantially simultaneous communications medium.[33] The mailbox rule hinges legal effectiveness on the time of dispatch, as opposed to the time of receipt, resulting in various anomalies. For example, an offeror may be bound by an acceptance he or she never received or by an acceptance mailed prior to a revocation of the offer. Although to date no court has explicitly applied section 64 to an e-commerce transaction, the trend of legal developments certainly points in that direction.[34] Jurisdictions adopting UCITA (or parties electing agreements to be governed by UCITA) eliminate uncertainty in this regard in transactions relating to digital information: Section 203 of UCITA provides that "[i]f an offer in an electronic message evokes an electronic message accepting the offer, a contract is formed: (A) when an electronic acceptance is received; or (B) if the response consists of beginning performance, full performance, or giving access to information, when the performance is received or the access is enabled and necessary access materials are received."

Not only must both parties to a contract assent to the agreement, but their assent must be to definite, specific terms,[35] and the acceptance must "mirror" the offer.[36] Acceptances that fail to mirror offers in any significant manner may be considered new offers or counteroffers. These counteroffers may be in the form of a writing or a nonconforming tender of goods. In conventional contracting, because both vendors and purchasers frequently use their own standardized invoices and order forms, the mechanics of offer and acceptance often boil down to a *battle of the forms* in which each party sends its own form with terms that may conflict with those of the other party's form.[37] To avoid needless hindrance of commerce, the UCC allows a contract to exist, notwithstanding nonmaterial disparities, and resolves differences in terms in favor of the offeror's form.[38] Some early commentators claimed that e-commerce would result in the obsolescence of such a rule because of its elimination of paper forms.[39] This has not proved to be true so far since e-commerce participants, particularly those without an ongoing relationship, tend to use their own standardized digital invoices and order forms, which simply result in a *digital battle of the forms.* Nevertheless, under current law, parties to e-commerce should be prepared to rely on the terms of the offeror's form or to establish other ground rules through specific provisions.[40]

Consideration

A valid contract also requires that the parties bargain for *consideration.* Consideration may consist of either actual performance, such as delivery of goods or services or payment for them, or a return promise.[41] Although e-commerce may involve novel methods of payment[42] and delivery, as long as a transaction includes a bargained-for exchange of adequately commensurate promises or performances, regardless of the manner of performance, the agreement will comply with the consideration requirement.

Statutes of Frauds

Although a valid contract may be established through oral offer and acceptance, courts in the United States and certain other jurisdictions typically do not enforce certain types of agreements unless they satisfy the statute of frauds.[43] For agreements of these types to be enforceable, the legal requirement that "the agreement . . . , or memorandum or note thereof, shall be in writing, and signed by the party to be charged therewith" must be satisfied.[44] The typical statute of frauds requires a writing and signature for the following classes of contracts, among others:[45]

- Contracts of an executor or administrator to answer for a duty of his or her decedent
- Suretyship contracts
- Contracts made upon consideration of marriage
- Contracts for the sale of interests in land
- Contracts that are not to be performed within one year from the making thereof
- Contracts for the sale of goods for the price of $500 or more.[46]

Moreover, thousands of other statutes in federal, state, and local jurisdictions in the United States also require (or are interpreted to require) certain types of transactions to be memorialized by writings and signatures.[47] Thus, if an electronic transaction falls into one of the classes covered by a statute of frauds or other statute requiring written documentation, parties seeking to create a binding contract must comply with the writing and signature requirements.

With respect to the writing requirement, the key issue is whether electronic communications constitute written material for the purposes of the applicable statute of frauds or other analogous legal rule. The current UCC defines writing to include "printing, typewriting, or any other intentional reduction to tangible form."[48] This implies that other forms of communication might suffice. The fact that courts in the past have held that new modes of communication, such as telegraph and fax, satisfy the writing requirement suggests that courts will be similarly willing to adapt the law to digital media.[49] A broader interpretation of the law may be required than was necessary for the novel media of the past since e-commerce, unlike telegraphs and fax machines, does not necessarily involve a "tangible form."[50] Nonetheless, we expect that the legal sufficiency of digital media will be sustained increasingly, assuming the widespread adoption of digital techniques and the production of a tangible record at any point when it becomes necessary.[51] In fact, at least one U.S. court to date has now ruled that Web-based contracts satisfy the "writing" requirement.[52] Courts may be similarly flexible, as they have been in the past for new modes of communication,[53] about signature requirements.[54] *The Restatement (Second) of Contracts,* section 134, provides that a signature may be "any symbol made or adopted with an intention, actual or apparent, to authenticate the writing as that of the signer." The current UCC defines *signed* to include "any symbol executed or adopted by a party with present intention to authenticate a writing."[55] Several possibilities might satisfy these definitions: answer-backs, use of network access codes, message headers, the sender's typed name at the close of a message, a digitized image of the sender's holographic signature at the close of a message, and digital signatures. A *digital signature* is a cryptographic-based mechanism that allows the recipient of a digitally signed message to determine the originator of that message and to confirm that the message has not been altered since being signed by that originator. This mechanism, the operation of which depends on the originator having sole possession of a secret data value called a *private key,* is described in detail in chapter 4. As discussed elsewhere in this book, *digital* signatures are a subset of *electronic* signatures.

Based on the legislative momentum of the last few years, the recognition and enforceability of electronic transactions does not only depend on the generous interpretations of courts. The U.S. federal government was among the first rule makers to recognize the validity of digital transactions involving federal procurement when the Office of the U.S. Comptroller General stated in 1991 that "[c]ontracts formed using Electronic Data Interchange technologies may constitute valid obligations of the government for purposes of 31 U.S.C. sec. 1501, so long as the technology used provides the same degree of assurance and certainty as traditional 'paper and ink' methods of contract formation."[56] The Government Paperwork Elimination Act, passed by Congress in 1998, permits federal agencies to make filings and submissions electronically "when practicable as a substitute for paper" and to use electronic authentication methods to verify the identity and integrity of such filings and submissions.[57] Additionally, the Electronic Signatures in Global and National Commerce Act (E-Sign) passed in 2000, further eliminates traditional legal barriers to e-commerce.[58]

UNCITRAL's efforts have also provided jurisdictions a model for the legal effectiveness of digital communications with respect to writings and signatures: the UN Model Law on Electronic Commerce, articles 5-7. Furthermore, most U.S. states have adopted legal reforms providing for the effectiveness of "electronic signatures"[59] and electronic communications as signatures and writings,[60] including legislation giving, in varying circumstances, a communication that is "digitally signed" the same legal validity "as if it had been written on paper."[61] In addition, both UETA (section 7) and UCITA (section 107) expressly provide for the legal recognition of electronic records and electronic signatures. The European Parliament has adopted a Directive, which requires EU member countries to ensure (1) that electronic signatures are not denied legal effectiveness or admissibility as evidence on the grounds that they are in electronic form (section 5.2) and (2) that "advanced electronic signatures" (electronic signatures uniquely linked to the signing party and possessing other enhanced security features) are in fact given as much legal effect and evidentiary weight as a "handwritten signature" on "paper-based data" [sections 5.1 and 2(2)].[62]

Provisions of the UCC Draft Revisions adopt the terms *record* instead of *writing*[63] and *authenticate* instead of *sign.*[64] These incremental changes in the UCC, if adopted, would bring digital documents further into legal compliance with the statute of frauds for the sale of goods. Another approach, one that the UCC Drafting Committee has debated in recent years, would simply repeal the statute of frauds.[65] In 1994, the UCC drafters repealed the statute of frauds in article 8 of the UCC relating to investment securities.[66] Repeal of the statute of frauds with respect to the sale of goods would be consistent with current law in England and various other jurisdictions and with the provisions of the UN Convention on Contracts for the International Sale of Goods (CISG), the principal treaty governing the international sale of goods.[67]

Accordingly, the combination of judicial acceptance of new technology, the development of trade usage, and legislative and administrative enactments suggests that electronically formed agreements will be found to constitute enforceable contracts for most statute-of-frauds purposes and under other similar legal requirements for writings and signatures. Nonetheless, given the varying applicability of legislation and regulation in different jurisdictions and situations, the lack of uniformity among these initiatives tends to leave e-commerce participants with some lingering uncertainty, particularly in the case of transactions involving parties in different jurisdictions. Therefore, until legislation and trade practices become sufficiently uniform and widespread in the jurisdictions in which they contract and otherwise conduct business, parties who desire greater certainty should execute written trading partner and other e-commerce agreements, thus establishing more concrete rules.[68]

Performance

Once a valid agreement has been reached, it is the duty of all parties to the contract to fulfill their respective end of the bargain; their efforts (and obligations to do so) are termed *performance.* For example, with Vera's lathe purchase, performance by the vendor, Danielle's Machine Makers, entails delivery of the lathe ordered by Vera, and payment by the purchaser, Vera, constitutes performance on her part. Performance by both sides is, of course, what the parties have bargained for—obtaining performance is their object in forming the valid and enforceable contract. Thus, when one party, in the absence of some permitted excuse,[69] fails to meet the legal requirements for satisfactory performance, there is a *breach* of the contract, and the nonbreaching party may have certain remedial rights against the breaching party.

In electronic transactions such as Vera's, performance does not necessarily involve digital media—Danielle's sends an *actual* lathe through *traditional* distribution channels (a *virtual* lathe does Vera no good), and Vera could, if she so desired (and if not precluded by contract with Danielle's), mail a check as her payment. Nonetheless, performance in many e-commerce transactions involves electronic media, especially in the payments process or where the contract is for the provision of online services such as access to information or download of software. Download of software and the access of billed information resources are examples of performance that can be completed without human mediation (beyond the initial programming).[70]

Compliance

Theoretically, a party's failure to perform completely and strictly in accordance with the terms of an agreement constitutes a breach of contract. Indeed, with respect to the sale of goods, the law has historically embraced the *perfect tender* rule, a standard entitling a buyer to reject goods unless the seller complies strictly with both quality and quantity provisions of a bargain.[71] Nevertheless, where one party has *substantially* performed in good faith, it would frequently be unfair to force that party to forfeit all of his or her efforts simply because he or she has not fully complied with the contract.[72] Thus, contract law softens the harshness of the perfect tender rule (or exact compliance) in some situations. For example, under the UCC, a buyer who chooses to retain a shipment of goods that does not strictly conform in quality or quantity waives his or her right to revoke such acceptance unless "the non-conformity *substantially* impairs" the value of the goods to the buyer.[73]

Breach

As stated earlier, a party's failure to perform as agreed results in a breach of contract. This includes both failure to perform substantially according to the terms of the contract once the time for performance has arrived and the refusal to perform even before the time for performance has arrived (termed *anticipatory repudiation*). Depending on the nature of the breach, a contract may be void on its face, voidable by the nonbreaching party, or severable, meaning that certain terms might be voided without affecting the validity of others. In a case of anticipatory breach, if the non-repudiating party has fulfilled its end of the bargain, the result is a total breach, giving the non-repudiating party various rights, including the right to terminate the contract and make claims for damages.[74]

3.4 Enforcement

A fundamental objective of contract law is to protect a party who accepts a promise in a properly formed agreement from injury as a result of a breach by the party who makes the promise. Accordingly, the law affords nonbreaching parties various avenues of recourse to enforce their rights under the contract. To take advantage of these remedies, a party who has been or stands to be injured as the result of a breach must be able to *prove* the injury and the damages that flow therefrom under the applicable rules of evidence. This section discusses the *liability* and *damages* a party might face for breach of contract and then addresses several rules of evidence that are particularly significant for the enforcement of e-commerce contracts.

Liability and Damages

A party who breaches an agreement may face various types of liability under contract law. In contracts for the sale of unique goods or other unique property, a plaintiff is typically entitled to *specific performance* of the contract by the defendant.[75] An award of specific performance requires a court order demanding the defendant to deliver the specific, contracted-for goods or services to the plaintiff. Because specific performance is an extraordinary remedy, the capability to accurately identify the person whose specific performance is demanded and the goods or other property that are the subject of the broken bargain is essential.

While various methods are used to set a proper amount of damages depending on the nature of the breach, the goal of the law is generally to either restore the injured party to its precontract position (*restitution*) or place the injured party in the economic position it would have been in had the contract been performed (*expectation* approach).[76] This may include an award of *incidental* or *consequential* damages to compensate for expenses or losses attributable to the breach.[77] Where a breach is committed in *bad faith* or through otherwise willful and malicious conduct, a court may award *punitive* damages.[78] Parties may limit their exposure to liability for damages for breach of contract by agreeing to clauses that *liquidate* or otherwise limit (or *cap*) the amount of damages a party would be entitled to receive upon breach by the other.[79]

Due to the dynamics of the systems and networks that businesses employ to conduct e-commerce, parties may find themselves liable for contracts that technically originated with them but, due to programming error, employee mistake, or deliberate misconduct, were executed and released unintentionally and without authority. Sound policy dictates that parties receiving messages be able to rely on the legal expressions of assent and authority from the sender's computer and thus be able legally to *attribute* these messages to the sender.[80]

The potential for liability due to statutory provisions establishing legal attribution (or case law analogs under the law of agency) provides additional incentive for e-commerce participants to employ adequate security measures. In addition to employing information security mechanisms and other technical and logical controls, techniques for limiting exposure to liability include[81]

- use of trading partner and operating agreements;
- compliance with recognized practices, procedures, and guidelines;
- satisfaction of appropriate audit and control objectives, programs, and reviews;
- accreditation or licensing;
- proper human resources management;
- demonstration of technical competence;
- insurance; and
- enhanced notice, disclosure, and warning mechanisms.

Many of these techniques are addressed later in this book.

Evidence

Rights and remedies are meaningless in the real world unless they can be enforced. Enforcement of a contract[82] requires that a party prove, in accordance with the rules of evidence, that a contract existed, what its terms were, how it was breached, and to what extent such party was damaged. For the contents of a document to be admissible in court, it must comply with several evidentiary rules, including (1) the rule of *authentication,* (2) the *hearsay* rule, and (3) the *best-evidence* rule. Both courts and rule-making bodies are currently attempting to apply these rules to computer-based and other digital information. UETA, for example, provides that "evidence of a record or signature may not be excluded because it is in electronic form."[83] Both the EU Directive (article 5) and the UN Model Law on Electronic Commerce (article 9) also provide expressly for the admissibility into evidence of electronically signed communications. However, until there is greater confidence that established legal rules are adequate to provide certainty of the evidentiary value of digital records, relevant provisions in trading partner agreements and other contracts that establish evidentiary rules between the parties are advisable.[84]

A precondition to the admissibility of a record in litigation is its authentication, a requirement that is satisfied by "evidence sufficient to support a finding that the matter in question is what its proponent claims."[85] Digital agreements, invoices and related electronic mail, and other digital communications must be authenticated in two respects: (1) their source and (2) the accuracy of their storage, retrieval, and printing or other visual display.[86] Although perceptions in the early days of e-commerce that "electronic files are particularly susceptible to purposeful or accidental alteration, or incorrect processing"[87] have generally been tempered, authentication of digital evidence may sometimes require a higher level of foundational proof than traditional evidence or, more likely, may require that counsel educate the judge or arbitrator regarding the strong probative value of digital evidence.[88]

Authentication of a document's source is clearly related to the issue of compliance with the signature requirement discussed earlier. Methods for authenticating electronic documents are discussed in chapter 4. Such authentication methods may require a trusted third-party record keeper.[89] As discussed in chapters 6 and 9, the use of certification authorities and notaries[90] in conjunction with certificate-based digital signatures can enhance authentication.

A party seeking to prove the contents of a digital record must not only establish the source of the record, but also demonstrate that the current state of the record is accurate and has a proper *chain of custody,* that is, its systems of receipt, storage, retrieval, and display do not result in deviations from the original message.[91] A typical standard that governs such a demonstration of accuracy for computer records is codified in U.S. Federal Rule of Evidence 901(9): "Evidence describing a process or system used to produce a result and showing that the process or system produces an accurate result." This standard requires that the party demonstrate the reliability of the hardware and software used, the methods of storage and retrieval, and the measures taken to ensure the integrity of the system.

Under Federal Rule of Evidence 902, certain types of documents or records do not require extrinsic evidence to authenticate. These *self-authenticating* documents include official publications, public documents, newspapers and periodicals, and acknowledged documents. Electronic records with digital signatures may possess at least as much protection as these documents with respect to data integrity. Legal reforms should ultimately provide that certain digitally signed documents are self-authenticating under Rule 902. In any event, e-commerce participants must employ business controls, including adequate security measures, designed to prove the integrity of their transactions.

According to the best-evidence rule, where there is any genuine concern regarding the authenticity of a "writing, recording, or photograph," its content can be proved only by production of the "original."[92] Federal Rule of Evidence 1001(3), which defines "original," provides that "[i]f data are stored in a computer or similar device, any printout or other output readable by sight, shown to reflect the data accurately, is an 'original.'"[93] Again, as with the authentication issue, questions may arise as to the integrity of the system and its ability to store, recall, and print out or display an accurate version of the record.[94] Parties should employ business practices, including adequate security measures (as discussed throughout this book), designed to prove reliability.

According to Federal Rules of Evidence 801, 802, and 803, *hearsay* is an out-of-court statement "offered in evidence to prove the truth of the matter asserted." Hearsay is not admissible unless specifically allowed under one of the listed exceptions to this rule. Accordingly, electronic messages or other digital communications regarding a party's understanding of contract terms or other relevant issues are not admissible in a case involving a breach of contract unless they can be shown to fall under such an exception. Most communications of this type, however, have the potential to be considered "records of regularly conducted activity," which are admissible under what is often referred to as the "business records exception."[95] Case law confirms that computer data compilations are indeed admissible as business records if a party can establish the reliability of the records.[96] To qualify, the records must be kept "in the course of a regularly conducted business activity" and as a "regular practice of that business activity."[97]

The risk of unenforceability of an obligation because of evidentiary problems may be reduced by formal *presumptions* regarding items of evidence relevant to the standards discussed earlier. An evidentiary presumption is a legal rule that requires a fact finder to recognize the existence of a presumed fact "unless and until evidence is introduced that could support a finding of its non-existence."[98] Currently, few presumptions in the law of evidence bear explicitly on e-commerce.[99] Nonetheless, analogies from paper-based documents can be drawn to certain presumptions that courts might eventually adopt in the case of digital information.[100] Some legislative initiatives have sought to enhance e-commerce certainty by providing various presumptions. Examples of such presumptions can be found in digital signature laws such as Utah's, which provides, among other things, that "[i]n adjudicating a dispute involving a digital signature, a court of this state shall presume that . . . the information listed in a valid certificate . . . and confirmed by a licensed certification authority issuing the certificate is accurate."[101] The EU Directive also mandates certain presumptions where "advanced electronic signatures" based on "qualified certificate[s]" created by "secure-signature-creation device[s]" have been employed.[102]

Parties engaging in e-commerce should consider the merits of establishing their own interparty presumptions through trading partner or other agreements. For example, the Model EDI Trading Partner Agreement (section 3.3.4) stipulates that certain electronic documents "will be admissible as between the parties to the same extent and under the same conditions as other business records originated and maintained in documentary form."

Aside from the legal issues affected by the evidentiary requirements of authentication and best evidence, parties engaged in e-commerce may find themselves facing the practical problem of proving that the version of the electronic document they possess as evidence of an agreement is the actual version to which the other party in fact agreed. This problem is especially pertinent where the terms of online agreements are incrementally resolved through multiple correspondence and edits and where multiple parties may edit and execute it. In such cases, how does one demonstrate definitively the terms to which a particular party agreed? As discussed in later chapters, appropriate security mechanisms, such as digital signatures and other technologies and techniques supporting non-repudiation can provide viable solutions to these potential evidentiary problems.

3.5   Other Legal Issues

Participation in e-commerce raises various other legal issues. The following subsections introduce some developments and practices particularly relevant to secure e-commerce law. Other important legal issues are raised in later chapters.

Notice and Conspicuousness

The accommodation of various requirements for legal notice and for conspicuousness via computer has been a source of continuing concern and uncertainty in e-commerce. Traditional law and legal practice are premised on the use of paper-based methods such as the mails, the availability of return receipts and other forms of tangible confirmed delivery, and semipermanent large type, capital letters, and other conventions to call the recipient's attention to particularly important matters and thereby diminish the ability of a recipient to later claim successfully that he or she was not (or did not have the opportunity to become) appraised of such matters.[103] Unfortunately, current legal standards lack clear guidance (or suffer from complexity) in this area; even some of the legal profession's most involved practitioners have characterized accommodation of computer-based notice and conspicuousness as requiring more of a "guess" than anything else.[104]

In the absence of established, uniform rules, parties must establish between themselves precise requirements for providing *notice* for each relevant application. The legal articulation of notice should include whether it should or must be communicated electronically or by other means (or both), such as certified or registered postal mail (and whether a return receipt should be requested) or a recognized courier service. The time at which notice is effective should also be defined; for example, upon transmission of the relevant message or upon receipt (possibly even *confirmed* receipt) of the message by the intended recipient.

When notice is sent electronically, the extent to which the recipient must verify its authenticity and acknowledge receipt should be determined. Because standard Internet e-mail protocols do *not* support a return receipt or message confirmation service, the typical sender of an electronic notice may only *request* an acknowledgment of receipt from the recipient. Each party (with the possible exception of consumers) generally has an underlying obligation to exercise commercially reasonable diligence in maintaining system availability for receipt of electronic notices. If the notice's originator does not receive an acknowledgment of receipt within a specified period (such as two business days from the time sent), arrangements should be made to use an alternative mode of communication, such as first-class postal mail, certified mail, or courier service.[105]

Conspicuousness is especially relevant for "Web-wrap" contracts—contracts to which a Web user agrees by consenting to the terms posted on a Web site.[106] Often the consent is obtained by a click in a dialog box or on a button stating "Yes," "OK," "I accept," or "I agree."[107]

NCCUSL has endeavored to reduce uncertainty regarding standards for conspicuousness in digital information transactions by adopting the following definition of *conspicuous* in UCITA:

> "Conspicuous," with reference to a term, means so written, displayed, or presented
> that a reasonable person against which it is to operate ought to have noticed it. A term
> in an electronic record intended to evoke a response by an electronic agent is conspic-
> uous if it is presented in a form that would enable a reasonably configured electronic
> agent to take it into account or react to it without review of the record by an individ-
> ual. Conspicuous terms include the following:
>
> (A) with respect to a person
>   (i)   a heading in capitals in a size equal to or greater than, or in contrasting type,
>   font or color to, the surrounding text;
>   (ii) language in the body of a record or display in larger or other contrasting
>   type, font or color or set off from the surrounding text by symbols or other
>   marks that draw attention to the language; and
>   (iii) a term prominently referenced in an electronic record or display which is
>   readily accessible or reviewable from the record or display; and
> (B) with respect to a person or an electronic agent, a term or reference to a term
>   that is so placed in a record or display that the person or electronic agent
>   cannot proceed without taking action with respect to the particular term or
>   reference.[108]

Privacy and Other Consumer Issues

The law generally views consumers as less sophisticated than commercial participants
and, as a matter of public policy, in need of a higher degree of protection. Consequently,
the law has traditionally provided enhanced protections for consumers[109] against fraud
and unfair trade practices by unscrupulous merchants. As e-commerce has proliferated,
consumers have become significant participants in e-commerce, and consumer advocates
have observed that various aspects of digital transactions, including the relative
anonymity of parties, heighten the potential for such problems and the need for appropriate protection.[110]

Accordingly, rule makers have generally been careful to preserve, and not preempt,
existing consumer rights. For example, the UN Model Law on Electronic Commerce
specifically notes that it does not supersede any consumer protection laws.[111] Current and
proposed UCC sections take a similar approach by providing that UCC transactions are
also subject to applicable consumer protection laws.[112]

Other initiatives have focused more squarely on consumer protection. For example, the Organisation for Economic Co-operation and Development (OECD) has promulgated Guidelines for Consumer Protection in the Context of Electronic Commerce and recommended that all member countries take steps to implement them through legislation, regulation, and promotion of business practices consistent therewith.[113] The OECD Guidelines include recommendations regarding effective protection for consumers in e-commerce contexts; fair business, advertising, and marketing practices; fair and accurate disclosures regarding the vendors, products, services, and transaction terms; easy-to-use and secure payment systems; meaningful access to fair and timely dispute resolution; and privacy of personal information.

Discussions and U.S. federal hearings regarding consumer protections in e-commerce have produced the following list of proposals from consumer advocacy groups:

1. Electronic disclosures should be permitted only when the transaction is initiated and consummated electronically.
2. When electronic signatures are required, the technologies used must be reasonable, reflect an actual intent to sign a document (not merely opening a package of shrink-wrapped software), and be attached only to documents that are unalterable after the signature is attached.
3. The consumer should be given the opportunity to accept or refuse disclosures electronically without surcharges.
4. The consumer must be able to obtain paper copies at a reasonable cost and in a timely manner.
5. The disclosures must actually be delivered to the consumer's e-mail address with a reply requested or must be retained on the seller's Web site for the duration of the contract.
6. When disclosures are provided to consumers through a seller's or creditor's Web site, they must be retained for the duration of the contract.
7. The electronic record must be accessible and retainable by the consumer. It must also be provided in a format that prevents alteration after it is sent, so it can be used to prove the terms of the record in a court of law.
8. The consumer's failure to respond to the consent request should trigger paper disclosures before it triggers default.[114]

In addition to concerns regarding disclosure, the capability for online businesses to easily gather and aggregate personal information (including financial and otherwise sensitive information) from e-commerce transactions has elevated information privacy issues to the forefront of consumer protection issues. In the United States, the Gramm-Leach-Bliley Financial Modernization Act imposes significant requirements and restrictions on the consumer and customer information practices of financial institutions.[115] The Health Information Portability and Accountability Act of 1996 (HIPAA) requires health plans, health care "clearinghouses," and other health care providers that transmit "individually identifiable" health information in electronic formats to maintain certain levels of confidentiality with respect to such information,[116] and the Children's Online Privacy Protection Act of 1998 (COPPA) requires online merchants to adhere to stringent regulations regarding the collection, use, or disclosure of personal information from and about children on the Internet.[117] The Federal Trade Commission has established an advisory committee on online access and security with specific proposals and focus on privacy issues,[118] and additional legislation has recently been proposed in both houses of the U.S. Congress to address consumer privacy concerns.[119] EU directives regarding data privacy have recently required U.S. diplomats to negotiate safe harbors for U.S. businesses and other compromise approaches consistent with the stronger EU rules, such as voluntary industry standards backed by some level of government enforcement, to avoid trade difficulties due to the absence of broad U.S. laws protecting consumer privacy.[120] Many of the U.S. states have also enacted laws that touch on the collection, use, or disclosure of consumer personal information.[121] U.S. courts and regulatory agencies have recently enforced various consumer rights to privacy against commercial parties who have disclosed such information to third parties without consent.[122]

Personal Jurisdiction

Another important legal issue is *personal jurisdiction,* which refers to the ability of one party to require another to answer to legal claims in the courts of a particular jurisdiction. Accordingly, personal jurisdiction affects not only where party A can sue party B, but also where party A can be sued by party B. U.S. constitutional law requires that a defendant must have a sufficient level of "minimum contacts" with a jurisdiction in order to justify his or her being summoned there.[123] In Europe, the Brussels Convention of 1968, which the European Union is currently in the process of revising, provides generally that defendants may be sued in the jurisdiction in which they are domiciled.[124] In e-commerce, messages relevant to a given transaction may pass through intermediaries in multiple jurisdictions across the world—even without the knowledge or express consent of the parties. If the simple relay of a message through a service provider in a remote jurisdiction is sufficient to constitute minimum contacts, e-commerce participants will be subject to enormous uncertainties. Even the more plausible possibility of being called into court in the distant jurisdiction of the other party to a digital transaction creates great uncertainty. Most rule-making bodies have adopted a "wait and see" approach, permitting experience in the judicial arena to show whether new rules are appropriate.[125] Until legal standards are crystallized in this respect,[126] parties engaged in e-commerce should agree upon jurisdictional issues before or at the time of their transactions. As a general rule, however, parties can typically be sued in the jurisdiction in which they are domiciled.

Negotiability

The law has yet to address sufficiently the effects of e-commerce on the *negotiability* of certain unique documents that the law recognizes as conferring rights upon their possessors. This type of document includes *negotiable instruments,* such as certain promissory notes and securities,[127] and negotiable *documents of title,* which include any "bill of lading, dock warrant, dock receipt, warehouse receipt, or order for the delivery of goods, and also any other document which in the regular course of business is treated as evidencing adequately that the person in possession of it is entitled to receive, hold and dispose of the document and the goods it covers."[128] For example, a negotiable bill of lading is intended to "adequately evidence that the person in possession of it is entitled to receive, hold and dispose of the documents and the goods it covers."[129]

Because a paper record manifests recognized attributes of its originality and uniqueness, it possesses intrinsic legal value to its holder. In contrast, digital documents do not possess an *inherent* uniqueness; indeed, one of their great advantages is their capacity for easy and precise duplication.

Nonetheless, because negotiability remains an important commercial practice, e-commerce participants must either develop acceptable alternatives to true negotiability or find methods of ensuring the negotiability of digital messages.[130] To date, the only recognized methods that can provide adequate proof are the use of trusted repositories (which maintain the "record copy" of the information)[131] and the use of tamper-proof or tamper-evident hardware, such as specific *smartcards* (which prevent or mitigate the disclosure and copying of "unique" information). The UN Model Law also addresses contracts for the carriage of goods and provides that digital communications may suffice in certain circumstances as bills of lading and other documents of title.[132] Bolero.net,[133] a joint venture of the Society for Worldwide Interbank Financial Telecommunication (S.W.I.F.T.) and TT Club (an insurance and risk management company for the transportation industry), has capitalized on this momentum by advancing an alternative to true negotiability using an electronic title registry maintained by Bolero.net as a neutral, trusted third party.

Parties to letter-of-credit transactions, common in high-value commercial dealings such as equipment leases or long-term inventory contracts, must deal with these same issues to conduct such transactions electronically. Article 5 of the UCC, which governs letter-of-credit transactions in most U.S. states, provides that a letter of credit must be "signed" by the issuer and "in writing."[134] The International Chamber of Commerce has advanced the law with respect to its *Uniform Customs and Practices for Documentary Credits (UCP)*[135] by providing that a letter of credit may take the form of a "teletransmission" to an advising bank and by employing the word "authenticated" in place of "signed" and "in writing."[136] Along these lines, UCC article 5 permits letters of credit to be issued in any form "that is a record and is authenticated (i) by a signature or (ii) in accordance with the agreement of the parties or the standard practice [of financial institutions]."[137]

Intellectual Property

Many of today's information-economy enterprises' most valuable assets are their intellectual properties—their patents,[138] trademarks,[139] copyrights,[140] trade secrets, and other intellectual rights. The open and efficient nature of information flows over the Internet has prompted commentators to assert that traditional intellectual property rights and rules should be jettisoned and rewritten. Intellectual property rights can be extremely vexing to enforce in cyberspace because of the ease of duplication and distribution of material and the vastness of the online environment. Accordingly, e-commerce systems demand greater vigilance (and yet may correspondingly create new liabilities) to ensure that parties do not violate or infringe upon existing copyrights, trademarks, patents, or other intellectual property rights.[141]

One area of particular focus (and controversy) has been the intersection of trademark rights and domain-name rights. For some time in the early days of the Web, Network Solutions, Inc., the entity responsible for registering the .com, .net, .org, and .edu top-level domain names, intervened in domain-name disputes; in the mid-1990s, Network Solutions established a policy of deferring to the courts for guidance. The frequency of cybersquatting, the practice of registering domain names without intent to use them except to extract a price from an obvious party using the name as a trade name or mark, prompted the U.S. federal government in 1999 to pass the Anti-Cyber-squatting Consumer Protection Act[142] to permit trademark holders to more easily enforce their trademark rights in such cases. The situation is now also governed by ICANN policy.

Taxation

As the volume of e-commerce has accelerated, taxing authorities reliant on transaction revenue (implemented through sales, use, value-added, and related taxes on consumption of goods and services) have witnessed their tax base erode and have become alarmed at the prospect of even greater future erosion. In the United States, for example, the states generally charge sales or use taxes on the purchase of most goods and services. If an e-commerce transaction is entirely intrastate and would have been taxable if it were not transacted electronically, the vendor in most cases is obligated to collect and remit a sales tax on behalf of the purchaser. Compliance with such tax rules is claimed to be particularly difficult for taxing authorities to police. Moreover, a significant portion of e-commerce transactions are not intrastate and therefore cannot, by virtue of the Commerce Clause of the U.S. Constitution, be taxed by a state except through a tax on the purchaser's "use" of the purchased item. Use taxes (and, in Europe and other jurisdictions, value-added taxes, or VATs[143]) are equally difficult for taxing authorities to enforce, particularly when the underlying transaction has been conducted online. Other traditional bases of tax revenue are being eroded due to the disintermediation and dematerialization inherent in many e-commerce transactions.[144]

To avoid stifling the growth of e-commerce, the U.S. Congress imposed a ban on e-commerce taxes.[145] Proposals to resolve taxation issues have been contentious and both policy- and technology-based.[146] E-commerce taxation has also been the subject of continuing debate internationally.[147] The controversy includes assertions that an Internet tax moratorium may effectively discriminate against *brick-and-mortar* enterprises—at least those that do not embrace and integrate the Internet into their businesses—and that the health and market caps of many of the largest e-commerce companies indicate that government subsidization is unwarranted.

Illegal Bargains and Criminal Law

While freedom of contract (also known as *party autonomy*) among parties to a transaction is the general rule, the law considers certain types of contracts as void or voidable because of conflict with the public interest. The list of problematic contracts include those that impair family relationships, restrain trade or the "alienation" of property, involve promises to commit a crime or a tort (a wrongful act), or implicate commercial bribery. Although none of these types of illegal bargains is unique to digital transactions, e-commerce participants should be aware of the potential invalidity or unenforceability of contracts against the public interest. Parties who engage in some particularly heinous classes of illegal bargains may even expose themselves to criminal liability.

E-commerce participants should also be aware of computer crime threats and methods to mitigate them. Even unsophisticated users have an increasing ability to gain access to, use, misappropriate, alter, or destroy information, records, or communications, including sensitive payment information or trade secrets. Every state in the United States has now enacted legislation (or modifications to existing statutes) addressing computer crimes.[148] In addition, several important federal statutes specifically address computer-related criminal activity: the Computer Fraud and Abuse Act of 1986,[149] the Electronic Communications Privacy Act of 1986,[150] and the Communications Assistance for Law Enforcement Act (CALEA).[151] Additionally, the background law of torts in most jurisdictions provides a basis for civil liability due to negligent or intentional abuses.[152] Nonetheless, legal systems around the world continue to struggle with the difficult tasks of defining computer abuse, both generally[153] and in terms of specific wrongs,[154] and enhancing rules to ensure that computer abuses fall under criminal and civil statutes[155] and that appropriate enforcement mechanisms are provided.

3.6 Dealing with Legal Uncertainties

As the preceding discussion of legal principles demonstrates, there are many issues relevant to e-commerce that remain (at least partially) unresolved in the law. Because the most efficient solutions are often best implemented on a systemic or global scale, these uncertainties, if left untreated at a high level, will prevent e-commerce from fully exploiting its technological efficiencies. Fortunately, rule makers have made progress and continue to advance their resolution.[156]

In chapter 8, we describe several existing and proposed legislative and regulatory initiatives and various published guidelines that address many of the legal uncertainties noted earlier on a systemic or global scale. Where these rules are undesirable, impractical, inadequate, or not implemented in the applicable jurisdictions or context, the parties must address the uncertainties through other means, such as contract[157] and internal business controls.

Agreements

Agreements play a particularly important role in e-commerce. In the absence of a rich complement of relevant law and trade practices, including robust security standards, agreements serve to bolster (and often ensure) the certainty of e-commerce. Agreements provide a first line of defense for parties trading over unsecured networks such as the Internet with partners with whom long-term, trusted relationships have not yet developed (or where trust among the parties is otherwise marginal). On the other hand, where parties do not contemplate engaging in an ongoing relationship, negotiation of an agreement may be inefficient or impractical.[158]

Agreements allow parties to benefit from freedom of contract. Without agreements, the rights and obligations of parties engaged in e-commerce are determined (whether by design or default) by the prevailing law—which often differs from the parties' specific intentions and expectations. Thus, even when legal rules in the e-commerce area are established with greater certainty, parties can use agreements to deviate from these rules when such deviation is to their advantage. In other words, agreements provide an important opportunity for parties to structure e-commerce relationships that are consistent with their precise business needs.

Agreements can be classified as either (1) documenting a single transaction or ongoing transactions among specified trading partners, such as for the purchase and sale of goods, or (2) providing general, systemic rules to facilitate e-commerce within a community of interest. Such facilitating e-commerce agreements include trading partner agreements (TPAs), value-added network (VAN) agreements, interconnection agreements,

Internet service provider (ISP) agreements, and payment agreements. These types of agreements are discussed in detail in appendix A.

Security Provisions in Model Agreements

Since treatment of security in both domestic and international e-commerce agreements has traditionally been quite modest, this book provides special focus on agreement provisions and related infrastructure supporting *secure* e-commerce. Some examples of the information security provisions in recognized model agreements are the following:

- *Model EDI Trading Partner Agreement:* "Each party shall properly use those security procedures, including those specified in the Appendix, if any, which are reasonably sufficient to ensure that all transmissions of Documents are authorized and to protect its business records and data from improper access."[159]
- *Model Electronic Payments Agreement:* "Each party shall employ reasonable security procedures [commensurate with the risks involved / sufficient to satisfy the requirements of Appendix sec. 4] to ensure that Transaction Sets, notices and other information specified in this Agreement that are electronically created, communicated, processed, stored, retained or retrieved are authentic, accurate, reliable, complete [and confidential]."[160]
- *European Model EDI Agreement:* "The parties undertake to implement and maintain control and security procedures and measures necessary to ensure the protection of messages against the risk of unauthorized access, alteration, loss, or destruction."[161]

None of these model agreements addresses how the parties should articulate their respective responsibilities for the implementation and use of information security techniques such as cryptography and digital signatures. Therefore, new model agreements (or addenda to model agreements) are needed, particularly as business communication infrastructure migrates toward Internet-based commerce. In these environments, trading relationships are often new, parties have not established trusted relationships, and the use of digital signatures is increasing.

Agreements specific to the use of public-key cryptography and digital signatures are discussed in chapter 10.

3.7 Two Business Models

Molding traditional paper-based practices into practices appropriate for e-commerce often proves difficult from the business perspective. For example, consider the uncertain kinship between traditional signatures and computer-based authentication methods. Most businesses have either purposefully or intuitively followed one of two alternative business models regarding signatures and authentication: the *formalistic* model or the *risk-based* model.[162] The implications of this choice are significant because the model chosen invariably affects the type and strength of information security techniques, practices, and procedures implemented, and the corresponding legal status of the digital information at issue.

The Formalistic Model

The formalistic model rests on two propositions: first, that legal requirements for both traditional and digital signatures are *de minimis*[163] and, second, that signatures and signature law are static, and therefore the security mechanisms necessary to satisfy signature requirements need not be dynamic (regardless of the value and risks involved in a particular transaction). Thus, the formalistic model dictates the use of the same signature procedures whether a transaction involves the low-risk purchase by Vera of one $200 lathe from Danielle's Machine Makers or the sale of $2 million worth of steel by Sharon's Steelcorp to a questionable manufacturer in a developing, politically unstable nation with an uncertain legal system.

   The formalistic model is most frequently justified by a modest requirement of signature laws, such as section 1, title 1, of the U.S. Code, which defines a signature as a mark "when the person making the same intended it as such [i.e., as a signature]." In fact, some of the formalistic model's supporters contend that signature requirements are so modest that, for e-commerce transactions, it is sufficient simply to include the signatory's name (as a character string), an *X*, a DUNS number, or the like, *without the use of any particular security mechanism or level of security.* Accordingly, the formalistic model discounts or dismisses requirements for strong computer-based authentication mechanisms, including digital signatures.

The Risk-Based Model

The risk-based model, on the other hand, rests on two propositions contrary to those underlying the formalistic model: first, that there are inherent differences between traditional and

computer-based signatures, requiring specific authentication and non-repudiation mechanisms, and, second, that signatures in e-commerce are necessarily dynamic and thus must
be *commensurate with the risks* of the subject transaction.

Thus, when the value of goods or the risk associated with a transaction is relatively
low (such as Vera's purchase of a lathe from the trustworthy Danielle's), the required controls are relatively minimal (or even nonexistent in some respects). But when the value or
risk is significant (for example, $2 million worth of steel to a questionable foreign manu-
facturer), the parties must implement more robust security mechanisms to ensure confidence in signature *enforceability.* Note, of course, that value and risk are relative—what is
extremely risky to a small business like Vera's may be of nominal risk to a large, wealthy
corporation like Sharon's Steelcorp.

Analysis of These Models

The most significant pitfall of the formalistic model is that it fails to recognize that traditional, paper-based signatures have *inherent* security attributes that bolster their forensic
utility (by providing important probative evidence), whereas computer-based information
that is not specially secured does not. The forensic attributes of traditional paper-based
signatures may include

- the chemical bonding of a particular ink to a particular paper's fibers;
- the biometric properties of a signature, such as stylus direction, pressure, and
  speed;
- the unique characteristics of a paper, including unique embossed letterhead,
  weight, style, and batch; or
- a typewriter's or printer's unique fonts or a seal's unique die and wax.

In contrast, computer-based information has no unique forensic attributes unless
supplemental information security technologies, practices, and procedures are applied.
That is, computer-based information is simply a series of zeros and ones that have no dis-
cernible uniqueness other than the content they apparently create. Therefore, there is no
simple analog between traditional and computer-based signatures[164]—not only because
the media are distinct, but also because the former enjoys critical inherent forensic attributes that the latter does not.

Under the formalistic model, where a single, static, security or authentication procedure is adopted for all transactions, small-risk or small-value transactions may result in unnecessarily large security or authentication measures (and unacceptable costs), whereas large-risk or large-value transactions may enjoy lower security or authentication costs but be inappropriately exposed to security compromise and resulting liability. Although the risk-based model involves an extra, incremental cost because it must be tailored to each situation, it is generally the more practical and efficient approach of the two.

3.8 Business Controls in a Digital Environment

Some of the most critical concerns of the secure e-commerce community include the need to control liability exposure and the need to ensure the enforceability of digital transactions. Although tremendous intellectual energy has been channeled into these issues, the community has not yet comprehensively addressed the full range of critical issues in the larger e-commerce controls environment. At a minimum, further guidance is needed to assist parties engaged in e-commerce in identifying, designing, and instituting the business controls that can protect their interests and facilitate electronic trading.

Experience has demonstrated that there are no shortcuts to achieving secure e-commerce. Rather, a rigorous, eclectic approach that weds technology to desirable and established business practices and procedures is required. Because e-commerce is an ever-changing field, it demands continuous oversight and proactive, creative innovation. Managers must not only acquire the appropriate knowledge and resources and apply the proper management techniques, but must also constantly invent or reformulate the appropriate control tools, techniques, and procedures. Such controls should, in turn, be reflected in e-commerce agreements and trade practices.

As an example of the work ahead of e-commerce participants in this regard, consider how an entity would undertake a risk analysis and security audit for e-commerce practices, including those for an e-commerce infrastructure that may have been neither fully built nor adequately tested. Adequate auditing tools and procedures for secure e-commerce must be developed further,[165] in part by altering and extrapolating them from existing audit programs and tools.[166]

3.9 Summary

This chapter has considered legal and business principles relevant to e-commerce, focusing on the validity and enforceability of e-commerce transactions. A combination of certain tools, including agreements, legal and business practices and policies, and security technologies, along with support for and refinement of these tools through legal reform, is essential to the success of e-commerce. Legal requirements and business policies should clarify and implement reasonable security measures without sacrificing needed flexibility. The past decade has witnessed great progress in developing the legal and security infrastructure necessary for conducting secure e-commerce. Careful planning and rigorous attention to these issues will contribute to a successful e-commerce environment short- and long-term.

E-commerce security is not only a business requirement, but also increasingly a legal necessity.

Notes

1. Examples of electronic auctions can be found at the following Web sites: eBay <http://www.ebay.com> (individuals engage in one-to-one trading in an auction format), LiveBid <http://www.livebid.amazon.com> (online participation of individuals in live auctions), and OffRoad Capital <http://www. offroadcapital.com> (auction system for participation by investors in private venture-capital fundings).

2. *Enforceability* means that a contract or transaction can overcome challenge, that is, that it can be proven by the applicable dispute resolution mechanism. In contrast, the *validity* of a contract means that it is not illegal or impermissible to have executed it in electronic form. Thus, enforceability is a more challenging proposition and may require greater evidence than merely demonstrating the validity of a contract or transaction.

3. Technology inevitably outpaces the law, which is necessarily reactive to societal developments. Nonetheless, the last few years have produced accelerating and sometimes breakneck efforts to legislate and regulate (or, in some cases, overregulate) in the areas of electronic communications and e-commerce.

4. For general resources on legal aspects of e-commerce, see Michael S. Baum and Henry H. Perritt, Jr., *Electronic Contracting, Publishing and EDI Law* (New York: Wiley, 1991), details at <http://www.wiley.com>; Michael S. Baum, "Analysis of Legal Aspects in EDI," in *EDI and the Law,* ed. Ian Walden (London: Blenheim Online, 1989); Olivier Hance, *Business and Law on the Internet* (New York: McGraw-Hill, 1997), details at <http://www.book-store.mcgraw-hill.com>; Chris Reed, *Internet Law: Text and Materials* (Evanston, IL: Northwestern University Press, 2000), details at <http://www.nupress.nwu.edu>; Thomas J. Smedinghoff, ed., *Online Law* (New York: Addison-Wesley Developers Press, 1996), details at <http://www.awlonline.com>.

5. By *functional equivalence* we mean that, although e-commerce transactions may involve a different sequence of legal, physical, and business actions between parties, the ultimate result is substantially equivalent to analogous paper transactions. Each mechanical step of the paper transaction does not necessarily have an identifiable and legally equivalent analog in the electronic transaction.

6. For example, in chapter 4 we introduce the technology of digital signatures. Legal infrastructure for digital signatures may benefit from new statutes but does not necessitate a fundamental revision of basic contract principles (see section 8.2 regarding digital signature legislation). Some commentators have argued that e-commerce is different enough to justify an entirely new and separate legal regime. See, for example, Raymond T. Nimmer and Patricia Kraut-house, "Electronic Commerce: New Paradigms in Information Law," 31 *Idaho Law Review* 937 (1995).

7. Generally, these choice-of-law rules refer a court to the law of the jurisdiction where the contract was formed. The locale of an e-commerce agreement may be difficult to determine without specific rules, but the law of contract formation is nearly uniform across U.S. jurisdictions. See Walter A. Effross, "The Legal Architecture of Virtual Stores: World Wide Web Sites and the Uniform Commercial Code," 34 *San Diego Law Review* 1263 (1998), available at <http://www.effross.com>.

8. Choice-of-law rules are themselves domestic in nature, and the actual application of these conflict rules in a particular jurisdiction may result in a different governing law than the law in which the contract was formed.

9. For participants in European Union countries in a sale-of-goods transaction, for example, the applicable law would likely be that of the country in which the *seller* is based, in accordance with the Rome Convention of 1980. This issue is complicated by questions of constitutional jurisdiction. For example, does a party have the ability to summon another party into the courts of state *X* or country *Y* simply because relevant digital communications passed through a service provider in state *X* or country *Y?* Under the Brussels Convention of 1968 (which the EU is currently in the process of revising), a defendant may generally be sued in the jurisdiction of his or her domicile. For further discussion, see "Personal Jurisdiction" in section 3.5.

10. The clause "without reference to its choice of law provisions" is included to prevent the problem of a chosen governing law (California law, in this case) having choice-of-law rules that would dictate the application of the law of another state, thereby defeating the parties' explicit choice of law.

11. For a general source on the common-law rules of contract in the United States, see the *Restatement (Second) of Contracts.* The *Restatement,* a persuasive text in most U.S. courts, is in large part an effort by the American Law Institute (an advisory group composed of legal practitioners and academics) to codify the common law of contracts as it exists in the majority of U.S. states. See <http://www.ali.org>. There are several extensive and detailed treatises on contract law, including Samuel Williston, *A Treatise on the Law of Contracts,* 4th ed. Richard A. Lord, ed. (St. Paul, MN: West Group, 1990). Arthur L. Corbin, *Corbin on Contracts,* rev. ed. Joseph M. Perillo, ed. (St. Paul, MN: West, 1993–1998).

12. The UCC itself is actually not a statute, but rather a *model* law drafted by a national committee of state legislators and experts. All U.S. jurisdictions have enacted their own UCC statutes based, at least in part, on the model law. Article 2 of the UCC governs "transactions in goods" and is therefore relevant to most e-commerce transactions involving the purchase and sale of items. For links to state statutes corresponding to sections of the UCC, see <http://www.law.cornell.edu/uniform/ucc.html>.

13. The United Nations Commission on International Trade Law (UNCITRAL) has adopted the *United Nations Model Law on Electronic Commerce,* UNCITRAL 29th Sess., UN Doc. A/51/17 (1996), available at <http://www.

uncitral.org/en-index.html>. Like the UCC, the UN Model Law on Electronic Commerce is not actually law until formally enacted in a particular state or country. Legislation based on the UN Model Law on Electronic Commerce has been adopted by many jurisdictions, including the countries of Australia, Bermuda, Colombia, France, Hong Kong Special Administrative Region of China, Mexico, Republic of Korea, and Singapore and the state of Illinois. The UN is currently advancing its model law treatment of e-commerce legal issues by developing model rules for electronic signatures. See the discussion in section 8.1 regarding the draft UN Model Law on Electronic Signatures.

14. See the discussion in section 8.1 regarding UETA. UETA can be found online at <http://www.law.upenn.edu/bll/ulc/fnact99/1990s/ueta99.htm>. A summary of UETA is online at <http://www.nccusl.org/uniformact_summaries/uniformacts-5-ueta.htm>.

15. As explained in section 8.1, UCITA covers transactions in computer information. For more information, see the "UCITA Online" Web site at <http://www.ucitaonline.com>.

16. Regulations frequently do so by referencing certain "technical or performance standards" and requiring that the parties comply with such standards in order to obtain or qualify for the desired treatment.

17. The UCC defines *course of dealing* as "a sequence of previous conduct between the parties to a particular transaction which is fairly to be regarded as establishing a common basis of understanding for interpreting their expressions and other conduct." A *usage of trade* is "any practice or method of dealing having such regularity of observance in a place, vocation or trade as to justify an expectation that it will be observed with respect to the transaction in question" (UCC sec. 1-205).

18. UCC sec. 1-102(3) ("The effect of provisions of this act may be varied by agreement, except as otherwise provided in this act. . . ."); UN Model Law on Electronic Commerce, article 4 ("Variation by agreement").

19. See, for example, American Bar Association, Electronic Messaging Services Task Force, *Model Electronic Data Interchange Trading Partner Agreement and Commentary,* 45 *Business Lawyer* 1717 (1990) (hereinafter Model EDI Trading Partner Agreement); American Bar Association, Section of Science and Technology, *Model Electronic Payments Agreement and Commentary (for*

Domestic Credit Transfers), 32 Jurimetrics 601 (1992) (hereinafter *Model Electronic Payments Agreement).*

20. For example, in section 8.3 we discuss the e-Terms international registry of such rules and practices.

21. For example, various statutes and principles of common law may be waived or preempted by contractual agreement.

22. In various circumstances, party autonomy is expressly foreclosed by statute or principles of constitutional or common law. For example, in certain states, a vendor dealing with consumers cannot disclaim warranties of merchantability. Another example would be that, as a matter of common law, parties cannot make an enforceable agreement to perpetrate an illegal act.

23. UCC sec. 1-205; UETA secs. 5, 6, and comments thereto; UN Model Law, article 4 and comments thereto. As with party autonomy, certain aspects of the course of trade between parties may not have legal effect if such practices are inconsistent with express provisions of applicable statutes or established principles of common law.

24. UCC sec. 1-205; UETA secs. 5, 6, and comments thereto; UN Model Law, article 4 and comments thereto. Statutory or common law can also preempt trade usage.

25. Directive 1999/93/EC of the European Parliament and of the Council of December 13, 1999, on a Community Framework for Electronic Signatures, available at <http://europa.eu.int/comm/internal_market/en/media/sign/Dir99-93-ecEN.pdf>. The EU Directive is discussed in greater detail in section 8.1.

26. For more information regarding NCCUSL, see <http://www.nccusl.org>. E-sign is presented in section 8.1.

27. In addition, enforceability is often closely related to the issue of non-repudiation, discussed in detail in chapter 9.

28. Unless noted otherwise, definitions in this section are from E. Allan Farnsworth, *Contracts* (Boston: Little Brown, 1990), chapter 3.

29. An example of a unilateral offer is a computer software vendor offering to pay a sum to anyone finding a bug in a product.

30. UCITA secs. 107 (use of electronic agents) and 206 (offer and acceptance, electronic agents). The NCCUSL Drafting Committee for revisions to UCC article 2 has proposed new sections to the UCC mirroring the provisions of UETA and UCITA: NCCUSL Reporter's Interim Draft for Comment—Revision of Uniform

Commercial Code Article 2—Sales, secs. 2-204(a), 2-204(e), 2-211 (March 2000) (hereinafter the UCC Draft Revisions), available at <http://www.law.upenn.edu/library/ulc/ulc.htm>.

31. For general reference materials regarding the laws of agency, see American Law Institute, *Restatement (Second) of Agency* (St. Paul, MN: American Law Institute Publishers, 1996); Legal Information Institute, "Agency: An Overview," <http://wwwsecure.law.cornell.edu/topics/agency.html>. Regarding Canadian law, see Ian R. Kerr, "Providing for Autonomous Electronic Devices in the *Uniform Electronic Commerce Act,*" available at <http://www.law.ualberta.ca/alri/ulc/current/ekerr.html>.

32. American Bar Association, Electronic Messaging Services Task Force, "Report: The Commercial Use of Electronic Data Interchange—A Report and Model Trading Partner Agreement," 45 *Business Lawyer* 1645 (June, 1990).

33. See, for example, *The Restatement (Second) of Contracts.* For a general criticism of the mailbox rule, see Beth A. Eisler, "Default Rules for Contract Formation by Promise and the Need for Revision of the Mailbox Rule," 79 *Kentucky Law Journal* 557 (1991).

34. For example, section 2-204(3) of the UCC Draft Revisions provides that "[i]n an interaction between individuals, if an offer evokes an electronic record in response, a contract is formed, if at all: (A) if the electronic message operates as an acceptance under Section 2-206, when the message is received; or (B) if the offer is accepted under Section 2-206 by an electronic performance, when the electronic performance is received." Again, until legal principles and trade practices are more certain, parties may wish to employ a trading partner agreement to establish their own concrete principles, for example, the Model EDI Trading Partner Agreement, secs. 2.1–2.3 (governing receipt and verification of transmissions, as well as acceptance).

35. Indefiniteness may not be fatal to the validity of an agreement if the vagueness in terms can be cured by implying more definite terms from the course of dealing between the two parties, from trade usage, or from "gap fillers" supplied by background law. Farnsworth, *Contracts,* sec. 3.28.

36. Farnsworth, *Contracts,* secs. 3.13 and 3.27.

37. See generally Michael J. Rustad, "Commercial Law Infrastructure for the Age of Information," 16 J. Marshall J. Computer Info. L., 255 (1997); Baum and

Perritt, *Electronic Contracting,* secs. 2.32, 6.7, and 6.16, pp. 91–93, 322–23, and 335–36.

38. UCC sec. 2-207. For general information, refer to Farnsworth, *Contracts,* sec. 3.21, pp. 170–79.

39. For example, see Dziewit, Graziano, and Daley, "The Quest for the Paperless Office," vol. 5, *Computer & Hi-Tech. Law Journal,* 78 (1989).

40. For example, see the Model EDI Trading Partner Agreement, sec. 3.1 (terms and conditions). See also UCC Draft Revisions, sec. 2-207, regarding battle-of-the-forms issues.

41. *The Restatement (Second) of Contracts,* sec. 71. For general information, refer to Farnsworth, *Contracts,* secs. 2.2–2.4, pp. 43–49. A simplistic view of the concept of consideration is that a contract must be supported by some real and reasonable value, to distinguish it from a gift. The value need not be specified in detail, as long as its existence can be supported in fact. Many contracts contain the clause "for One Dollar and other good and valuable consideration."

42. See section 5.8 regarding secure Internet payment schemes.

43. All states except Louisiana have adopted some form of the original English Statute of Frauds, either by statute or by case law.

44. An Act for Prevention of Frauds and Perjuries, 29 Car. 2, c. 3, sec. 17 (England 1677). Parliament repealed most of the Statute of Frauds in 1954, retaining its application only to agreements relating to suretyship and land (Law Reform (Enforcement of Contracts) Act, 1954, 2 & 3 Eliz. 2, c. 34).

45. *The Restatement (Second) of Contracts,* sec. 110; UCC sec. 2-201 (regarding the sale of goods provision). Note that the UCC statute of frauds for the sale of goods is undergoing intensive review and will likely be reformulated or, in certain circumstances, repealed (discussed later in this chapter).

46. The NCCUSL Drafting Committee has proposed that this amount be raised to $5,000. UCC Draft Revisions, sec. 2-201(a).

47. See NCCUSL's September 21, 1998, report on UETA, Task Force on State Law Exclusions, <http://www.webcom.com/legaled/ETAForum/docs/report4.html>.

48. UCC, sec. 1-201(46).

49. To date, no U.S. court has considered the issue directly in a published opinion, but several courts have intimated that a digital communication might be suffi-

cient to satisfy the writing requirement. See *Bains v. Piper, Jaffray & Hopwood, Inc.,* 497 NW2d 263 (Minn. App. 1993), which found that the letterhead of a computer-generated notice satisfies the writing requirement of the statute of frauds found in Minnesota's UCC sec. 8-319, and *Hessenthaler v. Farzin,* 564 A2d 990, 992 n. 3 (Pa. Super. Ct. 1989), which found a mailgram to constitute a writing and noted that "these types of questions are likely to occur with greater frequency in the future, as businesses and individuals increasingly rely on similar methods of negotiation such as electronic mail, telexes, and facsimile machines in conducting their business affairs." Nevertheless, see the case *Georgia Dep't of Transportation v. Norris,* 474 SE2d 216 (Ga. App. 1996), which held that faxed notice of claim did not satisfy Georgia's written notice requirements.

50. Nonetheless, see *Ellis Canning Co. v. Berstein,* 348 F. Supp. 1212 (D. Colo. 1972), which held that a tape recording of an oral contract constituted "tangible form."

51. This would typically be some moment after formation, such as when a dispute has arisen. However, courts have enforced contracts in the past that were memorialized after the fact. See, for example, *Crabtree v. Elizabeth Arden Sales Corp.,* 110 NE2d 551, 553 (N.Y. 1952), which found that payroll cards constituted memoranda. This approach obviously calls into question the integrity of the system's storage, retrieval, and printing functions, a question which goes to *authentication.* See the discussion of authentication in chapter 4.

    In the Model Trading Partner Agreement (discussed later in this chapter) and in other e-commerce agreements, the parties may specify that any document received electronically with adequate identifying characteristics and that is subsequently maintained in a form that allows it to be reduced to a paper copy will be effective between the parties as a signed writing.

52. For example, see *Parma Tile Mosaic & Marble Co. v. Estate of Fred Short,* 590 NYS2d 1019 (N.Y. Sup. Ct. 1992), which held that a facsimile transmission constituted an enforceable contract under the applicable statute of frauds despite the fact that the name of the party appeared only across the top of the fax; *Trevor v. Wood,* 36 NY 307 (1867), which approved telegraphed "signatures" for statute-of-frauds purposes; and *Howley v. Whipple,* 48 NH 487 (1869), which did the same.

53. See *ZEMCO Manufacturing, Inc. v. Navistar International Transportation Corporation,* 186 F3d 815 (7th Cir. 1999), which discussed generally whether computer printouts meet signature requirements, and *Wilkens v. Iowa Ins. Comm'r.,* 457 NW2d 1 (Iowa 1990), which held that computer-generated signatures in paper documents were permissible to meet the signature requirements of Iowa Code sec. 4.1(17) (1989).

54. See John Robinson Thomas, "Legal Responses to Commercial Transactions Employing Novel Communications Media," 90 *Mich. L. Rev.* 1145, 1161 (1992): 1145, 1161, available at <http://www.law. umich.edu/students/ orgs/mlr.htm>.

55. UCC sec. 1-201(39). Again, this leaves room for nontraditional types of signatures.

56. *Matter of National Institute of Standards and Technology—Use of Electronic Data Interchange Technology to Create Valid Obligations,* Comp. Gen. File B-245714 (December 13, 1991). This opinion arose from a request by NIST to determine "whether agencies can use Electronic Data Interchange (EDI) technologies to create valid contractual obligations that can be recorded consistent with 31 U.S.C. sec. 1501," which governs federal procurement. The Office of the Comptroller General is a branch of the U.S. General Accounting Office, as well as an arm of the Congress.

57. See the Office of Management and Budget's rules under the GPEA in 64 *Federal Register* (March 5, 1999): 10896.

58. E-sign is presented in Section 8.1.

59. "Electronic signature" under these acts is typically defined, if at all, as "any letters, characters, or symbols, manifested by electronic or similar means, executed or adopted by a party with an intent to authenticate a writing" [Florida Electronic Signature Act of 1996, general bill S942, 4(4)]. Electronic signatures are to be distinguished from digital signatures, as described more particularly in chapter 4.

60. See discussions in chapter 8. See also summaries at <http://www.pkilaw.com>, <http://www.bakerinfo.com/ecommerce>, and <http://cwis.kub.nl/~frw/ people/hof/ds-lawsu.htm>.

61. For example, see Utah Code sec. 46-3-403(1) (1996), available at <http://www.state.ut.us>; see also section 8.2.

62. The EU directive on a Community Framework for Electronic Signatures is presented in Section 8.1.

63. "'Record' means information that is inscribed on a tangible medium or that is stored in an electronic or other medium and is retrievable in perceivable form" [UCC Draft Revisions, sec. 2-102(a)(32)].

64. "'Authenticate' means: (A) to sign; or (B) execute or adopt a symbol, or encrypt a record in whole or in par[t], with present intent [to]: (i) identify the authenticating party; and (ii) either: (I) adopt or accept a record or term; or (II) establish the authenticity of a record or term that contains the authentication or to which a record containing the authentication refers" [UCC Draft Revisions, sec. 2-103(a)(1)].

65. See UCC Draft Revisions (November 1, 1996), sec. 2-201, <http://www.law.upenn.edu/library/ulc/ucc2/textd96.htm>. Depending on the form of the revision, the statute of frauds might nevertheless continue to apply to some digital commerce transactions, for example, those that contemplate performance of services in over one year's time. The current UCC Draft Revisions sec. 2-201(a) keeps the existing UCC sec. 2-201 intact but changes the threshold amount for applicability from $500 to $5,000.

66. UCC sec. 8-319 (statute of frauds), repealed by UCC Revised Article 8 (1994).

67. See article 12 of CISG. The CISG has been adopted by the United States and is thus a federal law. Although it is not applicable to transactions between domestic parties, the CISG generally preempts application of UCC article 2 in the sale of goods between parties of different nations that are signatories to the CISG. See *MCC-Marble Ceramic Center, Inc. v. Ceramica Nuova D'Agostino*, 144 F3d 1384 (11th Cir. 1998); *Claudia v. Olivieri Footwear Ltd.,* 1998 WL 164824 (S.D.N.Y. 1998); UCC Draft Revisions sec. 2-104 n. 1. Nonetheless, because of the exceptions to and other doubts regarding such preemption, parties who reside or do business in a jurisdiction where a statute of frauds still exists (or involved in transactions with such parties) may be uncomfortable in relying on the CISG without a signed writing until appropriate legal reform has occurred.

68. For example, see the Model EDI Trading Partner Agreement, sec. 1.5 ("Each party shall adopt as its signature an electronic identification consisting of symbol(s) or code(s) which are to be affixed to or contained in each Document

transmitted by such party ('Signatures'). Each party agrees that any Signature of such party affixed to or contained in any transmitted Document shall be sufficient to verify such party originated such Document. . . . ") and sec. 3.3.2 ("Any Document properly transmitted pursuant to this Agreement shall be considered . . . to be a 'writing' or 'in writing'; and any such Document when containing, or to which there is affixed, a Signature . . . shall be deemed for all purposes (a) to have been 'signed.' . . .").

69. Frequently, a party is permitted to delay performance if such delay arises from the occurrence of unforeseeable disasters in the general environment or marketplace (flood, earthquake, fire, war, rioting, etc.), sometimes called "acts of God" or "force majeure." See Farnsworth, *Contracts,* sec. 9.5.

70. In other words, the vendor's Web site can easily be programmed to download the purchased software or information to the buyer without any manual command or oversight by an individual.

71. UCC sec. 2-601.

72. Farnsworth, *Contracts,* sec. 8.12, pp. 616–22.

73. UCC sec. 2-608 (emphasis added). UCC sec. 2-508 also permits a seller who is not in strict compliance a reasonable time to *cure,* or correct, the nonconformity.

74. UCC sec. 2-610. For general information, refer to Farnsworth, *Contracts,* sec. 8.20, pp. 655–66.

75. UCC sec. 2-716. See also UCITA sec. 811.

76. *The Restatement (Second) of Contracts,* secs. 346–49. For general information regarding damages for breach of contract, see Farnsworth, *Contracts,* sec. 12.8, pp. 871–73.

77. UCC sec. 2-715. The ability of a plaintiff to claim an award for damages is limited by the extent to which the plaintiff has taken appropriate steps to *mitigate* damages.

78. Restatement, § 355 and Farnsworth, Contracts, § 12.8, pp. 874-79.

79. For example, see the Model EDI Trading Partner Agreement, sec. 4.6. Clauses limiting liability are not enforceable unless they are reasonable in light of the circumstances (UCC sec. 2-718). Under British law, the Unfair Contract Terms Act of 1977 and the Unfair Terms in Consumer Contracts Regulations of 1994 provide that unreasonable limitations are not enforceable against consumers.

80. UCC Draft Revisions, sec. 2-212 (electronic messages; attribution); UCITA secs. 213 and 214; UETA sec. 9; UN Model Law, article 13.

81. Not all of these measures are available or appropriate in all applications and situations. See chapter 4 concerning other technical controls.

82. Electronic records may also be important evidence in the enforcement of rights and remedies outside of contract law, such as cases involving negligence or intentional wrongs, that is, torts.

83. UETA sec. 13. See also UN Model Law, articles 8-10, which provide for the authentication and admissibility of digital transmissions under the best-evidence rule as long as certain standards for system integrity are satisfied; E-sign presented in section 8.1.

84. Model EDI Trading Partner Agreement, sec. 3.3.4, which provides for the admissibility of "Signed Documents" in the context of authentication, best-evidence, and hearsay rules; Trade Electronic Data Interchange System (TEDIS), European Model EDI Agreement, article 10 (1991): "messages [that] are transmitted in accordance with an authentication procedure such as a digital signature . . . shall have, between parties, a comparable evidential value to that accorded to a signed written document."

85. *Federal Rules of Evidence ("Fed. R. Evid.")* 901. See also Uniform Law Conference of Canada, Uniform Electronic Evidence Act (1998) sec. 3 <http://www.law.ualberta.ca/alri/ulc/acts/eeeact.htm>.

86. The physical storage and retrieval of a particular item of evidence often constitute what is termed that item's *chain of custody.*

87. U.S. Department of Justice, *Admissibility of Electronically Filed Federal Records as Evidence: A Guideline for Federal Managers and Counsel* (October 1990), 2.

88. There has been some case law to this effect. For example, see *United States v. Scholle,* 553 F2d 1109, 1124–25 (8th Cir.), *cert. denied,* 434 U.S. 940 (1977), stating that computer storage needs a more comprehensive foundation for admissibility, including testimony on procedures for input control, such as a test for ensuring accuracy and reliability. Some commentators argue that doubts as to the source and accuracy of a computer record should not affect its admissibility, but rather its credibility and therefore the weight

that the fact finder places on the record as evidence (*Manual for Complex Litigation Second,* sec. 21.446 [1985], Judiciary, Federal Judicial Center, Washington, D.C.).

89. A. Michael Froomkin, "The Essential Role of Trusted Third Parties in Electronic Commerce," 75 *Or. L. Rev.* 49 (1996); Sharon F. DiPaolo, Note, "The Application of the Uniform Commercial Code Section 2-201 Statute of Frauds to Electronic Commerce," 13 *Journal of Law & Commerce* 143, 152–54 (1993).

90. In particular, see section 8.2 regarding non-repudiation of origin, section 8.6 regarding trusted third parties (including notaries), and chapter 9 regarding the role of notaries in the certificate enrollment validation process.

91. See National Archives and Records Administration regulations 36 CFR sec. 1234 et seq. (2000); and *Armstrong v. Executive Office of the President,* 810 F. Supp. 335 (D.D.C.), *off'd in part, rev'd and remanded in part,* 1 F3d 1274 (D.C. Cir. 1993).

92. Federal Rules of Evidence 1002 and 1003. Where no genuine question about the authenticity of the original is raised, a duplicate is admissible. The best-evidence rule is common among many jurisdictions in both common and civil law.

93. See also the Utah Digital Signature Act, which provides that a "copy of a digitally signed message is as effective, valid, and enforceable as the original of the message" (Utah Code sec. 46-3-404, <http://www.le.state.ut.us/~code/TITLE46/46_03.htm>).

94. Case law has generally supported the reliability of computer data for purposes of the best-evidence rule in the context of contract and certain other disputes. *People of California v. Hernandez,* 64 Cal. Rprt. 2d 769 (Cal. Ct. of App. 1997); *United States v. Briscoe,* 896 F2d 1476, 1495 (7th Cir.), *cert. denied,* 111 S. Ct. 173 (1990); *In re Gulph Woods Corp.,* 82 B.R. 373 (E.D. Pa. 1988); *United States v. Greenlee,* 380 F. Supp. 652 (E.D. Pa. 1974), *aff'd,* 517 F2d 899 (3rd Civ. 1975). See also Deborah L. Wilkerson, "Electronic Commerce under the U.C.C. Section 2-201 Statute of Frauds: Are Electronic Messages Enforceable?" 41 *Kan. L. Rev.* 403, 423–24 (1992). The Canadian Uniform Electronic Evidence Act provides for presumptions of integrity under certain conditions (secs. 4 and 5).

95. Federal Rules of Evidence 803(6).

96. *Briscoe,* 896 F2d at 1494; Wilkerson, "Electronic Commerce," 424. The case law is bolstered by the adoption of the U.S. National Archives and Records Administration's Electronic Records Management regulations, which specifically permit the judicial use of electronic records under Federal Rule of Evidence 803(8), the "public records exception" to the hearsay rule. 36 CFR. sec. 1234.24 available at <http://law.house.gov/cfr.html>.

97. Federal Rules of Evidence 803 (6).

98. UCC sec. 1-201(31).

99. As explained later, the EU Directive and the UN Model Law on Electronic Commerce both contain presumptions regarding the evidentiary weight of certain electronic communications.

100. For example, see *Moore v. Arkansas,* 688 SW2d 733, 734 (Ark. 1985): "[T]here is a presumption that a letter mailed was received by the person to whom it was addressed."

101. Utah Code, sec. 46-3-406, <http://www.state.ut.us>.

102. EU Directive, sec. 5(1).

103. For example, UCC sec. 2-316(2) prohibits a merchant from disclaiming implied warranties in connection with a sale of goods unless the disclaimer is in "writing and conspicuous."

104. Ellen Kirsh, former general counsel for America Online, speaking at the Worldwide Electronic Commerce Conference, Bethesda, MD, October 20, 1995.

105. See the alternatives quoted in M. S. Baum, *Federal Certification Authority Liability and Policy,* NIST-GCR-94-654, June 94 (Gaithersburg, MD: National Institute of Standards and Technology, 1993), footnote 83, pp. 35–36, available at <http://www.verisign.com/repository/pubs>.

106. See Skip Sigel, Theo Ling, and Joshua Izenberg, "The Validity and Enforceability of Web-Wrap Agreements and Assessing the Need for Legislation," <http://www.law.ualberta.ca/alri/ulc/current/ewebwrap.htm>. See also the well-known shrink-wrap case *ProCD Inc. v. Zeidenberg,* 86 F3d 1447 (7th Cir. 1996) and *In Re RealNetworks, Inc. Privacy Litigation,* 2000 WL 631341 (slip May 8, 2000, N.D. Ill.), which held that Web-based contracts satisfy legal signature and writing requirements.

107. In this context, mechanisms can be deployed that require a user to take further affirmative actions to demonstrate consent, including, for example, typing out text stating "I agree," clicking on a secondary button that requests a response to the question "Are you sure?", requiring a response to a statement such as "by clicking here, you are signing the agreement," or even requiring the user to dictate a voice clip to be digitized and digitally signed by the user that restates the terms and willingness to enter into the proposed bargain. The possibilities for integrating other "notice-enhancing" mechanisms are boundless.

108. UCITA sec. 102(a)(14). See also the consumer provisions in E-sign in Appendix B.

109. By *consumer* we refer generally to a person who engages in commerce for his or her own personal or household (as opposed to business) use or purpose. UCITA sec. 102(a)(15) defines *consumer* as "an individual who is a licensee of information or informational rights that the individual at the time of contracting intended to be used primarily for personal, family, or household purposes."

110. For a summary of consumer protection issues in the context of e-commerce, see the Federal Trade Commission (FTC) Web site, <http://www.ftc.gov>, and regarding Canadian law, the report of Gowling, Strathy, and Henderson for the Office of Consumer Affairs, Industry Canada, at <http://strategis.ic.gc.ca/SSG/ca01031e.html>.

111. "This law does not override any rule of law intended for the protection of consumers" (UN Model Law, article 1, no.**). Delegates to the UNCITRAL drafting process for the UN Model Law in 1996 noted the lack of a common definition of *consumer* and the dearth of consistent legal treatment of consumers across jurisdictions (Guide to the Enactment of the UN Model Law, ¶ 27, available at <http://www.uncitral.org/english/sessions/wg_ec/ml-ec-bck-docs/wp-64.pdf>). The draft UN Model Law on Electronic Signatures employ identical language directly in the text of article 1.

112. UCC sec. 2A-104; UCC Draft Revisions sec. 2-104(a)(2); UCITA secs. 104 and 105.

113. A summary and the full text of these OECD Guidelines, as well as press releases and other related information, can be found at <http://www.oecd.org/dsti/sti/it/consumer/prod/guidelines.htm>.

114. Ralph Nader, "Digital Signature Legislation Must Protect Consumers," *Computerworld* (January 17, 2000), available at <http://www.computerworld.com/cwi/story/0,1199,NAV47_STO40753,00.html>. See also Consumers Interna-

tional, "Study for the European Commission on Practical Consumer Experiences with E-Commerce," available at <http://europa.eu.int/comm/dg24/library/surveys/sur12_en.html>.

115. See 15 U.S.C. secs. 6801 et seq. (enacted December 1999). Congress has targeted November 2000 as the effective date for the Financial Modernization Act privacy provisions.

116. HIPPA, Public Law 104-191 (August 21, 1996), 110 Stat. 1936, amended the Public Health Service Act, the Employee Retirement Income Security Act of 1974 (ERISA), and the Internal Revenue Code of 1986.

117. 15 U.S.C. sec. 6501 et seq. (1998). See also <http://www.ftc.gov>.

118. See the FTC Web site at <http://www.ftc.gov/acoas/index.htm>. See also the FTC's report on its enforcement activities in 1999 under the Truth in Lending Act and other financial services consumer protection statutes at <http://www.ftc.gov/os/2000/01/tlreporttofed2000.htm>. Additionally, the FTC has presented a report to Congress ("Privacy Online: Fair Information Practices in the Electronic Marketplace") in which it concludes that self-regulatory efforts alone are insufficient and recommends that Congress enact legislation that will ensure adequate protection of consumer online privacy. See <http://www.ftc.gov/reports/privacy2000/privacy2000.pdf>.

119. See the following three bills introduced in the U.S. Congress in 1999 and 2000: the Consumer Internet Privacy Enhancement Act, S. 2928 (July 26, 2000); the Consumer Privacy Protection Act, S. 2606 (May 23, 2000); and the Online Privacy Protection Act of 1999, S. 809 (April 15, 1999).

120. See the U.S. Department of Commerce Web site, <http://www.ita.doc.gov>. In mid 2000 the United States became recognized by the EU as having methods for protecting data privacy that meet the requirements of EU member states. See <http://europa.eu.int/comm/internal_market/en/media/dataprot>.

121. See Robert E. Smith, *Compilation of State and Federal Privacy Laws* (Privacy Journal 1992) available at <http://www.townonline.com/privacyjournal/>.

122. But see Volokh, "Freedom of Speech, Information Privacy and the Troubling Implications of a Right to Stop People from Speaking About You," available at <http://www.law.ucla.edu/faculty/volokh/privacy.htm>.

123. See *International Shoe Co. v. Washington,* 326 U.S. 310 (1945). See also its progeny, including *World-Wide Volkswagen Corp. v. Woodson,* 444 U.S. 286 (1980) and *Asahi Metal Indus. Co. v. Superior Court,* 480 U.S. 102 (1982).

124. See <http://europa.eu.int/eur-lex/en/lif/dat/1968/en_468A0927_01.html>.

125. See the following articles for additional information on personal jurisdiction issues: Effross, "Legal Architecture of Virtual Stores"; Christopher Gooch, note in "The Internet, Personal Jurisdiction, and the Federal Long-Arm Statute: Rethinking the Concept of Jurisdiction," 15 *Ariz. J. Int'l. & Comp. Law* 635 (1998); Michael MacClary, "Personal Jurisdiction and the Internet," 3 *Suffolk J. Trial & App. Adv.* 93 (1998); Richard S. Zembek, comment in "Jurisdiction and the Internet: Fundamental Fairness in the Networked World of Cyberspace," 6 *Alb. L.J. Sci. & Tech.* 339 (1996); Ogilvy Renault, "Jurisdiction and the Internet: Are Traditional Rules Enough?" <http://www.law.ualberta.ca/alri/ulc/current/ejurisd.htm>; Michel Racicot, Mark S. Hayes, Alec R. Szibbo, and Pierre Trudel, "The Cyberspace Is Not a No-Law Land," <http://strategis.ic.gc.ca/SSG/it03117e.html>.

126. The ubiquitous nature of the Internet complicates the application of traditional jurisdictional law. A posting is available in all jurisdictions simultaneously. Web storefronts may be construed as offers to conduct business in foreign jurisdictions under the applicable local law. The Internet is unique in being both local and global simultaneously. For examples of cases involving jurisdiction and e-commerce or other electronic communications, see *Intercon, Inc. v. Bell Atlantic Internet Solutions, Inc.,* 2000 U.S. App. Lexis 3592 (10th Cir. 2000); *GTE New Media Services, Inc. v. Bellsouth Corp.,* 199 F3d 1343 (D.C. Cir. 2000); *Mink v. AAAA Development, LLC,* 190 F3d 333 (5th Cir. 1999); *3D Systems v. Aarotech Labs, Inc.,* 160 F3d 1373 (Fed. Cir. 1998); *Online Partners.com, Inc. v. Atlanticnet Media Corporation,* 2000 U.S. Dist. Lexis 783 (N.D. Cal. 2000).

127. See UCC article 8.

128. UCC sec. 1-201(15) (documents of title). Article 7 of the UCC governs the ownership, transfer, and, together with UCC article 9, granting of security interests in documents of title.

129. UCC sec. 1-201(15).

130. See E-Sign Title II in Appendix B for additional thoughts on the problem of inherent uniqueness, see Walter A. Effross, "Notes on PKI and Digital Negotiability: Would the Cybercourier Carry My Luggage?" 38 *Jurimetrics* 385 (1998), available at <http://www.effross.com>.

131. For example, see the approach to electronic bills of lading taken in Comité Maritime International (CMI), "Rules for Electronic Bills of Lading," *Paris/ELECTRO* 15 (June 22, 1990). See also Baum and Perritt, *Electronic Contracting,* sec. 11.9, pp. 689–93, and appendix D, pp. 799–803; R. Kelly, "Comment: The CMI Charts a Course on the Sea of Electronic Data Interchange: Rules for Electronic Bills of Lading," 16 *Maritime Lawyer* 349 (1992); 349; J. Gliniecki and C. Ogada, "The Legal Acceptance of Electronic Documents, Writings, Signatures, and Notices in International Transportation Conventions: A Challenge in the Age of Global Electronic Commerce," 13 *Journal of International Law & Business* 117, 136–141 (1992).

132. UN Model Law, articles 16 and 17. The Canadian Uniform Electronic Commerce Act follows the UN Model Law example in sec. 25, <http://www.law.ualberta.ca/alri/ulc/current/euecafin.htm>.

133. See <http://www.bolero.net>.

134. UCC sec. 5-104. See also R. D. Whitaker, "Letters of Credit and Electronic Commerce," 31 *Idaho Law Review* 699 (1995).

135. International Chamber of Commerce, *Uniform Customs and Practices for Documentary Credits,* Pub. No. 500 (1993), <http://www.iccwbo.org>. Letters of credit between international parties commonly incorporate the *UCP* standards by reference.

136. *UCP,* article 11. Of course, institutions and other parties such as U.S. banks, which are also subject to the UCC, may not be comfortable with the enforceability of an electronic letter of credit until appropriate reforms have been adopted.

137. UCC Draft Revisions, sec. 5-104. Section 5-102(a)(14) of the Draft Revisions defines *record* as "information that is inscribed on a tangible medium, or that is stored in an electronic or other medium and is retrievable in perceivable form." See also Whitaker, "Letters of Credit and Electronic Commerce," 711–12; J. Rogers, "An Essay on Horseless Carriages and Paperless Negotiable Instruments: Some Lessons from the Article 8 Revision," 31 *Idaho Law Review* 687 (1995).

138. Patents grant an inventor the right to exclude others from producing or using the inventor's discovery or invention for a limited period of time. See <http://wwwsecure.law.cornell.edu/topics/patent.html>.

139. See generally <http://wwwsecure.law.cornell.edu/topics/trademark.html>.

140. A copyright gives the owner the exclusive right to reproduce, distribute, perform, display, or license his or her work. See <http://wwwsecure.law.cornell.edu/topics/copyright.html>.

141. See appendix A of this book regarding regulation of content by Internet service providers.

142. The Anti-Cybersquatting Consumer Protection Act added a new section 43(d) to the Lanham Act, 15 U.S.C. sec. 1125(d), providing for remedies against anyone who—with bad-faith intent to profit—registers, traffics in, or uses a domain name that (a) is identical or confusingly similar to a mark that was distinctive when the domain name was registered, (b) is identical or confusingly similar or dilutive of a mark that was famous when the domain name was registered, or (c) infringes marks and names protected by statute, such as the Olympic symbol. A separate section of the Anti-Cybersquatting Act that is not included in the Lanham Act provides protection against the unauthorized registration of personal names as domain names.

143. A VAT is an indirect tax applied to the value added at each stage of production (primary, manufacturing, wholesale, and retail). At the retail level, a VAT works as a tax on consumption, much like sales taxes in many U.S. states.

144. For example, the growth of e-commerce has resulted in a crisis-level tax-base erosion in Hong Kong, a traditional center for the physical distribution of goods. Gren Manuel, "Taxes Lost Through the Net," *South China Morning Post* (February 8, 2000), available at <http://www.technologypost.com/internet/DAILY/20000208093828357.asp?Section=Main>.

145. See the Internet Tax Freedom Act of 1998, Title XI of Public Law 105-277, the Omnibus Appropriations Act of 1998. The Web site of the Advisory Commission on Electronic Commerce, <http://www.ecommercecommission.org/about.htm>, details e-commerce taxation issues, including the Internet Tax Freedom Act.

146. For example, see a proposal by the National Governor's Association, <http://www.nga.org/Pubs/IssueBriefs/2000/Sum000202TeleCom.asp>. Also, sophisticated software is now available to compute and process sales and use taxes (as well as corresponding tax exemptions) over the Internet. Such soft-

ware can be combined with digital authentication techniques to produce even more powerful tools to facilitate Internet taxation. See, for example, <http://www.taxware.com>.

147. See, for example, the OECD and ICC Web sites, <http://www.oecd.org> and <http://www.iccwbo.org/home/menu_taxation.asp>.

148. For a general overview of federal laws in this area, see Baum, *Federal Certification Authority Liability and Policy,* 144–59 <http://www.usdoj.gov/criminal/cybercrime/fedcode.htm>. For state laws in this area, see Smedinghoff, *Online Law,* 477–89.

149. Codified at 18 U.S.C. sec. 1030. One of the key provisions of this act is section 1030(a)(5)(B), which prohibits "the transmission of a program, information, code, or command to a computer or computer system with reckless disregard of a substantial and unjustifiable risk that the transmission will damage, or cause damage to, a computer, computer system, network, information, data or program. . . ."

150. Codified at 18 U.S.C. secs. 2510–711.

151. Enacted in 1994, CALEA is codified at 47 U.S.C. 1001 et seq.

152. See generally W. Page Keeton et al., eds., *Prosser and Keeton on the Law of Torts* (St. Paul, MN: West, 1984). One of the landmark cases in tort law, *The T.J. Hooper v. Northern Barge Corp.,* 60 F2d 737 (2nd Cir. 1932), reinforced the principle that the standard of care required to avoid liability for negligence is not based necessarily on the general industry standard but on the availability of technology (whether or not the industry has adopted it generally).

153. For example, the OECD has promulgated a definition of computer abuse, but the definition is so broad and ambiguous as to be nearly meaningless: *computer abuse* means "any illegal, unethical or unauthorized behaviour relating to the automatic processing and the transmission of data" or "any illegal action in which a computer is a tool or object of the crime" <http://www.oecd.org>.

154. Take, for example, the oft-proposed crime of unauthorized use, which poses difficulties because, in practice, authorization is frequently so discretionary that it is difficult to codify.

155. This issue is artfully considered in "Government's Opposition to Defendant's Motion to Dismiss the Indictment," noted in *United States v. Morris,* 728 F. Supp. 95 (N.D.N.Y. 1990), *aff'd.,* 928 F2d 504 (2nd Cir.), *cert. denied,* 112 S. Ct. 72 (1991).

156. Overregulation can be as stifling to e-commerce as underregulation. Accordingly, it is important that the continual advance of regulation to reduce uncertainty in e-commerce transactions be deliberate and well conceived.

157. Even when effective regulation is in place, e-commerce participants generally benefit by the certainty and flexibility of a contract within the parameters of such regulation.

158. Due to the costs of negotiation, online consumers are often faced with requests to enter into a standard form (sometimes referred to as *adhesion*) contract with vendors and should be aware that such forms typically contain provisions that grant significant legal advantages to the vendor. See Michael J. Madison, "Legal-Ware: Contract and Copyright in the Digital Age," 67 *Fordham L. Rev.* 1025 (1998); 1025; Jerry C. Liu, Robert J. O'Connell, and W. Scott Petty, "Electronic Commerce: Using Clickwrap Agreements," 15 No. 12 *Computer Lawyer* 10, (1998); T. D. Rakoff, "Contracts of Adhesion: An Essay in Reconstruction," 96 *Harvard Law Review* 1174 (1983).

159. Model EDI Trading Partner Agreement, sec. 1.4 (security procedures).

160. Model Electronic Payments Agreement, sec. 7.1.

161. TEDIS, European Model EDI Agreement, article 6.

162. M. S. Baum, "Linking Security and the Law of Computer-Based Commerce," in *Workshop on Security Procedures for the Interchange of Electronic Documents,* NIST Internal Report NISTIR 5247, ed. Roy G. Saltman (Springfield, VA: National Institute of Standards and Technology, 1993), 23–34.

163. Indeed, some pundits claim that no security is needed to satisfy simple signature requirements.

164. We use *computer-based signatures* here in the same sense that we referred to *electronic signatures* earlier. Both should be distinguished from the use of a digital signature mechanism.

165. See, for example, the efforts and objectives of X9 at <http://www.x9.org> and of the American Institute of Certified Public Accountants (AICPA) at <http://aicpa.org>.

166. Auditors may do well to review the recognized audit controls in EDI and PKI as models. For the first nationally recognized, publicly developed EDI audit

program, including sections on electronic trade agreements and security, see Michael S. Baum, Gerald R. Bielfeldt, Joseph Coyle, Donald R. Loesch. Joyce A. Mornich, Philip Oddo, and Horton L. Sorkin, *A Model EDI Audit Program* (Data Interchange Standards Association, October 1995), <http://www.disa.org>. The first standardized PKI control objectives were developed in X 9.79: Public Key Infrastructure—Practices and Policy Framework, discussed in section 8.3.

Information Security Technologies

Thishis chapter introduces the special technologies that underlie secure e-commerce and explains the main security concepts and terms used in the remainder of the book. We commence with an explanation of some basic information security principles. This is followed by an introduction to the main technological elements used in providing information security, including symmetric cryptography, public-key cryptography, digital signatures, cryptographic key management techniques, and authentication mechanisms. Finally, the question of how to maximize justifiable trust in an implemented system is discussed. The topics addressed in this chapter are extremely complex when considered in depth, and the introductory material given here is kept to a high level. For the reader interested in the details, we provide sources of more comprehensive material.

4.1 Information Security Fundamentals

We commence by introducing some fundamental principles underlying information security and some general concepts used in designing and determining the need to use particular security mechanisms. For detailed coverage of this subject, see texts by Pfleeger or Ford.[1]

Basic Concepts

Information security has four main objectives:

- *Confidentiality:* ensuring that information is not disclosed or revealed to unauthorized persons
- *Integrity:* ensuring consistency of data, in particular, preventing unauthorized creation, alteration, or destruction of data
- *Availability:* ensuring that legitimate users are not unduly denied access to resources, including information resources, computing resources, and communications resources
- *Authorized use:* ensuring that resources are not used by unauthorized persons or in unauthorized ways

The main technological disciplines for achieving these objectives are *communications security* and *computer security.* Communications security relates to the protection of information while it is being transferred from one system to another. Computer security relates to the protection of information within a computer system, including such aspects as the security properties of operating system software and database management software. Communications security and computer security safeguards need to work in conjunction with safeguards in other security disciplines, including:

- *Physical security,* such as door locks, guards, guns, multitier building access controls, and tamperproofing of equipment
- *Personnel security,* such as employee screening and awareness, education, and training programs
- *Administrative security,* such as security audit, accountability controls, and incident response planning
- *Media security,* such as controlling the sensitivity-marking and reproduction controls on sensitive stored information and ensuring that discarded paper or magnetic media containing sensitive information are destroyed securely

To explain how communications security and computer security work, we need to first introduce a few basic concepts:

- A *security policy* is a set of rules which apply to all security-relevant activities in a *security domain*. A security domain is typically the set of computer and communications resources belonging to one organization. The rules are established by an *authority* for that security domain.
- *Authorization,* which is part of a security policy, is the granting of rights. It amounts to establishing who may do what to which resource.[2]
- *Accountability* is a fundamental principle underlying any security policy. Individuals who take actions that are governed by a security policy must be accountable for their actions. This provides an important link to personnel security.
- A *threat* is a person, thing, event, or idea which poses some danger to an asset in terms of that asset's confidentiality, integrity, availability, or legitimate use. Threats may result from deliberate actions, such as hacker penetration, or accidental actions, such as a message sent in error to the wrong address.
- An *attack* is an actual realization of a threat. A *passive attack* involves unauthorized monitoring, but not alteration of data, for example, wiretapping; an *active attack* involves deliberate alteration of information.
- *Safeguards* are controls, mechanisms, policies, and procedures that protect assets from threats.
- *Vulnerabilities* are weaknesses in safeguards or the absence of safeguards.
- *Risk* is an estimate of the cost of a vulnerability, taking into account the probability of a successful attack. Risk is highest when the value of a vulnerable asset is high and the probability of a successful attack is high. Conversely, risk is lowest when the value of the vulnerable asset is low and the probability of a successful attack is low.
- *Risk analysis* is a process which gives a quantitative or a qualitative assessment of whether expenditure on safeguards is warranted.

Threats

There are many potential threats to e-commerce information systems; the main categories are

- *Masquerade:* An intruder pretends to be a legitimate user. Many other types of attack are built on masquerade as the first stage. Masquerade can use both technological and nontechnological means, for example:

- *Sniffing:* Learning passwords by observing passing traffic on a LAN
- *Password cracking*: Using a computer to exhaustively guess passwords until the correct one is found
- *Trashing:* Learning secrets such as passwords from a victim's trash
- *Social engineering:* Duping an authorized person into disclosing account or password details in a telephone call

- *System penetration:* An unauthorized person gains access to a computer system and modifies system or application files, steals confidential information, or illegitimately uses resources. System penetration may result from masquerade or by exploiting system weaknesses.

- *Authorization violation:* A person authorized to use a system for one purpose uses it for an unauthorized purpose. This threat is manifested either by *insiders* misusing or abusing a system or by an external penetration. An authorization violation may exploit a system vulnerability to gain privileged access to a system, greatly increasing the potential impact of an initial penetration.

- *Planting:* Usually as a follow-up to a system penetration or authorization violation attack, an intruder leaves behind a planted capability to perpetrate or aid future attacks. Variations include

  - *Trojan horse:* Software which outwardly has a legitimate purpose but which, when executed, compromises the security of the user. An example of a Trojan horse is a screen-saver that, while creating a pretty screen image, surreptitiously scans a PC's memory and disk files for character strings formatted as credit card numbers and sends all such strings to an external network address accessible by the attacker.

  - *Virus:* A packaged, automated combination of system penetration and planting. The system penetration typically involves masquerade or exploiting a system weakness. The planting involves installing a capability to reperpetrate the original attack on other targets. The planted component may also cause local damage or mischief.

- *Communications monitoring:* Without penetrating the victim's computer, an attacker learns confidential information, some of which may facilitate a future attack, by monitoring communications on the communications path.

- *Data modification:* Without penetrating the victim's computer, an attacker tampers with communicated data or the communications process. For example, an attacker might deliberately change data fields in financial transaction messages in transit through a computer network.

- *Network spoofing:* A type of masquerade in which one network system is made to appear as another. Variations include
  - *Server spoofing:* An attacker installs a bogus server and dupes a user into voluntarily giving sensitive information to that system.
  - *DNS spoofing:* An attacker interferes with the operation of the DNS system, causing connections for a legitimate server to be rerouted to the wrong IP address.
- *Denial of service:* These attacks affect the *availability* objective. Legitimate access to information, services, or other resources is deliberately impeded. For example, a service access port is deliberately used so heavily that service to other users is disrupted, or an Internet address is *flooded* with packets.[3] A *distributed denial of service* attack is one in which many different sources are programmed to flood a target destination.
- *Repudiation:* A party to a communication later falsely claims that the communication did not take place.

Safeguards

Safeguards can be deployed to prevent or reduce the likelihood of threats being realized or to reduce the impact of a realized threat. Safeguards span all of the security disciplines, including communications security, computer security, physical security, personnel security, administrative security, and media security. A security regime is only as strong as its weakest link. For effective security, safeguards from the various disciplines should be used together. For example, a technically sound password system, designed to counter system penetration attempts, will be ineffective if users leave written passwords in an unsecured place or can be duped into revealing a password to an unknown telephone caller or to a rogue Web site's enrollment form. In communications security and computer security, safeguards are often referred to as *security services*. These are not services in the usual people-oriented sense; the terminology reflects that one part of a system provides a service (typically on demand) to another part of the system. There are five primary security services:

- *Authentication services* provide assurance of identity; that is, when someone or something claims to have a particular identity (such as a name), an authentication service can confirm the correctness of this claim. Authentication therefore counters masquerade threats. Authentication has two main variants:

1. *Entity authentication* authenticates an identity presented by a remote communicating party; passwords, for example, are an entity authentication mechanism.

2. *Data origin authentication* authenticates the claimed identity of the originator of a message or other data item.

- *Access control services* protect against unauthorized access to resources, such as processing, communications, or information resources. In this context, *unauthorized access* can mean unauthorized use, disclosure, modification, destruction, or invocation of operations. Access control is the primary means for enforcing authorization.

- *Confidentiality services* protect against information being revealed to unauthorized persons. Confidentiality generally involves hiding data items[4] by encrypting them. However, information can be leaked in other ways. For example, an observer may monitor the number, size, and frequency of messages delivered to a particular address, without necessarily seeing the contents of those messages.

- *Data integrity services* protect against data being changed inconsistently with the recognized security policy. Changing, in this sense, might include adding, deleting, or modifying data elements.

- *Non-repudiation services* protect against one party to a transaction or communication activity later falsely denying that the transaction or activity occurred.

These security services are not something newly conceived for electronic environments. Rather, they are electronic counterparts of checks and balances used in nonelectronic systems. Table 4.1 provides some examples of mechanisms used to implement nonelectronic analogs of these security services.

Non-repudiation

Non-repudiation is fundamentally different from the other security services. It serves to protect users against threats from other legitimate users, as much as from unknown attackers. Non-repudiation can be defined as the attribute of a communication that protects against a successful dispute of its origin, submission, delivery, or content.

Table 4.1   Examples of Nonelectronic Security Mechanisms

Security Service	Nonelectronic Mechanism Examples
Authentication	Photo identification card Knowledge of mother's maiden name
Access Control	Locks and keys Master key system Checkpoint guard
Confidentiality	Sealed letter Opaque envelope Invisible ink
Integrity	Indelible ink Hologram on credit card
Non-repudiation	Notarized signature Certified or registered mail

The word *non-repudiation* might be a misnomer, since this security service does not eliminate the threat of repudiation; that is, it does not prevent any party from repudiating a communication or transaction. Rather, non-repudiation facilitates the availability of evidence to support the speedy resolution of disputes.

The motivation for non-repudiation services is not just to prevent communicating parties from successfully cheating each other. It also reflects the reality that computer systems are imperfect and that circumstances can arise in which two or more parties may hold different views of an event.

Consider some of the problems that can arise in the world of traditional paper-based business transactions. Paper documents, such as quotations, bids, contracts, orders, invoices, and checks play a critical role in the conducting of business between organizations. However, many problems can occur in their handling, such as

- Document lost in the mail
- Document lost by recipient before processing
- Document generated by an unauthorized person
- Document accidentally corrupted within an organization or while in transit between organizations
- Document forged or fraudulently modified within an organization or while in transit between organizations
- Disputed filing time of a document

To aid in systematically dealing with such problems, various traditional mechanisms are employed, such as signatures, countersignatures, notarized signatures, receipts, postmarks, and certified and registered mail. If good business practices are followed, there is usually an adequate paper trail to facilitate dispute resolution. If necessary, persuasive evidence is available in the form of records held by the disputing parties plus third parties such as the post office, courier agents, and notaries. With the help of such evidence, parties may be able to resolve their differences themselves or, in some cases, with the assistance of third parties, such as mediators, arbitrators, or courts of law.

While many problems with traditional business transactions are shared by electronic transactions, there are differences that affect the methods and strength of proving the validity of such transactions. For example, in electronic transactions, fewer humans are involved, whereas in traditional paper-based transactions, interrogating these humans can assist greatly in resolving disputes. On the other hand, certain problems with electronic transactions are easier to resolve when digital signatures (described later in this chapter) and other security enhancing technologies are invoked.

In principle, non-repudiation disputes can arise in any of a variety of events that affect two or more parties. Such disputes concern whether a particular event occurred, when it occurred, what parties were involved, what information was associated with the event, and what actions were taken by each of the parties. Non-repudiation is discussed in detail in chapter 9.

4.2   Introduction to Cryptography

Cryptographic techniques, such as *encryption* and *digital signatures,* are important building blocks in the implementation of all of the security services introduced in the preceding section.

The most basic building block is called a *cryptosystem* or *encryption algorithm.* A cryptosystem defines a pair of data transformations called *encryption* and *decryption.* Encryption is applied to data, known as *plaintext,* that directly represents information such as the words or numbers constituting a message. Encryption transforms the plaintext data into unintelligible data called *ciphertext.* A decryption transformation, applied to cipher-text, results in the regeneration of the original plaintext.

An encryption transformation has two inputs: the plaintext and an independent data value known as an *encryption key.* Similarly, a decryption transformation requires a *decryption key.* A key is a seemingly random string of bits. The key length, as a number of bits, depends on the particular cryptosystem.

An obvious use of a cryptosystem is to provide confidentiality. The plaintext represents unprotected, sensitive data. The corresponding ciphertext may be transmitted in untrusted environments because, if the cryptosystem is a good one, it will be infeasible for anyone to deduce the plaintext from the ciphertext without knowing the decryption key. Cryptosystems also have uses other than confidentiality, as will become apparent later in the chapter.

There are two basic types of cryptosystems: *symmetric* systems, which are sometimes called private-key or secret-key systems, and *public-key* systems, which are sometimes called asymmetric systems. These have distinct characteristics and are used in different ways to provide security services.

For comprehensive reference texts on modern cryptosystems, see Schneier or Menezes et al. For more basic tutorials on cryptography, see Davies and Price or Stinson.[5]

Symmetric Cryptosystems

Symmetric cryptosystems, which have been in use in commercial networks since the early 1970s, are characterized by the fact that the *same* key is used in the encryption and decryption transformations (see figure 4.1).

To provide confidentiality, a symmetric cryptosystem works as follows: Two systems, *A* and *B*, need to communicate securely. By some process (discussed later), they both

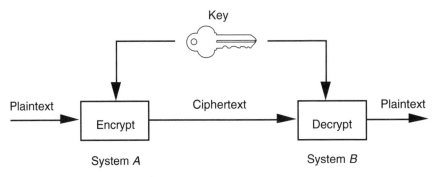

Figure 4.1   A Symmetric Cryptosystem

obtain a data value to use as a key. The key is kept secret from everybody except systems *A* and *B*. This enables either *A* or *B* to protect a message sent to the other system by encrypting the message using the key known only to them. Only these two systems can decrypt the message.

In a good symmetric cryptosystem, unless all bits of the key are correctly supplied to the decryption function, no information from the plaintext is revealed by the decryption function.

A symmetric cryptosystem operates either as a *block cipher* or a *stream cipher.* In a block cipher, the encryption function operates on a fixed-size block of plaintext, *n* bits in length, and generates a fixed-size block of ciphertext which is also *n* bits in length. (Typically, *n* is 64 or 128 bits.) The decryption function operates on an *n*-bit block of ciphertext and generates an *n*-bit block of plaintext. On the other hand, a stream cipher can operate over a plaintext message or stream of data of arbitrary size, generating ciphertext of the same size; a stream cipher typically processes the data as a sequence of characters, where a character can be considered to be one bit or a fixed number of bits.

Stream ciphers are often constructed using a block cipher as the basic building block. This has resulted in the definition of various *modes of operation* of block ciphers that enable them to function as stream ciphers. Two common modes of operation are *cipher block chaining* (CBC) and *cipher feedback* (CFB), both defined in U.S. federal government and ISO standards.[6] For technical details, see Davies and Price.[7]

These are the most common symmetric cryptosystems:

- *Data Encryption Standard (DES):* DES was adopted as a U.S. federal standard in 1977[8] and a financial industry standard in 1981[9] and served well as the primary

algorithm for protecting unclassified government information and financial industry transactions for roughly 20 years. DES is a block cipher which operates on
64-bit blocks of data and employs a 56-bit key. DES stood up well against attack,
at least by publicly disclosed means, until 1998, when the Electronic Frontier
Foundation constructed, for under $250,000, a DES-cracking hardware processor
known as "Deep Crack."[10] "Deep Crack" was able to solve a DES-cracking challenge issued by RSA Security in under three days. Later challenges of a similar
type have been solved more quickly. The demise of DES as a cryptosystem suitable for commercial use resulted primarily from its comparatively small key
space, that is, the number of possible key values, which, with a 56-bit key, is 2^{56},
or about 70 quadrillion. Technology has advanced to the point that it is now possible to build, without undue expense, processors that can try every key until they
find the one that successfully decrypts. This cryptanalytic approach is known as
an *exhaustive search.*

- *Advanced Encryption Standard (AES):* In recognition of the impending demise of
  DES, in 1997 the U.S. Department of Commerce launched the AES project,
  aimed at establishing a stronger standard algorithm to replace DES.[11] AES is a
  block cipher that can operate on 128-bit blocks of data and key sizes of 128, 192,
  and 256 bits. The algorithm definition, based on the Rijndael cryptosystem
  designed by Belgian cryptographers Dr. Joan Daemen and Dr. Vincent Riijmen, is
  targeted for formal adoption as a government standard in 2001, and widespread
  deployment is expected to ultimately result.[12]

- *Triple-DES:*[13] The effective key size of DES can be increased by using a
  multiple-encryption approach. Triple-DES involves an initial encryption of a
  64-bit block using key *a*, followed by a decryption of the result using key *b*,
  followed by an encryption of that result using key *c*. Two or three 56-bit keys are
  used (keys *a* and *c* are sometimes the same). The resultant algorithm is generally
  believed to be many orders of magnitude stronger than DES. A shortcoming of
  triple-DES is its comparatively high processor resource usage requirement, especially if implemented in software.

- *Rivest Ciphers:* The proprietary RC2, RC4, RC5,[14] and RC6 algorithms, attributed to Ron Rivest and RSA Security, Inc., are popular because of their relative
  simplicity and ease of implementation.

• *Other proprietary algorithms:* Several proprietary algorithms have been defined and are being used in commercial products. Examples are IDEA (International Data Encryption Algorithm) from Ascom-Tech in Switzerland, Bruce Schneier's Blowfish,[15] and CAST from Nortel.[16] While proprietary algorithms such as these may be good, it is difficult for the community at large to gain confidence in the strength of proprietary algorithms because of their limited exposure to public scrutiny.

Message Authentication Codes

Assume that a message is to be sent from its originator to a recipient with no requirement for confidentiality; however, the recipient needs confidence that the message was not modified en route. The necessary protection can be achieved using a *message authentication code* (MAC), also known as an integrity check-value or message integrity check. A MAC is an additional piece of data, generated by a message originator, that accompanies or is logically associated with the plaintext message in transit. The process is illustrated in figure 4.2. The value of the MAC depends on all bits of the input message; if any bit or bits of the message are changed after the MAC is generated, a different MAC value results, and the recipient is apprised that the message's integrity has been compromised.

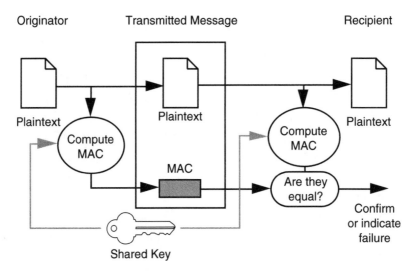

Figure 4.2   Message Authentication Code (MAC)

Upon receipt of the message, the recipient recalculates the MAC from the message content and checks that the two MAC values agree. This is similar to common error-detection procedures used in communications systems, for example, attaching a data field called a cyclic redundancy check (CRC) to a message. However, there is one major difference: The prospect of a deliberate attack must be taken into account. If an active attacker changes a message, there is nothing to prevent that attacker from also recalculating and replacing the CRC on the message so that the recipient cannot detect that data modification occurred. To protect against such attacks, the process for generating the MAC employs a secret key that is also known to the message recipient. The recipient can be confident that if the message contents and MAC are consistent upon receipt, someone who knows the key generated the MAC. Hence, message modification by an intruder can almost certainly be detected.

There are two common methods for generating MACs:

- *Hash-function based:* A method in which a hash function (discussed in section 4.3) is applied to a bit string that contains both the message data bits and the data bits of a secret key. This type of mechanism is known as a *keyed hash function* or an *HMAC.*[17]
- *Symmetric-cipher based:* A MAC generation method which uses a symmetric cryptosystem as a building block. This type of mechanism was standardized in 1986 and has been widely used by the financial industry.[18]

Public-Key Cryptosystems

The technology of public-key cryptography was introduced in 1976 by Whitfield Diffie and Martin Hellman of Stanford University.[19] In contrast to symmetric cryptosystems, a public-key cryptosystem uses a pair of related keys: one key for encryption and the other for decryption. Furthermore, we choose to consider the key pair as being linked to one of the systems involved. One key, the *private key,* is kept secret by that system, while the other key, the *public key,* can be publicly disclosed. The cryptosystem must have the property that, given knowledge of the public key, it is infeasible to determine the private key.

There are two basic modes in which public-key cryptosystems can be used, depending on whether the public key is used as the encryption key or decryption key. Consider first figure 4.3, which illustrates the *encryption mode.*

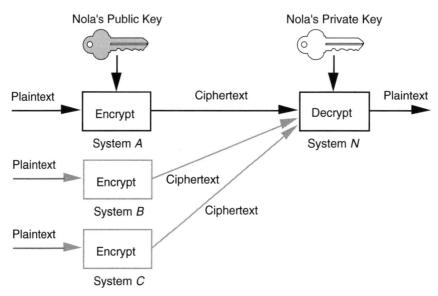

Figure 4.3   Public-Key Cryptosystem: Encryption Mode

Let us suppose that system *N* is part of Nola's Web server configuration supporting her e-market business. We choose to associate the key pair with Nola and to keep the private key securely hidden within system *N*. The public key is made known (by means we describe later) to all of Nola's customers and prospective customers. When Ali, the owner of system *A*, wants to send a confidential message to Nola, his system encrypts the message using Nola's public key. Only system *N* can successfully decrypt the message because it is the only place where the private key resides. The process is similar to symmetric encryption (as in figure 4.1), but with an important difference. Any of Nola's customers, such as Burt at system *B* and Charles at system *C*, can also send her a confidential message using only one key pair.

The other mode of use of a public-key cryptosystem, *authentication mode,* is illustrated in figure 4.4. System *V* is part of Vera's computer configuration that she uses to order supplies. In this case, we choose to associate the key pair with Vera and to keep the private key securely hidden within system *V*. The public key is made known to all of Vera's suppliers and anyone else who wants to know it. Suppose system *V* encrypts a message and sends it to Ali's system *A*. System *A* can decrypt the message using Vera's public key. We have not achieved any confidentiality here, since anyone can likely learn the public key and can

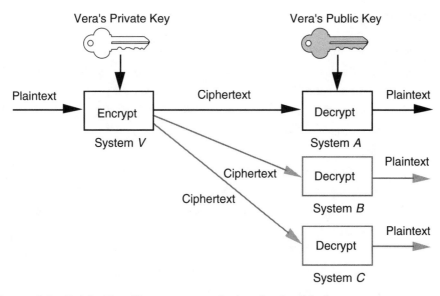

Figure 4.4 Public-Key Cryptosystem: Authentication Mode

decrypt the message. However, we have achieved something else. Anyone, such as Ali at system A, Burt at system B, or Charles at system C, who successfully decrypts the message can be certain that the message came from Vera, because the only place where the corresponding private key resides is in Vera's system V.

Hence, by using the private key as an encryption key, public-key cryptography can be used for data origin authentication and for ensuring the integrity of a message. This authentication mode of public-key cryptosystems provides the basis for building digital signature systems.

A public-key cryptosystem that can operate in both encryption and authentication modes is called a *reversible public-key cryptosystem.* Some public-key cryptosystems can operate in authentication mode but not encryption mode. They are known as *irreversible public-key cryptosystems.*

Public-key cryptosystems have characteristics that make them much more powerful than symmetric cryptosystems. However, public-key cryptosystems present a much greater challenge to the algorithm designer because the public key represents additional information that can be used in attacking the algorithm. Public-key systems in current use rely on the underlying assumption that a particular, known mathematical problem is difficult to solve.

RSA Algorithm

RSA is a reversible public-key cryptosystem, named after its inventors, Ron Rivest, Adi Shamir, and Len Adleman from the Massachusetts Institute of Technology (MIT). Its description was first published in 1978.[20] The RSA calculations, which are summarized in Appendix J, make use of a number called the public modulus, which forms part of the public key. The public modulus is obtained by multiplying two prime numbers[21] that form part of the private key.

The security of RSA depends on the fact that, while finding large prime numbers is relatively easy, factoring the product of two such numbers is difficult. If the numbers are sufficiently large, factoring requires enormous processing resources, to the extent that the problem is considered computationally infeasible.

To give an intuitive feel of what this means, suppose you were asked to find the two factors of the number 437, that is, find which two numbers multiplied together give 437. Most people find this a nontrivial task, requiring a calculator and numerous trial calculations to come up with the answer. However, if asked to multiply 23 by 19, the same people can very quickly get the answer (437); some are able to do the calculation in their heads. When the numbers are sufficiently large, for example, numbers requiring thousands of bits to represent them, even computers have difficulty performing the factoring.

The strength of RSA is often questioned. It has a very obvious way of being broken: Factor the modulus using any of several known factoring methods. The strength therefore depends on the time required and the cost of equipment that could perform the factoring. The continually decreasing cost of equipment and improvements in factoring techniques must be taken into account in considering RSA's strength in the future. The state of the art in factoring in 1999 was demonstrated by a well-publicized event: the factoring of a 155-digit (512-bit) RSA modulus, which had been posted as a public challenge by Rivest, Shamir, and Adleman 22 years earlier. This RSA-155 number was factored through the international collaboration of many scientists and students using spare processor time on roughly 300 computer workstations or PCs and a supercomputer. The total elapsed time for the factoring effort was 5.2 months. Since that event, further improvements to factoring techniques have been discovered, and of course, computer technology continues to become faster and cheaper.

What can give us confidence that RSA will continue to be a viable algorithm in the future is that a small increase in the size of the modulus results in a large increase in the effort required to factor it. (As a rule of thumb, with current factoring algorithms, increasing the size of the modulus by three digits doubles the difficulty of factoring it.) While 512-bit keys were once used for commercial purposes, that is no longer recommended. However, a 1,024-bit modulus is likely to be sufficiently strong for most commercial purposes for several years to come, with a 2,048-bit modulus being warranted for key pairs that are used repeatedly over periods of several years or for particularly security-critical purposes.

4.3 Digital Signatures

A digital signature is a data item which accompanies or is logically associated with a digitally encoded message and which can be used to ascertain both the originator of the message and that the message has not been modified since it left the originator. The overall process is illustrated in figure 4.5. Vera's system performs a *sign* operation that uses Vera's private key to generate the signature. Ali's system performs a *verify* operation that uses Vera's public key and allows Ali to be sure that the received message originated from Vera and that the message contents were not modified since leaving Vera. For example, if Ali is the order-processing clerk at Danielle's Machine Makers, the digital signature mechanism can be used to verify that Vera's electronic purchase order for a lathe is authentic and was not fabricated by a malicious Internet hacker.

In some respects, a digital signature is similar to a message authentication code (MAC). However, there is one major difference. A digital signature may need to support non-repudiation; that is, a recipient of a message may need to use the digital signature to

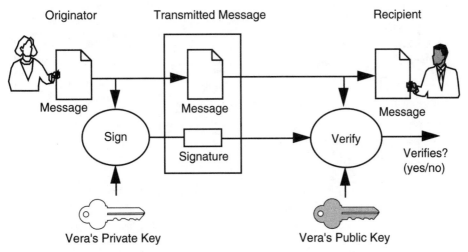

Figure 4.5 Digital Signature

convince a third party of the originator's identity. If a digital signature is used as the basis for resolving a dispute between the originator and recipient of an e-commerce transaction message, the party with the most to gain by falsifying the message may well be the recipient. Hence, the recipient must not be able to generate a digital signature that is indistinguishable from one generated by the originator. Therefore, a MAC cannot generally perform the function of a digital signature since the recipient knows the key used to generate the MAC.

Digital signature mechanisms that overcome this weakness of MACs can be built using public-key technology.[22] Discussion of three such mechanisms follows.

RSA Digital Signatures

A simplistic digital signature technique employing a reversible public-key cryptosystem, such as RSA, is illustrated in figure 4.6. The originator of a message generates an encrypted version of the message using RSA in the authentication mode (that is, the encryption key is the private key of the originator). This encrypted version of the message is sent attached to a copy of the plaintext message. The recipient's system, which needs to know the corresponding decryption key (the public key of the originator), decrypts the encrypted version of the message contents and compares it with the plaintext version. If

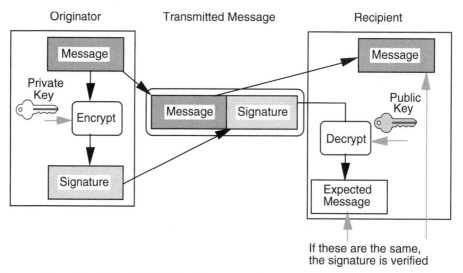

Figure 4.6   Simplistic RSA Digital Signature Scheme

the two are the same, the recipient can be assured that the originating system possessed the encryption key and that the message contents were not changed en route.

A public-key-based digital signature scheme like this one has the valuable property that any potential message recipient can check the signature, because the decryption key (the originator's public key) can be made publicly known without compromising security.

This scheme has some problems, in particular, its cost in terms of processing and communications overhead. Encryption and decryption have to be applied to the entire message contents, and the volume of data sent is at least double the original message size. To improve the scheme, a *hash function* is introduced into the processing. A hash function is a one-way function which maps values from a large (possibly very large) domain into a comparatively small range. For example, a typical message can be thousands or even millions of bits in length. A hash function can operate on the message and produce an output value which is, say, 160 bits in length. The hash function has the property that if the message is changed in any way, even by just one bit, an entirely different value is produced by the hash function. (Hash functions are discussed in more detail later in this section.)

The resultant digital signature process is shown in figure 4.7. The hash function is used to generate a fixed-length data item known as a *message digest* from the content of

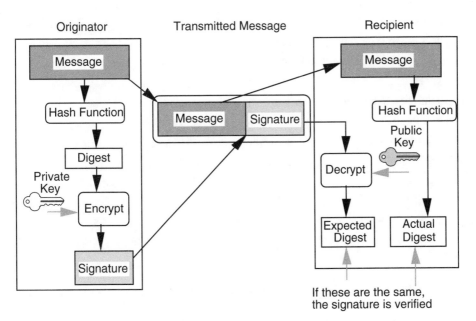

Figure 4.7   RSA Digital Signature Scheme Using Hash Function

the message to be signed. The digest has the property that, in general, any change to the message results in a different digest.

With this scheme, the originating system applies the hash function to obtain the digest, then RSA-encrypts the digest to give the signature that is transmitted with the message. Upon receiving the message, the recipient system recomputes the digest and also RSA-decrypts the signature. It then compares these two values. If they match, the recipient is assured that the originator knew the private key and that the message contents were not changed en route.

Digital Signature Algorithm (DSA)

In August 1991, the U.S. National Institute of Standards and Technology (NIST) issued for comment its proposed *Digital Signature Standard (DSS)*, which defines the Digital Signature Algorithm (DSA). After minor changes as a result of public review, the *DSS* was first published as a Federal Information Processing Standard (FIPS) in 1994.[23] DSA is based on a different mathematical problem than RSA: the *discrete logarithm problem*, relating to the difficulty of inverting a mathematical exponentiation operation in a finite field. The mathematics are summarized in appendix J.

From the perspective of the user of the algorithm, DSA differs little from RSA. The signing system generates a digest of the message to be signed using a hash function, as with RSA. The digest is then processed by a DSA signing operation, which requires the private key and which generates a signature comprising two 160-bit numbers. This signature accompanies the original message when it is communicated or stored. A recipient system that needs to verify the signature recomputes the digest by applying the hash function to the received message. It then feeds this digest, the signature, and the public key into a DSA verifying operation. The result of this operation is an indication of whether or not the signature correctly checks out.

The only important technical difference between RSA and DSA is that DSA's verification process is more processing-resource intensive than that of RSA. Their cryptographic strengths and other technical characteristics are not notably different. RSA has tended to dominate over DSA in the marketplace owing largely to much greater early penetration.

Elliptic Curve Digital Signature Algorithm

Elliptic curve cryptosystems represent an alternative to RSA and DSA as the basis of implementing digital signatures. Elliptic curve–based digital signature systems can perform basically the same functions as ones based on RSA and DSA, but with more efficient implementations. Elliptic curve digital signatures can be generated and verified more quickly than with RSA or DSA. Elliptic curve digital signatures may also be more readily deployed in small, limited-resource devices such as *smartcards* (plastic cards containing microprocessor chips).

Elliptic curve cryptosystems and DSA are both variants of cryptographic methods that depend on the discrete logarithm problem.[24] DSA is an algorithm based on the discrete logarithm problem in a (mathematical) multiplicative group comprising the set of integers modulo some prime p. Variants of this same algorithm can be obtained by using different finite groups. Elliptic curves are one basis for generating such groups. The main reason for looking at variants of algorithms like DSA in different groups is that the discrete logarithm problem may be more difficult in some groups than in others. Elliptic curves fall into the more difficult category. This means that it is considered possible to devise a stronger cryptosystem with a shorter key size using elliptic curves than a similar cryptosystem using the integers modulo p. With elliptic curve systems, the numbers operated upon are smaller, and therefore implementations tend to perform better.

A standard for an elliptic curve–based variant of DSA, called the Elliptic Curve Digital Signature Algorithm (ECDSA), was developed by the Institute of Electrical and Electronics Engineers (IEEE) and by the American National Standards Institute (ANSI) X9 committee on financial services.[25]

Hash Functions

A *one-way function* is a function which is easy to compute but difficult to reverse. In mathematical terms, given a value x, it is easy to apply the one-way function f to x to give the value $y = f(x)$, but, given y, it is not feasible to compute the corresponding $x = f^{-1}(y)$. *Hash functions,* used to generate message digests in digital signatures, are one-way functions that need to have the following properties:

- The function must be truly one-way; that is, it must be computationally infeasible to construct an input message which hashes to a given digest.
- It must be computationally infeasible to construct two messages which hash to the same digest.

Any weakness in these properties may result in a weakness in the digital signature process that uses the hash function. For example, if an active attacker can examine a message and its digest and deduce another message content with the same digest, the attacker can substitute that message content. The substitution will not be detected, regardless of the strength of the cryptosystem used in generating the signature.

Designing good hash functions has proven to be a difficult task. Researchers have proposed many different hash functions, but the majority of them have subsequently been shown to have weaknesses of some sort.[26] The most widely deployed hash function for e-commerce applications is the U.S. government's Secure Hash Algorithm (SHA-1), specified in FIPS PUB 180-1.[27] SHA-1 generates a 160-bit output (for compatibility with the DSA algorithm), which gives it a substantial advantage over earlier commercial algorithms with 128-bit output. Newer hash functions, soon to be published as U.S. government standards, have even larger output sizes. The MD5 algorithm from RSA Data Security, Inc., is still sometimes used but has some known theoretical weaknesses.[28]

4.4 Key Management

Fundamentals

All cryptographic techniques, whether used ultimately for encryption, MAC, or digital signature, depend on cryptographic keys. The management of these keys is itself a complex and crucial aspect of providing security. Key management includes ensuring that key values generated have the necessary properties, making keys known in advance to the particular systems that need them, and ensuring that keys are protected as necessary against disclosure or substitution. Key management methods vary substantially depending on whether the keys being managed are those of symmetric cryptosystems or public-key cryptosystems.

All keys have limited lifetimes. This is necessary for two reasons:

- *Cryptanalysis,* which is the thwarting of a cryptosystem by an attacker using mathematical analysis, is facilitated by having large amounts of ciphertext on which to work. The more a key is used, the greater the opportunity for an attacker to gather ciphertext.
- Given that a key can conceivably be compromised or that an encryption process with a particular key might be cryptanalyzed, limiting the lifetimes of keys limits the damage that can occur.

The period for which a particular key is intended to be used is called the *cryptoperiod* for that key.

The life cycle of a key typically includes the following phases:

- Key establishment, which involves key generation and key distribution
- Key backup/recovery or key escrow (where applicable)
- Key replacement/update (sometimes called *rekeying*)
- Key revocation
- Key expiration/termination, which may involve key destruction or key archiving

Key establishment for symmetric keys is generally accomplished via either *key transport* or *key agreement*; we explain these methods in subsequent subsections. However, having raised the subject of key establishment, this is a convenient time to emphasize the role of random number generators in key generation generally. The unpredictability of any key depends on the unpredictability of a random number, or seed, used in its generation. If there is any known bias in the random number, an attacker using an exhaustive cryptanalytic approach can benefit tremendously from trying the more likely candidates first. A truly random process, such as a (hardware) random noise source, is preferable. A pseudorandom software process operating on a secret random initial seed may be adequate, but the full characteristics of such a system need to be analyzed carefully before assuming that it is suitable for key generation.[29]

Key backup/recovery reflects the need to be able to recover a copy of a secret or private key should it be lost or otherwise unobtainable. In particular, if information is stored in an encrypted form and a particular key is needed to decrypt it, loss of the key may mean loss of the information. There are three main situations in which backup/recovery requirements arise:

1. A key might be lost accidentally by its holder. For example, the disk file that holds the key might be lost because of a hardware failure, or a user might forget the password needed to recover a key from a protected disk file or to activate a hardware token that holds a key. To recover from such situations, the user responsible for the information may require a backup/recovery mechanism.
2. An employer might be concerned about the loss of corporate information if an employee leaves a corporation, is disabled, or becomes disgruntled, and fails to return all keys needed to recover all corporate information encrypted by him or her.

3. Law enforcement or intelligence organizations might want the ability to recover encrypted information to support their investigations or other activities. For example, a law enforcement agency may have authorization, such as a court order, to wiretap the communications of a criminal suspect but needs access to encryption keys to recover the intercepted information.

The requirements here are all very different, but the *technical* mechanism to satisfy all requirements is essentially the same: Someone must hold copies of sensitive keys and release them under appropriate circumstances. The main difference lies in *who* holds the backed-up copies of the keys. Cases 1 and 2 are generally recognized as legitimate applications of key backup/recovery technology. Case 3 is much more controversial and is commonly referred to as *key escrow*, reflecting the fact that keys typically need to be held in trust by a third party.

Key replacement/update involves reexecuting a key establishment process when a key's cryptoperiod expires or under special circumstances.

Key destruction involves obliterating all traces of a key. The value of a key may persist long after it has ceased to be actively used. For example, an encrypted data stream recorded now may contain information which will still be confidential several years into the future; the secrecy of any key used for confidentiality purposes needs to be maintained until the protected information no longer needs to be considered confidential. Also, the ability to prove the legitimacy of a digital signature in a legal contest (possibly several years hence) materially depends on ensuring that the key or keys involved remain protected throughout the entire intervening period. This also makes it important to destroy securely all copies of certain secret or private keys after their active use terminates. For example, it must not be possible for an attacker to determine old key values by examining old data files, memory contents, or discarded equipment.

Key archiving may be required, for example, for digital signature public keys, in order to be able to validate an old digital signature for non-repudiation purposes. Such archiving may need to be entrusted to a third party.

In general, protection of a key needs to be enforced throughout its entire lifetime, from generation to termination. All keys need to be protected for integrity purposes, as an intruder's modifying or substituting a key can compromise the protection service for which the key is being used. Additionally, all keys, except public keys in public-key cryptosystems, need to be protected for confidentiality purposes. In practice, the safest way to

store a key is in a physically secure location. When physical security of a key is impractical, in particular, when it needs to be communicated from one place to another, the key
must be protected by other means, such as

- Assignment to a trusted party, such as a bonded courier, who will guarantee
  protection of items under his or her custody
- Use of a dual-control system, whereby a key is split into two or more parts, with
  each part entrusted to a separate person or environment for purposes of communication or intermediate storage
- Protection during communication by encryption under another key. This introduces the concept of *layers of keys* in network security.

RSA Key Transport

A common method of key establishment for symmetric encryption keys is RSA key transport. The symmetric key is generated in one system, then distributed to one or more other
systems, encrypted using RSA in its encryption mode.

A typical application of this approach, using a symmetric cryptosystem and RSA to
protect an e-mail message, is illustrated in figure 4.8. The message originator's system
generates a random symmetric key K, encrypts the message content using that key, and

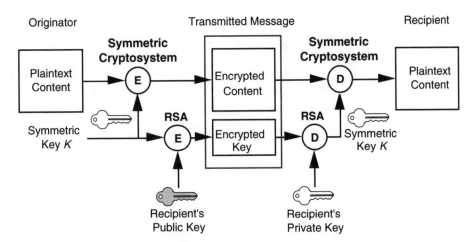

Figure 4.8   E-Mail Encryption Using RSA Key Transport

attaches to the message a copy of the symmetric key encrypted under the public key of the intended recipient. The recipient system that holds the correct RSA private key decrypts the RSA-encrypted symmetric key and then uses that key to decrypt the message content. Any eavesdropper who obtains a copy of the protected message can make no progress in decrypting it, assuming that the eavesdropper does not know the RSA private key.

One might well ask why we did not simply encrypt the message content with RSA. The main reason is that RSA is much more resource demanding than any of the common symmetric algorithms. For example, an RSA decryption operation typically uses at least 100 times the processing resources of DES to work on the same-sized data item. For this reason, RSA is rarely used for bulk data encryption.

The hybrid approach takes advantage of the best characteristics of both the symmetric and public-key cryptographic worlds. The message contents, which may be sizable, are encrypted using a comparatively fast symmetric algorithm. The symmetric key, which is a comparatively short data item, is transferred in an RSA-encrypted form using the public key of the intended recipient, taking advantage of the scalability of public-key cryptosystems.

An added attraction of this approach to e-mail protection is that the same encrypted message can be sent to multiple independent recipients without requiring a separately encrypted copy for each. It is simply necessary to attach, to the one encrypted message content, separate copies of the symmetric key encrypted under the RSA public keys of all the legitimate recipients. Each legitimate recipient is able to recover the symmetric key and consequently the message content.

Diffie-Hellman Key Agreement

Another method of key establishment, whereby two communicating systems can agree on a value for a secret symmetric encryption key, was devised by Whitfield Diffie and Martin Hellman and published in their seminal paper on public-key cryptography.[30] This ingenious technique, known as *Diffie-Hellman key agreement,* operates as follows: Systems A and B each generate a random secret value, x and y, respectively. From its secret value, each system then computes a corresponding public value, X and Y, respectively. The systems exchange public values. Each system can then compute, from one secret value and the other public value, the same key; that is, A can compute the key from x and Y, and B can compute the same key from y and X. Eavesdroppers, who may know the public values but neither secret value, cannot compute the key. The mathematics are summarized in appendix J.

As outlined here, Diffie-Hellman key agreement can be used by two systems communicating online to establish a session key. It can also be used to establish a shared key for an e-mail message, thereby providing an alternative to the RSA-encrypted symmetric key method for e-mail protection described earlier. For example, if system A is a message originator and system B is the recipient, system B might select one value of y for use over a period of time and publish the corresponding value Y for use by any other system, such as A, wishing to send encrypted messages to B. For a particular message, A generates a new x and X pair plus a new encryption key using x and Y. The value of X is sent along with the message so that system B can regenerate the same key using y and X. If B is the only message recipient, the Diffie-Hellman-derived key can be used to encrypt the message. If there are multiple recipients, the message is encrypted using a new random key, and copies of that key are attached for each recipient, each itself encrypted under a Diffie-Hellman-derived key for that recipient. Note that Y acts as a public key for B and needs to be distributed and otherwise managed in essentially the same way as an RSA public key (see discussion in next subsection).

ANSI standard X9.42 describes a range of variants of Diffie-Hellman key derivation suitable for use in various application scenarios.[31]

Recall our discussion in section 4.3 of how a digital signature system based on the discrete logarithm problem might have a more efficient variant using a mathematical group based on an elliptic curve rather than on the numbers modulo a prime number. The same discussion applies to the Diffie-Hellman technique. Elliptic curve variants of Diffie-Hellman have tremendous potential for efficiently establishing symmetric keys for protecting messages between pairs of distributed systems.

Distribution of Public Keys

The key distribution requirements of public-key cryptosystems are inherently very different from those of symmetric cryptosystems. With a symmetric cryptosystem, it is necessary to place copies of one key in the hands of two parties who will use it to protect communications between them, while keeping knowledge of the key secret from all other parties. With a public-key cryptosystem, it is necessary to place one key (the private key) in the hands of one party, keeping knowledge of it secret from all other parties. At the same time, an associated key (the public key) is typically made public knowledge to anyone who wishes to communicate securely with the holder of the private key.

When distributing a public key, confidentiality is not required. However, it is essential that the integrity of the public key be maintained. There must not be any opportunity for an attacker to substitute some other value for what one party believes to be the public key of another party; otherwise, the following type of attack might succeed. Suppose Ali's system *A* is verifying a digitally signed message purporting to be from Vera's system *V*. However, in the meantime, an imposter has generated the message and signed it using his or her own private key. The imposter also substituted his or her own public key for what Ali's system considers to be Vera's public key. Ali's system check of the digital signature (using the wrong public key) indicates that all is well; therefore, the attacker has succeeded in masquerading as Vera.

Distribution of public keys is not as simple as publishing them in a telephone directory, unless users have a high level of trust in that directory and the access paths to it, but such trust proves difficult to achieve. This leads to public keys' distribution in the form of *certificates*. A certificate, generally speaking, is a data structure that is digitally signed by some party in whom users of the certificate place their trust. A *public-key certificate* is a data structure that securely links together the identity of some party (the certificate's *subject*) and a public-key value. The technological and legal infrastructures built up around the issuance and management of certificates are known as public-key infrastructure (PKI). Public-key certificates and broader aspects of PKI are discussed in detail in chapters 6 and 7, respectively.

4.5   Authentication

Authentication is the means of gaining confidence that remote people or things are who or what they claim to be. It is the most essential of all the security services because reliable authentication is needed to enforce access control, to determine who is authorized to receive or modify information (thereby implicating confidentiality services), to enforce accountability, and to achieve non-repudiation.

The legitimate owner of an identity is known as a *principal*. Principals needing to be authenticated may include people, pieces of equipment, and online applications in computer systems. Someone or something attempting to be authenticated as a particular principal is called a *claimant*.

Many methods are used to provide authentication; some depend on cryptographic techniques and others do not. Authentication methods are generally based on any of the following factors:

1. The claimant demonstrates knowledge of something, such as a password.
2. The claimant demonstrates possession of something, such as a physical key or card.
3. The claimant exhibits some required immutable characteristic, such as a fingerprint.
4. Evidence is presented that the claimant is at some particular place or network address.
5. The party needing to be assured of the claimant's identity accepts that some other trusted party has already established authentication.

Depending on the attributes of a particular transaction, reliance on any one of the factors 1 through 4 alone is sometimes considered inadequate. *Multifactor authentication* methods employ a combination of these factors.

An authentication method also needs to relate to the context in which the identity is presented:

- *Entity authentication:* An identity is presented by a remote person, system, or application participating in a communication session.
- *Data origin authentication:* A principal's identity is presented along with a message. It is claimed that the message originated from that principal.

Entity authentication may be either *unilateral* or *mutual.* With unilateral authentication, just one party to a communication activity authenticates the other. With mutual authentication, the parties at both ends authenticate each other. The importance of mutual authentication is often underestimated. When a client connects to a server, the need for the client user to be authenticated is rarely questioned. But should the server not also authenticate itself to the client? An important reason for doing so is to prevent an intruder from setting up a *spoofing* system, which emulates a legitimate server so as to capture the user's password or other sensitive information.

Overviews of the more common authentication methods follow.[32]

Passwords and PINs

Passwords, pass-phrases, and personal identification numbers (PINs) are all variants of one type of mechanism; for the purposes of this chapter, we refer to them all as passwords.

Almost all personal authentication schemes depend on passwords to some extent. However, passwords constitute one of the major vulnerabilities of e-commerce systems and are at the root of many system compromises.

These are the major threats to password-based authentication:

- *External disclosure:* An attacker learns a password by means external to the electronic systems or network. For example, a user may write the password (PIN) on his or her plastic card, or an attacker may use such techniques as *shoulder surfing* of customers at banking terminals, *trashing* to find passwords in the trash, or *social engineering* to dupe an innocent party into revealing a password.
- *Guessing:* An attacker keeps trying different passwords until successful. If passwords come from a sufficiently large set of possible values, this should be impractical. However, with user-chosen passwords or PINs, there is a risk of a user choosing a particularly obvious value, such as that user's birth date or telephone number. An attacker may gain significant advantage by simply trying these more likely values first.
- *Communications eavesdropping:* An attacker who monitors communications may learn passwords if they are transmitted unprotected over a communication line or network.
- *Replay:* Even if a password is encrypted for transfer, it might be possible for an attacker monitoring communications to record the protected password and replay it later to masquerade as the legitimate principal.[33]
- *Host compromise:* An attacker penetrates a computer system containing a database of passwords.

Countering these threats requires effective password management procedures, awareness training, responsible user behavior, and careful authentication system design.

Authentication Protocols

Countering threats such as communications eavesdropping and replay depends on careful design of the *authentication protocol* that governs the communication of authentication-related data between the system associated with the party to be authenticated (typically a client system) and the system that makes, and usually depends on, the authentication decision (typically a server system). Authentication protocols are usually built into the surrounding communications protocol, such as the network-layer protocol or application-layer protocol.

Assuming a context in which a user at a client is authenticating to a server, the elements used to build the authentication protocol include these:

- *Transformed password:* The password presented by the user is processed through a one-way function in the client to give a transformed password, which is communicated to the server. The server applies the same function to its stored copy of the password and, if the two results are the same, concludes that the user supplied the correct value. However, an eavesdropper cannot recover the password from the transmitted value.[34]Alternatively, the server might only store the transformed password rather than the plain text password.

- *Challenge-response:* The server sends the client a random value called a challenge, which is different for each authentication request. This value must be incorporated into the client's response, for example, as an additional input to the one-way function that computes a transformed password. In processing the response, the server confirms that the right challenge was used. This gives protection against replay attacks.

- *Time stamp:* The authentication request from client to server has the current time of day embedded in it, for example, as an additional input to the one-way function that computes a transformed password. In processing the response, the server checks that the time supplied is reasonable. This is another method of protecting against replay attacks, but it has practical limitations because it depends on all systems having secure, synchronized clocks.

- *One-time password:* A one-time password is like a transformed password, but it protects against replay attacks as well as eavesdropping. An example is the Internet standard one-time password mechanism,[35] which was an evolution of Bellcore's S/KEY system.[36] This mechanism is essentially a transformed password scheme which generates a different online password each time by passing the user-entered password through a one-way function n times, where n decreases by 1 on each new login attempt. The server system keeps track of the values of n and the last online password used. An eavesdropper observing one online password cannot deduce a future online password because the one-way function cannot be inverted. The resultant system is comparatively simple to implement in both client and server systems and does not require either end to store plaintext passwords.

- *Digital signature:* Digital signatures are the basis of many modern authentication protocols. The client proves possession of a particular private key by signing a protocol message, or a field in a message, using that key. The signed data may contain a challenge value or a time stamp, thereby protecting against replay threats.

- *Zero-knowledge techniques:* Zero-knowledge techniques[37] are a cryptographic technology based on interactive proof systems. A zero-knowledge technique is a means by which possession of information can be verified without any part of that information being revealed. These techniques can be cryptographically stronger than more conventional cryptographic techniques and can use fewer processor resources. However, many of these techniques require more complex data exchange protocols that need to transfer more data, so they may consume greater communications resources.

Good authentication protocols, which typically combine several of these or similar elements, have proven to be a design challenge. In addition to threats such as eavesdropping and replay, the protocol may have to deal with such threats as spoofing, in which a bogus server system is inserted in a configuration, or a *man-in-the-middle* attack, in which an active attacker intervenes in a protocol exchange between two systems and reads and modifies the data items moving in both directions at will.

Authentication protocols are frequently combined with key establishment protocols, such as RSA key transport or Diffie-Hellman key agreement, to ensure that session keys are established between the correct parties. See Diffie *et al*[38] for the classic paper on the pitfalls of combining authentication protocols with Diffie-Hellman key agreement and how to avoid them.

Kerberos

Kerberos is an interesting example of a user authentication method, including sophisticated authentication protocols, based entirely on symmetric cryptosystems. Kerberos was designed as part of Project Athena at the Massachusetts Institute of Technology, a project focused on building a powerful client-server-based educational computer network. Kerberos provides the means for authenticating client workstation users to host servers, and vice versa. The Kerberos Version 5 specification was adopted by the Internet community for wider use.[39]

Kerberos uses DES symmetric cryptography and online authentication servers. Every principal (that is, legitimate workstation user) and every host server share a symmetric key with the authentication server. The client first communicates with the authentication server to obtain a protected data item, called a *ticket,* which it then passes to the target server. Communication between the client and authentication server is protected using their shared key. The ticket is constructed so as to be interpretable only by the correct target server, namely, the server that shares the right key with the authentication server (see figure 4.9).

The result of successful completion of both message exchange sequences is that the client and the target server share a secret session key generated for them by the authentication server. This knowledge provides the basis for mutual authentication and possibly encryption and integrity checking on a communication session to follow.

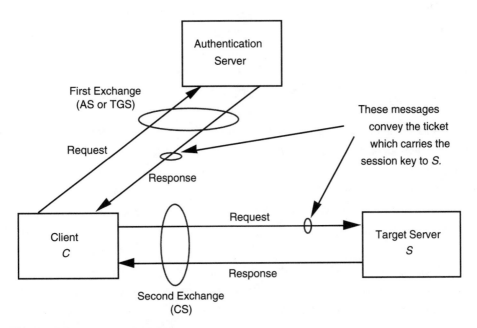

Figure 4.9   Kerberos Exchanges

The Kerberos architecture involves three message exchange sequences:

- *Authentication service (AS) exchange:* This is an initial exchange between a client and the Kerberos authentication server that knows the client's secret key. Through this exchange, the client obtains a ticket to be used to access some other (nominated) server. This exchange is typically used at the start of a login session, when the user provides a password to the client software; the password is input to a one-way function to produce the client's secret key. The nominated server is usually a ticket-granting authentication server, from which other tickets can be obtained subsequently in the login session.
- *Ticket-granting service (TGS) exchange:* This is an exchange between a client and an authentication server, known as a ticket-granting server, which does not use the client's secret key (hence the client system can erase all knowledge of this very sensitive key early in a login session). Instead, this exchange uses a ticket for the ticket-granting server, obtained earlier in an authentication service exchange. Through this exchange, the client obtains a further ticket to be used to access any other (nominated) server. The ticket-granting service exchange is typically used within a login session, whenever the client needs to access a new server.
- *Client-server (CS) authentication exchange:* This is an exchange between a client and a target server that authenticates the client to the server and, optionally, the server to the client. It makes use of a ticket obtained earlier in either an authentication service or a ticket-granting service exchange.

Kerberos includes procedures for use across multiple domains, called *realms,* that employ independent authentication servers, possibly under the control of separate organizations. A comprehensive administrative protocol is also defined.

The main attraction of Kerberos is that it provides a good level of protection and uses relatively inexpensive technology. Disadvantages, in comparison with more modern authentication schemes that employ digital signature technology, are

- The need for trusted (physically secured) online servers, with high availability
- Dependence on time stamps for replay detection (which implies that synchronized and secure time clocks are required)
- Difficulties in scaling to arbitrarily large user populations

Personal Tokens

Recall from our earlier discussion that authentication methods are based on one or more underlying factors. Personal tokens use the factor of the user's demonstrating possession of something, namely, a small hardware device which is normally held by an individual. This factor is commonly used in conjunction with the claimant demonstrating knowledge of something, namely, a password or PIN. To be able to masquerade as the legitimate user, it is not adequate for an attacker just to learn the PIN (as might be accomplished through social engineering) or to obtain the token (as might be accomplished by theft). Rather, it is necessary for the attacker both to learn the PIN *and* to obtain the token (thereby demonstrating *two-factor authentication*), making a successful attack much harder to engineer.

Personal tokens operate in a variety of ways, such as

- *Storage token:* A secret data value, such as a digital signature private key, is stored on a token and made available for use in an authentication protocol after the token has been *unlocked* by presenting the correct PIN.
- *Synchronous one-time password generator:* The token generates a new password periodically, such as every minute, and makes this password available to the token holder for use in authenticating to a host that supports this authentication method. The one-time password is computed by applying a one-way function to the current time of day and a permanent secret value stored within the token. Hosts and tokens must stay time-synchronized.
- *Challenge-response:* The token operates the client end of a challenge-response protocol, producing a response computed by applying a one-way function to a combination of a challenge value sent from a target host and a permanent secret value stored within the token.
- *Digital signature token:* The token holds a digital signature private key together with the logic necessary to compute a digital signature on a supplied data value using that private key. This digital signature may be employed in an authentication protocol. Before generating a signature, the token typically needs to be unlocked by presenting the correct PIN.

Tokens need to be tamper-resistant or tamper-evident to make it difficult for an attacker to learn and exploit the secret values stored within them or to manufacture a clone of a token. Tokens come in a variety of physical forms, such as

- *Human-interface token:* A handheld device with a digital display. The display shows a number which the holder subsequently enters into a network terminal, such as a desktop computer. If the authentication method requires the holder to enter data to the token, such as a PIN or a challenge value, the token may also contain a small keypad for this purpose.
- *Smartcard:* A microprocessor and storage system realized in a microcircuit embedded in a plastic card the size of a credit card. The card operates when inserted into an external terminal device with which it interfaces via electrical contacts. Through these contacts, the terminal provides electrical power and communicates with the card processor using a low-speed serial asynchronous character protocol. The basic physical, electrical, and communications aspects of the interface have been standardized by ISO/IEC.[40]
- *PCMCIA card:*[41] A pocket-size token for use with the standard multipin sockets commonly found on laptop PCs for interfacing to a modem or other accessories. A PCMCIA token can contain much more powerful processing and memory logic than a smartcard and has a much higher bandwidth interface.
- *USB token:* A keychain-sized physical token that connects to a Universal Serial Bus (USB) port, which is available on many contemporary PCs. The token can contain powerful processing and memory logic.

A major factor influencing a token's physical form is the type of interface needed, in particular, whether a special hardware interface, such as an electrical-contact interface, is required or whether a human interface is adequate. If a hardware interface is required, following a standard, such as a smartcard or PCMCIA standard, is important. With human interface tokens, overall costs may be lower because there is no need for special interface hardware. In general, with challenge-response tokens or synchronous one-time password generators, the volumes of data transferred to or from the token are so small that human interfaces are adequate.[42] However, for a digital signature token, a hardware interface is essential.

Biometrics

Biometric identification uses certain biological characteristics or behavioral traits of individuals to verify their identity electronically. A biometric reader measures physiological indicia and compares them to specified values, but unlike a cipher, it is not capable of securing information (including a biometric template or sample) communicated over an unprotected system such as the Internet.

Many biometric technologies have been developed with the objective of enhancing the authentication of individuals, including

- Fingerprint recognition
- Voice recognition
- Handwriting recognition
- Face recognition
- Retinal scan
- Hand geometry recognition

Although some biometric techniques possess unique strengths that make them well suited to specific narrow applications, by themselves they are insufficient to provide a complete basis for authentication in secure e-commerce—the strength and breadth of their security features are simply too limited.[43] Biometric technologies can be used to *supplement* authentication infrastructures, such as that provided by digital signatures, when particularly strong assurances of identity are essential.

In most respects, application of biometric technologies is equivalent to use of a special password which, unlike conventional passwords, cannot be used by others. Note that devices that measure biometric characteristics must be implemented as trusted components and that encodings of biometric characteristics must always be stored and communicated in a protected (encrypted and/or integrity-protected) form.

Roaming Protocols

One requirement that frequently arises in e-commerce scenarios is for a *roaming user* to be able to execute secure transactions from a wide range of different terminals. This might involve multiple terminals in a workplace setting or, in the case of a consumer, terminals at home, at the office, or at a public Internet kiosk in a shopping mall. An interesting challenge that arises is how to deliver to a client a set of private data such as private keys, account identifiers, and passwords needed to access particular services or servers when the client terminal holds no long-term state information about the user. For example, if digital signatures are to be used as the basis of authenticating users or securing transactions, how does the client obtain the private key required to generate the digital signature?

One approach to this problem is to have the roaming user carry a smartcard or similar personal token on which the private data are stored. However, this approach is not always cost effective or feasible because of the costs of procuring, installing, and supporting smartcards and smartcard readers as well as limitations in interoperability between a given smartcard and reader.

An alternative approach is to have a server hold a copy of a user's private data. The user authenticates to the server on the basis of a presented password, and the server downloads (via encrypted communications) the required private data to the client terminal for the limited period when the user is using that terminal. An attraction of this type of approach is that the server can monitor all attempts to recover the private data and cease responding when the number of unsuccessful tries in some particular time period is deemed excessive. The server is said to be operating a *lockout* or *throttling* mechanism. This obviates the prospect of a successful exhaustive password-guessing attack and makes it possible to use comparatively user-friendly passwords. The situation is comparable with the typical ATM, in which a four-digit PIN is adequately secure since an attacker has only a very limited number of tries at guessing the PIN.

Various protocols for supporting private-data servers for roaming users have been specified.[44] These are commonly known as password-based authentication and key exchange protocols. Prominent protocols of this type are Bellovin and Merritt's EKE protocol,[45] Jablon's SPEKE protocol,[46] and other proposed protocols.[47]

However, all of the aforementioned protocols suffer from one shortcoming: *The server represents a major vulnerability.* If the server operator or someone who compromises the server wishes to determine a user's password or private key (either of which will enable the attacker to masquerade as the user), viable attacks are possible, despite efforts in some of the designs to minimize the sensitivity of the data stored on the server. Anyone who can access the server database or can disable any throttling or lockout mechanism can try passwords exhaustively until an account is penetrated. Since the operational environment may have created the expectation that reasonably user-friendly passwords are secure, one can anticipate that attacks of this type might often be successful.

In some application scenarios, particularly those in which non-repudiation is a goal, this weakness can rule out the use of the private-data server approach entirely. The possible attack scenario virtually destroys non-repudiation properties otherwise inherent in digital signature technology. If a roaming user wishes to deny digitally signing a transaction after the fact, the user might plausibly claim that the server operator or someone who compromised the server obtained the user's private key as previously described and signed the transaction, posing as the user.

This shortcoming can be alleviated by spreading responsibility for recovering the user's private data across two or more servers. These servers can be operated in separately secured facilities by separate personnel, potentially under the control of independent organizations. A system can be put together in which it is infeasible for anyone not knowing the user's password to discover either the password or the user's private data, unless all of the server operators collude or are compromised by the same party.[48] Using such technology, an appropriately controlled and audited operational environment can be set up in which concerns about server compromise are greatly diminished. Nevertheless, the client terminal must always be trustworthy.

Address-Based Authentication

Address-based mechanisms assume the authenticity of a user on the basis of the originating address of a call. Indications of the calling address are available in most types of data networks and, to a limited extent, telephone networks. Where such indications are not available, the same basic effect can be achieved using an automatic call-back process. An authenticating system maintains a file of legitimate calling addresses for each principal; on an authentication attempt, the authenticating system either checks the calling address for legitimacy or clears the original call and calls back to what is known to be a legitimate address.

This type of mechanism faces several problems. One problem is the reliability of calling addresses notified by a network. Depending on the network technology, it may be easy for an attacker to modify the calling address seen by the host. Another problem is maintaining a continuing association of a principal (a person or a piece of equipment) with a network address. Address changes may occur so frequently that the change system is overly expensive, unmanageable, or insecure. Network features, such as call forwarding or redirection, create major problems with the call-back approach and open various opportunities for attack.

Address-based mechanisms cannot be considered authentication mechanisms in their own right but can be a useful supplement to other mechanisms.

4.6 System Trust

One of the most important characteristics of a security system implementation is its trust
or assurance level. To what extent can someone depending on that system be assured that
the system indeed performs the functions it claims to perform and does not perform any
unwanted functions? Software, in particular, is notorious for not reliably performing the
desired functions, usually as a result of design flaws or tampering.

As an example of system trust concerns, consider biometric authentication mechanisms. However good a biometric technique is at discriminating between subjects, it is
only as trustworthy as the device used to collect the information that the technique relies
on and the means used to communicate with that device.[49]

These are some measures which might be taken to maximize system trust:

- Use only products developed under appropriate quality controls and from reliable
  vendors. The attraction of free or low-cost software needs to be carefully balanced against the risks.
- Protect the environment in which critical software resides. Implement appropriate
  protection against intruders penetrating a system over a network, and capture
  information to support later analysis of penetrations. High-quality, reliable software components can often be easily patched by an intruder to serve the whim of
  that intruder.
- Use hardware components for critical functions, especially functions in which
  tampering might be difficult to detect. However, the much higher costs of hardware versus software have to be weighed against the risks.
- Use government-endorsed products. The U.S. government has programs to evaluate
  products for government use. The FIPS 140 standard[50] is used to evaluate hardware
  and software implementations of cryptographic modules. The international Common Criteria provides a basis for evaluating computer products generally on their
  functionality and trustworthiness.[51] The Common Criteria, which evolved from
  various national programs including the U.S. Trusted Computer System Evaluation
  Criteria (the *Orange Book*) and the European ITSEC standard,[52]

The most important point is that trust in a system can be assessed only through a
complete study of the system as a whole—not just the constituent parts. Any system is

only as strong as its weakest link, and it is folly to assume that potential intruders will not find that weakest link. A complete assessment of threats and analysis of risks are necessary to ensure that a system is secure for its intended purposes. This analysis needs to take into account all factors, including computer security, communications security, personnel security, physical security, administrative security, and media security.

4.7 Summary

Information security is a well-established discipline with the objectives of ensuring the confidentiality, integrity, and availability of information and protecting against illegitimate use of resources. E-commerce may be subject to many different threats, including system penetration, authorization violations, planting of malicious software, communications monitoring, communications tampering, denial of service, and false denial that a transaction occurred. To protect against these threats, information security provides various safeguards, such as authentication, access control, confidentiality, data integrity, and non-repudiation services.

Cryptography is an important tool in implementing all of these security services. There are two basic types of cryptographic system: symmetric and public-key cryptosystems. A symmetric cryptosystem employs a single cryptographic key and can be used for encrypting data for confidentiality purposes or for generating message authentication codes (MACs) to protect data integrity.

A public-key cryptosystem uses a key pair: a private key kept secret by one party and a corresponding public key that can be made known to anyone. Public-key systems are, in some respects, more powerful than symmetric systems. The RSA algorithm is the best-known public-key cryptosystem.

A digital signature is a data item which accompanies or is logically associated with a message and can be used to ascertain the originator of the message and to confirm that the message was not modified since it was digitally signed. Digital signature methods include an RSA-based method, the U.S. government Digital Signature Algorithm (DSA), and the Elliptic Curve Digital Signature Algorithm (ECDSA).

All encryption systems and digital signature systems depend on key management methods, which include appropriate procedures for key generation, distribution, update, backup/recovery, revocation, and termination. A symmetric cryptosystem key can be distributed in a form encrypted under an RSA public key. A symmetric key can also be established between two systems using the Diffie-Hellman key agreement technique.

Public keys do not have to be kept secret, but a user needs to be assured that he or she is using the right public key. Public keys are therefore generally distributed in the form of signed certificates. Issuance and management of such certificates are the core functions underlying public-key infrastructure (PKI).

Authentication is the means of gaining confidence that remote people or things are who or what they claim to be. Passwords constitute an important authentication mechanism but are vulnerable to several threats. Networks increasingly use sophisticated authentication protocols built from such elements as transformed passwords, challenge-response, time stamps, and digital signatures. Kerberos is an interesting example of a user-authentication method based on symmetric cryptographic techniques only. The use of personal hardware tokens substantially strengthens authentication systems. Roaming protocols support the downloading of private keys and other private data to designated client terminals for a user.

Underpinning the implementation of any security countermeasure is system trust or assurance. Measures must be taken to give users confidence that a system performs the functions it claims to perform and does not perform any unwanted functions.

Notes

1. C. Pfleeger, *Security in Computing,* 2nd ed. (Upper Saddle River, NJ: Prentice Hall PTR, 1997), details at <http://www.prenhall.com/013/337486/33748-6.html>; W. Ford, *Computer Communications Security: Principles, Standard Protocols and Techniques* (Upper Saddle River, NJ: Prentice Hall, 1994), chap. 2, details at <http://www.prenhall.com/013/799452/79945-2.html>.

2. In this context, a *resource* could be, for example, a computer system, data file, or record in a database.

3. See, for example, <ftp://info.cert.org/pub/cert_advisories/CA-96.21.tcp_syn_flooding>.

4. The difference between *information* and *data* needs to be noted. Information has meaning, or *semantics.* In a digital system, a piece of information is com-

monly represented for storage or transfer purposes as a *data item,* which comprises a string of binary digits (*bits*).

5. B. Schneier, *Applied Cryptography,* 2nd ed. (New York: Wiley, 1995), details at <http://www.wiley.com, http://www.webwares.com/books/slade/ bkapcryp.rvw>; A. J. Menezes, P. C. van Oorschot, and S. A. Vanstone, *Handbook of Applied Cryptography* (Boca Raton, FL: CRC Press, 1996), details at <http://www.crcpress.com, http://crypto2.uwaterloo.ca/~crypbook>; D. W. Davies and W. L. Price, *Security for Computer Networks,* 2nd ed. (New York: Wiley, 1989), details at <http://www.wiley.com>; D. Stinson, *Cryptography: Theory and Practice* (Boca Raton, FL: CRC Press, 1995), details at <http://www.crcpress.com>, <http://bibd.unl.edu/~stinson>.

6. U.S. Department of Commerce, *DES Modes of Operation,* Federal Information Processing Standards Publication FIPS PUB 81 (1980), available at <http://csrc.nist.gov>; International Organization for Standardization, *Information Technology—Security Techniques—Modes of Operation for an n-bit Block Cipher Algorithm,* ISO/IEC 10116.

7. Davies and Price, *Security for Computer Networks.*

8. U.S. Department of Commerce, *Data Encryption Standard,* Federal Information Processing Standards Publication FIPS PUB 46 (1977; republished as FIPS PUB 46-2, 1994), available at <http://csrc.nist.gov>.

9. American National Standards Institute, *ANSI X3.92: American National Standard, Data Encryption Algorithm* (American National Standards Institute, 1981).

10. Electronic Frontier Foundation, *Cracking DES: Secrets of Encryption Research, Wiretap Politics and Chip Design* (Sebastopol, CA: O'Reilly & Associates, 1998), details at <http://www.ora.com/catalog/crackdes/>.

11. "Notices." *Federal Register* 62, no. 1 (January 2, 1997): 93–94.

12. Up-to-date status information on AES is available at <http://www.nist.gov/aes>.

13. American National Standards Institute, *ANSI X9.52: Triple Data Encryption Algorithm Modes of Operation* (American National Standards Institute, 1997).

14. R. Baldwin and R. Rivest, *The RC5, RC5-CBC, RC5-CBC-Pad, and RC5-CTS Algorithms,* RFC 2040 (Internet Activities Board, 1996) <ftp://ftp.isi.edu/in-notes/rfc2040.txt>.

15. B. Schneier, "Description of a New Variable-Length Key, 64-Bit Block Cipher," in *Fast Software Encryption: Cambridge Security Workshop Proceedings* (Berlin: Springer-Verlag, 1994), 191–204, available at <http://www.counterpane.com/bfsverlag.html>.

16. For descriptions of these proprietary algorithms and others, see Schneier, *Applied Cryptography.*

17. Menezes et al., *Handbook of Applied Cryptography.*

18. American National Standards Institute, *ANSI X9.9: American National Standard for Financial Institution Message Authentication (Wholesale)* (American National Standards Institute, 1986).

19. W. Diffie and M. Hellman, "New Directions in Cryptography," *IEEE Transactions on Information Theory* IT-22, no. 6 (1976): 644–54; W. Diffie, "The First Ten Years of Public Key Cryptology" in *Contemporary Cryptology: The Science of Information Integrity,* ed. Gustavus J. Simmons (New York: IEEE Press, 1992), 136–75.

20. R. L. Rivest, A. Shamir, and L. Adleman, "A Method for Obtaining Digital Signatures and Public-Key Cryptosystems," *Communications of the ACM* 21, no. 2 (February 1978): 120–26.

21. A prime number is an integer that has no factors other than 1 and itself.

22. C. J. Mitchell, F. Piper, and P. Wild, "Digital Signatures," in Simmons G. J. (Ed.), *Contemporary Cryptology: The Science of Information Integrity,* (New York: IEEE Press, 1992), pp. 325–78 <http://www.ieee.org/bookstore/compbk.html>.

23. U.S. Department of Commerce, *Digital Signature Standard (DSS),* Federal Information Processing Standards Publication FIPS PUB 186-2 (2000), available at <http://csrc.nist.gov/fips/fips186-2.pdf>.

24. Other examples are the ElGamal and Schnorr digital signature schemes. T. ElGamal, "A Public Key Cryptosystem and a Signature Scheme Based on Discrete Logarithms," *IEEE Transactions on Information Theory* IT-31, no. 4 (1985): 469–72; C. P. Schnorr, "Efficient Signature Generation by Smart Cards," *Journal of Cryptology* 4, no. 3 (1991): 161–74 , available at <http://www.iacr.org/jofc/by volume.html>.

25. Institution of Electrical and Electronics Engineers, *Standard P1363: Standard Specifications for Public Key Cryptography,* details at <http://grouper.ieee.org/groups/1363/index.html>; American National Standards Institute, *ANSI X9.62: Public Key Cryptography for the Financial*

Services Industry: The Elliptic Curve Digital Signature Algorithm (ECDSA) (American National Standards Institute, 1997). For an introduction to the subject, see Stinson, *Cryptography: Theory and Practice.* For a detailed treatise, see A. Menezes, *Elliptic Curve Public Key Cryptosystems* (Boston, MA: Kluwer Academic, 1993), details at <http://www.math.uga.edu/~ntheory/names_m.html>.

26. Mitchell et al., "Digital Signatures."

27. U.S. Department of Commerce, *Secure Hash Algorithm,* Federal Information Processing Standards Publication FIPS PUB 180-1 (1995), available at <http://csrc.nist.gov>. Note that the originally published version of SHA, in FIPS PUB 180, was modified in the revised FIPS PUB 180-1 to remove an unexplained weakness. The modified hash function is commonly called SHA-1.

28. R. Rivest, *The MD5 Message-Digest Algorithm,* RFC 1321 (Internet Activities Board, 1992) <ftp://ds.internic.net/rfc/rfc1321.txt>. For discussion of the weaknesses, see RSA Data Security, Inc., H. Dobbertin, "The Status of MD5 after a Recent Attack," pp.1–6. *Cryptobytes* 2, no. 2 (Summer 1996): available at <http://www.rsa.com>.

29. The risks of poor random number generators were made apparent in a widely publicized event in 1995, when it was publicly demonstrated how encryption keys generated by Netscape's Navigator browser could typically be reproduced in one minute of processing time because the underlying random number generator used a seed from a range which could easily be guessed. Netscape quickly corrected the problem in the next product release. For a detailed description of why good random number generation is important and how good random numbers can be generated, see D. Eastlake, III, S. Crocker, and J. Schiller, *Randomness Recommendations for Security,* RFC 1750 (Internet Activities Board, December 1994) <ftp://ds.internic.net/rfc/rfc1750.txt>.

30. Diffie and Hellman, "New Directions in Cryptography."

31. American National Standards Institute, *ANSI X9.42: Establishment of Symmetric Algorithm Keys Using Diffie-Hellman* (American National Standards Institute, 1997).

32. For more detail, see Ford, *Computer Communications Security,* chap. 5.

33. Suitably designed authentication protocols can circumvent this type of attack; this is discussed further in the next subsection.

34. Typically, other data items such as the user's name or a random *salt,* or both, are input to the one-way function along with the password or PIN. This prevents an attacker from simply building a lookup table of transformed password values corresponding to commonly used passwords.

35. N. Haller, C. Metz, P. Nesser, and M. Straw. *A One-Time Password System,* RFC 2289 (Internet Activities Board, February 1998) <ftp://ftp.isi.edu/in-notes/rfc2289.txt>.

36. Neil Haller, *The S/KEY One-Time Password System,* RFC 1760 (Internet Activities Board, 1995) <ftp://ftp.isi.edu/in-notes/rfc1760.txt>.

37. J. Nechvatal, "Public Key Cryptography," in *Contemporary Cryptology,* 178–288; J.-J. Quisquater and L. Guillou, "How to Explain Zero-Knowledge Protocols to Your Children," in *Advances in Cryptology—CRYPTO '89 (Lecture Notes in Computer Science 435)* ed. G. Brassard (Berlin: Springer-Verlag, 1990), 628–31.

38. W. Diffie, P. C. van Oorschot, and M. J. Wiener, "Authentication and Authenticated Key Exchanges," *Designs, Codes and Cryptography* 2, no. 2 (June 1992): 107–26.

39. J. T. Kohl and B. C. Neuman, *The Kerberos Network Authentication Service (V5),* RFC 1510 (Internet Activities Board, 1993) <ftp://ftp.isi.edu/in-notes/rfc1510.txt>.

40. ISO/IEC 7816, *Identification Cards—Integrated Circuit(s) Cards with Contacts,* can be ordered from <http://www/iso.ch>.

41. Personal Computer Memory Card International Association, the standard interface for small external hardware modules commonly used in laptop PCs. The term *PC card* is often used synonymously.

42. Human interfaces need to be straightforward and not time-consuming; otherwise they are ineffective.

43. Dr. Jim Wayman, director of the National Biometric Test Center, notes that "DNA and all other 'forensic' identification techniques, including latent fingerprint identification, require extensive expert human processing and are not automatic. Therefore, they are not 'biometric identification techniques' according to the definition I use" (e-mail to Michael S. Baum, November 29, 1998, on file with author).

44. For a survey, see R. Perlman and C. Kaufman, "Secure Password-Based Protocol for Downloading a Private Key," in *Proceedings of the 1999 Network and Distributed System Security Symposium* (Internet Society, January 1999).

45. S. M. Bellovin and M. Merritt, "Encrypted Key Exchange: Password-Based Protocols Secure against Dictionary Attacks," in *Proceedings of the IEEE Symposium on Research in Security and Privacy* (IEEE, Oakland: May 1992, pp. 72–84, available at <http://www.alw.nih.gov/Security/FIRST/papers/crypto/aeke.ps>); S. M. Bellovin and M. Merritt, *Augmented Encrypted Key Exchange: A Password-Based Protocol Secure against Dictionary Attacks and Password File Compromise,* Technical Report (AT&T Bell Laboratories, 1994) available at <http://www.alw.nih.gov/Security/FIRST/papers/crypto/aeke.ps>).

46. D. Jablon, "Strong Password-Only Authenticated Key Exchange," in *ACM Computer Communications Review* (vol 26, no. 5, October 1996, available at <http://www.world.std.com/ndpi/isipuns.html>); D. Jablon, "Extended Password Protocols Immune to Dictionary Attack," in *Proceedings of the WETICE '97 Enterprise Security Workshop* (Cambridge, Mass.: June 1997).

47. L. Gong, T. M. A. Lomas, R. M. Needham, and J. H. Salzer, "Protecting Poorly Chosen Secrets from Guessing Attacks," *IEEE Journal on Selected Areas in Communications* 11, no. 5 (June 1993): 648–56; L. Gong, "Optimal Authentication Protocols Resistant to Password Guessing Attacks," in *Proceedings of the 8th IEEE Computer Security Foundations Workshop,* Ireland, June 13, 1995, pp. 24–29; T. Wu, "The Secure Remote Password Protocol," in *Proceedings of the 1998 Network and Distributed System Security Symposium* (Internet Society, January 1998), 97–111; S. Halevi and H. Krawczyk, "Public-Key Cryptography and Password Protocols," in *Proceedings of the Fifth ACM Conference on Computer and Communications Security, 1998,* available at <http://www.research.ib.com./security.pub-passwd.ps>

48. W. Ford and B. S. Kaliski, Jr., "Server-Assisted Generation of a Strong Secret from a Password," Proceedings IEEE 9th International Workshops on Enabling Technologies: Infrastructure for Collaborative Enterprises, June 14–16, 2000 (Los Alamitos, CA: IEEE Computer Society, 2000, pp. 176–180), available at <http://www.verisign.com/repository/pubs/roaming.pdf>.

49. If a biometric sampling device is intrinsically trustworthy (e.g., an ATM camera that transmits over a secure private network), it is possible to rely on the result to a high degree. It is not possible, however, to place a significant degree of trust in an arbitrary sampling device (e.g., a digital tablet) that may become compromised, or even in a trusted sampling device if it communi-

cates its data across an untrustworthy network (such as the Internet) in an unsecured fashion.

50. U.S. Department of Commerce, *Security Requirements for Cryptographic Modules,* Federal Information Processing Standards Publication FIPS PUB 140-1 (1994), available at <http://csrc.nist.gov>.

51. Common Criteria Editorial Board, *Common Criteria for Information Technology Security Evaluation* (Gaithersburg, MD: Computer Security Division, National Institute of Standards and Technology), available at <http://csrc.nist.gov>; also published as International Standard ISO/IEC 15408 (1999).

52. U.S. Department of Defense, *Department of Defense Trusted Computer System Evaluation Criteria,* DOD 5200.28-STD (Fort Meade, MD: National Computer Security Center, December 1985), available at <http://www.disa.mil/MLS/info/orange/intro.html>, <http://csrc.nist.gov/secpubs/rainbow/std001.txt>; Commission of the European Communities, *Information Technology Security Evaluation Criteria (ITSEC): Provisional Harmonized Criteria* (Brussels: Commission of the European Communities, 1991), available at <http://www.itsec.gov.uk>.

CHAPTER 5

Internet Security

Internet technologies and e-commerce applications go hand in hand. Unfortunately, the risks of using the Internet can be daunting. This chapter addresses how to exploit the Internet's capabilities without exposure to unacceptable risks. In particular, we describe how the principles and technologies introduced in chapter 4 can be applied to the Internet environment to give the protections that e-commerce requires. We start with a discussion of the three main areas into which Internet security can be divided: system security, which refers to the protection of end systems, communications security at the network layer, and application layer, respectively. Specific security methods and protocols for the Internet are then described, including firewalls, IPsec and virtual private networks, Web security, messaging security, and secure Internet-based payment methods.

5.1 Segmenting the Problem

From a technical perspective, the Internet security solution can be divided into three categories of safeguards: *network-layer security, application-layer security,* and *system security.* These safeguards must be implemented in conjunction with other safeguards, such as physical security, personnel security, and media security safeguards, with the goal of satisfying all the demands of a comprehensive security policy. Detailed coverage of security policies, which need to be carefully crafted by every organization to optimally satisfy its own business and risk-management objectives, is beyond the scope of this book.[1]

Network-Layer Security

Network-layer security refers to the protection of the communication of data items from one network end system to another. This topic excludes any coverage of security within end systems.

If an end system is connected directly to the Internet without appropriate network security measures, any packet of data it receives potentially

- may have been modified in transit,
- may not be from the source from which it appears to come, and
- may be part of a deliberate attack upon the system, including penetration and denial-of-service attacks.

Also, any packet sent potentially

- may not go where it is addressed,
- may get modified en route, and
- may be read by unknown people or systems.

While troublesome, this may not be a wholly untenable situation because application-layer security and system security safeguards tend to assume that the network is entirely unreliable and potentially hostile. These measures may therefore provide the required protection. Network-layer security, on the other hand, aims to improve the inherent security characteristics of the network as seen by an end system, which means that less reliance is needed on the protection measures in the end systems themselves. This may sometimes be very beneficial, especially with end systems that are not closely controlled by security-conscious and security-competent people, for example, a desktop computer in a typical business or home environment. Network-layer security also has the attraction that it works for all applications, without those applications needing to be *security-aware*.

Network-layer security services, or safeguards, typically include

- *Authentication and integrity:* Providing a receiving system with assurance of the source of a packet and assurance that any modification of the packet since leaving that source is detected

- *Confidentiality:* Protecting the contents of a packet from disclosure to anyone except the intended recipient of the packet
- *Access control:* Restricting communication with a particular end system to only particular applications or particular remote packet sources or destinations

Provision of these services is discussed in sections 5.2 and 5.3.

Another aspect of network security relates to protection of the core Internet infrastructure protocols, such as the protocols that manage the distribution of network routing information and the protocols associated with the Domain Name System (DNS). The latter, in particular, can present substantial security concerns to e-commerce participants, since manipulation of DNS servers or protocols can cause traffic sent to a DNS address (such as a particular .com address) to be redirected to a rogue server.[2] The IETF has developed security features to protect DNS through digital signing of DNS data.[3] Detailed coverage of these aspects of network security is beyond the scope of this book.

Application-Layer Security

Application-layer security refers to security safeguards that are built into a particular application and that operate independently of underlying network-layer security measures. Some application-layer security services constitute an alternative to or a duplication of network-layer security services. For example, application-layer encryption of messages between a Web browser and a Web server might achieve the same result as encryption of the traffic at the network (IP) layer. However, many applications have special security requirements that just cannot be satisfied by network-layer security.

Take e-mail, for example. An e-mail message may be transported over a series of different network sessions and stored in a variety of unknown systems in transit. Network-layer security cannot provide protection against the message tampering that might occur in a mail gateway that performs an e-mail store-and-forward function. Furthermore, such intermediate systems may represent a substantial risk—even if you trust the integrity of the service providers involved, it is much harder to be confident that someone else cannot penetrate their systems. Also, e-mail needs to be protected on a per-person basis, not a per-system basis. When an e-mail originator encrypts a message for a particular recipient, only that recipient should be able to recover the message contents—not other users who might share the use of a system with that recipient. E-mail therefore requires true *end-to-end* or *writer-to-reader* protection, which simply cannot be provided by network-layer security services.

Security characteristics of electronic payment protocols can be even more complex. For example, in a payment message from buyer to vendor to bank, different fields in the message might need to be kept confidential with respect to different parties. Some fields might need to be encrypted so that only the vendor can interpret the contents, but other fields might need to be encrypted so that the vendor cannot interpret the contents, but the acquiring bank, to which the message is subsequently forwarded, can interpret them. (See section 5.7.)

The complexities of the security requirements in modern application protocols have meant a progressive trend toward use of application-layer security measures in favor of network-layer security measures. The latter still have their place, but they cannot generally be assumed to serve as the primary means of protecting e-commerce applications.

Application-layer security measures span all the security services defined in chapter 4, including authentication, access control, confidentiality, data integrity, and non-repudiation. Particular application-layer security measures relating to the Web, messaging, and payments are described in sections 5.4 through 5.8.

System Security

System security is protection of a particular end system and its local environment, regardless of the communications protection afforded through network-layer or application-layer safeguards. System security involves such safeguards as these:

- Ensuring the absence of known security weaknesses in installed software. Someone must ensure that all security-related vendor software patches are promptly installed and that questionable software, which might contain a virus or Trojan horse, is not installed.
- Ensuring that a system is configured to minimize penetration risks. The system should be configured to listen for Internet packets only on those ports assigned to applications that are actively used on that system. Modems should not, in general, be configured to permit dial-in.[4]
- Ensuring that downloaded software is from a trusted, reliable source.

- Ensuring that a system is administered so as to minimize penetration risks. The currency of all access control data must be maintained. Passwords must be changed regularly, and easily guessed passwords must be avoided. Obsolete user accounts must be deleted, as system penetration using such an account is more likely to go undetected.
- Ensuring that appropriate audit mechanisms are in place so that successful penetrations will be detected and new preventive measures installed as appropriate.

Historically, most system damage attributed to Internet-originated attacks could have been averted through adequate attention to system security. All Internet system administrators and users need security-related training and awareness of current Internet security-related developments.[5]

The exploitation of known weaknesses in software products remains the main means by which external attackers penetrate systems, even though such weaknesses are usually identified quickly and corrective patches issued by the vendors. For example, a particularly common problem is the buffer overflow attack, in which an attacker sends a message too large for a data storage area, resulting in overwriting of the memory following that area.[6] The overwriting typically causes the program to execute code supplied by the attacker, enabling many different types of system compromise.[7] The attack is made possible because a careless programmer failed to include a routine check in the code. However, most of the risks are averted if the system administrator is diligent about timely installing all security-critical software patches from the product vendor.

System penetrations can be leveraged by attackers in diverse ways. For example, *distributed denial-of-service attacks* are attacks that bombard network servers with massive volumes of network traffic, rendering them inoperative. Such attacks typically generate the offensive traffic through attack tools implanted on large numbers of previously penetrated computers belonging to innocent parties.[8]

More detailed coverage of system security is beyond the scope of this book. System security, by its very nature, depends on the particular hardware platform, operating system software, and local security policy.[9] In concluding our discussion of this topic, we simply wish to reiterate that system security is an essential element in securing e-commerce. *No e-commerce application can be considered secure if the system on which it is running is not secure.*

5.2   Firewalls

A physical *firewall* protects against the spreading of a fire in one part of a building to another part. In a computer network, a firewall protects a benign part of a network from dangers (possibly spreading out of control) in another part of the network. Most commonly, a firewall is deployed between an organization's internal network and the public Internet backbone, which it is prudent to consider fraught with dangers such as malicious hackers and eavesdroppers.

Network firewalls may take different physical and logical forms and provide various functions. Their main purpose is to implement an organization's security policy. Security policies may vary widely from organization to organization. Functions typically provided by a firewall include these:

- Limiting the set of applications for which traffic can enter the internal network from the Internet, and limiting the internal addresses to which traffic for different applications can go. Typically, incoming traffic is permitted to go only to a system that is specially equipped to cope with the applicable threats. For example, incoming Web HTTP or FTP requests may be allowed to pass if directed to an internal server that has the necessary technical and administrative controls to support secure external access. However, such requests may not be permitted to go to any other internal network address.
- Authenticating the sources of certain classes of incoming traffic. For example, external interactive users seeking access to any internal network system via the TELNET protocol may be permitted entry only if they first authenticate using a personal token and the firewall determines that they are authorized persons.
- Limiting the ability of internal network systems to send traffic to the external Internet based on the identity of the application and other relevant parameters. For example, distributed denial-of-service attacks typically employ software agents implanted on compromised systems belonging to innocent parties. A properly configured firewall not only blocks network traffic originating from such a source but also draws the firewall administrator's attention to the existence of this unexpected source of network traffic.
- Acting as a *security gateway* and encrypting or integrity-checking all traffic over the Internet backbone to or from some other security gateway. Such a configuration is sometimes called a *virtual private network*.

Building a firewall generally requires a combination of policy setting, technical planning, product procurement or configuration, and customization. There are several commercial firewall products available. Elements in a firewall solution might include these:

- *Screening routers:* A router which selectively blocks packets, usually when routing them from one network to another. A screening router uses a set of preestablished rules that define the types of packets that may be passed (for example, those from or to a particular IP address and port number).[10] This process is also known as *packet filtering*.
- *Proxy servers:* Application-specific server programs that selectively forward users' requests for Internet services, such as Web HTTP or FTP, to the targeted external servers, provided that the requests conform with local security policy. A proxy server is intended to be transparent to both the internal network client and external Internet server, except for a possible performance impact. Instead of communicating directly with each other, both systems actually communicate with the proxy server. Note that the client software has to be cognizant of this proxy configuration so that it redirects requests to the proxy rather than trying to communicate with the external server directly.
- *Demilitarized zone (DMZ):* Network host computers located between the external network and internal network. Even if a host system in the demilitarized zone is compromised by an external intruder, this does not give direct access to the internal network; for example, it does not allow the intruder to monitor packets between two systems on the internal network. Certain server systems, such as Web servers that provide access to external users, may be configured in the demilitarized zone.[11]

5.3   IPsec and Virtual Private Networks

The network-layer protocol used on the Internet is the Internet Protocol (IP). IP defines a standard way of formatting a set of data items called *headers* and attaching them to the packet of data being communicated, to give what is called an *IP datagram*. The headers perform such tasks as identifying the source and destination system addresses and port numbers. IP is a connectionless protocol: Every packet of data is treated independently. Because of the way Internet packet switching works, packets can sometimes get lost or reordered in transit. Correction of such problems is not an IP concern but a concern of a higher-layer protocol, usually the Transmission Control Protocol (TCP), which can shuffle received packets into the right order and request retransmission of missing packets. The role of IP is simply to get a packet of data from source system to destination system.

IP is not inherently secure. For example, since 1994, many Internet systems have been subjected to an attack known as *IP spoofing*. This attack involves an attacker's generating packets that contain a false source address. Several applications, such as the X windows remote terminal application for UNIX, depend on the IP source address as the basis of authentication. The attacks proved to be very successful in allowing intruders to execute privileged (root access) commands on many systems. The ability to execute such commands gives an attacker complete control over a system and the data stored on it.[12]

In 1994, the IETF launched a project to add security features to IP. The challenges faced by this project extended far beyond information security technologies; for example, these concerns needed to be addressed:

- Existing network components would need to remain functional, even though many would never be upgraded to include security features.
- Export restrictions on cryptographic technologies could make it difficult to deploy good technical solutions globally.

The IETF working group that addressed this project was known as IPsec, and the same name is now commonly used for the protocol family that resulted. IPsec protects packet streams moving between pairs of systems, where a system may be either an end system (a client or server) or a security gateway (a router or firewall).

IPsec protection operates in two different modes: *transport mode* and *tunnel mode*. Transport mode is used to protect the upper-layer protocol (typically TCP) part of a packet and provides end-to-end protection between one network end system (client or server) and another. Tunnel mode protects an entire IP packet by enveloping it in a new packet with its own plaintext IP headers. The addressing information in the final packet may be different from that in the unprotected packet, to facilitate processing through security gateways. This allows some important secure network configurations to be built that are not protected purely end to end.

Here are some examples of IPsec configurations:

- *Multisite virtual private network (VPN):* IPsec protects all traffic between two or more private sites interconnected via the Internet. Tunnel-mode protection operates between a VPN gateway (router or firewall) on one site and a VPN gateway on another site. Traffic between any pair of end systems on different sites can thereby be protected, without requiring those end systems to implement IPsec and without requiring their operators or users to be cognizant of the use of the public Internet as the communications vehicle.
- *Road warrior remote access:* A roaming user with a laptop computer, for example, can access a trusted home network from an untrusted network such as the public Internet via an ordinary ISP. All traffic, such as e-mail retrieval and browser access to corporate Web servers, is protected. This allows the roaming user to operate in essentially the same manner as if directly connected to the home network. Tunnel-mode IPsec is implemented on the roaming terminal and a gateway router or firewall that gives access to the home network from the Internet. This IPsec configuration constitutes a cost-effective substitute for the previous generation of remote access systems for road warriors, which required expensive and performance-constrained dial-in lines and modem banks.
- *End-to-end security:* IPsec, operating in either transport or tunnel mode, protects all traffic between two end systems, such as a pair of redundant servers at separate sites. The protection is managed at the end-system level and resists all forms of intermediate system attack, including attacks instigated from local networks.

The IPsec protocols comprise two packet protection protocols: the *Authentication Header* protocol and the packet encryption or *Encapsulating Security Payload* protocol. We outline the features of these protocols later in this chapter, along with the concepts of security policy and security associations that govern the use of these protocols and the key management protocol that supports them.[13]

Security Policy and Security Associations

The IPsec protocols can provide confidentiality, data origin authentication, and data integrity services to packets. However, not all packets passing any IPsec-processing point (end system, router, or firewall) are treated equally. Security policy determines the security services afforded to a given packet, based on such criteria as source IP address, destination IP address, transport protocol, and port number (which generally maps to the application type). For example, security policy might dictate the following treatment:

- All e-mail traffic entering (or leaving) a site and destined for (or originating from) the corporate mail server is passed through without requiring IPsec protection.
- All traffic to or from a remote corporate site must be IPsec-protected for confidentiality, data origin authentication, and data integrity.
- All packets not covered by the preceding provisions are discarded.

Information defining the security policy is held in a *security policy database* (SPD).

A pair of IPsec systems that respectively generate and consume an IPsec-protected packet do so within the context of a *security association.* A security association is a set of parameters upon which both systems must agree. The parameters include identification of the protection protocol to be used, the mode (transport or tunnel), the cryptographic algorithms to be used for the various security services, the keys, and the duration for which the keys are valid. Every security association has an identifier, called a *Security Parameter Index,* to which the systems involved have preagreed. This identifier is included in the header of every IPsec-protected packet. The set of parameter values defined by a security association are stored in a security association database (SAD).

The ways security associations are established and managed are discussed later under "IPsec Key Management."

Authentication Header Protocol

The Authentication Header provides authentication and integrity protection to IP datagrams, but no confidentiality protection.[14] The absence of confidentiality makes the protocol easy to implement and efficient to operate and can facilitate product deployment internationally by averting controls on the export, import, or use of encryption. If confidentiality is required at the IP level, the packet encryption protocol described in the next subsection should be used in conjunction with or instead of the Authentication Header.

The Authentication Header protocol allows the recipient of an IP datagram to have confidence in its authenticity and its source. This mechanism depends on proof that the originator possesses a particular secret key. The mechanism is therefore much stronger than early Internet authentication approaches based on checking IP source addresses, which can be easily forged in IP spoofing attacks.

Generation of an Authentication Header involves computing a message authentication code (MAC) on those parts of the IP datagram that do not normally change as the datagram moves across the network.[15] This authenticates the source of the datagram and confirms that it was not modified in transit. The header also contains a security parameter index, which identifies a security association, and a sequence number to support replay detection at the receiver.

Different algorithms may be used for computing the MAC. The most common type of algorithm, preferred because of its comparatively high performance, is the keyed hash function. Two algorithms that must be implemented are *keyed SHA-1* and *keyed MD5*.[16]

Packet Encryption Protocol

Encryption at the IP level involves what is formally called the Encapsulating Security Payload (ESP) protocol—a protocol distinct from the Authentication Header protocol—which is designed to provide confidentiality, as well as authentication and integrity, to an IP packet.[17] As with the Authentication Header, this protocol can operate in either transport or tunnel mode.

This protocol uses a MAC for authentication and integrity purposes, similar to the Authentication Header protocol. However, this protocol also requires use of a symmetric encryption algorithm. In principle, different algorithms are available for selection. For interoperability, all products are required to implement the DES algorithm,[18] but specifications also exist for the Blowfish,[19] CAST,[20] and triple-DES algorithms. It is anticipated that the AES algorithm will be supported in due course.

Like the Authentication Header protocol, packet encryption uses the security association concept to determine algorithm, keys, and other such parameters. A security parameter index, which identifies a preestablished security association, is carried unencrypted in the Encapsulated Security Payload header. This field points to the information that is needed by a receiving system to decrypt the encrypted part of the datagram.

IPsec Key Management

Establishment of cryptographic keys for IPsec is part of the process of establishing security associations. Security associations can be established by either manual or automated means.

With manual security association establishment, a person manually configures a system with required security association parameter information, including its key and the keys of other systems with which it is expected to communicate securely. Because of the cost and error-prone nature of such processes and the inability to make changes dynamically, the manual approach is practical only in small, constrained configurations.

Automated security association establishment adds scalability and flexibility. The IETF has designed the Internet Key Exchange (IKE) protocol as a standard means of automated security association establishment for IPsec and potentially for other Internet protocols as well.[21]

Recall that a security association involves a pair of systems for which common parameter values (some of which are highly sensitive) must be established. IKE is a complex protocol that operates between these two systems.[22] It involves these processes:

- Establishing a shared secret between the two systems, using Diffie-Hellman key agreement. This shared secret is used to protect subsequent exchanges.
- Authenticating the two systems to each other. This may be based on preshared keys or, more generally, on a public-key cryptographic technique such as an RSA or DSA digital signature.
- Using the resulting authenticated and encrypted channel to negotiate characteristics of an IPsec security association and establish required secret keys for use in conjunction with that security association.

Using IKE (and consequently IPsec) on a large scale necessitates, at yet another level, the use of a public-key infrastructure (PKI). The PKI supports secure delivery of public keys to those systems that require them for authenticating remote systems. PKIs are addressed in detail in chapters 6 and 7.

5.4 Web Security with SSL/TLS

The Web presents a myriad of opportunities for innovative approaches to information dissemination and communication. The Web also presents a myriad of opportunities for misuse and abuse. Security concerns on the Web fall into two basic categories: The first category relates to the risk of compromise of a Web server, for example, databases being exposed to unauthorized persons, or attackers gaining the ability to execute malicious code on the server. Even though such problems tend to be Web specific, they are essentially a matter of system security. For advice in this area, see Stein or guidelines published by the International Computer Security Association.[23] The second category of concern relates to attacks perpetrated on the external network, such as collection of credit card numbers by electronic eavesdropping or diversion of client-originated traffic to bogus vendor Web sites. These problems need to be addressed through standard application security protocols supported by the common Web server and browser products.

The most widely used general-purpose secure Web protocols are the Secure Sockets Layer (SSL) protocol and its close relative, Transport Layer Security (TLS). SSL was developed by Netscape Communications Corporation.[24] Netscape contributed SSL to the IETF for standardization purposes, and the result, which incorporates some minor improvements, is the IETF TLS specification.[25]

While SSL/TLS is primarily thought of as a secure Web protocol, it is technically a new layer of protocol inserted in the protocol stack above the Internet TCP protocol. It can be used to protect the communication of any application protocol that normally operates over TCP, for example, HTTP, FTP, or TELNET. The most common use of SSL/TLS is in protecting HTTP communications; in particular, a URL commencing with "https://" indicates use of HTTP protected by SSL/TLS. The layer placement of SSL/TLS is compared with that of IPsec in figure 5.1.

SSL/TLS provides a range of security services for client-server sessions. To understand the value of these services, consider them in light of protecting the Web session in

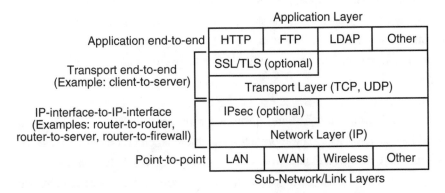

Figure 5.1 Architectural Layer Placement of SSL/TLS and IPsec

which Vera orders a lathe from Danielle's Machine Makers. Vera will know that the session is SSL-protected because of an indicator on her browser screen.[26] These are the security services:

- *Server authentication:* The server is authenticated to the client by demonstrating possession of a particular private key. This is important to Vera, to be sure that she is really communicating with Danielle's site and not some other site posing as Danielle's to gather credit card numbers or other private information from unsuspecting buyers.
- *Confidentiality:* Data items transferred in the session are encrypted to protect against disclosure to electronic eavesdroppers. This is particularly important, as it can protect against eavesdroppers' learning Vera's credit card number or other personal account information as it is transmitted to the server.
- *Integrity:* Data items transferred in the session are protected with a message authentication code (MAC) to ensure that any attempt to modify data in transit is detected. This protects both Vera and the vendor against an active attacker causing havoc, for example, by changing the order for one lathe into an order for 10 lathes or altering the shipping address.
- *Client authentication:* This optional security service authenticates the client to the server by demonstrating possession of a particular private key. Danielle's would prefer to have proof that the person at the client is actually Vera but may not be overly concerned, provided a valid credit card number has been presented and authorized successfully. Given that this service is not necessarily essential to the vendor and that many potential customers may not possess their own key pairs anyway, this service may, in the short term, find limited use with Internet shopping. However, for other applications, such as Internet banking and general contracting, it may be very important for the server site to strongly authenticate the client.

Every SSL/TLS communication is protected with server authentication, confidentiality, and integrity services. These protections, which depend on the use of a server-based key pair, are achieved essentially as illustrated in figure 5.2. The server sends its public key to the client in the form of a certificate, signed by a certification authority whose own public key is *a priori* known to and trusted by the client.[27] The client can

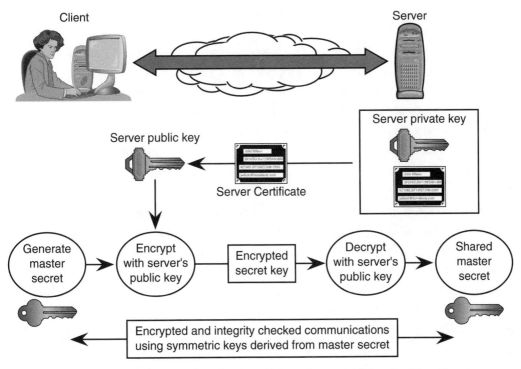

Figure 5.2   SSL Server Authentication, Encryption, and Integrity Checking

therefore have confidence it has received the correct server public key. The client generates a random master secret and sends that value to the server, encrypted with the
server's public key. Since only the legitimate server can decrypt that master secret, the
result is that the server and client now exclusively share a master secret. The master
secret is then used to generate symmetric encryption keys for confidentiality purposes
and MAC keys for integrity purposes.[28] Because only the correct server can decrypt the
master secret and thus the encrypted data from the client, the server is implicitly authenticated to the client.

Client authentication is an optional additional feature. It depends on the use of a
client-based key pair and a certificate for that key pair issued by a certification authority that the server trusts. The client uses its private key to generate a digital signature on
a fresh data item[29] and then sends this signed data item to the server along with its certificate. The server verifies the digital signature and uses the certificate to check that the

correct client public key has been supplied. This has the effect of authenticating the client to the server.

Internally, SSL/TLS consists of two sub-protocols: the Record Protocol and the Handshake Protocol. The Record Protocol defines the basic format for all data items sent in the session. It provides for compressing data, generating a MAC on the data, encrypting the data, and ensuring that the receiver can determine the correct data length, given that the input data may need to be padded out to give an integral number of blocks for use with a block cipher algorithm. The MAC is prefixed to the data as part of the Record Protocol prior to encryption. A record sequence number is included to protect against the reordering of data items by an active attacker. For the Record Protocol to calculate a MAC and to encrypt a data item, cryptographic keys must already be established in the client and the server. The protocol supports changing to a different set of protection algorithms and keys at any time.

The Handshake Protocol is used to negotiate which protection algorithms are used to authenticate the client and server to each other, to transmit required public-key certificates, and to establish the session keys for use in the integrity-check and encryption processes of the Record Protocol. Different key establishment algorithms are supported, including RSA key transport, Diffie-Hellman key agreement, and the U.S. government's KEA algorithm.

When a new session is established, it may be possible to reuse existing session keys from prior communications. Session keys have an associated session identifier for this purpose. Reuse of session keys reduces overheads and is usually acceptably secure, provided that the keys are not too old; in any case, the decision to reuse session keys is always a policy decision on the server's part.

The Handshake Protocol is a higher-level protocol than the Record Protocol; that is, the former is conveyed via the latter. In the first couple of messages exchanged in a session, the Record Protocol cannot encrypt or compute integrity-check values because the keys are not yet known; however, the protocol is designed in such a way that this does not present a security problem.

Prior to the U.S. federal government's liberalization of cryptographic policy in January 2000, encryption algorithms used in SSL/TLS products were a major concern.[30] U.S.-sourced SSL/TLS products had both domestic (for use within the United States) and generally exportable implementations. Both types of implementation used the same encryption algorithm, which typically has a key length of 128 bits. The difference between the two implementations lay in the Handshake Protocol implementation. In the exportable implementation, the *effective* key length was 40 bits; the actual encryption key was derived from a 40-bit secret value plus public information. In the domestic version, the effective key length could be as long as 128 bits. A mechanism existed that allowed some exportable browsers to operate with 128-bit strength encryption when communicating to specially licensed servers operated by financial institutions or other specially qualifying organizations. Since the liberalization of government cryptographic policy, concerns surrounding these issues are fading rapidly.

5.5   Other Web Security Protocols

Other than SSL/TLS, secure Web protocols that have been developed and deployed include these:

- *Wireless Transport Layer Security (WTLS):* Part of the Wireless Application Protocol (WAP) industry standards for the presentation and delivery of information to wireless phones and other wireless devices
- *Signed downloaded object protocols:* Protocols that authenticate the source and integrity of downloaded software or other content
- *Client digital signature protocols:* Protocols that support the digital signing of a transaction by a user at a client terminal
- *Platform for Privacy Preferences (P3P):* Protocols to support the expression and querying of Web site policies for protecting the privacy of user data

Wireless Transport Layer Security

The Wireless Application Protocol (WAP) is a set of standards for the presentation and delivery of wireless information and telephony services on mobile phones and other wireless terminals. The WAP specifications are being developed by the WAP Forum, a consortium of wireless handset manufacturers, service providers, infrastructure providers, and software developers.[31] The WAP 1.1 specifications were completed in 1999, and handset and infrastructure products implementing those specifications began shipping in early 2000. Since then, the specifications have been enhanced progressively.

WAP provides a complete set of protocols for the wireless Internet environment, designed to operate over any of the underlying wireless bearer technologies (GSM, CDMA, TDMA, etc.). The specifications include a hypertext markup language called Wireless Markup Language (WML), which is a relative of HTML but is oriented toward the special needs of mobile wireless devices and their limited-functionality user interfaces.

From the security perspective, the most significant WAP specification is the Wireless Transport Layer Security (WTLS) protocol. WTLS is a close relative of SSL/TLS, providing the same basic functionality, but with some built-in efficiencies designed with the limited-bandwidth wireless environment in mind.[32]

Signed Downloaded Objects

The Web experience is heightened by the use of software that is downloaded to and run in client systems. Java programs, called *applets,* are automatically downloaded from a server upon accessing certain Web pages, then interpreted and executed by the client's browser. Java examples, such as spinning text and animated icons, can be found throughout the Web. Java also supports communication by an applet back to its source server, enabling applications such as scrolling stock quotes or interactive chat programs.

Java applets create new risks for users of the Web. Instead of software running on a remote server, the execution of the applet occurs on the client's system, which shifts the security risk from the server to the client. Running executable code from an unknown source always raises legitimate security concerns.

Java applets run in their own trusted execution environment, called the *sandbox,* on the client platform.[33] By design, an applet should not be able to inspect or alter the client's file system, run system commands, or load system software libraries. A Java applet should also be able to contact only the server from which it was originally downloaded. Given these restrictions, applets *should* be able to do little damage to the client or server systems. However, many flaws in Java and its early implementations were found and generally fixed in due course.[34] However, it is possible that further flaws remain or will be introduced.[35]

One prospective flaw that has emerged is that of *hostile applets.* A hostile applet, when downloaded, may attempt to exploit a client's system resources inappropriately or maliciously. For example, an applet has access to the mail port of its host machine; therefore, it may send forged mail from the client. There are concerns that hostile applets might crash browsers, kill other running applets, or consume excessive resources of the host system. Various solutions to combating such attacks have been proposed, but foolproof defenses remain a challenge.

The preceding concerns are not limited to Java but include downloadable executable software generally. Microsoft's *ActiveX* system,[36] for example, raises the same types of concerns. ActiveX controls are reusable software components developed by software vendors. These controls can be used to add specialized functionality to Web sites, desktop applications, and development tools. For example, a stock ticker control can be used to add a live stock ticker to a Web page, or an animation control can be used to add animation features. In fact, the security concerns with ActiveX can be greater than with Java because ActiveX does not have a containment model like Java's sandbox.

The best remedy for these security concerns is reliable knowledge of the source of any software that is downloaded onto one's system. Applets or other software from questionable sources should be refused. Furthermore, in the event of a problem, the affected user should know, reliably, the source of the software in order to obtain recourse.

Systems for authenticating the source of downloadable executable software have been developed, for example, Microsoft's *Authenticode* system.[37] Authenticode enables developers to digitally sign their software code, allowing clients to verify the publisher of downloaded software before executing it. Verifying the digital signature also ensures that the software has not been tampered with during downloading. Authenticode uses PKCS #7 signed data standards (discussed later in this chapter). Signatures are verifiable using public-key certificates issued by recognized certification authorities (see chapter 6).

Client Digital Signatures

To bind a user to a transaction, such as a Web-based payment instruction or contractual commitment, the user may be required to digitally sign the transaction in the client using a local private key. Such a digital signature may be instrumental in achieving non-repudiation properties. Note that SSL/TLS and WTLS do not provide such a function and hence make little contribution to satisfying non-repudiation needs.

There is no universal standard protocol for this purpose, but the following approaches exist:

- *WAP Signtext function:* The WAP specifications include a specification for a standard digital signature mechanism that can be invoked from a WML script.[38]

- *Proprietary signature mechanisms:* Various Web security product vendors offer digital signature functions that can be invoked via a client software product or downloaded applet or control. Many use the PKCS #7 format for such signatures, making that format a de facto standard for this purpose.
- *XML digital signature standard:* The XML digital signature standard, developed by the World Wide Web Consortium (W3C) and the IETF, is suitable for digitally signing elements of XML documents.[39]

Platform for Privacy Preferences

The Platform for Privacy Preferences (P3P) is a W3C project.[40] It was motivated by concerns about possible compromise of consumers' privacy by Web sites that collect information regarding the browsing habits of their users and subsequently exploit that knowledge or disseminate it elsewhere.

P3P provides a basis for Web sites to express their privacy practices in a standard format that can be retrieved automatically and interpreted by software components, called user agents, that are built into or linked to a user's browser. P3P user agents permit users to be notified of site practices (in both machine- and human-readable formats) and to (optionally) automate decision making based on these practices. Thus, users need not read the privacy policies at every site they visit.

P3P does not *solve* the privacy problem, since it does not ensure that sites actually practice the procedures they preach in their disclosed privacy policies. However, it is a valuable contribution to the resolution of consumer privacy concerns on the Web.

5.6   Secure Messaging and S/MIME

Messaging Security Services

The security needs of messaging applications, including e-mail and mail-enabled applications, clearly cannot be satisfied by network security measures alone. Secure messaging demands writer-to-reader protection in environments in which messages may traverse multiple network connections and may be stored and forwarded through unknown application-level mail gateway systems. Furthermore, messages may be submitted and received through end systems that support many users. Before discussing messaging security protocols, let us present the vocabulary for messaging systems. Messages originate from and are ultimately received by *users,* which may be people or mail-enabled application programs. A message has one *originator* and one or more *recipients.* A user is supported by *mail client* software, sometimes called a *user agent,* which performs such tasks as preparing and submitting messages and receiving and preprocessing received messages for the user. The message transfer backbone comprises systems called message hubs, switches, gateways, or transfer agents (MTAs). When a message has multiple recipients, the message contents may be copied and sent via multiple paths at various points while traversing the network.

Various secure messaging protocols have been developed, some proprietary and some with a standards imprimatur. These protocols share various functions. There is one set of *basic security services* that any messaging security protocol must provide and that satisfies most user requirements. Beyond these basic security services, various *enhanced security services* might also be provided.

The basic messaging security services comprise protective measures applied to a single message as a stand-alone data object. They are, in general, independent from message submission, transfer, and delivery mechanisms and can be implemented entirely in user agents. The basic message-protection services include

- *Message origin authentication:* Provides a recipient with assurance that a message came from the claimed originator. For example, when the order department of Sharon's Steelcorp receives a message that appears to be a steel order from Danielle's Machine Makers, the order clerk wants assurances that the message has not been concocted by a malicious attacker. It is a very simple matter for an attacker to set the *From:* field in a message to any desired value. The message origin authentication service authenticates the originator on the basis of possessing a particular cryptographic key.
- *Content integrity:* Protects message contents against modification between the originator and recipient, including modification by an active attacker. This security service needs to be bound with message origin authentication for the latter to be meaningful.
- *Content confidentiality:* Protects message contents against disclosure to eavesdroppers between the originator and recipient. Sharon's and Danielle's conduct

their business under a nondisclosure agreement and require their technology to
support that agreement.

- *Non-repudiation of origin:* Provides a recipient with strong evidence of the origin
  of a message and its contents. When Nola's Electronic Market receives an order
  from a previously unknown customer and initiates the shipping of expensive
  products, Nola requires assurances that the customer will not later deny having
  placed the order and refuse to pay for it. (Nola's margins leave little room for
  absorbing the cost of returned items or litigating disputes, so she desires strong
  evidence immediately to convince *anyone* that an order was placed.)

Enhanced messaging security services typically transcend simply protecting a single
message as a stand-alone object. For example, *confirmation* services provide secure notifications to a message originator that the message was delivered to a recipient or at least
reached some specific point on the message path.[41] Other enhanced security services may
be provided by particular messaging security protocols to suit special needs of particular
environments. For example, protocols designed for use in military environments might
include a security labeling service, which allows a security label to be attached to a message to indicate the message's security classification or other authorization control information.

While various messaging security protocols have been developed, the industry has
rallied around the S/MIME protocol as its dominant standard.

S/MIME

The S/MIME protocol was first developed by a private group under the leadership of RSA
Security, Inc. S/MIME Version 2 was implemented by all the major e-mail product vendors, including Microsoft, Lotus, and Netscape.[42] The Version 2 specifications were submitted to the IETF and published in the IETF document series but were not endorsed as
IETF standards.[43] However, the IETF then assumed responsibility for S/MIME. Version 3,
which was developed under the IETF consensus process, entered the IETF standards
track.[44]

S/MIME gained popularity over competing secure e-mail proposals mainly because
it was built on an existing base of de facto standards called the Public-Key Cryptography
Standards (PKCS), for which many vendors had already implemented software.[45]

The main building block of S/MIME is a specification called Cryptographic Message Syntax (CMS), which defines data structures and procedures for cryptographically encapsulating (for example, digitally signing or encrypting) other data structures. The original version of CMS, which was part of PKCS, was known as PKCS #7.[46] S/MIME's fundamental approach to providing the basic protection services described previously is to apply CMS encapsulation to a base MIME body part, generating a new cryptographically protected data structure, which itself becomes a MIME content.

S/MIME defines a MIME content type called the *application/pkcs7-mime* type. The purpose of this content type is to convey a protected representation of any unprotected MIME body part. With S/MIME, the different types of protection, such as digital signing and encryption, are considered variants of one basic transformation or *enveloping* process using one of several different structured data types defined in CMS, such as

- *Signed data:* The representation of the body part to be protected is built into a data structure which includes one or more digital signatures over that data together with necessary algorithm identifiers and (optional) public-key certificates and other signer-related information.
- *Enveloped data:* The representation of the body part to be protected is symmetrically encrypted and then incorporated into a data structure which includes a copy of the encryption key for each recipient, encrypted under the public key of an RSA encryption key pair for that recipient, together with necessary recipient identifiers and algorithm identifiers. Alternatively, a Diffie-Hellman key establishment mechanism can substitute for RSA.

An S/MIME object can be reencapsulated into another S/MIME object if multiple types of protection need to be applied.

The process for generating the S/MIME content for a digitally signed MIME body part is illustrated in figure 5.3.

The first step is to *canonicalize* the message, or transform the message content to a *canonical form*. This step is necessary because the Internet messaging environment is built on an underlying *text-based* transport system that is designed to carry character-encoded messages, rather than a *binary* transport system that can transparently carry any data item encoded as a string of bits. Consequently, as a message progresses on its path from originator to recipient, the representation of the message text may change. Different

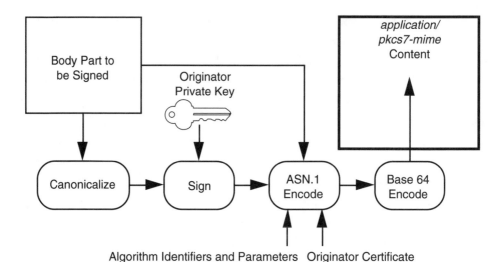

Figure 5.3   S/MIME Digital Signature Generation

systems use different character-encoding schemes.[47] Also, different systems use different conventions for representing the end of a text line, for example, the carriage return (CR) character, the line feed (LF) character, or a sequence of CR followed by LF. A message may be converted to use different character encodings or a different line-terminator convention as it enters a new system. While such conversions do not change the meaning of a message, they introduce the risk of a valid digital signature no longer verifying correctly. To avert such problems, it is necessary for all systems to compute digital signatures on a common, agreed-upon representation of a message, using an agreed-upon character encoding and an agreed-upon line-terminator convention. This standard representation of a message is called a *canonical form* of the message.

After canonicalization of the representation of the input body part, the S/MIME digital signature process involves cryptographic transformation and conversion of the resultant binary data string to a form which can traverse a text-string-oriented message transfer system. (The latter step usually follows a process called *base 64 encoding,* a common means of conveying binary data with MIME.) CMS data-structure processing involves encoding in accordance with the internationally standardized data-typing and -structuring notation called Abstract Syntax Notation One (ASN.1).[48]

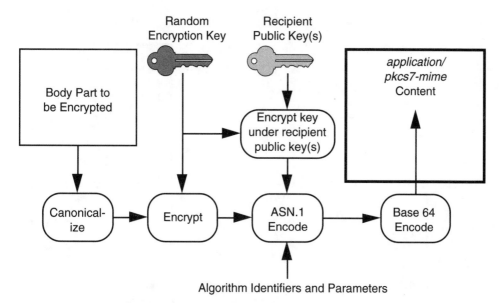

Figure 5.4   S/MIME Encryption Process

The process for generating an encrypted S/MIME content is illustrated in figure 5.4. The process is the same as that for S/MIME digital signing, except that the enveloped data variant of CMS is used in place of the signed data variant, resulting in a different crypto-graphic transformation.

The S/MIME digital signature process illustrated in figure 5.3 has one shortcoming. A mailer that is not S/MIME-capable cannot read the contents of the original body part of a signed message. The capacity to do so is sometimes considered a valuable feature: Recipients without a security-equipped mailer may benefit from reading signed messages even if they cannot verify the signatures.

S/MIME addresses this shortcoming with an alternative structure that uses the *multipart/signed* MIME type together with a different S/MIME type, called *application/pkcs7-signature*. The *multipart/signed* content type defines a structure com-prising two body parts. The first body part may contain any MIME content, such as a piece of text, sound clip, or structured type, that is, an instance of *multipart*. The digital signa-ture is computed over this first body part, including its MIME headers. The second body part contains the digital signature and any control information needed by a recipient user agent to verify that signature.

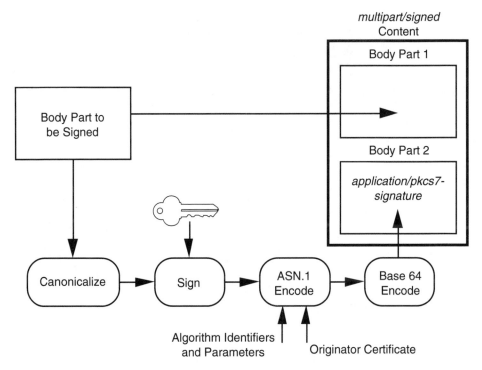

Figure 5.5   S/MIME Digital Signature Generation with *multipart/signed*

S/MIME defines the MIME type *application/pkcs7-signature* for use in the second body part of *multipart/signed.* The result is illustrated in figure 5.5. The contents of the *application/pkcs7-signature* type are a special case of the signed data variant of PKCS #7, which omits the copy of the plaintext signed data.

In addition to the message-protection formats we have discussed, S/MIME defines a format for conveying a request to have a public-key certificate issued. This involves another MIME content type, called *application/pkcs10,* which carries a certificate request message as defined in another of the PKCS standards, PKCS #10.[49]

S/MIME Version 3 also specifies a set of *enhanced security services,* which may optionally be provided.[50] These include signed receipts, security labels, and support for security-capable mailing list expanders.

5.7   Other Messaging Security Protocols

Web-Based Secure Mail

S/MIME's greatest competition today lies not in other mail client-to-mail client messaging protocols but in the Web-based approach to e-messaging. Web-based messaging differs from mail-client-based messaging in that the end user uses a standard Web browser rather than a mail client. Messaging services are provided through a mail hub based on Web servers. Communications between the client and server can be protected by SSL/TLS.

Web-based secure mail solutions vary in the extent to which the user is required to trust the mail hub to perform security-critical functions on his or her behalf. At one extreme, the mail hub is fully trusted by the originator and recipient users. The communication between the mail hub and a user is protected by standard SSL/TLS. The mail hub digitally signs, encrypts, decrypts, and verifies signatures on behalf of users. At the other extreme, the security is provided on a truly end-to-end basis, as with S/MIME. On origination, a message is digitally signed and encrypted within the originating client system, and on receipt, the signature is verified and the content decrypted in the recipient client. This approach requires some software to execute in the clients; such software, in the form of an executable module such as an applet or ActiveX control, can be downloaded from the server supporting the mail hub. Other variants exist between these two extremes, in which the mail hub is trusted to perform certain functions only. Any of these alternatives may be acceptable for specific environments, depending on the risk model.

The major appeal of the Web-based secure mail approach is that the user does not require a preinstalled mail client: he or she can communicate secure mail using a standard browser, potentially from various terminal systems. Web-based secure mail also provides much greater flexibility in enhancing the user experience and in integrating the e-mail function with the surrounding application environment.

Pretty Good Privacy

Pretty Good Privacy (PGP) is a message-protection software product which is popular within various niches of the Internet user community.[51] PGP was written by Phil Zimmerman, a well-known computer scientist turned political activist turned businessman. PGP's popularity has been aided by its being available free of charge, for example, from the Massachusetts Institute of Technology Web site.[52] A commercially supported version is also available from Network Associates, Inc.[53]

From a technical perspective, PGP is very similar to S/MIME. It uses digital signature and encryption functions to provide basic message-protection services. PGP defines its own message-protection format, which can be embedded in a MIME body part if required. An Internet standards-track specification for using a PGP protection envelope in conjunction with the *multipart/signed* and *multipart/encrypted* structured MIME types has been developed.[54]

The main aspect of PGP that distinguishes it from S/MIME is that PGP defines its own public-key-pair management system, including its own form of public-key certificates. This key management system is incompatible with recognized public-key infrastructure standards (discussed in chapters 6 and 7). PGP key management is based on loose, ad hoc relationships between the various parties who own PGP key pairs, rather than on a well-organized infrastructure designed to support accountability. Consequently, while PGP is a highly effective system for protecting casual e-mail between Internet users, it is not generally considered suitable for supporting wide-scale e-commerce. This aspect of PGP is discussed further in chapter 7.

Legacy Secure Messaging Protocols

Prior to the emergence of S/MIME as a universal, standard, secure messaging protocol, there were many different secure messaging protocols in use. These included proprietary protocols from various vendors plus other protocols, such as Privacy Enhanced Mail (PEM), MIME Object Security Services (MOSS), X.400 security, and Message Security Protocol (MSP), which were recognized to some extent as standards. Information on the latter set of protocols, all now of historical interest only, is provided in appendix G.

5.8   Secure Payments on the Internet

Electronic payments should be authenticated, resistant to forging, and confidential (to protect sensitive data such as credit card numbers and other payment instructions). These qualities can generally be obtained by applying the security features of the electronic messaging and Web protocols described in sections 5.4 through 5.6 to transactions that implement a payment process. Certain additional security requirements may sometimes arise, for example, the SET protocol (described later in this section) protects sensitive payment data from disclosure while traversing merchant server systems.

Secure Payment Data Capture

A common way for an Internet merchant to receive payment is to securely capture payment information data from the customer, then process the payment through a traditional, that is, non-Internet-based payment process. This is usually limited to bank card (credit or debit card) payments. A customer enters a bank card number into a field on a Web form, and that number is transported to the merchant server protected under SSL/TLS encryption. As described previously, this depends on the server having a key pair and a certificate that is trusted by the client. The server recovers the bank card number by decryption and the number is used to invoice payment via non-Internet-based means, like a bank card purchase by telephone.

Online Payment Processing

Several options now exist for an Internet merchant not only to capture the customer payment data via the Internet but also to have the payment processed online via a payment-processing service provider. Payment instruments supported include credit and debit cards, purchase cards, electronic checks, and automated clearinghouse (ACH) transactions. These payment methods are generally supported by a payment gateway service provider that switches transactions to a range of traditional payment processors as a service for Internet merchants.[55]

Electronic checks constitute an Internet-based online version of the paper check payment system. An important standardization initiative on electronic checks known as *eCheck*[56] was developed by the Financial Services Technology Consortium (FSTC) and is now managed by CommerceNet. In addition, several *electronic cash* proposals are undergoing trial or production operation.[57]

Another area in which systems are being developed is that of *micropayments*. These are systems designed to support large numbers of small payments; pennies rather than dollars per transaction. At present, an individual micropayment purchase is not large enough to be handled cost effectively as a traditional payment transaction via financial institutions. Many small transactions can be accommodated, but first they need to be aggregated for financial institution processing. These collection and batch processes tend to conflict with the real-time transactional requirements of Internet commerce. Micropayment systems and stored value cards seek to overcome these shortcomings.

The SET Protocol for Bank Card Payments

In 1996, MasterCard and Visa joined forces to promote the development of the Secure Electronic Transaction (SET) protocol and infrastructure specification to support bank card payments as part of Internet-based electronic shopping or service provision.[58] The goal of SET was to provide a more secure environment than that offered through traditional SSL/TLS-protected bank card payments on the Web.

These are the primary participants in the SET environment:

1. *Issuer:* A financial institution that issues bank cards (credit cards or debit cards), typically bearing a particular *brand* (examples of brands are Visa and MasterCard).
2. *Cardholder:* An authorized holder of a bank card who is registered with the corresponding issuer to perform electronic commerce.
3. *Merchant*: A seller of goods, services, or information who accepts payment electronically.
4. *Acquirer:* A financial institution that supports merchants by providing a service for processing bank card transactions.

These are secondary participants in the SET infrastructure:

5. *Payment gateway:* A system that provides online electronic commerce services to merchants. Such a system is operated by either an acquirer or some other party that supports acquirers; in the latter case, the payment gateway needs to interface to the acquirer to support the authorization and capture of transactions.
6. *Certification authorities:* Components of the infrastructure that certify public keys of cardholders, merchants, or acquirers or their gateways. (Discussion of the role of certification authorities is deferred to chapters 6 and 7.)

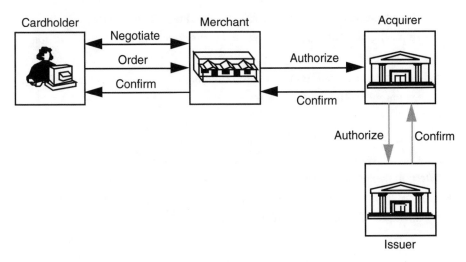

Figure 5.6 Purchase Sequence Using SET

In executing an electronic payment transaction, the primary participants typically interact as illustrated in figure 5.6. After a cardholder agrees to make a purchase from a merchant, the cardholder sends an online payment instruction to the merchant. The merchant communicates online with its acquirer via a payment gateway, typically forwarding all or part of the cardholder's payment instruction, to authorize and capture the transaction. The capturing, that is, the entry of a definitive transaction into the financial settlement network, is done by the acquirer. The authorization may require a query transaction back to the issuer; if so, this is done using existing financial networks, which are not typically Internet based.

In this environment, public-key technology is used to support various functions:

- Encryption of payment instructions so that a user's bank card number is never exposed during transfer on the Internet, nor is it exposed to merchant systems (where it could be at risk of compromise)
- (Optional) Authentication of cardholders to merchants and acquirers to protect against use of stolen cards by unauthorized individuals who initiate electronic transactions
- Authentication of merchants to cardholders and acquirers to protect against imposters establishing Internet sites where they pose as legitimate merchants and execute fraudulent transactions

- Authentication of acquirers to cardholders and merchants to protect against some-one posing as an acquirer to be able to decrypt sensitive payment instruction information
- Integrity protection of transaction information to prevent against tampering on the unprotected Internet

The global PKI that supports the SET environment is described in chapter 7.

SET has a sophisticated design and the benefit that credit card numbers do not need to be stored in databases in merchant servers, where they are susceptible to system pene-tration attack. However, because of SET's complexity compared with simpler Internet payment methods, it has not been widely deployed.

Secure EDI Transactions

In business-to-business applications, payments can sometimes be implemented using EDI interchanges conveyed over the Internet. Both the ANSI X12 and EDIFACT EDI formats define their own internal security mechanisms. For example, an ANSI X12 *interchange* is defined to be a doubly nested structure, built out of a sequence of data *segments,* as shown in figure 5.7. An interchange comprises one or more *functional groups,* each representing a collection of related business forms. A functional group comprises one or more *transaction sets,* each representing a business form. ANSI standard X12.58[59] specifies how secu-rity can be provided at either or both of the functional group and transaction set granularities. The security services provided are data origin authentication, confidential-ity, and integrity, with optional support for non-repudiation (if digital signatures are used). ANSI X12.58 defines the security segments to be inserted in functional groups or transac-tion sets as indicated in figure 5.7. These segments convey such data as key identifiers, integrity check-values, digital signatures, and time stamps.

Any protection provided that is internal to the interchange is independent of whether or not the interchange is transported via the Internet or other communications means. Regardless of the transport means, this type of protection may be important because dif-ferent transaction sets may need various protections, for example, to be signed by or encrypted for different parties.

In addition, when an EDI interchange is transported via the Internet, standard Inter-net messaging security protocols can be applied to the messages or their body parts. For instance, the EDI MIME content types mentioned in chapter 2 can be protected using

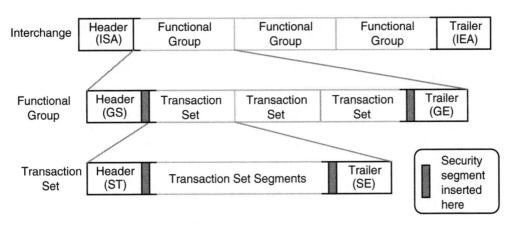

Figure 5.7 ANSI X12 Interchange Structure

S/MIME.[60] It is generally wise to use authentication and integrity protection at this level, and depending on the application, it may also be wise to use confidentiality protection. Such security services are recommended because the whole internal interchange may not be adequately protected, having been designed with a more benign communications environment than the Internet in mind.[61] Nevertheless, protecting a complete Internet message is not necessarily a substitute for securing individual transaction sets or functional groups using X12 or EDIFACT security options.

The emergence of XML, which greatly facilitates the definition and processing of forms, is replacing traditional EDI formats in at least some EDI environments. The IETF and W3C digital signature and encryption standards[62] can be used to provide the necessary protections of XML elements.

5.9 Summary

It is possible to exploit the Internet's capabilities without exposing oneself or one's organization to unacceptable risks.

Internet security involves three categories of technological security solutions: network-layer security, application-layer security, and system security. Network-layer security is the protection of the communication of data items from one network end system to another. Application-layer security involves security safeguards that are built into a particular application and that operate independently of network security measures. System security relates to protection of an end system and its local environment, regardless of the communications protection afforded through network-layer security or application-layer security measures.

As part of network-layer security, the Internet network-layer protocol (IP) has been extended to include the IPsec security protocols. The IPsec Authentication Header mechanism provides authentication and integrity protection to an IP datagram. The IPsec packet encryption mechanism (called Encapsulating Security Payload) adds confidentiality protection. Different key management options are available, ranging from manual key distribution to PKI.

A firewall protects a network from threats presented by that network's connection to another network. Most commonly, a firewall is built between an organization's internal network and the Internet backbone. Firewalls can limit and control network traffic passing in either direction. They involve various protection mechanisms, including network-level packet-filtering systems and application-level proxy systems. It is possible to build a virtual private network in which network sites communicate with each other via the Internet backbone with confidence that the private network traffic is not vulnerable to external attack.

Web communications may require application-level protection against such threats as electronic eavesdropping to collect credit card numbers or bogus Web sites masquerading as legitimate vendors or service providers. The predominant secure Web protocol is the Secure Sockets Layer (SSL) protocol, or its IETF-standardized derivative called Transport Layer Security (TLS). These protocols permit entity authentication, confidentiality, and integrity protection of Web client-server communications. Particular attention must be paid to downloadable executable software, such as Java or ActiveX; such software should be digitally signed by its source and verified before use.

Internet messaging, including e-mail, can be protected using an application-layer protection protocol, such as the industry standard S/MIME protocol, Web-based secure mail, or Pretty Good Privacy (PGP). All of these protocols provide the basic protection services of message origin authentication, content confidentiality, content integrity, and potential support for non-repudiation of origin via a digital signature. Some additional security services might also be provided.

Internet payments can be implemented using SSL/TLS-protected Web transactions. There are also several Internet-based payment methods, facilitated by service providers.

The Secure Electronic Transaction (SET) specifications, developed by Visa and MasterCard, define a protocol and infrastructure to support bank card payments as a part of Internet-based electronic shopping or service provision. Public-key technology is used to authenticate the various participants, including cardholders, merchants, and acquirers, and to protect sensitive payment information from unauthorized disclosure on the Internet or within merchant systems.

Notes

1. For some valuable guidance, see B. Fraser, ed., *Site Security Handbook,* Request for Comments (RFC) 2196 (Internet Activities Board, 1997) <ftp://ftp.isi.edu/in-notes/rfc2196.txt>.

2. Sound application-layer safeguards, however, still provide protection, even in the face of such attacks.

3. D. Eastlake, *Domain Name System Security Extensions,* RFC 2535, (Internet Activities Board, 1999) <ftp://ftp.isi.edu/in-notes/rfc2535.txt>.

4. If there is a pressing requirement for dial-in, there must also be an access control mechanism that strongly authenticates incoming callers.

5. The advisory and bulletin services from the Internet Computer Emergency Response Team (CERT), <http://www.cert.org>, are an excellent source of information on the latest security incidents. CERT advisories and bulletins are posted on the Usenet newsgroup comp.security.announce. To receive them automatically by e-mail, send a request to cert-advisory-request@cert.org.

6. C. Cowan, P. Wagle, C. Pu, S. Beattie, and J. Walpole, "Buffer Overflows: Attacks and Defenses for the Vulnerability of the Decade," *Proceedings of the DARPA Information Survivability Conference and Exposition* (Los Alamitos, CA: IEEE Computer Society, 2000) 130–44, available at <http://schafercorp-ballston.com/discex>.

7. For example, the code can assign the attacker root privilege, which effectively gives the attacker open access to the entire system.

8. For more details of how these attacks work, see "Results of the Distributed-Systems Intruder Tools Workshop" (CERT Coordination Center, December 1999), available at <http://www.cert.org/reports/dsit_workshop.pdf>.

9. A good reference text for the UNIX environment is S. Garfinkel and G. Spafford, *Practical UNIX & Internet Security,* 2nd ed. (Sebastopol, CA: O'Reilly & Associates, 1996), details at <http://www.oreilly.com/catalog/puis>.

10. Port numbers are used to distinguish between different applications running on a system.

11. For a broad-ranging analysis of the problems and solutions associated with firewalls, see William R. Cheswick and Steven M. Bellovin, *Firewalls and Internet Security: Repelling the Wily Hacker* (Reading, MA: Addison-Wesley, 1994), details at <http://www.aw.com/cp/ches.html>. For a detailed guide for practitioners, see D. Brent Chapman and Elizabeth D. Zwicky, *Building Internet Firewalls* (Sebastopol, CA: O'Reilly & Associates, 1995), details at <http://www.ora.com>. For coverage of Web proxy servers, see A. Luotonen, *Web Proxy Servers* (Upper Saddle River, NJ: Prentice Hall PTR, 1998), details at <http://www.phptr.com/ptrbooks/ptr_0136806120.html>.

12. The IP spoofing vulnerability was originally documented in S. Bellovin, "Security Problems in the TCP/IP Protocol Suite," *Computer Communication Review* 19, no. 2 (April 1989): 32–48. For further details of the attack, see <ftp://info.cert.org/pub/cert_advisories/CA-95:01>.

13. For the definitive overview of the IPsec architecture, see S. Kent and R. Atkinson, *Security Architecture for the Internet Protocol,* RFC 2401 (Internet Activities Board, 1998) <ftp://ftp.isi.edu/in-notes/rfc2401.txt>. For a detailed description of the technology, we recommend N. Doraswamy and D. Harkins, *IPSec: The New Security Standard for the Internet, Intranets, and Virtual Private Networks* (Upper Saddle River, NJ: Prentice Hall PTR, 1999), details at <http://vig.prenhall.com/acadbookpage?ISBN=0130118982>.

14. S. Kent and R. Atkinson, *IP Authentication Header,* RFC 2402 (Internet Activities Board, 1998) <ftp://ftp.isi.edu/in-notes/rfc2402.txt>.

15. A few header fields change as the packet moves from node to node, such as a time-to-live field, which progressively counts down. For calculation purposes, zeros replace the contents of these fields, and the check-value is computed on the entire datagram.

16. C. Madson and R. Glenn, *The Use of HMAC-SHA-1-96 within ESP and AH,* RFC 2404 (Internet Activities Board, 1998) <ftp://ftp.isi.edu/in-notes/rfc2404.txt>; C. Madson and R. Glenn, *The Use of HMAC-MD5-96 within*

ESP and AH, RFC 2403 (Internet Activities Board, 1998) <ftp://ftp.isi.edu/in-notes/rfc2403.txt>.

17. S. Kent and R. Atkinson, *IP Encapsulating Security Payload (ESP),* RFC 2406 (Internet Activities Board, 1998) <ftp://ftp.isi.edu/in-notes/rfc2406.txt>.

18. C. Madson and N. Doraswamy, *The ESP DES-CBC Cipher Algorithm with Explicit IV,* RFC 2405 (Internet Activities Board, 1998) <ftp://ftp.isi.edu/in-notes/rfc2405.txt>.

19. B. Schneier, "Description of a New Variable-Length Key, 64-Bit Block Cipher," in *Fast Software Encryption, Cambridge Security Workshop Proceedings* (Berlin: Springer-Verlag, 1994), 191–204, available at <http://www.counterpane.com/bfsverlag.html>.

20. C. Adams, *The CAST-128 Encryption Algorithm,* RFC 2144 (Internet Activities Board, 1997) <ftp://ftp.isi.edu/in-notes/rfc2144.txt>.

21. D. Harkins and D. Carrel, *The Internet Key Exchange (IKE),* RFC 2409 (Internet Activities Board, 1998) <ftp://ftp.isi.edu/in-notes/rfc2409.txt>.

22. IKE is built on the key management protocol known as ISAKMP. For details, see D. Maughan, M. Schertler, M. Schneider, and J. Turner, *Internet Security Association and Key Management Protocol (ISAKMP),* RFC 2408 (Internet Activities Board, 1998) <ftp://ftp.isi.edu/in-notes/rfc2408.txt>.

23. L. D. Stein, *How to Set Up and Maintain a World Wide Web Site: The Guide for Information Providers* (Reading, MA: Addison-Wesley, 1995), details at <http://www.aw.com/cp/stein-web.html>; International Computer Security Association (ICSA), White Papers, available at <http://www.icsa.net>.

24. For a copy of the SSL specification, consult the Netscape Web site, <http://www.netscape.com>.

25. T. Dierks and C. Allen, *The TLS Protocol Version 1.0,* RFC 2246 (Internet Activities Board, 1999) <ftp://ftp.isi.edu/in-notes/rfc2246.txt>.

26. For example, a closed yellow lock at the bottom of a Microsoft Internet Explorer window indicates that SSL/TLS protection is enabled.

27. We discuss mechanisms for achieving this *a priori* knowledge in chapters 6 and 7.

28. A different derived key is used for each purpose in each direction.

29. The fresh data must be unique to the particular SSL/TLS session and known to both parties in order to protect against replay attacks.

30. You can track progress on this subject at the Web site <http://www.bxa.doc.gov>.

31. For more information, see <http://www.wapforum.org>.

32. Differences include an option for a minimized certificate format, in comparison with the X.509 format used on the wired Web, and a simplified set of cryptographic algorithm suite options.

33. J. Steven Fritzinger and Marianne Mueller, "Java Security," in *Proceedings of the Network Security '96 Conference,* Washington, DC, November 1996, available at <http://java.sun.com/security>.

34. G. McGraw and E. W. Felten, *Java Security: Hostile Applets, Holes, and Antidotes* (New York: Wiley, 1997), details at <http://www.rstcorp.com/java-security.html>.

35. For updated information, refer to <http://java.sun.com/sfaq> and <http://www.cs.princeton.edu/sip/pub/secure96.html>.

36. For details, refer to <http://www.microsoft.com>.

37. For details, refer to <http://www.microsoft.com>.

38. See the latest WAP specifications at <http://www.wapforum.org>.

39. See the latest specification at <http://www.w3c.org>.

40. For the latest version of the P3P specification, refer to the W3C Web site, <http://www.w3c.org>.

41. Message confirmation services have different variations and descriptors, such as *signed receipt, proof of delivery, proof of submission, non-repudiation of delivery,* and *non-repudiation of submission.*

42. Mail clients are functionally distinct from Web browsers, although vendors sometimes choose to package them together and link their user interfaces.

43. S. Dusse, P. Hoffman, B. Ramsdell, L. Lundblade, and L. Repka, *S/MIME Version 2 Message Specification,* RFC 2311 (Internet Activities Board, 1998) <ftp://ftp.isi.edu/in-notes/rfc2311.txt>; S. Dusse, P. Hoffman, B. Ramsdell, and J. Weinstein, *S/MIME Version 2 Certificate Handling,* RFC 2312 (Internet Activities Board, 1998) <ftp://ftp.isi.edu/in-notes/rfc2312.txt>.

44. B. Ramsdell, *S/MIME Version 3 Certificate Handling,* RFC 2632 (Internet Activities Board, 1999) <ftp://ftp.isi.edu/in-notes/rfc2632.txt>; B. Ramsdell, *S/MIME Version 3 Message Specification,* RFC 2633 (Internet Activities Board, 1999) <ftp://ftp.isi.edu/in-notes/rfc2633.txt>.

45. The PKCS standards were developed by RSA Security, Inc., in the early 1990s. The specifications are published on the RSA Security Web site, <http://www.rsasecurity.com>, and the parts relevant to S/MIME Version 2 were also published as IETF RFCs 2313 through 2315.

46. RSA Security, Inc., *PKCS #7: Cryptographic Message Syntax Standard,* available at <http://www.rsasecurity.com> and as IETF RFC 2315 at <ftp://ftp.isi.edu/in-notes/rfc2315.txt>. The updated version of this specification published in conjunction with S/MIME Version 3 was called simply CMS; see R. Housley, *Cryptographic Message Syntax,* RFC 2630 (Internet Activities Board, 1999) <ftp://ftp.isi.edu/in-notes/rfc2630.txt>.

47. Such as ASCII, Unicode, or EBCDIC encoding.

48. ISO/IEC 8824, *Information Technology-Open Systems Interconnection-Specifications of Abstract Syntax Notation One (ASN.1),* also published as the ITU-T X.680 Recommendations series, at <http://www.itu.ch>. For an introduction to ASN.1, see appendix C.

49. RSA Security, Inc., *PKCS #10: Certification Request Format,* available at <http://www.rsasecurity.com> and as IETF RFC 2314 at <ftp://ftp.isi.edu/in-notes/rfc2314.txt>.

50. P. Hoffman, *Enhanced Security Services for S/MIME,* RFC 2634 (Internet Activities Board, 1999) <ftp://ftp.isi.edu/in-notes/rfc2634.txt>.

51. P. R. Zimmerman, *The Official PGP User's Guide* (Cambridge, MA: MIT Press, 1995); S. Garfinkel, *PGP: Pretty Good Privacy* (Sebastopol, CA: O'Reilly & Associates, 1995), details at <http://www.ora.com>.

52. PGP can be downloaded from <http://web.mit.edu/network/pgp.html>.

53. Refer to <www.pgp.com>.

54. M. Elkins, *MIME Security with Pretty Good Privacy (PGP),* RFC 2015 (Internet Activities Board, 1996) <ftp://ftp.isi.edu/in-notes/rfc2015.txt>.

55. Service providers in this area include CyberCash <http://www.cybercash.com>, CyberSource <http://www.cybersource.com>, and VeriSign Payment Services <http://www.verisign.com>.

56. For more information, refer to <http://www.echeck.com> or <http://www.commerce.net>.

57. Examples include eCash <http://www.digicash.com> and Mondex <http://www.mondex.com>. For more material on this subject, see Peter

Wayner, *Digital Cash: Commerce on the Net,* 2nd ed. (Chestnut Hill, MA: Academic Press, 1997).

58. The SET specifications are available online from <http://www.setco.org>.

59. ANSI X12.58, *Draft Standard for Trial Use for Managing Electronic Data Interchange: Security Structures* (1995), details at <http://www.disa.org>.

60. Note that S/MIME encapsulation protects the whole interchange, including interchange header and trailer, whereas X12.58 does not.

61. It is especially important that legacy EDI systems be reviewed when they are converted from communication over traditional, switched telecommunication services to the Internet.

62. For details of the XML digital signature standard, see <http://www.w3c.org>. At the time this book was published, the encryption standard was still in development.

CHAPTER 6

Certificates

W ebster's dictionary defines a certificate as "a document containing a certified statement, especially as to the truth of something."[1] In the electronic world, a certificate is a collection of information to which a digital signature has been affixed by an authority that is recognized and trusted by some community of certificate users. In e-commerce, certificates of various types can potentially serve various purposes. One of the most important types is a public-key certificate, in which a public-key value is securely associated with a particular person, role, device, or other entity. A public-key certificate is digitally signed by a person or entity, called a certification authority, that has confirmed the identity or other attributes of the corresponding private key's holder, whether person, device, or other entity. While public-key cryptography and digital signatures are essential elements of secure e-commerce, public-key certificates represent the key to wide-scale deployment of these technologies in large, potentially global, e-commerce communities. This chapter focuses on public-key certificates, how they are used, the applicable technical standards including X.509, and methods of certificate revocation. Use of certificates for another purpose—the distribution of authorization information—is also discussed.

6.1 Introduction to Public-Key Certificates

When a message originator wishes to send a confidential message using encryption based on public-key technology, that message originator needs a copy of the public key of each recipient. Also, when any party wishes to verify another party's digital signature, the verifying

181

party needs a copy of the signing party's public key. We call both the encrypting message originator and the digital signature verifier *public-key users.*

As described in section 4.4 under "Distribution of Public Keys," when a public-key value is communicated to a public-key user, it is not necessary to keep the value of the public key confidential. However, it is critical that the public-key user be assured that the public key used is the correct public key for the other party (that is, for the intended message recipient or the claimed digital signature originator). If an intruder can substitute a different public key for the valid one, encrypted message contents can be disclosed to unintended parties and digital signatures can be forged. In other words, the protections afforded by these technologies are compromised if intruders can substitute non-authentic public keys.

For small groups of cooperating parties, this requirement may be easily satisfied. For example, two personal acquaintances who wish to communicate securely with each other may obtain copies of each other's public key by exchanging diskettes containing the respective public-key values, then ensuring that these public-key values are subsequently stored securely on each user's respective local system. This approach is called manual public-key distribution. However, manual public-key distribution proves to be either impractical or inadequately secure in most public-key applications, especially if the user population is large or dispersed. Public-key certificates constitute the foundation for a systematic approach to public-key distribution that is highly scalable, keeps the burden on the system users to a manageable level, and has easily controllable security characteristics.

A public-key certificate system works by having a *certification authority* issue and manage certificates for a population of public-private key-pair holders. Each certificate contains a public-key value and information that unambiguously identifies the certificate's *subject,* that is, the person, device, or other entity that holds the corresponding private key (see figure 6.1). When the subject of a certificate is an individual or legal entity, the subject is typically referred to as a *subscriber* of the certification authority. The certificate is digitally signed with the certification authority's signing private key.

Establishment of such sets of certificates can greatly facilitate the distribution of authenticated public keys. Suppose that a public-key user has already obtained securely (for example, by manual public-key distribution) the public key of a certification authority and that the public-key user trusts the certification authority. That public-key user can now obtain the public key of any of the subscribers of that certification authority by obtaining a

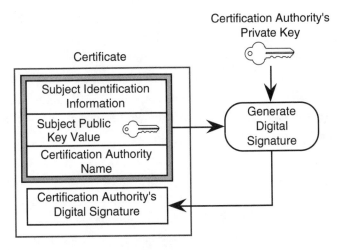

Figure 6.1   Simple Public-Key Certificate

copy of the certificate for that subscriber, extracting the public-key value, and verifying the certification authority's signature on the certificate using the certification authority's public key. A public-key user who uses certificates this way is known as a *certificate user* or a *relying party* of the certification authority.

The public-key certificate model is amenable to economical and automated deployment on a wide scale because of one important characteristic of certificates: *Certificates can be stored in and distributed via systems and channels that are not necessarily protected by confidentiality, authentication, and integrity services.* This is so for the following reasons:

- There is no fundamental need to keep the public key confidential; therefore, certificates are not inherently confidential.[2]
- The certificate is self-protecting: The certification authority's digital signature *inside* the certificate provides both authentication and integrity protection. If an intruder were to tamper with a certificate while in transit to public-key users, these users would detect such tampering because the certification authority's digital signature would no longer verify correctly.

Therefore, public-key certificates can be distributed by means such as unsecured file servers, unsecured directory systems, and unsecured communications protocols.

The primary benefit of certificates is that a public-key user can reliably obtain the public keys of a large number of other parties, starting with knowledge of only one party's public key—that of the certification authority. Certificates are therefore a means for efficiently achieving *scalability,* that is, *multiplying* the size of the population throughout which public-key technology can be employed.

Note, however, that a certificate is useful only if the public-key user *trusts* the certification authority for the purpose of issuing certificates.

Certification Paths

If it were feasible to establish one certification authority that could issue public-key certificates for all the world's holders of public-private key pairs and if all public-key users were prepared to unequivocally trust that certification authority, clearly we would have the problem of public-key distribution solved once and for all. Unfortunately, that is not feasible. It is impractical for a certification authority to have sufficient knowledge of and adequate relationships with all potential subscribers to allow it to issue and manage certificates that would be acceptable by all public-key users. Therefore, we need to accept that the world will have multiple certification authorities.

Given multiple certification authorities, it is not practical to assume that a public-key user already securely holds the public key of the particular certification authority that has issued a certificate for the party with whom that public-key user wishes to communicate securely. However, to obtain that certification authority's public key, the public-key user may be able to find and use another certificate—a certificate for that certification authority's public key issued by another certification authority whose public key is securely held by the public-key user.

Thus, theoretically at least, one can apply the certificate paradigm recursively to obtain the public keys of a progressively greater number of certification authorities and, accordingly, to obtain the public keys of a greater number of end key-pair holders. This leads to the general model, called a *certificate chain* or *certification path,* on which large-scale certificate-based public-key distribution systems are based. The model is illustrated in figure 6.2. A public-key user starts off acquiring, with high assurance, the public keys of one or more certification authorities called *trust anchors* or *root certification authorities.*[3] The public-key user can then obtain and use the public key of any key-pair holder, provided that a trusted certification path exists from a trust anchor of that public-key user to that key-pair holder, possibly via any number of intermediate certification authorities.

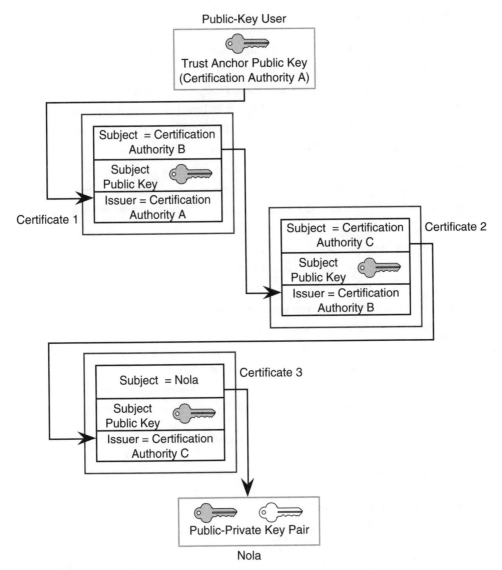

Figure 6.2   Certification Path

Note that, at this stage, we are not implying any restrictions on the structuring of relationships between certification authorities. Provided that any certification path can be found, the system will work. In chapter 7, we take up the issues of certification authority interrelationships and associated trust models and explore systematic ways of ensuring that certification authority chains exist and can be found.

Validity Periods and Revocation

The basic certificate and certification path models described earlier require some refinement for practical application. First, timeliness must be recognized; public-private key pairs should not be assumed to be operational forever. Good cryptosystem design principles require a key pair to have a restricted lifetime to limit cryptanalysis opportunities and constrain the period of vulnerability should a compromise occur. For this reason, and to facilitate enforcement of applicable business and legal policies, a certificate has a scheduled validity period, defined by a start date and time and an expiration date and time.

After a certificate expires, the binding between the public key and the certificate subject may no longer be valid, and the certificate should no longer be trusted. A public-key user should not use an expired certificate, unless it is to reconfirm an earlier action in the same way as it would have occurred within the certificate validity period, for example, to verify a digital signature on an old document. Upon certificate expiration, if the subject of that certificate still has a valid public key (either the same key or a new one), the issuing certification authority may issue a new certificate for that subscriber.

Furthermore, there are various circumstances under which a certification authority may wish to *revoke* a certificate prior to its expiration date. Examples of such circumstances are known or suspected compromise of the corresponding private key: It should be possible to protect public-key users against continuing to use the public key via a certificate issued prior to the compromise. Revocation procedures are discussed in section 6.6.

Legal Relationships

In some situations, a certification authority services exclusively a community of internal or affiliated persons; for example, a certification authority internal to an organization might manage certificates for employees of that organization.[4] In other situations, the certification authority services a broader community including unaffiliated persons. In the latter case, in particular, the certification authority generally owes specific obligations to the public-key users. These obligations are discussed in chapter 10.[5]

A digital signature verified using a certificate from an independent and trustworthy certification authority typically provides more compelling evidence than a digital signature verified on the basis of manual public-key distribution between trading partners. This is because an independent and trustworthy certification authority shares certain of the attributes of most *notaries:* being trusted and disinterested and attesting to designated facts.[6] This nexus underlies some legislative approaches in the digital signature field. For example, one digital signature law's commentary provides the following:

> Paper signatures have an intrinsic association with a particular person because they are made in the signer's unique handwriting. However, a key pair used to create digital signatures has no intrinsic association with anyone; such an association must be made by a certification authority identifying a person with a particular key pair. The reliability of every digital signature created by a private key will depend in part on the reliability of a certification authority's association of that key with a person.[7]

It is essential to have assurances that (a) only the subject of a certificate can exercise control over the corresponding private key and (b) certificate subjects have been properly validated, including validation that the holder of a private key corresponds to the certified public key. These issues are addressed further in sections 6.2 and 6.3, respectively, and in chapter 10.

6.2 Public-Private Key-Pair Management

Prior to detailed consideration of issuing, distributing, updating, suspending, revoking, and otherwise managing certificates, it is useful to revisit the requirements and processes for managing public-private key pairs. In particular, key-pair generation and certificate generation are often tightly integrated.

Key-Pair Generation

When a new key pair is generated, it is necessary to arrange for the secure transfer of

- the *private key* to the key-pair holder's system and, if backup or archiving is required, to the backup or archival system[8] and
- the *public key* to one or more certification authorities for certificates to be issued.

There are two basic alternatives for where a key-pair is generated:

- *Key-pair holder system:* The key pair is generated in the same system (possibly the same hardware token or software module) in which the private key will be subsequently stored and used. For digital signature key pairs used to meet non-repudiation requirements,[9] there is a strong case for this arrangement because the private key never in its lifetime leaves its native environment. This makes it easier to build confidence that no other party can obtain that private key. Such an approach is, in fact, a requirement under certain regulations and standards, such as the ANSI X9.57 standard.[10]

- *Central system:* The key pair is generated in some central key-management system, and the private key is transported securely to the key-pair holder system. This approach is sometimes essential with key-pair holder systems, such as certain smartcards, that have limited processing and memory resources; on such devices, key-pair generation may be impractical. Centralized key-pair generation is also beneficial under other circumstances; for example, a central system may have greater resources and stronger controls and therefore be able to generate a higher-quality (that is, less predictable or computable) key pair. Also, if the key pair is one for which the private key needs to be backed up or archived in a central system, centralized key-pair generation can be convenient because the same system or closely related systems perform the key generation and key backup or archive functions.

Both of these key generation alternatives need to be accommodated, and both lead to variances in the procedures for certificate generation and management. In fact, it is common that a certification authority and a particular subscriber might want to use different approaches for different key-pair types, for example, to generate a digital signature key pair in the key-pair holder system and an encryption key-establishment key pair in a central system.

It may prove convenient to combine into one central system or facility all of the functions of certification authority, key-pair generation, and key-pair backup or archiving. However, if practical, it is considered better security practice to separate the functions of certification authority and private-key management to better constrain the consequences of a compromise. Furthermore, a certification authority that does not know private keys may be a more convincing trusted third party to vouch for identity, authority, or other assertions in a certificate.

Private-Key Protection

Recall that public-key technology and public-key certificates depend on a private key's being usable only by the same person, device, or entity that is identified in the corresponding public-key certificate. Therefore, protection of the private key from unauthorized access is of paramount importance.

Private keys are typically protected by one of these methods:

(1) Storage in a tamper-resistant hardware module or token, such as a smartcard or PCMCIA card

(2) Storage in an encrypted data file on a computer hard drive or other data storage medium

(3) Storage on a *credentials server,* which delivers the private key to the user for a period of use after the user authenticates to the server

In all cases, access to the key needs to be protected via one or more personal authentication mechanisms, as discussed in section 4.5. Typically, a password or PIN is involved in this personal authentication. For example, with method 2, the encryption can employ a symmetric key that is derived mathematically from a password or PIN known only to the legitimate private-key holder. Other methods of personal authentication, such as possession of a physical token or a biometric check, can also be used, especially with method 1.

In general, method 1 affords greater security than methods 2 and 3, but it is more expensive. Method 2 suffers from vulnerability to offline exhaustive password-guessing attacks by anyone who can obtain a copy of the encrypted file. Method 3 can be implemented so as to resist exhaustive password-guessing attacks but, unless special technology is employed, can be vulnerable to attacks on the server.[11]

Methods 2 and 3 are sometimes used to protect one or more private keys or sensitive information in a data structure sometimes called a *digital wallet;* method 2 uses a *client-side wallet,* and method 3 a *server-side wallet.*

Key-Pair Update

Good security practices dictate that provision always be made for updating public-private key pairs on a regular, periodic basis and in response to exceptional conditions, such as known or suspected compromise of a private key. When a new key pair is generated, a new certificate needs to be generated for the new public key. Also, depending on the particular conditions surrounding the key-pair update, it may be necessary to revoke an earlier certificate. Key-pair and certificate life cycles are discussed further in section 6.8.

How Many Key Pairs Does a User Need?

A user often has more than one key pair and hence more than one certificate. From the technical perspective, keys and certificates can potentially be shared across applications, but the characteristics of the applications may make that impractical. For example, policy might dictate that a private key used to protect financial transactions be stored and protected in a smartcard, whereas for a private key used for protecting casual e-mail, a smartcard might be considered both unnecessary and overly burdensome on the user; therefore, distinct key pairs and certificates are warranted for these two applications. Furthermore, different keys and certificates are often needed for business or political reasons, just as many people use more than one credit card.

Aside from business and political reasons, users also sometimes need different keys and certificates for digital signature and encryption purposes to satisfy sound key life-cycle management principles. This issue arises in particular with the RSA algorithm. RSA has the property that one key pair can potentially be used for both encryption (such as for transporting a symmetric key) and digital signature purposes. For example, if parties A and B want to communicate securely and B has an RSA key pair, A can send an encrypted symmetric key to B by encrypting it under B's public key. Using the same key pair, B can sign a message to A; B generates the signature using B's private key, and A verifies the signature using B's public key. This simplifies some aspects of key management substantially, compared with a configuration in which a user has distinct key pairs for encryption and digital signature purposes. However, if one looks closely into the full range of key management implications, it becomes apparent that such double use of one key pair raises concerns, and *dual key pairs* for encryption and digital signature purposes for one user are sometimes advisable.

To understand why dual key pairs may be warranted, let us consider some of the key management requirements of the two key-pair types. First, for digital signature key pairs, the following requirements apply:

1. A digital signature private key must be stored for its entire life so that only its authorized holder can access it. This is a requirement to support non-repudiation. It is commonly recommended, and sometimes mandated,[12] that a digital signature private key never leave one device, in which it is created, used, and destroyed.

2. A digital signature private key does not generally need to be backed up as protection against accidental loss of the key; if the key is lost, a new key pair can be easily generated.[13] Furthermore, backup would conflict with requirement 1. Also, a digital signature private key should not be escrowed.[14]

3. A digital signature private key does not need to be archived; archiving would conflict with requirement 1. In fact, a digital signature private key should be securely destroyed when its active life terminates. If its value is disclosed, even a long time after it is no longer actively used, it may still be used to forge signatures on purportedly old documents.[15]

Looking now at key pairs used to support encryption, different key management requirements arise:

4. An encryption private key may need to be backed up, archived, or escrowed. Backup or archiving may be needed to recover encrypted information. If a key is lost (owing, for example, to equipment failure or a forgotten password), it is not acceptable that all information held encrypted under that key also be lost.

5. A private key used to support encryption does not need to be securely destroyed when its active life terminates. On the contrary, requirement 4 implies that it should *not* be destroyed.

Clearly, requirements 1-3 and requirements 4-5 are in conflict. If one uses the same key pair for establishing both digital signature and encryption keys, it is impossible to satisfy all the requirements. Dual key pairs can circumvent these problems.

6.3   Certificate Issuance

Registration Authorities

Interactions between a certification authority and its subscribers or certificate applicants are typically managed through intermediaries called registration authorities (RAs).[16] There might be multiple registration authorities for a certification authority, and they might be distributed. The value of such an arrangement is apparent, for example, where certificate issuance involves *personal presence* for verifying the applicant's identity through presentation of identifying documentation, exchanging physical tokens, or taking biometric measurements.

A registration authority does not itself issue certificates; however, the registration authority might validate and approve or reject certificate applications. The certification authority subsequently issues certificates to approved certificate applicants. The functions provided by a registration authority typically include these:

- Enrolling, de-enrolling, and approving or rejecting requested changes to the certificate attributes of subscribers
- Validating certificate applications
- Authorizing requests for key-pair or certificate generation and requests for the recovery of backed-up keys[17]
- Accepting and authorizing requests for certificate revocation or suspension (where supported by the applicable certification authority)
- Physically distributing personal tokens to and recovering obsolete tokens from people authorized to hold and use them

Registration authorities might be distinct legal entities from the certification authority. Alternatively, the term *registration authority* is sometimes used to refer to a set of technical and administrative functions performed by particular system components of an entity that acts as a certification authority.

Enrollment

A certification authority issues certificates to entities that have completed an enrollment process. In today's e-commerce environments, certificates are issued to many different types of entities, including people, organizations, and devices. Typically, the enrollment process starts with a certificate applicant requesting issuance of a certificate. (Considering a device to be a certificate applicant is often a stretch, but usually one can identify a human or organization that stands behind a certificate application for a device.)

Depending on the circumstances, enrollment may have various degrees of formality. For example, where an employer issues certificates to its employees, the registration process can be automatic. The relationship between employer and employee is well understood, and the employer-operated certification authority likely has automatic and reliable access to an employee database from which to obtain enrollment information on behalf of the employee and to facilitate its validation.[18]

There are different ways in which certificate enrollment might be achieved. In the Internet environment, these processes can be conducted partially or fully online, for example, through an online enrollment process between a subscriber using a Web browser and a server that acts as the front end for a certification authority service. However, a registration authority (or in some cases, the certification authority itself) must validate the subscriber and confirm that the public-key value and other subscriber information originate from that subscriber and have not been modified in transit from the subscriber. The registration authority may require further information about the subscriber, obtained either in an online dialog with the subscriber or by consulting relevant databases, possibly belonging to a third party. There are limitations to the assurances available by using a purely online registration system. In the more general case, some validation procedures occur through offline channels; for example, the certificate applicant presents identification credentials to a registration authority, or a registration authority sends a secret password via the postal service to the certificate applicant for later submission during an online exchange to request a certificate.

Certificate Generation

Generation of a certificate typically involves the following steps:

1. The certification authority is presented with the requisite certificate content information from the certificate applicant.
2. The certification authority confirms the accuracy of the information submitted by the applicant that is intended to be included in the certificate (in accordance with its recognized obligations and applicable policies and standards).[19]
3. The certificate is signed by a signing device that holds the certification authority's private key.
4. A copy of the certificate is forwarded to the subscriber, and if required, the subscriber returns an explicit confirmation of acceptance of the certificate.
5. A copy of the certificate may be submitted to a certificate repository, such as a directory service, for publication.[20]

6. As an optional service, a copy of the certificate may be archived by the certification authority or some other entity to provide enhanced archival, evidentiary, or non-repudiation services.

7. The certification authority records appropriate details of the certificate generation process in an audit journal, along with details of all other material events in the certificate issuance process.

Subject Authentication

Prior to approving and issuing a certificate, it is critical that the registration authority confirm the identity or other designated attributes (such as privileges, role, or authority) of the person, device, or entity whose private key corresponds to the public key contained in a certificate. The extent to which identity or other attributes must be confirmed depends on the level of assurances that a particular class or type of certificate purports to provide; this is typically expressed within the applicable certificate policy, certification practice statement, or user agreement. In general, the certification authority or some entity trusted by the certification authority must validate certain distinguishing characteristics of the certificate applicant.

Identity is confirmed through the use of one or more techniques and procedures:

• *Demonstrated knowledge of private information:* The subject presents private information that links that subject, with recognized assurances, to a persona reflected in an existing database. In some cases, the information might be as simple as an account number or name plus a password or PIN. In other cases, it might include other information, such as mother's maiden name or date of last account transaction.

• *Personal presence:* The physical appearance of a person before a trusted entity is widely recognized as important, if not indispensable, to a strong validation of identity. Personal presence permits a certification authority or its delegate to assess not only the certificate applicant's existence and distinguishing characteristics, but also the applicant's capacity and intent to apply for a certificate and to conform to applicable rules and practices. For example, sometimes it is possible to assess whether a person is intoxicated, is a minor or an adult, or understands the language and requirements of a certificate application. Once identity is established (through personal presence), the person's physical presence is generally unnecessary for most digital signature purposes (except possibly for notarial acts, such as those involving acknowledgments and affidavits in most jurisdictions, which must be sworn before a notary).

- *Identification documents:* A certification authority or its delegate can use identification documents to validate the applicant's identity, generally in conjunction with personal presence. The use of such documents (particularly those containing a photograph, such as a passport, employee badge, or driver's license) is widely recognized as trustworthy. Document identification requirements in commerce and government vary considerably. For example, one state's notarial law says that "'[s]atisfactory evidence,' as it pertains to identification on the basis of documents . . . means identification of an individual based on at least one current document issued by the federal or a state government with the individual's photograph, signature and physical description, or at least two documents issued by an institution, business entity, or federal or state government with at least the individual's signature."[21]

The use of identification documents, as is true of any identity validation mechanism, is wrought with potential risks that should be well understood by the validator. For example, one unsettling book describes the ease with which one can obtain and use fraudulent identification.[22] This book states that it "not only tells how to create a new identity, but also how to erase your past completely." The anonymous author continues:

> What has always surprised me is how simple it is to establish valid United States documentation under an assumed name and how much people rely on that piece of plastic or paper that says "I am John Doe." . . . One of the reasons the use of valid documentation and an assumed name works so easily is that this is one of the few countries in the world that does not have one unique national document, easily scrutinized, to identify the bearer. Consequently, documents not initially intended to serve as standardized I.D. are used as such in every state. The advantages of this system to you are obvious.

Certificate Update

Every certificate has a limited lifetime. Throughout that lifetime, the certification authority has certain obligations to fulfill, such as the processing of revocations. In general, certificates can be replaced upon expiration. Key pairs also need to be replaced periodically, and upon such replacement, a new certificate is needed. Expiration and update of certificates are often coupled with expiration and update of key pairs. (This is not always the case: Some certification authorities may issue an updated certificate for a continuing key pair.)

Certificate update can sometimes be accomplished as a process that is transparent to the subscriber concerned, for example, in a community of interest where the organization acting as certification authority effectively controls subscriber certificates or where the only cause for the certificate update is key-pair update. Regarding the latter update case, some cryptographic products can recognize automatically when a key pair has expired, update that key pair, and conduct the necessary communications dialog with a certification authority to effect the issue of a new certificate, all without requiring subscriber involvement.

If the certificate update has other ramifications, for example, if some of the subscriber identification information in the certificate has changed or if the certification authority has a policy of periodically requiring confirmation of certificate details from the subscriber, the subscriber must generally be involved in the update process. The subscriber is notified of the update and may need to explicitly confirm the content of an updated certificate application and accept the new certificate (see chapter 10 concerning "Certificate Acceptance").

6.4 Certificate Distribution

To encrypt data or to verify a digital signature, a public-key user needs a certificate for the corresponding party's public key, plus any certification authority certificates required to form a complete certification path. Recall that this is a data dissemination problem rather than a security problem: The certificates do not have to be delivered via secured systems or protocols because the certificates are self-protecting. This section describes different available means of distributing certificates.

Certificate Accompanying Signature

With a digital signature, there is a very convenient means for distributing certificates. The signer generally has a copy of its own certificate and can attach a copy of that certificate to the digital signature. If this is done, anybody who wants to verify a signature has the certificate in hand. Similarly, the signer can attach other certificates that might be needed in validating its own certificate, for example, certificates for the signer's certification authority issued by other certification authorities. Most communication protocols that employ digital signatures include a provision for attaching certificates to digital signatures in this way.

One objection to attaching certificates to digital signatures is a possible waste of communications or storage capacity because the signature verifier may already have the necessary certificates stored locally. For this reason, attachment of certificates is generally at the signer's discretion.

Also, it may not be obvious to a signer exactly which certificate or certificates a verifier needs, given that there might be different certification paths from different verifiers to the signer. Therefore, if there is no rigid certification authority structure that ensures a single certification path from all verifiers to a signer, it is not practical for a signer to ensure that all required certificates are attached to a signature. A verifier therefore may need a fallback method for retrieving missing certificates, such as a directory or repository.

Distribution via Directory Services

When using public-key technology to encrypt a message, a message originator must first obtain the certified public keys of all recipients. While the message originator might happen to have copies of required public-key certificates stored locally as a result of previous interactions with the parties involved, in the more general case, the message originator needs to find the required certificates. In this situation, a directory service or repository that can distribute certificates proves invaluable. The message originator retrieves the certificate for a recipient via a directory query, possibly in conjunction with other information, such as the recipient's e-mail address.

Standards for an online directory service model and supporting protocols were developed by the International Telecommunication Union (ITU) and the International Organization for Standardization (ISO).[23] These directory standards, commonly known by their ITU designator *X.500,* were designed to support multipurpose distributed directory services on a potentially global scale. Services supported range from simple name-to-address lookup to browsing or attribute-keyed searching. The X.500 directory can act as a source of information for people, communications network components, computer applications, or other automated systems. For computer network users, for example, a lookup of a person's name may return such information as telephone number, e-mail address, and details of the application protocols supported by that person's equipment.

When the X.500 standards were first developed in 1984-88, the potential for using X.500 directories for distributing public-key certificates was also recognized. Consequently, the standards include specifications for the data objects required for X.500 to fill

this role, together with a high-level description of the surrounding management procedures. This material is in the specification designated X.509.[24]

Adoption of X.500 in the marketplace generally has not met original expectations.
The technology is complex, hence costly to implement and deploy.

Based on X.500, the Internet community derived its own directory access protocol,
called Lightweight Directory Access Protocol (LDAP). LDAP is compatible with the
X.500 directory model but is simpler and more implementer-friendly than the standard
X.500 protocols.[25] LDAP is a useful standard protocol for accessing information stored in
a directory, including public-key certificates. Note that LDAP is nothing more than an
access protocol and does not require the underlying directory database to be based on any
particular technology. The IETF PKIX Working Group has specified procedures for
retrieving certificates via LDAP.[26]

Proprietary directory systems have also been used for distributing public-key certificates within particular software platform environments; however, these systems have now
largely migrated to support LDAP as a standard access protocol.

Other Distribution Methods

Any number of different means can be used to distribute certificates. Recall that certificates
do not need special security protection and can be distributed via untrusted systems using
unsecured protocols. For example, the IETF PKIX Working Group has specified protocols
for requesting and receiving certificates on the Web via HTTP or FTP.[27] Certificates that are
used repeatedly are also typically cached locally in systems that use public keys.

6.5   X.509 Certificate Format

The most widely recognized standard public-key certificate format is defined in the ITU
X.509 standard (also known as ISO/IEC 9594-8).

Base Certificate Format

The X.509 certificate format has evolved through three versions in different editions of the
standard: Version 1 format in the 1988 1st edition, Version 2 format in the 1993 2nd edition, and Version 3 format defined in the 1997 3rd edition and enhanced in the 2000 4th

Certificate

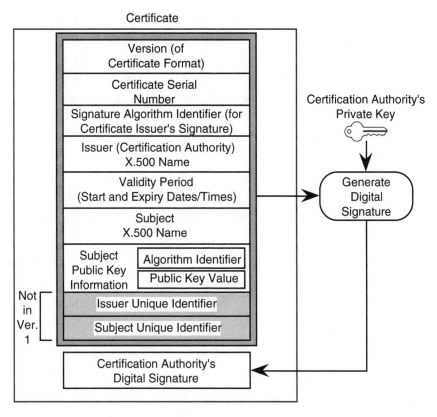

Figure 6.3   X.509 Versions 1 and 2 Certificate Format

edition. We first describe the basic X.509 certificate format reflected in the Version 1 and 2 specifications. Version 3 added an extension mechanism, which we discuss subsequently. The basic format is shown in figure 6.3.

The certificate fields are interpreted as follows:

(a) *Version:* Indicator of Version 1, 2, or 3 format, with allowance for possible future versions

(b) *Serial number:* Unique identifying number for this certificate, assigned by the issuing certification authority

(c) *Signature:* Algorithm identifier of the digital signature algorithm used by the certification authority to sign the certificate (this is discussed further in the later subsection "Object Registration")

(d) *Issuer:* X.500 name of the issuing certification authority (this is discussed further in the next subsection, "X.500 Names")

(e) *Validity:* Start and expiration dates and times for the certificate

(f) *Subject:* X.500 name of the holder of the private key for which the corresponding public key is being certified

(g) *Subject public-key information:* The value of a public key for the subject together with an identifier of the algorithm with which this public key is to be used

(h) *Issuer unique identifier:* An optional bit string used to make the issuing certification authority name unambiguous in the event that the same name has been reassigned to different entities through time (see the next subsection, "X.500 Names")

(i) *Subject unique identifier:* An optional bit string used to make the subject name unambiguous in the event that the same name has been reassigned to different entities through time

X.500 Names

Although X.509 certificates are not restricted to use in conjunction with X.500 directory systems, the Version 1 and 2 certificates employ X.500 names exclusively to identify subjects and issuers.[28]

An X.500 directory comprises a set of *entries.* Each entry is associated with one real-world object, such as a person, an organization, or a device, which has an unambiguous[29] name called a *distinguished name* (DN).[30] The directory entry for an object contains values of a set of attributes pertaining to that object. For example, an entry for a person might contain values of the attributes common name, telephone number, and e-mail address. To support the unambiguous naming requirement, all X.500 entries are logically organized as a tree structure called the *Directory Information Tree* (DIT). The Directory Information Tree has a single conceptual root and unlimited further vertices, with all vertices (except the root) subordinate to some other vertex. Each vertex (except the root) corresponds to a directory entry and has a distinguished name. The root has a null distinguished name.

The distinguished name for an entry is constructed by joining the distinguished name of its immediate superior entry in the tree with a *relative distinguished name* (RDN), which distinguishes the subordinate entry from other immediate subordinates of the same superior entry.

A relative distinguished name for an entry is a statement regarding the values of one or more attributes of that entry. More precisely, it is a set of attribute value assertions, each of which must be true, concerning the *distinguishing values* (attribute values intended to provide uniqueness) of the entry. In practice, a relative distinguished name is a statement of the equality of one attribute value; for example, a person might have the relative distinguished name *Common Name = Kimberly.*

Figure 6.4 provides an example of a global X.500 name structure. There is one tier of vertices under the root, with each vertex associated with one country. Another tier under each country has vertices associated with organizations in that country. Entries for people and other objects associated with an organization are subordinate to the organization entry. The construction of the distinguished name for Kimberly, chief executive officer of Sharon's Steelcorp in the United States, is shown.

The Version 2 X.509 certificate format contains two identifier fields that are not X.500 names: the issuer unique identifier and subject unique identifier fields. The main

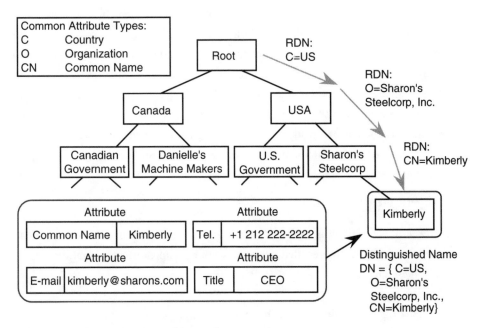

Figure 6.4   Example X.500 Name Construction

purpose of adding them to the Version 1 format was to support X.500 access control facilities, which were added to the X.500 standards at the same time. These fields address the concern that an X.500 name may be reused over time. For example, suppose a member of the staff of Sharon's Steelcorp has the X.500 name {*Country = US, Organization = Sharon's Steelcorp, Inc., Common Name = John Smith*}. Suppose further that this person leaves the corporation and the X.500 name is deassigned, but a year later someone else called John Smith joins the corporation and is reassigned the same X.500 name. This could cause authorization ambiguities in the access control lists that are attached to X.500 data objects and that may be very loosely administered.[31] In other words, the new John Smith may inadvertently be assigned some of the access privileges of the original John Smith. The unique identifier field permits a new value, such as a new number in sequence, to be associated with an X.500 name whenever that name is reused.

Unfortunately, unique identifiers do not constitute a very reliable solution to the problem because they are difficult to manage, tend to be hidden from view, and are too easily ignored or omitted from implementations. A better approach is to systematically ensure that all X.500 names are unambiguous. This can be achieved by including in a relative distinguished name an attribute value that will be unique throughout time. There is a problem with common names anyway; for example, Sharon's Steelcorp may well have more than one employee with the name John Smith. Organizations typically have an employee number system to deal with such ambiguities, and there is usually no difficulty in ensuring that employee numbers are not reused through time. Therefore, a better form of relative distinguished name for a Sharon's employee might be {*Common Name = John Smith, Employee Number = 0012345*}. Such an approach, which obviates the need for the unique identifier fields, is being adopted by many organizations that use X.500 or X.509. The X.500 Serial Number attribute may be used for this purpose.

Object Registration

The X.509 certificate format in figure 6.3 includes algorithm identifiers for the certificate issuer's signature and for the certified public key. For example, different identifiers can be defined for these algorithms:

- Digital signature using DSS with the SHA-1 hash function
- Digital signature using RSA with the SHA-1 hash function

- Encryption key establishment using RSA key transport
- Encryption key establishment using an authenticated Diffie-Hellman technique

These algorithm identifiers are one example of a class of objects requiring registration, that is, the assignment of unique object identifiers. Other examples of classes of objects requiring registration arise later in the chapter, including certificate extension types and name forms.

The object registration system used for algorithm identifiers and for many other object classes relevant to e-commerce is the *object identifier* mechanism specified in international standards and supported by a set of national object registration authorities.

An object identifier is a value, comprising a sequence of integer components, which can be assigned to a registered object and which has the property of being unique among all object identifiers. The object identifier works on the basis of a hierarchical structure of distinct value-assigning authorities; each level of the hierarchy has responsibility for one integer component of the value. Rules for the upper levels of the hierarchy are defined in annexes to the international standard for Abstract Syntax Notation One (ASN.1) and in a registration authority procedures standard.[32]

The values assigned at the top-most level are

- 0 (for ITU use),[33]
- 1 (for ISO use), and
- 2 (for joint ISO-ITU use).

Under the ISO arc, the second level takes the values 0 (for ISO standards), 2 (for ISO-recognized countries), and 3 (for recognized international organizations). Under the joint ISO-ITU arc, different values are assigned to the second level to satisfy different standards requirements. One important value is 16 (country), which is used for national registration authorities.[34]

The country arc {2 16} is particularly important. At the next level down, three-digit country codes are used to identify countries.[35] A nominated organization in each country acts as a national registration authority for object identifiers. For example, the country code for the United States is 840. The United States has chosen to make the American National Standards Institute (ANSI) its national registration authority. ANSI in turn has assigned, at the next level down, arc 1 for U.S. organizations that register with it.

Suppose, for example, ANSI assigns the value 15678 to Sharon's Steelcorp. Putting all the components together, this now means that Sharon's Steelcorp is uniquely assigned the object identifier with components {2 16 840 1 15678}. Sharon's Steelcorp then has the right to assign component values at lower levels for its own purposes, such as the value {2 16 840 1 15678 1} for its own tree of cryptographic algorithms and {2 16 840 1 15678 1 66} for a particular private cryptographic algorithm.

Figure 6.5 illustrates this object identifier assignment example. Note that it is the assigned numbers that are important: Each number also has associated with it a short text string to aid in readability, but the object identifier system is *not* a name assignment system. For example, the object identifier for the Sharon's Steelcorp algorithm may be written as {joint-iso-itu-t (2) country (16) us (840) organization (1) sharons (15678) algorithms (1) sharons-super-algorithm (66)}.

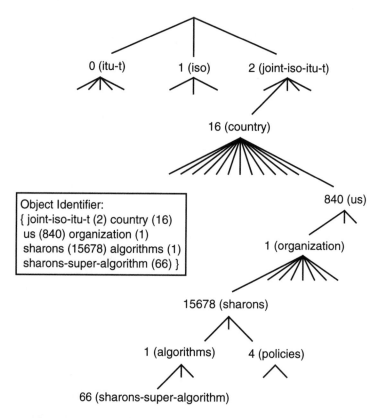

Figure 6.5   Object Identifier Example

Table 6.1   Some Common Algorithm Identifiers

Object identifier	Algorithm	Source of specification
{iso (1) member-body (2) us (840) rsadsi (113549) pkcs (1) pkcs-1 (1) sha-1WithRSAEncryption (5)}	Digital signature: RSA with SHA-1	RSA Security, Inc.
{iso (1) member-body (2) us (840) x9-57 (10040) x9cm (4) dsa-with-sha1 (3)}	Digital signature: DSA with SHA-1	ANSI X9.57
{iso (1) member-body (2) us (840) x9-62 (10045) signatures (4) ecdsa-with-sha1 (1)}	Digital signature: ECDSA with SHA-1	ANSI X9.62
{iso (1) member-body (2) us (840) rsadsi (113549) pkcs (1) pkcs-1 (1) md5WithRSAEncryption (4)}	Digital signature: RSA with MD5	RSA Security, Inc.

Table 6.1 provides some examples of registered algorithm identifiers in common use in X.509 certificates.

Extended (Version 3) Certificate Format

In the 1993-94 period, when large-scale commercial deployment of X.509 certificates was first attempted, it became apparent that the Version 1 and 2 certificate formats were deficient in several respects. There are several reasons why certificates need to carry additional information, such as these:

- Given that any one certificate subject is likely to have different certificates for different public keys used for different purposes and that key pairs need to be updated regularly, it is necessary to be able to distinguish conveniently the various certificates of one subject.
- Some applications need to identify users by application-specific name forms, rather than X.500 names. For example, in secure e-mail, it is generally more important to bind a public key to an e-mail address than to an X.500 name.
- Different certificates may be issued under different certification policies and practices, which often govern the extent to which a public-key user trusts a certificate.

For example, if a certificate has been issued to a subscriber on the expectation that it will be used for encrypting casual e-mail, the certification authority may not have performed all the identity and authorization checks that would be appropriate if the certificate were to be used in verifying digital signatures on high-value, business-to-business financial transactions. Certificate users need to know the assurances and practices applicable to each certificate.

To satisfy these and other requirements, additional fields were needed in the certificate format. In fact, it was apparent that a variety of different fields might need to be progressively added to certificates to satisfy known and unknown future requirements. The standards organizations working in this field (ISO/IEC, ITU, and ANSI X9) adopted a common position that a general extension mechanism should be added to the X.509 certificate. This resulted in the definition of the X.509 Version 3 certificate format.

The Version 3 certificate has the same format as Version 2 except that an *extensions* field is added, as shown in figure 6.6. The extensions field provides for the incorporation of any number of additional fields into the certificate.

Each extension field has a type, which needs to be *registered,* in the same way that an algorithm is registered, that is, by assigning an object identifier to it. Extension types can therefore, in principle, be defined by anyone. In practice, to achieve interoperability, common extension types must be widely understood by different implementations. The most important extension types are, in fact, standardized (see discussion under "Standard Certificate Extensions"). However, it is possible for communities of interest to define their own extension types to satisfy their own particular needs.

In a Version 3 certificate, each extension field contains an object identifier value indicating the extension type, a criticality indicator, and a value. The extension type governs the data type of the value (such as a text string, date, or complex data structure) and the semantics associated with this value.

The purpose of the criticality indicator is to accommodate environments in which different system implementations recognize different sets of extensions. This can occur as a result of certificates being designed to support the needs of multiple applications or as a result of new extensions being progressively introduced through technology migration. The criticality indicator is a simple flag that indicates whether an occurrence of an extension is *critical* or *noncritical.* If it indicates a noncritical extension, a system using the certificate is permitted to ignore that extension field if it does not recognize the extension type. If the flag indicates a critical extension, it is not safe for a system to use any part of

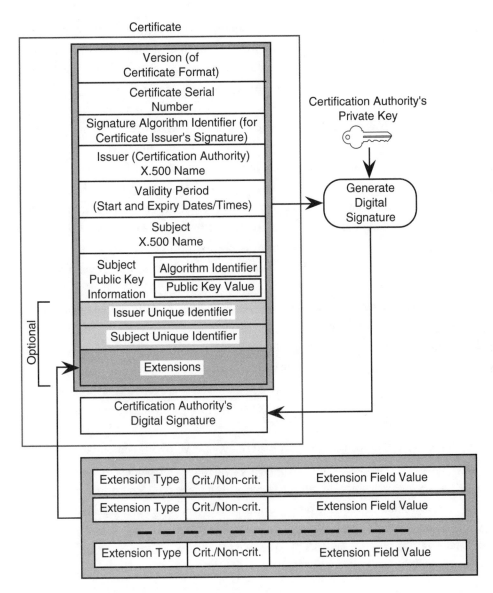

Figure 6.6   X.509 Version 3 Certificate

the certificate unless the system recognizes the extension type and invokes the associated function.

For example, suppose an extension field is designed to convey an alternative form of name for the certificate subject for use by a particular set of applications. Such a field can be flagged as noncritical because other applications that do not use the alternative name form may still be able to use the certificate effectively on the basis of the primary subject name field, even if they have no understanding of the alternative name extension. On the other hand, suppose an extension conveys information that limits the purposes for which the certification authority intends the certificate to be used. If a certificate-using system does not understand that extension and ignores it, it may be operating unsafely. In the latter case, the extension should be flagged as critical by the certification authority.

The criticality concept is frequently misunderstood. Although an extension is considered *important* by a certificate user, it is *not* essential that the extension be flagged as critical. A certificate-using system may require that certain extensions be present in a certificate or that certain information be present in certificate fields before the certificate is considered acceptable. Such a requirement is not related to criticality: The certificate-using system can require that particular noncritical extensions, as well as certain critical extensions, be present.

Noncritical extensions facilitate certificate sharing by different applications and graceful migration through progressively adding new extension types. Critical extensions lead to interoperability problems and should be avoided except to address security concerns. The majority of the extensions in common use are noncritical.

Naming in X.509 Version 3

One of the most important differences between X.509 Version 3 and previous versions relates to naming. Version 3 is no longer restricted to the X.500 naming system for identifying such entities as certificate subjects and certificate issuers.[36] Any entity can be identified by one or more names of a variety of different forms. Examples of name forms are X.500 names, Internet domain names, Internet e-mail addresses, and Uniform Resource Identifiers (URIs). For example, Kimberly, the CEO of Sharon's Steelcorp, might be identified in different contexts by these different names:

- The X.500 name {*Country = US, Organization = Sharon's Steelcorp, Inc., Common Name = Kimberly*}
- The X.500 name {*Country = US, Organization = Sharon's Steelcorp, Inc., Title = CEO*}
- The e-mail address *kimberly@sharons.com*

Each of these names unambiguously identifies the subject. Therefore, it is perfectly reasonable to issue a certificate containing all three names and for that certificate to be used by anyone who recognizes at least one of the names. Such a certificate is usable, for example, with an e-mail application that has no links with X.500 and simply wants to associate a public key with an e-mail address. The same scheme applies to certificate issuers: A certification authority can have one or more names of different forms, provided that each name unambiguously identifies the same entity.

These are the name forms explicitly recognized in the X.509 standard:

- Internet e-mail address
- Internet domain name
- X.400 e-mail address
- X.500 directory name
- EDI party name (comprising a name of a name-assigning authority plus a party name assigned by that authority)
- Web Uniform Resource Identifier (URI)
- Internet IP address (for associating public-key pairs with Internet connection end points)
- Registered identifier (a name that constitutes an object identifier, as described under "Object Registration" earlier in this section)
- Other name (any other name form; the name form is registered as an object following the approach described under "Object Registration" earlier in this section)

The only critical requirement of any naming system is that a name must unambiguously identify one entity within the context in which the naming system is used.

Standard Certificate Extensions

A set of standard extensions for the X.509 Version 3 certificate was developed by the ISO/IEC, ITU, and ANSI X9 standards organizations. The ISO/IEC and ITU extensions were incorporated into the 1997 edition of the standard and enhanced in the 2000 edition. The ANSI extensions are technically aligned with the ISO/IEC/ITU extensions but give additional attention to the use of these extensions in financial industry applications.[37]

The standard extensions can be separated into the following groups:

- Key information
- Policy information
- Subject and issuer attributes
- Certification path constraints
- Extensions related to certificate revocation lists (CRLs). (We explain the extensions in the other groups next but defer consideration of this group to section 6.7.)

The *key information* extensions convey additional information about the subject and issuer keys, such as key identifiers and indicators of approved key usage. These extensions allow administrators to limit the purposes for which certificates and certified keys are used. These are the key extensions:

- *Authority key identifier:* This field can be used to distinguish different certificate-signing keys used by the issuing certification authority (for example, different keys used over different time intervals). The key may be identified
  - by an explicit key identifier;
  - by a pointer to another certificate, in which another certification authority certifies the public key of the issuing certification authority (the other certificate is identified by its certificate issuer name and the certificate serial number); or
  - by both an explicit key identifier and a certificate pointer.

  This field assists certificate-using systems in efficiently finding certification paths, given that many certification authorities regularly update their key pairs as part of key life-cycle management. This field can help find the next certificate in a certification path when traversing in the direction toward the trust anchor.
- *Subject key identifier:* This field enables distinct keys used by one certificate subject to be differentiated. For example, the subject may replace its key pair periodically, and this field indicates which public key in the sequence is certified in a given certificate.
- *Key usage:* This field indicates the purpose for which the key is used: digital signature (other than for non-repudiation, certificate signing, or CRL signing), non-repudiation, key encipherment, data encipherment, Diffie-Hellman key agreement, certificate signing, CRL-signing, encipher only, or decipher only.

There are two variants of the field, with a subtle difference in their meaning. The field's being flagged as critical indicates the first variant. In this variant, the certification authority restricts the certificate and key for use only for the indicated purpose. If the certificate user were to use the key for another purpose, it would do so in violation of the certification authority's policy and would not be able to rely justifiably and reasonably on the certificate for such unauthorized purpose. The field's being flagged as noncritical indicates the second variant. In this case, the field is nothing more than an indicator for use by the certificate user as an aid in finding the right certificate. For example, a user may have different keys and certificates for digital signature and encryption key establishment, with both certificates stored in the user's directory entry; this field can help a certificate user find the right certificate. Both variants of the field have their uses, but certification authorities most likely choose to use the critical variant to assist in enforcing their policies and for risk management purposes.

- *Extended key usage:* This field allows key usage purpose to be refined, by the use of object identifiers registered in other standards or privately. For example, a certificate might contain an object identifier indicating use only for SSL/TLS server key certification.
- *Private-key usage period:* This field indicates the period of authorized use of the digital signature private key corresponding to a certified digital signature public key. The significance and usage of this field, which can limit the impact of a private-key compromise, are discussed in section 6.8.

The *policy information* extensions convey indicators of *certificate policy;* use of these extensions, which relate to certification authority practices, is explained in chapter 7 "Public-Key Infrastructure." These are the policy information extensions:

- *Certificate policies:* This field identifies the policies or practices that the certification authority associates explicitly with the certificate. The field may also convey optional policy qualifiers.
- *Policy mappings:* This field, which is applicable only when the subject of the certificate is also a certification authority, allows a certificate issuer to indicate that one or more of that issuer's certificate policies can be considered equivalent to another policy used in the subject certification authority's domain.

The *subject and issuer attribute* extensions support alternative names for certificate subjects and issuers. They can also convey additional attribute information about the subject to assist a certificate user in gaining confidence that the certificate applies to a particular person, organization, or device. These are the subject and issuer attribute extensions:

- *Subject alternative name:* This field contains one or more alternative, unambiguous names for the certificate subject, using any of a variety of name forms. This field allows the certificate to support applications such as e-mail or IPsec, which employ their own name forms and may not employ X.500 names. The name forms supported are those listed under "Naming in X.509 Version 3" earlier in this section.

- *Issuer alternative name:* This field contains one or more alternative names for the certificate issuer. The name forms are the same as for the subject alternative name extension. This field is particularly useful for certification authorities that must be identified and recognized by names that are more meaningful to specific application environments such as the Web or e-mail.

- *Subject directory attributes:* This field conveys any desired X.500 attribute values for the subject of the certificate. It provides a general means for conveying additional identifying information about the subject beyond what is conveyed in the name fields. Examples of useful identifying information could be the subject's position in an organization, telephone number, or postal address.

The *certification path constraint* extensions help different domains (such as different organizations) link their infrastructures together. When one certification authority certifies another certification authority, in the certificate it can include information advising the certificate users of restrictions on the types of certification paths that can stem from this point. These are the certification path constraint extensions:

- *Basic constraints:* This field indicates whether the certificate subject can act as a certification authority or is an end entity only. This indicator is important to prevent end users from erroneously or fraudulently emulating certification authorities. If the subject can act as a certification authority, a certification path length constraint may also be specified. For example, this field may indicate that certificate users must not accept certification paths that extend more than one certificate from this certificate: They may use end entity certificates issued by the subject certification authority but should not accept longer chains in which the subject certification authority certifies yet another certification authority.

- *Name constraints:* This field restricts the name space that is considered accept-able in subsequent certificates in a certification path through this certificate. Nam-ing and the use of this constraint field are discussed in detail in chapter 7.
- *Policy constraints:* This field specifies a set of constraints regarding explicit cer-tificate policy identification and policy mapping. Policy-related constraints are discussed in detail in chapter 7.
- *Inhibit any policy:* This field specifies a constraint which indicates that *any-policy* is not considered an explicit match for other certificate policies for all certificates in the certification path starting with a nominated certification authority. Policy-related constraints are discussed in detail in chapter 7.

The PKIX Certificate Profile

In 1994, the IETF established a working group called the Public Key Infrastructure (X.509) Working Group, known universally by the acronym *PKIX*. The purpose of this group was to

- refine X.509 so as to satisfy the needs of Internet protocols and applications, including, in particular, the Web, e-mail, and IPsec, and
- produce any additional specifications needed to build interoperable implementa-tions of Internet protocols and applications that employ X.509-based certificates.

The first major output of this group included a *profile* of the X.509 certificate for-mat, that is, a specification that both restricts the choices afforded by the base standard and also fills in some specific detailed specifications for features, such as private extensions, left wide open by that standard.[38]

The PKIX certificate profile is very extensive. These are some of its more substan-tial stipulations:

- Requirements on the types of attributes that need to be supported in X.500 direc-tory names[39]

- Conventions for specifying subject or issuer names using the name formats corresponding to IP addresses, Internet e-mail addresses, DNS names, and URIs
- Conventions for expressing and interpreting name constraints for the preceding name forms
- Rules clarifying how certificate policies are to be treated when processing certification paths
- Definitions of two standard certificate policy qualifiers—the CPS pointer and user notice qualifiers—for use in the certificate policies extension
- Definitions of extended key usage values to flag certificates intended for TLS server authentication, TLS client authentication, e-mail protection, signing of downloaded code, or time stamping
- Definition of two Internet-specific X.509 private extensions. The authority information access extension provides a pointer, in the form of a URI, to an address for accessing an online certificate status service (see section 6.6). The subject information access extension conveys an address for contacting the subject.
- Identification of supported cryptographic algorithms

The PKIX profile has been widely adopted and to many secure Internet applications is as important and authoritative a reference as the X.509 specification itself.

Qualified Certificates

In 2000, the IETF PKIX Working Group completed a specification of another profile, called the Qualified Certificates profile, which is a further refinement of the general PKIX certificate profile intended for certificates issued exclusively to natural persons represented by registered, unmistakable identities.[40] The term *qualified certificate* was coined by the European Commission to describe a certain type of certificate with specific relevance in European legislation. This PKIX specification is intended to support this class of certificates but also to be more broadly applicable to personal certificates used to support "legal signatures" falling under a wide range of governing laws.

The Qualified Certificates profile specifies conventions relating to issuer and subject name fields and special provisions regarding the use of some certificate extensions.

The issuer field must contain a registered name for the organization responsible for the certificate (i.e., the certification authority), expressed using a subset of the following naming attributes: Domain Component, Country Name, State Or Province Name, Organization Name, Locality Name, and Serial Number. Additional attributes may be present, but they should not be essential in identifying the issuing organization.

The subject field must contain a subset of the following naming attributes: Country Name, Common Name, Surname, Given Name, Pseudonym, Serial Number, Organization Name, Organizational Unit Name, State Or Province Name, Locality Name, and Postal Address. Various rules regarding use of these attributes are stipulated. Other attributes may be present but must not be necessary to distinguish the subject name from other subject names within the issuer domain. This subject name may or may not represent a complete (legal) *unmistakable identity* of the subject; a relying party may have to additionally examine information stored in the subject alternative name extension and the subject directory attributes extension in order to determine such an unmistakable identity.

The profile includes the following stipulations regarding certificate extensions:

- *Subject directory attributes:* This extension field may be used to convey additional naming attributes, to be used in conjunction with the attributes in the subject field, for specifying the complete (legal) unmistakable identity of the subject. Rules regarding use of the following attribute types are provided: Title, Date Of Birth, Place Of Birth, Gender, Country Of Citizenship, and Country Of Residence.
- *Certificate policies:* This extension field must be present and must contain the identifier of at least one certificate policy which reflects the practices and procedures undertaken by the certification authority.
- *Key usage:* This extension field must be present, and if the key usage non-repudiation bit in that extension is asserted, then it should not be combined with any other key usage bit. This eliminates some ambiguities otherwise present in the use of such bits.
- *Biometric information:* This extension field, defined in this profile, provides for inclusion of a hash of a biometric template plus an optional pointer (URI) to a location for obtaining the full biometric template. The biometric template might be, for example, a condensed representation of facial image, fingerprint, retina scan, iris scan, or handwriting characteristics.
- *Qualified statements:* This extension field, defined in this profile, provides for inclusion of statements by the issuer that a qualified certificate is issued in accordance with requirements of a particular legal system.

ASN.1 Notation and Encoding

The X.509 data formats (like the X.500 protocols generally) are expressed in the notation called Abstract Syntax Notation One (ASN.1), which was developed as part of the Open Systems Interconnection (OSI) standardization program.[41] While ASN.1 is very powerful, it is unpopular in many circles because of its complexity, the fact that its specifications have not historically been conveniently available,[42] and the lack of high-quality, low-cost implementation tools.

A brief introduction to ASN.1 is given in appendix C, and the full ASN.1 notation for the X.509 certificate is reproduced in appendix D.

6.6   Certificate Revocation

A public-key certificate has a limited valid lifetime, indicated by a start date and time and an expiration date and time, which are included in the signed part of the certificate. The length of the validity period is a policy matter for the issuing certification authority; values typically range from several months to several years.

When a certificate is issued, it is expected to be usable for its entire validity period. However, under some circumstances, users should stop relying on a certificate prior to the expiration of its validity period. Such circumstances include known or suspected compromise of the corresponding private key, change of name, and change of relationship between subject and certification authority (for example, a person ceases employment with an organization). Under such circumstances, the certification authority can *revoke* the certificate. Because revocation is possible, the *operational period* of a certificate may be shorter than its originally scheduled *validity period.*

Requesting Revocation

The decision to revoke a certificate is the responsibility of the certification authority, generally in response to a request from some authorized person. Who is authorized to revoke a certificate depends on the practices of the certification authority, which must be made known to various parties, including the subscriber. The subscriber generally is authorized to request revocation of his or her own certificate. Officers of the certification authority also typically are authorized to revoke a subscriber's certificate under prescribed circumstances, such as material breach of the subscriber's obligations (discussed in chapter 10) or death of a subscriber. In addition, other people may be authorized to request revocation, such as a subscriber's employer who can revoke an employment-related certificate.

The certification authority should generally authenticate the source of any revocation request. Responsibility for evaluating, approving, or denying revocation requests may be delegated to registration authorities.

Certificate Revocation Lists

After deciding that a certificate is to be revoked, a certification authority must apprise potential certificate users of the revocation. A common method for providing general notice of revocation involves the certification authority's periodically publishing a data structure called a *certificate revocation list* (CRL). The CRL concept is described in the X.509 standard. A CRL is a time-stamped list of revoked certificates that has been digitally signed by a certification authority and made available to certificate users. The CRL might be distributed, for example, by posting it at a known Web URL or by distributing it from the certification authority's own X.500 directory entry. Each revoked certificate is identified in a CRL by its *certificate serial number,* a unique number for the certificate generated by the issuing certification authority and included in the certificate. The main elements of a simple CRL are shown in figure 6.7.

When a system uses a certified public key (for example, to verify another user's digital signature), the certificate-using system not only checks the certificate signature and validity but also acquires a suitably recent CRL and confirms that the certificate serial number is not on that CRL. The meaning of "suitably recent" is not standardized and may vary with local policy; under most policies, it means the most recently issued CRL.

A certification authority issues CRLs regularly, such as hourly, daily, or weekly; the particular interval is a policy decision of the certification authority. A new CRL is issued each period regardless of whether or not any new revocations have been added to the list in the latest period; this is necessary so that a certificate-using system can be certain that it has an up-to-date CRL. An attractive feature of this revocation method is that CRLs can be distributed by the same means as public-key certificates themselves—namely, via communications and server systems that do not need to be rigorously trusted to preserve the

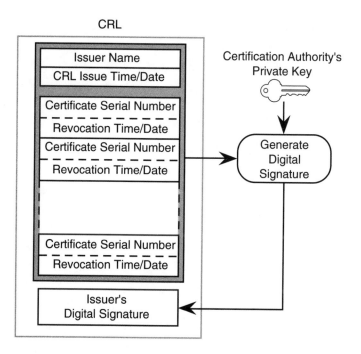

Figure 6.7   Simple Certificate Revocation List

integrity of data—since the CRL is digitally signed. This approach is thus economical to install and operate. In particular, there is no need for costly trusted servers or secure communications paths, as may be required with other methods of disseminating revocation information.

One limitation of this revocation method is that the time granularity of revocation is limited to the CRL issue period. For example, if a revocation is reported now, that revocation will not be reliably communicated to certification-using systems until the next periodic CRL is issued, for example, up to an hour, a day, a week, or longer. Note that there is nothing preventing a certification authority from generating and posting a new CRL immediately when a new revocation becomes known. However, it cannot be guaranteed that such *off-cycle* CRLs always reach certificate-using systems. For example, if an intruder deletes an off-cycle CRL from an unsecured server and leaves the previous periodic CRL in its place, this cannot be detected with certainty by the certificate-using system.

Broadcast CRLs

An important property of the *periodic* revocation list approach is that it can be used in a mode whereby a certificate-using system retrieves CRLs from a directory when it needs them. This is sometimes called a *pull* method of CRL distribution. An alternative distribution approach is a *push* method, in which a certification authority broadcasts revocation lists to certificate-using systems as new revocations are posted. Such broadcasts need to employ protected communications, such as secure e-mail or a protected transaction protocol; otherwise an attacker might be able to intercept and obliterate revocation notifications as they are distributed. The major advantage of the push approach is that more critical revocations, such as those resulting from key compromise or certification authority failure, can be distributed very quickly, without the time granularity delay problem inherent in the periodic revocation list approach.

However, there are several potential problems with this approach. First is the requirement for a protected distribution method to ensure that CRLs reach their intended destinations. Second is the potentially massive amount of traffic that would be generated if this method were to be used for all revocations; thus, it is practical only for notifying about the more critical revocations. Third is the problem of deciding, in an arbitrarily large infrastructure environment, which revocations need to be advised to which certificate-using systems. Fourth is the absence of standards for such methods, which militates against their widespread use.

This revocation approach was exploited by the U.S. Department of Defense in the Multi-level Information System Security Initiative (MISSI) program, in which a public-key infrastructure for the Defense Messaging System (DMS) was developed.[43] MISSI used a conventional periodic revocation list approach to advise of revocations generally, plus a broadcast approach for advising of the relatively small number of revocations resulting from compromised keys. The latter method used an additional revocation list, called a compromised key list, which was maintained centrally for an entire root domain network on the basis of compromise notifications advised by the various certification authorities in the network. The compromised key list was distributed via secure e-mail.

In the Defense Messaging System, the potential problems with broadcast revocation lists were averted. Availability of a protected distribution method was not a concern because the target application being supported was secure e-mail, hence all systems involved had ready access to secure e-mail services. Because the broadcast approach was used only for notifying about key compromises and because such compromises could be expected to be very rare in the well-controlled Defense Messaging System environment, the compromised key list was unlikely to ever gain significant size. Because one compromised key list was used for the entire network, there was no problem about who should receive which broadcast CRL.

However, the MISSI approach, like any broadcast CRL approach, does not scale well and cannot generally support the demands of a nationwide, much less a global, open commercial infrastructure.

Online Status Checking

One concern often expressed with the periodic CRL approach is that certificate-using systems cannot tolerate the delay in revocation notification resulting from the time granularity factor. Depending on the application environment, much damage can result from a compromised key in a day. In an ideal world, knowledge of a revoked certificate would be made available to a certificate user immediately when that user wants to use that certificate.

With online status checking, a public-key-using system that wishes to confirm the validity of a certificate executes an online transaction with a server associated with the issuing certification authority. The transaction returns an indication of the current revocation status of the certificate. The transaction must be secured to the extent that its timeliness and source must be assured to the public-key-using system. This typically requires generation of a digital signature by the certification authority and verification of that signature by the public-key-using system for each transaction. The certification authority must operate a high-availability online service, accessible by all potential users, and this service must be provided from within a secure environment.

As a standard method of implementing online status checking, the IETF PKIX group developed the Online Certificate Status Protocol (OCSP).[44] This protocol defines a standard format for request and response messages to ascertain whether or not a certificate is revoked. The OCSP responder is either the certification authority that issued the certificate or some other entity authorized by that certification authority to issue OCSP responses on its behalf.

The OCSP request message contains an identifier of the requester, plus one or more identifiers of certificates for which the status is sought, with provision for adding extension fields to the protocol (much as X.509 provided for adding extension fields). The request message may optionally be digitally signed. In many configurations, it may not be of concern to the OCSP responder who is requesting status, but in other configurations, such as when the OCSP service is made available only to authorized requesters or if the responder attaches semantic significance to responses from different requesters,[45] then the responder requires the digital signature to authenticate the requester.

The OCSP response, which is always digitally signed by the responder, contains an identifier of the responder, time of response generation, plus the following items for each certificate in the corresponding request:

- Certificate identifier (same as in request)
- An indication of status (good, revoked, or unknown)
- Start and finish time for a validity period for this response, expressed in This Update and Next Update fields, used similarly to the corresponding fields in an X.509 CRL. Responses whose Next Update value is earlier than the local system time value or responses whose This Update time is later than the local system time should be considered unreliable
- Provision for additional protocol extensions

OCSP can be used for real-time status checking, whereby each response is generated in real-time on the basis of a query to the database of the certification authority or another authoritative entity. However, the validity period feature in OCSP makes it possible to use the protocol in non-real-time modes, for example, generating OCSP responses from an existing CRL or reusing cached OCSP responses. Accordingly, anyone planning to procure OCSP products or services is cautioned to check the timeliness of the status information they will receive from the OCSP responder since it does not always represent an up-to-the-moment confirmation of status as recognized by the certification authority.

Online status checking can be very appealing for its timeliness but can be costly, especially as the environment scales. Trusted online servers with appropriate security controls and cryptographic processing resources capable of generating a digital signature per query transaction can be costly to acquire and operate. Like many other decisions about securing e-commerce systems, a decision to use online status checking should be based on a risk analysis that balances the costs of the safeguard against the costs of a successful attack.

Short-Lived Certificates

Short-lived certificates constitute another approach to revocation, which is particularly suitable for environments in which certificate-using systems are severely resource constrained, such as many mobile wireless systems. With this approach, a key-pair holder is validated once in a *long-term credentials* period—typically one year—with the expectation that the one key pair will be used throughout that period. However, instead of issuing a one-year-validity certificate, the certification authority issues a new short-lived certificate for the public key, with a lifetime of, say, 25 hours,[46] every day throughout that year. The server or gateway picks up its short-lived certificate daily and uses that certificate for client sessions established that day. If the certification authority wishes to revoke the server or gateway (for example, due to compromise of its private key), it simply ceases issuing further short-lived certificates. Clients will no longer be presented with a currently valid certificate and hence will cease to consider the server authenticated.

This approach has similar characteristics to a periodic (such as daily) CRL. However, the revocation-checking burden is removed from the client and placed, instead, in the infrastructure. This approach has been adopted by the WAP Forum as one option for dealing with revocation of WAP server or gateway certificates in Internet-capable mobile phones.[47]

Other Revocation Methods

Various other approaches to revocation status querying and notification have been proposed and in some cases deployed. Such approaches have not yet received wide industry endorsement but may prove to be a good fit in satisfying the needs of particular application environments. These are some proposed methods:

- *Removal from repository:* A simple approach is for the certification authority to immediately remove the certificate from the subject's directory entry when a certificate is revoked; public-key-using systems that are particularly concerned with timeliness perform a fresh certificate retrieval whenever they wish to use a certificate. While this is comparatively simple to implement, it is not generally secure because directory servers and directory communications are not generally adequately trusted. For example, an intruder in the communications path could insert a copy of an old certificate into a directory retrieval transaction, even if that certificate had been revoked. Furthermore, the approach does not accommodate protocols in which certificates are normally distributed by attachment to signed messages that require the certified key for their verification.

- *Trusted certificate server or directory:* To add strength to the preceding approach, we could ensure that the server that supplies the certificate is implemented as a trusted system and that the transaction response returning the certificate is digitally signed by that server and contains a current time stamp. For example, a Web transaction could use SSL/TLS to provide the required protection of the transaction response. Alternatively, the X.500 directory protocols contain an optional feature called *signed operations,* which could be employed to protect the transaction response. This may be an acceptable way of achieving immediate revocation, provided that all servers and clients involved implement the protection protocol and that the certificate-using system has confidence that the directory or certificate server is indeed operated under trusted conditions and under the policy of the certification authority involved. For this approach to satisfy all requirements, it becomes virtually equivalent to, and at least as costly as, real-time revocation checking.

- *Fine-granularity periodic CRLs:* Given that the issue cycle of periodic CRLs is a certification authority decision, is it possible to make this period sufficiently short that revocation notifications are timely enough using the basic periodic CRL approach without requiring trusted servers or protecting protocols? A CRL issue cycle can be set to one day, one hour, or 10 minutes, provided that the lists are not so large that processing and communications resource costs become unacceptable and that the directory system is able to cope with the distribution. Such granularity delays are likely to be acceptable for many applications. With such applications, there is typically a delay of hours or even days before a certification authority is notified of a suspected compromise; hence, the CRL granularity delay may be insignificant.

- *Certificate revocation trees:* This is a method of disseminating revocation information that is more efficient than a CRL but not generally more timely.[48]

All the preceding approaches to revocation—with their various performance characteristics, such as immediacy, response time, processing overhead, and cost—may find application in particular environments. The most appropriate approach depends on the assessed risk traded off against performance and cost.

Revocation Process Timeline

To understand some of the more subtle implications of periodic CRLs, including associated legal issues, it is helpful to consider a typical event timeline associated with revocation of a certificate (see figure 6.8).

The sequence of events is generally as follows:

(a) *Issue of CRL 1:* A CRL is issued prior to revocation of the certificate.
(b) *Compromise occurs:* An event occurs that triggers the revocation of the certifi-
    cate; for example, an intrusion into a sensitive workplace environment raises
    suspicion of the compromise of a private key stored on a workstation in that
    environment. The precise time of the event is not necessarily known. This
    event can precede or follow event (a).
(c) *Revocation request:* An authorized person sends a revocation request to the certi-
    fication authority or applicable registration authority that authenticates and either
    approves or rejects such request. This event can precede or follow event (a).
(d) *Revocation time:* The certification authority formally recognizes the revocation
    and records a revocation time.
(5) *Issue of CRL 2:* The CRL containing the revocation is issued and published.

If a certificate is used any time after event (b) to verify a public key, clearly the corresponding private key is not necessarily under the uninterrupted control of the listed subject

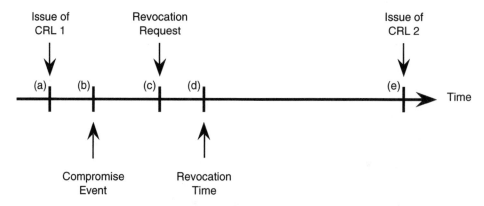

Figure 6.8   Revocation Timeline

of the certificate, and significant damage could potentially be done to the certificate user or another party. To be able to respond to such situations, the parties should apportion risk among themselves. The greatest risk is typically borne by the party best able to control that risk or otherwise having contracted for a particular apportionment of liability.[49]

In the CRL-based revocation scenario, identifying the party best able to control the risk is not straightforward. Suppose, for example, that the revocation results from the compromise of a private key. The situation in each of the aforementioned time periods might be as follows:

- *Period (b)-(c):* The compromise has occurred but notification of it has not been communicated to the certification authority. The relying party cannot be expected to know of the compromise. The subscriber may or may not know of the compromise. It may be reasonable that the subscriber bear greater risk for private-key misuse during this period.
- *Period (c)-(d):* The compromise has been communicated to the certification authority, but a CRL has not been published by the certification authority. The certificate user cannot be expected to know of the compromise. It may be reasonable that the certification authority bear greater risk of private-key misuse during this period.
- *Period (d)-(e):* The certification authority (or an associated repository) has published the revocation but the relying party may not yet know of the revocation. The risk allocation depends on the particular revocation mechanism used (and presumably agreed between the parties). With periodic CRLs, the certificate user will not know of the revocation until after CRL 2 is issued. It may be in the best interests of the certificate user to wait until CRL 2 is issued before concluding the transaction that used the key in question. With online status checking, it may be reasonable to expect the certificate user to know about the revocation during this period.
- *Period after (e):* The certification authority has now fulfilled its commitments in publishing revocation information. If a certificate user still uses a revoked certificate in this period, it is generally reasonable for that certificate user to assume greater responsibility for the consequences.

Dispute resolution upon revocation also depends largely on the accuracy with which timing of events is known and provable. The situation is improved significantly if signed transactions or messages bear trusted time stamps.

The obligations of the certification authority, subscriber, and relying party regarding a revocation situation and the corresponding apportionment of liability deserve rigorous attention in establishing certification authority practices. There is no monolithic and *absolute* best practice for fashioning the rights and responsibilities of each party. Rather, it is critical that definitive rules controlling revocation events be established and agreed upon. This subject is addressed further in chapters 9 and 10.

6.7   X.509 Certificate Revocation List

In addition to the standard certificate format described in section 6.5, the X.509 standard also defines a standard CRL format.

CRL Format

The X.509 CRL format, like the certificate format, has undergone some evolution since first appearing in 1988. In particular, when the extension mechanism was added to the certificate to create the Version 3 format, the same type of mechanism was added to the CRL to create the Version 2 CRL format.[50] This format is illustrated in figure 6.9. The IETF PKIX group subsequently specified a profile of the CRL format.[51]

The fields of the CRL are interpreted as follows:

(a) *Version:* Indicator of Version 1 or 2 format, with allowance for possible future versions. For Version 1, the version field is omitted and the CRL entry extensions and CRL extensions fields are not permitted.

(b) *Signature:* Indicator of the algorithm used in signing this CRL.

(c) *Issuer:* Name of the authority that issued this CRL and whose signature appears on this CRL. While this is most commonly the certification authority whose certificates are being revoked or suspended in this CRL, with the Version 2 CRL, this is not necessarily the case.

(d) *This update:* Date and time of issue of this CRL.

(e) *Next update:* Date and time by which the next CRL will be issued. This optional field may be omitted if the issue cycle is known to all CRL users. Nevertheless, it is recommended that this field always be included.

(f) *Certificate serial number:* Serial number of a revoked or suspended certificate.

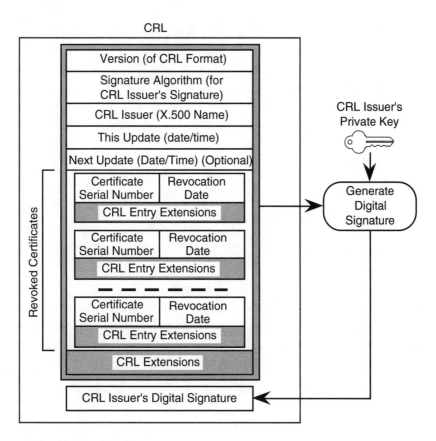

Figure 6.9 X.509 CRL Format

(g) *Revocation date:* Effective date of revocation or suspension of a particular certificate.

(h) *CRL entry extensions:* Additional fields (the types of which must be registered) that may be attached to each revocation entry.

(i) *CRL extensions:* Additional fields (the types of which must be registered) that may be attached to the full CRL.

The extension mechanism used for *h* and *i* is the same as for the X.509 certificate format, including the criticality indicator (see section 6.5).

A set of standard CRL extensions and CRL entry extensions has been developed by the ISO/IEC, ITU, and ANSI X9 standards organizations. They are published along with the standard certificate extensions.

The standard extensions can be separated into the following areas:

- General extensions
- CRL distribution points
- Delta-CRLs
- Indirect CRLs
- Certificate suspension
- Status referrals

General Extensions

The general extensions, which include some CRL extensions and some CRL entry extensions, are as follows:

- *CRL number:* This CRL extension field conveys an incrementing number for each CRL issued in sequence covering the same certificate population. This number can help a certificate-using system to determine whether any past CRLs were missed; it is also needed to support the delta-CRL feature (described later). While all extensions are optional in X.509, this extension is mandatory to implement in the PKIX CRL profile.
- *CRL stream identifier:* This CRL extension field distinguishes the certificate population for which the CRL number is unique.
- *Invalidity date:* This CRL entry extension field indicates a date when it is known or suspected that a private key was compromised.
- *CRL scope:* A CRL does not necessarily cover all certificates issued by a certification authority; for example, it might cover only a particular subrange of certificate serial numbers, a particular name subspace, or certificates containing a particular CRL distribution point name. This CRL extension field specifies precisely which set of certificates is covered by this CRL.
- *Ordered list extension:* This CRL extension field indicates whether the list is ordered by certificate serial number or revocation date. By default, a CRL is not necessarily ordered, but an ordered list may be more efficient to process.
- *Reason code:* This CRL entry extension field gives a reason for the certificate revocation. Some applications may be able to make direct use of the revocation

reason by feeding it back to the user or potentially by reacting differently to different reasons.

For the reason code extension, the following values are defined:

- *Key compromise:* An end entity's certificate is revoked owing to known or suspected key compromise.
- *CA compromise:* A certification authority's certificate is revoked owing to known or suspected key compromise.
- *Affiliation changed:* The subject's name or other information about the subject in the certificate has changed.
- *Superseded:* The certificate has been superseded.
- *Cessation of operation:* The certificate is no longer needed for the purpose for which it was originally issued.

There are also two special values: *Remove from CRL* is discussed in the later subsection "Delta-CRLs," and *certificate hold* is discussed in the subsection "Certificate Suspension."

Both the authority key identifier and issuer alternative name extensions, described in section 6.5 as certificate extensions, can also be used as CRL extensions. These serve to unambiguously identify the key used to sign the CRL and to allow the CRL issuer to be identified by name forms other than X.500 names.

CRL Distribution Points

The size to which a CRL can grow is a potential concern. With periodic CRLs, when any system uses a certificate, that system generally needs to fetch a CRL and process it (including verifying the signature over the complete CRL). If CRLs become very large, this presents performance problems in terms of both communications overhead and processing overhead for certificate-using systems.

Entries are added to CRLs as revocations occur. An entry may be removed when the certificate expiration date is reached. The rate at which revocations occur is generally unpredictable but clearly depends on the number of subjects covered. The two main factors that can be used to control CRL sizes are therefore the size of the subject population and the certificate validity period.

It is often undesirable to force shorter certificate lifetimes to limit CRL sizes. Shorter certificate lifetimes can have negative ramifications, such as higher operational costs, more user inconvenience, and higher demands on archive resources.

In the 1988 and 1993 versions of X.509, each certification authority had two CRLs: one for all the end users that it certified and one for the other certification authorities that it certified. The latter list could be expected to be very short, usually empty. This was very valuable in reducing CRL processing overhead when verifying certification paths; of all the certificates in the chain, only the one end-user certificate would be likely to encounter a CRL of significant size. However, the concern remained that the CRL for the end-user certificate needed to cover the entire population of end users for one certification authority. It is highly desirable to allow such populations to be in the range of tens of thousands, hundreds of thousands, or possibly even millions of users. The end-user CRL is therefore at risk of growing to an unacceptable size.

This problem was addressed with the Version 3 certificate and Version 2 CRL. With these new formats, it is possible to arbitrarily divide the population of certificates for one certification authority into a number of partitions, each partition being associated with one *CRL distribution point.* Therefore, a certification authority can control the maximum size to which a CRL can grow. CRL distribution points may be identified by any of a variety of name or address forms, including X.500 names, URIs, or e-mail addresses.

These X.509 extensions also permit separate CRL distribution points to exist for different revocation reasons; in particular, routine revocations (for example, those resulting from a name change) can be placed on a different CRL from revocations due to security compromises. Depending on the application environment and policy, it may be acceptable for some applications to check only the list of compromise revocations. It is also possible to update the compromise CRL more frequently than the routine CRL. With the right infrastructure, the CRLs covering compromise situations can be kept small and can be issued with a very finely grained cycle, such as hourly or even more frequently. CRLs for routine revocations, which are likely to be much larger, can be issued with a coarser granularity, such as daily.

The following extensions are defined:

- *CRL distribution points:* This certificate extension field identifies the CRL distribution point or points that distribute CRLs on which a revocation notification for this certificate would appear if this certificate were to be revoked. To check for possible revocation, a certificate-using system should fetch and check a CRL from one of these distribution points or from another known source, such as a directory entry of the issuing certification authority itself. A distribution point may distribute a CRL that contains certificate revocation notifications regardless of revocation reason, or it may distribute a CRL containing revocation entries for a limited set of revocation reasons; the extension field indicates which applies. This extension does not need to be flagged as critical. If a certificate-using system does not recognize this field, the system should accept the certificate only if it can check revocation status by other means.

- *Issuing distribution point:* This CRL extension field gives the CRL distribution point name or names for this particular CRL and indicates whether the CRL is limited to revocations for end-entity certificates only, for certification authority certificates only, or for a limited set of reasons only. All of these fields need to be in the signed part of the CRL and need to be checked by the user; they protect against an attacker's substituting the wrong CRL at a distribution point. For example, without these checks, an attacker could replace a non-empty CRL from distribution point *A* with an empty CRL from distribution point *B* and cause some revoked certificates to be considered valid. The CRL is signed by the CRL issuer (usually a certification authority itself); CRL distribution points do not have their own key pairs.

Delta-CRLs

The delta-CRL mechanism, which is distinct from the CRL distribution point mechanism, is another way to reduce CRL distribution overheads. A delta-CRL is a digitally signed list of the changes that occurred since the issuance of the prior base CRL. Delta-CRLs are designed to reduce communications overhead for systems that can maintain their own databases or caches of revoked certificate information. The delta-CRL can be used to update the current state of the database without the need for processing a full CRL. Operating in this mode requires the use of secure storage facilities; this is not generally practical in the typical desktop computing environment but may be appropriate in a large server environment.

Delta-CRLs are indicated either using the CRL scope extension or the following CRL extensions:

- *Delta-CRL indicator:* This CRL extension field identifies a CRL as a delta-CRL only. A delta-CRL contains only the new CRL updates since an earlier CRL issue. The extension carries the CRL number of the *base CRL,* that is, the CRL to which the changes in this delta-CRL need to be applied to produce an equivalent of the current full list of revocations.
- *Base update:* This CRL extension field, in a delta-CRL that contains the delta-CRL indicator extension, gives the date and time after which this delta-CRL provides updates to the revocation status.

There are also a certificate extension and a CRL extension to help in finding delta-CRLs:

- *Freshest CRL:* This certificate extension field gives addresses where delta-CRLs for the particular certificate can be obtained.
- *Delta information:* This CRL extension is for use in CRLs that are not delta-CRLs and indicates that delta-CRLs are also available for the CRL containing this extension. The extension tells where the related delta-CRLs can be found and optionally the time at which the next delta-CRL is to be issued.

Delta-CRLs also employ a special value in the reason code extension. The *remove from CRL* reason code indicates that an entry that was present in the base CRL or a subsequent delta-CRL should now be removed because a certificate suspension has been released.

Indirect CRLs

The indirect CRL feature allows a CRL to be issued by a different authority from the one that issued the certificate concerned. The most important consequence of this feature is that one CRL can now contain revocations from multiple certification authorities.

This feature can provide performance benefits by reducing the number of CRLs to be fetched and processed in various operational situations. These are some typical uses:

- In a community involving multiple certification authorities, notifications of all compromise revocations (as opposed to routine revocations caused by name changes, etc.) can be put on one list for the entire community. This list needs to be distributed and checked frequently and can be expected not to grow excessively large.[52]

- When processing any certification path, a CRL needs to be checked for every certificate in the path. All certificates except one are certification authority certificates. Significant performance improvements can result from creating one (indirect) CRL that contains all the revocations of certification authority certificates throughout a large enterprise or community.

Indirect CRLs are indicated using the certificate and CRL extensions for CRL distribution points. The CRL distribution points extension in a certificate has an optional field to identify the CRL issuer when the CRL issuer is different from the certificate issuer. This field (which is, of course, signed by the certificate issuer) serves as the means by which the certificate issuer delegates authority to the CRL issuer to issue revocation notifications on its behalf; it is important that the certificate user check that any CRL used is signed by an approved CRL issuer.

In an indirect CRL, a special indicator is set in the issuing distribution point extension. This indicator warns the certificate user to check the certificate issuer for every entry in the CRL; the user cannot assume that all entries relate to certificates issued by the CRL issuer as with ordinary CRLs. To support this function, one additional CRL entry extension is defined:

- *Certificate issuer:* This field indicates the certificate issuer for the CRL entry with which it is associated. If this extension is not present in the first entry in an indirect CRL, the default certificate issuer for that entry is the CRL issuer. If this extension is not present in subsequent entries in an indirect CRL, the default certificate issuer for that entry is the certificate issuer for the preceding entry. These default rules give a convenient way for structuring an indirect CRL to contain groups of entries for distinct certificate issuers with minimal data overhead.

Certificate Suspension

Sometimes the question of whether or not a certificate should be revoked is not black and white. For example, suppose that a bank is acting as a certification authority for its customers and that an automated monitoring system detects suspicious activity in the account of a particular customer, pointing to possible compromise of that customer's private key. Under such circumstances, the bank may not want to revoke the customer's certificate, possibly leading to a customer relations faux pas and an unnecessary recertification process should it subsequently be found that nothing untoward had actually occurred. However, prospective users of such a certificate need to be advised of its special status since they might even be held responsible for relying on it.

To satisfy this requirement, the ANSI X9 committee introduced a certificate suspension mechanism as an extension to the CRL mechanism. An item on a CRL may be *held,* rather than revoked. On a later CRL, the status of the entry may be changed to revoked or the entry for the certificate may be removed from the CRL entirely (the hold is released).

The *held* status is indicated by a special value, *certificate hold,* in the reason code CRL entry extension. There is also a supporting CRL entry extension:

- *Instruction code:* This field can convey a registered instruction identifier to indicate the action to be taken upon encountering a held certificate. Possible instructions are "call the certification authority before using the certificate" or "repossess the user's card/token."[53]

Status Referrals

The *status referrals* extension allows the CRL data structure to specify a *status referrals list,* a fundamentally different data structure from a CRL per se. A status referrals list is a signed, time-stamped list of CRLs and their respective CRL scopes that a certification authority currently issues. A relying party can fetch and inspect a status referrals list in order to determine exactly which CRL it should be using to check the status of any given certificate.

For example, a certification authority may periodically issue a new status referrals list, typically with a relatively high reissue frequency (in comparison with other CRL reissue frequencies). The list might include a last-update time and date for every referenced CRL. A certificate user, on obtaining this list, can quickly determine whether cached copies of CRLs are still up to date. This can eliminate unnecessary retrieval of CRLs. Furthermore, by using this mechanism, certificate users become aware of CRLs issued by the authority between its usual update cycle, thereby improving the timeliness of the CRL system.

This extension also provides a mechanism to redirect a relying party from a preliminary location—for example, one pointed to in a CRL distribution point extension or the directory entry of the issuing authority—to a different location for revocation information. It can also accommodate new revocation methods, such as OCSP, as well as CRLs.

The status referrals mechanism was invented by the IETF PKIX group as a work-around for a significant deficiency in the CRL distribution points mechanism, namely, that the revocation approach for any certificate had to be hardwired into that certificate. The status referrals mechanism allows a certification authority to flexibly modify its revocation status notification regime for an existing certificate population.

6.8   Key-Pair and Certificate Validity Periods

Key pairs, regardless of their purpose, need to be updated periodically. This effectively restricts time windows for cryptanalytic attacks and limits the exposure of a key compromise to a well-defined period. A certificate's lifetime must not exceed the viable lifetime of its certified public key. Because the subject of key-pair and certificate lifetimes has some subtleties, let us explore it in some depth.

The validity period of an unrevoked certificate indicates to a certificate user the period for which the following can generally be assumed:

- The public key is valid for use for its designated purpose.
- The binding between the public key and other information in the certificate (notably, the identification information) is trustworthy.
- The certification authority will publish revocation notifications (assuming this is required under the applicable certificate policy).

Given that key pairs are generally updated periodically, consider the relationship between certificate validity periods and the periods for which the public key and private key of a given pair can be reliably used. The situation varies, depending on the purpose for which the key pair was created.

Encryption-Related Key Pairs

With a key pair used for encryption or encryption key establishment, the public key should be used only while a valid certificate exists. If the public key is used by an encrypting system without checking a valid certificate, there is a risk of encrypting data for an unintended party, thereby compromising confidentiality. The period for which the corresponding private key is used by a decrypting system may be quite different from that for which the public key is used. For example, the private key may be used for decryption purposes long after all certificates for the public key have expired; this is essentially a local matter for the private key holder and does not need to be reflected in certificates.

Digital Signature Key Pairs

With a key pair used for digital signature purposes, two basic situations, which deserve independent consideration, arise:

- *Historic validation:* In some situations, the certificate user (that is, the signature verifier) is not concerned with certificate revocations that occur after the time a signature was created using the private key. This can be the case, in particular, for non-repudiation scenarios. In such scenarios, it is necessary to preserve as evidence the full set of certificate state information associated with a signature (that is, all certificates in the applicable chain, plus all CRLs or other revocation state information) *as it existed at the time of signing,* without regard for revocations that occur after the time of signing. In this case, the certificate validity period need not extend beyond the period of use of the private key, except, most likely, for a short extension to ensure that at least one periodic CRL is published after signing and before the certificate validity expires.
- *Real-time validation:* In other situations, the certificate user is concerned with certificate revocations that occur up to the time of signature verification, regardless of how long ago the signing may have occurred. Examples of this situation are verifying a software publisher's signature on a copy of its software electronically distributed from an Internet server, verifying a certification authority's signature on a public-key certificate, or verifying a time-stamping server's time stamp on a third-party document. In these situations, the signature verifier generally wants to check that a valid, unrevoked certificate exists *now.* In this situation, the certificate validity period generally extends somewhat longer (possibly a great deal longer) than the period over which the private key is still used for signing.

In the real-time validation situation, it can sometimes be beneficial for the public-key certificate to carry an indication of the period in which the private key is valid to use for signing (note that this may be a period somewhat less than the certificate validity period). For this purpose, the X.509 Version 3 certificate includes an extension field for the private-key usage period.

This field can sometimes provide added security to the public-key user. Consider the case where a digital signature key pair is updated every year (that is, the private key is used only for a year), but certificates are issued supporting use of the corresponding public key for up to two years (because the certification authority commits to the notification of certificate revocations for two years). In this scenario, a certificate is issued with a two-year validity period, but the private key validity field indicates that the private key can be validly used only for the first year of that period. Depending on the application, this may reduce exposure to undetected or unreported private-key compromise. Some applications can apply an independent check that a signature was generated within the validity period of the private key and reject the signature otherwise. Suppose, for example, that the private key for 2001 is compromised. It is possible for the attacker to forge only 2001 signatures, even though an unrevoked certificate covering both 2001 and 2002 is in circulation.

Certification Authority Signature Key Pairs

Certification authority signature key pairs are, in essence, just one case of digital signature key pairs as previously discussed. However, a certificate signature is likely to span both of the digital signature scenarios discussed earlier. Historic validation is often needed to resolve disputes, but real-time validation is often needed too. Certificate users often demand and are entitled to receive up-to-date revocation status information on all certification authority certificates still in active use. Therefore, use of the X.509 private-key validity period field is an appropriate way for certification authorities to limit exposure to compromise (and to limit their consequent liability).

Note that the valid lifetime of a public-key certificate is limited not only by its stated validity period but also by the validity of the affixed certification authority signature. Therefore, a certification authority should ensure that the validity period of its own public key (and some corresponding certificate) extends over the intended validity period of any certificate it is signing.

6.9   Certificate Formats Other than X.509

The X.509 certificate has been very broadly accepted as the industry standard public-key certificate format. A few alternative formats have been specified and are used in niche environments, including these:

- *The WAP WTLS certificate format:* For WTLS, the WAP Forum specified a new certificate format, which is logically equivalent to an X.509 Version 1 certificate but which uses a simple octet-string encoding instead of ASN.1. The WTLS protocol may use this format or X.509. The new certificate format is commonly used for WTLS server certificates because it is more efficiently transported to and processed by limited-resource client devices such as mobile phones. X.509 is more commonly used for WTLS client certificates because of interoperability advantages and the absence of resource concerns in the servers that process these certificates.
- *PGP certificates:* PGP has its own certificate format, discussed in chapters 5 and 7.
- *DNSSEC:* The IETF standard for DNS security contains the logical concept of certified public keys, but the certification is represented in the form of a combination of DNS *resource records.* This type of "certificate" is limited to use in the DNS environment only.
- *Simple PKI (SPKI and SDSI):* This project defines its own certificate format. These certificates, which are used as much for conveying authorization information as for binding public keys to people or other entities, are discussed in the next section.

6.10   Certification of Authorization Information

The fundamental purpose of a public-key certificate is to bind a public key to a person, device, or other entity by way of a name or other identifying information included in the certificate. When using a public key to verify a digital signature, other information about the signer is also sometimes needed before relying on the signature. In particular, it is often necessary to know expressly that the signer is *authorized* to sign for a particular purpose, for example:

- Is a particular individual authorized to commit a corporation to spending a given dollar amount? Is a cosigner required?
- Is a digital signature on a signed acknowledgment of a filed tax return a duly authorized official signature?
- Is a digital signature on a received software file the signature of an entity authorized to guarantee the authenticity of that copy of the software (as a form of protection against malicious software tampering during the software distribution process)?

Distribution of authorization information can also be accomplished using certificates; a recognized authority can issue a certificate declaring expressly that a particular person, role, or object possesses particular privileges or authority. In the remainder of this section, we outline some different ways to distribute authorization information via certificates.

Authorization Information in X.509 Public-Key Certificates

In an environment in which public-key certificates are used for binding public keys to people, devices, or other entities, the same certificates can also convey authorization information about the certificate subjects. In fact, some of the X.509 certificate extension fields implicitly carry authorization information; for example, the basic constraints field authorizes certain entities to act as certification authorities. It is clearly possible to carry other, general subject authorization information in certificates, for example, in attributes in the subject directory attributes extension or in nonstandard extensions defined especially for that purpose.

However, there are two reasons why caution should be taken in using public-key certificates for conveying authorization information:

- Often, the authority who is most appropriate for certifying the identity of a person associated with a key pair is *not* appropriate for certifying authorization information. For example, the corporate security department may be the appropriate authority for certifying the identities of persons holding public keys, but the corporate finance office may be the only appropriate authority for certifying permission to sign on behalf of a corporation. Such *separation of duties* is sometimes a firm policy requirement.

- The dynamics of the two types of certification may not be compatible. For example, the persons authorized to perform a particular function in an organization may vary monthly, weekly, or even daily. However, public-key certificates are typically designed to be valid for a year or more. If it becomes necessary to revoke and reissue public-key certificates frequently because of changing authorizations, this may have a severe impact on the performance characteristics of the public-key certificate system.

There are some circumstances in which these concerns do not apply and system implementations can take advantage of public-key certificates to convey authorization information. A good example is the public-key certificates of the U.S. Department of Defense, in which fields are used to carry information on the security clearance of the certificate subject. The certification authority can be readily trusted to attest to the accuracy of the security clearance information, and this information does not change frequently enough to cause problems with the dynamics of the overall certificate system.

Attribute Certificates

Recognizing that public-key certificates are not always the best vehicles for securely distributing authorization information, the U.S. financial industry's ANSI X9 committee developed an alternative approach, known as *attribute certificates.* This approach was refined by ISO/IEC and the ITU and incorporated into X.509. The IETF is developing a profile for the attribute certificate similar to that for the X.509 public-key certificate.

An attribute certificate binds one or more pieces of attribute information to the certificate's subject. Anyone can define and register attribute types and use them in attribute certificates. The certificate is digitally signed and issued by an *attribute authority* (which may also act as a certification authority or registration authority). Apart from differences in content, an attribute certificate is managed the same way as a public-key certificate. In particular, an attribute authority can use the X.509 CRL-based revocation mechanism to revoke attribute certificates.

The fields of an attribute certificate are as follows (see appendix D for full ASN.1 notation):

- *Version:* Indicator of the particular certificate format. Version 1 was defined in the 3rd edition of X.509 (1997) and version 2 was defined in the 4th edition (2000).

- *Holder:* Identification of the person or entity with which the attributes are associated. Identification can be either (1) by name, (2) by reference to an X.509 public-key certificate (such reference comprises a combination of X.509 issuer name and X.509 certificate serial number), or (3) by direct binding to a data object's value (by incorporating a hash of that value in the certificate).
- *Issuer:* Name of the attribute authority issuing this attribute certificate. While X.509 allows different name forms to be used or the issuer to be identified by reference to a public-key certificate or by direct binding using a hash value, the PKIX profile requires that the issuer be identified by a single directory name.
- *Signature:* Identifier of the digital signature algorithm used to sign the certificate.
- *Serial number:* Unique number for this certificate, assigned by the issuing attribute authority and used in a CRL to identify this certificate.
- *Attribute certificate validity:* Start and expiration dates and times for the certificate. This period defines the operational period of the certificate, unless the certificate is revoked prior to its expiration.
- *Attributes:* Information concerning the entity referred to in the *holder* field or concerning the certification process. This information may be supplied by the subject, the attribute authority, or a third party, depending on the particular attribute type.
- *Issuer unique identifier:* An optional bit string used to make the issuing attribute authority name unambiguous in the event that the same name was reassigned to different entities through time. Note that the same concerns mentioned earlier for unique identifiers in public-key certificates apply equally to attribute certificates.
- *Extensions:* This field allows the addition of new fields to the certificate format. It works the same way as the extensions field of the X.509 public-key certificate.

The X.509 *privilege management infrastructure* (PMI) model is complex and attempts to cover diverse authorization requirements, including role-based authorization and delegation of authorizations. It defines several extensions to the basic attribute certificate. While the X.509 privilege management model and attribute certificate may prove important in the future of e-commerce, the lack of commercial deployment to date restrains us from covering it further in this book. Attribute certificates represent an important area of e-commerce technology that is yet to be fully explored or developed.

Simple Public-Key Infrastructure

Another authorization certificate scheme was developed by the IETF *Simple Public-Key Infrastructure* (SPKI) Working Group.[54] The SPKI approach is novel in that an SPKI certificate grants specific authorizations, or privileges, to a public key without necessarily requiring identity binding to the person or entity that holds the corresponding private key. For example, an SPKI certificate might grant permission for a given public key to authenticate Internet logins using the TELNET protocol by a particular user identifier to a nominated server over a particular time interval.

The SPKI project also promoted implementation simplicity by adopting a less rich and less costly to implement data-encoding scheme than the (arguably implementer-unfriendly) ASN.1 notation used in X.509.

One of the main inputs to the SPKI effort was a proposal by Ron Rivest and Butler Lampson for a public-key certificate design called *Simple Distributed Security Infrastructure* (SDSI).[55] The SDSI proposal was, in part, a reaction to the perceived growing complexity of X.509; the needs of many application environments could be satisfied with something simpler. SDSI, by and large, defines a subset of X.509 functionality. It omits several of the more complex X.509 features, such as certificate policies, constraints, and key life-cycle management, that simpler application environments can do without. It also proposes a simpler representation and encoding syntax than the ASN.1 notation used in X.509. The SPKI proposal from the IETF SPKI Working Group and the SDSI proposal (further developed by the Massachusetts Institute of Technology) were eventually merged.

A valuable contribution of SDSI is a particular name-structuring arrangement based on linked local name spaces. For example, Danielle's Machine Makers can assign local names to all its employees, such as *ali* for the order processor, Ali. Another organization which recognizes Danielle's as a unique entity and trusts Danielle's to assign unique names to all its employees can recognize Ali by the unambiguous name *danielle's ali*. This approach can be used recursively to build names that are unambiguous in the context in which they are used, without having to resort to a formal hierarchical name structure.[56]

SDSI also addresses the authorization issue by providing for the definition of some simple types of authorization certificate. For example, an SDSI certificate could contain a definition of a group of individuals. The certificate assigns the group a name which can be used in access control lists that govern access to resources. SDSI also defines a *delegation certificate,* which gives the delegated party the authority to sign statements of certain types on behalf of the delegator.

The SPKI/SDSI design has interesting potential, especially for use in protecting access to resources in closed environments. However, it currently presents several unanswered questions in terms of ensuring accountability, policy enforcement, and auditability in e-commerce environments.

Certified distribution of authorization information is an active development area and, at the time of publication of this book, the best approach is uncertain.

6.11 Summary

When a public key is used in message encryption or to verify a digital signature, it is critical that the public-key user be assured that the public key used really is the correct public key for the message recipient or signer. A public-key certificate is a data structure that securely associates a public-key value with a particular person, device, or other entity, called the certificate subject. A certification authority that has confirmed the identity of the subject digitally signs the certificate.

With certification paths, multiple certificates are used to progressively confirm the values of public keys of certification authorities and ultimately the public keys of end entities. A certificate system therefore allows a public-key user to reliably obtain the public keys of a large number of other parties, starting with knowledge of only one certification authority public key.

The certificate system depends on protection of the private key that corresponds to a certified public key in a way that allows only the authenticated certificate subject to use that key. Depending on the application, it may be preferable that an end entity use different key pairs for encryption and digital signature purposes.

A person or other legal entity requiring a certificate generally needs to register with a certification authority and to explicitly request issuance of a certificate. Certificate issuance can use online procedures but often requires some offline exchanges, such as communication of validation information or a secret password. Confirmation of identity may require the personal presence of the applicant or the presentation of suitable identification documents. A registration authority is a person or organization that acts as an intermediary between certification authority and subscribers, for example, by representing the certification authority in procedures that require personal presence. Certificates are distributed to their eventual users via directory services, certificate servers or repositories, or attachment to digitally signed data items.

The most widely recognized standard public-key certificate format is defined in the X.509 standard from ISO/IEC and the ITU. The X.509 certificate format has evolved through three versions. Version 3, which was completed in 1997, introduced many new, optional features. While earlier versions supported only the X.500 name system, Version 3 supports a variety of name forms, including e-mail addresses and URLs. X.509 Version 3 also provides certificate extensions, including standard extensions and private or community-defined extensions. Standard extensions are defined for various purposes, including key and policy information, subject and issuer attributes, and certification path constraints.

A certificate is issued with the expectation that it will be operational until a scheduled expiration date. However, under circumstances such as compromise of the corresponding private key, the certificate needs to be revoked. The most common method of revocation notification involves the certification authority periodically issuing a certificate revocation list (CRL), which is a digitally signed, time-stamped list of revoked certificates. Other revocation notification methods are available, including direct communications with a trusted server to confirm the current status of a certificate.

Standard X.509 includes a definition of a standard CRL format. The Version 2 CRL format includes the same extensibility mechanism as the X.509 Version 3 certificate format and has standard extensions that are compatible with the X.509 Version 3 certificate standard extensions. This CRL standard includes provision for temporarily suspending a certificate, as well as permanently revoking a certificate. The Online Certificate Status Protocol (OCSP) is a standard for requesting and receiving certificate status online and potentially in real time.

Distribution of authorization information has different requirements from those of associating a public key with an identity, but these requirements can also be satisfied using certificates. A recognized authority can issue a certificate declaring that a particular person or thing possesses particular privileges or authority. Alternatively, the privileges or authority can be directly associated with a public key, without identifying the associated person or thing. Different ways of realizing authorization certificates include adaptations of X.509 Version 3 public-key certificates, X.509 attribute certificates, and the Simple Public-Key Infrastructure (SPKI) proposal.

Notes

1. *Webster's New Collegiate Dictionary* (Springfield, MA: G. & C. Merriam, 1980).

2. Access to certificates may, of course, be restricted to parties needing to use them. This may be required, for example, to prevent knowledge of the staff and organization structure of a corporation from being made public.

3. Because *root certification authority* is used in different ways throughout the industry, for example to denote the certification authority at the apex of a hierarchical structure of certification authorities, we favor the term *trust anchor* in this book to denote the more general concept of a certification authority whose public key is already trusted in a certificate-using application.

4. An affiliated person is sometimes understood to include an officer, director, employee, partner, contractor, intern, another person within the organization, or a person maintaining a contractual relationship with the organization when the organization has business records providing strong assurances of the identity of such person.

5. See Information Security Committee, Section of Science and Technology, American Bar Association (ABA), *Digital Signature Guidelines* (Chicago: American Bar Association, 1996), sec. 3.7 (certification authority representations in certificate), available at <http://www.abanet.org/scitech/home.html>.

6. This is discussed further in chapters 8 and 9. See also Michael S. Baum and Henry H. Perritt, Jr., *Electronic Contracting, Publishing, and EDI Law* (New York: Wiley, 1991), secs. 4.33–4.36, 208–26.

7. State of Utah, *Utah Digital Signature Law,* Utah Code Annotated Title 46, chap. 3, Utah Administrative Code R154-2-101 et seq. Commentary, November 1995, p. 19, available at <http://www.gvnfo.state.ut.us/ccjj/digsig/dsut-act.htm>.

8. The distinction between *backup* and *archiving* is as follows: Backup is short-term storage of a copy of a data item as protection against its accidental loss during its normal operative life. Archiving is long-term storage of a data item, intended to persist well after its normal operative life, for use in the event that historical records need to be referenced at an unknown future time. Typically, different technologies and procedures are used to implement backup and archiving.

9. Non-repudiation is discussed in detail in chapter 9.

10. American National Standards Institute, *ANSI X9.57: American National Standard, Public-Key Cryptography for the Financial Services Industry: Certificate Management* (American National Standards Institute, 1997).

11. Except that strong resistance against attacks on a server can be achieved with a multiserver design as outlined in W. Ford and B. S. Kaliski, Jr., "Server-Assisted Generation of a Strong Secret from a Password," *Proceedings of the IEEE 9th International Workshops on Enabling Technologies: Infrastructure for Collaborative Enterprises,* National Institute of Standards and Technology (NIST), Gaithersburg, MD, June 14–16, 2000. (Los Alamitos, CA: IEEE Computer Society, 2000) pp. 176–180.

12. For example, in the ANSI X9.57 standard.

13. Private-key backup may be warranted in situations where the public key is widely distributed and hard to replace. This can sometimes occur with certification authority keys.

14. While there may be a sustainable argument for an authorized government agency to eavesdrop on encrypted communications, there is *no* legitimate requirement for a government agency to be able to forge citizens' signatures.

15. Secure time stamping of signed documents reduces the risks of such forgeries' going undetected, but secure time stamping is not in widespread use.

16. Various terms are used elsewhere for essentially the same function: *Local registration agent* (LRA) is used in ANSI X9 standards; *organizational registration agent* (ORA) is used in certain U.S. government specifications. We prefer *authority* over *agent* because this entity is not necessarily an agent in the legal sense; for example, it could be an independent contractor. Nevertheless, the term *registration authority* needs to be used with care because it is often used for other purposes, such as to refer to an organization that assigns names or unique identifiers.

17. A recovered private key should not be made available to the registration authority in such a way that the registration authority could use that key as if it were the subscriber. The registration authority simply approves recovery of the key, which is then delivered securely to the subscriber.

18. Nevertheless, if employees are to be held accountable for their acts using digital signatures, they should knowingly accept their key pairs and certificates and knowingly be accountable for their private-key use. Generally, the employer

should require the employee to sign a *subscriber agreement* that obligates an employee to use digital credentials in accordance with company policies and designated practices.

19. Such policies and standards are typically enunciated within a *certificate policy* and *certification practice statement,* as described in chapter 10.

20. There is no universal agreement on whether this should be an optional or mandatory requirement of a certification authority. The ABA *Digital Signature Guidelines,* for example, imply that publication with a repository should be mandatory.

21. Oregon Revised Statutes sec. 194.50(8) (1989). The Uniform Law on Notarial Acts notes that identification documents are "documents containing pictorial identification and signature, such as local drivers' licenses and U.S. passports and military identification papers, issued by authorities known to exercise care in identification of persons requesting such documentation" (Uniform Law on Notarial Acts sec. 2 cmt. [1990]). For an example of a practical implementation of comparable requirements by a certification authority, see <http://www.verisign.com/repository/NotaryFAQ>.

22. Anonymous, *How to Create a New Identity* (New York: Carol Publishing Group, 1991). Previously published under the title *New I.D. in America: How to Create a Foolproof New Identity* (Boulder, CO: Paladin Press, 1983).

23. ISO/IEC 9594, *Information Technology—Open Systems Interconnection—The Directory,* also published as the ITU-T X.500 Recommendations series, details at <http://www.itu.ch>.

24. ISO/IEC 9594-8, *Information Technology—Open Systems Interconnection—The Directory: Public-Key and Attribute Certificate Frameworks,* also published as ITU-T X.509 Recommendation, details at <http://www.itu.ch>.

25. M. Wahl, T. Howes, and S. Kille, *Lightweight Directory Access Protocol (v3),* Request for Comments (RFC) 2251 (Internet Activities Board, 1997) <ftp://ftp.isi.edu/in-notes/rfc2251.txt>.

26. S. Boeyen, T. Howes, and P. Richard, *Internet X.509 Public Key Infrastructure Operational Protocols-LDAPv2,* RFC 2559 (Internet Activities Board, 1999) <ftp://ftp.isi.edu/in-notes/rfc2559.txt>; S. Boeyen, T. Howes, and P. Richard, *Internet X.509 Public Key Infrastructure LDAPv2 Schema,* RFC 2587 (Internet Activities Board, 1999) <ftp://ftp.isi.edu/in-notes/rfc2587.txt>.

27. R. Housley and P. Hoffman, *Internet X.509 Public Key Infrastructure Operational Protocols: FTP and HTTP,* RFC 2585 (Internet Activities Board, 1999) <ftp://ftp.isi.edu/in-notes/rfc2585.txt>.

28. With the Version 3 certificate, virtually all ties to X.500 are relaxed, and other name forms are supported. This is discussed further in a later subsection, "Extended (Version 3) Certificate Format."

29. By *unambiguous,* we mean that any name identifies exactly one real-world object within the domain of objects covered by the directory in question. Optional rules are defined that enable X.500 to be used on a global scale; if these rules are followed, the name will be *globally unambiguous.*

30. *Distinguishing name* would be a better term. This is one example of the contorted terminology that sometimes results from linguistic concerns in the development of international standards.

31. In particular, if an X.500 user is removed from the system, there is no way to systematically find all the access control lists that grant privileges to that user's name.

32. ISO/IEC 8824-1, *Information Technology—Open Systems Interconnection—Abstract Syntax Notation One (ASN.1): Specification of Basic Notation,* also published as the ITU-T X.680 Recommendation, details at <http://www.itu.ch>; ISO/IEC 9834-1, *Information Technology—Open Systems Interconnection—Procedures for the Operation of OSI Registration Authorities: General Procedures,* also published as the ITU-T X.660 Recommendation, details at <http://www.itu.ch>.

33. The arm of the ITU involved in this work is the ITU Telecommunication Standardization Sector, known by the abbreviation ITU-T.

34. The ISO arc {1 2} is effectively equivalent to the joint arc {2 16}, but the latter is becoming more commonly used.

35. These country codes are defined in ISO 3166, *Codes for the Representation of Names of Countries.*

36. Other types of entities to which the same naming conventions apply are certificate revocation list issuers and certificate revocation list distribution points. These are described in section 6.7.

37. ANSI X9.55, *American National Standard: Public Key Cryptography for the Financial Services Industry: Extensions to Public Key Certificates and Certificate Revocation Lists* (American National Standards Institute, 1997).

38. R. Housley, W. Ford, T. Polk, and D. Solo, *Internet X.509 Public Key Infra-structure Certificate and CRL Profile,* RFC 2459 (Internet Activities Board, 1999) <ftp://ftp.isi.edu/in-notes/rfc2459.txt>. Note that this document is currently undergoing updating, and a replacement RFC is anticipated in 2001.

39. Attributes that must be supported include country, organization, organizational unit, state or province name, common name, distinguished name qualifier, serial number, and domain component. The latter is used in representing an Internet DNS name as an X.500 name and is specified in S. Kille, M. Wahl, A. Grimstad, R. Huber, and S. Sataluri, *Using Domains in LDAP/X.500 Distinguished Names,* RFC 2247 (Internet Activities Board, 1998) <ftp://ftp.isi.edu/in-notes/rfc2247.txt>.

40. S. Santessan, W. Polk, P. Barzin, and M. Nystrom, *Internet X.509 Public Key Infrastructure Qualified Certificates Profile,* RFC [number to be assigned] (Internet Activities Board, 2000).

41. ISO/IEC 8824-1, *Information Technology—Open Systems Interconnection—Abstract Syntax Notation One (ASN.1).* Also published as ITU-T X.680 series Recommendations <http://www.itu.ch>.

42. ASN.1 specifications have proved elusive and expensive in the past. The full ASN.1 specifications are now readily available from ISO or the ITU at <http://www.itu.ch>. For a good overview of ASN.1, focusing on what needs to be understood to implement X.509-based protocols, see B. S. Kaliski, Jr., *A Layman's Guide to a Subset of ASN.1, BER, and DER,* RSA Laboratories Technical Note (1993) <ftp://ftp.rsasecurity.com/pub/pkcs>.

43. U.S. National Security Agency, *MISSI Phase 1 Program Overview,* Version 3.3, October 17, 1994; U.S. National Security Agency, *MOSAIC Key Management Concept,* Rev. 2.5, February 28, 1994.

44. M. Myers, R. Ankney, A. Malpani, S. Galperin, and C. Adams, *X.509 Internet Public Key Infrastructure Online Certificate Status Protocol (OCSP),* RFC 2560 (Internet Activities Board, 1999) <ftp://ftp.isi.edu/in-notes/rfc2560.txt>.

45. For example, in the Identrus architecture (discussed in chapter 7), all OCSP requests must be signed since the responder views each of its responses as a guarantee of available funds to cover payment for a particular e-commerce transaction.

46. We suggest 25 rather than 24 hours so that there is a one-hour overlap of certificate lifetimes, thus avoiding a critical instant at which no certificate is valid, but this is a function of the applications to be supported.

47. See the latest version of the WAP PKI specification at <http://www.wapforum.org>.

48. Promoted by ValiCert, Inc., <http://www.valicert.com>.

49. For example, a party might be able to pay a premium for a favorable apportionment of risk.

50. The Version 2 CRL format can be used for advising not only about revocation of certificates but also about *suspension* of a certificate. Certificate suspension is discussed later in this section.

51. In RFC 2459.

52. This is the scenario encountered with the U.S. Department of Defense's compromised key list. In fact, the compromised key list design was the primary motivator for including the indirect CRL feature in the standard.

53. These instruction codes are defined in the ANSI X9.57 standard.

54. C. Ellison, *SPKI Requirements,* RFC 2692 (Internet Activities Board, 1999) <ftp://ftp.isi.edu/in-notes/rfc2692.txt>; C. Ellison, B. Frantz, B. Lampson, R. Rivest, B. Thomas, and T. Ylonen, *SPKI Certificate Theory,* RFC 2693 (Internet Activities Board, 1999) <ftp://ftp.isi.edu/in-notes/rfc2693.txt>.

55. Documentation on SDSI is available at <http://theory.lcs.mit.edu/~cis/sdsi.html>.

56. X.509 Version 3 supports a virtually unbounded set of name forms, which could include the SDSI model of linked local name spaces. However, the particular naming model proposed in SDSI is not normally used in the X.509 context; therefore, it represents a significant new development.

Public-Key Infrastructure

$\mathbf{A}$ public-key infrastructure (PKI) can be loosely defined as the set of infrastructural services that support the wide-scale use of public-key-based digital signatures and encryption. In this book, we consider this term to cover certification authorities and certification authority structures, repositories or directories associated with certification authorities, the means of interfacing applications to the foregoing infrastructural components, and the legal infrastructures required to underpin all of the foregoing. These concepts were introduced in previous chapters. In this chapter, we discuss in more detail some of the fundamental issues encountered in building PKIs that can support large and diverse user communities. We also describe some of the tools available to assist in building large PKI communities, especially some of the more advanced features of X.509. First, we outline the issues faced by an enterprise intending to implement PKI. We then discuss ways to structure relationships between multiple certification authorities, ways to associate different certification policies and practices with different certification paths, name constraints, and certificate management protocols used in interfacing application products to a supporting PKI. We discuss PGP's web of trust and compare it with X.509-based PKI. We conclude with some examples of notable real-world multienterprise PKI designs.

7.1 PKI for the Typical E-Commerce Enterprise

PKI is what enables public-key encryption and digital signature technology to be used effectively on a wide scale and relates primarily to the provision of certification authority services. Most significantly, PKI generally involves multiple certification authorities cooperating to satisfy the needs of communities of arbitrary size.

For an enterprise, the need to deploy or use PKI may materialize in various ways, including these:

- As a transparent technology underlying a procured application. Lotus Notes customers, for example, have used PKI for years, without the typical user realizing it.
- As a standard adjunct to another product. For example, to enable SSL data protection on an SSL-capable Web server, one must obtain an SSL server certificate, most commonly through a commercial certification authority.
- As part of doing business in a particular community, such as a business-to-business exchange that includes PKI-enhanced protections integral to its exchange infrastructure.
- As a means of achieving the requisite security properties or supporting non-repudiation demands in a particular business application. Examples include the authentication of parties participating in Internet-based supply chain management or the encryption of sensitive data such as consumer credit card numbers sent to a merchant Web site.
- As an optional addition to an enterprise-internal application, such as e-mail or a virtual private network (VPN) used for remote employee access, to enhance security or improve scalability.
- As part of an enterprise-wide strategy whereby PKI is made ubiquitously available to leverage diverse future applications.

In some of these situations, the enterprise needs to make few major deployment decisions since some other party is providing the core PKI services. However, in the latter three situations, the enterprise is deploying its own PKI and must make some fundamental decisions regarding that deployment, such as these:

- *Scope and structure of community:* It is important to plan a PKI up front with a view to its ultimately serving as large a community as practical. (We discuss later in this chapter how difficult it is to later link together preexisting PKI islands.) For example, it might be possible to design a PKI to logically span a whole corporate conglomerate rather than a single department or application, or better still, it might be possible to join an existing larger PKI community, such as one operated on behalf of an entire vertical industry sector. In any case, it is necessary to resolve how the PKI community is structured and how its entities, in particular, the participating certification authorities, relate to each other.

- *Practices:* The practices to be followed by all participants in the PKI must be established up front. This starts with the decision of whether to join an existing PKI community or start a new one. With an existing community, such as an industry-specific community or an existing horizontally oriented community managed by a commercial certification authority, practices generally have been pre-established. With a private PKI, the enterprise may specify its own practices.[1]

- *Service provider versus in-house:* An enterprise deploying PKI faces a fundamental choice of either subscribing to a managed service (partial or complete outsourcing) or building the PKI in-house using software products from a PKI software vendor. With the managed service approach, the service provider provides the secure facility, the cryptographic hardware and software, the specialized know-how, the redundant operational infrastructure, and risk sharing. With an in-house approach, the enterprise does all this itself and bears all the risk, which generally means higher cost of ownership and much longer time to deploy, but which benefits by greater independence.

- *Vendor choice:* Having made the preceding decisions, the choice of vendor remains to be made. Factors to be considered, in addition to price and features, should include scalability, user experience, ease of support,[2] ease of application integration, and application product independence.

In the remainder of this chapter, we explore various fundamental aspects of PKI, with a view to providing background material to help in making such procurement and deployment decisions.

7.2 Certification Authority Structures: Traditional Models

To use a remote party's public key, a certificate user (relying party) must find and validate a complete certification path traversing one or more certification authorities from that public key to a *trust anchor* certification authority—one whose public key is already held and trusted by the certificate user. To build a large, scalable PKI, a major challenge is to make the finding and validating of certification paths simple, convenient, and efficient. This depends largely on establishing rules or conventions for structuring the relationships whereby certification authorities certify other certification authorities. These structuring conventions are sometimes called *trust models,* although this term is misleading, since PKI trust depends on many other factors as well.

In this section and the next, we discuss the main structuring models that have been proposed or used. In this section we describe the traditional models: hierarchies and forests of hierarchies. Most real-world PKI deployments use these models. Their implementation in certificate-using systems is comparatively straightforward, allowing them to be readily realized in a wide range of application products, including commodity products. More complex models, which are more costly and difficult to implement but may be required to satisfy the demands of special application environments, are then described.

Before proceeding, however, let us consider the term *cross-certification*—one of the most confusing terms in the industry. In this book, we adopt the meaning of cross-certificate that was painstakingly agreed upon by the IETF PKIX Working Group:

> A cross-certificate is a certificate issued by one CA [certification authority] to another
> CA which contains a CA signature key used for issuing certificates.[3]

In other words, cross-certification is simply the issuance of a certificate by one certification authority to another for use in a certification path, regardless of the resulting structure (such as hierarchical and nonhierarchical).

Hierarchies (Trees)

Reducing the certification path problem to its simplest form, we need a systematic means of linking members of a large community of end entities to a small number of trust anchors via acceptably short paths, with each path traversing a series of trusted certification authorities. In mathematical graph theory, tree structures, or hierarchies, provide a well-known optimal solution to this problem.

Consider the structure in figure 7.1. In this diagram, the entities with uppercase identifiers (such as Z, X, and Y) are certification authorities. The entities with lowercase identifiers (such as a, b, and c) are end entities, or subscribers. An arrow means that the source entity has issued a certificate for the public key of the target entity.

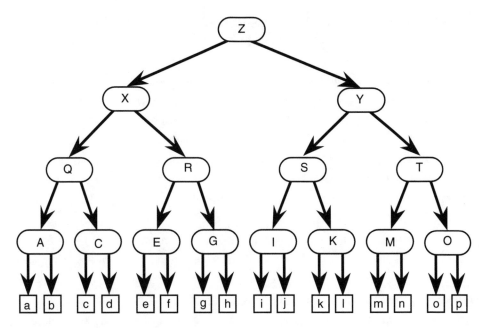

Figure 7.1   Hierarchical Structure

All certification paths start from the *root certification authority* Z. Certificate users need to have only the root certification authority as a trust anchor; in other words, they must hold a reliable copy of the root certification authority's public key, validated by independent means. It is easy to construct a certification path to any end entity. For example, any certificate user can obtain a validated copy of *a*'s public key using a certification path of four certificates:

- A certificate for X, issued by Z (note that the certificate user inherently trusts Z's public key)
- A certificate for Q, issued by X
- A certificate for A, issued by Q
- A certificate for end entity a, issued by A

This model scales well. There can obviously be many more than two entities subordinate to any other. Suppose, for example, that every certification authority can certify up to 100 subordinate certification authorities or up to 10,000 end entities. A four-tiered structure, as in figure 7.1, could then support up to 10 billion end entities, with no certification path exceeding four certificates.

Also, most significantly, there is only one certification path for any end entity, so certification paths are very easy to find. For example, any end entity such as a can store the path of certificates from root Z to itself and distribute that path as one data structure to any other end entity needing it. For example, a can attach these certificates to any object it has digitally signed so that the signature verifier will always have all required certificates on hand. The certification path can also be stored in a's directory entry so that anyone needing it to send an encrypted message to a can fetch all the needed certificates in one directory access.

When using any certification path, a certificate user must trust every certification authority on that path to have exercised due diligence in issuing its certificates and to have taken appropriate precautions to ensure that no other party might forge certificates that purport to be from that certification authority. All participants in the structure typically commit to adhere to practices associated with, and often defined by, the PKI community based on that hierarchy.

In a hierarchical structure, the root certification authority Z is particularly critical from a trust perspective, since all certification paths depend on trust in Z. If an attacker were to compromise Z's private key, that attacker could forge digital signatures for any signer in the structure and likely convince any signature verifier that the forged signature is legitimate. Furthermore, depending on how trust anchors are established, it may be difficult to revoke the root certification authority.

Accordingly, the root's private key must be exceptionally well protected, for example, by keeping it offline and disabled in a secure facility and only enabling it under highly supervised and audited conditions. This is usually not an unreasonable burden, since the root certification authority certifies only other certification authorities (not end entities) and so generally issues certificates infrequently.

Correspondingly, most certification authorities that certify end entities generally issue certificates frequently and must be online. Hence, there is generally a strong case to construct any PKI as a hierarchy of at least two levels, with at least one offline root certification authority and at least one online certification authority. A PKI involving just a single, isolated certification authority is not generally viable, except in a PKI supporting a very small community or a low-trust application environment.

Forests of Trees

In a hierarchical PKI structure, all participants in the structure must commit to meeting a minimum standard of trustworthiness and must adhere to a common set of practices. This is not difficult to achieve in a PKI designed up front for a particular community, such as the employees of a corporation, the customers of a business-to-business exchange, or the broader community in a particular vertical industry sector.

However, it is not always practical to build one all-embracing hierarchy for all parties participating in a secure application environment. An alternative approach is to configure a certificate-using system to recognize multiple hierarchies, as illustrated in figure 7.2. Situations that lead to this configuration might include, for example,

- where the certificate user is prepared to trust certificates issued by certain external organizations to their own local communities, for example, their employee or customer communities, or
- where the certificate user is prepared to trust certificates issued by multiple independent commercial certification authorities.

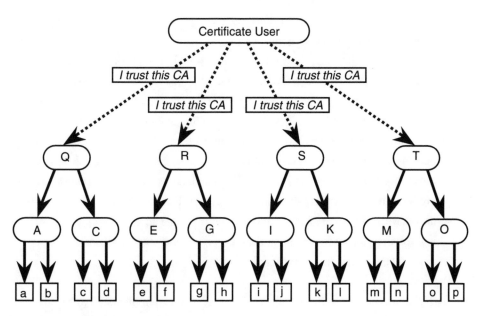

Figure 7.2   Forest of Hierarchies

Various mechanisms exist for establishing roots of hierarchies as points of trust. Such mechanisms, which are primarily a matter of product vendor or customer choice (rather than something requiring industry-wide standardization), include these:

- *User-controlled direct:* The user operating the certificate-using application explicitly enables certain roots to be trusted for the application in question. Typically, application software is shipped with a default list of roots preinstalled. The user may disable particular default roots or install additional trusted roots in the list. This is the model employed with the typical Web browser as shipped. It is appealing in that it gives the individual total control, but it can be problematic in that individuals are often not adequately trained or authorized to exercise such control.

- *Domain-controlled direct:* The domain administrator forces all certificate-using systems (such as browsers or mail clients) in the local domain to recognize a particular set of trusted roots. This approach is appropriate within an enterprise. It places policy decisions and enforcement in the hands of the domain administrator while making root management transparent to the end user. Certain networking product suites support this option.

- *User-controlled cross-certification:* The user operating the certificate-using application conceptually acts as a mini-certification authority and issues locally signed certificates for the recognized set of root certification authorities. This essentially inserts a new level of root certification authority above the original set of roots, converting the forest structure into a single hierarchy. Certificate-using products then need to recognize only one root and can find and process certificate chains straightforwardly, as they would with a simple hierarchy.[4] This mechanism has been used, for example, in Lotus Notes.

- *Domain-controlled cross-certification:*[5] This model is the same as user-controlled cross-certification, except that the top-level certification authority is operated by an enterprise for all the users in its domain. It has the advantages of placing policy decisions and enforcement at the enterprise rather than end user level and of making root management transparent to the end user.

All of these mechanisms are well tried and have been demonstrated to be effective in practice. In fact, the vast majority of deployed PKIs use these structuring models and mechanisms. However, a more general model exists and is introduced in the next section. Readers who are not interested in the finer details of this subject may skip to section 7.4.

7.3   Certification Authority Structures: The Generalized Model

When the X.509 Version 3 certificate format was developed, it was felt that trees and forests of certification authorities might not satisfy all application environment requirements and that more complex structuring models might sometimes be required. Requirements were envisaged, for example, for interoperation of separately established PKIs that implement nonidentical policies and for construction of PKIs that could simultaneously support different applications with different policy demands.[6] Consequently, the X.509 standardization committee resolved to specify a rich set of tools that would allow any user community to structure the certification authority relationships of its PKI any way it saw fit (at the possible expense of complexity in the implementation of relying parties' systems). In this section we describe the main features of this *generalized* structuring approach.

The complexities of the generalized model lie in the resolution of two core problems: how to find a suitable certification path and, having found it, how to validate it. These functions must be implemented in every certificate-using system (or in a server that supports that system). It is helpful to consider these as two separate tasks; their implementations may well be quite separate because certification path discovery is not a security-critical function, whereas certification path validation is.

Certification Path Discovery

Procedures for certification path discovery are not stipulated in X.509 but are left to the implementer. The certification path discovery problem is as follows: *I need to find a certification path between a target user's public key and any one of my set of trust anchor keys.*

Assuming that some certification path exists and all its certificates are openly available in accessible directories, it is generally possible to find that path through standard directory technology. Let us consider the most general case, where nothing is known other than the name of the target user and the names of the trust anchor certification authorities.[7] The problem is illustrated in figure 7.3.

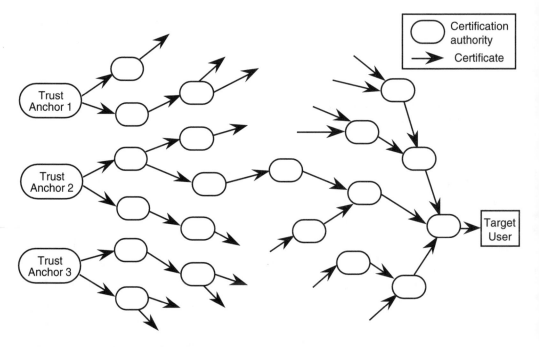

Figure 7.3   General Certification Path-Finding Problem

If a path exists and is not unreasonably long, we can find that path if certain information retrieval services are available. First, we need to assume that we can retrieve a certificate for the target user's public key issued by some certification authority. This is a reasonable assumption. With a digital signature, a certificate for the target user's public key is usually delivered with the signature; with encryption, a certificate for the target generally can be easily obtained: either a cached copy of a certificate from prior communications with that user or from a simple directory lookup that delivers user certificates.

This leaves us with two other information retrieval service requirements:

1. Given a certification authority's name, a service to retrieve certificates for that certification authority's public keys issued by other certification authorities

   2. Given a certification authority's name, a service to retrieve certificates issued by that certification authority for the public keys of other certification authorities

If service 1 is available, we can find a certification path by working back progressively from the target user's certificate toward a trust anchor, as follows:

- *Step 1:* Given a certificate issued by certification authority X, determine the set of certification authorities that have issued certificates for the public key of X.
- *Step 2:* If one of the certification authorities from step 1 is a recognized trust anchor, we have found the required certification path; otherwise, proceed to step 3.
- *Step 3:* For each certification authority found in step 1, repeat the step 1 procedure, treating that certification authority as certification authority X.

If a certification path exists, this procedure will eventually find it.[8]

If service 2 is available, we can apply a similar (but inverted) procedure, starting from each known trust anchor and searching outward until we find a path to the certification authority that issued the target user's certificate.

If both services 1 and 2 are available, we have even more flexibility. We can, for instance, start searching from both the target user's certification authority inward and from the trust anchors outward, aiming to meet in the middle. Given both services, there are many ways to search for certification paths and much room for innovation by product vendors.

How reasonable is it to assume that service 1 or 2 exists? If we can assume a ubiquitous directory service—employing, for example, X.500 or LDAP—then these services are certainly technically feasible. However, widely accessible private directory services have proved elusive in the past, largely due to concerns regarding exposure of private information. Furthermore, the expectation of 24/7 availability of directory services from diverse organizations can be difficult to meet. In today's Internet environment, this is neither an unsolvable problem nor a high-confidence assumption. Deployment of the generalized model of certification authority structuring therefore seems questionable outside controlled, contained environments, such as enterprise-internal or government communities, owing to certification path discovery issues. Imposed structural rules that simplify the directory search problem might, however, alleviate the concerns.

Certification Path Validation

After finding a suitable certification path, it is necessary to validate that path. This involves such actions as these:

1. Verifying the digital signature on each certificate and checking that basic constraints are followed.
2. Checking that the names in the certificates are consistent with a valid certification path, that is, that the subject of every certificate (except the last) is the issuer of the next certificate.
3. Checking that the validity periods of all certificates correctly span the time for which validity is being checked. (Note that this generally requires an accurate local clock, which may not be a good assumption in the typical client terminal.)
4. Checking that each certificate has not been revoked. This may be a complex process involving, for example, retrieving, validating, and checking the correct CRL or executing an online status-checking transaction.
5. Checking that the required certificate policies are indicated in the certificates. (We explain certificate policies in section 7.4.)
6. Checking that name constraints are followed. (We explain name constraints in section 7.5.)

Path validation is a process that must be performed before accepting an end-entity certificate, regardless of the PKI model. However, in the hierarchical and forest of trees models, policy and name constraint extensions are often not used, therefore actions 5 and 6 may not be required or only a subset of these actions may need to be performed.

It is important that this entire process be conducted securely. If an intruder can somehow subvert this process or the result, the effect can be the same as if that intruder substituted the wrong public key—the intruder may be able to forge digital signatures and decrypt encrypted data intended for others.

The X.509 Version 3 specification and PKIX profile give detailed attention to this security requirement. Both include a detailed description of an algorithm that implements the chain validation process in a way that allows the process to be implemented within a *secure boundary* (this could be a hardware or software boundary). Anyone implementing certification path validation logic should study one of these specifications carefully.

7.4 Certificate Policies

When a certification authority issues a certificate, it is providing a statement to a certificate user that a particular public key is bound to a particular entity (the certificate subject). But to what extent and for what purposes can the certificate user *rely* on that statement by the certification authority? Authenticating the identity or other attributes of a person and checking the corporate credentials of a company are nontrivial tasks; they can be performed at different quality levels, and high quality will probably not come without a price. For some applications, high quality tops the requirements list; for others, low cost is paramount. Therefore, different certificates may be issued following different practices and procedures and may be suitable for different purposes.

A certification authority publishes a statement of the practices and procedures it follows in a document called a *certification practice statement* (CPS). CPSs range in complexity and length, but they focus on disclosing what a certification authority does, as opposed to more general requirements imposed on a PKI. CPSs are discussed in detail in chapter 10.

In response to the need for a more general document describing applicable requirements and policies within a PKI, the *certificate policy* (CP) concept was introduced in X.509 Version 3. A certificate user can use a reference to a CP in a certificate when deciding whether or not the certificate is suitable for use for a particular purpose. A PKI can be designed to support diverse certificate policies and thus satisfy the needs of various applications and assurance or trust models. Any individual certificate typically is associated with a single certificate policy or possibly is consistent with a small number of different policies.

The Certificate Policy Concept

A *certificate policy* (CP) is defined in X.509 as

> A named set of rules that indicates the applicability of a certificate to a particular community and/or class of application with common security requirements. For example, a particular certificate policy might indicate applicability of a type of certificate to the authentication of electronic data interchange transactions for the trading of goods within a given price range.[9]

CPs need to be recognized by both the issuer and users of a certificate. A CP is registered and assigned a unique object identifier, as described under "Object Registration" in section 6.5. In this case, the registered object is a published statement. In a communications protocol, only the object identifier needs to be conveyed; it serves as a *reference* to the certificate policy statement.

For example, Sharon's Steelcorp might define the following two policies for use within its own corporate PKI:

- *Sharon's general-use policy:* This policy is intended for use in day-to-day data protection by all corporate employees, for example, for authenticating and encrypting casual e-mail and connections to corporate Web servers. The certified key pairs may be generated, stored, and managed using low-cost, software-based systems. A certificate is automatically issued to anybody identified in the corporate directory who submits a signed certificate request form to a network administrator. Sharon's assigns this policy the object identifier *{joint-iso-itu-t (2) country (16) us (840) organization (1) sharons (15678) policies (4) general-use (1)}*.
- *Sharon's financial policy:* This policy is intended for use in protecting financial transactions with a value over $10,000. The certified key pairs must be generated and stored in cryptographic hardware tokens. A token is given to, and a certificate issued for, only management staff and designated individuals on a specially approved list. To be issued such a token, an authorized individual must personally appear at the corporate security office and present his or her corporate identification badge. Sharon's assigns this policy the object identifier *{joint-iso-itu-t (2) country (16) us (840) organization (1) sharons (15678) policies (4) financial (2)}*.

Certificate Policies Extension

In X.509 Version 3 certificates, CP references are conveyed in the certificate policies extension field. X.509 assumes a model in which certificate-using systems have been preprogrammed with the policy references that the user is prepared to accept for a given application. Under this model, certificate users can process and accept certificates automatically and efficiently, provided that one of the foreseen policies is in use. The policy acceptance decision may be made by the user (or an administrator in the user's organization) in advance, that is, at the time of the preprogramming. On the basis of this model, the X.509 standard describes how a certificate-using system must process the certificate policies extension field.

This extension field has two variants: one with the field flagged as noncritical and one with it flagged as critical. It is important to understand the subtle difference between these two cases.

A noncritical certificate policies field lists policies that the certification authority declares applicable. However, the certification authority is not mandating that the certificate be *restricted* to use in accordance with these policies; the certificate may be used for other purposes and under other policies. In the Sharon's Steelcorp example, the certificates issued to Sharon's staff generally might contain in this field the object identifier for Sharon's general-use policy. The certificates issued to Sharon's management staff, certifying the keys in their hardware tokens, might contain the object identifiers for both Sharon's financial and Sharon's general-use policies.

The noncritical certificate policies field is designed to be used by applications as follows: Each designated application is preconfigured to know what policy it requires. For example, the Sharon's Steelcorp e-mail applications and Web servers are configured to require *Sharon's general-use* policy. Sharon's Steelcorp financial applications could be configured to require *Sharon's financial* policy for certificates used in validating transactions over $10,000 or *Sharon's general-use* policy for transactions of lower values.

When processing a certification path, a policy that is acceptable to the certificate-using application must be present in every certificate in the path: certification authority certificates as well as end-entity certificates. The standard also defines a special value *any-policy* that a certification authority may use to indicate that a certificate may be used regardless of policy.

If the certificate policies field is flagged as critical, it serves the same purpose as a noncritical field but also has an additional role. It indicates that use of the certificate is *restricted* to one of the identified policies. In other words, the certification authority is declaring that the certificate must not be used under any policy other than those identified. The field therefore serves to protect the certification authority against liability exposure if some party uses the certificate for an unintended purpose. For example, a credit card company might issue certificates to its cardholders for the purpose of protecting credit card transactions. The credit card company understands the risks associated with credit card transactions and can readily assess its exposure should a defective certificate accidentally be issued, for example, to an erroneously authenticated person. However, suppose someone used a credit card certificate as the basis of encrypting multimillion-dollar trade secrets that subsequently fell into the wrong hands because of an error in issuing the credit card certificate. Under such circumstances the credit card company might conceivably be held responsible for damages caused by a certificate used for a purpose for which it was not intended. The critical-flagged certificate policies extension is intended to mitigate the risk in this type of situation.

Regardless of whether noncritical or critical, the certificate policies extension field can convey, along with each certificate policy identifier, additional policy-dependent information in a *qualifier* field. The standard does not mandate the purpose for which this field must be used. In fact, it does not even mandate the syntactic data type of this field. Anyone can define a qualifier type and can register it in the way described under "Object Registration" in section 6.5. Whenever a certificate policy is defined, the policy definition should state the qualifier types that can be used with the policy.

In practice, policy qualifiers are not particularly useful unless prior agreement is reached, outside the standard, on the purposes for which they will be used and on the syntaxes that will represent them. This is not to suggest that there is only one way to format and use qualifiers; rather, a collection of common qualifier types will most likely emerge. For example, these are some important purposes for which qualifiers are used (and standardized in the PKIX profile):

- *CPS pointer:* For providing a robust link back to a location from which a copy of the full certification practice statement can be retrieved (the qualifier conveys a Web URL)
- *User notice:* For conveying textual information regarding legal obligations (such as limitation of liability) for display (disclosure) to certificate users whenever certificates are used[10]

Policy Mappings Extension

X.509 also defines a policy mappings extension field, designed for optional use in a certificate that links two separate domains, that is, a cross-certificate between infrastructures operated by different organizations. This field allows a certification authority to indicate that certain policies in its own domain can be considered equivalent (or adequate) to certain other policies in the subject certification authority's domain.

For example, suppose that under Sharon's Steelcorp's business alliance with Danielle's Machine Makers, the two corporations agree to cross-certify each other's PKIs for the purposes of mutually protecting e-mail. Danielle's existing policy for e-mail protection is *Danielle's general-use* policy. One can see that simply generating cross-certificates between the two domains will not provide the necessary interoperability, as all of Sharon's e-mail applications are configured to require the *Sharon's general-use* policy. One possible solution is to reconfigure all the e-mail applications to require either *Sharon's general-use* or *Danielle's general-use* policy. Another solution, which is likely to be easier to administer, uses the policy mapping field. This field, in a cross-certificate for Danielle's certification authority issued by Sharon's certification authority, can provide a statement that Sharon's certificate users can consider *Danielle's general-use* policy to be equivalent, for practical purposes, to *Sharon's general-use* policy. The policy mapping field is always noncritical.

It is not yet clear how important this field will prove in practice. The whole subject of linking infrastructures operated by different organizations needs further experimental deployment before we can be confident in implementing policy mapping broadly.

Policy Constraints and Inhibit-Any-Policy Extensions

The policy constraints extension contains two optional indicator fields that serve separate purposes as follows:

- *Require explicit policy indicator:* A certification authority can use this flag to indicate that an explicit, acceptable policy identifier must be present in every further certificate in the certification path. This option is useful under the following circumstances: Within a certificate user's home domain, the certificate user's application may trust the local certification authorities sufficiently that it does not require *any* particular certificate policy to be present in certificates. For example, in Sharon's Steelcorp, transactions that are wholly internal to the company may not need policy checking; the application trusts any certificate that the certification authority issues. In this case, the using application tells its certificate-processing logic to accept any policy; this can significantly simplify certificate administration. However, if a certification path includes a certificate for a certification authority *outside* Sharon's Steelcorp, the rules may need to change. The administration of Sharon's may require that outside certification authorities always have explicit, acceptable policy identifiers in their certificates. This can be enforced by having Sharon's certification authority set the r*equire explicit policy* indicator in the certificate for the outside certification authority.

- *Inhibit policy mapping indicator:* A certification authority can use this indicator to stipulate that policy mapping is not permitted in the remainder of the certification path. Again, this indicator is most likely to be set in a certificate for an outside organization's certification authority. It is a worthwhile precaution because policy mapping is difficult to administer and could be subject to inappropriate use.

The *inhibit any-policy* extension is closely related to the policy constraints extension. It is used to stipulate that the special value *any-policy* ceases to apply at some point in the certification path—generally a point outside the certificate user's home domain.

Contents of a Certificate Policy

There is no standard definition of what topics should be covered by a certificate policy. A certificate policy is simply the set of topics that a certification authority deems necessary to include and that satisfy certificate users as to the acceptability of particular certificates. The IETF provides some guidance in RFC 2527,[11] which is discussed in chapters 8 and 10. Based on this RFC, these topics are typically included:

- *Introduction:* Whether this certificate policy is intended for use only by members of a particular community, for example, employees of an organization or subscribers to a certification authority service; whether this policy is intended only for a specific purpose
- *General provisions:* Provisions relating to warranties provided by certification authorities, registration authorities, and others; disclaimers of warranties; limitations of liability; confidentiality and privacy matters; intellectual property protection; and general legal matters
- *Identification and authentication policy:* The requirements governing the certification authority's practices relating to identifying and authenticating certificate subjects
- *Operational requirements:* The practices followed by the certification authority in operating its services, for example, the frequency with which CRLs are issued and the procedures for audit trails

- *Physical, procedural, and personnel security controls:* The measures taken by a certification authority, registration authority, or end entity to ensure that its environment is secure, including protective measures relating to physical security, personnel security, product assurance, and network-access security
- *Technical security controls:* Requirements for measures taken by a certification authority, registration authorities to protect its cryptographic keys; possibly also requirements placed on subscribers regarding the extent to which and how they must protect their cryptographic keys
- *Certificate and CRL profiles:* Requirements regarding the content of certificates and CRLs issued by the certification authority
- *Specification administration:* The name and contact details of the policy defining authority and details of how the policy definition is maintained and published

Certification authority practices are discussed in detail in chapter 10. In that chapter, we also explore the relationship between the X.509 CP concept and other statements of certification practices.

7.5 Name Constraints

One of the more complex parts of the generalized certification path validation model is the X.509 name constraint mechanism. This mechanism allows any certification authority, when it certifies another certification authority, to specify exactly what names are allowed in subsequent certificates in the certification path. Certificate-using systems mechanically check that name constraints have been followed. This mechanism can potentially limit the damage that can result from certification authority mistakes or from the actions of malfunctioning or malicious certification authorities.

For example, when the certification authority of Danielle's Machine Makers cross-certifies the central certification authority of Sharon's Steelcorp, Danielle's certification authority can specify that the only acceptable subject names that may appear in subsequent certificates in the certification path are X.500 names in either of the subtrees

{*Country* = *US*, *Organization* = *Sharon's Steelcorp, Inc.*, . . . } or

{*Country* = *UK*, *Organization* = *Sharon's Steelcorp, Ltd.*, . . . }.

This does not mean that these are the only names for which Sharon's Steelcorp can issue certificates: Sharon's certification authority may issue certificates to other foreign subsidiaries or may even issue certificates to different corporations with which it does business. However, Danielle's wants to limit its certifications to the two subtrees identified because these span the only people in Sharon's with which Danielle's does business. Danielle's is reducing its risks by not allowing certification paths to those parts of Sharon's that it does not know and does not need to know.

In fact, the model is much more powerful than the preceding example shows. It is possible to customize name-space specifications much more precisely than just using complete X.500 subtrees. A name constraint is specified by lists of both permitted subtrees and excluded subtrees. A permitted subtree specifies a name space in which names are permitted to fall (the preceding example used two permitted subtrees). An excluded subtree specifies a name space in which names are not permitted to fall. If necessary, excluded subtree rules override permitted subtree rules. For example, Danielle's may want to permit certification paths to all of Sharon's in the United States except the Industrial Machines division, which is the only part of Sharon's that competes with Danielle's. Danielle's can arrange this with a permitted subtree {*Country = US, Organization = Sharon's Steelcorp, Inc., . . .* } plus an excluded subtree {*Country = US, Organization = Sharon's Steelcorp, Inc., Organizational Unit = Industrial Machines Div., . . .* }.

Even finer tree pruning is available if needed. It is possible to specify that only certain levels of a naming subtree apply, with either permitted or excluded subtrees.

Name constraints can also be used with name forms other than X.500 names, provided that they are name forms that have a defined hierarchical structure. Other name forms with such structure include Internet e-mail addresses and Internet domain names. The rules for using these types of names in X.509 name constraints are specified by the IETF. For example, if Danielle's uses the PKI to support secure e-mail with Sharon's, Danielle's might include in its certificate for Sharon's certification authority a permitted subtree name constraint using the e-mail address name form that permits only the name space *sharons.com*. This constraint means that Danielle's users can use Sharon's certificates that associate public keys with e-mail addresses of the form *someone@sharons.com*. However, a certificate from a Sharon's certification authority certifying *president@ whitehouse.gov* would be automatically rejected by the e-mail applications at Danielle's.

7.6   Certificate Management Protocols

Standards are essential if PKI is to develop its full potential. There are multiple suppliers of infrastructure products and many more suppliers of application products that use that infrastructure. The scalability advantages of public-key technology cannot be realized unless all these products can interoperate. For example, one vendor's digital-signing client must be able to communicate with another vendor's certification authority to have a certificate issued. Standardized certificate management protocols are therefore essential.

PKCS Standards

The PKCS standards, developed by RSA Security, include two specifications that have proved particularly useful in certificate management. PKCS #10 defines a format for a message to request issuance of a certificate from a certification authority; it allows the requesting entity to supply its public key and other values requested for inclusion in the certificate. (The certification authority may but is not required to use such values.)

PKCS #7 specifies an enveloping format for protecting messages such as e-mail messages. However, a degenerate form of PKCS #7 has proved popular for delivering issued certificates back to an entity that requests a certificate using PKCS #10. The degenerate PKCS #7 contains just the issued certificate plus superior certificates in a hierarchy in an ASN.1 wrapper; it does not really envelope a message at all.

The combination of PKCS #10 and degenerate PKCS #7 has been a popular protocol for certificate request and issuance since the earliest PKI deployments, largely because the software to generate and parse these data structures is widely available in common software developer toolkits.

Certificate Management Protocol (CMP)

In the mid-1990s, the IETF PKIX Working Group launched a project to develop a more comprehensive certificate management protocol than was afforded by the PKCS specifications. Two proposals were put forward: The first was a totally new design for a quite complex protocol called Certificate Management Protocol (CMP), and the second was a proposal to augment the PKCS specifications by adding required new features incrementally. Unfortunately, it proved impossible politically to agree on one approach. The vendors with substantial investment in installed Internet-based PKI preferred to build incrementally on the PKCS software they were already using. Other vendors favored adoption of the new CMP. The unfortunate result was adoption of two different standards-track specifications that are virtually identical in their technical characteristics but incompatible. The PKCS-based protocol evolved to become CMC (Certificate Management Over CMS), described in the following subsection.

CMP[12] specifies a set of message formats for use in management communications between systems that support various PKI functions, such as certification authority and registration authority, or between such infrastructure systems and application systems that use the PKI services. Message formats are defined to support the following functions:

- *Initialization/certification:* An end entity is registering with a PKI provider for the first time, generating a key pair or having the key pair generated by the infrastructure provider, and requesting issuance of a certificate for the public key. Request and response messages are specified for use in various scenarios. The request format generally employed is known as the Certificate Request Message Format (CRMF), which is specified in a companion standard.[13] PKCS #10 formatted requests are also permitted but discouraged.

- *Proof of possession:* When issuing a certificate, a certification authority or its registration authority needs to be confident that the certificate applicant indeed possesses the private key corresponding to the public key that will be in the certificate. Otherwise, various risks arise.[14] With certification requests for digital signature key pairs, this is usually accomplished by requiring the certificate applicant to sign the request. However, with encryption key pairs, other mechanisms are required.[15] CMP includes message formats to support exchanges that may be required for this purpose.

- *Key update:* A certificate subject requests issuance of a new certificate as an update of an existing certificate, either for the same key pair or simultaneously with the establishment of a new key pair.

- *Key recovery:* An end entity is requesting recovery of a lost private key (or possibly a private key history) that has been backed up by a key recovery system, along with copies of corresponding certificates.

- *Revocation request:* A certificate subject or other authorized party is requesting revocation of a certificate (or possibly multiple certificates).

- *Cross-certification:* A certification authority requests that another certification authority issue it a certificate for use in certification paths. The existence of this exchange has caused confusion, since it suggests that establishment of a cross-certification arrangement between certification authorities comprises little more than a mechanistic exchange of public keys. In commercial practice, cross-certification is primarily a nontechnical process involving resolution of legal, business, and practices issues. Communication of a public key value more commonly involves a simple, manual (and audited) procedure.
- *Announcements:* Message formats are specified for announcing update of a certification authority's key pair, availability of a new certificate, revocation (or impending revocation) of a certificate, or issuance of a CRL.

When it is necessary to protect a message for authentication, integrity, or encryption purposes, CMP defines its own protection envelope format.

The design goals for CMP were ambitious. CMP supports a broad range of PKI architectures and permits registration authorities to participate in issuing and revoking certificates. Registration authorities can perform bulk transactions, requesting certificates for many different users from the certification authority in a single message.

This new functionality is attractive but introduces new complexity as well. CMP defines 25 message types, including 6 flavors of certificate requests and 4 responses. In addition, CMP specifies complete transactions with response and confirmations. The increase in complexity over PKCS #7 and PKCS #10 has proved to be an impediment to many implementers.

Certificate Management Over CMS (CMC)

The Certificate Management Over CMS (CMC) specification[16] defines a set of message formats that focus primarily on the process whereby applications enroll for issuance of certificates. Two alternative request formats are supported (corresponding response formats are also defined):

- *Simple request:* The request uses the original PKCS #10 object format.
- *Full request:* The request can use PKCS #10 or the same CRMF format as used by CMP in a general envelope.

These objects may be wrapped in CMS protection envelopes to add authentication or encryption protection. Nested enveloping can occur, for example, when a registration authority adds its approval to a user's signed certificate application by further enveloping the user's registration request prior to forwarding to the certification authority. Key updating, key recovery, and cross-certification are all supported but viewed as simple variants of the registration protocol. Message elements to support proof of possession are also defined. CMC also includes such functions as revocation requests, which were not standardized at all in earlier PKCS #7-based and PKCS #10-based systems. In fact, CMC provides all the functions of CMP but employs much more of a box-of-tools approach in comparison with CMP's message enumeration approach. In particular, it is designed to be simple to implement in systems that already have software libraries that implement PKCS #7 or CMS.

There are also two other PKCS-derived certificate management protocols, which were developed as interim specifications in the period when CMC was produced: *Cisco's Certificate Enrollment Protocol* (CEP) and the *Certificate Request Syntax* (CRS) protocol developed jointly by Microsoft, Cisco, Netscape, and VeriSign. The reader may encounter these protocols since they were both implemented in commercial products. Most likely, such products will migrate to CMC in due course.

Server-Based Public-Key Validation

The most challenging part of implementing PKI support in a secure application or communications product is usually the implementation of public-key validation, for example, the processing that needs to occur when a digital signature is being verified and the public key needs to be validated through validation of a certification path. With hierarchical or forest PKI structures, this problem is generally manageable, but with more general structures, the complexity grows enormously. This raises the potential need to off-load the process of validating a public key to a server that specializes in performing this function.

The IETF PKIX Working Group recognized the need for standards to support this approach and currently has an active project on the topic. It may prove possible to provide this function through an extension to the OCSP protocol.

Proposals have also been put forward to facilitate PKI deployment for XML-based applications by defining XML-based message exchanges to support public-key registration and validation. This type of PKI interface is emerging quickly and may eventually supplant the less implementer-friendly protocols of the IETF PKIX community. Server-based validation of public keys will be inherent to this type of solution.

7.7   PGP's Web of Trust

Pretty Good Privacy (PGP),[17] at least in its early realizations, does not use X.509 certificates. It has its own concept of a certificate, which involves a mechanism for taking a PGP public key, computing a PGP signature on that key using another PGP private key, and attaching the signature to the original public key. There is no concept of a certification authority, as such; any PGP user can certify any other PGP user's public key. However, such a certificate is used by a relying party's PGP software only if the relying party has explicitly recognized the signer as a *trusted introducer.*[18]

PGP users can build up certification paths arbitrarily through the entire worldwide community of PGP users. If I, as a PGP user, decide that I have a reliable copy of Vera's public key and that I trust Vera to introduce other users by certifying their public keys, then, on the basis of certificates from Vera, I can build a community of PGP users with whom I can communicate. Conversely, I might be prepared to certify the public keys of my own community of acquaintances to allow people who already have a reliable copy of my public key (and who trust me) to obtain reliable copies of the public keys of my acquaintances. Given that such certifications can be chained or nested, we achieve an ad hoc system for building large communities of PGP users who can communicate with each other, without introducing any formal structure such as a hierarchy of certification authorities. The PGP certification model is known as a *web of trust.*[19]

PGP certificate management is a manual process, in the hands of every PGP user. As a PGP user, I hold in a local stored file called a *key ring* a set of other users' public keys. Stored with each such key are the following indicators:

- Whether or not I consider the key to be valid
- The level of trust that I place in this key for the purpose of its owner certifying other users' public keys

When I decide a key is valid (for example, because its owner gave it to me personally) and accept it into my key ring, I make an independent decision as to whether or not I trust that key for certifying other keys. In fact, I can rate my trust in the key, for certification purposes, at any of four levels:

- *Don't know:* If I flag a key this way, PGP will expressly ask me whether I trust this key for this purpose each time it needs to use this key to verify a certification on another key.
- *No:* PGP will not use a certificate that depends on this key for its verification.
- *Usually:* This flags my trust in the key as being *marginal.* By default, PGP interprets this as follows. One marginal certificate for a public key is not by itself adequate to consider the certified public key to be valid. However, if my PGP software can find two separate marginal certificates for that public key, my PGP software will consider the public key certified as valid.
- *Yes:* PGP will automatically accept and use a certificate that is verified by this public key.

The PGP web of trust allows any entity to act as a certification authority and to issue certificates for any other entity. This model can work well for loosely interacting communities, such as individuals seeking to protect their Internet personal e-mail communications. However, it suffers from the problem of requiring too many individuals to make important decisions regarding trust, leading to a high risk of bad decisions being made in haste or without proper understanding of the consequences. Furthermore, this loose model makes it very difficult to enforce accountability or to efficiently resolve disputes.

A unique feature of PGP is the option of having multiple certifiers certify a public key. This comes into play with *marginal certificates;* typically, two (optionally, more than two) marginal certificates are needed to validate a key. In comparison, X.509 certificates are always signed by a single certification authority. Multiply signed certificates would appear to be advantageous, in that risk is spread across multiple certifiers rather than depending entirely on the diligence and trustworthiness of one certification authority. However, the PGP model is questionable, as there is no mechanistic way of ensuring that the certifiers are independent. Trusting two colluding certifiers, such as two members of the same crime organization, only gives a false sense of security (unless you are also a member of that crime organization). In the casual PGP environment, where the public-key user has the opportunity to personally reflect on the trustworthiness of all certifiers before using a key, the system can work well. However, its utility does not extend to use for e-commerce and other more risk-intensive, automated applications.

X.509 has not moved to include multiply signed certificates, mainly because of many resulting complexities. Suppose different certification authorities are prepared to vouch for different subject attributes, but neither is prepared to vouch for all attributes? Would all certification authorities recognize the same policies for the certificate? What if different certification authorities want to specify different constraints? Could one certification authority revoke the certificate, or would all certification authorities have to revoke simultaneously? It is generally believed that multiply signed X.509 certificates would be so complex that no vendor would be prepared to implement them and no user organization would be able to administer them.

7.8   Some Multienterprise PKI Examples

Many PKIs have been successfully deployed, the majority of them controlled by a single enterprise and used by that enterprise and its affiliated entities. Scalability, however, depends on the establishment of PKIs spanning multiple enterprises. These are some notable real-world examples of multienterprise PKIs:

- Privacy Enhanced Mail (PEM)
- Secure Electronic Transaction (SET)
- Identrus
- The VeriSign Trust Network
- The Federal Bridge Certification Authority
- The Government of Canada PKI

Privacy Enhanced Mail

In 1993, the Internet community completed the development of a set of proposed Internet standards for the Privacy Enhanced Mail (PEM) secure e-mail protocols and supporting PKI.[20] The PEM infrastructure, illustrated in figure 7.4, was hierarchical. While the PEM application did not prove successful in the marketplace, the PKI design is significant since it is the foundation on which most subsequent large-scale PKI development has been based.

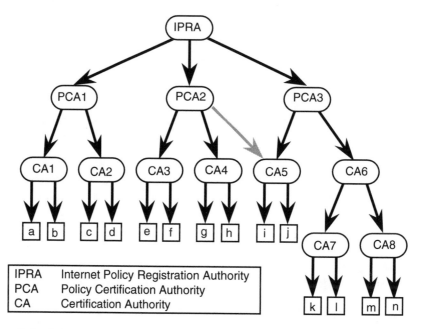

Figure 7.4   Privacy Enhanced Mail (PEM) Infrastructure

The PEM model has three types of certification authority:

- *Internet Policy Registration Authority (IPRA):* This is the top-level certification authority. It was operated under the auspices of the Internet Society, an international, nonprofit organization.
- *Policy certification authorities (PCAs):* Policy certification authorities, at the second level of the hierarchy, are the only certification authorities certified by the IPRA. A PCA must register with the IPRA and publish a statement of its policy on certifying users or subordinate certification authorities. Different policy certification authorities aim to satisfy different user needs. For example, an *organizational* policy certification authority might support the internal security needs of certain commercial organizations, and a *high-assurance* policy certification authority might have a more stringent policy designed for satisfying high-value or high-risk financial transaction requirements. Because every PEM certification path contains exactly one PCA, a certificate user can associate a policy with every certification path.

- *Lower-level certification authorities (CAs):* These certification authorities represent, for example, particular organizations, particular organizational units (such
  as departments, groups, or sections), or particular geographical areas.

There is one variation from the pure hierarchical structure. A certification authority
at the third level of the hierarchy can be certified by more than one PCA (for example,
CA5 in figure 7.4 can be certified by PCA2 as well as PCA3). This makes it possible to
build multiple certification paths, with different policies, for one end entity.

The PEM specification identifies three types of policy that may be associated with
lower-level certification authorities (the policy reflected in a PCA policy statement):

- An *organizational* certification authority issues certificates to individuals affiliated with an organization, such as a corporation, government body, or educational
  institution. *Affiliation* might mean being employed by a corporation or government body or being a student of an educational institution.
- A *residential* certification authority issues certificates to individuals on the basis
  of a geographical address. It was envisioned that civil government entities would
  assume responsibility for such certification in the long term.
- A *persona* certification authority is a special case: A certificate issued by this type
  of certification authority does not claim to associate the name in the certificate with
  a particular person or entity. Such a certificate is designed for a user who wishes to
  conceal his or her identity while making use of PEM data protection services.

The development of the PEM infrastructure raised many important issues and presented solutions to some important problems. One can see in this design, for example, the
forerunner of the certificate policy concept. However, the attempt at real-world deployment of the PEM infrastructure was not successful on a significant scale for various reasons, including the emergence at the time of new e-mail technologies such as MIME.

Secure Electronic Transaction (SET)

The major credit card companies, led by Visa and MasterCard, combined to develop
Secure Electronic Transaction (SET), a comprehensive protocol and infrastructure specification to support bank card payments for Internet-based retailing.[21] The SET environment

includes card issuers, cardholders, merchants, acquirers (financial institutions that support merchants in bank card processing), payment gateways (systems operated by acquirers or other parties to process payments for merchants), and certification authorities.

Public-key technology is used to support authentication of all parties of a transaction to each other plus encryption of all sensitive transaction data. The latter includes protection of payment instructions from cardholder to payment gateway in such a way that bank card numbers are not exposed to merchant systems (where they could be at risk of compromise).

The hierarchically structured SET PKI, which is illustrated in figure 7.5, includes these types of certification authorities:

- *Root certification authority:* The root certification authority is kept offline and is used only to issue certificates for brand certification authorities. The root is out-sourced to an industry-wide trusted third party.
- *Brand certification authority:* Brand owners, such as Visa and MasterCard, oper-ate certification authorities at this level. Each brand has considerable autonomy as to how it manages certificates from this point down.

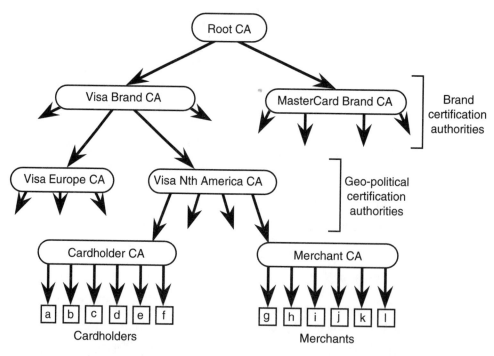

Figure 7.5   SET Public-Key Infrastructure

- *Geopolitical certification authority:* This (optional) level allows a brand to distribute responsibility for managing lower-level certificates across different geographic or political regions. Policies may vary in different regions because of financial system variations.
- *Cardholder certification authority:* These certification authorities issue certificates to cardholders. Certificate requests can be submitted via e-mail or the Web. Depending on brand rules, the certification authority may be operated by an issuer or other party; in the latter case, it is generally necessary for the certification authority to communicate with the issuer to validate cardholder details before issuing a certificate.
- *Merchant certification authority:* These certification authorities issue certificates to merchants, based on approval by an acquirer.

While the success of SET as a commercial application is highly questionable today (at least on a global basis), its supporting PKI architecture represents a copybook example of sound, large-scale PKI design.

Identrus

Identrus, LLC,[22] was formed in 1999 through a partnership of leading international financial institutions, including ABN-AMRO, Citibank, Industrial Bank of Japan, Bank of America, Commerzbank, Natwest Group, Barclays, Deutsche Bank, Sanwa Bank, Chase, Dresdner Bank, Scotiabank Group, CIBC, HSBC, Wells Fargo, and HypoVereinsbank. Identrus's purpose is to enable trusted business-to-business e-commerce, with financial institutions playing the main trust provider role. Identrus aims to foster a seamless commercial process with a single identity, create a means for non-repudiation, and make financial products and services e-commerce ready.

The core of the Identrus solution is an international-scale PKI through which businesses are certified via their financial institutions. The PKI is hierarchically structured, with levels as follows:

- *The Identrus root certification authority:* The root is operated by an outsource provider on behalf of Identrus. Standard systems, procedures, and risk management policies are established at this level. There is an associated repository that provides real-time status of level 1 participants.

- *Level 1 authority:* Major financial institutions that certify level 2 institutions and their own commercial clients
- *Level 2 authority:* Smaller financial institutions that are sponsored by level 1 institutions and that certify their own business clients
- *Businesses:* Commercial customers of level 1 or level 2 institutions that transact business with each other, making use of the Identrus trust services

The Identrus infrastructure provides on-line status of all certificates via OCSP responders operated by all certification authorities.

VeriSign Trust Network

The largest commercial certification authority network, the VeriSign Trust Network,[23] involves VeriSign, Inc., in the United States and a continually expanding network of worldwide affiliates, including such major service providers as British Telecommunications, KPN Telecom, Telia, and CIBC. The network comprises many distinct hierarchical PKIs, of which some are public structures (for example, ones that support SSL Web servers on the public Internet) and the rest are private structures operated on behalf of various private enterprises. The public structures all operate under certificate policies developed and published by VeriSign.

Federal Bridge Certification Authority

The U.S. Government's Federal Bridge Certification Authority[24] represents an experiment that fully exploits the generalized PKI structuring model. The goal is to provide a basis for interoperation among independently established and operated PKIs belonging to various federal departments and agencies and possibly nongovernment entities. The intention is that the Bridge Certification Authority not be a root certification authority, in that it does not start certification paths. It simply connects PKIs (which represent *trust domains*) through the establishment of cross-certificate pairs between the Bridge Certification Authority and a designated principal certification authority in each domain. The Bridge Certification Authority is operated by a Federal Policy Management Authority, which also establishes the requirements for cross-certifying with the Bridge Certification Authority. The architecture is illustrated in figure 7.6.

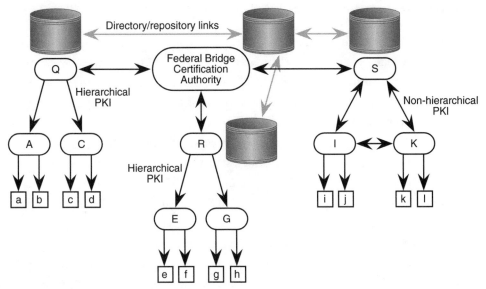

Figure 7.6   Federal Bridge Certification Authority

This project represents one of the first serious attempts to link up *existing* PKIs into a larger structure. The idea is that an agency can cross-certify with just the Bridge Certification Authority, rather than with each agency. Any two agencies that are cross-certified with the bridge can establish trust paths. Subject to certain conditions (such as policy consistency across the domains, which is questionable in practice), this is achievable theoretically. However, it faces many practical difficulties, in particular, the need for special certificate-processing logic in all certificate-using products. In particular, this model demands full implementation of the policy-processing extensions described in section 7.4. Most commercial products are designed to operate with hierarchical and forest models only, where functions such as policy mapping and policy constraints are not used. This concern might eventually be overcome through government-sector market pressures on product vendors. Alternatively, it might be overcome by the emergence of server-based public-key validation, given that inserting special policy rules processing in a server is much easier than in clients.

Government of Canada PKI

The Canadian government has spent several years designing and building a government-wide PKI called the Government of Canada PKI (GOCPKI).[25] This is a hierarchical structure with a root certification authority called the Canadian Central Facility (CCF) and a lower tier of certification authorities operated by departments and agencies. Overall policy is set by a central Policy Management Authority.

The Canadian approach has been more successful than the U.S. approach since it was designed for a large community from day one, with provision for a community-wide policy. This has obviated the need to link up disparate PKIs to establish a government-wide structure, as is being attempted in the United States. However, the GOCPKI still suffers from the limitation that it is a PKI island, whereas requirements arise for interoperation with external PKIs, such as foreign government PKIs or private commercial PKIs. Therefore, the GOCPKI is also exploring ways to establish cross-certification links with other PKIs at the CCF level. The longer-term success of such endeavors remains to be seen.

7.9 Pragmatics of PKI Interoperation and Community Building

PKI interoperation is a complex and groundbreaking undertaking. Its complexity is a function of both technical requirements and legal issues. Given the PKI industry's limited experience with interoperation of *preexisting* PKIs, a modest, incremental approach is suggested. The best starting point is the implementation of interoperation structures based on communities of interest, with a view to eventually extending coverage to global public communities. Regardless of the technical structuring model, meaningful interoperation will find greater relative success if the technical, security, and business controls and other attributes of the interoperating PKIs are more similar than not.

With the experience gained from such implementations, more generalized interoperation practices can be developed and implemented with greater confidence and scope in the future. The emergence of certification authority accreditation and certification infrastructures should simplify harmonized reliable interoperation. Such developments are discussed in chapter 11.

7.10   Summary

A range of infrastructural services of both a technological and legal nature are needed to effectively exploit public-key technologies to their fullest potential in support of e-commerce. These services center around certification authorities and related certificate management facilities. Many issues arise when these services embrace highly diverse organizations and communities that need to work together.

Anyone using a remote party's public key needs to find and validate a certification path, potentially traversing multiple certification authorities, from that public key to a *trust anchor* certification authority whose public key is already held and trusted. The ease of finding and validating certification paths depends on the structuring conventions that govern how certification authorities certify other certification authorities.

The hierarchical model involves a tree structure of certification authorities, with each node certifying nodes at the level below. Each end entity has only one certification path, which starts from the root certification authority. Most real-world PKI deployments use the hierarchical model or a forest model comprising multiple hierarchies.

When the X.509 Version 3 certificate format was developed, a generalized model for PKI structuring was designed, and X.509 now contains a rich set of tools intended to allow any user community to structure the certification authority relationships of its PKI as it sees fit. The two basic challenges faced in the generalized model are how to find a suitable certification path and, having found it, how to validate it. Path finding can be automated, provided that the necessary information retrieval services, such as a directory service, are available. Path validation needs to follow carefully a precise algorithm and needs to be implemented securely.

The generalized model involves advanced features relating to certificate policies and name constraints. Certificate policy (CP) refers to the way a certificate indicates to a certificate user whether or not the certificate is suitable for a particular application purpose. X.509 Version 3 certificates have fields for specifying applicable policies and for mapping one policy to another when a certification path crosses the boundary of an administrative domain. Policy qualifier fields can contain additional information, such as a pointer to the applicable certification practice statement.

When one certification authority certifies another, name constraints allow the former to specify exactly what names are allowed in subsequent certificates, if any, in the certification path. This helps a certificate user by limiting the damage of an erroneous or malicious certification by a distant certification authority.

Various protocols are used for implementing the communications between an application and infrastructural components such as certification authorities. These protocols include RSA Security's PKCS and the IETF standards track protocols CMP and CMC.

Pretty Good Privacy (PGP) specified its own type of certificate, rather than using X.509. PGP also uses a web of trust, in which any user in the community can certify any other user's public key.

Many PKIs have been successfully deployed, the majority of them controlled by a single enterprise and used by that enterprise and its affiliated entities. Some notable real-world examples of multienterprise PKIs are the Privacy Enhanced Mail (PEM) design, the Secure Electronic Transaction (SET) architecture, Identrus, the VeriSign Trust Network, the Federal Bridge Certification Authority, and the Government of Canada PKI.

Notes

1. We discuss PKI practices in detail in chapter 10. Note that the choice of practices is generally independent of the choice of insourcing or outsourcing PKI service. PKI service providers typically offer an option to support a private PKI in which the enterprise specifies its own practices.

2. Requirements for installing and maintaining proprietary software on desktops must be considered.

3. R. Housley, W. Ford, T. Polk, and D. Solo, *Internet X.509 Public Key Infrastructure Certificate and CRL Profile,* Request for Comments (RFC) 2459 (Internet Activities Board, 1999) <ftp://ftp.isi.edu/in-notes/rfc2459.txt>. Note that this document is currently being updated, and a replacement RFC is anticipated in 2001.

4. A minor complication is the possible need to find the highest-level certificate and add it to the presented certificate path, but since such certificates are all issued and managed locally, this is generally straightforward.

5. Another PKI structuring model that has been espoused in the past is *fully meshed top-level cross-certification,* in which the set of root certification authorities of a group of domains all cross-certify each other. This permits building a large, homogeneous community from existing hierarchies. Note, however, that from the perspective of any of the constituent domains, this

model is identical to the domain-controlled cross-certification model described here. Also note that the model cannot be applied recursively, so it does not represent a scalable means of building large PKI communities from smaller ones. Consequently, we consider this model to be of only limited practical utility.

6. For example, a user might trust a certification authority for certifying the commercial Web servers with which he or she regularly transacts low-dollar-value business but not trust that same certification authority with information that could reveal the user's chest of trade secrets. This suggests requirements for the ability to associate different policies with different certification paths, to enforce these policies, and to permit different users to recognize different policies as being acceptable for different applications.

7. The problem can be simpler if structuring restrictions, such as hierarchies, are in force.

8. Readers familiar with computer programming know that we must augment this simplistic description with some checks, including a check to ensure that the algorithm does not enter a loop and a check to ensure that it terminates after searching sufficiently deeply. Furthermore, the search needs to be implemented on a *breadth-first* rather than *depth-first* basis to avoid unnecessarily expending resources to explore unproductive and possibly lengthy paths. In addition, note that this process is impractical if the certification authority population is too large.

9. ISO/IEC 9594-8, *Information Technology—Open Systems Interconnection— The Directory: Public-Key and Attribute Certificate Frameworks,* also published as the ITU-T X.509 Recommendation, details at <http://www.itu.ch>.

10. See appendix H which presents the *PKI Disclosure Statement,* the framework of which can be referenced for such purposes.

11. S. Chokhani and W. Ford, *Internet X.509 Public Key Infrastructure Certificate Policy and Certification Practices Framework,* RFC2527 (Internet Activities Board, 1999) <ftp://ftp.isi.edu/in-notes/rfc2527.txt>.

12. C. Adams and S. Farrell, *Internet X.509 Public Key Infrastructure Certificate Management Protocols,* RFC 2510 (Internet Activities Board, 1999) <ftp://ftp.isi.edu/in-notes/rfc2510.txt>. Note that this document is being updated, and a replacement RFC is anticipated in 2001.

13. M. Myers, C. Adams, D. Solo, and D. Kemp, *Internet X.509 Certificate Request Message Format,* RFC 2511 (Internet Activities Board, 1999) <ftp://ftp.isi.edu/in-notes/rfc2511.txt>.

14. For example, if Tim requested and obtained a certificate in his own name for Louisa's digital signature public key, Tim might subsequently claim convincingly that an item of original intellectual property signed by Louisa was in fact his.

15. For example, the certificate applicant proves the ability to successfully decrypt an encrypted random challenge sent from the registration authority.

16. M. Myers, X. Liu, J, Schaad, and J. Weinstein, *Certificate Management Messages over CMS,* RFC 2797 (Internet Activities Board, 2000) <ftp://ftp.isi.edu/in-notes/rfc2797.txt>.

17. P. R. Zimmerman, *The Official PGP User's Guide* (Cambridge, MA: MIT Press, 1995), details at <ftp://net-dist.mit.edu/pub/PGP>; S. Garfinkel, *PGP: Pretty Good Privacy* (Sebastopol, CA: O'Reilly & Associates, 1995), details at <http://www.ora.com>.

18. As a practical matter, some prominent key holders are widely recognized (even sought after) as particularly trustworthy introducers—effectively, sound root authorities from which to get one's key signed.

19. The web does not necessarily grow in an unbounded way, as users are encouraged to use discrimination in determining which other users they trust as introducers and to limit the depth to which introductions can be nested.

20. S. Kent, "Internet Privacy Enhanced Mail," *Communications of the ACM* 36, no. 8 (August 1993): 48-59; S. Kent, *Privacy Enhancement for Internet Electronic Mail, Part II: Certificate-Based Key Management,* RFC 1422 (Internet Activities Board, 1993) <ftp://ftp.isi.edu/in-notes /rfc1422.txt>.

21. Visa International and MasterCard International, *Secure Electronic Transaction (SET) Specification,* available at <http://www.setco.org>.

22. For information on Identrus, see <http://www.identrus.org>.

23. For information on the VeriSign Trust Network, see <http://www.verisign.com>.

24. For information on the Federal Bridge Certification Authority, see <http://csrc.nist.gov/pki>.

25. For more information on the GOCPKI, see <http://www.cse.dnd.ca/cse/english/gov.html> or <http://www.cio-dpi.gc.ca>.

Legislation, Regulation, and Guidelines

T he widespread deployment of public-key technology and PKI in the e-commerce arena depends as much on the resolution of legal uncertainties as it does on the resolution of technical issues. There are many issues relevant to e-commerce that are at least partially unresolved in the law. Because the most efficient solutions are often best implemented on a systemic or global scale, these uncertainties, if left untreated, will prevent e-commerce from fully exploiting its technological efficiencies. Fortunately, rule makers have made progress and continue to advance their resolution. This chapter discusses recent efforts to reduce remaining legal uncertainties, including U.S. domestic law, international conventions and model laws, guidelines, and model agreements and provisions. First, we describe several legislative and regulatory initiatives, in the United States and elsewhere, that affect e-commerce generally. Then we discuss recent moves to enact legislation regarding digital signatures and the supporting PKI used to protect commercial and governmental transactions. Finally, we discuss various guidelines that articulate usages of trade and recommended conduct and that possess the authority of their sponsoring organizations. Such guidelines are exercising increasing influence within the e-commerce community.

8.1   General E-Commerce Legislation and Regulation

In the early days of the Internet and Web, policy makers were generally slow to recognize the potential and inevitability of e-commerce, but that has since changed dramatically. The focus on these issues is now intensive.

Initially, legislative and regulatory attention on computer-based transactions in the United States focused on electronic funds transfers, through promulgation of and modifications to the federal Electronic Funds Transfer Act, Regulation E thereunder, and UCC Article 4A (funds transfers). The initial focus on funds transfers reflected the financial services industry's early use of computers. Since then, computerization has become prevalent in most sectors, and the development of rules has progressed from exclusively sectoral enablement to general, horizontal e-commerce enablement.

The most widely adopted initiatives contributing to the advance of e-commerce globally focus on ensuring that transactions and records conducted electronically are not the subject of discrimination, that is, are not denied legal effect or enforceability solely because of their electronic form. These initiatives are often referred to as *electronic signature* laws. The first of these international initiatives, the UN Model Law on Electronic Commerce, promulgated by the UN Commission on International Trade Law (UNCITRAL) in 1996, has proved to be extremely influential. Many jurisdictions worldwide have adopted rules based on this model law. In the United States, a majority of the states have now adopted legislation or regulations fairly categorized as electronic signature laws,[1] and many jurisdictions are now considering a model law influenced by the UN Model Law, the Uniform Electronic Transaction Act (UETA).[2] The remainder of this section provides further detail on electronic signature rules.

Beyond the general technology-neutral electronic signature rules are those that address specifically *digital signatures* and provide a framework for and assurances of the reliable use of public-key cryptography and trusted third parties, including certification authorities (discussed at length in other chapters of this book). Digital signature and related rules are addressed in section 8.2.

Electronic Funds Transfer Act and Regulation E

The Electronic Funds Transfer Act (EFTA), enacted in 1978, governs the electronic transfer of funds to or from consumer accounts within the jurisdiction of the United States.[3] Regulation E[4] is the set of provisions that the Federal Reserve System has promulgated to implement the EFTA's regulation of electronic funds transfers.[5] In general, the EFTA and

Regulation E provide consumer protection and allocate liability among e-commerce participants, including financial institutions and the holders of physical tokens such as ATM cards. The EFTA and Regulation E pioneered the development of payment-related e-commerce rules in the consumer realm.[6]

Specifically, the EFTA and Regulation E impose requirements of disclosure and documentation, allocate risk for various mishaps, and establish a dispute resolution scheme. In terms of disclosure, the EFTA mandates that consumers be apprised of their legal rights and remedies regarding electronic funds transfers and the applicable charges. The EFTA and Regulation E give consumers the right to receive documented information on each transfer and periodic statements of account activity.

The EFTA and Regulation E explicitly subject financial institutions to liability for certain mistakes or other mishaps and limit their liability for bona fide unintentional errors. The EFTA and Regulation E also govern the liability of consumers for unauthorized transfers. In general, a consumer's liability for an unauthorized transfer is capped at the lesser of $50 or the aggregate amount of unauthorized transfers occurring prior to the time the consumer gives notice to the financial institution, unless the consumer fails to give timely notice of loss or theft or to report unauthorized transfers appearing on a periodic statement in a timely manner. Apart from these notification requirements, the EFTA and Regulation E impose *no* duty of care on consumers with respect to the safeguarding of access devices.[7] In the absence of other applicable laws, the consumer protections provided by the EFTA and Regulation E obviously have significant implications for e-commerce and its corresponding use of digital signatures and other authorization and authentication mechanisms.[8]

In May 1996, the Federal Reserve proposed revisions to Regulation E that would permit electronic communications to satisfy requirements for *written* disclosure and adopted a version of these proposals as interim rules in March 1998.[9] In late 1999, the Federal Reserve proposed final versions of these rules, as well as similar rules under Regulations B (Equal Credit Opportunity), M (Consumer Leasing), DD (Truth in Savings), and Z (Truth in Lending).[10]

UCC Article 4A: Funds Transfers

Article 4A of the Uniform Commercial Code (UCC) was first promulgated by the National Conference of Commissioners on Uniform State Laws (NCCUSL) in 1989 to address funds transfers, specifically "wholesale wire transfers,"[11] which are often, though not necessarily, effected by electronic communications.[12] The drafters of Article 4A recognized certain problems associated with the extensive use of nonwritten, legally operative communications and accordingly defined and conferred formal significance upon security procedures. Accordingly, Article 4A provided an initially useful model for dealing with the allocation of risk for substantially instantaneous transactions of potentially enormous value. Due to its recognition and focus on electronic media and its emphasis on security, UCC Article 4A has influenced the content and policies implemented in diverse model laws and e-commerce agreements.[13]

In general, Article 4A places considerable responsibility on customers to protect the integrity of security procedures[14] agreed upon with banks. Thus, a payment order is "effective" as the order of a customer, even if it is in fact unauthorized by the customer, if a security procedure is in place that is "commercially reasonable and the payment order is accepted in good faith and in compliance with the security procedure."[15]

Electronic Signature Legislation

Rule-making bodies worldwide have proposed or taken action to give legal effect to e-commerce through *electronic signature laws*. Some of the proposals and laws simply grant *electronic signatures*[16] and electronic records legal validity to an extent no less than traditional signatures and writings. Nonetheless, it is unclear how effective (at least as to their relative enforceability) many of these rules will be unless such electronic signatures provide at least comparable levels of assurances regarding security, authentication, support for non-repudiation, and other reliability attributes provided by traditional signatures.

UCC Draft Revisions

NCCUSL has proposed e-commerce-relevant revisions to various articles of the UCC.[17] Following is a summary of some of the more significant proposals that potentially bear on e-commerce:

- *Article 2—Sale of Goods:* As discussed in chapter 3, the current UCC Article 2 contains a statute of frauds which provides that "a contract for the sale of goods for the price of $500 or more is not enforceable by way of action or defense unless there is some writing sufficient to indicate that a contract for sale has been made between the parties and signed. . . ."[18] The UCC drafters initially proposed a revision essentially repealing the statute of frauds for sales of goods by providing instead that a "contract or modification thereof is enforceable, whether or not there is a record signed by a party against whom enforcement is sought, even if the contract or modification is not capable of performance within one year of its making,"[19] but are now championing a revision that would simply raise the statute of frauds threshold to $5,000.[20] As also discussed in chapter 3, additional proposed revisions would provide for use of the terms *record* instead of *writing* and *authenticate* instead of *sign*,[21] contractual formation in the absence of direct human involvement,[22] and attribution and authentication of electronic messages.[23]

- *Article 2A—Leases:* The UCC drafters are currently considering revisions to Article 2A regarding leases of personal property, which in large part mirror those just described for Article 2 in the context of sales of goods. These include raising the statute of frauds threshold to $1,000,[24] use of the terms *record* in place of *writing* and *authenticate* in place of *sign*,[25] and contract formation in the absence of direct human interaction.[26]

- *Article 5—Letters of Credit:* As discussed in chapter 3, section 3.5, under "Negotiability," proposed revisions to UCC Article 5 would accommodate electronic letters of credit by broadening the definition of *record* and by permitting authentication by means other than a traditional signature.[27]

UCITA

Promulgated in July 1999 by NCCUSL, the Uniform Computer Information Transactions Act (UCITA) was originally drafted to be a new Article 2B of the UCC and was eventually finalized as a stand-alone model law.[28] UCITA governs transactions relating to computer information,[29] for example, transactions in which rights to data or software are licensed or sold. Accordingly, UCITA applies only to these types of transactions, unlike UETA or the UN Model Law, both of which apply to all electronic transactions. With certain exceptions, parties may opt in or out of UCITA.[30] UCITA defines *conspicuous, record* (in place of *writ-*

ing), and *sign*,[31] formation of contracts without direct human involvement,[32] and attribution and authentication of electronic messages.[33]

Whether UCITA will be widely adopted in the United States remains uncertain. Its promulgation by NCCUSL in 1999 (and its first legislative adoptions in March and April 2000 in the states of Virginia and Maryland, respectively) prompted boisterous objections from various groups, including consumer advocacy groups, who asserted that UCITA inappropriately favors software licensers and harms consumers.[34] In any event, UCITA serves as a bellwether for many vexing e-commerce policy issues.

UN Model Law on Electronic Commerce

A 1996 product of UNCITRAL, the UN Model Law on Electronic Commerce seeks to advance the legal standing of e-commerce by removing barriers to computer-based trade. In 2000, legislation based on the UN Model Law on E-Commerce was adopted by numerous jurisdictions worldwide, including the countries of Argentina,[35] Bermuda,[36] Colombia,[37] Hong Kong, South Korea, and Singapore,[38] and the Model Law on E-Commerce influenced legislation in various other jurisdictions, including Australia,[39] Canada,[40] France,[41] and the United States. For commercial parties in jurisdictions that have not adopted the Model Law on E-Commerce, the Model Law on E-Commerce is not binding (unless its terms are incorporated by reference in a trading partner agreement or other contract). Nonetheless, due to its influence, the Model Law on E-Commerce has greatly affected the law of e-commerce and the conduct of e-commerce participants. An outline of the Model Law on E-Commerce appears in figure 8.1 together with a few critical observations about each section, and the complete Model Law on E-Commerce is reproduced in appendix E. *A Guide to Enactment of the Model Law* has been prepared by the UNCITRAL Secretariat and provides particularly useful information about the scope of the Model Law on E-Commerce and its specific provisions.[42]

UETA

The Uniform Electronic Transactions Act (UETA) was formally adopted by NCCUSL at its annual meeting in July 1999.[43] Versions of UETA have since been enacted or proposed in many states.[44] Like the UN Model Law, UETA takes a technology-neutral approach to

Part One. Electronic Commerce In General

Chapter I. General Provisions
Article 1. Sphere of application
Article 2. Definitions
Article 3. Interpretation
Article 4. Variation by agreement

Chapter II. Application Of Legal Requirements To Data Messages
Article 5. Legal recognition of data messages
Article 6. Writing
Article 7. Signature
Article 8. Original
Article 9. Admissability and evidential weight of data messages
Article 10. Retention of data messages

Chapter III. Communication Of Data Messages
Article 11. Formulation and validity of contracts
Article 12. Recognition of parties of data messages
Article 13. Attribution of data messages
Article 14. Acknowledgment of receipt
Article 15. Time and place of dispatch and receipt of data messages

Part Two. Electronic Commerce In Specific Areas

Chapter I. Carriage Of Goods
Article 16. Actions related to contracts of carriage of goods
Article 17. Transport documents

[Future Provisions]

Figure 8.1   Outline of UN Model Law on Electronic Commerce

electronic signatures.[45] Accordingly, jurisdictions adopting UETA ensure that writing and signature requirements will not be barriers to electronic transactions by expressly providing that communications not be denied legal effect because they are transmitted or signed electronically and that courts accept electronic records into evidence on at least the same footing as paper records.[46] An outline and description of UETA's key provisions appear in figure 8.2.

Section 1. Short Title
Section 2. Definitions
Section 3. Scope
Section 4. Prospective Application
Section 5. Use of Electronic Records and Electronic Signatures;
         Variation by Agreement
Section 6. Construction and Application
Section 7. Legal Recognition of Electronic Records, Electronic Signatures,
         and Electronic Contracts
Section 8. Provision of Information in Writing; Presentation of Records
Section 9. Attribution and Effect of Electronic Record and
         Electronic Signature.
Section 10. Effect of Change or Error
Section 11. Notarization and Acknowledgment
Section 12. Retention of Electronic Records; Originals
Section 13. Admissibility in Evidence
Section 14. Automated Transaction
Section 15. Time and Place of Sending and Receipt
Section 16. Transferable Records
Section 17. Creation and Retention of Electronic Records and
         Conversion of Written Records by Governmental Agencies
Section 18. Acceptance and Distribution of Electronic Records by
         Governmental Agencies
Section 19. Interoperability
Section 20. Severability Clause
Section 21. Effective Date

Figure 8.2 Outline of UETA's Key Provisions

U.S. Federal Legislation

Until the enactment of the Federal Electronic Signatures in Global and National Commerce Act (the "Federal E-Sign Act," see appendix B)[47] in 200 0, e-commerce legislation in the U.S. was largely the domain of the individual states. The Federal E-Sign Act prohibits discrimination against electronic signatures and records. It represents a congressional compromise on prolonged discussion and debate regarding various issues, including trade facilitation, federal preemption of state laws, and consumer protection.

The Federal E-Sign Act provides that a "signature, contract, or other record relating to such transaction may not be denied legal effect, validity, or enforceability solely because it is in electronic form..."[49] In addition, it provides that record retention requirements may be satisfied by electronic means, so long as the electronic records are accurate, accessible to persons entitled to access them, and capable of accurate reproduction for later reference, whether communicated by transmission, printing, or otherwise.[50] The Federal E-Sign Act also contains a complex set of consumer disclosure and consent provisions that permit contracting electronically so long as specified procedures are observed.[51]

The Federal E-Sign Act does not address many areas of the law, including wills and trusts; family law matters; much of the Uniform Commercial Code; court orders, notices and official court documents; and essential notices such as for utility services, health insurance and product recalls.

Title III of the Federal E-Sign Act expressly requires the U.S. Secretary of Commerce to "promote the acceptance and use, on an international basis, of electronic signatures in accordance with [certain specified principles] and in a manner consistent with section 101 of [the Federal E-Sign Act]." The principles specified include "(a) the removal of paper-based obstacles to e-commerce by adopting relevant principles from the UN Model Law on E-Commerce, (b) the ability for parties to a transaction to "determine the appropriate authentication technologies and implementation models for their transactions, with assurance that those technologies and implementation models will be enforced," (c) the ability for parties to a transaction to "have the opportunity to prove that their authentication approaches and their transactions are valid," and (d) a "nondiscriminatory approach to electronic signatures and authentication methods from other jurisdictions."[52]

Although the basic intent of the Federal E-Sign Act is admirable, the extent to which it was needed, its scope, and its approach have been debated within the legal and e-commerce communities. Some of the issues of interest to the PKI community include:

- *Preemption of State Digital Signature Laws*—Some legislators and legal pundits argue that the Federal E-Sign Act's preemption provisions are broad and would therefore preempt most, if not all, of the digital signature laws in the various U.S. states.

> **Implications**: If such broad preemption were successful, the PKI oversight and assurance mechanisms provided by the individual states would be scrapped without corresponding Federal substitutes. However, broad preemption is unlikely to happen. The Federal E-Sign Act provides expressly that a "State [law] may modify, limit, or supersede ... *Section 101* ... only if such [law does] not require, or accord greater legal status or effect to, the implementation or application of a specific technology..."[53] The reference to Section 101 in the above sentence qualifies expressly the scope of preemption such that preemption affects only state laws that deny effect to electronic records solely because they are electronic or where they mandate exclusively a particular technology. That is, the preemption provision only affects laws that violate the basic non-discrimination provisions of Section 101. Since most digital signature laws do not discriminate as defined in Section 101, they should not be preempted and should not otherwise interfere with U.S. state certification authority licensing regimes.[54]

• *Preemption and Confidentiality*: More than 10 U.S. states have enacted "digital signature" or "certification authority" licensing or approval regimes. Most of these regimes serve to advance the trustworthiness of certificates that enable at least *two* important and distinct technologies: (1) digital signatures *and* (2) encryption for confidentiality. Although the Federal E-Sign Act addresses only electronic signatures, an overzealous interpretation of its preemption provisions could be used as a pretext to destroy the current licensing/approval infrastructures that support the use of digital certificates to support confidentiality/privacy.

> **Implications:** This may diminish the trustworthiness and effectiveness of the primary (if not the most viable) tool available to ensure confidentiality of Internet communications, resulting in diminished public trust and a corresponding reduction in Internet use. This is a questionable direction to take at a time when privacy vulnerabilities and corresponding concerns of citizens are at an all-time high.[55]

• *Notarial Integrity*: Traditional notary laws are intended to enhance the legal status accorded to notarized documents. Such laws are steeped in controls intended to mitigate fraud and to advance public trust. Examples include requirements for seals, wet signatures, hand stamps, and sealed envelopes. The Federal E-Sign Act not only enables notarial acts to be undertaken electronically (a useful provision), but may remove analogous requirements for trustworthiness (in contrast to traditional practices) when undertaken in electronic form.[56]

> **Implications:** This invites fraud, diminishes legal effect and the *perception of trust* of notarized documents. Consumers could be injured to the extent that they will not be able to prove effectively their documents. Also, since the Federal E-Sign Act endorses electronic signatures without imposing any requisite level of security, it may cause discrimination against notarized paper-based signatures because, unlike electronic notarizations under the Federal E-Sign Act, their paper-based counterparts have the burdens (and benefits) of fraud controls.

- *Oral Communications*: The Federal E-Sign Act does not provide that an oral communication or a recording of an oral communication would satisfy the Act's consumer consent requirements (that is, oral communications are not considered electronic records). (See Federeal E-Sign Act, sec. 101(c)(6).)

> **Implications:** The future of electronic commerce will invariably utilize more voice recording and recognition, particularly in communications with cell phones, PDAs, and automobiles. Nonetheless, the Federal E-Sign Act fails to recognize fully these increasingly important e-commerce technologies.

- *Evidence of Forged or Erroneous Signatures*: The Federal E-Sign Act does not require the retention of information whose sole purpose is to enable a contract or other record to be sent, communicated or received.[57]

> **Implications:** This exclusion would tend to apply to digital certificates and to other vital information (including "meta" data) that would allow false or fraudulent signatures to be detected. This invites fraud to the extent that the traditional tools used in tracing the origin and assuring the integrity of a document are not required to be retained. The victim of a forgery may no longer have important evidence to protect himself or herself.

EU Electronic Signature Directive

In December 1999, the European Parliament adopted the EU Directive on a Community Framework for Electronic Signatures.[58] The EU Directive requires EU member states to ensure that their respective national legal regimes comply with the principles established in the EU Directive. The EU Directive incorporates the broad, technology-neutral approach of the UN Model Law on Electronic Commerce but also addresses specifically "secure-signature" technologies (such as digital signatures). The EU Directive provides for, among other things, the legal effectiveness and admissibility of electronic signatures (with

Article 1. Scope
Article 2. Definitions
Article 3. Market access
Article 4. Internal market principles
Article 5. Legal effects of electronic signatures
Article 6. Liability
Article 7. International aspects
Article 8. Data protection
Article 9. Committee
Article 10. Tasks of the committee
Article 11. Notification
Article 12. Review
Article 13. Implementation
Article 14. Entry into force
Article 15. Addresses

Annex   I. Requirements for qualified certificates
Annex II. Requirements for certification-service-providers issuing
           qualified certificates
Annex III. Requirements for secure signature-creation devices
Annex IV. Recommendations for secure signature verification

Figure 8.3 Outline of the EU Directive

favorable presumptions applying where "advanced electronic signatures" are based on "qualified certificate[s]" and created by "secure-signature-creation device[s]"[59]), limitations on liability for certification authorities,[60] and privacy of personal information.[61] An outline of the EU Directive appears in figure 8.3.

Standards to implement the EU Directive are under development.[62]

UN Draft Model Law on Electronic Signatures

The UNCITRAL Working Group on Electronic Commerce has drafted a Model Law on Electronic Signatures.[63] UNCITRAL's purposes in preparing the UN Model Law on

Article 1. Sphere of application
Article 2. Definitions
Article 3. Equal treatment of signatures technologies
Article 4. Interpretation
Article 5. Variation by agreement
Article 6. Compliance with a requirement for a signature
Article 7. Satisfaction of article 6
Article 8. Conduct of the signatory
Article 9. Conduct of the certification service provider
Article 10. Trustworthiness
Article 11. Conduct of the relying party
Article 12. Recognition of foreign certificates and electronic signatures

Figure 8.4   Outline of the Draft UN Model Law on E-Signatures

E-Signatures include the international harmonization of laws "supporting certification processes, including emerging digital authentication and certification technology; the applicability of the certification process; the allocation of risk and liability of users, providers and third parties in the context of the use of certification techniques; the specific issues of certification through the use of registries; and incorporation by reference."[64] The UN Model Law on E-Signatures transcend the UN Model Law on Electronic Commerce by addressing issues that are primarily relevant to certification series providers and PKIs despite the express media-neutrality of the rules.[65]

The draft UN Model Law on E-Signatures currently contains the provisions shown in figure 8.4.[66]

Article 1 is consistent with other e-commerce initiatives such as the UN Model Law on Electronic Commerce in that it expressly provides that the UN Model Law on E-Signatures does not preempt consumer protection laws. Article 5 also follows prior e-commerce initiatives by advancing party autonomy, or the ability of particular contracting parties to "contract around" certain provisions of the UN Model Law on E-Signatures.

In addition, the UN Model Law on E-Signatures break new ground at the international policy level in several notable respects. Most importantly, although prior initiatives provided a framework for the legal rights and obligations of signatories, certification authorities, and relying parties in the context of digital signatures,[67] Articles 8 through 11 of the UN Model Law on E-Signatures address essential aspects of the conduct of the parties. These provisions may be of particular importance as general "gap fillers" for diverse forms of secure e-commerce. Finally, Article 13 of the UN Model Law on E-Signatures explicitly provides for the recognition of electronic signatures across jurisdictional boundaries. These policy innovations are influencing the international debate and the substance of national rule making.

8.2 Digital Signature Laws

New legislation such as UETA, UCITA, and the Federal E-Sign Act in the United States can effectively resolve many legal uncertainties, for example, whether certain electronic communications satisfy "writings" requirements. Incremental modifications to existing law, such as definitive court rulings[68] and proposed revisions in the United States to the UCC, also contribute to resolving such uncertainties. Nonetheless, aside from explicit contractual provisions among transacting parties and service providers, the most unequivocal method of addressing the legal uncertainties of digital signatures and PKI is *digital signature legislation.* Various jurisdictions have enacted or proposed such legislation. At a minimum, such legislation stipulates that electronic communications and records that are signed with digital signatures are, under certain circumstances, at least as legally valid and enforceable as traditionally signed documents. Other digital signature laws not only address the validity, enforceability, and evidentiary value of digitally signed messages and records but also establish comprehensive PKI legal regimes that address such issues as certification authority quality and trustworthiness, liability of the parties, and specific PKI component requirements, such as for repositories.

In the United States, the state of Utah was the first jurisdiction to enact digital signature legislation.[69] California followed not long thereafter.[70] Many other U.S. states subsequently enacted digital signature legislation of one sort or another or have digital signature law proposals pending in some form.[71] Most of these initiatives were influenced by early work produced by the American Bar Association (ABA) Information Security Committee in the form of its Digital Signature Guidelines, a set of unifying principles underlying digital signature legal issues.[72] Despite the ABA Guidelines' caveat that they are not drafted as model legislative provisions, legislators have given and are likely to continue to give considerable weight to the language and policies of the ABA Guidelines in drafting their own proposals.

Various branches of the U.S. federal government have implemented, studied, or otherwise considered digital signature initiatives.[73] After much consideration, the U.S. Congress declined to adopt a federal digital signature law,[74] opting instead in 2000 to pass the Federal E-Sign Act, a technology-neutral act enabling electronic signatures in general.[75]

Internationally, Germany,[76] Italy,[77] and Singapore[78] were among the first countries to adopt digital signature legislation, and many others have since followed by enacting or proposing statutes, regulations, or executive orders relating to digital or electronic signatures.[79] Many of these initiatives have been influenced by the work of the United Nations, such as the United Nations Model Law on Electronic Commerce and later by its draft Model Law on Electronic Signatures. These efforts have been supplemented by the European Union's Directive on a Community Framework for Electronic Signatures. Although the EU Directive may grant some level of heightened legal effect where digital signatures and public-key infrastructure are employed, neither initiative fully exploits the specific benefits enabled by digital signatures and PKI to the extent that they struggle with the vagaries of *technology neutrality.*[80]

Because e-commerce is a global phenomenon and efficient transjurisdictional secure business benefits by harmonization among relevant laws, the highly divergent legislative approaches to PKI rules (discussed later) create ongoing challenges to global harmonization and interoperation. The following discussion presents an overview of important policy issues addressed by various existing and proposed digital signature laws.

Scope and Detail

Policy makers have espoused different approaches regarding the scope and detail of digital signature legislation. As noted earlier, some legislators and pundits have urged (often successfully) that electronic signature legislation should not be *so* comprehensive and detailed that it becomes burdensome and unworkable, but rather prefer a so-called *minimalist* approach which tends to simply prohibit discriminatory treatment against electronic sigantures and records and perhaps delegates some limited rule-making authority to an appropriate administrative entity. In addition, some states have opted to create digital signature rules limited only to public-sector matters.

An example of the minimalist approach is provided by the California Digital Signature Act. This very brief law reads simply as follows:

16.5. Use of digital signature.

(a) In any written communication with a public entity, as defined in Section 811.2, in which a signature is required or used, any party to the communication may affix a signature by use of a digital signature that complies with the requirements of this section. The use of a digital signature shall have the same force and effect as the use of a manual signature if and only if it embodies all of the following attributes:

(1) It is unique to the person using it.

(2) It is capable of verification.

(3) It is under the sole control of the person using it.

(4) It is linked to data in such a manner that if the data are changed, the digital signature is invalidated.

(5) It conforms to regulations adopted by the Secretary of State.

(b) The use or acceptance of a digital signature shall be at the option of the parties. Nothing in this section shall require a public entity to use or permit the use of a digital signature.

(c) Digital signatures employed pursuant to Section 71066 of the Public Resources Code are exempted from this section.

(d) "Digital signature" means an electronic identifier, created by computer, intended by the party using it to have the same force and effect as the use of a manual signature.[81]

The California Digital Signature Act illustrates how, despite the flexibility of minimalist legislation, it tends to leave many important issues unaddressed. For example, restricting the effect of digital signature legislation only to certain public-sector activities or interaction between private and public entities limits the benefit and leaves some of the most significant barriers and problems unresolved or even untouched. The California Digital Signature Act, in an effort to be more technology neutral, has adopted a definition of *digital signature* that is inconsistent with any generally accepted technical definition. Digital signature technology is simply too new and complex to assume that existing law provides an adequate legal framework for the coordinated and controlled implementation of a reliable public-key infrastructure.

A comprehensive approach to digital signature law was first enacted as the Utah Digital Signature Act, an outline of which follows:

Part 1. Title, Interpretation, and Definitions

Part 2. Licensing and Regulation of Certification Authorities

Part 3. Duties of Certification Authority and Subscriber

Part 4. Effect of a Digital Signature

Part 5. State Services and Reorganized Repositories

The breadth of coverage of the Utah act and other comprehensive legislation such as the Washington Electronic Authentication Act is presented in the following subsections.

Perhaps a widely acceptable compromise to these divergent legislative approaches might be to create some PKI-specific "gap-filler" provisions that would be akin in approach to those included within Article 2 of the UCC or the Draft U.N. Model Law on Electronic Signatures. Such gap fillers would at least address the most essential (and widely recognized) rights and obligations of certification authorities, subscribers, and relying parties. Examples of possible gap-filler provisions that appear in the UN Model Law on Electronic Signatures provide that, absent agreement to the contrary,

- a certification service provider would be required to act in accordance with its representations and utilize trustworthy systems,[82]
- subscribers would be required to exercise reasonable care to avoid unauthorized use of their private keys,[83] and
- relying parties would be required to bear the legal consequences of failing to take reasonable steps to verify an electronic signature's reliability.[84]

Writings and Signatures

At a minimum, a digital signature act grants validity and enforceability to electronic messages or records transmitted or archived using digital signature technology. Beyond this threshold objective, policy makers must determine what strength and assurances of the digital signatures should be required to satisfy the legal form requirements for such diverse records and transactions as an electronic offer, acceptance of contract, an electronic filing, or the notice of other electronic records or documents. Furthermore, rule makers must resolve requirement to evoke presumptions regarding the enforceability and strong evidentiary value of such messages and records.

Sections 300, 320, and 330 of the Washington act are representative of various digital signature laws:[85]

> Satisfaction of signature requirements. (1) Where a rule of law requires a signature, or provides for certain consequences in the absence of a signature, that rule is satisfied by a digital signature if: (a) the digital signature is verified by reference to the public key listed in a valid certificate issued by a licensed certification authority; (b) the digital signature was affixed by the signer with the intention of signing the message; and (c) the recipient has no knowledge or notice that the signer either: (i) breached a duty as a subscriber; or (ii) does not rightfully hold the private key used to affix the digital signature.
>
> Digital message as written on paper. . . . A message is as valid, enforceable, and effective as if it had been written on paper, if it: (1) bears in its entirety a digital signature; and (2) that digital signature is verified by the public key listed in a certificate that: (a) was issued by a licensed certification authority; and (b) was valid at the time the digital signature was created.
>
> Digital message deemed original. A digitally signed message shall be deemed to be an original of the message.

The significance of granting statutory validity to electronic messages. records, and signatures as valid writings and signatures was highlighted in chapter 3 in the discussion regarding statutes of frauds. Digital signature legislation should address this subject so long as statutes of frauds continue to exist (and create uncertainty and unintended legal disabilities).[86] The laws of most jurisdictions provide other legal requirements for traditional paper writings and signatures such as for certain notices to consumers.[87] Regarding evidentiary value, presumptions may also be added to shift burdens of proof to a designated party.[88]

Certification Authority Quality and Standards

Certain digital signature laws, such as the original Utah act, initially sought to address certification authority quality by restricting licensure of certification authorities to governmental entities, attorneys, financial institutions, and other fiduciaries. Most statutes and proposals recognize, however, that such restrictions inappropriately exclude most of the information technology industry. Thus, they do not restrict licensure to such parties, but rather restrict it on the basis of general trustworthiness,[89] which is typically a function of risk management including security standards; proper financial resources; bonding; and insurance.[90] As an alternative to (or in support of) licensing, many jurisdictions are considering the benefits of assessment and accreditation regimes to determine the quality and trustworthiness of certification authorities, PKIs, and certificates. This is discussed in chapter 11.

The more comprehensive digital signature rules address, among other things, the publication of policies and practice statements,[91] record retention,[92] representations and warranties implied by a certificate,[93] and revocation, suspension, and expiration of certificates.[94]

Subscriber Requirements

Digital signature legislation may address the duties of and rules applicable to PKI subscribers as well as to certification authorities. For example, legislation of this sort typically imposes duties on subscribers to use trustworthy systems,[95] to safeguard their private keys,[96] and to initiate suspension or revocation upon private key compromise.[97]

Apportionment of Liability

Perhaps the most significant and controversial issue of digital signature legislation is who should bear liability, and to what extent, for the damages resulting from reliance on erroneous certificates. The potential bearers of these costs, or liabilities, include certification authorities, subscribers, and parties who rely on the erroneous certificates.[98] As the party that issues certificates, the certification authority may often be one of the primary targets for redress. This burden may be shifted (to some extent) to other parties by statute, case law, and contract.[99] Two related questions are: Should liability be apportioned by statute, and if so, in what manner?

Some commentators and policy makers have contended that it is premature to address liability issues because digital signature technology and the PKI industry are so new that the implications of allocating costs are not sufficiently understood.[100] Such a position has parallels to that taken by certain advocates of a minimalist (or, in some cases, a technology-neutral) approach to e-commerce rules.[101]

To the extent that PKI warrants promotion or fair use through legislated apportionment of liability, the issue then becomes what allocation schemes will be most efficient to encourage the deployment of PKI and distribute risk fairly. The Utah act provided one model under which a licensed certification authority that complies with "all material requirements" of the act enjoys a "safe harbor" from consequential damages specifically and from all other liability in excess of reliance limits stated in the certificate, even if the certification authority itself has been negligent. Other initiatives, including the Washington act, have followed:

> [U]nless a licensed certification authority waives application of this subsection, a licensed certification authority is:
>
> (a) Not liable for any loss caused by reliance on a false or forged digital signature of a subscriber, if, with respect to the false or forged digital signature, the certification authority complied with all material requirements of this chapter;
>
> (b) Not liable in excess of the amount specified in the certificate as its recommended reliance limit for either: (i) a loss caused by reliance on a misrepresentation in the certificate of any fact that the certification authority is required to confirm; or (ii) failure to comply with [the statutory rules regarding issuance of certificates];
>
> (c) Not liable for (i) punitive or exemplary damages . . . or (ii) damages for pain and suffering.[102]

In similar style, the EU Directive states:

> As a minimum, Member States shall ensure that by issuing a certificate . . . a certification-service-provider is liable for damage caused to any [party] who reasonably relies on that certificate . . . unless the certification-service-provider proves that he has not acted negligently.[103]

This provision effectively amounts to a legislative determination that the duties established in the statute for certification authorities constitute a complete recitation of the duties of a certification authority so as not to be held negligent in the performance of its services.[104] Accordingly, if a certification authority complies with the material requirements of the statute, it will have satisfied its obligations and therefore should not be further subject to liability for its acts or omissions.[105]

Various commentators have questioned the propriety of this approach. They suggest, for example, that the Utah model does not adequately protect the interests of consumers or unsophisticated users, particularly regarding damages resulting from the compromise of the subscriber's private key.[106] This requires scrutiny of what precautions are reasonable to expect a subscriber to take to safeguard the private key and the effectiveness of those precautions, among other issues.

Various analogies can be drawn to existing liability schemes, including those imposed by the Electronic Funds Transfer Act (EFTA). The EFTA and Regulation E thereunder incorporate policy determinations that, in the context of credit card and other transactions involving financial institutions, consumers should be asked to bear only $50.00 of loss due to fraud (as long as they take proper steps to report). Some commentators have suggested that a similar limitation should be adopted in the allocation of liability in PKIs. Nonetheless, most recognize that significant differences between the institutions and transactions that the EFTA was designed to govern and those involved in PKI justify a modified, if not altogether different, approach. These differences include the ready availability of insurance (including federal insurance) for financial institutions, the fact that certification authorities may have neither comparable control over nor financial interest in the underlying transactions, and that certification authorities can be information utilities that are exploited for diverse applications that may not necessarily share common attributes, risk models, economics, and technologies with credit card services.[107]

Ultimately, the widespread implementation of PKI may depend, in part, on how these concerns are addressed. If the liability risks are too high or uncertain for certification authorities, they will be unwilling to enter the market or provide PKI services at reasonable costs. On the other hand, if consumers (or even sophisticated subscribers) perceive that use of the technology will subject them to unacceptable risks, they will not become involved until they perceive that such risks have been satisfactorily mitigated.

Some nations and U.S. states continue to advance digital signature legislation. Ultimately, private market needs for harmonization will likely lead to greater uniformity among jurisdictions in their different policy approaches. In the interim, the development of digital signature legislation will continue to challenge the legal treatment of secure e-commerce.

8.3   General E-Commerce Guidelines

Various guidelines are influential in the e-commerce community. Guidelines articulate usages of trade and recommended conduct and possess the authority of their sponsoring organizations. In fact, in the "light-speed" world of e-commerce, where the technology has generally outpaced the law, guidelines have been remarkably influential and have arguably served as *de facto* rules. They have sometimes served as industry-based initiatives to preempt government regulation. Various e-commerce guidelines may address, for example, general on-line business principles, advertising, consumer protection, or dispute resolution, or may focus on the needs of a particular market, technology, or sector. Also, guidelines may address the conduct of particular parties in different relationships, such as business-to-business, business-to-consumer, consumer-to-consumer, or government-to-consumer. The following guidelines exemplify important contributions and initiatives:

- *The Uniform Rules of Conduct for Interchange of Trade Data by Teletransmission (UNCID):*[108] This document, published in 1988, was the product of a collaborative effort directed by the International Chamber of Commerce (ICC). Of historical significance, UNCID constitutes a code of conduct or set of guidelines for EDI users, with specific focus on security and other communications aspects of trade data such as verification of a sender's identity, acknowledgment of receipt, confirmation of content, encryption or other methods of confidentiality, and storage of data. In many respects, UNCID influenced the development of the early significant EDI trading partner agreements and basic e-commerce principles.

- *OECD Guidelines:* The Organisation for Economic Co-operation and Development (OECD) has developed a number of guidelines and guideline-like documents addressing a broad range of e-commerce issues, including "Building Trust for Users and Consumers," "Establishing Ground Rules for the Digital Marketplace," "Enhancing the Information Infrastructure for Electronic Commerce," and "Maximising the Benefits."[109]

- *Better Business Bureau BBB OnLine Code of Online Business Practices:* These are guidelines "designed to guide ethical 'business to customer' conduct in electronic commerce [and] represent sound online advertising and selling practices that the Better Business Bureau (BBB) and BBB OnLine believe will boost customer trust and confidence in online commerce."[110] The guidelines contain five sections: truthful and accurate communications, disclosure, information practices and security, customer satisfaction, and children.

- *Guidelines for Merchant-to-Consumer Transactions:* The Electronic Commerce and Consumer Protection Group, an e-commerce industry group, has produced consumer protection guidelines to advance industry self-regulation. The guidelines contain the following sections: scope and definitions; merchant contact information; marketing practices; information about goods and services; information about the transaction; cancellation, return, and refund policies; packaging; security; customer service and support; warranty; privacy; self-regulatory programs; dispute resolution; and effective enforcement.[111]
- *E-Terms:*[112] E-Terms is an initiative within the ICC to develop an Internet-accessible registry of e-commerce trade rules and provisions to serve both as a source for particular legal provisions and definitions that parties may specifically reference and incorporate into agreements and as a codification of standard, worldwide e-commerce trade practices.[113] Additionally, the e-Terms repository can enhance assurances that terms are available and accessible since the repository can supplement e-commerce company repositories as a redundant source of such terms. To an extent, e-Terms extends the concept of the existing *Incoterms* program of the ICC for traditional, paper-based trade.[114]

8.4   PKI-Related Standards and Guidelines

This section introduces other guidelines and standards that have contributed to or promise to contribute to trustworthy PKI and secure e-commerce.[115] Some of these specifications relate to particular vertical markets only.

American Bar Association Digital Signature Guidelines

The American Bar Association's Information Security Committee, Section of Science and Technology, published the Digital Signature Guidelines (ABA Guidelines) in 1996.[116] Although widely recognized as the seminal source of PKI law and practices, the ABA Guidelines do not purport to be a model PKI law, but rather "general statements of principle, intended as a common framework of unifying principles that may serve as a common basis for more precise rules in various legal systems."[117] The ABA Guidelines have most likely influenced *all* digital signature legislation and guidelines[118] and certification policies and practices. An outline of the ABA Guidelines is provided in figure 8.2. Several of its specific provisions are discussed or annotated in this book.

General Usage for International Digitally Ensured Commerce

In 1997, the International Chamber of Commerce published the document General Usage for International Digitally Ensured Commerce (GUIDEC).[119] In many respects, the GUIDEC extended the ABA Guidelines and sought to "serve as a guide to background, core concepts and best practices in the use of digital signatures, viewed from an international business perspective." The GUIDEC claims to provide "insight into the growth and use of the medium, its relationship to differing legal systems, and application in an international context."

IETF Certificate Policy and Practices Framework

In 1999, the IETF published a checklist of the categories of information that might be addressed in a certificate policy (CP) or certification practice statement (CPS) in Informational Request for Comments (RFC) 2527, titled *"Internet X.509 Public Key Infrastructure Certificate Policy and Certification Practices Framework."*[120] The stated purpose of this document is not to define particular CPs or CPSs per se. Rather, RFC 2527 aims to identify the elements of a CP or CPS that, taken together, facilitate a comprehensive expression of PKI trustworthiness. It also facilitates comparisons of certification practices for interoperation purposes. The RFC 2527 framework has become a widely adopted industry guideline.

RFC 2527 divides CP or CPS provisions into eight major sections:

1. Introduction
2. General Legal and Business Provisions
3. Initial Validation of Identity and Authority
4. Certificate Life Cycle Operational Requirements
5. CA Facility and Management Controls
6. Technical Security Controls
7. Certificate and CRL Profiles

Part 1: Definitions
Part 2: General Principles
Part 3: Certification Authorities
Part 4: Subscribers
Part 5: Relying on Certificates and Digital Signatures

Figure 8.5   Outline of ABA Digital Signature Guidelines

8. Specification Administration

American Bar Association PKI Assessment Guidelines

The PKI Assessment Guidelines (PAG)[121]—an ongoing work product of the ABA Information Security Committee, Section of Science and Technology—address the development of PKI policy and assessment criteria and provide a framework and intellectual underpinnings for assessing a PKI and its components, both PKI products and managed services. It also promotes interoperation between PKIs, introduces basic PKI assessment models including relevant terminology advances the legal-technical interface, provides guidelines for drafting and assessing CPs and CPSs and user agreements, and provides a rich interdisciplinary educational resource valuable to both specialists and neophytes.[122] The PAG is neither a CP nor a profile governing a particular PKI implementation. Rather, it serves as a restatement of developing and recognized policy and practices governing the PKI environment. The PAG is intended to become a living resource that will be updated to reflect new PKI developments and practices.

British Standard BS 7799-1:1999: A Code of Practice for Information Security Management

British Standard BS 7799 presents a "comprehensive set of controls comprising the best information security practices in current use . . . in industry and commerce."[123] Articulating more than 100 controls, it contains the following 10 sections:

1. Security policy

2. Security organization

3. Asset classification and control

4. Personnel security

5. Physical and environmental security

6. Communications and operations management

7. Access control

8. System development and maintenance

9. Business continuity management

10. Compliance

Regarding security for application systems and PKIs, BS 7799 includes general guidance for data encryption, digital signatures, message authentication, and non-repudiation.[124] Its requirements have been increasingly reflected in certification practice guidelines, standards, and audit control objectives standards.[125]

Standard Qualified Certificate Policy for Certification Service Providers Issuing Qualified Certificates

The mandate of the European Union's Directive on a Community Framework for Electronic Signatures[126] identifies a special form of electronic signature that is based on a *qualified certificate*. The qualified certificate provides the underpinnings for a class of signatures that are attributed special legal status and that are deemed to satisfy the requirements for traditional paper-based signatures. Annex II of the directive specifies requirements on certification service providers (CSPs) issuing qualified certificates. These requirements are further articulated in a draft European Telecommunications Standard Institute (ETSI) standard, the Standard Qualified Certificate Policy for Certification Service Providers Issuing Qualified Certificates,[127] in accordance with the Directive. It is intended to have broad applicability and deliberately focuses on requirements that are purportedly unbounded by specific technical solutions. The standard's importance transcends the European theater because of its impact on foreign recognition and interoperation between the EU and foreign entities and their certificates.

Federal Information Processing Standard Publication 140

FIPS PUB 140-1, *Security Requirements for Cryptographic Modules,* (or its successor FIPS PUB 140-2) is of core importance to PKI security, particularly for the assured protection of private keys.[128] This standard specifies the security requirements that are to be satisfied by a cryptographic module that protects sensitive information in computer and telecommunication systems. Four security levels are specified for each of 11 requirement areas. Each security level offers incrementally increased security to allow cost-effective solutions that are appropriate for different degrees of data sensitivity and application environments.

CS2: Practical Commercial Protection

The CS2 protection profile specifies "near-term achievable, security baselines using commercial off-the-shelf (COTS) information technology." CS2 couples this functionality with assurances selected to provide a maximum amount of confidence consistent with (1) existing best practices for COTS development and (2) no extensive (and hence costly) third-party evaluation."[129] CS2 is highlighted because of its early adoption as the primary security assessment criteria under some governmental PKI licensing and approval regimes, such as under the Washington Digital Signature Act's regulation.[130] Nonetheless, the overall trend in PKI assessment and licensing is toward more robust and PKI-specific regimes.

WebTrust Principles and Criteria for System Reliability

American Institute of Certifed Public Accountants (AICPA) WebTrust[131] is a framework for practitioners licensed by WebTrust to assess the adequacy and effectiveness of the controls employed by certification authorities. These principles and criteria are intended to provide assurance services that are ultimately manifested in a WebTrust seal to be displayed by accepted entities.

Illustrative practitioner's reports are also included. WebTrust, an adaptation of the AICPA's Statement on Standards for Attestation Engagements (SSAE 1), seeks to replace the Statement of Auditing Standards No. 70 (SAS 70)[132] as the current top-tier standard for high-trust assessment of PKIs.

Financial Services Industry Documents

Standards or guidelines targeted at financial services applications include these:

- *X9.79: Public Key Infrastructure—Practices and Policy Framework:* This standard describes PKI components and "sets a framework of practices and policy requirements for deploying PKI *within the financial services industry.* It further identifies control objectives and procedures for the operational practices relative to industry accepted information systems control objectives."[133] This standard will most likely become influential and adopted widely.
- *Certification Authority Rating and Trust (CARAT):* Developed under the auspices of the National Automated Clearing House Association, these guidelines seek to govern the use of identity-based public key certificates.[134] They give particular focus to (and advocacy for) "closed" business models and PKI architectures.

Health Care Industry Documents

E-commerce in health care is receiving increasing attention because of statutory mandates for the protection of personally identifiable health information. While this is a developing area, its requirements are solidifying. In the United States, the most critical health care guidelines and standards activities focus on interpreting and implementing the impending privacy, security, and electronic signature regulations under the Health Insurance Portability and Accountability Act (HIPAA).[135] Significant documents include these:

- *Electronic Transactions Criteria for the Healthcare Industry; EHNAC Security Criteria:* The Electronic Health Network Accreditation Commission (EHNAC)[136] has developed various health care-related criteria and assessment regimes for the assessment of health information systems and networks. EHNAC offers a specific accreditation regime to satisfy the proposed security and privacy regulations under HIPAA.

- *Model Certificate Policy for Healthcare PKI:* This certificate policy, developed by the American Society for Testing and Materials (ASTM)'s E31 committee (on Healthcare Information) subcommittee E31.20 seeks to assure secure and interoperable PKI within the healthcare environment.[137] This draft standard seeks to be responsive to the draft security regulations under HIPAA.

8.5 Summary

There are many issues relevant to e-commerce that currently are at least partially unresolved in the law. Recent efforts to reduce remaining legal uncertainties have been made through U.S. domestic and foreign law, international conventions and model laws, guidelines, and model agreements and provisions.

U.S. legislative and regulatory attention was focused initially on electronic funds transfers, through promulgation of and modifications to the federal Electronic Funds Transfer Act, Regulation E under that act, and UCC Article 4A (funds transfers). There have also been several influential global initiatives that focus on ensuring that electronic transactions and records are not denied legal effect or enforceability solely because of their electronic form. These initiatives, often called electronic signature laws, include the UN Model Law on Electronic Commerce, developed by UNCITRAL. In the United States, many states have adopted legislation or regulations fairly categorized as electronic signature laws, and many jurisdictions have adopted or are considering the adoption of a model law influenced by the UN Model Law and the Uniform Electronic Transaction Act (UETA). The Federal Electronic Signatures in Global and National Commerce Act (the Federal E-Sign Act), which was enacted in 2000, includes the provision that transactions in or affecting interstate or foreign commerce may not be denied "legal effect, validity, or enforceability solely because [they] are in electronic form." In 1999, the European Parliament adopted the EU Directive on a Community Framework for Electronic Signatures, requiring EU member states to ensure that their respective national legal regimes comply with its principles. UNCITRAL is completing a Model Law on Electronic Signatures.

Various jurisdictions have enacted or proposed digital signature legislation. At a minimum, such legislation stipulates that electronic communications and records that are signed with digital signatures are, under certain circumstances, at least as legally valid and enforceable as traditionally signed documents. Some digital signature laws also establish comprehensive PKI legal regimes that address such issues as certification authority quality and trustworthiness, liability of the parties, and specific PKI component requirements, such as for repositories. Jurisdictions with such legislation include many U.S. states and many nations.

Various other guidelines articulate usages of trade and recommended conduct and possess the influence and authority of their sponsoring organizations.

Notes

1. In this context, *electronic signature* typically includes *any* letters or symbols in electronic form executed by a party with intent to authenticate a record. See the discussion of electronic and digital signatures in section 3.3 under "Statutes of Frauds."
2. Adopted by the National Conference of Commissioners on Uniform State Laws in 1999. See <http://www.nccusl.org>.
3. 15 U.S.C. secs. 1693 et seq.
4. 12 C.F.R. part 205, "Electronic Funds Transfers."
5. Defined by the EFTA as "any transfer of funds, other than a transaction originated by check, draft, or similar paper instrument, which is initiated through an electronic terminal, telephonic instrument, or computer or magnetic tape so as to order, instruct, or authorize a financial institution to debit or credit an account" [15 U.S.C. sec. 1693a(6)]. This section goes on to provide an illustrative list of electronic funds transfers, which includes point-of-sale (POS) transfers, ATM transactions, direct deposits or withdrawals of funds, and transfers initiated by telephone. A series of exempt transactions is also enumerated. See also 12 C.F.R. secs. 205.3; Board of Governors of the Federal Reserve System, *Official Staff Commentary on Regulation E* (Electronic Funds Transfers) Washington D.C., Federal Reserve; <http://www.bog.frb.fed.us/> and<http://woodrow.mpls.frb.fed.us/info/sys>.
6. For discussion of the applicability of Regulation E to stored-value cards, see Walter A. Effross, "Putting the Cards before the Purse? Distinctions, Differences, and Dilemmas in the Regulation of Stored Value Card Systems," 65 *University of Missouri-Kansas City Law Review*, 319(1997).

7. Thus, a consumer who writes his or her access code on an ATM card or on a piece of paper kept with the card would not impair his or her rights under EFTA. See Regulation E Staff Commentary Q6-6.5. Washington D.C., Federal Reserve, "The extent of the consumer's liability is determined by the promptness in reporting loss or theft of an access device or unauthorized transfer appearing on a periodic statement. Negligence on the consumer's part cannot be taken into account to impose greater liability than is permissible under the act and Regulation E." Compare this with typical subscriber obligations to protect private keys.

8. Updates, references, and links to news and source materials regarding e-commerce law and policy as they relate to electronic financial services can be found at the Web site of the American Bar Association subcommittee on Electronic Financial Services, <http://www.abanet.org/buslaw/efss>.

9. 61 *Federal Register* 19696 (May 2, 1996); 63 *Federal Register* 14,528 (March 25, 1998).

10. See <http://www.federalreserve.gov/boarddocs/press/Board-Acts/1999/199909012>.

11. Prefatory Note to Article 4A, U.L.A. 28 (1991): 455, 457, available at <http://www.nccusl.org>.

12. Article 4A defines *funds transfer* as "the series of transactions . . . made for the purpose of making payment to the beneficiary of the order" [UCC sec. 4A-104(a)]. Apart from purely financial settlement matters, funds transfers consist principally of payment orders from the originator (or payer) to the originator's bank and thence, with or without the use of intermediary banks, to the beneficiary's bank and ultimately to the beneficiary (UCC secs. 4A-103, 4A-104). A payment order may be "transmitted orally, electronically, or in writing" [UCC sec. 4A-103(a)(1)]. A version of Article 4A has been adopted in all 50 states. See <http://www.nccusl.org/uniformact_factsheets/uniformacts-fs-ucca4a.htm>.

13. For example, Article 4A was influential in the crafting of the UNCITRAL Model Law on International Credit Transfers, U.N. Doc. E.95.V.17 (1992), available at <http://www.uncitral.org>. In addition, section 1.2 of the Model Electronic Payments Agreement incorporates many of the definitions of Article 4A by reference.

14. Section 4A-201 defines *security procedure* to mean "a procedure established by agreement of a customer and a receiving bank" that is implemented "for the purpose of (i) verifying that a payment order or communication amending or canceling a payment order is that of the customer, or (ii) detecting error in the transmission or the content of the payment order or communication." Section 4A-201's illustrative list of security procedure features arguably tend to support the use of public-key cryptographic security mechanisms, although such technology was not specifically contemplated at the time of drafting.

15. UCC sec. 4A-202(b). Interestingly, the "commercial reasonableness" of a given security procedure is a "question of law" [UCC sec. 4A-202(c)]. The Official Comments state that this designation is appropriate because procedures are likely to become standardized and "a question of law standard leads to more predictability concerning the level of security that a bank must offer to its customers" (UCC sec. 4A-203 comment 4. It should be noted, however, that in granting commercial reasonableness "questions of law" status does not reduce the need for plenary trials because the bank must still prove good faith and compliance.

16. Note that a *digital signature* is only one type of *electronic signature.*

17. Many of the UCC Draft Revisions are available online, together with reports and commentary on the debates and progress of the Draft Revisions. See <http://www.law.upenn.edu/library/ulc/ulc.htm>.

18. UCC sec. 2-201.

19. UCC Draft Revisions, sec. 2-201. Note also the accommodation of electronic letters of credit, as discussed in chapter 3 with reference to the UCC Draft Revisions to Article 5.

20. UCC Draft Revisions, sec. 2-201(a).

21. UCC Draft Revisions, sec. 2-102(a)(33) (discussed in chapter 3, section 3.3, under "Statutes of Frauds").

22. UCC Draft Revisions, sec. 2-208 (electronic transactions, formation; discussed in chapter 3, section 3.3, under "Offer and Acceptance").

23. UCC Draft Revisions, sec. 2-212 (electronic messages, attribution).

24. UCC Draft Revisions, sec. 2A-201 (September 1996).

25. UCC Draft Revisions, secs. 2A-103(a)(1) and 2A-103(a)(31).

26. UCC Draft Revisions, sec. 2A-206B.

27. UCC Draft Revisions, secs. 5-102(a)(14) and 5-104.

28. The full text and comments of UCITA are at
    <http://www.ucitaonline.com/ucita.html> or
    <http://www.law.upenn.edu/library/ulc/ucita/cita10st.htm>. For the status of
    state adoption of UCITA, see <http://www.ucitaonline.com/whathap.html>.
    For general information, see George L. Graff, ABA Section of Science and
    Technology, "The Evolution of the Uniform Computer Information Transaction
    Act" (1999). Published by ABA Chicago. Available at <http://www.abanet.org/
    scitech/uccarticle2b.html>.

29. UCITA sec. 103.

30. UCITA sec. 104.

31. UCITA sec. 102(6) ("Authenticate"), 102(14) ("Conspicuous"), and 102(54)
    ("Record"). See discussion in chapter 3, section 3.5, regarding conspicuous-
    ness, particularly in the context of Web-wrap licenses.

32. UCITA sec. 202.

33. UCITA secs. 107 (attribution of electronic records and performance, electronic
    agents) and 108 (authentication procedure).

34. See, for example, Ed Foster, "UCITA Threatens Rights of Consumers in the
    New Age of Electronic Commerce," *Infoworld* (January 7, 2000), available at
    <http://www.infoworld.com/articles/op/xml/00/01/10/000110opfoster.xml>.

35. Presidential Decree No. 427/1998, available at
    <http://www.sfp.gov.ar/decree427.html>.

36. Electronic Transactions Act of 1999, available at
    <http://www.bmck.com/ecommerce/bermuda-eta.doc>.

37. Electronic Commerce Law 527 (August 1999), available at
    <http://www.qmw.ac.uk/~tl6345/colombia_en_final.htm>.

38. 1998 Singapore Electronic Transactions Act, available at
    <http://www.cca.gov.sg/cta/framecontent.html>. For general information, see
    <http://www.uncitral.org/english/status/status.pdf>.

39. Electronic Transactions Bill of 1999 (no. 162, 1999), available at
    <http://www.law.gov.au/ecommerce>.

40. Uniform Electronic Commerce Act, available at
    <http://www.law.ualberta.ca/alri/ulc/current/euecafin.htm>.

41. Electronic Signature Bill (Sept. 1999), available at <http://www.legifrance.gouv.fr/citoyen/actua.htm>.

42. Available from the Secretariat at <http://www.uncitral.org>.

43. The full text and comments of UETA can be accessed at <http://www.law.upenn.edu/bll/ulc/fnact99/1990s/ueta99.htm>. A summary is online at <http://www.nccusl.org/uniformact_summaries/uniformacts-s-ueta.htm>.

44. For a listing of legislative adoptions of UETA, see NCCUSL's Web site at <http://www.nccusl.org/uniformact_factsheets/uniformacts-fs-ueta.htm>.

45. See Amelia H. Boss, "The Uniform Electronic Transactions Act in a Global Environment" (unpublished; a copy is on file with the authors). See <http://www.temple.edu/lawschool/boss.html>.

46. UETA secs. 7 and 13.

47. A copy of this Act appears in Appendix B.

48. Federal E-Sign Act, sec. 101(a).

49. Id. Secs. 101(d), 101(h).

50. Id. Sec. 101(c).

51. Id., Title III.

52. Id., sec.102(a) (emphasis added).

53. This topic warrants much greater treatment. The following white papers analyze extensively the preemption issues: Raymond T. Nimmer, *Electronic Signatures in Global and National Commerce Act of 2000: Effect on State Laws* (Aug. 2000). Available at < http://www.verisign.com/respository/esign >; Amy Carlson, *E-SIGN* (Oct. 2000). Available at < http://www.pkiforum.org >.

54. Nonetheless, the Federal E-Sign Act's performance standards provisions (section 103(3)) may provide at least some modest assistance in support of digital signature standards.

55. The notary provision states, "[I]f a ... law requires a signature or record ... to be notarized ... that requirement is satisfied if the [notarization] is attached to or logically associated with the signature or record." Federal E-Sign Act section 101(g).

56. Federal E-Sign Act, sec. 101(d)(1).

57. EU Directive, article 5.

58. The EU Directive, article 6, uses the term "certification-service-provider."

59. EU Directive, article 8.
60. UNCITRAL Working Group on Electronic Commerce, 36th Sess., U.N. Doc. A/CN.9/467 (2000), available at <http://www.uncitral.org>.
61. UN Model Law on Electronic Signatures, p. 2.
62. See www.etsi.org/sec/el-sign.htm.
63. "None of these Rules, except article 5, shall be applied so as to exclude, restrict or deprive of legal effect any method of creating an electronic signature that satisfies the requirements referred to in article 6(1) of these Rules or otherwise meets the requirements of applicable law" (UN Model Law on Electronic Signatures [February 14–25, 2000], article 3).
64. Articles 2 and 13 of the UN Model Law on E-Signatures were not considered in the March 2000 meetings of the working group and are not included in the document cited earlier as A/CN.9/467. They are available in their December 1999 draft form in UN Doc. A/CN.9/WG-IV/WP.84 (1999), available at <http://www.uncitral.org/en-index.htm>.
65. The multiple-class regime, the debate over and drafting of the rules regarding generic electronic signatures versus "enhanced signatures" has served to advance the international policy discussion on the topic.
66. For example, the ABA Digital Signature Guidelines, discussed in section 8.4, and the Utah Digital Signature Act, discussed in section 8.2, both address these items.
67. See, for example, *In Re RealNetworks, Inc. Privacy Litigation,* 2000 WL 631341 (slip May 8, 2000, N.D. Ill.), which held that Web-based contracts satisfy legal signature and writing requirements.
68. Utah's digital signature bill became law in May 1995. It was subsequently amended in 1996 and 2000. The current version is codified as Utah Code secs. 46-3-101 et seq. (2000), available at <http://www.commerce.state.ut.us/digsig/legal.html>.
69. The California legislature passed its digital signature act in September 1995. It is codified as section 16.5 of California's Government Code.
70. These other states include Georgia, Illinois, Michigan, Minnesota, Nebraska, Nevada, North Carolina, Oregon, Texas, and Washington. For citations and links to these statutes and proposals, see <http://www.mbc.com/ecommerce.html> and <http://www.bakerinfo.com/ecommerce>.

71. See American Bar Association, Information Security Committee, Section of Science and Technology, Digital Signatures Guidelines (1996), at 19, available at <http://www.abanet.org/scitech/home.html>.

72. For example, the first initiative on a federal level was the Decision of the Comptroller General in the Matter of National Institute of Standards and Technology (NIST)-Use of Electronic Data Interchange Technology to Create Valid Obligations, Comp. Gen. File VB-245714 (December 13, 1991). See <http://www.softwareindustry.org/issues/docs-org/cg-opinion.pdf>. Subsequently, in 1994, the NIST commissioned a study of the liability and other policy issues implicated by a possible "federal certification authority." See M. S. Baum, *Federal Certification Authority Liability and Policy,* NIST-GCR-94-654 (Gaithersburg, MD: National Institute of Standards and Technology, 1994), available at <http://www.verisign.com/repository/pubs/>.

73. Much of the behind-the-scenes discussion and delay focused on peripheral issues directly implicated by a federal law, such as the extent to which a federal law would preempt state laws regarding privacy, consumer protection, and writing and signature requirements in interstate commerce, and perhaps most importantly, a policy favoring technologically neutral rules.

74. The theory behind technology neutrality is to enable current authentication technologies without precluding the use of other, yet-to-be-developed but currently unidentified authentication technologies that are equally or more adequate than current ones. Unfortunately, some policy makers with technology-neutral objectives have failed to take advantage of opportunities to give appropriate support and certainty to methodologies and infrastructures (such as digital signatures and PKI) that already exist and are available widely to support the legal and technical security needs of e-commerce. See Michael S. Baum, "Technology Neutrality and Secure Electronic Commerce: Rulemaking in the Age of 'Equivalence,'" available at <http://www.verisign.com/repository/pubs/techneutralityv1_1.doc>.

75. Adopted in 1997. See <http://www.kuner.com> for English translations and explanations of the German ordinances. Revisions are currently under discussion. See <http://www.sicherheit-im-internet.de/download/SigGEckpunkte_eng.pdf>.

76. Italian Law No. 59, article 15, c. 2 (1997) See <http://www.aipa.it>.

77. 1998 Singapore Electronic Transactions Act.

78. These other countries include Argentina, Australia <http://www.ogit.gov.au>, Austria, Bermuda, Brazil, Canada <http://www.cio-dpi.gc.ca>, Chile, China, Colombia, Denmark, Ecuador, Finland, France, Great Britain, Hong Kong, Hungary, India <http://caselaw.delhi.nic.in/incodis/newacts/itbl.htm>, Ireland, Japan, Malaysia, Mexico, Netherlands, New Zealand, Peru, Philippines, Russia, South Korea, Spain, Sweden, and Thailand. See <http://www.mbc.com/ecommerce.html> and <http://www.bakerinfo.com/ecommerce> for a comprehensive summary of electronic signature and digital signature rules.

79. See footnote 74 (considering technology neutrality).

80. California Government Code sec. 16.5.

81. UN Model Law on E-Signatures (2000), articles 9(1)(a) and 9(1)(f).

82. UN Model Law on E-Signatures, article 8(1)(a).

83. UN Model Law on E-Signatures, article 11(a).

84. Rev. Code Wash. secs. 19.34.300, 19.34.320, and 19.34.330. See also UN Model Law, articles 6-9 (discussed earlier in section 8.1), and ABA Guidelines 5.1, 5.2, and 5.5.

85. See comment 5.1.3 to ABA Guidelines 5.1 regarding erosion of statutes of frauds.

86. See, for example, Utah Code Annotated sec. 46-3-401, comment b, which lists numerous statutory requirements for signatures in the Utah Code. Also, see the consumer notice provisions in the Federal E-sign Act.

87. For example, see Rev. Code Wash. sec. 19.34.340, which makes digital signatures self-authenticating by providing that a certificate is an "acknowledgment" under Washington law, and Rev. Code Wash. sec. 19.34.350 (adjudicating disputes-presumptions). See also ABA Guideline 5.6 (presumptions in dispute resolution). The resolution of such presumptions continues to be controversial within law-reform groups.

88. Most digital signature statutes contain provisions to the effect that a "licensed certification authority shall use only a trustworthy system to issue, suspend, or revoke a certificate" Rev. Code Wash. sec. 19.34.200(1). "Trustworthy system" means "computer hardware and software that (a) are reasonably secure from intrusion and misuse; and (b) conform with the requirements established [by

regulations]" Rev. Code Wash. sec. 19-34-020(43). See also ABA Guidelines 3.1 and 1.35 (trustworthy system).

89. For example, ABA Guidelines 3.3 (financial responsibility) provides that a "certification authority must have sufficient financial resources (1) to maintain its operations in conformity with its duties, and (2) to be reasonably able to bear its risk of liability to subscribers and persons relying on certificates issued by the certification authority and digital signatures verifiable by reference to public keys listed in such certificates." Typical of many statutes is Utah's requirement that to obtain and retain a license, a certification authority must, among other things, file with the state a "suitable guaranty" and "present proof to the [state] of having working capital reasonably sufficient . . . to enable the applicant to conduct business as a certification authority" Utah Code sec. 46-3-201(4) and (6). See also Rev. Code Wash. sec. 19.34.100.

90. See chapter 10 regarding certification policies and practice statements. See also Utah Code sec. 46-3-301(2) and ABA Guidelines 3.2 (disclosure) and 3.4 (employees and contractors).

91. See ABA Guideline 3.5 (records).

92. Utah Code sec. 46-3-303 (warranties and obligations of certification authorities upon issuance of a certificate) and sec. 46-3-304 (representations and duties upon acceptance of a certificate). See also Rev. Code Wash. secs. 19.34.220 and 19.34.230; ABA Guideline 3.7.

93. See, for example, Utah Code secs. 46-3-306 through 308, Rev. Code Wash. secs. 19.34.250 through 270, and ABA Guidelines 3.9 through 3.12.

94. See Utah Code sec. 46-3-301(1) and ABA Guideline 4.1 (generating the key pair).

95. See Utah Code sec. 46-3-305 (control of the private key); Rev. Code Wash. sec. 19.34.240 (private key-control-public disclosure exemption); and ABA Guideline 4.3 (safeguarding the private key).

96. See Utah Code sec. 46-3-306 and ABA Guideline 4.4 (initiating suspension or revocation). See also ABA Guideline 4.2 (subscriber's obligations), which sets forth additional duties of a subscriber in various circumstances.

97. One might add certain third-party beneficiaries and society at large to this list under some liability schemes.

98. Certification authorities can shift risk of liability to subscribers directly through subscriber agreements and certification practice statements. Certification

authorities may also seek to shift liability to the relying parties either through disclosures in the certificate itself or through certification practice statements and relying party agreements. The success of this strategy will depend on the extent to which the relying party received "notice" of the reallocation. See chapter 10 regarding certification practice statements and the PKI disclosure statement and section 3.5 regarding notice.

99. For a summary of the arguments on both sides of this issue, see A. M. Froomkin, "The Essential Role of Trusted Third Parties in Electronic Commerce," 75 *Oregon Law Review* 49, (1996): available at <http://www.law.miami.edu/~froomkin/articles/trustedno.htm>.

100. Objections to legislated apportionment of liability do not always stem from a lack of understanding or conviction regarding the value of public-key infrastructure. Devout believers in free-enterprise economics might contend that we ought to allow the market, not policy makers, to determine whether PKI is socially valuable. If it is indeed valuable, competitive market forces will suffice to apportion liability through practices initiated by competing PKIs themselves. Also, certification authorities can offer subscribers different classes of certificates that have differing liability schemes determined by contract. To some extent, this is already occurring. See section 10.1

101. Rev. Code Wash. sec. 19.34.280(2). See also Utah Code sec. 46-3-309(2) (recommended reliance limits and liability) and ABA Guideline 3.14 (liability of complying certification authority): "A certification authority that complies with these Guidelines and any applicable law or contract is not liable for any loss which (1) is incurred by the subscriber of a certificate issued by that certification authority, or any other person, or (2) is caused by reliance upon a certificate issued by the certification authority, upon a digital signature verifiable with reference to a public key listed in a certificate, or upon information represented in such a certificate or repository."

102. EU Directive, article 6.

103. The EU Directive sets forth the *minimum* requirements for EU member states; member states may in fact implement legislation that is more strict.

104. To the knowledge of the authors, no certification authority to date has been the subject of litigation arising from harm suffered by subscribers or relying parties.

105. For example, a hacker might conceivably obtain the private key of a subscriber by means of a virus over the Internet and then employ the private key to transact thousands of dollars of business on the account of the subscriber.

106. These issues are further explored in Michael S. Baum, "Technology Neutrality."

107. ICC, *UNCID: Uniform Rules of Conduct for Interchange of Trade Data by Teletransmission,* ICC Pub. No. 452 (Paris: ICC Publications, 1988).

108. OECD guidelines and reports are available at the OECD Web site, <http://www.oecd.org/subject/e_commerce/>.

109. <http://www.bbbonline.org/businesses/code/draft/index.htm>.

110. See <http://www.ecommercegroup.org/guidelines.htm>.

111. See <http://www.iccwbo.org/home/news_archives/1999/electronic_ contacts.asp>.

112. Recall from discussion in chapter 3 the importance of established trade practices as legally recognized sources of law under the UCC and other commercial laws.

113. International Chamber of Commerce (ICC), *Incoterms,* Pub. No. 460 (Paris: ICC Publications, 1990). *Incoterms* is an international registry of commercial trading rules and contract provisions, for example, the term *F.O.B.* used to specify delivery provisions. The 1990 revision was undertaken primarily to adapt terms to the increasing use of EDI. The ICC has announced a 2000 revision. See <http://www.iccwbo.org/home/incoterms/pdf/English.pdf>.

114. In addition to the standards and guidelines described in this section, other documents that are noteworthy in their influence over PKI developments include the VeriSign certificate policy, certification practice statement, and user agreements at <http://www.verisign.com/repository>; CobiT, "Control Objectives for Information and Related Technology," <http://www.isaca.org/cobit.htm>; "Generally Accepted System Security Principles (GASSP)-Pervasive Principles" <http://web.mit.edu/security/www.gassp1.html>; OECD, *Guidelines for the Security of Information Systems* (Paris: OECD, 1997), <http://www.oecd. org//dsti/sti/it/secur/prod/e_secur.htm>.

115. The ABA Guidelines derive from the ABA's Resolution No. 115 of 1992, which required the ABA to support public and private efforts to "facilitate and promote the orderly development of legal standards to encourage use of infor-

mation in electronic form . . . ; encourage the use of appropriate and properly implemented security techniques, procedures and practices to assure the authenticity and integrity of information in electronic form; and recognize that information in electronic form, where appropriate, may be considered to satisfy legal requirements regarding a writing or signature to the same extent as information on paper or in other conventional forms when appropriate security techniques, practices and procedures have been adopted"
<http://www.abanet.org/scitech/home.html>.

116. ABA Guidelines, Introduction, p. 19.

117. For example, the Certification Authority Guidelines of the Electronic Commerce Promotion Council of Japan (ECOM) (1998). See <http://www.ecom.or.jp>.

118. See <http://www.iccwbo.org/home/guidec/guidec.asp>.

119. S. Chokhani and W. Ford, *Internet X.509 Public Key Infrastructure Certificate Policy and Certification Practices Framework,* Request for Comments (RFC) 2527 (Internet Activities Board, 1999) <ftp://ftp.isi.edu/in-notes/rfc2527.txt>.

120. See <http://www.abanet. org/scitech/home.html>.

121. See draft PAG sec. A.3, version 17 (November 2000).

122. BS 7799, Foreword (1998).

123. BS 7799 secs. 8.2.4-8.2.7. BS 7799 has progressed to an international standard: ISO 17799.

124. For example, ANSI X9.79.

125. Directive 1999/93/EC. The directive was introduced in chapter 3.

126. See <http://www.etsi.org/sec/el-sign.htm>.

127. "This standard specifies the security requirements that are to be satisfied by a cryptographic module utilized within a security system protecting sensitive information. The standard provides four increasing, qualitative levels of security: Level 1, Level 2, Level 3, and Level 4. These levels are intended to cover the wide range of potential applications and environments in which cryptographic modules may be employed. The security requirements cover areas related to the secure design and implementation of a cryptographic module. These areas include cryptographic module specification; cryptographic module interfaces; roles, services, and authentication; finite state machine model; physical security; operating system security; cryptographic key management; electromagnetic

interference/electromagnetic compatibility (EMI/EMC); self-tests; design assurance; and mitigation of other attacks. (FIPS 140-2, Introduction). FIPS 140-2 draft is available at <http://csrc.nist.gov/fips/dfips140-2.pdf>.

128. Gary Stoneburner, "CSPP—Guidance for COTS Security Protection Profiles," Version 1.0 (CS2)(NIST: Gaithersburg, MD, 1999), available at <http://csrc. nist.gov/publications/nistir/ir6462.pdf>.

129. See <http://www.aicpa.org>.

130. CS2 recognizes "two forms of legitimate access, namely, public access and 'authorized users.' With public access, the user does not have a unique identifier and is not authenticated prior to access. An example is access to information on a publicly accessible web page. Such users have legitimate access but are differentiated from 'authenticated' users who are (1) uniquely identifiable by the system, (2) have legitimate access beyond publicly available information, and (3) are authenticated prior to being granted such access." CS2, section 1.2. CS2 claims that compliant products will

- provide the functionality appropriate for controlling a community of benign (i.e., not intentionally hostile nor malicious) authorized users;
- protect against unsophisticated technical attacks by individuals other than authorized users;
- enforce an access control policy between active entities (subjects) and passive objects based on subject identity, allowed actions, and environmental constraints such as time of day and port of entry;
- perhaps enforce information flow control policies at the macro (e.g., domain to domain) level;
- be resistant to resource depletion by providing resource allocation features;
- provide mechanisms to detect insecurities;
- provide mechanisms for trusted recovery in the event of system failure or detection of insecurity; and
- Support these capabilities in a distributed system connected via an insecure network.

131. See Version 1.0 (February 9, 2000) at <http://www.aipca.org>.

132. Accredited Standards Committee (ASC), *X9* (American Bankers Association, Secretariat), section 1 "Scope" (emphasis added). See <http://www.aba.org>.

133. See <http://www.nacha.org>.

134. Public Law 104-191 (August 21, 1996), 110 Stat. 1936, amended the Public Health Service Act, the Employee Retirement Income Security Act of 1974 (ERISA), and the Internal Revenue Code of 1986. See <http://www.hhs.gov>.

135. See <http://www.ehnac.org>.

136. ASTM (American Society for Testing and Materials) E31.20 subcommittee, ASTM Draft Standard 2.1 (ASTM: West Conshohocken, PA) ASTM E31 Committee on Healthcare Informatics, 2000). "This Policy is intended to define minimum requirements that must be satisfied by CAs issuing certificates to healthcare persons for those certificates to be generally acceptable to autonomous healthcare Relying Parties. This Policy assumes that all parties which will participate in the PKI all have healthcare industry roles and responsibilities [such as] mandated [by HIPAA]. This Policy is supplemented by a second more restrictive Policy that is less dependent upon industry oversight for the assurances that it provides." The ASTM E31 Committee on Healthcare Informatics has also developed provisional standards covering access privileges, audit logs, and individual rights, among other things. See <http://www.astm.org>.

Non-repudiation

A communication has the attribute of non-repudiation if it is protected against a successful dispute of its origin, submission, delivery, or content.[1] In other words, non-repudiation offers a party to a communication protection against a false claim by another party that the communication never took place. As a practical matter, non-repudiation is not absolute: It depends on supporting technical, procedural, and legal protocols or mechanisms, including the services provided by a trusted third party. This chapter explains the role of non-repudiation in secure e-commerce and describes how non-repudiation can be supported. The chapter begins by exploring the development of the concepts of repudiation and non-repudiation in both the legal and technological spheres. It continues by examining three major non-repudiation mechanisms in the digital communications context: non-repudiation of origin, non-repudiation of delivery, and non-repudiation of submission. Methods of implementing non-repudiation for secure e-commerce are then discussed, taking into account the roles of public-key infrastructure, time stamping, notaries, and archiving. The chapter concludes with a discussion of issues pertinent to non-repudiation in dispute resolution, with a focus on current evidentiary standards.

9.1 Concept and Definition

In his well-known philosophical treatise on government, Thomas Hobbes declared that without legal or other normative rules imposed by some authoritative entity, the "life of man" would be "solitary, poore, nasty, brutish and short."[2] If legal norms have succeeded in making life any less nasty and brutish than Hobbes supposed, at least part of the improvement stems from the law's ability to restrict deceitful individuals from gaining unfair advantage or from exculpating themselves from wrongdoing through dishonest repudiation of their own statements or actions. The law attempts to circumscribe the unfortunate traits of human nature through

- preventive rules and norms imposed by prescriptive and prohibitory statutes, regulations, and case law;
- the legal recognition of certain practices; and
- enforcement mechanisms designed to prove and penalize deceit according to the rules of evidence and procedure.

An example of a preventive practice recognized by law is the handwritten signature affixed to a written document that is both a cultural norm and a legal requirement.

The human participants in commerce lack perfection in ability and memory, resulting in errors through accident or forgetfulness. Furthermore, some people may lie or attempt deceptive repudiation toward their own ends. For these reasons, non-repudiation has always been essential to the security of traditional commerce. But because of the astonishing transformations of the information age, non-repudiation has become vastly more urgent for the world of e-commerce.

The term *non-repudiation* came into widespread use in the information security field in the 1980s. It was coined in the landmark 1988 ISO standard *Open Systems Interconnection Security Architecture*[3] and has been used since by many international standards. In these technical standards, non-repudiation is typically described as a *security service* that counters repudiation, where repudiation is defined as "denial by one of the entities involved in a communication of having participated in all or part of the communication."

The legal concept of repudiation can be traced through various alternative meanings back to ancient times. A historical analysis of the use of this term in law is presented in appendix I.

Non-repudiation in E-Commerce

For the purposes of this book, we define non-repudiation as an attribute of a communication that protects a party to the communication against false claims by another party that the communication never took place. A correlative meaning of non-repudiation becomes the legal or practical effect of this attribute.

This definition is intentionally broad. For example, compare the definition of *non-repudiation* in the ABA Guidelines:

> Strong and substantial evidence of the identity of the *signer* of a *message* and of *message integrity,* sufficient to prevent a party from successfully denying the origin, submission or delivery of the *message* and the *integrity* of its contents.[4]

The definition in the ABA Guidelines understandably focuses on that which is most significant to the legal community, namely, non-repudiation's evidentiary value in the resolution of a potential dispute. Nonetheless, the term has a much broader meaning for the business and technical communities.

Non-repudiation can be viewed in two ways:

1. A message or party either has or does not have non-repudiation; in a legal context, a party would like to be able to meaningfully ask, "Can we achieve non-repudiation if a dispute arises?"
2. A message or party possesses various degrees of non-repudiation.

In practice, view 2 is more realistic. Accordingly, when considering their legal and practical position in real-world digital transactions, parties are better advised to ask themselves not, "Will we have non-repudiation?" but rather, "Will we have credible evidence to persuade the third-party dispute-resolution authority (for example, judge, jury, or arbitrator) that we have *enough* non-repudiation?" The ultimate dispute-resolution authority must reach a binary yes/no decision—but only after accumulating and weighing multiple pieces of non-repudiation evidence, which may weaken or partially contradict each other.

A legal claim of non-repudiation based on a digital signature relies, in part, on the technology producing a logical and credible inference of non-repudiation. That inference is at least akin to "strong and substantial evidence" of non-repudiation in the dispute-resolution process under ABA Guideline 1.20. The legal regime defines the extent of the procedural advantage of that inference, which includes the following:

- At least an assurance that the inference can be introduced into evidence in the proceeding under the European Union's Electronic Signature Directive[5]

- A presumption that is expressly made rebuttable in the Illinois Digital Signature Law[6] and in the ABA Guidelines[7]
- At most something arguably approaching a nonrebuttable presumption in the case of the Utah Digital Signature Law[8] and the German Digital Signature Law[9]

The relationship of non-repudiation to authentication and data integrity also warrants clarification. As discussed in chapter 4, authentication provides assurance of the identity of someone or something, such as the person at the other end of a communication session or the originator of a message. Data integrity protects against alteration of data in a manner inconsistent with the recognized security policy, for example, the unauthorized modification of a message in transit. While non-repudiation depends on authentication and data integrity, it is fundamentally different by virtue of its role in resolving legal disputes. Non-repudiation consists of the ability to prove successfully *to a third party* and *after the fact* that a specific communication originated with, was submitted by, or was delivered to a certain person.[10]

Consider, for example, the types of protection that can be provided by applying a message authentication code (MAC) to a message, as described in section 4.2. Recall that a MAC is a symmetric cryptographic mechanism—both the originator and recipient of a message share a common key. The originator uses the key to generate the MAC, and the recipient uses the same key to verify the MAC. This mechanism can provide *authentication* and *data integrity:* The recipient (one of the two parties with the key) can be confident of who originated the message and that the message was not modified, provided that it is known that only the two parties possessed the key. However, a MAC cannot generally provide *non-repudiation* of the origin of a message because it does not have technical attributes that can demonstrate *and convince a third party* as to who originated the message; since two parties possessed the key, either one can accuse the other of secretly originating the message or secretly enabling another person to have done so.

To illustrate how authentication, data integrity, and non-repudiation can be provided to differing degrees, consider the following types of communications:

- *Traditional signed writing delivered via postal mail:* A traditional signed writing supports a moderate degree of non-repudiation. Handwritten, or *holographic,* signatures contain attributes that may permit moderately strong authentication—they are difficult to forge, and they permit some binding of the signer's identity to the message because the physical qualities of ink on paper binds the wet signature to the message . Notarial acknowledgment of the signature enhances such authentication. With respect to integrity, a recipient who receives a sealed envelope (without obvious signs of tampering) can be reasonably confident that the message inside is that which the sender actually enclosed; alternatively, an examination of the writing may reveal evidence of tampering or modification because the physical qualities of ink on paper prevent easy modification of the writing's contents. The postmark may provide evidence of the message's origination and the approximate date it was dispatched. A return receipt, or certified mail, can confirm delivery.

- *Unprotected digital message with a symbolic signature:* An example of a symbolic signature on a digital message is the mere appearance of one's name within or appended to the message, or perhaps the inclusion of a digitized image of a handwritten signature. Data integrity may or may not be present, depending on the communications environment and technologies in use. Due to its comparatively weak probative value in confirming the identity of the sender of the message, the unprotected signature generally contributes, at best, only modestly to authentication and non-repudiation.[11]

- *Digitally signed message:* When properly implemented, a digital signature can provide very strong authentication, very strong data integrity, and strong to very strong non-repudiation. Among other features, the digital signature (in contrast with other types of electronic signatures) is logically bound to the message. Non-repudiation via a digital signature can be further enhanced by using protocols that include time stamps and automatic or mandatory acknowledgment of receipt.[12]

No attribute of a communication can prevent a party from refusing to perform; similarly, even the strongest non-repudiation attributes cannot prevent a participant from denying transmission or receipt of a communication. Rather, non-repudiation guards against a *successful* false denial by exposing wrongful repudiation with strong evidence to support speedy and effective dispute resolution before a neutral third party. Non-repudiation can also deter parties from attempting acts of wrongful repudiation.

9.2 Types of Non-repudiation

Communication, whether bilateral or multilateral, involves two primary types of parties: originators and recipients.[13] Correspondingly, non-repudiation has two primary types: non-repudiation of origin and non-repudiation of delivery. Another case is non-repudiation

of submission, which helps to prevent or resolve disagreements as to whether a party submitted (meaning dispatched) a specific message with specific content to a specific destination. In this section we explore these three variants of non-repudiation.

Non-repudiation of Origin

Non-repudiation of origin aids resolution of disagreements over whether or not a particular party originated a particular message, the time this origination occurred, or both. For
explanatory purposes, let us assume that origination equates to sending a message.[14] Non-
repudiation of origin protects recipients by providing proof for use in resolving disputes
such as:

- A recipient claims to have received a message, but the party identified as sender
  claims not to have originated the message.
- A recipient claims to have received a message different from that which the
  sender claims to have originated.
- A recipient claims to have received a particular message originated on a specific
  date and at a specific time, but the party identified as sender claims not to have
  originated that particular message at that specific time and date.

The reality in each of these cases is at least one of the following:[15]

1. The originator is lying (or misinformed).
2. The recipient is lying (or misinformed).
3. A computer or communications error has occurred.
4. An intervening third party has deceived the two parties.

Only non-repudiation allows the parties involved in an e-commerce transaction to
effectively rule out situations 3 and 4 in a dispute. Let us consider an example. Suppose
that Nola has secured the right to market and sell Sammy's Sensational Spark Plugs as one
of several worldwide licensed distributors. On her Electronic Market Web site, Nola establishes online order mechanisms for the retail and wholesale purchase of spark plugs by
visitors to the Web site. Nola's Web site employs secure e-commerce techniques, including the use of digital signatures.

One day, Nola receives an order from a Fred Smiley in Fargo, North Dakota, by e-mail. The order message is not digitally signed. The order is for 10 thousand spark plugs at Nola's listed price for that quantity of $1 each. Against her better judgment, Nola ships the order despite Fred's failure to employ a digital signature. The next day, Louisa's Manufacturing, a competitor of Sammy's, announces that it has developed a method of manufacturing spark plugs at one-fifth the cost incurred by other manufacturers. Louisa's will now sell an order of 10 thousand spark plugs for less than 20 cents each.

Two days later, Nola receives the shipment of 10 thousand spark plugs back from Fred Smiley. She locates a phone number for Mr. Smiley and calls him. "Look, Fred," she starts. "You placed an order. I shipped the spark plugs, all quality tested. We had a contract. You have no right to go back on the deal. If you don't accept the shipment and pay the contract price as agreed, my lawyer will see you in court!" Fred replies, "I did receive your spark plugs. They looked like sensational plugs. Unfortunately, I never placed such an order. I have no idea how you got my name and address. Some hacker kids must have thought it was an amusing prank."

Depending on the law in the applicable jurisdiction regarding the requirements for writings and signatures, Nola may or may not have a valid and enforceable contract with the originator of the order.[16] Nonetheless, even assuming that the order that was not digitally signed satisfies the formal legal requirements for a valid acceptance, Nola has a serious enforceability problem on her hands because she does not possess sufficiently persuasive evidence that Fred originated the order as she asserts. A clever online attacker might have sent a message that looked as if it came from Fred. In other words, Fred's e-mail order provides weak support for non-repudiation of origin.

The evidence Nola needs to achieve non-repudiation of origin must persuasively associate, or link together, various pieces of information, including at least

- the identity of the originator and
- the content of the message.

In addition, in many cases she may need other information, such as

- the date and time when origination occurred,
- the identity of the intended recipient or recipients, and
- the identities of any trusted third parties involved in generating or retaining records.[17]

Had Nola implemented mechanisms that required Fred to provide her with these evidentiary items, she would have been in a stronger position to prevail in a dispute concerning the origin of the order and to recover damages on her contract.

Non-repudiation of Delivery

Non-repudiation of delivery aids resolution of disagreements as to whether a particular party received a particular data item, the time the delivery occurred,[18] or both. In other words, non-repudiation of delivery protects originators[19] by providing proof for use in resolving disputes such as the following:

- An originator claims to have sent a message, but the party identified as recipient claims not to have received the message.
- An originator claims to have sent a message different from that which the recipient claims to have received.
- An originator claims to have sent a particular message on a specific date and at a specific time, but the party identified as recipient claims not to have received that particular message at a time and on a date consistent with the claimed time and date of sending.

As with the disputes over origination, the reality in each case is that one party is lying, a computer or communications error has occurred, or both parties are telling the truth and an interloper has deceived them. Again, non-repudiation evidence can aid in ruling out the possibilities of computer errors or third-party intervention to strengthen a complaining party's claim.

Suppose that Vera needs to replenish her supply of grease to lubricate the equipment in her machine shop. She surfs the Web and finds the site of Greasy Gary, a lubrication distributor. Gary apparently has an overabundance of grease inventory; he is offering a very low price for the type of grease Vera needs. Vera fills out Gary's online order form and submits it. Unfortunately, Gary's site does not implement secure e-commerce techniques.

Two weeks later, Vera has not received any shipment from Greasy Gary, and her equipment is starting to squeak and slow down, so she does some quick investigating. She learns through the Grease Grapevine, an e-auction site devoted exclusively to the grease market, that a day or two after she transmitted her order, Gary received a proposal from a third party to purchase his entire inventory of grease at a premium price. Gary accepted the proposal and now has no grease to sell to Vera at the bargain prices he promised.

Vera calls Gary and exclaims, "Listen, Gary, you owe me a shipment of grease at your incredible price of two weeks ago, and if I don't see your grease at my shop in two days, you'll be hearing from my lawyer about a breach of contract!" Gary responds, "First of all, my grease is always at an incredible price. Second, I can tell you that I received no order from you two weeks ago, and I have no grease to sell you at that price even if I wanted to."

Depending on the applicable law regarding the requirements for writings and signatures, Vera may or may not have a valid contract with Gary. Nonetheless, assuming that the order that was not digitally signed constitutes a valid acceptance, Vera has a serious enforceability problem on her hands because she cannot effectively prove that Gary received the order on the date she asserts. In other words, her e-mail order provides weak support for non-repudiation of delivery.

The evidence Vera needs to achieve non-repudiation of delivery must adequately associate, or link together, various pieces of information, including at least

- the identity of the recipient and
- the content of the message.

Additionally, in some cases, she may need other information, such as

- the date and time at which delivery of the message occurred,
- the identity of the originator, and
- the identities of any trusted third parties involved in generating supporting records.

As the situation now stands, Vera has little or no evidence that her order went through at all, much less that Gary received and opened it. Had Vera refused to deal with Gary until he implemented secure mechanisms to provide her with such evidence, she would have been better positioned to prevail in a dispute concerning the delivery of the order.

Non-repudiation of Submission

Non-repudiation of submission is sometimes considered to be sufficiently distinct from non-repudiation of origin and of delivery to classify it as a third basic type of non-repudiation. Non-repudiation of submission helps prevent or resolve disagreements as to whether a particular party transmitted, or *submitted,* a particular data item, the time the submission occurred, or both. In other words, non-repudiation of submission protects originators by providing proof sufficient to resolve one or more of the following disputes:

- An originator claims to have sent a message, but the intended recipient claims not only that he or she did not receive the message but also that the originator did not send the message.
- An originator claims to have sent a particular message on a specific date and at a specific time, but the intended recipient claims that the message was not sent at that time on that date.

If both originator and recipient are being truthful in their allegations, then either an interloper has deceived the parties or a fault has occurred in the computer or communications systems.

Non-repudiation of submission is particularly useful in cases where the timing of the transmittal of a message is critical to its legal effect.[20] For example, in the context of an acceptance of an offer to contract, an originator may need strong evidence that his or her acceptance was submitted (assuming that mere submission, as opposed to actual delivery, is sufficient for effective acceptance) prior to the recipient's submission or delivery of a revocation of his or her initial offer.[21] In other contexts, parties executing online securities transactions or submitting court filings or reports with regulatory agencies may also need strong evidence that their filings or reports were submitted in a timely manner or in a particular order.[22]

In several respects, non-repudiation of submission is similar to non-repudiation of delivery and is sometimes classified as a variant thereof.[23] In particular, both types primarily protect originators, as opposed to recipients, and the implementation methods for both types are similar. Implementation is discussed in section 9.5.

9.3   Activities and Roles

Having established the purpose, definition, and types of non-repudiation, we next examine the technical model for implementing non-repudiation in support of secure e-commerce. This section describes the activities and roles involved in providing non-repudiation.

Mechanistically, the sequence of events associated with providing non-repudiation services for a particular communication involves five distinct activities, occurring in the following order:[24]

1. Non-repudiation request
2. Record generation
3. Record distribution
4. Record verification
5. Record retention[25]

Different participants in a digital communication may play different roles in each of these phases, depending on whether the parties seek non-repudiation of origin or non-repudiation of delivery (or submission). Non-repudiation, as a legal and practical result, necessarily depends on each of these activities being undertaken in connection with the communication or transaction they are meant to support, not after the fact.[26]

Non-repudiation Request

To achieve non-repudiation, one or more of the participants to a communication must somehow agree, prior to its origination and delivery, to use non-repudiation services and to generate the necessary record to provide the desired degree of non-repudiation. This may require that one of the parties, or an interested third party, make an explicit advance request that non-repudiation services be applied to the communication. Such explicit requests are not always necessary, as there may be a standing arrangement (such as a trading partner agreement or an existing course of dealings among the parties) establishing that non-repudiation services always apply to certain types of events. Such agreements can serve as or reflect *system rules* applicable to the members of a community of interest or regulation.[27]

To illustrate how commercial parties employ non-repudiation practices in traditional contexts, consider the following example. Suppose Nola desires to accept an offer to enter into a contract with Vera, and this acceptance is to be communicated via typewritten letter. Non-repudiation of origin is accomplished, in part, by Nola's signature on the acceptance letter. In general, it is not necessary for Vera to request explicitly that Nola sign the letter, as there is a well-established practice of doing so. However, in some circumstances, Vera or Vera's lawyer might explicitly request specific non-repudiation evidence from Nola—for example, an attestation (such as an additional signature by a witness to the first signature) or a notarial acknowledgment of the acceptance letter.

In the digital environment, Nola's Web site (or messages originating from Nola) should state clearly that non-repudiation techniques are applied, or must be applied, to all orders and that no order will be deemed to create a valid and enforceable contract unless it employs proper non-repudiation protocols.[28] Vera, on the other hand, would have to make a specific request of Greasy Gary that non-repudiation of delivery apply, and she should refrain from engaging in any high-value or otherwise significant transactions unless Gary complies.

Accordingly, the role associated with this preliminary phase is that of service requester. The service requester is usually one of the primary parties to the communication, but it could alternatively be someone representing the interests of one of those parties.

To achieve non-repudiation of origin, the recipient, or a party representing the recipient's interests, is typically the service requester; in non-repudiation of delivery, the originator, or a party representing the originator's interests, is the service requester. In the acceptance letter example, Vera or Vera's lawyer assumes the service-requester role. In the other examples, Nola (a recipient desiring non-repudiation of origin) and Vera (an originator desiring non-repudiation of delivery) are the service requesters.[29]

Record Generation

A non-repudiation record captures data regarding the origination or receipt of a communication in a form suitable for prospective use as evidence in the event of a repudiation dispute. The party who is considered a potential repudiator of the communication must play a role in record generation. The record may contain a copy of part of the communication content (such as filled-in electronic forms fields) or information that is supplied separately from the primary communication. The party generating the record may do so autonomously,[30] or a trusted third party may participate in the process. For non-repudiation of origin, the originator (or third party attesting the origination) must act as record generator; for non-repudiation of delivery, the recipient (or third party attesting to the delivery to the recipient) must act as record generator.

In our acceptance letter example, Nola (the originator) generates the record by computing the necessary signature and, if requested or required, obtaining an attestation or acknowledgment. If Nola desired non-repudiation of delivery, Vera (the recipient) might be required to perform record generation by signing a return receipt included with the letter in the presence of a postal clerk.[31] Note that the record generated might include time and date information via the notary's acknowledgment or the postal service's postmark.

Record Distribution

After the execution of the communication and the generation of the appropriate record, the record generator must make the record available to the party or parties who may ultimately need to use it. In the acceptance letter example, Nola transfers the signature, attestation, or acknowledgment to Vera. In the digital context, Fred Smiley and Greasy Gary could transmit their records to Nola and Vera, respectively.

The principal participants may, however, use trusted third parties to receive, verify, and store the record. In the acceptance letter example, Nola might transmit the letter directly to Vera's attorney. Attorneys in all jurisdictions operate under ethical obligations to maintain client escrow accounts properly (at least when holding client funds). In the digital environment, Nola and Vera could have their respective trading partners transmit non-repudiation records directly to a trusted third party that operates under moral and legal obligations analogous to escrow accounts that ensure confidentiality and trustworthiness.

Record Verification

After receiving the non-repudiation record from its generator, the service requester or its designee must verify that the record supplied is sufficient to provide support for non-repudiation in the event a dispute arises. Secure e-commerce practices and business controls mandate that such verification generally should be a normal part of the communication process, rather than merely a consequence of a dispute.[32]

In the traditional context, this phase might involve the recipient's confirmation that the document is signed by the appropriate party, correctly dated, and if necessary, properly attested or notarized. In the digital environment, the parties (or trusted third parties designated by them) would confirm that the non-repudiation evidence satisfied established protocols and standards.

Record Retention

After verifying the sufficiency of the record, the service requester or its designee must retain the record for possible future retrieval and use. The service requester may retain, or archive the record itself, but the strength of non-repudiation evidence (for some purposes, even digitally signed evidence) is bolstered if a trusted third party undertakes the archiving role, since that may diminish any doubts regarding the trustworthiness of the evidence. In the handwritten letter example, Vera would store the signed acceptance letter, with its acknowledgment, if any, in her files. Nola would do likewise with the return receipt. If the paper or digital communication involved a conveyance of an interest in real property, a legal security interest in or lien on personal property, or one of a host of other important transactions, the parties would most likely seek to record the deed or file the document with an appropriate government entity, acting as a trusted third party.[33]

The five activities and various roles outlined create and preserve records that will generally support non-repudiation by providing strong evidence that origination or receipt of a particular communication occurred. Additional information about the communication may also be included, if the parties employ appropriate requests and mechanisms, such as the date and time the communication was originated, transmitted, or received. The following two sections present various approaches to executing these activities and fulfilling these roles, first for the case of non-repudiation of origin and then for non-repudiation of delivery.

9.4 Mechanisms for Non-repudiation of Origin

Originator's Digital Signature

One mechanism for providing non-repudiation of origin is for the originator of a message to digitally sign the message. This is illustrated in figure 9.1. The digital signature constitutes the non-repudiation record. The record verification phase involves a recipi-

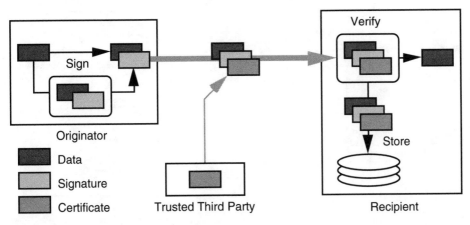

Figure 9.1   Originator's Digital Signature

ent's verifying the digital signature. The digital signature and the corresponding message are then retained by the recipient. In the event that the originator later denies sending the message, the recipient can furnish the retained digitally signed message for
non-repudiation purposes.

A recipient's claim to possess the correct public key to verify the digital signature
may not, by itself, satisfy the burden of proving origin. Rather, a trusted third party is
required to validate the public key. Therefore, for a mechanism in which the verification
of digital signatures supports non-repudiation, the involvement of trusted third parties is
essential.[34]

Key revocation also requires particularly careful attention. If a public-key certificate
is revoked (for such reasons as suspected compromise of the private key), the precise time
of revocation must be communicated to all potential users of non-repudiation records. A
record generated using a certificate prior to its revocation is generally considered probative and valid, but a record generated after such revocation is not. Thus, users of non-repudiation records need to check stringently for possible revocation of any applicable
certificate.

Furthermore, non-repudiation may demand real-time revocation status notification.
The possibility of a certificate's being revoked after it has been used to verify a signature
is particularly problematic because revocation may impair the ability of a party to rely
effectively on the certificate in enforcing a contract. The consequences of such an event

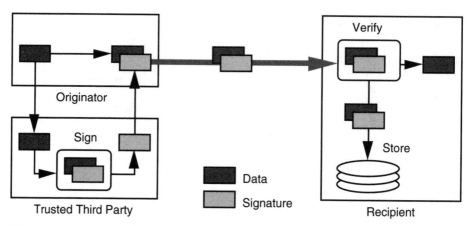

Figure 9.2 Trusted Third-Party Digital Signature

depend on non-repudiation practices. It may be necessary to store copies of applicable certificate revocation lists to resolve such a dispute effectively. The use of the Online Certificate Status Protocol (OCSP) may provide a more suitable and robust solution.

Digital Signature of a Trusted Third Party

Another mechanism employs the digital signature of a trusted third party, alone or in concert with the originator's own digital signature (see figure 9.2).

When using the digital signature of a trusted third party alone, in one scenario, the trusted third party is vouching for the source of the message on the basis of having authenticated the originator by some independent means. In this case, the originator transmits the message to a trusted third party, who generates a digital signature over a data item containing the message content, the identity of the originator, and other required or optional information such as a time stamp. The trusted third party returns this digitally signed data item to the originator, who in turn forwards it to the recipient for use as a non-repudiation record.

Prior to adding its digital signature, the trusted third party must authenticate the content and source of the record to confirm that it is authentic. Therefore, the record from the originator must have authentication and integrity protection.[35]

This mechanism has some advantages over the originator's digital signature method. One advantage is that a relatively small number of trusted third-party signers can support a large community of originators and recipients, thereby minimizing the number of certified public keys that need to be managed. Another advantage is that, as long as the signing trusted third party is recognized as maintaining a trustworthy timekeeping device, a time stamp can be easily associated with the signature, providing recipients with a non-repudiable time of origination or dispatch.[36]

This method can be extended by having the originator digitally sign the message prior to sending it to the trusted third party for an additional signature. In this case, the trusted third party is vouching for the validity of the originator's digital signature. The signed data item from the trusted third party is sometimes referred to as a *transactional certificate,* a special form of certificate relating to a specific communication or transaction.[37]

Digital Signature of Trusted Third Party on Digest

In a variation of the preceding trusted third-party signature method, the originator may first generate a digest, or digital fingerprint, of the communication by applying a hash function to its content. The digest is then sent to the trusted third party, who computes a digital signature over a data item containing the digest, the identity of the originator, and other required or optional information such as a time stamp.[38] This digital signature becomes a non-repudiation record; it is returned to the originator and then forwarded to the recipient as discussed earlier.

There are advantages to having a trusted third party sign a digest of a message instead of the full message content. This approach reduces the volume of data that must be transmitted to the trusted third party, and it preserves the confidentiality of the original data. Hence, under this scheme, the trusted third party need be trusted only for signature purposes, not for confidentiality purposes as well.

If there is any possibility of the originator's using more than one hash function, it is important to attach to the digest an unambiguous identifier of the particular hash function used. This identifier must also be included in the value signed by the trusted third party. If this is not done, there is an arguable case that someone might be able to find two different messages which, under two different hash functions, generate the same digest.[39] Therefore, failure to include the hash function identifier in the signed evidence could affect the strength of that evidence.

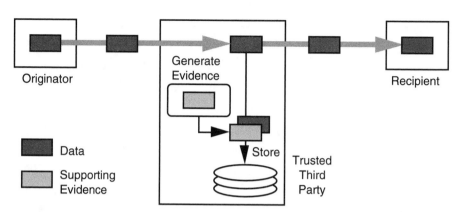

Figure 9.3   Inline Trusted Third-Party Evidence Stored

Inline Trusted Third Party

Another type of mechanism for providing non-repudiation of origin involves the insertion of a trusted third party into the communication path between the originator and recipient. There are different ways this trusted third party might operate; figure 9.3 illustrates the simplest option. In this method, referred to as an *inline trusted third-party* method, the trusted third party simply captures and retains a non-repudiation record to support the resolution of future disputes regarding the origin, submission, and content of communicated data. Such a record typically includes a copy or digest of the data, the identities of the originator and the intended recipient, and a time stamp.

This type of mechanism has the advantage of not affecting the format of the application protocol fields.[40] However, it requires the use of other security services. In particular, integrity and data-origin authentication services must apply to the communications between originator and trusted third party and between trusted third party and recipient.

Figure 9.4 represents another variation of the inline trusted third-party mechanism. In this case, the trusted third party generates a digital signature as the non-repudiation record and forwards it to the recipient for verification and retention.

Combinations of Mechanisms

Participants can augment the strength of a non-repudiation record by using multiple mechanisms in combination or by adding other enhancements. For example, digital-signature-based

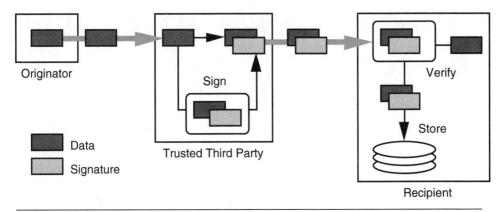

Figure 9.4 Inline Trusted Third-Party Evidence Forwarded

mechanisms can be enhanced by involving multiple parties in the signing process. This typi-cally involves affixing multiple independent signatures, such as those of witnesses and notaries or additional trusted third parties. These measures greatly improve resistance to the compromise of keys and reduce dependence on individual parties. Furthermore, any of the mechanisms described earlier can be combined. For example, a non-repudiation record can include the originator's signature plus multiple trusted third-party signatures, all produced in different systems.

9.5 Mechanisms for Non-repudiation of Delivery

Recipient Acknowledgment with Signature

One mechanism for supporting non-repudiation of delivery is for the recipient of a mes-sage to send to the originator a digitally signed acknowledgment containing a copy or digest of the contents of the original communication and other required or optional infor-mation, such as the time of delivery. The signature must be generated by the recipient or by a party acting on behalf of the recipient. Figure 9.5 illustrates the operation of this mechanism for cases where the recipient employs its own digital signature.

In most respects, this mechanism is equivalent to the application of non-repudiation of origin techniques to an acknowledgment message that contains the necessary evidence

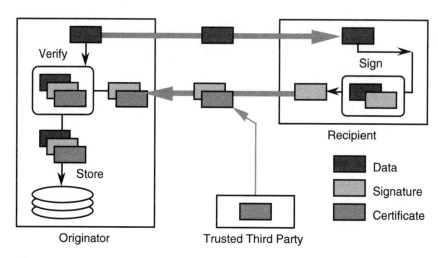

Figure 9.5   Non-repudiation of Delivery Using Recipient's Signature

required by the originator of the original message.[41] The same requirements regarding certificates and key revocation that apply to the non-repudiation-of-origin mechanisms discussed in section 9.4 also apply to this non-repudiation-of-delivery mechanism.

For Internet-based e-commerce, one mechanism of this type is standardized. This is the digitally signed receipt mechanism in S/MIME Version 3, which provides valuable support for non-repudiation of delivery.

Trusted Delivery Agent

This mechanism involves the intervention of a trusted third party acting as a *delivery agent.* The delivery agent intervenes in the communication path between originator and recipient. The originator transmits the message to the delivery agent, who acknowledges its final receipt by means of a signature-based mechanism as described earlier (or alternatively maintains a trustworthy record of final deliveries[42]), but not until the delivery agent has completed final delivery to the recipient.

This mechanism resolves one of the problems that can arise with mechanisms that depend on acknowledgment from the recipient himself or herself. Such mechanisms provide no inherent protection against a *reluctant recipient* who chooses not to acknowledge a particular delivered communication (typically after having seen its contents) or not to do so in a timely fashion.[43] Thus, in a sense, the trusted delivery agent approach is roughly akin to the use of a *process server,* such as a deputy or police officer who delivers certain legal documents (such as a summons or subpoena), although the legal effect of each approach may vary considerably.[44]

Progressive Delivery Reports

Many distributed communications applications, such as e-mail, involve forwarding of messages through multiple distinct administrative domains. In such applications there is the risk of losing data en route and not being able to attribute the loss to any particular party or domain: a loss of accountability. Consequently, it may be agreed to apply non-repudiation of delivery at multiple points along a communication path, for example, at each point where a message enters a different administrative domain. This results in a system in which responsibility for a message is securely associated with a particular administrative domain at all times.[45]

Non-repudiation of Submission

Non-repudiation of submission applies in communication environments in which messages are transported by a third party, such as a commercial e-mail service provider. Non-repudiation of submission provides strong evidence that the message has been dispatched and accepted by the transporting party for transfer to the intended recipient or recipients.

Non-repudiation of submission can be considered a subspecies of non-repudiation of delivery; it amounts to non-repudiation of delivery of a message to the transporting party, the intermediary, rather than to the recipient. The mechanism most typically used for non-repudiation of submission is the recipient's signature mechanism shown in figure 9.5, with the transporting party replacing the recipient. Given the expectation that the independent transporting party would have no interest in the message content, more robust mechanisms for non-repudiation of delivery are not necessary and generally are not implemented in the non-repudiation-of-submission context.

9.6   Trusted Third Parties

Because a decision maker presented with non-repudiation evidence in a dispute between participants will likely give greater weight to evidence generated and retained by a trusted third party, the involvement of trusted third parties in non-repudiation may be critical for secure e-commerce. Accordingly, this section addresses the functions and necessary attributes of trusted third parties in facilitating non-repudiation. Without reference to any specific setting, a trusted third party is "an independent, unbiased third party that contributes to the ultimate security and trustworthiness of computer-based information transfers."[46]

In connection with non-repudiation in e-commerce applications, trusted third parties perform or assist in performing various functions, including (a) public-key certification, (b) identity and authority validation, (c) time stamping, (d) records retention, (e) delivery intermediation, and (f) dispute resolution.

Public-Key Certification

By issuing a public-key certificate, a trusted third party certifies that a particular public key corresponds to a particular private key held by a particular entity and that the key pair is valid or was valid at a specific time.

In addition to transaction or message content (including associated time stamps, digital signatures, and transactional certificates), public-key certificate content also significantly affects features of non-repudiation:[47]

- *Validity period:* Transactions must be digitally signed within the validity (operational) period of a certificate and before the revocation (or suspension) of the certificate as a precondition to such transactions' support for non-repudiation.
- *Certificate policy:* The designated certificate policy (and applicable certification practice statement) is generally a primary place to present the various parties' mutual expectations with respect to using a certificate in support of non-repudiation for a digitally signed message.
- *Key usage field:* In an X.509 certificate, the key usage extension defines the purposes and restrictions (such as encipherment, digital signature, certificate signing) of the key contained in a certificate and is employed when a key that could be used for more than one operation is to be restricted. Since the meaning of the non-repudiation bit is not necessarily specified in the technical standards, the significance of that bit should be stipulated clearly within the applicable certificate policy.[48]

In the Vera and Gary example in section 9.2 regarding non-repudiation of delivery, had Vera submitted Gary's online order form exclusively to solicit a quote (that is, only to confirm availability and price from Gary and not to commit to purchase anything yet), and had Vera's transaction implied a request for use of non-repudiation services, Gary might have argued (not necessarily with success) that Vera was bound to the transaction. If this transaction were combined with the use of a third-party time-stamping service, further confusion (and dilution of non-repudiation support) might result, at least where the applicable certificate policy did not clarify the significance of such service.[49]

Identity Confirmation

Under some non-repudiation mechanisms, the trusted third party vouches for the identity or authority of a message's originator by signing (or cosigning) the message on behalf of the originator. Identity confirmation is also a function of the certification of public keys.

Time Stamping

A *time stamp* is a notation that specifies the date and time that an activity occurred and is typically associated with the identity of the person or agent that created the notation. Such notation is typically appended to, or logically associated with, a message.[50] Time stamps are created for many purposes by parties to a transaction, trusted third parties, and telecommunications service providers. In the traditional paper context, notaries often perform time-stamping functions for important transactions by confirming the date on which a document was signed. In the digital context, a trusted third party generates a time stamp for a given message by having a time-stamping service append a time value to the message or a digest of the message, and then digitally sign the result. Such a digital time stamp serves as evidence in support of non-repudiation. The significance of a time stamp is a function of the context in which it is used, its relative trustworthiness, and applicable law. Digital signature regulations or legislation often includes a specific treatment of time stamping for such purposes.[51]

Parties may combine the time-stamping function with other non-repudiation signature functions. For example, a trusted third party may attest to both an originator's identity and the correct time. Alternatively, a dedicated time-stamping service may be employed for the sole purpose of securely appending the time and date, without confirming any attributes of the originator or the content.

Time stamps serve important functions in many applications. Parties making regulatory, business, or court filings may employ time stamps to confirm the times of their filings. Where the timing of contractual offers, acceptances, and revocations is at issue, time stamping can provide definitive evidence to resolve disputes.

In addition, some non-repudiation mechanisms use trusted time stamping as evidence of message *transmission* or *delivery,* distinct from evidence of the *time* of transmission or delivery. For example, where the originator's digital signature mechanism is employed for non-repudiation of origin, a devious originator could seek to repudiate transmission of a message by

- causing its own signature to become invalid by deliberately publicizing its private key and then instigating revocation and
- claiming that an interloper originated the message with the compromised key pair.

Trustworthy time stamps associated with signatures and revocation requests would reduce or counter such false claims by a devious originator, since the recipient could demonstrate that the originator transmitted the message prior to certificate revocation.[52]

Many factors affect the trustworthiness of a time stamp, the most significant of which include the following:

- *Resistance to forgery:* A time stamp should provide assurance against undetected tampering or deletion. Trustworthy digital signatures and trusted third-party databases are primary methods of ensuring resistance to forgery. A quality associated with resistance to forgery is durability, the property that once a time stamp is applied, it remains intact and provable for at least the intended period of time.[53]
- *Auditability:* The property that the source of the time can be traced to its origin and the time stamp can be associated with the corresponding data for which it represents a time event.
- *Independence:* The impartiality of a time stamp maker can significantly affect its trustworthiness and thus the support that it provides for non-repudiation. As alternatives to simple digital signatures that combine a message and time value, some innovative technologies for time stamping have been developed that enhance the provability of independence.[54]

- *Accuracy:* Reflects the extent to which the stated time consistently reflects the time as maintained by a national timing center or standards laboratory.[55] Accuracy implicates compensation for time deviations, including clock drift and network delays.[56] The accuracy of time communicated over the Internet may be degraded by network vulnerabilities, including denial of service and asymmetry in the delay through the channel between the user and the reference clock.[57] Table 9.1 illustrates, at a coarse level, differences in the accuracy of various time-stamping sources typically used in commerce.
- *Granularity (or resolution):* Describes the smallest unit of time recorded by a time stamp. Prior to e-commerce, commercial time stamps typically had a granularity of a day, hour, or minute. E-commerce makes much finer-grained time stamps possible and desirable due to the increasing time sensitivity of many online applications.[58]

In some environments, the sequence of events is more important than exact time that an event occurred. Of course, knowing the exact time of an event would allow one to determine the sequence. However, a much simpler mechanism is also sufficient if all parties use the same trusted third party. That mechanism would simply be a monotonically increasing integer in lieu of the date and time.

Table 9.1   Approximate Time-Source Accuracy[59]

Time source	Accuracy
Mechanical time piece	A few minutes
Quartz time piece	A few seconds
Typical uncorrected network time	0.1 seconds
Network Time Protocol (NTP)	0.05 seconds
Typical server clock	5 milliseconds
GPS	1 microsecond
Atomic clock	1 nanosecond

Competing and conflicting time-stamping patent claims as well as subtle (and not so subtle) threats by patent holders and licensees have deterred the widespread deployment of time-stamping technologies. The patents in dispute cover aspects of time stamping that range from the simple act of digitally signing a time stamp to complex time-stamping protocols.[60]

Records Retention

When a participant employs a trusted third party to generate non-repudiation records, that participant may benefit by having the trusted third party archive those records. Certain records retained by a trusted third party will typically be deemed more reliable than records archived by a primary participant to a communication. Of course, participants may desire assurances against the trusted third party's failure to perform. Such assurances may include the trusted third party's executing a sufficient bond in connection with its archiving services, insurance, or an apportionment of liability among the primary parties and the trusted third party that favors the primary parties. In addition, an attestation from an auditor to all parties as to the successful completion of a compliance audit may be particularly helpful.

One aspect of system design deserves special attention in the non-repudiation context. Non-repudiation records often need to be retained for a long period, possibly years.[61] As explained in sections 9.4 and 9.5, regardless of the specific mechanism used to support non-repudiation, such evidence is computed on a data string, which represents certain information. Therefore, in addition to establishing and preserving digitally signed messages as evidence, it is necessary to establish and preserve a common view of the data representation scheme. In other words, participants in a communication must, for example, agree on and preserve throughout the lifetime of the evidence the particular data encoding or the precise application program (such as spreadsheet or word processor) format used.[62]

Delivery Intermediation

In some circumstances, as described in section 9.5, a trusted third party may act as an intermediary, or delivery agent, between an originator and a recipient, providing assurances to the originator that a particular message has been or will be delivered to the recipient.

Dispute Resolution

A trusted third party may act as an arbiter in resolving disputes.[63] This function differs from those identified earlier in that it is a role that is performed primarily in the legal, as opposed to the technical, arena.

Required Attributes of Trusted Third Parties

The basic attributes that a trusted third party must possess are independence, neutrality, reliability, and acceptance by all participants.[64] Acceptance may be explicit, as expressed in a formal contract between the parties themselves, implied in contract, or required by statute, regulation, or treaty. For some applications, it may be appropriate for a government agency to assume trusted third-party functions. For others, a private organization may assume the functions, typically in conjunction with other communication service functions.[65]

Notaries

A notary serves as a trusted third party to the extent that he or she is independent and unbiased and contributes to the ultimate security and trustworthiness of an information transfer. Nonetheless, most notaries who perform functions of traditional identity confirmation essential to secure e-commerce are not technology-based trusted third parties (such as certification authorities), in that they neither perform the technology-based functions listed earlier in this section nor make digital communications a material part of their notarial activities. Notaries are geographically dispersed, ubiquitous,[66] commissioned officers of governments, vested with specific authority to perform trust-enhancing functions. Therefore, they constitute a cost-effective and logistically practical institution for assisting in certain non-repudiation services and performing other activities that bolster e-commerce security. This section briefly introduces selected notarial functions and addresses the utility of notaries as trusted third parties in support of non-repudiation services.

U.S. notaries generally have authority to engage in the following acts:

- *Taking an acknowledgment:* This act establishes the identity of the person acknowledging a document and the genuineness of the signature attached to the document.
- *Taking a verification:* This act involves a sworn statement as to the truth of the facts stated within a document.
- *Witnessing or attesting a signature*
- *Certifying or attesting a copy of a document*
- *Making a protest:* This act requires the notary to issue a challenge as to the validity of a negotiable instrument or deed.[67]

Several of these notarial acts directly contribute to non-repudiation. Historically, in many jurisdictions, legal restrictions and practical realities have prevented notaries from performing most notarial acts, such as acknowledgments and verifications, online.

Notarial acts traditionally require that all affidavits or acknowledgments be made in the physical presence of the notary,[68] that the notary obtain physical proof of identity,[69] that the notary administer an oath in many cases,[70] that the notary impress his or her seal upon the document or certificate,[71] and that the notary *sign* a *written* certificate.[72]

Many barriers could be overcome by straightforward legal reforms, including these:

- Recognizing the sufficiency of certified digital signatures and other secure digital media to fulfill at least a subset of notarial requirements in substitution for paper-based notarial acts.
- Creating a new class of e-savvy notaries with heightened qualifications (or raising the requirements for all notaries across the board).

As with the contractual and evidentiary issues discussed in chapter 3, traditionally legal requirements for notarial acts are being scrutinized and, in some cases, liberalized in response to technological advances. Legal reform affecting various notarial processes is well underway globally and will increasingly facilitate the reliability of digital transactions and records.[73] Nonetheless, a lack of technical knowledge among most notaries,[74] including Latin-law notaries,[75] presents a considerable challenge. Various information security specialists and attorneys have advanced a new type of notary, called the *Cyber-Notary*.[76] A CyberNotary would most likely be a lawyer, would be required to have training in reliably creating and verifying digital signatures, and would be a *transna-tional* legal specialist, that is, an expert in international commercial law. In the meantime, traditional notarial acts still serve valuable but limited functions in e-commerce.[77]

9.7   Dispute Resolution

The ultimate goal of non-repudiation services and mechanisms is to avoid disputes among parties to digital communications and commerce and, in the event that disputes do arise, to provide means of resolving them efficiently. The non-repudiation procedures described earlier for both origin and delivery provide considerable preventive protection due to their ability to deter participants from attempting to deceive other participants by falsely deny-ing dispatch or receipt of a communication.

When a dispute arises, however, the non-repudiation services and mechanisms pre-sented in this chapter should provide as much or more *ex post,* or after the fact, evidence in support of enforceability. As a matter of mechanics, such dispute resolution involves (1) retrieval of the non-repudiation records (from storage), (2) presentation of the records to the involved parties, (3) presentation of the matter before the arbiter of the dispute, and (4) the dispute resolution mechanism's decision.

Disputes that remain unresolved after the presentation of records to the repudiat-ing party are typically resolved by a dispute resolution process, such as mediation, arbi-tration, or adjudication. As a legal matter, the strength of the *ex post* ability of non-repudiation evidence to support the enforcement of one's rights depends on the extent to which the non-repudiation evidence is admissible and persuasive under the governing rules. Admissibility (and even the weight and effect of evidence) may be stipulated in trading partner agreements,[78] certification practice statements, or industry practices.

The following subsections address the current state of the law with respect to "crypto-evidence," or state-of-the-art technical evidence, a category that encompasses evidence generated for non-repudiation purposes in the e-commerce context.[79] Two groups of issues are significant in this discussion: first, whether the evidence itself is admissible and, if so, the extent of credibility it should be accorded, and second, whether expert testimony regarding the evidence is admissible and what weight the decision maker should grant it.[80]

Technology-Based Evidence

As discussed in chapter 3, authentication of an item of evidence is a prerequisite to its admissibility. Unless an item is legally self-authenticating, the party seeking to introduce a record into evidence must be able to demonstrate its reliability with respect to both origin and integrity. Accordingly, in a dispute involving repudiation, the aggrieved party must be able to show who generated the evidence (whether itself or a trusted third party) and that the evidence, if transmitted, was transferred in a proper chain of custody.[81] Even after a party overcomes the threshold obstacles of authentication, best evidence, and hearsay,[82] the same issues of reliability regarding origin and integrity bear on the degree of weight or credibility that a decision-making body may assign to the evidence.

There is some indication that implementation of enhanced technology, such as that based on XML, may assist in the creation of viable electronic records that satisfy evidentiary requirements. In particular, an XML schema proposed to the W3C in 1998, XFDL (Extensible Forms Description Language), was developed specifically to address the body of issues associated with digitally representing e-commerce forms on the Internet. This language supports a precision layout, fine-grained internal business rules and computations, input validation, multiple overlapping digital signatures (for witnessing and other purposes), and transaction records that encapsulate the entire content, context, and structure of an e-commerce document.[83]

A flaw in many e-commerce systems is the inability to digitally sign, or even capture, a complete record of a transaction. For example, when a user fills out and submits the HTML form found on typical e-commerce Web sites, only the data entered by the user is captured. The rendered HTML content, which provides the context and structure of the agreement itself, is not bound to the user-entered data. In other words, the form's questions and answers are separated, thereby seriously hampering the ability to prove what a user saw and agreed to at the time of submission or signing.

Accordingly, it may be advisable for organizations to investigate enhanced technology, such as XFDL, for the creation of electronic records that provide non-repudiation evidence.

As the law develops greater recognition for public-key technology, the burdens associated with the process of authenticating non-repudiation evidence and assisting it through the hurdles of the best evidence and hearsay rules will be reduced and will become smaller than those currently faced by parties dealing with non-repudiation evidence in traditional (non-PKI-secured) electronic transactions. Legislation or judicial rulings may recognize trustworthy digital signatures as self-authenticating and may provide certain presumptions regarding the admissibility of digital evidence. Likewise, lawmakers and judges who understand public-key technology will likely grant digital signatures the appropriate enhanced weight and credibility that they deserve in comparison to other types of evidence.

Expert Testimony Regarding Technology-Based Evidence

Due to the technical nature of the evidence in an e-commerce dispute, the overwhelming majority of decision makers, whether arbitrators, judges, or jurors, cannot fully understand the significance of the evidentiary record without expert testimony regarding that record and its significance in the case.[85] For this reason, the rules of evidence permit the testimony of qualified expert witnesses where erudition in "scientific, technical, or other specialized knowledge" would be helpful to the decision makers.[86] Persons capable of serving as expert witnesses regarding the use of digital signatures as non-repudiation evidence include cryptographers (specialist mathematicians) and cryptographic systems professionals (computer scientists with knowledge of and experience with cryptographic techniques applicable to information security systems).

Before an expert witness may testify in judicial proceedings under this rule, the court must determine whether the witness is proposing to testify with respect to scientific, technical, or other specialized knowledge that will assist the trier of fact in understanding evidence or determining a fact at issue.[87] According to the U.S. Supreme Court, unless a scientific principle has received judicial notice as a scientific law,[88] determinations regarding expert witnesses involve "a preliminary assessment of whether the reasoning or methodology underlying the testimony is scientifically valid."[89] The reasoning or methodology at issue in the case of repudiation in a secure e-commerce context includes public-key cryptography.[90] Certain aspects of secure time- and date-stamping technology also require demonstration of scientific validity of reasoning and methodology. As of

2000, no U.S. court had published an opinion addressing the qualifications of expert witnesses to testify regarding public-key cryptography.

Although one might infer from this dearth of cases that non-repudiation mechanisms employing digital signatures are functioning successfully to deter parties from litigation, it is more probable that public-key cryptography is new enough that no case involving it has been filed and finalized. As a result, parties desiring to introduce expert testimony with respect to non-repudiation evidence must look to cases and rules for more general guidelines.

The four principal factors that U.S. courts currently consider significant in making an assessment regarding the scientific validity of an expert's reasoning or methodology were elaborated by the U.S. Supreme Court case of *Daubert v. Merrell Dow Pharmaceuticals, Inc.* The Court's exposition in *Daubert* explicitly addressed only "scientific" knowledge, leaving unanswered the questions of whether these factors are relevant to "technical" or "other specialized" knowledge and whether there is a difference (and, if so, what it might be).[91] Subsequently, however, in *Kuhmo Tire Co., Ltd. v. Carmichael,* the Supreme Court extended the application of these principal factors to technical testimony.[92] This is particularly important where the use of expert testimony addresses technical PKI implementations, rather than simply the underlying cryptography. Consequently, we assume here that testimony regarding non-repudiation evidence in secure e-commerce would likely face judicial scrutiny under the *Daubert* standard.

The four factors set forth in the *Daubert* case are as follows:

- Whether the methodology can be (and has been) tested
- Whether the methodology has been subjected to peer review and publication
- The methodology's known or potential rate of error
- Whether the methodology has received "general acceptance" within the relevant scientific community[93]

Other factors that courts have considered to be significant to the determination of reliability include the following:

- Whether the methodology is the subject of *standards* that control its operation[94]
- Whether there is an explicitly identified relevant scientific community[95]
- Whether the methodology appears to lend itself to abuse[96]

Public-key cryptography and digital signatures satisfy each of the four *Daubert* factors (particularly as extended by *Kuhmo*), as well as the other factors. The predominant algorithms used can be and have been successfully tested.[97] These algorithms have unquestionably been subjected to extensive peer review and have been the subject of elaborate scholarly publication. Many articles in academic and scientific journals, as well as many conference proceedings and domestic and international standards organizations, have reviewed and accepted public-key algorithms such as RSA.[98] Given the argument that public-key cryptography and cryptosystems have an infinitesimally small possibility of error in their application, as long as the technology is implemented properly, courts should find that they pass scrutiny in this regard.[99]

Having discussed the current judicial approach to qualification of technical experts, we must note that courts engage in a *Daubert*-type analysis only when a party challenges the admissibility of expert testimony. Typically, parties have raised such challenges in cases involving novel or alternative scientific methodologies and theories, frequently termed by the challenging parties as "junk science."[100] Given the widespread use of public-key cryptography and cryptosystems among e-commerce participants and the very high likelihood that public-key cryptography and cryptosystems would satisfy *Daubert* and the other current legal standards, it is unlikely that parties would object to the admission of expert testimony regarding public-key cryptography and cryptosystems on the grounds that it is "junk science."[101]

9.8 Summary

Non-repudiation services provide a communications user with protection against another user's later successful denial that a particular transaction took place. This protection is provided through the collection of persuasive evidence to support dispute resolution by a third party. Non-repudiation of origin foils a party's false denial that it originated a message. Non-repudiation of delivery foils a party's false denial that it received a message. Non-repudiation of submission protects a sender against false claims that it did not transmit a message.

From the technical perspective, there are five phases in the process of establishing and supporting non-repudiation. The service-request phase may be explicit or implicit but must precede the critical action (origination, delivery, or submission) to which non-repudiation is to apply. The record-generation phase occurs in conjunction with the critical action. In the record distribution phase, the record is transmitted to a party who may ultimately need it. In the record-verification phase, the record is checked by the party to whom it is transferred or entrusted for retention. Finally, the record-retention phase involves the archiving of the evidence for future retrieval and use, if necessary, to resolve a dispute.

Non-repudiation of origin can employ the originator's digital signature or the digital signature of a trusted third party who vouches for the originator, computed either on the message itself or on a digest of that message. Non-repudiation of origin may also employ an inline trusted third party, which generates required evidence and either stores it or forwards it to the recipients. When the time of origination is significant, the record generated in support of non-repudiation should include a time stamp, signed by a trusted third party. For added protection, multiple mechanisms can be used in combination.

Non-repudiation of delivery can employ a recipient's acknowledgment, containing a signature computed on the contents of the delivered data. The signature can be generated by the recipient or by a trusted third party vouching for the recipient. Alternatively, parties may employ a trusted delivery agent. In applications in which messages are forwarded through multiple administrative domains, non-repudiation of delivery can be applied at multiple points on the message path.

Non-repudiation of submission can be supported through employment of non-repudiation of delivery mechanisms between the originator and the transporting party.

The non-repudiation process involves the performance by trusted third parties of various functions, including public-key certification, identity or authority confirmation, time stamping, records retention, delivery intermediation, and dispute resolution. Parties assuming these functions must at least be neutral and reliable if their actions are to be effective.

The goal of non-repudiation in secure e-commerce can be achieved only if the people responsible for resolving disputes recognize, by presumption or through the advocacy of the parties, the legitimacy of public-key cryptography as evidence that is both admissible and persuasive. Given the accelerating use and acceptance of digital signatures in commerce and the modern approaches taken by courts to evaluate evidentiary issues, there seems little doubt that non-repudiation evidence generated using these technologies will ultimately gain judicial acceptance as admissible and persuasive evidence.

Ultimately, e-commerce will fail as an effective means of transacting business if participants cannot overcome the problems presented by repudiation and protect themselves from false claims. E-commerce becomes secure only with non-repudiation services, as achieved through implementation of the methods described in this chapter.

Notes

1. The term *non-repudiation* has more than one prevailing definition. Various definitions of the term are presented throughout this chapter.
2. Thomas Hobbes, *Leviathan* (Buffalo, NY: Prometheus Books, 1988, first published 1651) pt. I, chap. 13, p. 65.
3. ISO 7498-2, *Information Processing Systems—Open Systems Interconnection—Basic Reference Model—Part 2: Security Architecture,* also published as the ITU-T Recommendation X.800, details at <http://www.itu.ch>.
4. American Bar Association (ABA), Information Security Committee, Section of Science and Technology, *Digital Signature Guidelines* (1996), Guideline 1.20. Comment 1.20.1 notes that the definition does not include the technical security service, but rather "is intended to express a legal conclusion or result which flows from the use of digital signatures verified by certificates in the manner provided in these Guidelines."
5. See Directive 1999/93/EC of the European Parliament and of the Council of December 13, 1999, on a Community Framework for Electronic Signatures, Article 5.2, available at <http://europa.eu.int/comm/internal_market/en/media/sign/Dir99-93-ecEN.pdf>; European Electronic Signature Standardization Initiative (EESSI), Final Report of the EESSI Expert Team (July 20, 1999) "qualified electronic signatures" under Article 5.2, available at <http://www.ict.etsi.org/>.
6. Section 10-120, Illinois Electronic Commerce Security Act (1998), available at <http://mbc.com/ecommerce/legis/ill-esca2.html>.
7. ABA Guideline 5.6.

8. Utah Code Ann. sec. 46-3-406 (1996), available at <http://www.le.state.ut.us/ ~code/TITLE46/htm/46_03025.htm>.

9. See German Digital Signature Law, *Signaturegesetz,* secs. 14(2) and 126 BGB, trans. Christopher Kuner, available at <http://www.kuner.com/data/sig/digsig4. htm>.

10. In the context of contractual non-repudiation, substantial evidence of the contracting parties may become indispensable. See section 3.3 on basic contract formation. Non-repudiation in consumer transactions has been the subject of controversy to the extent that non-repudiation of consumer transactions is viewed as abrogating consumer rights by creating strict liability of the consumer or otherwise fostering injustice by preventing a consumer from disavowing transactions that he or she claims not to have executed. The classic case is the "Grandma inadvertently sells her house" scenario. Interestingly, the subscriber in such scenarios is typically the consumer rather than the relying party. One must distinguish among the security service of non-repudiation (which can enhance certainty and reliability, thereby benefiting all parties) and whatever legal remedies are available to certain classes of citizens.

11. Where strong authentication is unavailable, greater reliance on extrinsic evidence (tending to demonstrate the general reliability of the e-commerce environment), including contextual information about the message, is needed to successfully demonstrate non-repudiation. In the Internet environment, such evidence is typically more difficult, resource intensive, and less efficient to produce reliably.

12. Enhanced forms of private-key protection for digital signature keys are generally recognized to support strong non-repudiation. See section 4.5 (describing personal tokens and roaming protocols), section 10.7 (discussing technical security and private-key protection) and section 11.1 (describing trusted and certified cryptomodules and operating systems).

13. Additionally, third-party beneficiaries may have particularly important legal interests in the non-repudiability of communications between the originators and recipients, such as a beneficiary of a will or a tax authority to determine taxes due on commercial transactions.

14. The term *originate* should be interpreted broadly. Originate simply implies that a party held the data item at some time; it does not necessarily connote legal ownership. Non-repudiation mechanisms are generally applicable to data-item creation and subsequent storage of the data item in a database, as well as to transmission of the item to a second party. In the storage case, the party storing the data item is typically the originator, and the party ultimately retrieving the data item is in the role of recipient.

15. List suggested by Dario Tarentelli, director of Veridial, in an interview with Michael S. Baum, Paris, October 26, 1992.

16. See chapter 8 (providing an overview of e-commerce legislation). U.S. legislation (both state and federal law) tends to validate such click-wrap e-contracts notwithstanding the absence of paper-based traditional writing and signature.

17. For example, Nola may request and retain a copy of a digitally signed purchase order from Fred. To be able to verify the signature later, she should also retain a copy of a certificate for Fred's public key, signed by a trusted certification authority, plus a copy of the current CRL (certificate revocation list) from that certification authority.

18. This form of non-repudiation does not necessarily extend beyond "physical" delivery of the information; it does not necessarily imply that the recipient read the data or acted on it in any particular way. In this regard it is somewhat analogous to signing for receipt of a certified letter, where such signature implies nothing about whether the signer has read the contents or not. Compare the similar rules under section 15, "Time and Place of Sending and Receipt," of the Uniform Electronic Transactions Act, available at <http://www.law.upenn. bll/ulc/fnact99/1990s/ueta1999.htm>, and section 102(52) (defining *receipt*) of the Uniform Computer Information Transactions Act (October 15, 1999), available at <http://www.law.upenn.edu/bll/ulc/ucita/ucitaFinal00.htm>.

19. It may also protect recipients to the extent that the recipient was obligated (at least) to take delivery.

20. See "Time Stamping" in section 9.6.

21. See discussion of the mailbox rule in section 3.3.

22. Like many agencies, the Environmental Protection Agency (EPA) has firm deadlines regarding filing reports or appeals to decisions. For example, the

EPA's Y2K Enforcement Policy encouraged companies to promptly test computer-related equipment involved in monitoring environmental problems for Y2K compliance. To encourage this, the EPA agreed to waive 100% of civil penalties and recommend against civil prosecutions for Y2K-related violations reported by February 1, 2000. See EPA 99-12-25, March 12, 1999; see also E. Lynn Grayson, *Chicago Daily Law Bulletin* (March 22, 1999): 6. However, some agency regulations allow for hardship exemptions from filing deadlines where reports are to be filed electronically and computer or communications failures prevent timely filing. For example, see SEC Regulation S-T, 17 C.F.R. sec. 232.201(a), which provides a temporary hardship exemption for SEC filers via the EDGAR system in cases of "unanticipated technical difficulties." Where problems in delivery occur in the transmission path or with the recipient's system, non-repudiation of submission certainly bolsters a party's claim for such an exemption. Moreover, the availability of mechanisms for non-repudiation of submission might lead to agency regulations providing that timely transmittal (as opposed to actual delivery) of a filing is sufficient to make a filing timely. The IRS, for example, provided penalty relief for taxpayers and businesses who made reasonable efforts to comply with the tax laws but were unable because of Y2K problems beyond their control. See 1999 WL 124481 (I.R.S.) or IR-99-104, December 22, 1999.

23. Indeed, non-repudiation of submission may in some cases be thought of as non-repudiation of delivery to a trusted third party.

24. This list of activities is based on a list of phases of non-repudiation in ISO/IEC 10181-4, *Information Technology—Security Frameworks in Open Systems—Non-repudiation Framework,* also published as ITU-T Recommendation X.813, details at <http://www.itu.ch>.

25. In ISO/IEC 10181-4, dispute resolution is listed as the final phase in the provision of non-repudiation, simply because one of the purposes of non-repudiation is to provide evidence sufficient to resolve disputes efficiently. Nonetheless, since avoiding disputes is the other principal goal of non-repudiation mechanisms, this chapter addresses dispute resolution as a relevant but separate activity. In this sense, non-repudiation acts as a tool to facilitate dispute resolution, as opposed to dispute resolution's acting as a phase of non-repudiation.

26. Attorneys and businesspersons have engaged in record generation, transfer, verification, and record retention for centuries—they merely may not have consciously considered their actions in these terms.

27. Ultimately, the use of non-repudiation services will become a recognized industry practice in e-commerce, provided that the technology is available at a reasonable cost, adds value, and is widely deployed. Associated PKI practices would then become implied terms or usages of trade unless the parties explicitly agreed to the contrary. See chapter 3 regarding usages of trade.

28. In practice, a clear statement that non-repudiation techniques are applied might take one or more of the following forms: (a) To participate in a transaction, you must present a certificate that can be authenticated by you or a trusted third party, and you are responsible for maintaining sole access to your account or (b) You will receive a password and account designation upon registering. You are responsible for maintaining the confidentiality of the password and account and are fully responsible for all activities that occur under your password or account.

29. Where trade practices or course of dealing between participants obviates explicit service requests, the service-requester role becomes more of a conceptual abstraction than a reality as far as requesting non-repudiation is concerned. However, the service-requester role may still exist for requesting the use of particular protocols or heightened non-repudiation mechanisms.

30. See UETA sec. 14, "Automated Transactions": "In an automated transaction . . . [a] contract may be formed by the interaction of electronic agents of the parties, even if no individual was aware of or reviewed the electronic agents' actions or the resulting terms and agreements."

31. Return receipt service provides a mailer with evidence of delivery (to whom the mail was delivered and the date of delivery). A return receipt also supplies the recipient's actual delivery address if it is different from the address used by the sender. A return receipt may be requested before or after mailing (U.S. Postal Service, *Domestic Mail Manual,* S915, which describes and defines "return receipt").

32. See Federal Rules of Evidence, Rule 803(6) (Business Records Exception): "The following are not excluded by the hearsay rule: [records] kept in the

course of a regularly conducted business activity." See "Evidence" under section 3.4 regarding business records.

33. Of course, for such transactions, the electronic recording would need to be valid and available.

34. For this reason, the responsibilities assumed by a certification authority that issues public-key certificates for non-repudiation purposes may be somewhat greater than the responsibilities of one that issues such certificates for basic authentication, confidentiality, or information integrity purposes. Correspondingly, the trustworthiness of the end-user cryptomodule and other dimensions of the infrastructure may need to be somewhat greater.

35. This authentication may be based on local domain security services, such as a client-server network with public-key or Kerberos authentication and key establishment.

36. Whether the time is of origin or dispatch depends on the deployed protocol. That is, the time is generally of dispatch when the originator sends the message to the trusted third party who then transfers it directly to the intended recipient, whereas the time is generally of origin when the originator sends the message to the trusted third party who time-stamps, digitally signs, and returns it to the originator before the originator then transmits it to the intended recipient. The applicable policy, contracts, or system rules should clearly indicate the intended meaning of a given time stamp and digital signature. See draft ETSI Standard, *Electronic Signature Standardization for Business Transactions,* ETSI ES 201 733 V1.1.4 (1999-11-25), available at <http://www.etsi.org/sec/el-sign.htm>, which proposes a "commitment type" that "can be indicated in the electronic signature either: explicitly using a 'commitment type indication' in the electronic signature, implicitly, or explicitly from the semantics of the signed data. If the indicated commitment type is explicit using a 'commitment type indication' in the electronic signature, acceptance of a verified signature implies acceptance of the semantics of that commitment type. The semantics of explicit commitment types indications shall be specified either as part of the signature policy or may be registered for generic use across multiple policies."

37. ABA Guideline 1.34 defines *transactional certificate* as a "certificate for a specific transaction incorporating by reference one or more digital signatures."

38. The design of a standardized time-stamping token has been the subject of considerable debate. Such token standard should address (a) what the token components are, (b) what trust model services the token requires or is bound to, (c) the state of the token itself, and (d) the token's use models (policies and practices under which it will be deployed) (contribution by Todd Glassy to the ietf-pkix@imc.org mailing list [November 13, 1999]).

39. This would be considered infeasible with one hash function, provided that the hash function is well designed. However, if one hash function can be substituted transparently for another (however unlikely), the claim of infeasibility is much more difficult to make.

40. For example, it can be used with an ordinary e-mail protocol that has no provision for attaching special signatures, certificates, or tokens to messages.

41. Subject to the specific requirements of the transaction, the PKI used by the recipient to digitally sign an acknowledgment message should be of materially equivalent trustworthiness. UCC sec. 2-207 states that a "definite and seasonable expression of acceptance or a written confirmation which is sent within a reasonable time operates as an acceptance even though it states terms additional to or different from those offered or agreed upon, unless acceptance is expressly made conditional on assent to the additional or different terms."

42. See <http://www.tumbleweed.com> for an example of such a confirmed delivery service.

43. A good trading partner agreement can provide only limited protection in this case. For example, section 2.2 of the ABA Model Electronic Data Interchange Trading Partner Agreement requires the receiving party to "promptly and properly transmit a functional acknowledgment in return." But the undertaking of such transmittal remains within the exclusive power of the receiving party.

44. Moreover, since the police officer physically forces the document onto the recipient's property or person, it can be distinguished from a communications protocol which, at best, is a precondition for the generation of a mandatory acknowledgment of the recipient's willingness to download the subject communication.

45. Traditional *registered mail* provides an analogous type of service. In the digital environment, this mechanism is available with the X.400 Message

Handling System; see W. Ford, *Computer Communications Security: Principles, Standard Protocols and Techniques* (Upper Saddle River, NJ: Prentice Hall PTR, 1994), chap. 13, details at <http://www.prenhall.com/013/799452/79945-2.html>.

46. M. S. Baum, "Trusted Entity Debate Needs User Participation," *Network World* (May 3, 1993): 32; see also Francis Fukuyama, *Trust: The Social Virtues and the Creation of Prosperity* (Tampa, Fl: Free Press Paperbacks, 1995), which provides an enlightening analysis of attributes of trust.

47. Although every attribute of a certificate may have some impact on non-repudiation, the three listed attributes have particularly acute operative impact.

48. Standards specifiy the following explicit certificate purposes: digitalSignature (0), *non-repudiation* (1), keyEncipherment (2), dataEncipherment (3), keyAgreement (4), keyCertSign (5), cRLSign (6), encipherOnly (7), and decipherOnly (8). See RFC 2459 (emphasis added).

49. Imagine if the originator certificate's key usage extension was set for non-repudiation, but the originator's corresponding digitally signed transaction did not indicate intended support for non-repudiation, the trusted third party's time stamp had a policy field in the time-stamp token that indicated use exclusively for non-repudiation purposes, and that time-stamping entity's certificate failed to include a critically set KeyPurposeID with the value id-kp-timeStamping and failed to indicate whether it was intended to support non-repudiation. The bottom line is that overuse and lack of coordination and clarity regarding non-repudiation can diminish its effective use.

50. ABA Guideline 1.33 defines *time-stamp* as "(1) To create a notation that indicates, at least, the correct date and time of an action, and the identity of the *person* that created the notation; or (2) Such a notation appended, attached or referenced"; compare the German Digital Signature Law, *Signaturegesetz,* sec. 126.2.4 BGB, sec. 2: "(4) A time stamp within the meaning of this law is a digital attestation of a certifier marked with a digital signature that certain digital data was presented to it at a certain time."

51. Several state statutes define time stamping without requiring it and some note that the times recorded are presumptively valid in court. See, for

example, Missouri Revised Statutes sec. 28.669 (1994); Utah Code Ann. sec. 46-4-406 (1994); Washington Revised Code sec. 19.34.350 (1994). Malaysia's 1997 Digital Signature Bill was one of the laws to address time stamping the most specifically, providing for the recognition of date and time services when the certifying third party ("controller") determines that the requirements prescribed in the act have been satisfied and the services are on a list of recognized date- and time-stamp services that the controller has published.

52. Such use of a time stamp would provide further evidentiary support of the efficacy of a digital signature created within the validity period of its corresponding certificate, consistent with ABA Guideline 1.33, which states: "Where a rule of law requires a signature, or provides for certain consequences in the absence of a signature, that rule is satisfied by a digital signature which is

    1. affixed by the signer with the intention of signing the message and
    2. verified by reference to the public key listed in a valid certificate."

    See also Hans Nilsson and Denis Pinkas, *Validation of Electronic Signatures,* white paper (March 19, 1999), available at <http://www.evidian.com>. Nonetheless, subject to applicable rules, a devious originator could subsequently claim that the key had been compromised without its knowledge prior to the key's use by the originator.

53. Time stamps can later be re-time-stamped and notarized (even where certificate revocation lists are unavailable).

54. For example, see S. Haber and W. S. Stornetta, "How to Time-Stamp a Digital Document," *Journal of Cryptology* 3, no. 2 (1991): 99–111. For further discussion, see A. J. Menezes, P. C. van Oorschot, and S. A. Vanstone, *Handbook of Applied Cryptography* (Boca Raton, FL: CRC Press, 1996), chap. 13. Compare the commercial initiative to digitally sign data from government-operated authoritative time sources at <http://www.certifiedtime.com>.

55. See generally NIST Time and Frequency Division at <http://www.bldrdoc. gov/timefreq/>, which explains and provides accurate time. See also "Definitions of Time" at <http://tycho.usno.navy.mil/systime.html>.

56. See the NIST Network Time Service at <http://www.bldrdoc.gov/timefreq/service/nts.htm>, which allows users to synchronize computer clocks via the Internet. The time information provided by the service is directly traceable to UTC (NIST). The service responds to time requests from any Internet client in several formats, including the DAYTIME, TIME, and NTP protocols.

57. Note that GPS time does not include additional leap seconds beyond the 19 that were defined when the GPS time scale was initialized. The number of leap seconds since that epoch is transmitted from each satellite as part of the navigation message. In addition, some GPS receivers (especially the handheld units designed to determine the user's position) do not compensate for processing time of the signals once received, resulting in up to several seconds discrepancy between the time that is displayed and the datum that was received from the satellite.

58. As an example of the rapid advance of timing precision requirements, in 1980, data timing used mostly 1-second resolution. After the advent of microprocessor-based timing, 1 millisecond became the standard. In the 1990s with GPS, 1 microsecond became the standard, and several nanoseconds became possible under laboratory conditions (a contribution from Bill Lattin to the ietf-pkix@imc.org mailing list [1999]).

59. Patents issued include "Public/Key Date-Time Notary Facility" (Fischer, 1991), "Electronic Notary" (Durst et al., 1991), "Public/Key Date-Time Notary Facility" (Fischer, 1992), "Digital Document Time-Stamping with Catenate Certificate" (Haber et al., 1992), "Method for Secure Time-Stamping of Digital Documents" (Haber et al., 1992), "Method of Extending the Validity of a Cryptographic Certificate" (Haber et al., 1994), "Personal Date/Time Notary Device" (Fischer, 1995), and "Digital Document Authentication System" (Haber et al., 1998).

60. In *Surety Technologies, Inc. v. Entrust Technologies, Inc.,* 74 F. Supp. 2d 632 (E.D. Va., 1999) (No. Civ. A. 99-203-A), in essence, the court ruled that Entrust (and any other party) was free to use hash-and-sign timestamping. This case, which denied Surety some fundamental patent claims on time stamping, may have brought partial resolution of intellectual property issues.

61. For example, the temporal terms of certain commercial leases and contracts often exceed 25 years, certain trust instruments can be in effect to the outer limit of the rule against perpetuities, and, of course, statutes of limitations periods, which provide a defense to actions arising from such transactions or documents, often extend seven or more years. Additionally, digital signature laws often include considerable retention periods.

62. See National Archives and Records Administration, *Electronic Records Management,* 36 C.F.R. 1234 (1998), which provides an overview of methods and requirements for reliable long-term archiving of electronic-based information resources.

63. The term *arbiter* is used loosely here and is not meant to refer exclusively to formal arbitration proceedings. For additional information, see M. S. Baum, "Alternative Dispute Resolution Mechanisms," in *Federal Certification Authority Liability and Policy,* NIST-GCR-94-654 (Gaithersburg, MD: National Institute of Standards and Technology, 1994), 378, available at <http://www.verisign.com/repository/pubs>.

64. In practice, the only party that must accept the authority of the trusted third party is the final dispute resolution mechanism, since it is only that party that ultimately determines non-repudiation. Nonetheless, having all parties trust and recognize the role of the trusted third party will mitigate disputes, speed dispute resolution, and enhance the value of the infrastructure.

65. For example, a value-added network (VAN) operator may provide some trusted third-party functions as part of its service offerings. For example, the online auction site eBay offers arbitration services in its user agreement. See eBay, "User Agreement," at <http://pages.ebay.com/help/community/png-user.html>: "Arbitration. Any controversy or claim arising out of or relating to this Agreement or our services shall be settled by binding arbitration in accordance with the commercial arbitration rules of the American Arbitration Association. Any such controversy or claim shall be arbitrated on an individual basis, and shall not be consolidated. . . . The arbitration shall be conducted in San Jose, California, and judgment on the arbitration may be entered into any court having jurisdiction thereof. Either you or eBay make seek any interim or preliminary relief from a court of competent jurisdiction in San Jose, California, necessary

to protect the rights or property of you or eBay pending the completion of arbitration."

66. There are currently more than four million notaries public in the United States (Baum, *Federal Certification Authority Liability and Policy,* 283). According to The International Union of Latin Notaries (UINL) data from questionnaires in 1994 and 1996, there were in excess of 85,000 notaries public reported by the 43 countries that responded. See <http://www.uinl.org>.

67. Uniform Law on Notarial Acts (ULNA), sec. 2, 14 U.L.A. 1, available at <http://www.law.upenn.edu/bll/ulc/fnact99/1980s/ulna82.htm>. For a general summary of computer-based notarial issues, see Michael S. Baum and Henry H. Perritt, Jr., *Electronic Contracting, Publishing and EDI Law* (New York: Wiley, 1991) 208–11. In Argentina, for example, a document does not have legal effect without a notarial act such as an acknowledgment or verification. See Notarial Law 12990, Cod. Civ. articles 997–1011. Each notarial act typically includes the date of the notarial act.

68. The official comment to section 2 of the ULNA provides that "personal physical appearance of the acknowledging party before the notarial officer is required." The personal presence requirement is of great importance and value.

69. "[A] notarial officer [must have] satisfactory evidence that a person is the person whose true signature is on a document . . ." [ULNA sec. 2(f)].

70. ULNA sec. 1(3).

71. ULNA sec. 6(d). *Seal* is not defined.

72. ULNA sec. 7.

73. One significant U.S. legislative reform is the Uniform Electronic Transaction Act, available at <http://www.law.upenn.edu/bll/ulc/fnact99/1990s/uetna99.htm>, which provides in section 11, "Notarization and Acknowledgment": "If a law requires a signature or record to be notarized, acknowledged, verified, or made under oath, the requirement is satisfied if the electronic signature of the person authorized to perform those acts, together with all other information required to be included by other applicable law, is attached to or logically associated with the signature or record." See also the notary provisions of The Federal E-Sign Act discussed above in section 8.1; Quebec Civil Code section II, article 281, "Preuve des faits inscrits ou con-

statés par l'officier": "The recital, in an authentic act, of the facts which the public officer had the task of observing or recording makes proof against all persons."

74. Baum and Perritt, *Electronic Contracting*, 211–12.

75. The Latin or civil law notary is a qualified attorney who has trained, passed special notarial examinations, and been admitted to the notarial profession. A Latin-law notary may often act as a legal advisor, prepare documents, and appear before courts in uncontested and other routine matters (Comité Franco-Italian du Notariat Ligure Provençal, *The Function of the Latin Law Notary,* Hommage au XiX° Congrés Internationale du Notariat Latin [Amsterdam, 1989]; Baum, *Federal Certification Authority Liability and Policy,* note 1066).

76. The ABA Guidelines (comment 1.6.3) define CyberNotary as an attorney at law "admitted to practice in the United States and qualified to act as a Cyber-Notary[SM] pursuant to specialization rules." CyberNotary infrastructure is under development in various forums.

Florida accepted the CyberNotary in its 1996 Electronic Signature Act. See David Sommer, "New Legal Code: Sign It by Modem: Florida's Electronic Signature Act Has Become Law, How It Will Be Implemented Isn't Clear Yet," *Tampa Tribune* (June 3, 1996): 1. However, the Florida provisions were eventually repealed in 1999 (F.S.A. sec. 117.20, repealed by Laws 1999, c. 99-251, sec. 165, effective July 1, 1999).

Although no jurisdiction has developed a true CyberNotary, several states have modified the traditional requirements for notaries to accommodate electronic signatures, some going beyond the notary provisions in UETA (presented in footnote 73, above). For example, the Utah Code develops the most sophisticated requirements for allowing the suspension of the formality of a seal on proper digital signature and sufficient information [Utah Code Ann. sec. 46-1-16 (7) (1999)]. Arkansas has suspended the formal requirement of a seal, passing a definition of notary that states, "Any rule of law which requires a witness or notary shall be deemed satisfied by the electronic signature of the witness or notary" (Ark. Code Ann. sec. 24-31-104b3 [Michie 1999]). Similarly, a provision in the Georgia code states almost the same definition (Ga. Code Ann. 10-12-4j [1999]).

77. For example, for notarial acknowledgments to support digital certificate applicant validation. See "Notary FAQ" at <http://www.verisign.com/repository>.

78. For example, section 6-2 of the American Bar Association's Model Electronic Payments Agreement provides that "[t]he receipt by the sender of an Acknowledgment from the recipient shall constitute *conclusive evidence* that the subject communication was received and is syntactically correct" (emphasis added). Nonetheless, public policy and other government interests may limit or preclude the enforcement of such stipulations, although, of course, party autonomy principles (particularly among business partners) will generally be respected under the law. See section 3.2 on party autonomy.

79. This section builds on the discussion in chapter 3 regarding electronic evidence in the context of enforceability of contractual promises.

80. The discussion focuses primarily on the law in U.S. jurisdictions, generally modeled after the Federal Rules of Evidence. Nonetheless, many of the same issues bear similar importance in other legal regimes.

81. This constitutes a classical requirement for proof of the integrity of documentary evidence. Typically, a party must show proper chain of custody by demonstrating that a record was properly maintained (including that it was protected from alteration or loss) from the time of its creation or receipt until it is presented in court. The custodians of traditional as well as computer-based records have faced the burdensome (and sometimes impossible) task of proving in detail the sufficiency of the procedures they have used to protect the subject records at every relevant moment of time (and their compliance with such procedures). Because digital signatures can "seal" records and render them unforgeable without detection, public-key technology should substantially reduce the custodian's burden in this context.

82. See chapter 3. To ensure that non-repudiation evidence qualifies for the business records exception to the hearsay rule, participants should make requests for non-repudiation services and subsequent archiving of evidence as part of their standard procedures.

83. For an advanced discussion of XML, XFDL, and the issue of non-repudiation as it relates to the integrity of e-commerce documents, see Barclay T. Blair and

John Boyer, "XFDL: Creating Electronic Commerce Transaction Records Using XML," This is a single reference in a journal published by Elsevier?: *International Journal of Computer and Telecommunications Networking, Computer Networks* 31 (1999): 1611–22, available at <http://www8.org/w8-papers/4d-electronic/xfdl/xfdl.html>.

84. For general information, see Cohasset Associates, "Electronic Commerce Forms: Requirements, Issues, and Solutions," <http://www.cohasset.com/comm_forms.html>, which provides an in-depth overview of the issues surrounding the content, context, and structure of electronic records.

85. Exceptions include some industry arbitrators or evidentiary panels of magistrates, who specialize in resolving disputes involving technical evidence.

86. In U.S. law, this principle is codified in Federal Rule of Evidence 702: "If scientific, technical, or other specialized knowledge will assist the trier of fact to understand the evidence or to determine a fact in issue, a witness qualified as an expert by knowledge, skill, experience, training, or education, may testify thereto in the form of an opinion or otherwise."

87. U.S. courts must make these determinations pursuant to Federal Rule of Evidence 104(a) (or some analogous state rule): "Preliminary questions concerning the qualification of a person to be a witness, the existence of a privilege, or the admissibility of evidence shall be determined by the court, subject to [the relevancy conditioned on fact]. In making its determination it is not bound by the rules of evidence except those with respect to privileges."

88. Federal Rule of Evidence 201.

89. *Daubert v. Merrell Dow Pharmaceuticals, Inc.,* 113 S. Ct. 2786, 2796 (1993).

90. In addition to demonstrating scientific validity, presumably a foundation would need to be laid under Fed. R. Civ. Proc. Rule 901(a) and 901(b)(9) to demonstrate that the digital signature creation and verification process "worked" accurately before the results of a signature verification could be admitted into evidence in support of the proposition that the digital signature was made by the private key corresponding to the public key contained in the sender's certificate:

Rule 901. Requirement of Authentication or Identification. (a) General provision. The requirement of authentication or identification as a condition precedent to admissibility is satisfied by evidence sufficient to support a finding that the matter in question is what its proponent claims. (b) Illustration. By way of illustration only, and not by way of limitation, the following are examples of authentication or identification conforming with the requirements of this rule: . . . (10) Process or system. Evidence describing a process or system used to produce a result and showing that the process or system produces an accurate result.

91. *Daubert,* 113 S. Ct. 2800.

92. *Kuhmo Tire Co., Ltd. v. Carmichael,* 119 S. Ct. 1167, 1171 (1999). Nonetheless, the court recognized that a "trial court should consider the specific factors identified in Daubert where there are reasonable measures of the reliability of expert testimony" (*Kuhmo,* 1176). The court noted that the failure to apply *Daubert* factors in such cases would constitute an abuse of discretion (*Kuhmo,* 1179). See *General Electric Company v. Joiner,* 522 U.S. 136 (1997), which confirmed the abuse-of-discretion standard.

93. *Daubert,* 113 S. Ct. 2796–98.

94. *Kuhmo,* 1173.

95. *Kuhmo,* 1176.

96. *Kuhmo,* 1175, which cited necromancy and astrology as examples of less credible methodologies.

97. See RSA Data Security, Inc., "Frequently Asked Questions About Today's Cryptography," question 3.6.7, "What Are Some Other Block Ciphers?" (January 26, 1999), available at <http://www.rsa.com/rsalabs/faq/html/3-6-7.html>.

98. See chapter 4 for further discussion about RSA.

99. The assertion that the technology is implemented properly is the most difficult aspect here. More work is yet needed on systematic approaches to ensuring that specific implementations can be assumed reliable. See Arjen K. Lenstra and Eroc R. Verjei, "Selecting Cryptographic Key Sizes in Commercial Applications," 3 *CCE Quarterly Journal* 4 (1999), which presents comprehensive cryptographic key size guidelines within the context of "three quantifiable parameters": life span of the information that needs protection, the acceptable security margin as a function of the resources and capability of the contemplated attacker, and the effectiveness of the attacks (cryptanalysis).

100. For a general overview of problems faced by courts in this area, see "Case Comment: *Daubert v. Merrell Dow Pharmaceuticals*," 107 *Harvard Law Review* 254–64 (1993); Tracey A. Paulauskas, "Note, Volume III of the Daubert Trilogy: *Kuhmo Tire Co. v. Carmichael*," 39 *Jurimetrics Journal* 443–54 (1999).

101. "There is apprehension that abandonment of 'general acceptance' as the exclusive requirement for admission will result in a 'free-for-all' in which befuddled juries are confounded by absurd and irrational pseudoscientific assertions. [This claim] seems overly pessimistic about the capabilities of the jury and of the adversary system generally" (*Daubert*, 2798 [Blackmun]).

CHAPTER 10

Certification Policies and Practices

$\mathbf{D}$igital signatures and encryption can be used with confidence if a trusted certification authority ensures the authenticity and integrity of public keys.[1] However, a certification authority can do so only if its services are recognized as being practical, trustworthy, and legally effective. Such recognition depends, in part, on the efficacy of the certification authority's practices. Certification practices can be expressed in various forms, including certificate policies (CPs), certification practice statements (CPSs), user agreements such as subscriber and relying party[2] agreements, and guidelines and laws governing the rights and responsibilities of the parties that provide and use certification services.

This chapter discusses certification policy and practices. We begin with an overview of the CP and CPS concepts and explain their purposes, content, and interrelationship. We then discuss practices issues that are typically addressed (or should be addressed) in one or more of the policy or practices documents.

10.1 Concepts

Privacy Enhanced Mail (PEM) Policy Statement

The CP and CPS concepts are rooted in the concepts of policy certification authorities (PCAs) and their policy statements that were introduced in the Internet Privacy Enhanced Mail (PEM) project.[3] These concepts are described in Internet RFC 1422,[4] which states:

It is important that a certificate management infrastructure for use in the Internet
community accommodate a range of clearly-articulated certification policies for both
users and organizations in a well-architected fashion. Mechanisms must be provided
to enable each user to be aware of the policies governing any certificate which the
user may encounter. This requires the introduction and standardization of procedures
and conventions that are outside the scope of X.509.[5]

Although PEM gained neither broad acceptance nor wide deployment, a few PEM
policy certification authorities were established, and they published policy statements.[6]
More importantly, PEM catalyzed in-depth consideration of the legal and practice issues
surrounding PKI. PEM deserves recognition as a major pioneering activity in exploring
the legal-technical boundaries of PKI.

Many experts concluded, however, that the PEM policy statement model needed
refinement to satisfy contemplated commercial and government use of PKI. This led to the
development of the CP and CPS concepts.

Certification Practice Statement

The term *certification practice statement* (CPS) originated in the American Bar Association's *Digital Signature Guidelines* (ABA Guidelines), where it is defined as a "statement
of the practices which a certification authority employs in issuing certificates."[7] A CPS
articulates the measures taken by a certification authority to manage certificate life-cycle
operations, to validate certificate applicants, and to describe underlying technical, procedural, and legal requirements contributing to a certification authority's trustworthiness.
The precise coverage of a CPS varies as a function of the applications and services supported, the environment, the security architecture, and many other factors.

A CPS can be valuable, if not indispensable, as a primary expression of PKI practices.[8] Because of deficiencies in PKI legislation and regulation, supporting case law, and
recognized usages of trade,[9] and without a cadre of "gap-filler" provisions[10] as exists in
the codified commercial law, a rigorously drafted CPS and ancillary agreements can provide the legal certainty needed to satisfy the intended purposes of certification services.

In e-commerce environments, the potential involvement of many entities with
diverse relationships creates complex legal issues that deserve attention. A responsive and
comprehensive CPS therefore might include

• a clear and complete articulation of the parties' legal rights and obligations,

- a systematic description of pertinent aspects of the operational environment, and
- an encapsulation of current industry knowledge and accepted practices.[11]

The form taken by a CPS can vary widely. According to the ABA Guidelines:

> A certification practice statement may take the form of a declaration by the certifi-
> cation authority of the details of its trustworthy system and the practices it
> employs in its operations and in support of issuance of a certificate, or it may be a
> statute or regulation applicable to the certification authority and covering similar
> subject matter. It may also be part of the contract between the certification author-
> ity and the subscriber. A certification practice statement may also be comprised of
> multiple documents, a combination of public law, private contract, and/or declara-
> tion. . . . [12]

The "combination of public law, private contract, and/or declaration" implies that a certification authority may use a variety of complementary mechanisms to advance legal certainty. These mechanisms can include, for example, a CP, a primary CPS document, a subscriber agreement,[13] and ancillary documents such as a security policy specification, technical manuals, and user guides.

Certificate Policy (CP)

We introduced the X.509 certificate policy concept in chapter 7. With the advent of the X.509 Version 3 certificate format, PEM PCAs and their policy statements were effec-tively superseded by the CP concept. To reiterate, an X.509 certificate policy is defined as a "named set of rules that indicates the applicability of a certificate to a particular commu-nity and/or class of application with common security requirements."[14]

The Relationship between a CPS and a CP

The PKI technical and legal communities have worked hard at distinguishing and clarify-ing the respective purposes and uses of a CP and a CPS. Although this distinction is still a subject of debate, we can observe the following characteristics of these documents:

- *Requirements versus procedures:* Generally, a CP is viewed as a statement of requirements (what needs to be achieved), whereas a CPS is viewed as a statement of procedures (how such requirements are to be satisfied). Thus, for example, a CP may specify the level of assurance associated with a particular class of certificate, and a corresponding CPS specifies the attributes and infrastructure that it purports will satisfy the level of assurance specified in the CP.

- *Specificity:* Generally, a CPS is a more detailed, comprehensive treatment of a certification authority's practices than the CP to which it corresponds.[15] In some environments, it may be appropriate to publish a short form or summarized CPS (as a CPS supplement) particularly geared toward consumers, such as a PKI disclosure statement.[16] More detailed CPS provisions might be incorporated by reference into such a document or otherwise published in widely available documents.

- *Scope:* The precise and proper scope of a CPS and other referenced documents are generally subject to the discretion of the publishing certification authority, taking into account the law,[17] including usage of trade, and the requirements of the community of interest[18] served by the CPS. Common approaches will inevitably be further shaped by industry and consumer forces and by continuing dialog within the PKI legal and controls community. A CP potentially covers many of the same types of provisions as a CPS (generally a subset of them) but is typically higher level or less precise because it may target interoperation among a broader community or disparate communities.

- *CP-CPS relationship:* One CP can be referenced in more than one CPS, and the CPS then describes the precise practices by which the requirements of the policy are implemented by that organization. Similarly, one CPS may reference multiple CPs if the certification authority supports multiple different applications and communities. On the other hand, multiple certification authorities (with differing CPSs) may adhere to the same CP.

- *Authorship:* A CP is not necessarily associated with a particular certification authority or PKI. Rather, it may have been created by a community of interest that consumes third-party PKI services.

- *Document architecture:* It may or may not be optimal to present a certification authority's practices in a single, comprehensive document. Despite the obvious virtues of managing and communicating a single, clearly identified CP or CPS, multiple documents may be required or preferable.

- *Certificate policy identifier:* It is possible to use an identifier of a CPS as the value of a CP identifier in an X.509 certificate. In this case, a CPS also constitutes a CP definition, and the presence of the identifier in the certificate typically constitutes a declaration that the certificate was issued in accordance with the terms of the CPS.
- *Facilitation of relying party acceptance:* Even if a CP is a less precise statement than a CPS, many certificate users may be prepared to use a certificate after inspecting only the CP identifier. In this regard, a CP may serve as a basis for accepting certificates in locally approved application scenarios, and application software might be configured to automatically accept certificates bearing that CP identifier. Conversely, such users might not want to accept a certificate that does not contain a recognized CP identifier.
- *Interoperation:* Writing CPs and CPSs following a common template has the advantage of making it easier to compare such documents to identify their similarities and differences. This can be particularly beneficial when organizations need to recognize the practices of other organizations in relation to their own. For example, if X.509 certificate policy mapping were to be deployed, the task of deciding whether a mapping is acceptable would be facilitated by the CPs' using the same template.[19]

Assurance Levels

Assurances refer to statements and conduct of a certification authority to provide and maintain a specified level of service.[20] The terms of the CP or CPS and associated agreements should state the precise scope and meaning of assurances.[21] Assurances may refer to the quality and security provided by a PKI, its certificates, and other designated data items, services and products.[22] Various PKIs have developed their own ways to describe the relative assurances of their certificates and infrastructures. For example, the U.S. government has created CPs intended to facilitate interoperation in sensitive but unclassified government-related applications.

An example of specified assurance levels is the set of four levels presented in the draft Certificate Policy for the U.S. Federal Bridge Certification Authority. These assurance levels include the following attributes:[23]

- *Rudimentary:* The applicant may apply for a certificate through an open network such as the Internet and need only provide an e-mail address. The private signature key may exist in software or hardware.
- *Basic:* The applicant may apply in person or through a network (via comparison with trusted information in a database or through other trusted means).
- *Medium:* The applicant must appear in person before a registration authority, trusted agent, or an entity certified by a state or Federal agency as being authorized to confirm identities. The applicant must present one Federal-government-issued picture ID, or at least two forms of non-Federal-government-issued identification (at least one of which must be a picture ID).
- *High:* The applicant must appear in person before a registration authority or trusted agent. The applicant identity validation requirements are consistent with *Medium.* The private signature key must exist in hardware.

Assurances are handled differently in different PKI communities. Ultimately, assurance levels or other manifestations of a certificate's trustworthiness cannot be assessed meaningfully without consideration of the overall systems, applications, and supporting technical, operational, and management infrastructures.

Certificate Classes

In the commercial PKI service industry, assurances are sometimes expressed in the context of certificate classes using a system of numbered levels. A PKI and designated components may support one or more levels in its role of issuing and managing certificates, providing other trust services, and maintaining trustworthiness. Each certificate class provides specific functionality and security features, as required by different applications. Like the assurance levels outlined earlier, certificate classes typically differ in terms of these requirements:

- Validation requirements, for example, validation of identity of a certificate's subject (such as through personal presence before a registration authority or a notary)
- Private-key protection requirements, for example, the strength of the methods employed to prevent key compromise (such as appropriate protection of crypto-modules, smartcards, and evaluated products) and to ensure appropriate key usage
- Requirements for operational, management, and physical controls

For example, the VeriSign Trust Network (VTN) CP definition[24] recognizes certificate classes 1, 2, and 3. Higher-numbered classes generally provide greater assurances than lower-numbered classes, but class numbers do not represent a strict ordering with respect to security services and trustworthiness. This is because the differences between classes can be multidimensional—classes can contain distinct attributes that are not precisely comparable to other classes, and classes can contain subclasses that are product specific or service specific.

Because the service offerings of PKI providers necessarily evolve, along with practices suitable to differing communities, any scheme to differentiate services using a system of simple numerical levels has limitations. Nonetheless, the certificate class paradigm generally maps well to the CP concept.

Organization of CP or CPS Content

The appropriate subject matter, organization, and logical presentation of CP or CPS content depend on many factors, including the applications supported, the applicable community of interest, the intended security, and the legal results demanded of the certification services. Generally, one of the following approaches is used:

- Detailing the rights and obligations of each party (such as certification authorities, subscribers, and relying parties) separately in series. This approach is particularly familiar to lawyers in their drafting and review of contracts.

- Addressing the rights and obligations of parties in the order that they would naturally arise throughout a typical certificate life cycle, for example, certification authority establishment and start-up procedures and then general certification authority operations, including enrollment (registration for a certificate), validation of certificate applicant information, certificate issuance, certificate acceptance, certificate use, certificate suspension, certificate revocation, and certificate expiration. This approach is perhaps most intuitive.
- Conforming to the structure in the leading international guideline, RFC 2527.[25] This approach might be best where interoperation among disparate PKIs is anticipated or where required by a particular community of interest.

Because of the widespread adoption of RFC 2527 as a common structure for a CP or CPS, in the rest of this chapter, policy and practices issues are addressed in the approximate order that such issues appear within RFC 2527.

A few observations are warranted regarding use of the RFC 2527 outline for a CP or CPS:

- Since PKI environments and implementations may vary widely, strict adherence to the structure of RFC 2527 may not always make sense. It may sometimes be better to use RFC 2527 as a checklist only.
- E-commerce business models, technology, and the law are changing rapidly. RFC 2527 was developed before many of these changes occurred. The outline and content of CPs and CPSs should track these changes, which may make it difficult to rigidly follow the RFC, unless that document is updated regularly.
- RFC 2527 notes that many of its items need not be completed for various reasons, including a subject that is redundant and treated elsewhere in the CP or CPS or is irrelevant to a particular implementation. In such cases, the item can be omitted; for completeness, it is recommended that a "no stipulation" statement be included.

The following sections serve as an introduction to certification practice development and interpretation.

10.2 CP and CPS Topics: Introduction of a CP or CPS

RFC 2527 Section 1—Introduction

This component identifies and introduces the set of provisions and indicates the types of entities and applications for which the specification is targeted. This component has the following subcomponents: overview; identification; community and applicability; and contact details.

A comprehensive introduction can be particularly helpful to set the stage and provide an overview of the infrastructure, its players, components, services, and important practices. We encourage drafters to use this part of the document freely to convey a clear message as to the intended community and applications, even if this duplicates material in later sections.

Community Membership and Interoperation

It may be useful to clarify the requirements for accepting a new certification authority or other component into the PKI community and to state how a certification authority terminates its relationship with that community.

Furthermore, the need for interoperation among disparate PKIs is increasing. Thus, a CP or CPS should indicate the extent to which and how interoperation is supported. Effective interoperation is challenging and requires great discipline and rigor if definitions, certificate content, applications and platforms, audit regimes, security, and liability practices of PKIs vary greatly. Successful interoperation requires skill, effort, and, most of all, advance planning.

Certificate Usage

Certain rules may be stated in a CP or CPS to support the effective use of certificates in verifying digitally signed messages or encrypting messages. Use-related provisions of a CP or CPS may also specify the obligations of a party who has received but has not yet relied on such messages. These provisions may also seek to resolve many classic e-commerce validity and enforceability issues, such as the satisfaction of formalistic writing and signature requirements.[26]

Digital Signature Verification Process

The recipient of a digitally signed message verifies the digital signature to determine whether or not it was created using the private key corresponding to the public key in the signer's certificate and whether or not the message has been altered since it was signed.[27] Assurance as to both of these conditions is indispensable to secure e-commerce.

To create affirmative obligations on the part of the user, a CP or CPS may describe the signature validation process in detail. In particular, it may state that verification of a digital signature requires verification of a complete certification path from the signer's certificate to an acceptable root public key, which must have been distributed by independent and secure means. The CP or CPS may also state the process of verifying a certification path covering, in more or less detail, the steps identified under "Certification Path Validation" in section 7.3 of chapter 7.

Subject to the verification process, a digital signature created during the operational period of a certificate is generally considered binding[28] unless

- the subscriber named as the subject of the certificate can establish that the certificate has incorrectly identified the subscriber as such subject[29] or
- the subscriber can establish that he or she lost control of the private key without violating his or her duty to safeguard the private key.[30]

This also assumes that

- the relying party has no knowledge or notice of a breach of the requirements of the CP or CPS by the signer and
- the relying party has complied with all material requirements of the CP or CPS (or corresponding relying party agreement), and the relying party's reliance on the certificate (and on the digital signatures verifiable using the certificate) is reasonable under the circumstances.[31]

Writings and Signatures

As discussed in chapter 8, the legal efficacy of electronic writings and signatures is not yet universally or uniformly regonized and facilitated globally. A CP or CPS might include provisions intended to advance the legal efficacy of e-commerce by serving as default provisions, that is, provisions that are intended to be effective in the absence of agreement between the parties to the contrary; for example:

- *Writings:* A message bearing a digital signature verified by the public key in a valid certificate shall not be denied legal effect solely because it is in electronic form.
- *Signatures:* Where a rule of law or applicable practice requires a signature or provides for certain consequences in the absence of a signature, that rule is satisfied in relation to a message by a digital signature affixed by a signer with the intention of signing a message and subsequently verified using the public key in a valid certificate.

If trading partners desire some treatment of these issues other than by default rules, they may contract for different rules among themselves. At a minimum, the inclusion of such default provisions may provide evidence of the parties' intent.

Identification

The CP or CPS should declare any ASN.1 object identifiers used to reference the CP or CPS, or subsets of it, in X.509 certificates. Similarly, any identifiers used in other protocols or applications should be stated.

10.3   CP and CPS Topics: General Provisions

RFC 2527 Section 2—General Provisions

This component specifies any applicable presumptions on a range of legal and general practices topics. This component contains the following subcomponents: obligations; liability; financial responsibility; interpretation and enforcement; fees; publication and repositories; compliance audit; confidentiality, and intellectual property rights.

Obligations

A CP or CPS should state the rights and obligations of all parties. In this section we identify some of the more important topics that are typically addressed. The enforcement of these rights and obligations depends on a sufficient legal regime that may include various rules, ancillary agreements, or other mechanisms intended to ensure that the parties are bound.

Certification Authority's Representations to Subscribers

Upon certificate issuance, a certification authority makes certain representations to a subscriber. The certification authority may make the following promises to the subscriber named in the certificate:

- There are no misrepresentations of fact in the certificate known to or originating from the certification authority.
- There are no transcription errors in data as received by the certification authority from the certificate applicant that result from a failure of the certification authority to exercise reasonable care in creating the certificate.
- The certificate meets all material requirements of the CP or CPS.

The certification authority may also promise to the subscriber to make reasonable efforts

- to promptly revoke or suspend certificates (under circumstances as stipulated) and
- to notify subscribers of any facts known to it that materially affect the validity and reliability of the certificate it has issued to such subscribers.[32]

Certification Authority's Representations to Relying Parties

To rely on a digital signature means to receive a digital signature and act in a manner that could be detrimental to oneself were the digital signature to be ineffective. By issuing a certificate, a certification authority may typically make the following representations to all who reasonably rely on a digital signature verifiable by the public key in the certificate:

- All information in the certificate or incorporated by reference is accurate (to the extent that the certification authority is obligated to check the accuracy of particular data fields).

- The certification authority has substantially complied with its published practices in issuing the certificate.

Representations by Subscriber upon Acceptance

The CP or CPS should present representations by the subscriber that constitute the subscriber's promises to the certification authority, other subscribers, and all who reasonably rely on the certificate's contents (relying parties). For example, the CP or CPS might stipulate that by accepting a certificate the subscriber promises that, at the time of acceptance and throughout the operational period of the certificate, until notified otherwise by the subscriber:

- All representations made by the subscriber to the certification authority (including, without limitation, those made in the certificate application) regarding the certificate contents are true.
- All information in the certificate is true to the extent that the subscriber has knowledge or notice of such information and does not promptly notify the certification authority of any material inaccuracies therein.
- In the case of a certificate for a digital signature key, each digital signature created using the private key corresponding to the public key in the certificate is the digital signature of the subscriber.
- No unauthorized person has ever had access to the subscriber's private key.
- The certificate is being used exclusively for authorized and legal purposes, consistent with the CP or CPS.
- The subscriber is an end-user subscriber—not a certification authority—and will not use the private key corresponding to the public key in the certificate for signing any certificate (of any format) or CRL, as a certification authority or otherwise, unless expressly agreed in writing between the subscriber and certification authority.[33]

A CP or CPS may also state that, by accepting a certificate, the subscriber

- acknowledges agreement to the terms and conditions contained in the CP or CPS or other applicable documents (such as a subscriber agreement) and

- assumes a duty to retain control of his or her private key and to take reasonable precautions to prevent its loss, disclosure, modification, or unauthorized use.

Indemnity by Subscriber

Indemnification by the subscriber of the certification authority may be included in a CP or CPS to make it clear that the subscriber is responsible for at least exercising reasonable care to safeguard his or her private key and for the accuracy of the information provided to the certification authority and used in issuing the certificate.

Liability

Risk Management

A certification authority's warranties of its services and apportionment of liability tremendously affect its assurances and role and the user community's perception of its trustworthiness. Invariably, the extent to which certification authorities agree to be or are held liable depends on one or more of the following factors:

- The certification authority's costs of operation and, if applicable, fees charged
- The understanding of PKI risks[34]
- The availability and use of proven tools to mitigate compromise and fraud
- The enactment of legislation that provides (or fails to provide) a safe harbor, favorable presumptions, or obligations of the exercise of reasonable care by certification authorities and users for certification activities
- The availability of robust and cost-effective insurance and related risk management vehicles
- Agreements between the user community and the certification authority
- Competition

No certification authority can sustain unlimited exposure and still remain solvent and competitive. Commercial certification authorities are generally adopting a liability position that is consistent with that of most ASPs, ISPs, software and hardware vendors, regulated telecommunications providers, and VANs—they are limiting their liability, often to direct damages.[35] This may change as the industry matures and the conditions affecting the aforementioned factors evolve.

Warranties

Most commercial certification authorities embrace, as a base line, a liability position premised in whole or in part on the safe harbor principle espoused in the ABA Guidelines:[36]

> A certification authority that complies with these Guidelines and any applicable law or contract is not liable for any loss which
>> (1) is incurred by the subscriber of a certificate issued by that certification authority, or any other person, or
>> (2) is caused by reliance upon a certificate issued by the certification authority,
> upon a digital signature verifiable with reference to a public key listed in a certificate, or upon information represented in such a certificate or repository.

By following this principle, a certification authority can disclose its performance obligations, complete such performance obligations, and correspondingly seek to limit its liability to those stated obligations. For example, a CP or CPS may state that certification authorities in their applicable documents warrant and promise to[37]

- provide the infrastructure and certification services, including the establishment and operation of a repository;
- provide the controls and foundation for the certification authority's PKI, including certification authority key-pair generation and key protection procedures;
- perform the stated validation procedures for certificate applications of the indicated class;
- issue certificates in accordance with the CP or CPS and honor the various representations to subscribers and to relying parties;
- publish accepted certificates;
- perform the obligations of a certification authority and support the rights of the subscribers and relying parties who use certificates;
- suspend and revoke certificates;
- provide for the expiration, reenrollment, and renewal of certificates; and
- comply with any other material obligations stated in its operative documents.

Additionally, certification authorities may warrant that their own private keys are not compromised unless they provide notice to the contrary.

Disclaimers and Limitations on Obligations

Just as a certificate user needs to understand the limits of its exposure for the use of certificates, a certification authority needs to understand its exposure in providing certification services. Consequently, one approach is to disclaim certain warranties, such as a warranty of merchantability and warranty of fitness for a particular purpose, and to otherwise seek to limit the certification authority's liability in accordance with the CP or CPS, the certification authority having presented (and adhered to) the various performance obligations or warranties (as described earlier under "Warranties").[38]

Damage and Loss Limitations

A CP or CPS can attempt to quantify the extent of the claimed limitations of liability by providing express caps on liability.[39] A cap is a contractual or legislative ceiling on the damages for which a party would otherwise be responsible in the event that a liability materializes (and the cap is held enforceable). If damages exceed the cap amount, other parties must bear the excess. A liability cap can be tied to a particular class of certificate, which in turn is tied to a particular set of assurances and to a corresponding cost structure. In such a model, the various caps are a function of the relative assurances of the particular certificate classes.

Financial Responsibility

Financial Resources

Certification authorities must be solvent. They must have sufficient financial resources to maintain their operations and perform their current and future duties. They must also be reasonably able to bear the risk of liability, to the extent required by applicable rules, to subscribers and relying parties.

The precise amount of available funds that are sufficient in the event of a major failure, such as the compromise of a root private key or other significant liability event, remains uncertain because of a lack of loss experience data in the insurance industry and a lack of legal decisions. Nonetheless, certification authorities should at least maintain insurance that covers PKI-specific and information technology-specific events (such as key compromise) and cybercrime or otherwise self-insure where possible.[40]

No Fiduciary Relationship

A department of motor vehicles is not the agent of drivers to whom it issues licenses, and an employer does not agree to be the agent of an employee to whom an identification badge has been issued. Similarly, a certification authority does not generally serve as an agent of or play such a fiduciary role for subscribers (unless required by contract or law). This is particularly true where certification authorities are removed from the transactions that are digitally signed by subscribers, that is, where they are not parties to such transactions and do not participate in the signing, time stamping, or communication of such messages. In such cases, a CP or CPS can provide that a fiduciary relationship is not established between a certification authority and subscriber.[41]

Interpretation and Enforcement

Conflict of Provisions

The CP or CPS can seek to declare its primacy by stating that it shall supersede other documents. Clear recognition of the authority of a CP or CPS as the central document within the PKI has the likely benefit of bolstering certainty and harmony.

Governing Law

A CP or CPS should make a choice of governing law, recognizing that information transferred via networks such as the Internet traverses an uncertain number of jurisdictions, since the paths that messages take are not deterministic.

PKI participants need to rely on traditional and developing principles for choosing the law of a particular jurisdiction and relying on a choice of law.

Dispute Resolution

Disputes can be resolved by litigation or by alternative dispute resolution (ADR) mechanisms such as arbitration. A CP or CPS should specify how disputes are to be resolved. Given the complexity of PKIs and the widespread lack of familiarity with them, there is most likely also benefit in providing some type of initial, informal mediation mechanism to assist the parties in framing the issues and in providing some technical and other informational assistance.

Publication and Repository

Publication of certificates and certain related information is a defining moment controlling fundamental obligations of certification authorities and certificate users. For example,

- publication of a certificate typically signals that it has been accepted by its subject;

- publication of revocation data is intended to put the relevant PKI community on notice that designated certificates cannot be trusted and that a relying party cannot justifiably rely on such certificates; and
- publication of a certification authority's CPS is intended to put the relevant PKI community on notice of its practices and may seek to bind both the certification authority and relevant PKI community to its practices.[42]

It is normal business practice for a certification authority to provide a repository[43] to make publicly available certain information (sometimes called disclosure records), such as certificates, CRLs, or other revocation or suspension information, and the CP or CPS. The repository is the focal point for all material information resources pertaining to a certification authority. The deployment of a robust, easy-to-use repository not only advances customer satisfaction but also may ensure more reliable and meaningful communication with all parties. Most important, it serves as a critical mechanism to provide notice of its practices to subscribers and relying parties.[44]

Compliance Audit

Operational compliance audits are essential to sustain the viability of a certification authority. Compliance audit reports are a well-recognized way to demonstrate a certification authority's due diligence, trustworthiness, and proper operation. Such audits may help reduce a certification authority's exposure.

PKIs should preserve an audit trail for all material certificate life-cycle events. Standardized PKI audit programs and procedures are now available, although preliminary.[45] Consequently, PKI auditing is typically undertaken using increasingly recognized and available audit procedures[46] and, in part, audited against more generally accepted auditing principles and standards.[47] Note that a PKI audit's requirements will typically exceed those of a conventional information services audit, in part, because of the inclusion of cryptographic key management control objectives.

A CP or CPS should reference the audit obligations of each relevant PKI component, such as registration authorities, repositories, and directories. A CP or CPS may state that a certified public accountant with demonstrated expertise in computer security or an accredited computer security professional will audit the operations of each certification authority and each other relevant entity at least annually (and at whose expense) to evaluate its compliance with the CP or CPS and other applicable agreements, guidelines, procedures, and standards.

Confidentiality

Depending on the attributes of a particular certificate, a certification authority sometimes obtains confidential or personal data from certificate applicants to validate identity, authority, or other attributes of applicants essential to the issuance of certificates in a trustworthy fashion. Then, consistent with its procedures, the certification authority might include a specified subset of that information within the certificate. Given the sensitivity of the release of such information, certification practices should address how the confidentiality of information will be maintained.[48]

For example, a CP or CPS may state which types of information are received and generated in confidence and must not be disclosed, except as specifically provided by the CP or CPS, authorized by the subject of such information, or required by law. This information may include these items:

- Certificate application records, whether approved or disapproved
- Subscriber agreements (except for information placed in a certificate or repository per the CP or CPS)
- Transactional records (both full records and the audit trail of transactions)
- Audit trail records created or retained by the certification authority
- Audit reports created by the certification authority, its repository, or their respective auditors (whether internal or public)
- Contingency planning, disaster recovery, and business resumption plans
- Security measures controlling the operations of certification authority hardware and software and the administration of certificate services and designated enrollment services, to the extent that their disclosure does not compromise security

Regarding authorization or legal requirements for the disclosure of confidential information, the CP or CPS could provide, for example:

> Certification authorities shall not release or be required to release any confidential information without an authenticated, reasonably specific request prior to such release from (i) the person to whom the certification authority owes a duty to keep information confidential and (ii) the person requesting confidential information (if not the same person), or a court order.

The certification authority may require that the requesting person pay a reasonable fee before disclosing such information. The PKI should also publish a privacy policy.[49]

Right to Investigate Compromises

Because the right of a certification authority to investigate compromise[50] (and purported lack of trustworthy operations) can be indispensable for that certification authority to perform its duties, a CPS may provide for an explicit power to investigate with flexibility and authority.

Criminal Activity

While a CP or CPS may prescribe conduct and set the rights and obligations of the parties as a civil matter, it also relies on the prohibition of certain conduct proscribed by criminal law. The latter, of course, is enforced by the government rather than by the certification authority. A number of criminal laws appear both applicable to and supportive of PKI trustworthiness (although such laws were not generally enacted with PKIs in mind). Examples include laws intended to counteract fraud generally and computer fraud or wire fraud specifically.[51]

A CP or CPS can contain an explicit warning regarding the illicit use or abuse of the certification services covered by that CP or CPS. The CP or CPS can also seek to encourage successful detection and prosecution as deterrence to criminal behavior by offering a reward for information leading to the arrest and conviction of anyone committing a crime that directly affects the certification services.[52]

10.4 CP and CPS Topics: Identification and Authentication

RFC 2527 Section 3—Identification and Authentication

This component describes the procedures used to authenticate a certificate applicant to a certification authority or registration authority prior to certificate issuance. It also describes how parties requesting rekey or revocation are authenticated. This component also addresses naming practices, including name ownership recognition and name dispute resolution.

The up-front validation of a certificate applicant through an identification and authentication process is fundamental to the assurances provided by a certificate. Therefore, it might be helpful to also summarize this process in the introduction of the CP or CPS.

Initial Registration: Naming

Historically, few issues in the development of PKIs (or distributed applications in general) have been more contentious than that of naming. Indeed, the complexities and politics of naming—such as privacy, philosophy of name management, and whether names should be managed at all—have created great problems for the Internet generally.

Names used to identify subjects in certificates range from the extremes of being intentionally descriptive of the subscriber to being intentionally anonymous. For example, the name might be a representation of an account number, or it might be an alias or handle, meaningful to the subscriber's local community but meaningless otherwise. A PKI should explain the significance of subject names contained in its certificates, which may vary with the service class or certificate policy.

In e-commerce, a name is sometimes intended to identify the subscriber in terms of some widely recognized naming system, such as personal name and address, e-mail address, or registered corporation name. Names are assigned by naming authorities. An organization that operates a certification authority can also optionally act as a naming authority. If so, the CP or CPS should describe the policies associated with the name registration service, including policies regarding the resolution of disputes over ownership of a particular name.[53] Note that if the certification authority does not itself also act as a naming authority, it needs to rely on external naming authorities to ensure that the naming information in certificates is unambiguous.

Initial Registration: Authentication

The authentication process typically involves one or a combination of the following processes:

- *Personal presence:* Individuals applying for certificates are required to appear personally before a trusted entity (such as a registration authority or notary) to facilitate the confirmation of their identities. (Some variants of processes requiring personal presence are noted later.)

- *Out-of-band validation:* The use of out-of-band validation checks, such as presentation of a PIN distributed by a personal telephone call or confirmed postal delivery to the applicant's address of record, can contribute to validation assurances. The assurances of such out-of-band validations vary as a function of the underlying confidence in the address information and the method of confirmation (such as by return receipt request or certificate of mailing), among other factors.

- *Third-party confirmation of personal data:* A third party confirms personal information provided by the certificate applicant by comparing it with information in databases maintained by that third party for such purposes. For example, online investigation can provide some modest assurance of identity by comparing a certificate applicant's identity information against credit bureau or organizational databases.

Depending on the environment, other processes may be appropriate.

Note that when personal presence is required, depending on the particular CP or CPS, there are several variants of the process:

- *Documentation presentation:* The certificate applicant can be required to present designated credentials, such as a government-issued photo ID, an employer ID, utility bills, professional credentials, or a court decree indicating a legal change of name.

- *Investigation:* The registration authority can be required to affirmatively investigate and confirm the validity of the documentation presented by the certificate applicant. The rigor of such investigations can vary.

- *Temporal variations of personal presence:* Usually personal presence involves the certificate applicant's physically appearing before the registration authority within a reasonable time after submitting a certificate application but prior to the issuance and delivery of a certificate. However, the personal presence requirement can in some cases be time-shifted to support an earlier trustworthy instance of personal presence. For example, subject to the applicable rules of the certification authority, a certificate applicant could personally apply for a bank account on

July 5, and then on November 5 apply for a certificate supported by the instance of personal presence on July 5. While the registration authority's use of the earlier instance of personal presence is weaker than if personal presence were undertaken concurrently with the certificate application process, it may still provide sufficient assurances for the purposes of the certification.

10.5 CP and CPS Topics: Operational Requirements

RFC 2527 Section 4—Operational Requirements

This component is used to specify requirements imposed upon issuing CA, subject CAs, RAs,[54] or end entities with respect to various operational activities. This component consists of the following subcomponents: certificate application; certificate issuance; certificate acceptance; certificate suspension and revocation; security audit procedures; records archival; key changeover; compromise and disaster recovery; and certification authority termination.

Certificate Application

Sound certificate application procedures are critical to a viable and credible certification service. The application procedures should obtain reliable information from certificate applicants as required, should provide for the certification authority's validation of such information, and should advise and caution certificate applicants of their rights and obligations.

Registration authorities are trusted entities delegated that role by a certification authority to assist subscribers in applying for certificates, to approve or reject certificate enrollment applications, or to assist in revoking (or, where applicable, suspending) certificates. A CP or CPS typically establishes minimum requirements for a registration authority, depending on the class of certificate application that the registration authority is authorized to service. Since the initial validation of a certificate applicant's information is critical to the trustworthiness of the issued certificate, registration authorities play an indispensable role in ensuring certification authority trustworthiness. Consequently, a clear articulation of registration authority requirements and procedures is essential.

Table 10.1   Sample Registration Authority Requirements

- Background check: Search criminal records (local, county, state or provincial, and national) and check credit or financial records of registration authority employees.

- Education confirmation: Confirm required educational credentials, typically proof of graduation at highest education level of registration authority employees.

- Training: Train personnel in the following areas: updates specific to functions served, such as security principles, general operation of the PKI, and operations specific to the worker's environment; hardware and software versions in use; all duties that personnel are expected to perform; incident and compromise reports and handling; and disaster recovery and business continuity procedures.

- Bonding: Performance bond

- Employment history check: For past 7 to 10 years

- Professional references: From at least three people

- Motor vehicle records: For past seven years

- Social security trace

Table 10.1 presents an example of the *trusted-entity* attributes of registration authorities that service certificates for moderate-risk commercial applications.

The CP or CPS should indicate the categories of information required from the certificate applicant prior to the registration authority's validating and approving or rejecting a certificate application.

Validation procedures may vary greatly, depending on the assurances, perceived risks, business model, and application for a particular certificate. For example, a registration authority may have obligations when validating certificate applications to corroborate the following items:[55]

- The certificate applicant is the person named in the certificate application (if and to the extent required by the applicable CP or CPS).
- The certificate applicant holds the private key corresponding to the subject public key in the certificate. (This obligation may be satisfied by a formal statement to

this effect from the certificate applicant, and/or demonstration of proof-of-possession of the private key, such as a digital signature on the certificate application.)

- The information to be included in the certificate is accurate, to the extent that the CP or CPS obligates the certification authority or registration authority to check such information.
- Any agent who applies for a certificate for a particular public key is duly authorized to make such a request.

Once a certificate is issued, the certification authority does not typically have a continuing duty to monitor and investigate the accuracy of the information in a certificate, unless subsequently notified of that certificate's compromise. In any event, such obligations are specified in the CP or CPS. Also, a subscriber is typically obligated to notify the certification authority of any material change in the information status of the certificate.

Certificate Issuance

Upon successful validation of a certificate application, a registration authority approves the application. The certification authority issues a certificate and notifies the certificate's subject of its contents. In so doing, the certification authority makes various representations to subscribers and relying parties, thereby assuming further obligations.

An issued certificate has an operational period, which can be reflected, for example, in an X.509 validity period field. A certificate's operational period is the period starting with the date and time the certificate is issued (or on a later date and time if so stated in the certificate) and ending with the date and time on which the certificate expires or is earlier suspended or revoked.[56] These periods vary; operational periods of one to three years are typical for end-user certificates. The actual operational period may be shorter than this because of revocation or suspension. A valid certificate, as defined in the ABA Guidelines, is one issued by a certification authority and accepted by the subscriber.

Certificate Acceptance

Acceptance of a certificate defines when many of the subscriber's critical obligations go into effect. Acceptance typically means a certificate applicant's demonstrating approval of a certificate while knowing or having notice of its contents, in accordance with the CP or CPS.[57] Consequently, a CP or CPS should seek to define precisely the moment of acceptance.

Much has been written about how to achieve contractual acceptance online, and legislative efforts are also addressing this issue. A prudent commercial certification authority will deal with this issue by providing as much disclosure about the content of the certificate as is practical and by requiring one or more affirmative acts by the subscriber to demonstrate acceptance.[58] For example, the subscriber may be required to affirmatively enter a private code (such as a PIN) during an online certificate retrieval or download process, in conjunction with other acts, or simply to use the certificate.

Certificate Suspension and Revocation

As discussed in chapter 6, suspension places a hold on a certificate, rendering it temporarily inoperable without permanently revoking it, whereas revocation permanently renders a certificate inoperable from a specified time forward. Rendering a certificate inoperable makes it unreasonable for any party to rely on the contents of that certificate, including its subject public key.[59]

Certificate revocation can be a consequence of events such as the following:[60]

- A loss, theft, modification, unauthorized disclosure, or other compromise of the private key of the certificate's subject
- The certification authority's determination that a certificate was not issued in accordance with the procedures required by its CP or CPS
- The subscriber's revocation request (and the certification authority's confirmation that the person requesting the revocation is in fact the subscriber)
- Breach of a material obligation of the CP or CPS by the certificate's subject
- Delay or prevention of the performance of an entity's obligations under the CP or CPS by an act of God, natural disaster, computer or communications failure, or

other cause beyond the entity's reasonable control that as a result materially threatens or compromises another entity's information

Confirmation of a subscriber's revocation request is important. On one hand, proof of the authenticity of a revocation request is needed to protect against a denial-of-service attack. On the other hand, requiring too much proof could create unnecessary damages due to delays in revoking compromised certificates. Consequently, an appropriate balance must be drawn between these competing interests. A CP or CPS can provide, for example, that revocation requests from subscribers must be in the form of a suitably authenticated digital or paper record or voice message from the subscriber or its agent.

A certification authority must notify its user community of the suspension or revocation of a certificate. Notification might use any of the revocation methods discussed in section 6.6, such as CRLs or online status checking. Note that a push method (such as broadcast revocation lists) obligates the certification authority to promulgate information, whereas a pull method (such as OCSP) typically obligates the relying party to query the certification authority or applicable repository for certificate status. The nature and type of notification services will invariably change as PKI and risk models evolve.

The duty of a key holder to protect his or her private key may extend beyond the operational period of his or her certificate to include any period of suspension or revocation. The reason for extending the protection period is to mitigate the potential for further damage or misuse of a compromised key.[61] (Of course, if the revocation is a result of private-key compromise, further protection of that key may well be irrelevant.)

Record Archiving

Documentation of events and activities is indispensable to the operation of a trustworthy PKI. PKI participants must be able to evidence their proper operations both before and after the fact to support certificate-based security services for communications and transactions. Accordingly, PKI participants should disclose generally the nature of material retained records.

Records that typically should be maintained and disclosed upon authorized request include documentation of a PKI participant's compliance with the applicable CP or CPS and documentation of information material to each certificate application and to each certificate issued. For each certificate, the records should extend to the complete certification life cycle, including creation, issuance, use, revocation, expiration, and renewal or reenrollment activities. These records should include the following information where relevant:

- The names of certificate subjects (unless the subject is expressly not authenticated and the name not obtained)
- The identity of persons requesting certificate suspension or revocation
- Other material facts represented in certificates
- Time stamps
- Other foreseeably relevant facts related to the life cycle of certificates

Records may be kept in either computer-based or paper-based form, provided that their indexing, storage, preservation, and reproduction are accurate and complete.

Time stamping of records by an independent trusted party or using a trustworthy mechanism enhances the integrity of PKIs and contributes to the non-repudiation of digitally signed messages.[62]

The retention of certification authority activity records for a designated period of time is indispensable for many reasons including:

- Support for non-repudiation of digitally signed messages
- Evidence of a certification authority's proper performance to rebut claims of misfeasance (or worse)
- Satisfaction of legislative and regulatory requirements where applicable
- Conforming to good industry practices

Although it may in some circumstances be optimal to retain records forever, this goal may be unrealistic because of technical and resource limitations. Few archivists will commit to the permanent retention of electronic records because of the impracticality of maintaining equipment to read historical data and the prohibitive expense of transferring data to new media and standards indefinitely.[63] Consequently, it might be reasonable (subject to the particular supported application) to expect certification authorities to commit to the retention of records for a period of 30 years or more after the date a certificate is revoked or expires.[64]

Compromise and Disaster Recovery

Contingency planning and disaster recovery (collectively known as *business resumption services*) are particularly important for a PKI because secure e-commerce increasingly demands them for competitive, legal, and public perception reasons. Consequently, a CP or CPS should indicate a PKI's undertaking to implement, document, and periodically test business resumption services.

Planning should extend, in particular, to the contingency of root private-key compromise. If an infrastructure's root key is compromised, recovery cannot be effected using the usual end-user certificate revocation processes. All affected users, including not only subscribers but also relying parties who may not necessarily be registered with the infrastructure, require notification of the situation. A new root key pair must then be established or a preestablished, redundant rollover root key invoked, and the new root made available to the user community.

Certification Authority Termination

Certification authorities will not operate forever. Consequently, PKI practices should address how a certification authority will terminate its operations. To reduce the impact of a termination of service, a CP or CPS can provide for timely notice, transfer of responsibilities to succeeding entities, ongoing maintenance of records, and possibly certain remedies.

For example, prior to cessation of operation, the CP or CPS may require a discontinuing certification authority to perform the following duties:

- Notify other certification authorities in the PKI of its intention to cease acting as a certification authority at least 90 days before cessation.

- Provide to the subscriber of each unrevoked or unexpired certificate it has issued at least 90 days' notice of its intention to cease acting as a certification authority.
- Revoke all certificates that remain unrevoked or unexpired at the end of the 90-day notice period, whether or not revocation has been requested by the subscribers.
- Give notice of revocation to each affected subscriber.
- Make a reasonable effort to minimize disruption from cessation of certification services to its subscribers and to persons duly needing to verify digital signatures by reference to the public keys contained in outstanding certificates.
- Make reasonable arrangements for preserving its records.
- In the case of a commercial certification authority, pay reasonable restitution (not to exceed the certificate purchase price) to subscribers for premature revocation of their certificates.[65]

To provide uninterrupted certification authority services to its certificate applicants and subscribers, a discontinuing certification authority may be required to arrange with another certification authority, for reissuance of its outstanding subscriber certificates. Unless a contract between the discontinuing certification authority and a subscriber provides otherwise and subject to the succeeding certification authority's approval, it may be possible to keep the original CP or CPS in effect under the succeeding certification authority.

10.6   CP and CPS Topics: Physical, Procedural, and Personnel Security Controls

RFC 2527 Section 5—Physical, Procedural, and Personnel Security Controls

This component describes nontechnical security controls (that is, physical, procedural, and personnel controls) used by the issuing CA to perform securely the functions of key generation, subject authentication, certificate issuance, certificate revocation, audit, and archival. This component can also be used to define nontechnical security controls on repository, subject CAs, RAs, and end entities.

A PKI must necessarily be trustworthy.[66] To ensure trustworthy operations, participants must use procedures, practices, and technologies that provide a reasonable degree of security and reliability. To describe these requirements, the ABA Guidelines introduce the concept of a trustworthy system.[67] A trustworthy system consists of computer hardware, software, and procedures that

- are reasonably secure from intrusion and misuse;
- provide a reasonable level of availability, reliability, and correct operation;
- are reasonably suited to performing their intended functions; and
- adhere to generally accepted security principles.

Physical, procedural, and personnel security requirements for PKIs are critical to ensuring a trustworthy system. The CP or CPS should address these matters, possibly by referencing other operative security documents. Nonetheless, it may be imprudent to disclose the details of internal security countermeasures publicly. Such countermeasures and their associated procedures might therefore be documented separately, and their access restricted appropriately.

All communications and operations, especially those affecting the security of the PKI, must be protected using security mechanisms commensurate with the attendant risks. Facilities must also be physically secured to an appropriate extent. PKI participants must also formulate and follow personnel management practices that provide reasonable assurance of the trustworthiness and competence of their employees and the satisfactory performance of their duties.

Most important, a certification authority must securely generate and protect its own private keys using a trustworthy system and must take necessary precautions to prevent their loss, disclosure, modification, or unauthorized use.

This subject is very broad, and extensive coverage is beyond the scope of this book.[68] However, at a high level, the CP or CPS should address (or appropriately reference) both local security policy and technical security policy. Local security policy addresses the following topics:

- *Physical controls:* Measures taken to secure the facility housing PKI components and systems, including use of guards, monitoring devices, locks, and access control devices (such as keys, tokens, and biometric access devices).
- *Procedural controls:* Measures include recognition of trusted positions, namely, roles that involve control over cryptographic keys, validation processes, and other operations that may materially affect the issuance, management, and use of certificates or privileged access to a repository. Protection of private-key values or other secret values that control access to private keys should involve split knowledge or

secret sharing, whereby secret shares are distributed to a number of independent individuals.[69] Secret-sharing provisions need to address a range of issues, including representations of hardware protection by the certification authority, acceptance of secret shares by secret share holders, safeguarding secret shares, availability and release of secret shares, record keeping by secret share issuers and holders, liability of secret share holders, and indemnity by the secret share issuer.

• *Personnel controls:* Personnel controls include measures such as background checks, training and retraining, job rotation, sanctions in the event of unauthorized actions, and special controls for contracting personnel (such as bonding, monitoring, auditing, and special contractual provisions). In particular, a certification authority has affirmative obligations to investigate and oversee persons who serve in trusted positions and to remove them if circumstances so dictate.

Technical security policy is addressed in the next section.

10.7   CP and CPS Topics: Technical Security Controls

RFC 2527 Section 6—Technical Security Controls

This component is used to define the security measures taken by the issuing CA to protect its cryptographic keys and activation data (e.g., PINs, passwords, or manually-held key shares). This component may also be used to impose constraints on repositories, subject CAs, and end entities to protect their cryptographic keys and critical security parameters. Secure key management is critical to ensure that all secret and private keys and activation data are protected and used only by authorized personnel. This component also describes other technical security controls used by the issuing CA to perform securely the functions of key generation, user authentication, certificate registration, certificate revocation, audit, and archival. Technical controls include life-cycle security controls (including software development environment security, trusted software development) and operational security controls. This component can also be used to define other technical security controls on repositories, subject CAs, RAs, and end entities.

As a commercial discipline, cryptographic key management is not widely practiced or understood. However, key management and associated security controls are of unforgiving importance to the operation of a trustworthy PKI.

Key-Pair Generation and Installation

Certificate application procedures should take into account key-pair generation procedures. In the case of key pairs used for digital signature purposes, potential compromise is minimized if subscribers generate their own key pairs and never disclose their private keys to any other entity, including a certification authority. In the case of key pairs used for encryption purposes, where key recovery or key escrow mechanisms are implemented, the situation is different. The key pair may be generated by a service provider, with the private key transferred securely to the subscriber, or it may be generated by the subscriber, with the private key transferred securely to the service provider for recovery or escrow purposes.

Private-Key Protection

Subscribers must take care to safeguard their private keys.[70] This is particularly important where key-pair generation or private-key storage is implemented in software because the risks are usually greater than with hardware modules or tokens. These obligations should be considered together with the security assurances and obligations of the end-user application or the security software vendors whose products generate and store such keys.[71]

A CPS may require that each certificate applicant (and, upon approval, each subscriber) acknowledge that such party, and not the certification authority, is responsible for protecting its private keys from compromise, loss, disclosure, modification, or unauthorized use. Furthermore, the delegation of authority to generate key pairs, if it occurs, does not relieve the delegator of its responsibilities and liabilities concerning the use, retention, or proper destruction of the private key. Nevertheless, certification authorities and software providers should be proactive in advancing the security of private keys.

Other Technical Security Controls

Other technical security controls include these:

- *Cryptographic module engineering controls:* Measures regarding the functions and assurance characteristics of hardware or software cryptographic modules, for example, conformance to the U.S. government standard FIPS PUB 140[72]

- *Computer security controls:* Measures such as the use of government-endorsed security products that meet recognized criteria for security functionality and assurance (see section 4.6 and chapter 11)
- *Life-cycle technical controls:* Measures addressing the security of the development environment, development facility, development personnel, configuration management during product maintenance, and software engineering practices

10.8   CP and CPS Topics: Certificate and CRL Profiles

RFC 2527 Section 7—Certificate and CRL Profiles

This component is used to specify the certificate format and, if CRLs are used, the CRL format. Assuming use of the X.509 certificate and CRL formats, this includes information on profiles, versions, and extensions used.

A profile is a set of restrictions or refinements applied to a base standard for use in a particular environment. A profile might specify, for example, use or nonuse of particular optional features of the base standard or additional extensions to the standard for the environment concerned. Certificate and CRL profiles enable users to parse, understand, and effectively use the contents of certificates. A CP or CPS typically describes the profile of certificates issued, including any special interpretations of certificate fields. Using a standardized, general-purpose format, such as X.509, greatly facilitates this task. Most commercial PKIs currently use X.509, but that is not necessarily essential from a business or legal perspective. New certificate formats are likely to find commercial application over time.[73]

Even with X.509, it is necessary for a certification authority to address how the certificate fields are to be used, especially the certificate extension fields. Extension fields may convey information about the public key being certified, the certificate issuer, the subscriber, relying parties, and the certification process. From a legal perspective, extensions can be used to provide enhanced notice and disclosure of a certification authority's practices to the user community. However, they should be used for this purpose with care because not all end-user applications (such as Web browsers) can be assumed to be capable of properly reading, displaying, or acting on even the standard X.509 extensions. This legacy problem will diminish as new versions of mass-market products are released. Some X.509 certificate extensions of particular significance to certification practices are described in chapter 7.

10.9 CP and CPS Topics: Specification Administration

RFC 2527 Section 8—Specification Administration

This component is used to specify how this particular certificate policy definition or CPS will be maintained. It contains the following subcomponents: specification change procedures; publication and notification procedures; and CPS approval procedures.

Most of the applications that derive (or will derive) benefit from PKIs are developing rapidly. Similarly, the PKI industry is undergoing dramatic changes that are impossible for any CP or CPS to fully capture and support for long durations. Furthermore, technology generally outpaces the law. Therefore, a CP or CPS greatly benefits from specifying a dynamic change process.

The change process should give an appropriate PKI authority the right to amend or modify the CP or CPS from time to time (prospectively, and not retroactively) after giving adequate advance notice of such changes to

- users (including subscribers and relying parties),
- affiliated subdomains within the PKI, and
- other PKIs with which interoperation occurs, or at least where there is an obligation to do so.

One approach would permit the notice requirement to be waived if failure to make the proposed change immediately might result in a compromise of the PKI or any portion of it. In such a case, the proposed change could become effective immediately on publication in the PKI's repository.

10.10   Systematizing CP and CPS Development

The early approaches of handcrafting individual CPs and CPSs and considering acceptance of the terms and conditions of another party's CPS on a case-by-case basis will progressively evolve into more efficient methods that exploit automation in various forms.
These are some ways in which automation is anticipated to affect certification practices:

- *CP and CPS reuse:* Examples of RFC 2527-compliant CPs and CPSs are being
  published as new PKIs are deployed. These documents serve as worked examples
  for later PKI deployments. CP and CPS authors will generally find advantages to
  iterating a published document describing a similar policy as their first draft.
  Over time, standard text and nomenclature may emerge.
- *CP and CPS development tools:* CP and CPS templates containing modularized certificate policy references and clauses to simplify development and deployment will
  become available on the Internet and via other media. Also, XML-based tools will
  facilitate machine-readable policy expression. Additionally, internationalization,
  translations, and localization tools will enhance CPS development. Such resources
  will be made available by PKIs, industry consortia, and private publishers.
- *Certificate policy negotiation and mapping:* One objective of CPs is to automate the communication and interoperability of participants in a PKI community. If a sufficiently small set of CPs become widely agreed upon, this will
  facilitate increased use of the CP-related features in X.509 and reduce the need
  for human intervention in deciding if a presented certificate is suitable for a
  given purpose.
- *Online policy and practice negotiation:* Ultimately, it may become possible to
  dynamically construct and agree upon CP and CPS terms and conditions that satisfy the needs of concerned parties, potentially on a per-transaction basis. This
  will necessitate standardized CP and CPS modules, specialized negotiation protocols and tools,[74] and an appropriate legal framework.

Automation is anticipated to become increasingly sophisticated and accepted—
particularly in light of facilitating law reforms and as the industry further develops usages of
trade.

10.11   Summary

The role of certification authority is important in making secure e-commerce possible. However, the effectiveness of a certification authority depends on its services being recognized as practical, trustworthy, and legally enforceable. Such recognition depends on the certification authority's practices being well-documented and such documentation being made available to the applicable community of interest. This documentation typically takes the form of a certificate policy (CP), a certification practice statement (CPS), and user agreements.

The CPS concept is rooted in the earlier concepts of policy certification authorities (PCAs) and their policy statements in the Internet Privacy Enhanced Mail (PEM) design. These concepts were effectively superseded by the CP concept introduced with X.509 Version 3 certificates. The precise relationship between a CP and CPS varies. Typically, CPs state requirements at a high level, and CPSs state in detail how such requirements are satisfied. Multiple CPSs may be written that satisfy a particular CP. Certificates issued under any of these CPSs can assert the same CP in an X.509 certificate. CPs are sometimes used as the basis of a decision to use a particular certificate, but recourse to a more detailed CPS is often also necessary. Certificate classes typically distinguish between distinct levels of service and map to a CP or CPS in various ways. One possibility is to have different CPs represent different certificate classes.

The provisions in a CPS depend on the community in which it will be used. The format, list of topics, and organization of a CPS vary, although CPSs increasingly mirror the ordering and format of corresponding CPs. This tends to facilitate the writing and comparing of different CPs or CPSs.

Before a commercial certification authority can commence providing service, it should establish its business and legal practices and describe the controls that it will use to ensure trustworthy operations. A CP or CPS typically identifies the service levels available in terms of certificate classes or similar concepts. Certificate formats may be described, usually with reference to a recognized standard such as X.509. Any particular structure that applies to the relationships between certification authorities, such as a hierarchical structure, may be identified. If a certification authority provides a name registration service, the CP or CPS may describe the policies associated with that service, including dispute resolution procedures. The use of a repository should also be described.

Certification authorities must use technologies and procedures that provide a reasonable degree of security and reliability, consistent with the attendant risks and suitable for the applications supported by its services. A CP or CPS, or other document referenced by the CP or CPS, typically describes the information, physical, and personnel security measures. Certification authorities must also have sufficient financial resources to maintain their operations and perform their duties, and they must be reasonably able to bear the applicable risk of liability to subscribers and relying parties. Certification authorities must keep adequate records and make them available on authorized request. Certification authorities must produce and preserve adequate audit trails and should be regularly audited using recognized information system audit standards. Other areas to be addressed by a CP or CPS include business resumption planning and disaster recovery, protection of confidential information, requirements imposed on registration authorities, and termination of operations of a certification authority.

To properly validate certificate applications and issue certificates, certificate application procedures must not only obtain reliable information from the certificate applicant but must also advise and caution certificate applicants of their rights and obligations. A certificate applicant must protect its private keys from compromise, loss, disclosure, modification, or unauthorized use. A certification authority validates a certificate application following designated procedures that may depend on the particular level of service (or certificate class) requested.

Certificate issuance refers to the actions performed by a certification authority in creating a certificate and notifying the certificate's subject of its contents. Upon the successful completion of validation and upon the certificate applicant's consent (or, where applicable, that of the applicant's superior or agent), the certification authority approves the certificate application by issuing a certificate. In so doing, the certification authority makes various representations to subscribers and relying parties.

Acceptance of a certificate is a defining moment that typically requires one or more affirmative acts by the subscriber. By accepting a certificate, the subscriber typically acknowledges several obligations.

Use-related provisions of a CP or CPS may specify the parties' obligations with regard to the verification of a digital signature before it is deemed to have been justifiably relied upon. Such provisions may also seek to resolve many of the classic e-commerce enforceability and validity issues, such as the satisfaction of formalistic writing and signature requirements. A CP or CPS may describe procedures for and implications of certificate suspension, revocation, and expiration.

A CP or CPS typically describes the manner in which certification authorities warrant their services and apportion their liability. This may include general warranties, disclaimers of warranty, and limitations of liability. Enhanced warranty protection or insurance programs may also be described.

Miscellaneous CP or CPS provisions might address issues such as conflict of provisions, governing law, dispute resolution, and change procedures.

The CP and CPS concepts will evolve further as more practical experience is gained with the use of PKI services. There are ongoing activities to harmonize these concepts in the technical, legal, and business communities, and certification authorities are increasing their efforts to create a disciplined, interoperable environment. Methods of writing and using CPs and CPSs will advance, and automation will be increasingly exploited.

Notes

1. For the purposes of this chapter, the definition of a *certification authority* includes registration authorities, repositories, and other supporting PKI components unless otherwise stated.
2. A party who acts (or is in a position to act) in reliance upon a certificate and its subject public key. This is equivalent to the term *certificate user* used in X.509. See American Bar Association, Information Security Committee, Section of Science and Technology, *Digital Signatures Guidelines* (1996), sec. 1.27, available at <http://www.abanet.org/scitech/home.html>.
3. See chapter 7.
4. S. Kent, *Privacy Enhancement for Internet Electronic Mail, Part II: Certificate-Based Key Management,* Request for Comments (RFC) 1422 (Internet Activities Board, 1993) <ftp://ftp.isi.edu/in-notes/rfc1422.txt>.
5. The structure and content of PEM policy statements are outlined in section 3.4.3 of RFC 1422. Eight subject areas for such a policy statement are identified: PCA

identity, PCA scope, PCA security and privacy, certification policy, management of certificate revocation lists, naming conventions, business issues, and other. See M. S. Baum, *Federal Certification Authority Liability and Policy,* NIST-GCR-94-654 (Gaithersburg, MD: National Institute of Standards and Technology, 1994) 353-56, available at <http://www.verisign.com/repository/pubs>, which presents a detailed expansion of these eight policy subject areas.

6. Two examples are Computer Security Technologies (Sweden), "Certification Policies in the COST Certification Infrastructure" <http://www.cost.se/cost_pol.htm>; N. Berge, *UNINETT PCA Policy Statements,* RFC 1875 (Internet Activities Board, 1995) <ftp://ftp.isi.edu/in-notes/rfc1875.txt>.

7. ABA Guidelines, sec. 1.8. A CPS is understood to include the *management* of, rather than only the *issuance* of, certificates.

8. Nonetheless, the form and content of a CPS and associated practices documents depend on the intended purposes of and applications supported by a certification authority. Throughout this chapter, when we refer to "CPS provisions," other vehicles for communicating certification practices may be equally or more suitably employed.

9. *usage of trade* is "any practice or method of dealing having such regularity of observance in a place, vocation or trade as to justify an expectation that it will be observed with respect to the transaction in question" [UCC sec. 1-205(2)].

10. A gap-filler provision is typically a contract term that is incorporated as a matter of law into a contract that otherwise did not address such terms but is determined to have been reasonable and necessary to effect the intention of the parties. In this regard, a gap-filler provision facilitates commerce. In particular situations, it is used as a supplement or clarification to the background common law or code.

11. See Baum, *Federal Certification Authority Liability and Policy,* 358-59.

12. ABA Guidelines, sec. 1.8.1.

13. A *subscriber agreement* is an agreement executed between a subscriber and a certification authority for the provision of designated certification services.

14. ISO/IEC 9594-8, *Information Technology-Open Systems Interconnection—The Directory: Public Key and Attribute Certificate Frameworks,* also published as the ITU-T X.509 Recommendation.

15. However, there are demonstrable exceptions. For example, the VeriSign CP is generally at least as detailed as its corresponding CPSs because it presents a detailed description of services that are available in cooperation with one or more of its affiliated certificate authorities to ensure that the affiliates within the VeriSign Trust Network (VTN) provide highly consistent and interoperable services. The CP is structured to include (with some exceptions) the detailed and precise language that must be published within an affiliate's CPS. The reasons for its comprehensiveness and detail include that (a) it seeks to ensure the highest possible degree of interoperation, (b) it is assumed that each affiliated certification authority conforming to the CP will provide consistent (if not identical) branded products and services, and (c) it contemplates that language translation and national localization requirements demand the highest degree of consistency possible.

16. For example, a draft PKI disclosure statement (PDS) template is available at <http://www.verisign.com/repository/pds.txt>, and an example of its deployment is available at <http://www.verisign.com/repository/disclosure.html>. See appendix H.

17. For example, the law places some restrictions on how far a party's bargaining power can advance its position in terms of an adhesion contract, such as many software shrink-wrap agreements which the purchaser "accepts" but does not read until after its purchase. For example, see *ProCD Inc. v. Zeidenberg,* Civ. No. 96-1139 (7th Cir. June 20, 1996); *In re Real Networks, Inc. Privacy Litigation,* 2000 WL 631341 (slip May 8, 2000, N.D. Ill.). These issues are discussed further in chapter 3.

18. *Community* (or *community of interest*) means the membership of some demographic, economic, legal, political, social, or other group. It may include constituents of academic, business, consumer, financial, social, or other special-interest organizations.

19. However, see chapter 2 regarding XML. Markup languages can facilitate the automated and dynamic comparison of practices documents without imposing a flat document structure.

20. Another dimension of assurances that manifests dependencies on PKI is that of critical information protection assurances, that is, protections against cyber threats. Indeed, if PKIs are to provide or enhance trustworthy e-commerce,

they must contemplate the vulnerabilities of the broader infrastructure (e.g., since PKIs themselves depend on telecommunications mechanisms). Presidential Decision Directive 63 (May 22, 1998) established a public-private partnership to address vulnerabilities. President Clinton signed Executive Order 13010 establishing the President's Commission on Critical Information Infrastructure Protection to examine and produce responsive recommendations on national policy. Its initial findings recognized the need for best practices to enhance protections, the private sector's indispensable role, and the essential role of PKI. See <http://www.ciao.gov>. "To date there are no shared list of infrastructure interdependencies for information security" (Institute of Internal Auditors, "Information Security Management and Assurance: A Call to Action for Corporate Governance" [April 2000] <http://www.theiia.org>). At the Critical Infrastructure Assurance Conference, Washington Summit, held at the White House on April 17, 2000, Secretary of Commerce William M. Daly noted that it is "the first time in history that the Federal Government cannot protect infrastructure alone." At the same conference, William Murray, an executive consultant at Deloitte Touche, noted that this is "the first infrastructure where users were peer to the infrastructure. For 30 years we've been operating systems like toys."

21. Assurances often express a general intention, supported by a good-faith effort to provide and maintain such services. Assurances do not inherently imply a guarantee that the services will be performed fully and satisfactorily. Assurances are generally distinct from insurance, promises, guarantees, and warranties.

22. Some participants within the Authentications Working Group of Asia Pacific Economic Conference (APEC) have urged that the accreditation of PKIs should be manifested by the accreditation of *certificates* because, they urge, certificates are the ultimate product of a PKI.

23. Draft (Oct. 5, 2000), available at < http://gits-sec.treas.gov >.

24. The VeriSign Trust Network CP and the VeriSign CPS can be viewed online or downloaded at <http://www.verisign.com/repository/>.

25. S. Chokhani and W. Ford, *Internet X.509 Public Key Infrastructure Certificate Policy and Certification Practices Framework,* RFC 2527 (Internet Activities Board, 1999) <ftp://ftp.isi.edu/in-notes/rfc2527.txt>.

26. See chapter 8 for a discussion of formalistic legal issues in e-commerce.

27. See ABA Guidelines, sec. 1.37 (verify a digital signature and message integrity). The technical verification process is presented in chapter 7.

28. ABA Guidelines, sec. 5.6 (where this is "rebuttably presumed" to be the case).

29. ABA Guidelines, sec. 5.6.1 through 5.6.4.

30. ABA Guidelines, secs. 4.3 and 5.6.1 through 5.6.4.

31. ABA Guidelines, sec. 5.3 and 5.4.

32. ABA Guidelines, sec. 3.7.

33. ABA Guidelines, sec. 4.2.

34. The industry is simply too new to have developed reliable actuarial data.

35. *Direct damages* are those that flow *directly* from a breach of contract, a wrongful act, or failure to act, as opposed to *consequential damages, punitive damages,* and other indirect damages.

36. ABA Guidelines, sec. 3.14 (liability of complying certification authority).

37. Paraphrased from the VeriSign Trust Network CP (version 1), using the general terminology of this book.

38. See ABA Guidelines, sec. 3.14; see chapter 8 for a review of certain policy issues affecting a certification authority's liability.

39. Baum, *Federal Certification Authority Liability and Policy,* 271-73, on various liability cap issues in the context of VANs.

40. Baum, *Federal Certification Authority Liability and Policy,* 337-47, concerning PKI insurance issues.

41. However, where a certification authority holds the private key of a subscriber, there is a compelling basis for the establishment of a fiduciary relationship. See ABA Guidelines, sec. 2.4 (fiduciary relationship).

42. The ABA Guidelines obligate certification authorities to "disclose any material certification practice statement" (sec. 3.2 Disclosure).

43. A *repository* is a database of certificates and other relevant information accessible online. See ABA Guidelines, sec. 1.28. See also chapter 6.

44. The ABA Guidelines comment that "the duties that a certification authority owes to a relying person are generally based on the certification authority's representations, which may include a certification practice statement" (sec. 1.8.2). "Whether a certification practice statement is binding on a relying person . . . depends on whether the relying person has knowledge or notice of [it].

A relying person has knowledge (or at least notice) of the contents of the certificate used by the relying person to verify a digital signature, including documents incorporated into the certificate by reference. . . . It is therefore advisable to incorporate the CPS into a certificate by reference" (ABA Guidelines, sec. 1.8.3).

45. See Chapter 11.

46. For example, American Institute of Certified Public Accountants (AICPA), Statement on Auditing Standards No. 70 (SAS 70) *Reports on the Processing of Transactions by Service Organizations, Professional Standards,* 1, AU sec. 324. Many IT auditors have found the SAS 70 appropriate for providing sufficient information to interested parties when assessing the reliability and trustworthiness of certificates and certification services. The value of the SAS 70 report, as compared with other reporting mechanisms (such as those provided by ISO 9000), includes its rigor and the recognized professional standards of the AICPA members who test and opine on the effectiveness of transactional controls. See <http://www.aicpa.org>.

47. Proprietary audit tools typically seek to integrate diverse security audit control objectives and principles. See IIA, The Institute of Internal Auditors, *Systems Auditability and Control* (The Institute of Internal Auditors: Altamonte Springs, FL 1991), available at <http://www.theiia.org>. Mar et al., *Understanding and Auditing EDI and Open Network Controls* (1991), see Baum et. al., ASC X12, *Model EDI Audit Program* (Data Interchange Standards Association, 1995).

48. "A Certification Authority should establish and make available to subscribers and relying parties, a policy with respect to the collection, use and disclosure of information about a subscriber ('personal information')" (PAG, sec. 2.8). Privacy issues are considered in chapter 3. See notes 120 and 121 in Chapter 8 on PAG.

49. As an example of such a policy, see <http://www.verisign.com/truste/index.html>.

50. A compromise can be defined as a violation (or suspected violation) of a security policy in which an unauthorized disclosure of or loss of control over sensitive information may have occurred.

51. Examples of U.S. laws that might be so referenced are 18 U.S.C. sec. 1030 (Computer Fraud and Abuse Act of 1986, as amended in 1996); 18 U.S.C. sec. 1343 (Federal Wire Fraud Act); 18 U.S.C. sec. 2701 (Unlawful Access to Stored Communications-the Electronic Communications Privacy Act of 1986); and 18 U.S.C. sec. 1029 (Fraud and Related Activity in Connection with Computers). One of the most important criminal laws that protects PKI is the Computer Fraud and Abuse Act's section 1030(a)(5)(B), which prohibits "the transmission of a program, information, code, or command to a computer or computer system with reckless disregard of a substantial and unjustifiable risk that the transmission will damage, or cause damage to, a computer, computer system, network, information, data or program. . . . " See *United States v. Morris,* 928 F2d 504 (2d Cir. 1991), sec. 3.5 under *Illegal Bargains and Criminal Law.*

52. Because PKI is necessarily complex, the need for specialized expertise in protecting against and prosecuting PKI crime is vitally important. Various law enforcement agencies and computer infrastructure organizations have established special units to detect, counteract, and prosecute computer abuse. PKI participants should implement procedures to respond effectively to PKI crime threats and to recover from a successful criminal attack. In the United States, entities that have demonstrated an interest in protecting public-key infrastructure and that appear to have special (and developing) competence in this area include the Federal Bureau of Investigation Computer Crime Squad, the U.S. Justice Department's Computer Crime Division, the Computer Emergency Response Team (CERT) at Carnegie-Mellon University, and various state computer crime prosecutorial SWAT teams.

53. See chapter 2 for dispute resolution rules, including those for ICANN.

54. CA and RA stand for certification authority and registration authority.

55. Many such obligations are discussed in the ABA Guidelines, sec. 3.7.

56. See ABA Guidelines, sec. 1.22. The *operational period* is similar to the X.509 *validity period,* except that the operational period can terminate earlier than the X.509 validity period as a consequence of revocation. Under the ABA Guidelines, the end of the operational period, even if by revocation, does not terminate the validity of the certificate (ABA Guidelines, sec. 3.12.3).

57. See ABA Guidelines, sec. 1.1.

58. See "Notice and Conspicuousness" in section 3.5.@QQ AU: As intended?:

59. See generally ABA Guidelines, secs. 3.9-3.12.

60. See ABA Guidelines, secs. 3.9-3.12.

61. See ABA Guidelines, sec. 4.3 (safeguarding the private key).

62. See ABA Guidelines, sec. 1.33, concerning time stamping.

63. Procedures have been developed to facilitate permanent records retention, although these methods can be fully evaluated only in hindsight. See National Archives and Records Administration, Electronic Records Management Regulations, 36 C.F.R. 1234.28, concerning selection and maintenance of electronic record storage media. Also, certain electronic records must be maintained permanently for federal government archival purposes. See Federal Records Act, 44 U.S.C. secs. 2101 et seq.; *Armstrong v. Executive Office of the President,* 1 F3d 1274 (D.C. Cir. 1993).

64. Records retention requirements for PKIs among the U.S. states typically range from a few years to several decades.

65. See generally ABA Guidelines, sec. 3.13 (termination of business with minimal disruption).

66. See ABA Guidelines, sec. 3.1. *Trustworthy* involves the concept of reasonableness and is not an absolute. Rather, it requires controls that are commensurate with the attendant risk.

67. ABA Guidelines, sec. 1.35.

68. For comprehensive coverage, see Philip Fites and Martin P. J. Kratz, *Information Systems Security: A Practitioner's Reference* (New York: Van Nostrand Reinhold, 1993).

69. Secret sharing can also be used to protect a copy of a key that can be recovered (where appropriate) in the event that the primary key is lost or destroyed. A secret share is a portion of a cryptographic secret split among a number of tokens.

70. For some guidance, see <http://www.verisign.com/repository/PrivateKey_FAQ/index.html>.

71. See generally, PAG Appendix 5 ("Proposed Criteria for Development of Compatible End-User Product").

72. U.S. Department of Commerce, *Security Requirements for Cryptographic Modules,* Federal Information Processing Standards Publication FIPS PUB 140-2 (2001), available at <http://csrc.nist.gov/fips>.

73. See, for example, chapter 6 regarding the WTLS certificate format.

74. See, for example, the description of the e-Terms project in section 8.3.

Public-Key Infrastructure Assessment and Accreditation

Rigorous assessment and accreditation of public-key infrastructures (PKIs) and their components are essential to the continued growth of secure electronic communications and e-commerce. Assessment and accreditation not only promote PKI quality and trustworthiness but also facilitate interoperation between PKIs by aiding policy makers and others in ensuring objective oversight and permitting mutual trust. Various public- and private-sector PKI rules mandate assessment and accreditation as prerequisites to licensure or approval. Even where these processes are not mandated, they are rapidly becoming a necessity for commercial PKIs and certification authorities striving to remain competitive. Furthermore, assessment and accreditation are useful risk management tools that can help demonstrate due diligence, satisfy insurance requirements, and reduce legal exposure. Nonetheless, approaches to assessment and accreditation have yet to converge, and these processes generally are complex and expensive. One problem is the lack of a common, industry-wide understanding of assessment and accreditation processes. Various standards and professional organizations are currently working on clarifying the issues. This chapter is targeted at readers who are intimately associated with the development, procurement, deployment, or regulation of large-scale PKIs.

11.1 The Role of Assessment in Public-Key Infrastructure

Assessment refers to a prescribed procedure for determining whether a system (such as a PKI) or one of its components (such as a certification authority or a directory server) satisfies defined criteria for trustworthiness and quality. Assessment plays an important role in PKI for a variety of reasons:

- *It can invoke favorable legal presumptions.* In some jurisdictions, digital signatures validated using certificates issued by assessed and licensed certification authorities enjoy enhanced legal status compared with those corresponding to certificates issued by certification authorities that have not been assessed and licensed.
- *It is necessary for licensure and accreditation.* A successful assessment is typically a precondition for accreditation and licensure of a PKI or component thereof.
- *It is sometimes necessary for PKI interoperation and for operation in specific jurisdictions.* Assessment may be a precondition for formal interoperation, including cross-recognition, among PKIs and for operation within specific jurisdictions. It can also affect policy regarding cross-certification.
- *It enhances PKI support for non-repudiation.* Assessment provides strong evidence of a PKI's trustworthiness and therefore of the reliability of the transactions and records it supports.
- *It enhances public perceptions of PKI.* Assessment, especially if it includes licensure or approvals, is often perceived by the public as bestowing a "Good Housekeeping-like seal of approval" on a PKI, certifying its trustworthiness.
- *It aids risk management.* Assessment can provide important information with which to make essential risk management decisions.
- *It may be required for insurance purposes.* Assessment is sometimes a prerequisite for insurance coverage or at least for premium discounts or enhanced coverage.

Notwithstanding the many benefits of assessment and the many rationales for practicing it, assessment is sometimes undertaken only when it is forced on a PKI by law, by the need to interoperate, or by the need to maintain competitiveness. This is due to its costs, complexities, and time to complete. Nonetheless, most PKIs undertake at least some type of compliance audit.

Users of Assessments

Users are an important consideration in the assessment process, as they generally define the nature, timing, and extent of assessments. Typical users of an assessment report include the following:

- *Subscribers:* Subscribers need assurances that the PKI services they use are secure and trustworthy, that the service provider is bound to its commitments, and that their privacy is protected.
- *Relying parties:* Relying parties depend on the accuracy and integrity of certificates throughout the certificate life cycle. In particular, relying parties determine a certificate's trustworthiness based on their confidence in the certification authority's representations, and assessments provide evidence that such representations are truthful.
- *Policy management authorities:* Policy management authorities (or *policy authorities*) often use assessments in determining whether candidate certification authorities qualify (1) to be certified within a PKI's certificate chain and (2) to issue certificates under a specific policy. Further, policy management authorities may make periodic assessments a condition of ongoing service provision by accredited certification authorities.
- *Certification and registration authorities:* Certification authorities and registration authorities are both subjects and users of assessment reports. An assessment completed by an independent third party provides a certification authority or registration authority with an objective, independent assessment of its operations, which it can use to strengthen its risk management program. For commercial certification authorities, a robust assessment report may also serve as a marketing asset.
- *Licensing and regulatory authorities:* Most certification authority legislation requires some type of assessment as a precondition for licensing or approval.

Qualifications of Assessors

The proper qualifications for PKI assessors have yet to be comprehensively and uniformly defined. Some laws require that certified public accountants (CPAs) perform certification authority assessments, while other laws provide only general guidelines (for example, that assessors should have been in the security profession a certain number of years). Members of such organizations as the American Institute of Certified Public Accountants (AICPA), the Institute of Internal Auditors, and the Information Systems Audit and Control Association (as well as several for-profit organizations without professional accreditation) may possess the skill sets or qualifications to perform PKI assessments. Assessor qualifications will continue to be debated and to evolve. Until a comprehensive and uniform standard is achieved, the following criteria should be considered in selecting an assessor:

- *Independence:* Assessors' independence—and the appearance of that independence—must be strictly maintained. Many CPAs, for example, are well established as independent auditors with no financial interests or management roles in the organizations they audit.
- *Quality assurance:* Assessors should have a mechanism for ensuring the quality of the work they perform. This quality assurance process could include reviews of work performed by lower-level staff, reviews by a second assessor, or the performance of specific assessment steps.
- *Qualifications:* The exact skills or qualifications required by individual assessors or their firms or organizations are a matter of subjective judgement. Skills that are generally required include knowledge of and experience with PKI, cryptography, computer security, the platforms in use, and auditing and assessment procedures. An understanding of the applicable certification practice statement (CPS) or certificate policy (CP) is also necessary.

Assessment Targets

PKI assessments vary considerably in scope, focusing on any or all of the following elements:

- *The overall PKI environment:* This represents the broadest type of PKI assessment. It includes an analysis of an organization's general use of information tech-

nology, its personnel, its facilities, and its policies and procedures, in addition to
its PKI-specific technologies and processes.

- *Systems and subsystems:* A PKI organization's information technology systems
  and subsystems may be assessed independently or collectively. A functional part
  of a PKI, such as a registration authority or repository, might be viewed as a sub-
  system or a discrete component.[1]
- *Discrete components:* A component assessment might focus on an organization
  within the PKI, such as a registration authority, or on an element of the PKI's
  technology, such as software used by a certification authority or a server that a
  certification authority has specified as secure.
- *PKI cryptomodules:* Cryptomodules include hardware and software used to
  secure cryptographic keys and perform other cryptographic processes.[2]

While a broader scope of assessment provides better assurances of trustworthiness,
it is also more expensive and challenging.[3]

Assessments can focus on a PKI's performance as of a specific date (such as July 1,
2001) or over an extended period of time (such as January 1, 2001, to December 31,
2001). Generally, assessments of new PKIs or their components cover specific dates, such
as their initial operational date. After a PKI or component thereof has been operating for
an extended period, assessments of it typically cover a longer period of time.

Often a diagnostic audit, or *pre-audit,* is performed prior to an assessment. This facilitates the assessment by familiarizing the subject, such as a certification authority or registration authority, with assessment procedures and applicable criteria. Typically, the results of a
diagnostic audit are provided to managers as a detailed report with observations and recommendations regarding internal controls that will be examined in the formal assessment.

Assessment of a PKI must consider diverse issues and should reflect the complex,
multidisciplinary nature of PKI products and services. Specific subjects or targets of PKI
assessments include the following:

- *Primary certification authority controls (general information technology controls):* A PKI assessor might review a certification authority's security policies,
  security organization, asset classification system, personnel security measures,

physical security measures, network management processes, system access controls, system development and maintenance processes, business continuity planning, and event journals. Primary certification authority controls include both environmental controls and general information services controls (such as how the certification authority is networked to other PKI components and what security implications may arise from such networking). They are referred to as primary controls because they must be in place for a PKI to be considered trustworthy. Without strong primary certification authority controls, it is unlikely that a PKI can provide trustworthy services. Thus, in cases where primary certification authority controls are found to be lacking, assessing additional components is probably not warranted.

- *Key and device management controls:* An assessor might review a certification authority's practices pertaining to key-pair generation; private-key storage, backup, and recovery; public-key distribution; private-key usage; private-key destruction; and cryptographic device management. A certification authority's key management practices are critical to its trustworthiness and rely on several primary controls (specifically, physical and personnel controls).
- *Certificate life-cycle controls:* An assessor might review practices pertaining to initial subscriber registration; certificate issuance, validation, updating, revocation, and renewal; and publication of certificate status information, including certificate revocation lists (CRLs). Because certificate life-cycle controls rely on strong primary and key management controls, this evaluation takes place only after those other elements have been assessed. Certificate life-cycle controls may include the practices of a certification authority, those of registration authorities, or both.

When assessment is intended to confirm the proper mapping of important details between two PKIs (or their components), particular consideration should be given to the following factors:[4]

- *Certificate life-cycle events:* Recognized events within a certificate's life cycle, including the creation and termination of trustworthy PKI components[5]
- *Actors: Who* or *what* executes or controls those events: people, organizations, systems, and devices

- *Event constituents:* The discrete components, dependencies, and assumptions that make up life-cycle events
- *Evaluation documents:* The documents that record or describe the aforementioned events and constituents
- *Evaluators:* The individuals who produce the evaluation documents
- *Criteria and risk factors:* The criteria to be used for the evaluation or assessment
- *Outcome of the evaluation:* The report from the evaluator, including descriptions of any qualifications or conditions
- *Applicability:* The degree to which the evaluation satisfies business and user requirements

Assessment Criteria

The criteria used to assess PKIs and their components originate from various sources, including communities of PKI users, domestic and international standards organizations, governments, and PKI providers. Irrespective of their origin, PKI assessment criteria should (and generally do) share certain important attributes:

- *Appropriateness:* They should address relevant security threats affecting the target application.
- *Objectivity:* They should be capable of objective evaluation.
- *Clarity:* They should be written so that they can be uniformly and accurately used for assessments by diverse qualified assessors.
- *Ubiquity:* They should be embraced by the entire community of interest.
- *Extensibility:* Assessors should be able to adjust and update the criteria to apply them to future implementations.

Assessment criteria can consist of procedures created specifically for a particular assessment (in which case they must be described in the assessment report so that the users of the assessment report can understand the nature of the assessment), or they can be publicly available measures approved by an open standards body or industry association and accepted by the users of the assessment. Such criteria, at least the higher-level criteria, may appear in a CP.[6]

Assessment Types and Requirements

PKI assessment can take various forms:

- *Self-assessments:* Typically, these are (or should be) carried out by operational or line management personnel.
- *Internal audits:* These should be performed by qualified internal individuals not directly involved in day-to-day PKI operations.
- *External audits:* These are performed by independent third parties, usually external to the organization (but they may include inspectors general in government agencies).

Often a combination of these different forms is employed.

PKI assessments also have varied requirements. For example:

- *Provision of certain documents:* Some assessment regimes require organizations to present professional licenses and credentials (for example, for an engineer certified on a particular product) and educational degrees, or to provide proof of purchase of a performance bond.
- *Certification of technical systems:* For example, an accrediting body may require evidence that designated computing resources, such as hardware or software, have been evaluated by an appropriate body.
- *Review of specified policies and practices:* An organization undergoing assessment may have to submit its privacy policy for review by a privacy advocacy organization, for example, or demonstrate good business practices in specific areas.

These examples represent just a few of the possible types and requirements of PKI assessments, and these elements are not mutually exclusive. For example, suppose that Sharon's Steelcorp wants its certification authority to be accredited by the hypothetical Association of Manufacturers (the AoM). The AoM may require that Sharon's certification authority be assessed by a specific AoM-defined regime that includes a self-assessment, an external audit, a review of specific policies and practices, and certification of technical systems.

Models of Assessment

The best way to ensure that PKI assessment is both efficient and meaningful worldwide is to limit the number of assessment methodologies and programs to a few widely recognized models. The challenge is to ensure that a limited number of assessment models are responsive to all potential assessment needs and targets. It is not surprising to observe a healthy competition among assessment models and programs.

The best model for a particular assessment varies, depending on many factors:

- The purpose or purposes of the PKI
- The required level or levels of assurance for the certificates issued by the PKI
- The perceived risks
- Statutory, regulatory, and contractual requirements
- Interoperation requirements
- The availability of assessment mechanisms
- The availability of qualified assessors
- Assessment costs
- Public perceptions and recognition

The different roles of individuals or organizations that execute these processes include the following:

- *Criteria developers* set the criteria used in an assessment.
- *Assessors* ascertain whether the target of the assessment satisfies the designated criteria.
- *Evaluators* perform the same basic function as assessors but generally within a more formal structure. Evaluation refers generally to the examination by an objective party of a specific hardware or software device to ascertain (to some designated level of confidence) that it satisfies specific criteria (e.g., certifying that a specific cryptographic device conforms to a FIPS PUB 140 level 3 standard).
- *Auditors* are professionals who perform assessments according to prescribed accreditation regimes.
- *Accreditors* are entities that approve the results of assessments.

An accrediting body might authorize different assessors to confirm compliance with different assessment criteria. As depicted in table 11.1, the accrediting organization (such as the hypothetical AoM) can use various assessors, including itself, for certain functions. Assessors can be specified *inclusively* (by stating the qualifications for participation as an assessor) or *exclusively* (either by mandating the use of a particular assessor or by requiring the accreditor's prior approval of a requested assessor).

11.2 Evolution of Information System Assessment Criteria

A possible model of assessment can be found in the information technology security evaluations used by governments to assess certain information technology products, including some PKI products. Formal criteria for these assessments have been evolving over the past two decades, from the U.S. Trusted Computer System Evaluation Criteria (TCSEC) introduced in 1985 to the European Information Technology Security Evaluation Criteria (ITSEC) published in 1991 and the International Common Criteria for Information Technology Security Evaluation in 1999. TCSEC, embodied in the *Orange Book*,[7] focused on confidentiality to protect national security secrets. ITSEC was developed primarily within the European Union and specifies assurances separate from functionality.[8] Since these criteria were released, there has been solid progress in evaluation techniques. The Common Criteria provide a common language for specifying and understanding what a product does and does not do.[9]

Some of the nomenclature of the Common Criteria is as follows:

- *Protection profile (PP):* A protection profile is a document that defines a security capability to be provided to satisfy a particular business need, the security environment in which this capability must be provided, a set of objectives that will result in the desired capability, and a set of security measures that will accomplish these objectives. These are defined in an implementation- or product-independent manner to provide the requirements for a category of products or systems. Generally speaking, a customer prepares or uses a protection profile.[10]
- *Security target (ST):* A security target is a document that contains information similar to that in a protection profile, yet extends it to provide the needed security capability for a specific implementation or product. One security target may conform to one or more protection profiles. The security target is probably the

Table 11.1 Components of a PKI Assessment

Assessment elements	Assessor and qualifications	Proof of compliance	Costs/benefits
Self-assessment	An internal individual knowledgeable about the areas and items to be assessed	Submission of the completed self-assessment	Prepares all parties for formal assessments and helps identify problems.[11]
Independent audit	An independent third party who conforms to the applicable audit procedure, such as the Statement of Auditing Standards 70 (SAS 70), CATrust, or equivalent.[12] Third-party auditors should be licensed by a professional accounting body (e.g., CPAs or chartered accountants); certified as a CISSP[13] or CISA (Certified Information Systems Auditor); demonstrate experience in computer security, Internet technologies, and PKI; be skilled in PKI auditing procedures; or hold *certified engineer* status for the assessed systems or products.[14]	Auditor's attestation report	Provides valid, reliable information. In addition, there may be an apportionment of risk between the accreditor and an independent auditor and possible liability benefits.
Verification of trusted personnel and performance bond	Any assessor or evaluator laboratory or a commercial	Certified copy of bond	Risk management and demonstration of suitability; possible liability benefits
Review of technical components	Common Criteria-accredited licensed evaluation facility (CLEF)	Copy of signed certificate	Rigorous; recognized internationally; provides input to an audit[15]
Review of privacy policy	Privacy advocacy organization, e.g., TRUSTe[16]	Proof of privacy policy licensing	Supports branding and reputation; provides input to audit
Review of business practices	Business practices groups, e.g., Better Business Bureau (BBB)[17]	Proof of good standing	Provides branding, recognized role, and input to audit

most important document in that it defines what is actually evaluated. Its intended audience is any user of the product. Most evaluators urge, "If you read no other document, read the security target!"

- *Target of evaluation (TOE):* This is the information technology security product or system (including hardware, software, and documentation) that is the subject of the evaluation.
- *Evaluation assurance level (EAL):* The levels of evaluation defined in the Common Criteria range from EAL1 to EAL7, as presented in table 11.2. Each level represents a different level of trust in the target of evaluation.
- *Commercial licensed evaluation facilities (CLEFs):* These are private-sector, independent technical laboratories that have been accredited by the applicable national Common Criteria evaluation and certification scheme to perform Common Criteria evaluations.
- *Evaluation technical reports:* These are reports of an evaluation's findings provided by the evaluation facility. They are usually presented in confidence, although a *sanitized* report is normally available to a wider audience.

The Common Criteria aligned and replaced various source materials and earlier standards and is now the recognized international standard for information technology security evaluation. The various evaluation assurance levels (EALs) defined in the Common Criteria represent incrementally higher levels of assurance from a risk management perspective.

An approximate correspondence between the assurance levels of these three standards is presented in table 11.2. It should be noted that even at the highest levels of assurance, it is not possible to provide 100% security against all threats, since doing so is likely to be technically infeasible, financially prohibitive, or both.

Features and Use of the Common Criteria

The Common Criteria are prescriptive in terms of the assurance tasks required at specific assurance levels. However, the Common Criteria do not mandate any particular security functionality. Rather, they provide a toolbox of generally accepted security functions that can be mixed and matched to meet the needs of a particular product. So, for example, a product developer can justify in a protection profile or security target the particular security functionality and assurance level that he or she has used, and both the functionality and assurance level must be justified in terms of the threats faced by the system.

Table 11.2 Comparison of Formal Evaluation Criteria

Common Criteria	ITSEC	TCSEC
	E0	D Minimal protection
EAL1 Functionality tested		
EAL2 Structurally tested	E1	C1 Discretionary security protection
EAL3 Methodically tested and checked	E2	C2 Controlled access protection
EAL4 Methodically designed, tested, and reviewed	E3	B1 Labeled security protection
EAL5 Semiformal designed and tested	E4	B2 Structured protection
EAL6 Semiformal verified design and testing	E5	B3 Security domains
EAL7 Formally verified design and testing	E6	A1 Verified design

The Common Criteria are not PKI specific; rather, a PKI-specific version of a protection profile or security target must be drafted to represent its specific information security requirements or capabilities.

The Common Criteria enable the comparison of results among independent security evaluators by providing a common set of requirements and evaluation processes for the security functions of various information technology products and systems (including operating systems, database and network systems, PKIs, firewalls, smartcards, and applications). Such evaluations can originate from any commercial licensed evaluation facility (CLEF) or accredited security testing laboratory within a country that is the subject of a mutual recognition arrangement (discussed later). The Common Criteria seek to resolve conceptual and technical differences between existing criteria and contribute to the development of an international standard that advances the foreign recognition of evaluation results.[18] Nonetheless, the foreign recognition of Common Criteria evaluations is limited to those undertaken for EAL1 through EAL4. Beyond EAL4, national security considerations of particular nations generally complicate, and in some cases preclude, foreign recognition of evaluation results. Such concerns have consequently bolstered the popularity and use of EAL4 for commercial PKI evaluations, since it is the highest level that ensures widespread foreign recognition.[19]

There is a considerable learning curve for non-evaluators regarding the meaningful use of Common Criteria. Consider the following:

- *Completeness:* The security of the target of evaluation must be complete with respect to the claims made in the security target. However, if no claim is made regarding the ability of the target of evaluation to counter a particular threat, then the evaluation may not have considered that threat. Note that even if no claim is made, the evaluators may still consider the threat in their evaluation. The evaluation report provides information on this.
- *Justification:* Evaluations depend on justification that the requirements are appropriate (both necessary and sufficient).[20] This is subjective, and material dependencies are not justified,[21] at least from a legal-technical perspective.
- *Reuse of evaluation results:* The permissibility of reusing the results from an evaluation is an explicit goal of the Common Criteria. Nonetheless, the practicality of reusing internationally recognized results is unresolved. Given the rapid revision of systems, products, and services and the corresponding costs of Common Criteria evaluation, reuse will invariably become a major issue—and perhaps create further confusion. The Common Criteria include components that address maintenance of assurance to mitigate the need for and expense of reevaluating products by maintaining a level of security assurance without formal reevaluation.
- *Alternative methods of assurance:* ISO is considering alternative methods of Common Criteria assessment.[22]

The Common Criteria are gaining some industry and government acceptance for information technology security system evaluation. The Common Criteria are the result of more than five years of development among the governments of more than six countries. In the United States, the NIST and the NSA have spearheaded Common Criteria development and implementation.

Mutual Recognition of Common Criteria Certificates

An *Arrangement on the Recognition of Common Criteria Certificates* (CCRA) has been completed between the United States, Canada, the United Kingdom, France, Germany, Australia, New Zealand, the Netherlands, Italy, Spain, Greece, Norway, and Finland.[23] Under the CCRA, once a product or system is certified, foreign recertification is unnecessary to sell it to other member countries, except in certain instances involving national security.

Liability of the Commercial Licensed Evaluation Facility

Typically, the agreements between the evaluator and the accreditation entity disclaim generally any liability on the part of the commercial licensed evaluation facility. For instance, one such agreement states that it "is not a guarantee of freedom from security vulnerabilities; there remains a small probability (smaller with higher evaluation levels) that exploitable vulnerabilities may be discovered after a certificate has been awarded."[24]

11.3   Noteworthy Assessment and Accreditation Schemes

Following are PKI assessment and accreditation regimes that have been deployed or are under consideration for national, regional, or sectoral adoption and that collectively provide a snapshot of important contributions and developments in this field.

National Schemes

Australia: Gatekeeper

Gatekeeper is the Australian government's primary initiative to enhance secure service delivery, streamline secure intragovernmental transactions, establish a "rational voluntary mechanism for the implementation of PKI by government agencies,"[25] and facilitate interoperability. It allows users to choose from a panel of service providers whose products and methods of delivery have been evaluated and accredited to meet prescribed government standards for integrity and trust. It also is intended to provide an interoperational mechanism to manage Australia's activities and interests concerning PKI.[26] Gatekeeper accreditation is mandatory for certification authority vendors who wish to supply PKI services to federal government agencies.

The Gatekeeper program is managed by the Office for Government Online, advised by the Government Public Key Authority (GPKA). It is charged with evaluating and accrediting entities under the prevailing requirements. The GPKA recognizes two levels of accreditation: *entry-level* and *full accreditation.* Entry-level accreditation entails largely a policy and practices review with a commitment to use evaluated products at the Common Criteria EAL4 level.[27] Full accreditation requires satisfaction of entry-level requirements, includings Common Criteria certification.[28] Gatekeeper accreditation requires a satisfactory evaluation of a PKI's or component's financial viability, operational policies and procedures, hardware and software configurations, facility (if applicable) and operations management, communications confidentiality mechanisms, applicable products, and functioning applicable gateways. Noteworthy Gatekeeper developments include the following:

- The GPKA is considering implementing an *accreditation certificate* that would authenticate all certification authorities that have satisfied Gatekeeper requirements. Gatekeeper certificates are currently issued in paper form. Each Gatekeeper-accredited (intermediate) certification authority serves as the root authority for its subordinate certification authorities and registration authorities.
- End-user platforms (such as browsers and other clients) are not evaluated. Diskettes, smartcards, PCMCIA cards, and removable hard disks are considered acceptable for storing a user's private key.[29]
- Gatekeeper accreditation is available separately for registration authorities. Accredited registration authorities can service more than one accredited certification authority. However, the permissible functionality of a registration authority is constrained to basic validation functions[30] (though it may be expanded in the future). It is currently anticipated that Gatekeeper II rules will address discretely the increasingly diverse roles played by registration authorities and other critical PKI components.

The strength or severity of Gatekeeper has created some confusion in the marketplace. Some experts view it as overkill. One commercial view places it somewhere "between the European 'tight' regulatory control of certification authorities and the U.S. light touch approach."[31] In any event, the rigor of Gatekeeper-like approaches and policy-mapping methodologies has provoked some modest debate within the international community.

Canada: The Government of Canada PKI

Canada has been a global leader in advancing policy initiatives and bilateral agreements on assessment and accreditation.[32] The Government of Canada PKI (GOCPKI) was introduced in section 7.8.[33] There is a federal government-wide implementation team, in which the Communications Security Establishment (CSE) is responsible for information technology security. The GOCPKI provides a valuable and influential example of a procedural framework for accreditation.

The Government of Canada is endeavoring to enable non-GOCPKI links in the GOCPKI via cross-certificates. Furthermore, rather than simply requiring such PKIs to observe the GOCPKI practices as stipulated in its CP, the Government of Canada is exploring ways to assess and accredit other CPs with a view to recognizing that such an external CP can "map" to the GOCPKI CP. If this approach proves successful, it may lend credibility to the practicality of the X.509 policy-mapping mechanism.

Accreditation of PKI components by the Government of Canada is within the GOC's exclusive discretion. A requesting organization must demonstrate its compatibility with the GOC's political, economic, social, or cultural policies and objectives or demonstrate that its request supports government secure e-commerce initiatives.[34] A departmental sponsor is required if the requesting organization is not covered by the *Policy for Public Key Infrastructure Management*[35] ("external candidates"). The request must state the government interests that compel cross-certification and must be executed by a senior official of the requesting organization. Requests from commercial and other organizations are considered when the likelihood of sufficient government interactions is demonstrated and Canadian interests are advanced. Candidates (subject to certain exemptions for governmental entities) may be requested to provide evidence of legal status and financial capacity,[36] among other information.[37]

A requester's CP is examined by a cross-functional, interdisciplinary expert team to establish *tables of concordance* between the requester's CP and the corresponding GOCPKI CP.[38]

The GOCPKI describes policy mapping as an exercise in which each section of a candidate certification authority's CP is examined to identify similar or equivalent sections in the GOCPKI CP.[39] The categories and the corresponding similarities or differences between the policies are found in the *mapping sheets*—the result of the mapping exercise. The mapping sheets demonstrate correspondence between the two organizations' CPs at a particular assurance level, with exceptions noted and described as critical or requiring further examination. Sections of the mapping sheets that are flagged as critical or requiring further examination undergo additional analysis, often involving additional documentation.

The trustworthiness of a cross-certified certification authority is determined by a presumption of trust that the candidate certification authority complies with its CP and security regime based on the aforementioned documentation, policy mapping, and testbed trials. This presumption is enforced contractually (via a cross-certification agreement).[40] The GOCPKI presumes trust but reserves the right to request site inspections. The responsibility for maintaining the trust relationship lies with the parties to the cross-certification arrangement.

Germany

Germany was the first country to legislate the use of digital certificates nationally. The rigor with which its rules have been interpreted has been controversial, with allegations that the rules either (a) discriminate against foreign certification authorities because the strenuous requirements are unnecessary, commercially infeasible, favor German vendors and will not be satisfied by foreign certification authorities, or (b) are necessary to ensure strong support for non-repudiation and for the protection of the public. The Digital Signature Ordinance[41] (*Signaturverordnung-SigV*) implementing the German Digital Signature Act[42] (via publication in the German Federal Gazette) requires certification authorities to satisfy ITSEC E2 (comparable to EAL3). However, key generation, key storage, and signature functions, as well as terminals for commercial services, must be evaluated against ITSEC E4 (comparable to EAL5). Revision of the Act is currently under consideration.

Italy

Technical regulations were issued by the Authority for Information Technology in the Public Administration (AIPA); the most relevant provisions affect interoperation.[43] The security of the key-generation and signing devices must be verified at the ITSEC E3 level or greater. Operative systems must conform to the ITSEC E2 or TCSEC C2 norms except for signing devices.[44]

South Korea

Under the Korean Digital Signature Act,[45] the Minister of Information and Communication may license certification authorities. The act has raised considerable controversy because it limits foreign recognition (via cross-certification) exclusively to certification authorities that have been certified under their respective "national roots." This has been viewed as a serious trade barrier.[46]

United Kingdom

The stakeholder-led nonprofit organization tScheme[47] provides a self-regulation scheme for the assessment and approval of electronic trust services. Assessments by tScheme measure assessment targets against predefined profiles specific to the type of service provided (such as registration, certificate issuance, and key generation). tScheme sets minimum criteria for such issues as organizational fitness, appropriate technology, and appropriate procedures.

A service provider wishing to be approved by tScheme must submit a self-declaration to tScheme, submit information on other applicable approvals, and complete an independent audit against the applicable profile. Upon approval by tScheme, an agreement is executed setting the conditions of approval and the use of the tScheme mark.

United States: Federal Government

The U.S. Federal Bridge Certification Authority (FBCA) model was introduced in section 7.8. The associated PKI assurance levels—rudimentary, basic, medium, and high—were introduced in chapter 10. The rudimentary level is appropriate for low-risk applications where non-repudiation is not a requirement. The highest level is intended to apply to high-risk applications where the environment is hostile and users may be malicious. The FBCA operates under the highest level of assurance. At a minimum, an agency PKI that wishes to be integrated with the federal PKI must satisfy assurance requirements at the rudimentary level. While the issue of policy mapping that pervades the FBCA is unproven as a pragmatic commercial model, this project has resulted in some potentially valuable procedures for assessing the policies and practices of external PKI components with a view to integration into the U.S. structure.

An agency seeking to interoperate with the federal PKI must file an application with the Federal PKI Policy Authority (FPKIPA), recommending parity in the levels of assurance provided by its certificates with those of the federal PKI. The FPKIPA acts on the recommendation by accepting the proposed mappings or proposing alternative mappings. If the agency and the FPKIPA can agree on those mappings, then a memorandum of agreement is struck between the agency and the FPKIPA, laying out their respective responsibilities. For the agency, these include complying with its CP and CPS, pledging not to materially revise either document without notifying the FPKIPA, and presenting the results of periodic independent audits that demonstrate compliance with the memorandum of agreement.

Once the agency certification authority effects interoperation with the federal PKI, the agency needs to determine how to constructively employ the cross-certificates now in place. Doing this requires the agency to decide how to interoperate appropriately with the federal PKI directory and other agency directories, using X.500 or LDAP. Agencies are required to employ naming mechanisms that do not harm interoperability, but beyond this, what they do is left to their discretion and hopefully is driven by their desire to effect substantive interoperability.

The FPKIPA does not serve as a guarantor. Agencies are not compelled to use the FBCA, and they may elect to impose restrictions on their acceptance of certificates issued by other agencies that have cross-certified with the FBCA. Thus, an agency need not agree with every determination of the FPKIPA in order to join the federal PKI.

Among other responsibilities, the FPKIPA is charged with working with private industry toward implementing the federal PKI design in commercial off-the-shelf (COTS) products.[48]

The FPKIPA maps each agency's CP to one of the federal PKI policies to facilitate trust decisions. This model avoids each agency's having to develop multiple bilateral relationships and CP mappings. "The Federal PKI will support transactions between Federal agencies and state governments, local governments, businesses and the general public."[49] The government's stated intention is to eventually make the federal PKI available to support interoperability between federal and nonfederal entities.

The current Federal Bridge prototype includes a small number of certification authority products that interoperate, via cross-certification, within the FBCA's "membrane." Interoperating with these products allows any agency certification authority to interoperate indirectly with all agency certification authorities cross-certified with the FBCA. Separate from the FBCA, the federal government has sponsored various agency uses of PKI, with over 40 production and pilot applications.[50]

United States: State Governments

Some U.S. states have enacted laws and regulations pertaining to digital signatures and PKI. While each state law varies, most share important similarities, in part because they were derived from or highly influenced by the Utah or Washington state digital signature laws. Since U.S. federal legislation does not specifically address digital signatures and secure e-commerce,[51] the immediate responsibility for advancing PKI interoperation among the states falls on the states. The first formal interoperation regime took the form of a reciprocity agreement between the states of Minnesota, Utah, and Washington, in which Minnesota agreed to recognize certification authorities licensed in Utah and Washington. The Minnesota Rules presume satisfaction of signature requirements "if the certification authority is licensed by a governmental entity other than the state of Minnesota and the secretary determines that the requirements for licensure in that jurisdiction are *substantially similar* to those in Minnesota. . . ."[52]

Some U.S. states that have adopted digital signature rules have embraced (or are considering) reciprocity of rules and bilateral agreement with other states. These arrangements generally provide for the recognition of the certificates issued by a foreign licensed certification authority within the jurisdiction of that state, as long as the following conditions are met:

- The certification authority holds a foreign certification authority license.
- The certification authority is registered to do business in the corresponding state with which this state desires reciprocity.
- The certification authority submits an application for the recognition of its foreign license.
- The foreign state's certification authority licensing rules are substantially similar to the rules of that state.
- The certification authority uses trustworthy systems, maintains insurance, and employs trustworthy operative personnel.

These are some of the states whose rules accommodate reciprocity:

- *California:* "In lieu of completing the auditing requirement in Section 22003(a)(6)(c), Certification Authorities may be placed on the 'Approved List of Certification Authorities' upon providing the Secretary of State with proof of accreditation that has been conferred by a national or international accreditation body, that the Secretary of State has determined utilizes accreditation criteria that are consistent with the requirements of Section 22003(a)(1)-(5)."[53]

- *Minnesota:* "[A]uthorizes the Secretary of State to determine whether the requirements for licensure as a certification authority in another jurisdiction are substantially similar to those in Minnesota. The Secretary has received requests from interested parties, has reviewed and found similar the laws of the following jurisdictions: The State of Washington; The State of Utah."[54]

- *Nevada:* "The secretary of state may recognize a foreign license, in whole or in part, if: (a) The certification authority who holds the foreign license, in addition to complying with any other legal requirements for the transaction of business in this state, submits to the secretary of state: (1) An application for the recognition of his foreign license; (2) A certified copy of his foreign license; and (3) The [fees required by Nevada regulations]; and (b) The secretary of state determines that the governmental entity that issued the foreign license imposes requirements substantially similar to the requirements of this chapter."[55]

- *North Carolina:* "The Secretary is hereby authorized to enter into reciprocal arrangements with appropriate and duly authorized public agencies of other jurisdictions having a law substantially similar to this Article so as to further the purpose of this Article."[56]

- *Oregon:* "Authentication Authorities, which are licensed, registered or otherwise under the statutory oversight of the United States, a foreign country or by a state, province, or political subdivision or agency of the United States or foreign country ('governmental unit') will be registered as an Authentication Authority in Oregon provided . . ."[57]

- *Utah:* "(1) A certification authority licensed as such by a governmental entity other than the State of Utah, may act as a licensed certification authority in Utah only if, in addition to meeting any other requirements established by law for the transaction of business, it either:

    "(a) obtains a license as a certification authority from the Division; or (b) provides to the Division a certified copy of a license issued by a governmental entity

whose licensing or authorization requirements the Division has found to be substantially similar to those of Utah, together with the fee required by Utah Administrative Code R154-10-102. A license recognized under this subsection shall be
valid in Utah only during the time it is valid in the issuing jurisdiction."[58]

- *Washington:* "The secretary may recognize by rule the licensing or authorization
  of certification authorities by other governmental entities, in whole or in part,
  provided that those licensing or authorization requirements are substantially similar to those of this state."[59]

A draft interstate digital signature reciprocity agreement has been developed within
the Government and Reciprocity Work Group of the Information Security Committee of
the American Bar Association.[60]

Regional Schemes

APEC

Established in 1989, Asia-Pacific Economic Cooperation (APEC) is the primary regional
vehicle for promoting open trade, practical economic cooperation, and Asian-Pacific sense
of community. Its 21 member economies have formed a series of committees and corresponding task groups, including those addressing telecommunications and authentication
issues.[61] APEC established its Electronic Authentication Task Group (EATG) in March
1997. It has prepared an issues paper on the various technologies that can be used for electronic authentication, including PKI.[62] Its current focus is PKI interoperation, and its
major project, "PKI Interoperability Project," put forward *cross-recognition* as an alternative to cross-certification.[63] The EATG approach has been described as

> not to specify criteria but to compare various criteria, licensing requirements, etc. to
> ensure there are no obstacles to cross border authentication. There is no suggestion in
> the APEC work that governments be required to accredit private sector activity. The
> work we have been doing and will continue to do is aimed at achieving cross recogni-
> tion, or cross certification if desired, with an approach flexible enough to accommo-
> date those who license with those who adopt other approaches such as accreditation or
> independent audit.[64]

The EATG initiatives are progressing with support and cooperation among its participating countries. It has gained deserved attention in the major PKI-related organizations worldwide.

European Union

The European Union's PKI assessment and interoperation initiatives are derived from the European Union Directive on a Community Framework for Electronic Signatures (EU Directive, discussed in section 8.1).[65] Under the EU Directive, member states have until July 2001 to adapt or adopt national laws. Article 5 of the EU Directive gives different levels of legal effect to *electronic signatures* and *qualified electronic signatures*. Article 6 establishes liability rules for issuers of *qualified certificates*. Article 7 provides a framework for cross-border recognition with "third countries of services and electronic signatures." Article 13 states that "Member States may decide how they ensure the supervision of compliance with the provisions laid down in this Directive; this Directive does not preclude the establishment of private-sector-based supervision systems; this Directive does not obligate certification-service-providers to apply to be supervised under any applicable accreditation scheme."

The European Electronic Signature and Security Initiative (EESSI)[66] coordinates a collaborative program to identify requirements for standardization to support the coherent implementation of the EU Directive. The program is being implemented principally by the European Committee for Standardization (CEN)[67] and the European Telecommunications Standardization Institute (ETSI).

The EESSI Steering Group includes market players, administrations, and formal and informal standards organizations. EESSI has also developed extensive contacts internationally with other organizations active in the PKI industry. It claims that its "objective is clearly not to build a 'Europe-only' framework, but to contribute to the implementation of global solutions." Nonetheless its role in promoting European industrial policy cannot be discounted.

Among the most controversial technical requirements of the EU Directive that are being implemented within the standards community are those of the EU Directive's Annex III. Because of their significance, they are presented here in full.

Annex III of the EU Directive (requirements for certification service providers [CSPs] that issue qualified certificates) requires that

> Secure signature creation devices shall at least ensure, by appropriate technical and procedural means, that
>
> > (a) the signature creation data used for signature generation can practically occur only once, and that its secrecy is reasonably assured;
> > (b) the signature creation data used for signature generation cannot be derived with reasonable assurance and that the signature is protected against forgery using currently available technology;

> (c) the signature creation data used for signature generation can be reliably pro-
> tected by the legitimate holder against the use of others.

> Secure signature creation devices shall not alter the data to be signed nor prevent that
> those data are presented to the signatory prior to the signature process.

In this context, "signature creation data" should be interpreted as a private key. The other annexes address requirements for qualified certificates, requirements for secure signature creation devices, and recommendations for secure signature verification.

EESSI is also proposing a conformity assessment scheme for products and services for electronic signatures, the purpose of which is to ensure the widespread acceptance of the compliance evaluation of products and services as a function of ensuring their alignment with the legal requirements and the corresponding standards.

The compliance assessment is mandatory for secure signature creation devices. It may also be used for voluntary accreditation of CSPs and for their subsequent supervision, for the use of signature creation and verification devices, and for trustworthy systems and mechanisms. In other words, both the evaluation and certification aspects of conformity assessment may be useful for all EESSI deliverables.

One of EESSI's work items is therefore to define general principles for conformity assessment and for an overall coordination of the conformity assessment process for electronic signature products and services. It is anticipated to result in a "prestandard" CEN/ISSS Workshop Agreement (CWA) in the form of guidelines titled *Guidelines for Conformity Assessment of Electronic Signature Products and Services*.[68] The work will be performed in collaboration with the European Co-operation for Accreditation (EA), and other recognized bodies working in this field.

Sectoral Schemes

Health Care

The U.S. Department of Health and Human Services has issued draft *Security and Electronic Signature Standards*[69] and *Standards for Privacy of Individually Identifiable Health Information*[70] pursuant to the Health Information Portability and Accountability Act (HIPAA).[71] Collectively, these draft regulations are broad initiatives intended to ensure the integrity and confidentiality of health information. Affecting any entity that transmits or maintains individually identifiable health information, these draft regulations have a profound impact on the health care industry.

The regulations are far-reaching, approach security systemically, and require responsive security controls to ensure the integrity and confidentiality of Internet communications. The regulations require *certification*[72] of computer systems and networks by either an internal or external *accrediting agency.* At least one external organization has advanced HIPAA security regulation certification.[73]

External, industry-based accreditation may moderate concerns about HIPAA's purportedly draconian requirements. Such external accreditors tend to promulgate assessment standards that appear to satisfy materially HIPAA's regulations while demonstrating reasonableness, sensitivity to e-commerce processes and constraints, and the principle that *security should be commensurate with perceived risk* (rather than absolute). If HIPAA regulators accept such an approach, then the satisfaction of such accreditation programs will likely be viewed as evidence of good-faith compliance to HIPAA, and the net risk to covered entities will likely be (at least somewhat) moderated, thereby encouraging covered entities to become accredited. Furthermore, implementing an industry-wide accreditation system that demonstrates compliance with specific HIPAA regulations will mitigate risk and liability to the industry and may curtail overregulation.[74]

Financial Services

Financial services industry initiatives pertinent to assessment and accreditation include the following:

- *BITS Financial Services Security Laboratory:* BITS is the technology group for the Financial Services Roundtable. BITS hosts the BITS Financial Services Security Laboratory, which is developing criteria profiles to assist in defining internal security, building proprietary products, developing RFPs (requests for proposals), and evaluating the security of e-commerce products.[75]
- *SETCo:* The SET architecture for Internet-based credit card payments was introduced in chapter 5, and its PKI was described in chapter 7. SETCo manages the specification, oversees software compliance testing, and coordinates efforts related to the adoption of SET as the global payment standard. SETCo participants encourage payment brands, financial institutions, merchants, cardholders, and software vendors to adopt SET as a payment solution for global Internet commerce.[76] SETCo also awards the SET Mark to vendors of products that complete SET compliance testing and interoperability testing, sign the necessary licensing agreements, and maintain their products within the current specification.

- *Identrus:* Identrus, which was introduced in section 7.8, has developed a proprietary audit and certification program using an external auditing firm to undertake
assessments.[77]

11.4   Rationalization of Assessment Schemes

The number of assessment regimes in arenas affecting e-commerce grows continually.
While this may seem beneficial, it creates confusion on the part of e-commerce users. Relevant assessment programs, some of which have an associated *seal of approval,* are shown
in table 11.3.

Table 11.3   Typical Assessment Programs

Assessment element	Sponsor	Assessment program/seal
Audit	AICPA	SAS 70
	AICPA	WebTrust/CATrust
Product evaluation (including cryptographic module security)[77]	Common Criteria evaluation and validation scheme	Validation certificate
	BITS Financial Services Security Laboratory	BITS Security Laboratory Certification Process Seal
Business practices	Better Business Bureau	BBBOnLine Reliability Program
SSL security	VeriSign	SecureSite seal
Privacy	TRUSTe	TRUSTe seal
	International Information Systems Security Certification Consortium	Certified Information Security Personnel
Professional	International Computer Security Association	ICSA Professional Certification Program

The varying requirements and assurances of each assessment regime—which are often quite subtle and not appreciated by consumers—dilute their public appreciation and therefore their effectiveness. Consequently, harmonized, modular, flexible, and widely recognized PKI assessment and accreditation regimes could be valuable. Such regimes would advance a limited number of recognized global seals.

Perhaps the best summary of this subject is provided by the director of NIST's National Information Assurance Partnership:

> Gaining assurance about complex systems is difficult. It cannot be accomplished in a cost-effective manner using any single approach but rather must employ a variety of recognized assessment techniques by competent individuals and organizations. Developing a flexible and open assessment regimen with national and international recognition is the first step toward giving consumers the assurance needed for the critical information technologies that comprise their systems and networks.[78]

Only time will tell how the global PKI community will respond to the challenges of global PKI assessment and accreditation. There is a tremendous amount of work ahead. Indeed, some aspects of PKI assessment continue to be more of an art than a science. We can expect that both private- and public-sector organizations will focus much attention on this subject.

11.5 Summary

Because trust is the foundation of PKI-based secure e-commerce, comprehensive, reliable, globally recognized assessment and accreditation are essential to its continued growth. At present, the assessment and accreditation of PKIs and their components are undergoing constant change and adaptation. But as the pressures for robust PKI interoperation continue to mushroom—across sectors, governments, and organizations—standardization in this area is becoming essential. Achieving this standardization will not be easy, however. First, assessment and accreditation are necessarily multidisciplinary endeavors, involving technology, law, auditing standards, economics, politics, and national sovereignty and security. Second, the requirements of scores of governments and organizations have to be satisfied. Thus, the future holds considerable debate, experimentation, and innovation in this area. Educating the public about the meaning and benefits of assessment and accreditation is also imperative.

Notes

1. Indeed, if such elements did not function as discrete components, the overall PKI probably could not function properly.

2. The most widely recognized standard for cryptomodule assessment is U.S. Department of Commerce, *Security Requirements for Cryptographic Modules,* Federal Information Processing Standards Publication FIPS PUB 140-2 (and its predecessor FIPS PUB 140-1). This standard is particularly important because the Common Criteria (discussed in section 11.2) do not include a cryptographic module standard (although the European Electronic Signature and Security Initiative [EESSI] has been influenced by, may incorporate this FIPS as a European standard). Thus, this FIPS serves as a de facto protection profile, and its practical use for assessment and evaluation is widely accepted globally.

3. It may also be more vexing because of a lack of mature standards, uncertainty, and the difficulty of establishing a reliable base line for comparison, among other things.

4. See generally Australian Government Solicitor, *PKI Accreditation Methodology* (Melboure: March 15, 2000).

5. These life-cycle events are presented in a typical CP and are also included in RFC 2527, discussed in chapters 8 and 10. A rigorous PKI assessment should include comprehensive examination of life-cycle events.

6. A CP generally includes or incorporates by reference all requirements associated with ensuring that certificates provide adequate assurance for a particular community. Accordingly, requirements for specific technical evaluations and assessments (e.g., Common Criteria) may be specified in a CP that requires compliance audits that correspondingly verify specific elements of a general PKI assessment. This may create a hierarchy of requirements for assessments and audits that focus on one or more elements, such as (1) component technical requirements and assessment (via a Common Criteria Protection Profile) and (2) subcomponent technical requirements and assessment (e.g., conformance to FIPS PUB 140-2). In other words, a protection profile or security target (discussed later in this chapter) is an *element of,* rather than an *alternative to,* an overall compliance audit of CP requirements.

7. Department of Defense, Trusted Computer System Evaluation Criteria (TCSEC), DoD document 5200.28-STD (Department of Defense: 1985), available at <http:www.radium.ncsc.mil/tpep/library/rainbow/5200.28-STD.html>.

8. During the 1980s, the United Kingdom, Germany, France and the Netherlands produced versions of their own national criteria, which were then harmonized and published as the Information Technology Security Evaluation Criteria (ITSEC). Version 1.2, was published by the European Commission in June 1991. It is available at <http://csrc.nist.gov/secpubs/itsec.txt>.

9. *Common Criteria for Information Technology Security Evaluation,* available at <http://csrc.nist.gov>; also published as International Strandard ISO/IEC 15408:1999.

10. An international repository of PPs is being established. A single, internationally recognized PP registry will promote the use and availability of protection profiles and packages. The U.S. National Institute of Standards and Technology has developed a PP that presents four levels of assurance for certificate issuance and management components (CIMC). See <http://csrc.nist.gov/pki/documents>.

11. A self-assessment is generally less expensive than other forms of assessment but is also typically less effective. The specific trust requirements of a particular PKI may not require the rigor and independence of a third-party audit. But in most cases, self-assessment is best exploited as only one component of a comprehensive PKI assessment regime.

12. The SAS 70 is explained in chapter 10. For information on CATRUST see <http://www.aicpa.org>

13. The CISSP is administered by the International Information Systems Security Certification Consortium $(ISC)^2$, an international certification consortium headquartered in the United States. The $(ISC)^2$ was established in 1989 as a nonprofit corporation to develop a certification program for information systems security practitioners. See <http://www.isc2.org/isc2faq.html>.

14. For example, a Microsoft Certified Professional <http://www.microsoft.com/Seminar/1033/GSMC-English/Seminar.htm>, a Novell Certified Network Engineer <http://www.novel.com/education/cerinfo>, or a VeriSign Certified Engineer <http//:www.verisign.com/training/pki/vce.html>.

15. Reviews of technical components may be done in a laboratory, in which case they do not consider specific deployment issues or manual procedures. Audits, by contrast, include assessments of the actual implementation of technical components.

16. See <http://www.truste.org>.

17. See <http://www.bbb.org>.

18. See Communications Security Establishment (CSE), *The Canadian Common Criteria Evaluation and Certification Scheme-What You Need to Know,* available at <http://www.cio-dpi.gc.ca/pki>.

19. Nonetheless, France is publishing PPs and doing evaluations that include assurances beyond EAL4. Additionally, the U.S. National Security Agency is developing operating system PPs that go beyond EAL4 as a short-term requirement.

20. Common Criteria, ASE_REQ 1-7, and 1-8.

21. Common Criteria, ASE_REQ. 1-14.

22. See, for example, Assurance Approaches Working Group Task 1 Report, "An Alternative Assurance Package (AAP3) to the CC's EAL3 Assurance Level," draft version 0.9 (August 1997), available at <http://csrc.nist.gov/cc/aa/>.

23. *Arrangement on the Recognition of Common Criteria Certificates in the Field of IT Security,* available at: <http://niap.nist.gov/>.

24. Service Central de la Sécurité des Systèmes d'Information, *French Certificates-French IT Security Evaluation and Certification Scheme,* available at <http://www.scssi.gouv.fr>. Note that there are standards initiatives under way to ensure that the incremental assurances added at EAL3 and EAL4 reduce the probability of exploitable vulnerabilities over those added at EAL2.

25. National Office for the Information Economy of Australia, "Gatekeeper Executive Summary" <http://www.govonline.gov.au/projects/publickey/gpkaGatekeeper ExecutiveSummary.htm>

26. Office of Government Information Technology, Commonwealth of Australia, "Gatekeeper-A Strategy for Public Key Use in the Government" (1998), available at <http://www.ogit.gov.au>. Australia has also established a National Electronic Authentication Council (NEAC) as a focal point to "enhance business and consumer confidence in systems for authenticating electronic commerce transactions." Available at <http://www.dca.gov.au>. The NEAC will

- provide policy advice to government,
- monitor market developments,
- oversee the development of a framework of relevant technical standards and codes of business practice by industry bodies and Standards Australia,
- provide information, advice, and encouragement to industry and consumers to follow best practices, and
- facilitate the wider use of authentication products issued by government agencies for other transactions (Ministry for Communications, Information Technology and the Arts, press release (June 22, 1999), available at <http://www.dca.gov.au>).

Note that licensing of certification authorities is *not* one of the listed functions.

27. Entry-level accreditation involves evaluation of the infrastructure *supporting* a product or technology, *not* evaluation or certification of the technologies or products themselves. Certification authorities are required to arrange evaluation of those aspects of their operations that they want certified. Some elements of evaluation may require only the submission of relevant documentation to the evaluators; others may require site visits. Certification authorities bear the costs of the evaluation. The evaluators provide the certification authority with a certificate that details what has been evaluated and the standard achieved. Certification authorities must enter into a prescribed Head Agreement for the Provision of Telecommunications Services to the Commonwealth via the Office for Government Online. Finally, certification authorities submit their certificates of evaluation and proof of signing the Head Agreement to the GPKA with a request for accreditation.

28. Full accreditation requires completion of entry-level accreditation requirements and the evaluation and certification of certification authority technologies to the EAL4 or ITSEC3 standard under the Australasian Information Security Evaluation Programme (AISEP). A certificate is then issued that details what has been evaluated and the standard achieved. Note that only the Australian Defense Signals Directorate working with an approved AISEP can evaluate or certify technologies under applicable criteria for government use. The technology provider or certification authority submits its EAL4 certificate to the GPKA with a request for full accreditation.

29. The Gatekeeper standards suggest that the Australian Defense Signals Directorate should be consulted on "appropriate standards for securing tokens." The Gatekeeper report identifies tokens as the preferred means for key storage.

30. The Gatekeeper requirements state that a registration authority does not have key-generation responsibilities.

31. E-mail from Greg Rowley, CEO of eSign, to Michael Baum (May 22, 2000).

32. For example, an agreement between Canada and the United States to establish the GOC/U.S. Government PKI Liaison Group; see <http://www.cio-dpi.gc.ca/pki/Documents/TOR_e.html>.

33. The Government of Canada established the GOCPKI Secretariat to develop policy; resolve technical, legal, and operational issues; and deploy a federal PKI. The GOCPKI Secretariat Task Force forms part of the Treasury Board of Canada Secretariat, with overall stewardship provided by the Secretary of the Treasury Board; see <http://www.cio-dpi.gc.ca>.

34. Otherwise, cross-certification requests must be associated with governmental activities and undertaken via the Canadian Central Facility (CCF), unless authorized by the GOC's Policy Management Authority.

35. Treasury Board of Canada, Policy for Public Key Infrastructure management in the Government of Canada (1999), <http:www.tbs-sct.gc.ca/pubs_pol/ciopubs/pki/pki1_e.html>.

36. Nonetheless, the GOC recognizes foreign sovereign immunity laws that may limit or preclude the rights of recovery to injured parties.

37. Required documentation includes a CP, security policy, or equivalent; compliance inspection; description of technology; request for appropriate level or levels of assurance; a nondisclosure agreement (with external candidates) for GOC organization candidates; certification or accreditation as required under the Government Security Policy; and proper OID (Object Identifier) registration.

38. Since policy mapping between two or more certificate policies is a subjective exercise, it is important to document any differences in philosophical approach to risks and risk management. Different approaches do not necessarily mean less security. For example, some certification authorities may use the lowest common technology but have a high degree of audit and risk management,

whereas other certification authorities may use highly trusted COTS (commercial off-the-shelf) products but a lesser degree of risk management.

The Candidate must identify which of its CPs are to be considered for Cross-Certification with the GOC PKI. It must be recognized that the CP and CPS may or may not be combined into one document (CP/CPS). In any event, the Cross-Certification Team will examine specific elements within the CP and CPS to determine the highest level of assurance supported (Government of Canada, *Cross-Certification Methodology and Criteria*, Treasury Board of Canada: draft Sept. 1999.

39. The GOC's approach to mapping is quite detailed. For example:

> There is a column in the Mapping Sheets marked "C" that flags a section. Each Category and Element are mapped to corresponding sections on the Candidate CA's CP. If the Candidate CA's CP section does not meet the specification or is not similar to the corresponding interpretation of the GOC PKI CP section for the equivalent level of assurance then it is marked with a "C" for critical flag. This can potentially cause a reduction in the level of assurance or a failure of the cross-certification depending on the severity of the risk. An "F" is a warning flag where further examination is required such as information that may be located in the CPS. A "W" is a warning flag where the section(s) has a small difference but it is not critical. No mark indicates the section is OK (i.e. equivalent or similar).

> Each section of the Candidate CA's CP being mapped must be recorded in the Comparable Section of the Mapping Sheets. A section may contain more information and be mapped against several Elements. Any section that does not meet the minimum requirements and has a flag must have a comment to explain the flag. If there is a requirement for additional information to support or detail the comment, additional documentation may be used as long as the information is referenced correctly.

> The examination is continued until all Categories and Elements have been mapped. In many cases there may be additional sections where the organization has placed additional conditions. These need to be identified and eventually a risk assessment performed. At this stage any additional section should be identified, with headings and any special conditions on a separate form.
>
> (Treasury Board of Canada: draft Sept. 1999; Annex 5.)

40. The GOC has adopted this presumption-of-trust approach on an interim basis.

41. See <http://www.iid.de/iukdg/sigve.html>.

42. See <http://www.iid.de/iukdg/iukdge.html#a3>.

43. See <http://www.interlex.com/testi/regtecn.htm>.

44. Additionally, consider the Italian Draft Regulation that limits recognition to European states: "The same authentication procedures . . . can be followed by

another CA operating on the bases of a license or of an authorisation released by another country member of the EC or of the European Economic Area, on the bases of equivalent requirements. . . ." The European Commission's response will be of particular importance in light of the EU Directive, discussed later in this chapter and in section 8.1.

45. See <www.rootca.or.kr>.

46. The Asia-Pacific Economic Cooperation's Authentication Work Group is monitoring the Korean situation carefully. Also, consider the impact of the trade and commerce memorandum of understanding executed between South Korea and the United States, which, among other things, focuses on conformity assessment:

> The memorandum of understanding between the National Institute of Standards and Technology, an agency of the Commerce Department's Technology Administration, and the Korean Agency for Technology and Standards will pave the way for closer technical cooperation in three key areas: documentary standards, conformity assessment (the procedures required to show that products meet the standards and regulations of an export market) and measurements-all of which influence market access and flows of imports and exports (NIST, "United States and Republic of Korea Sign Standards Agreement to Enhance Trade and Commerce" [May 9, 2000], available at <http://www.nist.gov/public_affairs/releases/g00-78.htm>).

47. See <http://www.tscheme.org.uk>; <http://www.fei.org.uk/fei/news/tscheme.html>.

48. The extent to which this will happen on a broad scale is uncertain. Product vendors may resist adding complexity to their commercial products purely to satisfy special demands of the government sector.

49. Electronic Messaging Association, *Federal Bridge Certification Authority (FBCA) Initiative and Demonstration, Electronic Messaging Association (EMA) Challenge Project Plan* (April 6–8, 2000), sec. 2.0. See <http://www.ema.org>.

50. *The Evolving Federal PKI,* issued by the Federal PKI Steering Committee under the Federal CIO Council, is available electronically at <http://gits-sec.treas.gov>.

51. Federal law addresses only electronic signatures generally. See the Electronic Signatures in Global and National Commerce Act (the Federal E-Sign Act), discussed in chapter 8. See <http://www.ema.org>.

52. Minnesota Secretary of State, "Foreign or Non-Minnesota Licensed Certification Authorities," available at <http://www.sos.state.mn.us/business/digital/nmlc.html> (emphasis added).

53. California Code of Regulations, sec. 22003(a)(6)(D), available at
<http://www.ss.ca.gov/digsig/regulations.htm>.

54. Minnesota Rules, part 8275.0135, available at
<http://www.sos.state.mn.us/business/digital/nmlc.html>. Nebraska has a virtu-
ally identical provision in Nebraska Administrative Code, title 437, chap. 4,
sec. 001.06c-001.06d, available at <http://www.nol.org/home/SOS/digitalsig/
t437.htm>.

55. Nevada Administrative Code, sec. 720.420 (recognition of foreign license),
available at <http://www.leg.state.nv.us/nac/nac%2D720.html>. See also
<http://sos.state.nv.us/digsig/>.

56. North Carolina General Statutes, sec. 66-58.11 (reciprocal agreements), available at <http://www.ncga.state.nc.us/statutes/statutes_in_html/chp0660.html>.

57. Oregon Electronic Signature Act, Administrative Rules, sec. 441-780-0060
(reciprocity), available at <http://www.cbs.state.or.us/external/dfcs/e_
commerce/digsig/rules.html>.

58. Utah Administrative Code, R154-10-404 (recognition of foreign licenses),
available at <http://www.commerce.state.ut.us/digsig/ForeignRecog.htm>.
This regulation further provides that:

> (2) The Division may certify that the requirements of another jurisdiction are
> substantially similar to those of Utah if, in order to obtain a license, the control-
> ling law of the other jurisdiction requires that a licensed certification authority:
>
> a. issues certificates based upon a system of public key cryptography using a
>   trustworthy system;
>
> b. provides for a suitable guaranty in an amount of at least $25,000;
>
> c. employs as operative personnel only individuals who have demonstrated
>   knowledge and proficiency in the requirements of the law regarding digital
>   signatures, and who are free of felony criminal conviction for a minimum of
>   fifteen years; and
>
> d. is subject to a legally established system of enforcement of licensure
>   requirements.
>
> (3) The Division shall make available upon request, a list of those jurisdictions
> which the Division has certified pursuant to paragraph (2) of this section. If a
> jurisdiction is not included in the list, the Division shall consider whether certi-
> fication of such jurisdiction should be added, upon request of either the juris-
> diction or a certification authority licensed by that jurisdiction and upon receipt
> of an English language copy of the applicable laws and regulations of that
> jurisdiction.

59. Washington Electronic Authentication Act, Revised Code of Washington, sec. 19.34.100(5), available at <http://www.secstate.wa.gov/ea/ealaws.htm>.

60. As noted in section 8.2, there is an issue of preemption of state law resulting from the Federal E-Sign Act. We can expect challenges regarding states with digital signature legislation but no UETA and states, like California, with digital signature legislation that have adopted nonstandard versions of the UETA.

61. See <http://www1.apecsec.org.sg/97brochure/97brochure.html>, which provides general information about APEC.

62. See <http://apii.or.kr/telwg/eaTG/eaTG-cont.html>, which includes an annex on PKI.

63. Its initiative seeks to map approximately 60 to 70 "key elements for a PKI" that would support a hypothetical $1,000 transaction and also a nonfinancial (customs clearinghouse) transaction.

64. E-mail from Steve Orlowski to Richard Guida (March 1, 2000; copy on file with authors).

65. See <http://europa.eu.int/comm/internal_market/en/media/sign/Dir99-93-ecEN.pdf> and <http://www.ict.etsi.org/eessi/e-sign-directive.pdf>.

66. See <http://www.ict.etsi.org/eessi/EESSI-homepage.htm>.

67. See <http://www.cen.org>.

68. The CEN/ETSI standards will include an annex for Common Criteria-based protection profiles for CSPs that issue qualified certificates for compliance assessment.

69. Proposed Rule 63 FR 43241 (1998).

70. Proposed Rule 64 FR 59918 (1999).

71. Public Law 104-191 (August 21, 1996), codified at 42 U.S.C. sec. 1320d.

72. Security and Electronic Signature Security Standards, Proposed Rule 63 FR 43251. "Through 2004, Public Key Infrastructure (PKI) will be the only cost-effective technology available to meet proposed DHHS standards for electronic signatures to guarantee the confidentiality, authenticity, integrity and non-repudiation of stored or transmitted patient-identifiable healthcare information (0.9 probability)" (Gartner Group, "Information Security in Healthcare" [May 24, 1999], available at <http://www.gartner.com>).

73. The Electronic Health Network Accreditation Commission (EHNAC). EHNAC is an independent, nonprofit accrediting body whose mission is to "promote standards, quality service, innovation, cooperation and open competition within the healthcare EDI industry"; establish minimum criteria for industry self-regulation; encourage firms in the industry to improve performance; facilitate open market access and competition; foster consistency in transmitted information; and enhance customer service and satisfaction. See <http://www.ehnac.org>.

74. See, for example, the E31.20 Committee of the American Society of Testing and Materials <http://www.astm.org>, which developed a model CP and profiles; the Working Group on EDI <http://www.wedi.org>; and AFEHCT (Association for Electronic Healthcare Transactions) <http://www.afehct.org>, which undertook a Healthcare Security Interoperability Pilot.

75. See <www.bitsinfo.org>.

76. See <http://www.setco.org/about.html>.

77. See <http://www.identrus.com/index2.htm>.

78. Statement of Ron S. Ross, director of the National Information Assurance Partnership, NIST (July 18, 2000; copy on file with authors).

Forms of Agreement

Agreements play a particularly important role in e-commerce. Agreements serve to bolster (and indeed are an "anchor" to assure) the expectations of the parties. As such, they enhance the certainty of e-commerce, particularly where relevant law, including usages of trade and security standards, is uncertain. Indeed, agreements also provide a first line of defense for parties trading over unsecured networks such as the Internet, and with partners with whom longer-term, trusted relationships have not yet developed, or where trust among the parties is otherwise marginal. Also, where parties do not contemplate engaging in an ongoing relationship, standard agreement forms become important because the negotiation of an agreement may be inefficient or impractical.[1]

Agreements allow parties to benefit from freedom of contract. Without agreements, the rights and obligations of parties engaged in e-commerce will be determined (whether by design or default) by the prevailing law—which often differs from the parties' specific intentions and expectations. Thus, even when legal rules in the e-commerce area are established with great certainty, parties can use agreements to deviate from these rules when such deviation is to their advantage. In other words, agreements provide an important opportunity for parties to structure e-commerce relationships that are consistent with and support their precise business needs.

Agreements can be classified as either (1) documenting a single or ongoing transactions among specified trading partners, such as for the purchase and sale of goods, or (2) providing general, system rules to facilitate e-commerce within a community of interest.

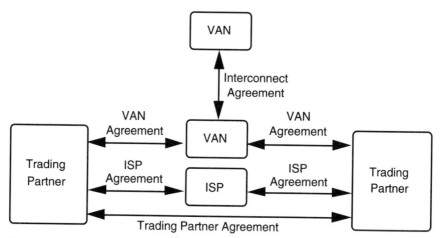

Figure A.1   Some Forms of E-Commerce Agreements.

Such facilitating e-commerce agreements include trading partner agreements (TPAs), Value-Added Network (VAN) agreements, interconnection agreements, Internet Service Provider (ISP) agreements, and payment agreements.[2] These types of agreements are discussed in this appendix. In Chapter 10 we introduced certification authority subscriber and relying party agreements.

One model of the relationships involved in some of these arrangements is presented in Figure A.1.

A.1 Trading Partner Agreements

Trading Partner Agreements (TPAs) are agreements between two (bilateral) or more (multilateral) parties who wish to trade electronically. Such electronic trading was traditionally accomplished using EDI, but it now includes HTML- and XML-based protocols (among various other protocols) over the Internet. Certain TPAs are sometimes called interchange agreements, EDI agreements, or preauthorization agreements. TPAs can:

- Enhance the validity and enforceability of underlying trade transactions by, among other things, agreeing on the effectiveness of electronic communications as signed writings;

- Reduce misunderstandings and uncertainty between parties;
- Apportion risk between trading partners, including liability for the acts of VANs, ASPs or ISPs;
- Define the parties' privacy and security obligations;
- Serve as an educational tool and implementation checklist; and,
- Serve as important audit and control tools.

Model TPAs to support EDI were prepared in the early 1990s by the American Bar Association, domestic and foreign governments, and industrial and international organizations.[3] Such TPAs attempt to provide a balanced treatment of legal and control issues, including at least a subset of the following issues.

- *Recitals*: TPAs generally express the parties' intentions to contract electronically and their acknowledgment that computer-based transactions are as valid and enforceable as comparable paper-based transactions.
- *Communication mechanisms*: TPAs generally state which methods of communication the parties will use—such as via ISPs or VANs.
- *System operations:* TPAs typically state that each party must pay its respective operational and data communications expenses (generally each party pays for messages that it originates).
- *Verification*: TPAs generally state the procedures that must be followed to verify the integrity of messages upon receipt. They might also detail the actions to be taken upon receipt of illegible (such as garbled) information—typically retransmission of or notification to the originating party.
- *Guidelines and user manuals*: As a matter of course, TPAs will list applicable technical and procedural guidelines and implementation manuals and profiles.
- *Signature and writing requirements*: Generally, TPAs will describe the nature and adequacy of signature substitutes (such as designated codes, keys, and authentication protocols).
- *Validity and enforceability*: TPAs will usually declare the parties' intentions to create valid and enforceable obligations using e-commerce mechanisms. They also may state the parties' intentions regarding the admissibility of evidence, attribution of messages, and presumptions.
- *Security requirements*: TPAs often require the trading partners to use such methods as necessary to support enforceable transactions, and to protect the confidential nature of inter-party communication.

- *Receipt:* Many TPAs define what constitutes "receipt" for purposes of contract law. In our example of Vera's lathe purchase, Danielle's receipt of Vera's purchase order can be designated to occur at various points, including: (1) when Vera sends the message to Danielle's; (2) when the message arrives at Danielle's ISP or VAN (as applicable); (3) when the message arrives at Danielle's computer system; (4) when Danielle's reads or processes the message; and (5) when Danielle's communicates a response (such as a communication acknowledgment or a substantive business document that references the message). TPAs also often detail specific time parameters regarding when trading partners must check their e-mail in-boxes or send acknowledgments. Due to the lack of automatic, explicit message acknowledgments (in the absence of using an enhanced delivery confirmation service), this is particularly important for Internet-based transactions.
- *Acceptance:* Similarly, TPAs often state what constitutes legal acceptance and when such acceptance is deemed to occur for contract formation purposes. Many of the issues noted in the receipt discussion above are equally applicable here.
- *Battle of the forms*: TPAs can provide a contractual solution to the problem of the "battle of the forms," in which, after the trading partners have reached agreement, one or both of the parties sends additional terms, attempting to modify the agreement.[4]
- *Record retention*: TPAs may identify which records must be retained by the parties, in what manner, and for how long.
- *Confidentiality:* TPAs generally state whether some or all of the information communicated is intended to be kept confidential and under what conditions, if any, it may be disclosed.
- *Apportionment of liability*: TPAs often apportion liability between the trading partners, including the acts of their respective third-party service providers, such as ISPs, ASPs or VANs.
- *Dispute resolution*: Many TPAs specify whether disputes will be resolved through traditional channels (such as litigation), or through an alternative dispute resolution mechanism (such as mediation or arbitration).
- *Notice*: Usually TPAs indicate where and how to send legally effective notice to the parties. Some TPAs also include provisions that permit or require electronic notice.
- *General boilerplate*: TPAs also generally address issues such as assignability, severability, survivability, termination, governing law, and force majeure (acts of god).

A.2   Value-Added Network (VAN) Agreements

VAN agreements are executed between a value-added data communications service provider, or "VAN," and a party desiring data communications services. These bilateral agreements generally describe the data services to be provided, obligate the customer to pay, and include warranty disclaimers and liability limitations. VAN agreements may also include technical information regarding the use and processing of formatted messages (such as EDI interchanges) and acknowledgments. These agreements also detail each party's responsibility for maintaining information security. The Internet Service Provider (ISP) agreement (discussed in more detail below) is a variant of the VAN agreement. Some application service provider (ASP) agreements and business-to-business exchange agreements can also be viewed as variants. VAN agreements typically address the following issues:

- *Service description:* A VAN agreement generally provides a description of the basic services to be provided by the VAN, such as data communications, format translation, and data mining.
- *Unauthorized access*: A VAN agreement often states what constitutes authorized access and prohibits unauthorized VAN access with respect to both general communications services and certain value-added services.
- *Customer service:* A VAN agreement typically states which customer support services are available, details of hours of operation, proper ways to communicate with customer service, and maximum wait periods. It also describes and distinguishes the VAN's regular customer service functions and services.
- *Ownership and use of customer data*: A VAN agreement often describes the extent to which the VAN may use customer data for unrelated purposes. Perhaps the greatest such use is aggregation of marketing data by the VAN for resale or reuse. VAN agreements also describe the extent to which a customer may obtain his or her archived data (including after termination of the agreement), and the fees a VAN may charge for such services. They also state whether the customer can use materials and products supplied by the VAN following termination of the agreement.
- *Data retention*: A VAN agreement often defines which data the VAN may or must retain and sets the retention period for defined types of data.
- *Availability*: A VAN agreement generally states that the VAN must perform in accordance with its published user documentation. The provider also may guarantee that

the system/service will be available for a specified time period (for example, 99.6% of the total hours for which services are contracted on a periodic basis). Sometimes such provisions are entitled "service level agreements" or "SLAs".

- *Fees and surcharges:* Fee and service provisions state which fees and services are chargeable to the user and establish the basis upon which such charges will be made (such as time and material, cost plus, etc.). Sometimes the VAN is permitted to adjust certain fees according to market conditions and inflation. The parties' respective obligations to pay taxes are also sometimes included. When price increases are greater than a stated amount or rate, customers are sometimes permitted to terminate the agreements without penalty.

- *Termination of service:* A VAN agreement frequently states that the agreement may be terminated without cause upon written notice by the service provider or customer within a stated time period (for example, 30 to 60 days); or, in the case of default by either party, if such default is not cured within a stated time period (for example, 10 days) the agreement may be terminated.

- *Third-party audits:* A VAN agreement sometimes states the right of the customer to obtain a copy of the VAN's independent third-party audit report, or to otherwise review designated documents describing the VAN's internal controls and adherence to such controls.

- *Reporting:* A VAN agreement often states the obligations of the VAN to undertake various types of reporting, including, for example, system availability, customer access and use of data, and system/security compromises.

- *Processing schedules:* A VAN agreement sometimes indicates the frequency with which the VAN will process specified types of data or transmit data to other service providers (such as on a batched basis).

- *Data recovery and business resumption capabilities*: Most VAN agreements describe the VAN's obligations in the event of system failure or other problems that require contingency planning. For example, such provisions may guarantee the customer's access to a "hot" or "warm" standby site or other backup facility, detailing when, where, for how long, and any guaranteed prioritization of the facility's resources.

- *Dispute resolution:* In some cases, a VAN agreement sets the method by which disputes will be resolved and the choice of law or forum applicable to resolving disputes between the parties. Typically, the VAN will choose the courts within its local jurisdiction as the exclusive venue for resolution of disputes or will require disputes to be submitted to binding arbitration.

- *Apportionment of liability:* A VAN agreement typically apportions liability between the VAN and its customers. Also, a VAN agreement typically includes disclaimers of warranty.

A.3   Interconnection Agreements

To facilitate reliable communications between trading partners connected to different VANs, many VANs interconnect their systems or networks. VANs execute *interconnection agreements* (also known as *interconnect* agreements) with other VANs to state how their interconnections will operate, to enhance reliability, and to control liability. The precise terms of an interconnection agreement are a function of the parties' respective bargaining power, business needs, and technical protocols. These protocols vary in their capacity to communicate acknowledgments, transmit billing information, and provide security. Interconnection agreements typically apportion liability between the VANs, indicate how and when data are to be exchanged, and facilitate inter-VAN communications generally. Interconnection agreements typically also include provisions addressing message transfer responsibilities, message acknowledgments, error identification and resolution, levels of service, billing and reimbursement practices, charges and settlement procedures.

A.4   Internet Service Provider (ISP) Agreements

ISP agreements define the rights and obligations of ISPs and users of various types of Internet services (as discussed in Chapter 2). Unlike traditional commercial EDI and VAN provider agreements, which respond to the needs of comparatively closed systems, ISP agreements typically address Internet-related communications and services, including content, abuse, and security issues. Common provisions of ISP agreements are as follows:[5]

- *Use and Acceptance:* Notice and agreement to ISP terms are typically executed online by consumers.[6] ISPs establish standardized services that are typically manifested in non-negotiated, standard-form agreements.[7] As with any non-negotiated agreement, there are concerns about enforceability. The practical necessity of signing up large numbers of users in real time bolsters the legitimate need for (and the law's acceptance of) legal presumptions favoring such enforceability.

- *Service Definitions:* ISP agreements generally describe the services to be provided by the ISP, which typically include Internet access, host services (such as e-mail and web hosting), and database/information services. For example, an ISP agreement might provide for "services on [the ISP's] host computing systems, including computing, telecommunications, software, and information services, as well as access to similar services provided by others via the Internet."

- *Lawful Use and Service Provider Control over Content:* Transmitting or otherwise making available certain information can subject the originator to legal liability on the basis of the content of such information.[8] Three of the grounds for liability based on content that are most relevant to e-commerce are defamation, copyright infringement (or interference with trademark or other intellectual property rights), and obscenity:

  - *Defamation:* A defendant may be held liable for defamation if he or she has originated a communication that is false and has resulted in harm to the plaintiff's reputation. Defamation may occur in written or visual media, in which case it is referred to as *libel*, or by oral or auditory media, in which case it is frequently termed *slander*.[9]

  - *Copyright infringement:* To prevail in litigation for copyright infringement,[10] a plaintiff must prove (a) its ownership of a valid copyright, and (b) that the defendant has "copied" "a protectable expression."[11]

  - *Obscenity:* Various U.S. state and federal laws (and similar laws in other jurisdictions) prohibit the distribution of "obscene" or otherwise "indecent" materials.[12] The difficulty of defining what is "obscene" or "indecent" contributes considerably to the significant uncertainty in the application of these laws.

Because ISPs play a role in the transmission and distribution of content, the possibility exists that an ISP can be held liable for harm caused primarily by, or for violations resulting primarily from, content posted by subscribers. Courts have already imposed such liability in various cases. Nonetheless, legislatures and courts are still attempting to define the extent to which, and the circumstances under which, ISPs might bear such responsibility. Cases in the early 1990s left ISPs with the dilemma that if they screened content, they might be held liable for the content that they fail to delete or restrict, but if they chose not to screen content, they might be held liable for not doing so.[13] Most ISPs currently take the approach that they do not screen content and are, accordingly, not responsible for that content, and it appears that ISPs have generally succeeded in avoiding liability through this approach.[14]

The confusion of the law regarding the secondary liability of ISPs is further compounded by the uncertainty of the law relating to *underlying* causes of action or violations, such as those relating to obscenity. For example, the law is far from settled regarding what constitutes obscene material and to what extent government may regulate its creation and distribution. For example, the U.S. Congress passed the Communications Decency Act of 1996,[15] which was signed into law by President Clinton in February, 1996. Section 223(a)(1)(B) of the Act provides for criminal sanctions against a party who, "by means of a telecommunications device," "knowingly . . . makes, creates, or solicits" and "initiates the transmission" of "any comment, request, suggestion, proposal, image or other communication which is obscene or indecent, knowing that the recipient of the communication is under 18 years of age." Section 223(d)(1) of the Act makes it a crime to use an "interactive computer service" to "send" or "display in any manner available" to a person under age 18, "any comment, request, suggestion, proposal, image or other communication that, in context, depicts or describes, in terms patently offensive as measured by contemporary community standards, sexual or excretory activities or organs, regardless of whether the user of such service placed the call or initiated the communication." In June of 1996, a federal district court held that these provisions were unconstitutional because the terms "indecent" and "patently offensive" were so vague that they violated the free speech and due process protections of the U.S. Constitution.[16] In 1998, Congress passed the Child Online Protection Act (COPA), making it illegal to knowingly make available to minors material that is "harmful to minors" (sexually explicit material meeting definitions set forth in COPA).[17]

Many U.S. states and international jurisdictions have addressed online obscenity through statute. State laws range from expanding existing laws prohibiting child pornography to restricting electronic transmissions in some states to prohibiting messages "with intent to harass, annoy, or alarm another person."[18] Despite some early legislation imposing liability on ISPs for permitting subscriber violations of pornography laws,[19] uncertainty in this area has generally been resolved in favor of not holding ISPs liable for such violations.

Due to the uncertainty of legal principles in these areas, ISPs typically attempt to limit their liability, as secondary participants, for violations relating to defamation, copyright infringement, distribution of obscene materials, or other legal harms or offenses by a subscriber. ISPs respond to this risk by attempting to limit exposure through the ISP agreement. Many ISP agreements therefore provide that ISP services "may be used only for lawful purposes" and that "transmission of any material in violation of any law is prohibited, including copyrighted material, material legally found to be threatening or obscene, or material protected by trade secret." Other ISP agreements simply put the subscriber on notice that the ISP does not attempt to restrict content, but that he or she will bear ultimate responsibility for all information posted. Most ISPs currently appear to follow the view that refraining from editorial activity is the best course of action. Accordingly, most ISP agreements contain explicit statements similar to the following provision from America Online's Membership Terms and Conditions relating to that organization's proprietary services, including Internet access:

> Most content on the AOL service is provided by AOL, our members, our affiliates, or independent content providers under license. In general, AOL does not pre-screen content available on the AOL service. AOL does not assume any responsibility or liability for content that is provided by others. AOL does reserve the right to remove content that, in AOL's judgment, does not meet its standards or does not comply with AOL's current Community Guidelines, but AOL is not responsible for any failure or delay in removing such material. Keep in mind that AOL is not responsible for content available on the Internet, although we reserve the right to block access to any Internet area containing illegal or other harmful content or otherwise being used for purposes that are unlawful or injurious to AOL or its members.

The law will undoubtedly undergo various initiatives and reforms in this area before electronic commerce participants can enjoy a relative level of certainty. Until then, parties must proceed with caution in these areas and understand their rights and potential liabilities.

Quality of Information

An ISP agreement typically states that the use "of any information, programs or data obtained from or via the ISP is at [the subscriber's] own risk. The ISP specifically denies any responsibility for the accuracy or quality of information obtained through its services."

Use of Other Networks

Most ISP agreements mandate that users who access other networks connected to the ISP must comply with the rules of those networks. Correspondingly, some ISP agreements hold their users responsible for determining whether or not specific data that they originate will be carried on another network—this is sometimes a daunting task. The availability of the other network's rules to the customer is generally relevant to the enforceability of this term.

Security

As previously explained, security provided by the Internet backbone is very limited; therefore, ISPs attempt increasingly to shift the responsibility for security to their customers and correspondingly, limit their own responsibility for security compromises. Because end-user obligations for information security are increasingly important, information security issues are presented in measured detail in ISP agreements.

Some ISP agreements include a customer acknowledgment that "the Internet is inherently insecure and that [the ISP] cannot protect against security breaches created by persons on the Internet (external to the ISP)." Although it is unclear to what extent an ISP can shift its liability by use of such disclaimers, they are common and it is prudent for ISPs to include them. Some ISP agreements agree to provide security at "the currently accepted industry level." Such a clause is of questionable value because: (1) it assumes that there is such a standard; and, (2) that such a level of security, if it exists, is adequate.

ISPs often require customers to maintain a secure password to be used to gain access to their account and to change their password on a regular basis. Customers are prohibited from using the ISP's services to obtain other customers' passwords and from making unauthorized attempts to access the systems and networks of others. Some proactive ISPs agree to check their password files periodically—if the ISP successfully cracks any password, it will notify the customer and request or require the customer to change it. Customers are required to refrain from sharing their passwords with anyone. Also, if suspicious activity is noticed, some ISPs will unilaterally change a customer's password and notify the customer accordingly.

Finally, although it is premature to find public-key infrastructure addressed in ISP agreements, the creation, issuance, use, and revocation of public-key certificates will soon be addressed in ISP agreement clauses because certificate management services are being bundled with ISP software and services.

Abuse and Misuse

Various activities, consolidated into the category of "abuse and misuse," are prohibited by ISP agreements. These activities are generally not clearly illegal, but rather characterized as "disrupting the system's normal use for others." Examples of this type of behavior include the mass posting of a message (including chain letters) to diverse newsgroups and mailing lists (*spamming*), sending junk e-mailings, improperly posting advertising, contravening *netiquette, flaming* other users, posting irrelevant materials to a mailing list, spawning multiple, unnecessary processes which consume excessive memory or processor resources for long periods, reverse-engineering of software supplied by the ISP and, for certain noncommercial systems, staying attached when not actively using the network.

Abuse and misuse provisions in ISP agreements generally focus on harassment, sabotage, or any unlawful activities (whether attempted or successful), including:

- Accessing information without authorization;
- Applying for or using a password under false pretenses;
- Securing a higher level of access privilege without the proper authority;
- Copying system files;
- Creating, using, or distributing malicious software;
- Decrypting system or user password files;
- Deleting, examining, copying, or modifying files and/or data belonging to other users without prior consent;
- Evading or changing resource quotas;
- Forging messages;
- Crashing network systems or programs;
- Posting or using copyrighted material without authorization; and
- Sharing, disclosing, or compromising passwords or other authenticators.

Other Provisions

Other provisions in an ISP agreement may include:

- *Availability*: ISPs generally do not warrant the availability of their services and often explicitly provide that service interruptions do not relieve customers of their obligation to pay.[20]
- *Access to users' private data*: Some ISP agreements prohibit the ISP from accessing any private user files unless such files threaten the integrity of the ISP's network or the Internet itself. In such cases, the ISP agreement typically allows the

ISP to access private files only after making (at least) a good faith attempt to contact the customer.

- *Account termination*: ISP agreements sometimes stipulate that the use of the Internet is a privilege, not a right,[21] and that inappropriate use may result in a loss of that privilege. In such cases, the ISP will determine in its own discretion what is inappropriate use and its decision is final. Some ISP agreements permit the ISP to close or suspend a specific user account, with or without notice or cause. ISP agreements generally provide that a customer may terminate an account by providing a request to the ISP. The customer is responsible for all fees up to the date of termination, except when the ISP is unable to provide services through the customer's own negligence.

- *Term*: ISP agreements generally provide that they shall remain in effect until a customer terminates his or her account, or until the ISP cancels it.

- *Amendments*: Most ISP agreements contain provisions permitting amendments to terms and conditions, including changes in prices and changes to services offered, upon notice to the subscriber (published online or in writing). Use by the customer after the effective date of such changes constitutes acceptance of them.

- *Fees*: Subscribers are typically invoiced monthly, net 30. Payment (often on a preauthorized basis) by credit card and electronic funds transfers is now commonplace.

- *Disclaimer of warranties*: Consistent with the ever-increasing focus on information content, many ISP agreements contain disclaimers of warranty such as the following:

"THE SERVICES AS WELL AS THE MATERIALS AND INFORMATION YOU FIND ON THE ISP'S DATA BASES ARE PROVIDED 'AS IS,' WITHOUT WARRANTY OF ANY KIND, EITHER EXPRESS OR IMPLIED, INCLUDING WITHOUT LIMITATION ANY WARRANTY FOR INFORMATION, SERVICES, OR PRODUCTS PROVIDED THROUGH OR IN CONNECTION WITH THE ISP'S SERVICE AND ANY IMPLIED WARRANTIES OF MERCHANTABILITY, FITNESS FOR A PARTICULAR PURPOSE, EXPECTATION OF PRIVACY OR NON-INFRINGEMENT."

Thus, a customer's typical recourse in the event of dissatisfaction is termination.

- *Limitations of liability*: Also consistent with the ISP focus on content issues in their warranty disclaimers, an ISP agreement might disclaim responsibility for:

any damages or injury caused by any failure of performance, error, omission, interruption, deletion, defect, delay in operation or transmission, computer virus, communication line failure, theft or destruction or unauthorized access to, alteration of, or use of records, whether for breach of contract, tortious behavior, negligence, or under any other cause of action. Customer specifically acknowledges that ISP is not liable for Customer's defamatory, offensive, infringing or illegal materials or conduct or that of third parties, and ISP reserves the right to remove such materials without liability."

- *Indemnification*: These provisions state that the customer agrees to reimburse or protect the ISP from any losses or claims resulting from the customer's use of the service that damages the customer or a third party.

A.5   Payments Agreements

Payments agreements enable or enhance the certainty of success in making payments electronically. Payments agreements take various forms, including:

- *Internet Payment Agreements*: These agreements are executed by consumers or merchants with third-party financial institutions with respect to on-line payment systems.[22]
- *Financial EDI Electronic Commerce Payments Agreements*: These agreements are executed between trading partners. They state the rights and responsibilities of the parties for making credit- or debit-based trade payments electronically. Some of the issues addressed include the effect of partial payments, timing of payments, and the use of funds clearinghouses. Such forms of agreement are sometimes integrated into standard TPAs or other e-commerce agreements.
- *Credit card and Internet payment service provider agreements*: These are agreements executed between a financial institution and a card or account holder.[23]
- *Electronic Funds Transfer (EFT) agreements*: These agreements are executed between a financial institution and its customers. They typically define the rights and obligations of the customer and the bank and are associated with credit- and/or debit-based electronic payments transactions.

Notes

1. Consumers are often presented with standard form contracts (sometimes referred to as *adhesion contracts*) by vendors and should be aware that such forms will typically contain provisions that grant significant legal advantages to the vendor. See Michael J. Madison, "Legal-Ware: Contract and Copyright in the Digital Age," 67 Fordham L. Rev. 1025 (1998); Jerry C. Liu, Robert J. O'Connell, W. Scott Petty, "Electronic Commerce: Using Clickwrap Agreements," 15 No. 12 Computer Lawyer 10, (1998); T.D. Rakoff, "Contracts of Adhesion: An Essay in Reconstruction," 96 Harvard Law Review 1174 (1983).

2. Another form of agreement is the *application service provider agreement* ("ASP Agreement"). ASP Agreements are noted for completeness but are not detailed in this book because of their widely diverse forms and because they do not necessarily address security issues.

3. These include the ABA's *Model EDI Trading Partner Agreement* and the TEDIS *European Model EDI Agreement*. The content and analysis of such model agreements remains relevant and useful today despite the fact that the use of intermediaries to translate or otherwise process message content has evolved or diminished.

4. See discussion of the "battle of the forms" under *Offer and Acceptance* in Section 3.3.

5. These provisions are iterated from diverse national, regional, and local ISP agreements.

6. On the other hand, more complex, negotiated, commercial and expensive commercial ISP agreements are not executed in that manner. See Section 3.5 regarding notice and conspicuousness.

7. The availability of many competitive Internet service offerings has tended to diminish certain concerns about ISP contractual over-reaching.

8. For comments on how these issues fit into the legal environment of e-commerce generally, see *Intellectual Property* in Section 3.5. The following discussion focuses principally on potential liabilities based on information content. Nonetheless, it is important for e-commerce participants to be aware that parties may also have intellectual property rights that they wish to enforce against infringing parties.

9. See Timothy Arnold-Moore, "Legal Pitfalls in Cyberspace: Defamation on Computer Networks," 5(2) *Journal of Law and Information Science* 165 (1994), available at <http://www.mds.rmit.edu.au/law/defame.html>.

10. Computer-related copyright issues are complex and rapidly changing. A detailed examination of them is beyond the scope of this book. For general information, see the following Web sites: <http://lcweb.loc.gov/copyright\> (U.S. Copyright Office), <http://www.copyright.com\> (Copyright Clearance Center), and <http://www.kindone.com/html/ip.html>.

11. *Baxter v. MCA Inc.*, 812 F.2d 421, 423 (9th Cir. 1987).

12. For example, most U.S. states have laws against pornography, many of which are enforceable in the setting of online distribution. In early 1996, Congress passed the Communications Decency Act, but the Supreme Court struck the law down in 1997 as unconstitutional under the First Amendment. See *Reno v. American Civil Liberties Union,* 117 S.Ct. 2329 (1997).

13. In the 1991 case of *Cubby v. CompuServe, Inc.*, 776 F. Supp. 135 (S.D.N.Y. 1991), the court exonerated CompuServe from liability for a defamatory message posted by one of its subscribers because CompuServe did not exercise editorial control over the messages posted on its service. The 1995 case of *Stratton Oakmont, Inc. v. Prodigy Services Co.,* 23 Media L. Rep. 1794 (N.Y. Sup. Ct. 1995), found that the Prodigy service could be held liable for defamatory postings because it had promulgated and implemented content screening guidelines and procedures. On the other hand, a federal court in 1993 held a bulletin board operator liable for infringement on the basis that it distributed content copyrighted by Playboy Magazine, even though the operator was unaware of the infringing nature of the content and played no affirmative role in screening or editing content. *Playboy Enterprises, Inc. v. Frena*, 839 F. Supp. 1552 (M.D. Fla. 1993).

14. As of May 2000, there had not been any court decisions in the United States addressing the issue on its merits since 1996.

15. 47 U.S.C. § 223(a) to (h).

16. *American Civil Liberties Union v. Reno*, 929 F. Supp. 824 (E.D. Pa. 1996). One judge opined, "Just as the strength of the Internet is chaos, so the strength of our liberty depends upon the chaos and cacophony of the unfettered speech the

First Amendment provides." 929 F. Supp. at 883 (Dalzell, J.). The government appealed this decision, but the United States Supreme Court upheld the district court's decision that the law is unconstitutional. See *Reno v. American Civil Liberties Union,* 117 S.Ct. 2329 (1997).

17. Pub.L. 105-277, Div. C, ,Title XIV, Oct. 21, 1998, 112 Stat. 2681-736; see also <http://www.copacommission.com>; and testimony of Michael S. Baum to the Commission on Online Child Protection (explaining the possible role of digital signatures in support of COPA—June 9, 2000) <http://www.verisign.com/repository/pubs/copa >.

18. General Statutes of Connecticut § 53a-182b(a) (1995).

19. Florida Statutes 847.0135 (1996).

20. Even if ISPs desired to warrant availability they are severely curtailed by the disclaimers of warranty in their respective telecommunications provider agreements and the inherent lack of reliability of the Internet. The denial of service problems experienced by various notable Web sites, including E*TRADE and Yahoo!, in March 2000, serve as one example of the risks to ISPs, ASPs and other Web providers of guaranteeing access.

21. Michael S. Baum, *Federal Certification Authority Liability and Policy* (Gaithersburg, Md.: National Institute of Standards and Technology, 1994), NIST-GCR-94-654, p. 17 (considering privileges versus rights with regard to PKI). Available at: <http://www.verisign.com/repository/pubs>.

22. See, for example, <http://www.verisign.com/payment/index.html>.

23. See, for example: the explanatory material regarding the Visa agreement <http://www.visa.com> and the CyberCash general terms and conditions <http://www.cybercash.com>. See also Section 5.6 regarding Internet payment schemes.

The U.S. Federal E-Sign Act

S. 761

One Hundred Sixth Congress
of the
United States of America

AT THE SECOND SESSION

Begun and held at the City of Washington on Monday,
the twenty-fourth day of January, two thousand

An Act

To facilitate the use of electronic records and signatures in interstate or foreign commerce.

Be it enacted by the Senate and House of Representatives of the United States of America in Congress assembled,

SECTION 1. SHORT TITLE.

This Act may be cited as the "Electronic Signatures in Global and National Commerce Act".

TITLE I—ELECTRONIC RECORDS AND SIGNATURES IN COMMERCE

SEC. 101. GENERAL RULE OF VALIDITY.

(a) IN GENERAL.—Notwithstanding any statute, regulation, or other rule of law (other than this title and title II), with respect to any transaction in or affecting interstate or foreign commerce—

(1) a signature, contract, or other record relating to such transaction may not be denied legal effect, validity, or enforceability solely because it is in electronic form; and

(2) a contract relating to such transaction may not be denied legal effect, validity, or enforceability solely because an electronic signature or electronic record was used in its formation.

(b) PRESERVATION OF RIGHTS AND OBLIGATIONS.—This title does not—

(1) limit, alter, or otherwise affect any requirement imposed by a statute, regulation, or rule of law relating to the rights and obligations of persons under such statute, regulation, or rule of law other than a requirement that contracts or other records be written, signed, or in nonelectronic form; or

(2) require any person to agree to use or accept electronic records or electronic signatures, other than a governmental agency with respect to a record other than a contract to which it is a party.

(c) CONSUMER DISCLOSURES.—

(1) CONSENT TO ELECTRONIC RECORDS.—Notwithstanding subsection (a), if a statute, regulation, or other rule of law requires that information relating to a transaction or transactions in or affecting interstate or foreign commerce be provided or made available to a consumer in writing, the use of an electronic record to provide or make available (whichever

S. 761—2

is required) such information satisfies the requirement that such information be in writing if—

    (A) the consumer has affirmatively consented to such use and has not withdrawn such consent;

    (B) the consumer, prior to consenting, is provided with a clear and conspicuous statement—

        (i) informing the consumer of (I) any right or option of the consumer to have the record provided or made available on paper or in nonelectronic form, and (II) the right of the consumer to withdraw the consent to have the record provided or made available in an electronic form and of any conditions, consequences (which may include termination of the parties' relationship), or fees in the event of such withdrawal;

        (ii) informing the consumer of whether the consent applies (I) only to the particular transaction which gave rise to the obligation to provide the record, or (II) to identified categories of records that may be provided or made available during the course of the parties' relationship;

        (iii) describing the procedures the consumer must use to withdraw consent as provided in clause (i) and to update information needed to contact the consumer electronically; and

        (iv) informing the consumer (I) how, after the consent, the consumer may, upon request, obtain a paper copy of an electronic record, and (II) whether any fee will be charged for such copy;

    (C) the consumer—

        (i) prior to consenting, is provided with a statement of the hardware and software requirements for access to and retention of the electronic records; and

        (ii) consents electronically, or confirms his or her consent electronically, in a manner that reasonably demonstrates that the consumer can access information in the electronic form that will be used to provide the information that is the subject of the consent; and

    (D) after the consent of a consumer in accordance with subparagraph (A), if a change in the hardware or software requirements needed to access or retain electronic records creates a material risk that the consumer will not be able to access or retain a subsequent electronic record that was the subject of the consent, the person providing the electronic record—

        (i) provides the consumer with a statement of (I) the revised hardware and software requirements for access to and retention of the electronic records, and (II) the right to withdraw consent without the imposition of any fees for such withdrawal and without the imposition of any condition or consequence that was not disclosed under subparagraph (B)(i); and

        (ii) again complies with subparagraph (C).

    (2) OTHER RIGHTS.—

    (A) PRESERVATION OF CONSUMER PROTECTIONS.— Nothing in this title affects the content or timing of any disclosure or other record required to be provided or made

S. 761—3

available to any consumer under any statute, regulation, or other rule of law.

(B) VERIFICATION OR ACKNOWLEDGMENT.—If a law that was enacted prior to this Act expressly requires a record to be provided or made available by a specified method that requires verification or acknowledgment of receipt, the record may be provided or made available electronically only if the method used provides verification or acknowledgment of receipt (whichever is required).

(3) EFFECT OF FAILURE TO OBTAIN ELECTRONIC CONSENT OR CONFIRMATION OF CONSENT.—The legal effectiveness, validity, or enforceability of any contract executed by a consumer shall not be denied solely because of the failure to obtain electronic consent or confirmation of consent by that consumer in accordance with paragraph (1)(C)(ii).

(4) PROSPECTIVE EFFECT.—Withdrawal of consent by a consumer shall not affect the legal effectiveness, validity, or enforceability of electronic records provided or made available to that consumer in accordance with paragraph (1) prior to implementation of the consumer's withdrawal of consent. A consumer's withdrawal of consent shall be effective within a reasonable period of time after receipt of the withdrawal by the provider of the record. Failure to comply with paragraph (1)(D) may, at the election of the consumer, be treated as a withdrawal of consent for purposes of this paragraph.

(5) PRIOR CONSENT.—This subsection does not apply to any records that are provided or made available to a consumer who has consented prior to the effective date of this title to receive such records in electronic form as permitted by any statute, regulation, or other rule of law.

(6) ORAL COMMUNICATIONS.—An oral communication or a recording of an oral communication shall not qualify as an electronic record for purposes of this subsection except as otherwise provided under applicable law.

(d) RETENTION OF CONTRACTS AND RECORDS.—

(1) ACCURACY AND ACCESSIBILITY.—If a statute, regulation, or other rule of law requires that a contract or other record relating to a transaction in or affecting interstate or foreign commerce be retained, that requirement is met by retaining an electronic record of the information in the contract or other record that—

(A) accurately reflects the information set forth in the contract or other record; and

(B) remains accessible to all persons who are entitled to access by statute, regulation, or rule of law, for the period required by such statute, regulation, or rule of law, in a form that is capable of being accurately reproduced for later reference, whether by transmission, printing, or otherwise.

(2) EXCEPTION.—A requirement to retain a contract or other record in accordance with paragraph (1) does not apply to any information whose sole purpose is to enable the contract or other record to be sent, communicated, or received.

(3) ORIGINALS.—If a statute, regulation, or other rule of law requires a contract or other record relating to a transaction in or affecting interstate or foreign commerce to be provided,

S. 761—4

available, or retained in its original form, or provides consequences if the contract or other record is not provided, available, or retained in its original form, that statute, regulation, or rule of law is satisfied by an electronic record that complies with paragraph (1).

(4) CHECKS.—If a statute, regulation, or other rule of law requires the retention of a check, that requirement is satisfied by retention of an electronic record of the information on the front and back of the check in accordance with paragraph (1).

(e) ACCURACY AND ABILITY TO RETAIN CONTRACTS AND OTHER RECORDS.—Notwithstanding subsection (a), if a statute, regulation, or other rule of law requires that a contract or other record relating to a transaction in or affecting interstate or foreign commerce be in writing, the legal effect, validity, or enforceability of an electronic record of such contract or other record may be denied if such electronic record is not in a form that is capable of being retained and accurately reproduced for later reference by all parties or persons who are entitled to retain the contract or other record.

(f) PROXIMITY.—Nothing in this title affects the proximity required by any statute, regulation, or other rule of law with respect to any warning, notice, disclosure, or other record required to be posted, displayed, or publicly affixed.

(g) NOTARIZATION AND ACKNOWLEDGMENT.—If a statute, regulation, or other rule of law requires a signature or record relating to a transaction in or affecting interstate or foreign commerce to be notarized, acknowledged, verified, or made under oath, that requirement is satisfied if the electronic signature of the person authorized to perform those acts, together with all other information required to be included by other applicable statute, regulation, or rule of law, is attached to or logically associated with the signature or record.

(h) ELECTRONIC AGENTS.—A contract or other record relating to a transaction in or affecting interstate or foreign commerce may not be denied legal effect, validity, or enforceability solely because its formation, creation, or delivery involved the action of one or more electronic agents so long as the action of any such electronic agent is legally attributable to the person to be bound.

(i) INSURANCE.—It is the specific intent of the Congress that this title and title II apply to the business of insurance.

(j) INSURANCE AGENTS AND BROKERS.—An insurance agent or broker acting under the direction of a party that enters into a contract by means of an electronic record or electronic signature may not be held liable for any deficiency in the electronic procedures agreed to by the parties under that contract if—

(1) the agent or broker has not engaged in negligent, reckless, or intentional tortious conduct;

(2) the agent or broker was not involved in the development or establishment of such electronic procedures; and

(3) the agent or broker did not deviate from such procedures.

SEC. 102. EXEMPTION TO PREEMPTION.

(a) IN GENERAL.—A State statute, regulation, or other rule of law may modify, limit, or supersede the provisions of section 101 with respect to State law only if such statute, regulation, or rule of law—

S. 761—5

(1) constitutes an enactment or adoption of the Uniform Electronic Transactions Act as approved and recommended for enactment in all the States by the National Conference of Commissioners on Uniform State Laws in 1999, except that any exception to the scope of such Act enacted by a State under section 3(b)(4) of such Act shall be preempted to the extent such exception is inconsistent with this title or title II, or would not be permitted under paragraph (2)(A)(ii) of this subsection; or

(2)(A) specifies the alternative procedures or requirements for the use or acceptance (or both) of electronic records or electronic signatures to establish the legal effect, validity, or enforceability of contracts or other records, if—

(i) such alternative procedures or requirements are consistent with this title and title II; and

(ii) such alternative procedures or requirements do not require, or accord greater legal status or effect to, the implementation or application of a specific technology or technical specification for performing the functions of creating, storing, generating, receiving, communicating, or authenticating electronic records or electronic signatures; and

(B) if enacted or adopted after the date of the enactment of this Act, makes specific reference to this Act.

(b) EXCEPTIONS FOR ACTIONS BY STATES AS MARKET PARTICIPANTS.—Subsection (a)(2)(A)(ii) shall not apply to the statutes, regulations, or other rules of law governing procurement by any State, or any agency or instrumentality thereof.

(c) PREVENTION OF CIRCUMVENTION.—Subsection (a) does not permit a State to circumvent this title or title II through the imposition of nonelectronic delivery methods under section 8(b)(2) of the Uniform Electronic Transactions Act.

SEC. 103. SPECIFIC EXCEPTIONS.

(a) EXCEPTED REQUIREMENTS.—The provisions of section 101 shall not apply to a contract or other record to the extent it is governed by—

(1) a statute, regulation, or other rule of law governing the creation and execution of wills, codicils, or testamentary trusts;

(2) a State statute, regulation, or other rule of law governing adoption, divorce, or other matters of family law; or

(3) the Uniform Commercial Code, as in effect in any State, other than sections 1–107 and 1–206 and Articles 2 and 2A.

(b) ADDITIONAL EXCEPTIONS.—The provisions of section 101 shall not apply to—

(1) court orders or notices, or official court documents (including briefs, pleadings, and other writings) required to be executed in connection with court proceedings;

(2) any notice of—

(A) the cancellation or termination of utility services (including water, heat, and power);

(B) default, acceleration, repossession, foreclosure, or eviction, or the right to cure, under a credit agreement secured by, or a rental agreement for, a primary residence of an individual;

S. 761—6

(C) the cancellation or termination of health insurance or benefits or life insurance benefits (excluding annuities); or

(D) recall of a product, or material failure of a product, that risks endangering health or safety; or

(3) any document required to accompany any transportation or handling of hazardous materials, pesticides, or other toxic or dangerous materials.

(c) REVIEW OF EXCEPTIONS.—

(1) EVALUATION REQUIRED.—The Secretary of Commerce, acting through the Assistant Secretary for Communications and Information, shall review the operation of the exceptions in subsections (a) and (b) to evaluate, over a period of 3 years, whether such exceptions continue to be necessary for the protection of consumers. Within 3 years after the date of enactment of this Act, the Assistant Secretary shall submit a report to the Congress on the results of such evaluation.

(2) DETERMINATIONS.—If a Federal regulatory agency, with respect to matter within its jurisdiction, determines after notice and an opportunity for public comment, and publishes a finding, that one or more such exceptions are no longer necessary for the protection of consumers and eliminating such exceptions will not increase the material risk of harm to consumers, such agency may extend the application of section 101 to the exceptions identified in such finding.

SEC. 104. APPLICABILITY TO FEDERAL AND STATE GOVERNMENTS.

(a) FILING AND ACCESS REQUIREMENTS.—Subject to subsection (c)(2), nothing in this title limits or supersedes any requirement by a Federal regulatory agency, self-regulatory organization, or State regulatory agency that records be filed with such agency or organization in accordance with specified standards or formats.

(b) PRESERVATION OF EXISTING RULEMAKING AUTHORITY.—

(1) USE OF AUTHORITY TO INTERPRET.—Subject to paragraph (2) and subsection (c), a Federal regulatory agency or State regulatory agency that is responsible for rulemaking under any other statute may interpret section 101 with respect to such statute through—

(A) the issuance of regulations pursuant to a statute; or

(B) to the extent such agency is authorized by statute to issue orders or guidance, the issuance of orders or guidance of general applicability that are publicly available and published (in the Federal Register in the case of an order or guidance issued by a Federal regulatory agency). This paragraph does not grant any Federal regulatory agency or State regulatory agency authority to issue regulations, orders, or guidance pursuant to any statute that does not authorize such issuance.

(2) LIMITATIONS ON INTERPRETATION AUTHORITY.—Notwithstanding paragraph (1), a Federal regulatory agency shall not adopt any regulation, order, or guidance described in paragraph (1), and a State regulatory agency is preempted by section 101 from adopting any regulation, order, or guidance described in paragraph (1), unless—

(A) such regulation, order, or guidance is consistent with section 101;

S. 761—7

(B) such regulation, order, or guidance does not add to the requirements of such section; and

(C) such agency finds, in connection with the issuance of such regulation, order, or guidance, that—

(i) there is a substantial justification for the regulation, order, or guidance;

(ii) the methods selected to carry out that purpose—

(I) are substantially equivalent to the requirements imposed on records that are not electronic records; and

(II) will not impose unreasonable costs on the acceptance and use of electronic records; and

(iii) the methods selected to carry out that purpose do not require, or accord greater legal status or effect to, the implementation or application of a specific technology or technical specification for performing the functions of creating, storing, generating, receiving, communicating, or authenticating electronic records or electronic signatures.

(3) PERFORMANCE STANDARDS.—

(A) ACCURACY, RECORD INTEGRITY, ACCESSIBILITY.— Notwithstanding paragraph (2)(C)(iii), a Federal regulatory agency or State regulatory agency may interpret section 101(d) to specify performance standards to assure accuracy, record integrity, and accessibility of records that are required to be retained. Such performance standards may be specified in a manner that imposes a requirement in violation of paragraph (2)(C)(iii) if the requirement (i) serves an important governmental objective; and (ii) is substantially related to the achievement of that objective. Nothing in this paragraph shall be construed to grant any Federal regulatory agency or State regulatory agency authority to require use of a particular type of software or hardware in order to comply with section 101(d).

(B) PAPER OR PRINTED FORM.—Notwithstanding subsection (c)(1), a Federal regulatory agency or State regulatory agency may interpret section 101(d) to require retention of a record in a tangible printed or paper form if—

(i) there is a compelling governmental interest relating to law enforcement or national security for imposing such requirement; and

(ii) imposing such requirement is essential to attaining such interest.

(4) EXCEPTIONS FOR ACTIONS BY GOVERNMENT AS MARKET PARTICIPANT.—Paragraph (2)(C)(iii) shall not apply to the statutes, regulations, or other rules of law governing procurement by the Federal or any State government, or any agency or instrumentality thereof.

(c) ADDITIONAL LIMITATIONS.—

(1) REIMPOSING PAPER PROHIBITED.—Nothing in subsection (b) (other than paragraph (3)(B) thereof) shall be construed to grant any Federal regulatory agency or State regulatory agency authority to impose or reimpose any requirement that a record be in a tangible printed or paper form.

S. 761—8

(2) CONTINUING OBLIGATION UNDER GOVERNMENT PAPER-
WORK ELIMINATION ACT.—Nothing in subsection (a) or (b)
relieves any Federal regulatory agency of its obligations under
the Government Paperwork Elimination Act (title XVII of
Public Law 105–277).

(d) AUTHORITY TO EXEMPT FROM CONSENT PROVISION.—

(1) IN GENERAL.—A Federal regulatory agency may, with
respect to matter within its jurisdiction, by regulation or order
issued after notice and an opportunity for public comment,
exempt without condition a specified category or type of record
from the requirements relating to consent in section 101(c)
if such exemption is necessary to eliminate a substantial burden
on electronic commerce and will not increase the material risk
of harm to consumers.

(2) PROSPECTUSES.—Within 30 days after the date of enactment of this Act, the Securities and Exchange Commission
shall issue a regulation or order pursuant to paragraph (1)
exempting from section 101(c) any records that are required
to be provided in order to allow advertising, sales literature,
or other information concerning a security issued by an investment company that is registered under the Investment Company Act of 1940, or concerning the issuer thereof, to be
excluded from the definition of a prospectus under section
2(a)(10)(A) of the Securities Act of 1933.

(e) ELECTRONIC LETTERS OF AGENCY.—The Federal Communications Commission shall not hold any contract for telecommunications service or letter of agency for a preferred carrier change,
that otherwise complies with the Commission's rules, to be legally
ineffective, invalid, or unenforceable solely because an electronic
record or electronic signature was used in its formation or authorization.

SEC. 105. STUDIES.

(a) DELIVERY.—Within 12 months after the date of the enactment of this Act, the Secretary of Commerce shall conduct an
inquiry regarding the effectiveness of the delivery of electronic
records to consumers using electronic mail as compared with
delivery of written records via the United States Postal Service
and private express mail services. The Secretary shall submit a
report to the Congress regarding the results of such inquiry by
the conclusion of such 12-month period.

(b) STUDY OF ELECTRONIC CONSENT.—Within 12 months after
the date of the enactment of this Act, the Secretary of Commerce
and the Federal Trade Commission shall submit a report to the
Congress evaluating any benefits provided to consumers by the
procedure required by section 101(c)(1)(C)(ii); any burdens imposed
on electronic commerce by that provision; whether the benefits
outweigh the burdens; whether the absence of the procedure
required by section 101(c)(1)(C)(ii) would increase the incidence
of fraud directed against consumers; and suggesting any revisions
to the provision deemed appropriate by the Secretary and the
Commission. In conducting this evaluation, the Secretary and the
Commission shall solicit comment from the general public, consumer
representatives, and electronic commerce businesses.

S. 761—9

SEC. 106. DEFINITIONS.

For purposes of this title:

(1) CONSUMER.—The term "consumer" means an individual who obtains, through a transaction, products or services which are used primarily for personal, family, or household purposes, and also means the legal representative of such an individual.

(2) ELECTRONIC.—The term "electronic" means relating to technology having electrical, digital, magnetic, wireless, optical, electromagnetic, or similar capabilities.

(3) ELECTRONIC AGENT.—The term "electronic agent" means a computer program or an electronic or other automated means used independently to initiate an action or respond to electronic records or performances in whole or in part without review or action by an individual at the time of the action or response.

(4) ELECTRONIC RECORD.—The term "electronic record" means a contract or other record created, generated, sent, communicated, received, or stored by electronic means.

(5) ELECTRONIC SIGNATURE.—The term "electronic signature" means an electronic sound, symbol, or process, attached to or logically associated with a contract or other record and executed or adopted by a person with the intent to sign the record.

(6) FEDERAL REGULATORY AGENCY.—The term "Federal regulatory agency" means an agency, as that term is defined in section 552(f) of title 5, United States Code.

(7) INFORMATION.—The term "information" means data, text, images, sounds, codes, computer programs, software, databases, or the like.

(8) PERSON.—The term "person" means an individual, corporation, business trust, estate, trust, partnership, limited liability company, association, joint venture, governmental agency, public corporation, or any other legal or commercial entity.

(9) RECORD.—The term "record" means information that is inscribed on a tangible medium or that is stored in an electronic or other medium and is retrievable in perceivable form.

(10) REQUIREMENT.—The term "requirement" includes a prohibition.

(11) SELF-REGULATORY ORGANIZATION.—The term "self-regulatory organization" means an organization or entity that is not a Federal regulatory agency or a State, but that is under the supervision of a Federal regulatory agency and is authorized under Federal law to adopt and administer rules applicable to its members that are enforced by such organization or entity, by a Federal regulatory agency, or by another self-regulatory organization.

(12) STATE.—The term "State" includes the District of Columbia and the territories and possessions of the United States.

(13) TRANSACTION.—The term "transaction" means an action or set of actions relating to the conduct of business, consumer, or commercial affairs between two or more persons, including any of the following types of conduct—

(A) the sale, lease, exchange, licensing, or other disposition of (i) personal property, including goods and intangibles, (ii) services, and (iii) any combination thereof; and

S. 761—10

(B) the sale, lease, exchange, or other disposition of any interest in real property, or any combination thereof.

SEC. 107. EFFECTIVE DATE.

(a) IN GENERAL.—Except as provided in subsection (b), this title shall be effective on October 1, 2000.

(b) EXCEPTIONS.—

(1) RECORD RETENTION.—

(A) IN GENERAL.—Subject to subparagraph (B), this title shall be effective on March 1, 2001, with respect to a requirement that a record be retained imposed by—

(i) a Federal statute, regulation, or other rule of law, or

(ii) a State statute, regulation, or other rule of law administered or promulgated by a State regulatory agency.

(B) DELAYED EFFECT FOR PENDING RULEMAKINGS.—If on March 1, 2001, a Federal regulatory agency or State regulatory agency has announced, proposed, or initiated, but not completed, a rulemaking proceeding to prescribe a regulation under section 104(b)(3) with respect to a requirement described in subparagraph (A), this title shall be effective on June 1, 2001, with respect to such requirement.

(2) CERTAIN GUARANTEED AND INSURED LOANS.—With regard to any transaction involving a loan guarantee or loan guarantee commitment (as those terms are defined in section 502 of the Federal Credit Reform Act of 1990), or involving a program listed in the Federal Credit Supplement, Budget of the United States, FY 2001, this title applies only to such transactions entered into, and to any loan or mortgage made, insured, or guaranteed by the United States Government thereunder, on and after one year after the date of enactment of this Act.

(3) STUDENT LOANS.—With respect to any records that are provided or made available to a consumer pursuant to an application for a loan, or a loan made, pursuant to title IV of the Higher Education Act of 1965, section 101(c) of this Act shall not apply until the earlier of—

(A) such time as the Secretary of Education publishes revised promissory notes under section 432(m) of the Higher Education Act of 1965; or

(B) one year after the date of enactment of this Act.

TITLE II—TRANSFERABLE RECORDS

SEC. 201. TRANSFERABLE RECORDS.

(a) DEFINITIONS.—For purposes of this section:

(1) TRANSFERABLE RECORD.—The term "transferable record" means an electronic record that—

(A) would be a note under Article 3 of the Uniform Commercial Code if the electronic record were in writing;

(B) the issuer of the electronic record expressly has agreed is a transferable record; and

(C) relates to a loan secured by real property.

S. 761—11

A transferable record may be executed using an electronic signature.

(2) OTHER DEFINITIONS.—The terms "electronic record", "electronic signature", and "person" have the same meanings provided in section 106 of this Act.

(b) CONTROL.—A person has control of a transferable record if a system employed for evidencing the transfer of interests in the transferable record reliably establishes that person as the person to which the transferable record was issued or transferred.

(c) CONDITIONS.—A system satisfies subsection (b), and a person is deemed to have control of a transferable record, if the transferable record is created, stored, and assigned in such a manner that—

(1) a single authoritative copy of the transferable record exists which is unique, identifiable, and, except as otherwise provided in paragraphs (4), (5), and (6), unalterable;

(2) the authoritative copy identifies the person asserting control as—

(A) the person to which the transferable record was issued; or

(B) if the authoritative copy indicates that the transferable record has been transferred, the person to which the transferable record was most recently transferred;

(3) the authoritative copy is communicated to and maintained by the person asserting control or its designated custodian;

(4) copies or revisions that add or change an identified assignee of the authoritative copy can be made only with the consent of the person asserting control;

(5) each copy of the authoritative copy and any copy of a copy is readily identifiable as a copy that is not the authoritative copy; and

(6) any revision of the authoritative copy is readily identifiable as authorized or unauthorized.

(d) STATUS AS HOLDER.—Except as otherwise agreed, a person having control of a transferable record is the holder, as defined in section 1–201(20) of the Uniform Commercial Code, of the transferable record and has the same rights and defenses as a holder of an equivalent record or writing under the Uniform Commercial Code, including, if the applicable statutory requirements under section 3–302(a), 9–308, or revised section 9–330 of the Uniform Commercial Code are satisfied, the rights and defenses of a holder in due course or a purchaser, respectively. Delivery, possession, and endorsement are not required to obtain or exercise any of the rights under this subsection.

(e) OBLIGOR RIGHTS.—Except as otherwise agreed, an obligor under a transferable record has the same rights and defenses as an equivalent obligor under equivalent records or writings under the Uniform Commercial Code.

(f) PROOF OF CONTROL.—If requested by a person against which enforcement is sought, the person seeking to enforce the transferable record shall provide reasonable proof that the person is in control of the transferable record. Proof may include access to the authoritative copy of the transferable record and related business records sufficient to review the terms of the transferable record and to establish the identity of the person having control of the transferable record.

S. 761—12

(g) UCC REFERENCES.—For purposes of this subsection, all references to the Uniform Commercial Code are to the Uniform Commercial Code as in effect in the jurisdiction the law of which governs the transferable record.

SEC. 202. EFFECTIVE DATE.

This title shall be effective 90 days after the date of enactment of this Act.

TITLE III—PROMOTION OF INTERNATIONAL ELECTRONIC COMMERCE

SEC. 301. PRINCIPLES GOVERNING THE USE OF ELECTRONIC SIGNATURES IN INTERNATIONAL TRANSACTIONS.

(a) PROMOTION OF ELECTRONIC SIGNATURES.—

(1) REQUIRED ACTIONS.—The Secretary of Commerce shall promote the acceptance and use, on an international basis, of electronic signatures in accordance with the principles specified in paragraph (2) and in a manner consistent with section 101 of this Act. The Secretary of Commerce shall take all actions necessary in a manner consistent with such principles to eliminate or reduce, to the maximum extent possible, the impediments to commerce in electronic signatures, for the purpose of facilitating the development of interstate and foreign commerce.

(2) PRINCIPLES.—The principles specified in this paragraph are the following:

(A) Remove paper-based obstacles to electronic transactions by adopting relevant principles from the Model Law on Electronic Commerce adopted in 1996 by the United Nations Commission on International Trade Law.

(B) Permit parties to a transaction to determine the appropriate authentication technologies and implementation models for their transactions, with assurance that those technologies and implementation models will be recognized and enforced.

(C) Permit parties to a transaction to have the opportunity to prove in court or other proceedings that their authentication approaches and their transactions are valid.

(D) Take a nondiscriminatory approach to electronic signatures and authentication methods from other jurisdictions.

(b) CONSULTATION.—In conducting the activities required by this section, the Secretary shall consult with users and providers of electronic signature products and services and other interested persons.

(c) DEFINITIONS.—As used in this section, the terms "electronic record" and "electronic signature" have the same meanings provided in section 106 of this Act.

S. 761—13

TITLE IV—COMMISSION ON ONLINE CHILD PROTECTION

SEC. 401. AUTHORITY TO ACCEPT GIFTS.

Section 1405 of the Child Online Protection Act (47 U.S.C. 231 note) is amended by inserting after subsection (g) the following new subsection:

"(h) GIFTS, BEQUESTS, AND DEVISES.—The Commission may accept, use, and dispose of gifts, bequests, or devises of services or property, both real (including the use of office space) and personal, for the purpose of aiding or facilitating the work of the Commission. Gifts or grants not used at the termination of the Commission shall be returned to the donor or grantee.".

Speaker of the House of Representatives.

Vice President of the United States and
President of the Senate.

ASN.1 Notation

C.1   Introduction

ASN.1 is a data-typing language, designed for specifying application layer communications protocols. What makes ASN.1 special, in terms of data-typing languages, is that it has accompanying rules for encoding data-type values into bit string representations, suitable for transfer by lower-layer protocols. The ASN.1 notation is defined in the multi-part standard ISO/IEC 8824.

ASN.1 provides a way to specify data types and values for the types. Types may be arbitrarily complex, because ASN.1 includes features for constructing new types out of simpler types that are already defined. ASN.1 also has extensive features to support the modularization of specifications, such that pieces of specification can be readily reused for different purposes.

Following is an abbreviated introduction to ASN.1's basic features, aimed at making the unfamiliar reader sufficiently comfortable to follow the limited use of ASN.1 notation in this book. For a more complete tutorial, see Kaliski or Steedman references in Section C.6.

C.2   The Basic Notation

The main elements of the notation are:

- *Keywords*: Defined in the standard, and generally distinguishable by being all upper-case alphabetic characters, e.g., **INTEGER**.
- *Type-references*: Used to name a type; the first letter must be an upper-case alphabetic character, and usually at least some of the remaining characters are lower-case alphabetics, e.g., **CurrentMonth**.
- *Value-references*: Used to name a value of a type; the first letter must be a lower-case alphabetic character, e.g., **december**.
- *Identifiers*: Used to name various items in an ASN.1 specification, including a component of a structured type; the first letter must be a lower-case alphabetic character, e.g., **dateField**. (A value-reference and an identifier can always be differentiated by virtue of the context in which the string occurs.)
- *Various special items*: The assignment item **::=**, bracketing items for different contexts (e.g., {, }, [,]), and others.
- *Comments*: The start of a comment field is signaled by two hyphens; the end of the field is signaled by two more hyphens or the end-of-line.

Certain basic (or unstructured) types are defined in the ASN.1 standard. They are known as either *simple types* or *useful types*. Simple types include:

- **BIT STRING**: Each value is an ordered sequence of bits.
- **BOOLEAN**: Takes two possible values, **TRUE** and **FALSE**.
- **CHARACTER STRING**: Each value is a string of characters from some defined character set.
- **ENUMERATED**: A set of values, each with a distinct identifier (for example, the set of 12 months in a year).
- **INTEGER**: Takes any integer value.
- **OBJECT IDENTIFIER**: (See *Object Identifiers and Registration* below).
- **OCTET STRING**: Each value is an ordered sequence of eight-bit values.
- **NULL**: Used where several alternatives are possible, but none apply.
- **REAL**: Takes any real-number value.

Useful types defined in the standard include:

- **GeneralizedTime**: Local date/time, plus local time differential factor.
- **UTCTime**: Coordinated Universal Time (GMT).

Additionally, several special cases of character strings are defined, including **NumericString**, **PrintableString**, **TeletexString**, **VideotexString**, **VisibleString**, **IA5String**, and **GraphicString**.

Constructed Types

The main constructed types are **SEQUENCE, SET**, and **CHOICE**.

A value for a **SEQUENCE** type is a concatenation of values from other types. A **SEQUENCE** type is defined by referencing an ordered list of existing types (some of which may be designated optional). Each value of a new type is an ordered list of values, one from each component type. An illustration of the notation is as follows:

```
NewType ::= SEQUENCE
{
        component1        [0]        Component1Type,
        component2        [1]        Component2Type,
        component3        [2]        Component3Type
}
```

Here, **NewType** identifies the new type being defined. The fields **component1**, **component2**, and **component3** are identifiers for the three components. The fields **Component1Type**, **Component2Type**, and **Component3Type** are type specifications or type-references. A value of the new type consists of a collection of three values—one of type **Component1Type**, one of type **Component2Type**, and one of type **Component3Type**. For example, a value of the following **SEQUENCE** type would comprise an integer plus a character string plus another integer:

```
TaxPayerInformation ::= SEQUENCE
{
        taxpayerId   [0]        INTEGER,
        name         [1]        IA5String,
        age          [2]        INTEGER
}
```

Any of the component specifications could be optionally followed by the keyword **OPTIONAL,** or the keyword **DEFAULT** and a value, which would indicate that this component could be omitted. The fields **[0], [1]**, and **[2]** are *tags*, which may be required to ensure that the different components can be distinguished in an encoding. They can be omitted, if the encoding would be unambiguous anyway (e.g., if no components were optional, as in the above example).

A value of type **SEQUENCE OF** is a collection of values, all of the same type. For example, a value of type **SEQUENCE OF INTEGER** is an ordered collection of integer values. (Note that there may be a set size limit inserted between **SEQUENCE** and **OF**.)

A **SET** type is essentially the same as a **SEQUENCE** type, except that the order of the components is insignificant and need not be preserved. The notation is the same as for the **SEQUENCE** type, but the keyword **SET** replaces **SEQUENCE**.

A **CHOICE** type is defined by referencing a list of existing types. Each value of the new type is a value of one of the component types. The notation for **CHOICE** is the same as for **SEQUENCE**, with the keyword **CHOICE** replacing **SEQUENCE**, and without the **OPTIONAL** or **DEFAULT** options. For example, a value of the following type is either an integer or character string:

```
TaxPayerLocator ::= CHOICE
{
        taxpayerId   [0]        INTEGER,
        name         [1]        IA5String
}
```

Example of ASN.1 Usage

Following is an example of the use of ASN.1 to define a structured type which constitutes a complete transaction specification. The transaction syntax contains two message types for use in accessing a (simplified) time server. The first message type is used for a client-to-server request; the second for a server-to-client response.

```
TimeServerTransactionSyntax ::= CHOICE
{
        request      [0]        Request,
                     -- From client to server
        response     [1]        Response
}                    -- From server to client
Request ::= SEQUENCE
{
```

```
        clientName                    [0]        GraphicString,
                    -- The server checks this for legitimacy
        transactionReference          [1]        INTEGER OPTIONAL
}                   -- This is used by the client
                    -- to correlate a response with a request


Response ::= SEQUENCE
{
        resultCode              [0]         ResultCode DEFAULT success,
        transactionReference [1]            INTEGER OPTIONAL,
        time                    [2]         GeneralizedTime
                    -- GMT time returned

}


ResultCode ::= ENUMERATED
        { success (0), formatError (1), unrecognizedClient (2) }
```

C.3   Advanced Features of ASN.1 Notation

The 1993 revision of the ASN.1 standards introduced some major extensions to the original notation, including the following advanced features:

- *Information object classes*: A facility to support the definition of conglomerates
  of ASN.1 types and/or values, which relate to some particular application concept. Examples of information object classes in this book include algorithms and
  certificate extensions.
- *Constraints*: Notation to constrain values of any type in any particular instance of use.
- *Parameterized types*: Notation to support partial specification of ASN.1 types in
  different specification modules. The definition of a parameterized type may
  include types and/or values in the form of dummy parameters. Specific types
  and/or values are substituted for these parameters when the parameterized type is
  referenced from another specification.

C.4   ASN.1 Encoding Rules

Standard ISO/IEC 8825 specifies encoding rules that may be applied to any data item
defined using ASN.1, giving a straightforward method of deriving a transfer syntax (i.e.,
representation bit-string) for that abstract syntax item. The original version of ISO/IEC

8825 defined the Basic Encoding Rules (BER) for ASN.1. These rules generate encodings using a simple tag-length-value scheme.

One shortcoming of the BER is that they permit multiple different representations for some values. The 1993 extensions to ISO/IEC 8825 added new encoding alternatives, the Distinguished and Canonical Encoding Rules, which generate a unique encoding for every data value.

C.5   Object Identifiers and Registration

Object Identifiers

The ASN.1 *object identifier* concept was introduced in Section 6.5, under *Object Registration*. An object identifier is a value, comprising a sequence of integer components, which can be conveniently assigned for some specific purpose and which has the property of being unique within the space of all object identifiers. The object identifier works on the basis of a hierarchical structure of distinct value-assigning authorities, with each level of the hierarchy having responsibility for one integer component of the value. Rules for the upper levels of the hierarchy are defined in annexes to the ASN.1 standard and in the Registration Authority Procedures Standard ISO/IEC 9834-1.

Registration Procedures

The three main objectives of registration procedures are:

  (a) Assigning a globally unique identifier (an ASN.1 object identifier) to a specification;
  (b) Encouraging common use of previously registered specifications (in general, the same specification should be registered only once); and,
  (c) Providing a generally available listing of registered items.

From the technical viewpoint, the only essential objective is (a). Almost anyone can register specifications which satisfy this objective. All that is needed is an object identifier subtree root, which can be obtained from a national registration authority, in accordance with ISO/IEC 9834-1. However, in the interests of (b) and (c), it may be desirable to register specifications in a way that makes them most publicly visible. Also, a new specification should not be registered unless it is reasonably certain that a suitable specification has not already been registered by someone else.

C.6 References

B.S. Kaliski Jr., *A Layman's Guide to a Subset of ASN.1, BER, and DER*, RSA
 Laboratories Technical Note, November 1993 <http://www.rsa.com/pub/pkcs>.

D. Steedman, *Abstract Syntax Notation One (ASN.1): The Tutorial and Reference*,
 Technical Appraisals Ltd., Isleworth, U.K., 1990.

ISO 3166: *Codes for the Representation of Names of Countries*.

ISO/IEC 8824-1: *Information Technology—Open Systems Interconnection—
 Abstract Syntax Notation One (ASN.1): Specification of Basic Notation* (Also
 ITU Recommendation X.680).

ISO/IEC 8824-2: *Information Technology—Open Systems Interconnection—
 Abstract Syntax Notation One (ASN.1): Information Object Specification* (Also
 ITU Recommendation X.681).

ISO/IEC 8824-3: *Information Technology—Open Systems Interconnection—
 Abstract Syntax Notation One (ASN.1): Constraint Specification* (Also ITU
 Recommendation X.682).

ISO/IEC 8824-4: *Information Technology—Open Systems Interconnection—
 Abstract Syntax Notation One (ASN.1): Parameterization of ASN.1 Specifications* (Also ITU Recommendation X.683).

ISO/IEC 8825-1: *Information Technology—Open Systems Interconnection—ASN.1
 Encoding Rules: Specification of Basic Encoding Rules (BER), Canonical
 Encoding Rules (CER) and Distinguished Encoding Rules (DER)* (Also ITU
 Recommendation X.690).

ISO/IEC 9834-1: *Information Technology—Open Systems Interconnection—
 Procedures for the Operation of OSI Registration Authorities: General Procedures* (Also ITU Recommendation X.660).

X.509 in ASN.1 Notation

T his Appendix presents the ASN.1 specifications
of X.509, 2000/2001 Edition, including the X.509 Version 3 certificate format and its standard extensions.[1]

AuthenticationFramework {joint-iso-itu-t ds(5) module(1) authenticationFramework(7) 4}
DEFINITIONS ::=
BEGIN

-- EXPORTS All --
-- *The types and values defined in this module are exported for use in the other ASN.1 modules contained*
-- *within the Directory Specifications, and for the use of other applications which will use them to access*
-- *Directory services. Other applications may use them for their own purposes, but this will not constrain*
-- *extensions and modifications needed to maintain or improve the Directory service.*

IMPORTS
    id-at, id-nf, id-oc, informationFramework, upperBounds, selectedAttributeTypes,
    basicAccessControl, certificateExtensions
        FROM UsefulDefinitions {joint-iso-itu-t ds(5) module(1) usefulDefinitions(0) 4}

    Name, ATTRIBUTE, OBJECT-CLASS, NAME-FORM, top
        FROM InformationFramework informationFramework

    ub-user-password, ub-content
        FROM UpperBounds upperBounds

    UniqueIdentifier, octetStringMatch, DirectoryString, commonName
        FROM SelectedAttributeTypes selectedAttributeTypes .

certificateExactMatch, certificatePairExactMatch, certificateListExactMatch,
KeyUsage,   GeneralNames,   CertificatePoliciesSyntax, algorithmIdentifierMatch,
CertPolicyId
          FROM CertificateExtensions certificateExtensions ;
--public-key certificate definition--

Certificate	*::=*	*SIGNED { SEQUENCE {*	
version	*[0]*	*Version DEFAULT v1,*	
serialNumber		*CertificateSerialNumber,*	
signature		*AlgorithmIdentifier,*	
issuer		*Name,*	
validity		*Validity,*	
subject		*Name,*	
subjectPublicKeyInfo		*SubjectPublicKeyInfo,*	
issuerUniqueIdentifier	*[1]*	*IMPLICIT UniqueIdentifier OPTIONAL,*	
			-- if present, version must be v2 or v3
subjectUniqueIdentifier	*[2]*	*IMPLICIT UniqueIdentifier OPTIONAL,*	
			-- if present, version must be v2 or v3
extensions	*[3]*	*Extensions OPTIONAL*	
			-- If present, version must be v3 -- } }

Version	*::=*	*INTEGER { v1(0), v2(1), v3(2) }*

CertificateSerialNumber	*::=*	*INTEGER*

AlgorithmIdentifier	*::=*	*SEQUENCE {*
algorithm		*ALGORITHM.&id ({SupportedAlgorithms}),*
parameters		*ALGORITHM.&Type ({SupportedAlgorithms}{ @algorithm})*
OPTIONAL }		

--Definition of the following information object set is deferred, perhaps to standardized
--profiles or to protocol implementation conformance statements. The set is required to
--specify a table constraint on the parameters component of AlgorithmIdentifier.

SupportedAlgorithms	*ALGORITHM*	*::=*	*{ ... }*

Validity	*::=*	*SEQUENCE {*
notBefore Time,		
notAfter Time }		

SubjectPublicKeyInfo	*::=*	*SEQUENCE {*
algorithm		*AlgorithmIdentifier,*
subjectPublicKey		*BIT STRING }*

Time ::= CHOICE {	
utcTime	*UTCTime,*
generalizedTime	*GeneralizedTime }*

Extensions ::= SEQUENCE OF Extension
-- For those extensions where ordering of individual extensions within the SEQUENCE is significant, the
-- specification of those individual extensions shall include the rules for the significance of the order therein

Extension ::= SEQUENCE {
       extnId   EXTENSION.&id ({ExtensionSet}),
       critical   BOOLEAN DEFAULT FALSE,
       extnValue OCTET STRING
                  -- contains a DER encoding of a value of type &ExtnType
                  -- for the extension object identified by extnId -- }

ExtensionSet EXTENSION ::=   { ... }

EXTENSION ::= CLASS {
       &id   OBJECT IDENTIFIER UNIQUE,
       &ExtnType }
WITH SYNTAX {
       SYNTAX   &ExtnType
       IDENTIFIED BY   &id }

-- other PKI certifiate constructs

Certificates   ::=   SEQUENCE {
       userCertificate   Certificate,
       certificationPath   ForwardCertificationPath OPTIONAL}

ForwardCertificationPath   ::=   SEQUENCE OF CrossCertificates

CrossCertificates   ::=   SET OF Certificate

CertificationPath   ::=   SEQUENCE {
       userCertificate   Certificate,
       theCACertificates   SEQUENCE OF CertificatePair OPTIONAL}

CertificatePair ::= SEQUENCE {
       forward   [0]   Certificate OPTIONAL,
       reverse   [1]   Certificate OPTIONAL
                    -- at least one of the pair shall be present -- }
       (WITH COMPONENTS {..., forward PRESENT} |
       WITH COMPONENTS {..., reverse PRESENT})

-- certificate revocation list (CRL)

CertificateList ::= SIGNED { SEQUENCE {
       version   Version OPTIONAL,
                    -- if present, version must be v2
       signature   AlgorithmIdentifier,
       issuer   Name,

```
        thisUpdate          Time,
        nextUpdate          Time OPTIONAL,
        revokedCertificates SEQUENCE OF SEQUENCE {
            serialNumber                     CertificateSerialNumber,
            revocationDate                   Time,
            crlEntryExtensions               Extensions OPTIONAL } OPTIONAL,
        crlExtensions       [0]     Extensions OPTIONAL }}
```

-- information object classes --

```
ALGORITHM   ::=  TYPE-IDENTIFIER
```
-- parameterized types --
```
HASH {ToBeHashed}          ::=          SEQUENCE {
    algorithmIdentifier                 AlgorithmIdentifier,
    hashValue                           BIT STRING ( CONSTRAINED BY {
    -- must be the result of applying a hashing procedure to the DER-encoded octets --
    -- of a value of --ToBeHashed } ) }
```

```
ENCRYPTED-HASH { ToBeSigned }   ::=        BIT STRING ( CONSTRAINED BY {
    -- must be the result of applying a hashing procedure to the DER-encoded (see 6.1) octets --
    -- of a value of -- ToBeSigned -- and then applying an encipherment procedure to those octets -- })
```

```
ENCRYPTED { ToBeEnciphered }      ::=       BIT STRING ( CONSTRAINED BY {
    -- must be the result of applying an encipherment procedure --
    -- to the BER-encoded octets of a value of -- ToBeEnciphered})
```

```
SIGNATURE { ToBeSigned }              ::=      SEQUENCE {
    algorithmIdentifier                 AlgorithmIdentifier,
    encrypted                           ENCRYPTED-HASH { ToBeSigned }}
```

```
SIGNED { ToBeSigned }                 ::=      SEQUENCE {
    toBeSigned                          ToBeSigned,
    COMPONENTS OF                       SIGNATURE { ToBeSigned }}
```

-- PKI object classes --

```
pkiUser     OBJECT-CLASS ::= {
    SUBCLASS OF        {top}
    KIND               auxiliary
    MAY CONTAIN        {userCertificate}
    ID                 id-oc-pkiUser }
```

```
pkiCA OBJECT-CLASS      ::= {
    SUBCLASS OF        {top}
    KIND               auxiliary
    MAY CONTAIN        {cACertificate |
                       certificateRevocationList |
```

```
                                authorityRevocationList |
                                crossCertificatePair }
        ID                      id-oc-pkiCA }


cRLDistributionPoint                    OBJECT-CLASS ::= {
        SUBCLASS OF                     { top }
        KIND                            structural
        MUST CONTAIN                    { commonName }
        MAY CONTAIN                     { certificateRevocationList |
                                        authorityRevocationList |
                                        deltaRevocationList }
        ID                              id-oc-cRLDistributionPoint }


cRLDistPtNameForm  NAME-FORM    ::= {
        NAMES                           cRLDistributionPoint
        WITH ATTRIBUTES                 { commonName}
        ID                              id-nf-cRLDistPtNameForm }


deltaCRL   OBJECT-CLASS ::= {
        SUBCLASS OF             {top}
        KIND                    auxiliary
        MAY CONTAIN             {deltaRevocationList}
        ID                      id-oc-deltaCRL }


cpCps      OBJECT-CLASS ::= {
        SUBCLASS OF             {top}
        KIND                    auxiliary
        MAY CONTAIN             {certificatePolicy |
                                certificationPracticeStmt}
        ID                      id-oc-cpCps }


pkiCertPath   OBJECT-CLASS         ::= {
        SUBCLASS OF             {top}
        KIND                    auxiliary
        MAY CONTAIN             { pkiPath }
        ID                      id-oc-pkiCertPath }
```

--PKI directory attributes --

```
userCertificate                 ATTRIBUTE       ::=       {
        WITH SYNTAX                             Certificate
        EQUALITY MATCHING RULE                  certificateExactMatch
        ID                                      id-at-userCertificate}


cACertificate                   ATTRIBUTE       ::=       {
        WITH SYNTAX                             Certificate
        EQUALITY MATCHING RULE                  certificateExactMatch
        ID                                      id-at-cAcertificate }
```

crossCertificatePair   *ATTRIBUTE*   *::=*   *{*
    WITH SYNTAX   *CertificatePair*
    EQUALITY MATCHING RULE   *certificatePairExactMatch*
    ID   *id-at-crossCertificatePair }*

certificateRevocationList   *ATTRIBUTE*   *::=*   *{*
    WITH SYNTAX   *CertificateList*
    EQUALITY MATCHING RULE   *certificateListExactMatch*
    ID   *id-at-certificateRevocationList }*

authorityRevocationList   *ATTRIBUTE*   *::=*   *{*
    WITH SYNTAX   *CertificateList*
    EQUALITY MATCHING RULE   *certificateListExactMatch*
    ID   *id-at-authorityRevocationList }*

deltaRevocationList A   *TTRIBUTE ::= {*
    WITH SYNTAX   *CertificateList*
    EQUALITY MATCHING RULE   *certificateListExactMatch*
    ID   *id-at-deltaRevocationList }*

supportedAlgorithms ATTRIBUTE ::= {
    WITH SYNTAX   *SupportedAlgorithm*
    EQUALITY MATCHING RULE   *algorithmIdentifierMatch*
    ID   *id-at-supportedAlgorithms }*

SupportedAlgorithm ::= SEQUENCE {
    algorithmIdentifier   *AlgorithmIdentifier,*
    intendedUsage   *[0]*   *KeyUsage OPTIONAL,*
    intendedCertificatePolicies   *[1]*   *CertificatePoliciesSyntax OPTIONAL }*

certificationPracticeStmt   *ATTRIBUTE*   *::=*   *{*
    WITH SYNTAX   *InfoSyntax*
    ID   *id-at-certificationPracticeStmt }*

InfoSyntax ::=   *CHOICE {*
    content   *DirectoryString {ub-content},*
    pointer   *SEQUENCE {*
    name   *GeneralNames,*
    hash   *HASH   { HashedPolicyInfo } OPTIONAL } }*

POLICY   ::= TYPE-IDENTIFIER

HashedPolicyInfo   ::=   POLICY.&Type({Policies})
Policies POLICY ::= {...} -- Defined by implementors --

```
certificatePolicy    ATTRIBUTE         ::=       {
        WITH SYNTAX          PolicySyntax
        ID                   id-at-certificatePolicy }


PolicySyntax  ::= SEQUENCE {
        policyIdentifier        PolicyID,
        policySyntax            InfoSyntax
        }


PolicyID     ::= CertPolicyId


pkiPath      ATTRIBUTE        ::= {
        WITH SYNTAX          PkiPath
        ID                   id-at-pkiPath }


PkiPath      ::= SEQUENCE OF CrossCertificates


userPassword ATTRIBUTE  ::=        {
        WITH SYNTAX                    OCTET STRING (SIZE (0..ub-user-password))
        EQUALITY MATCHING RULE    octetStringMatch
        ID                             id-at-userPassword }
```

-- object identifier assignments --

--object classes--

```
id-oc-cRLDistributionPoint        OBJECT IDENTIFIER ::=              {id-oc 19}
id-oc-pkiUser                     OBJECT IDENTIFIER ::=              {id-oc 21}
id-oc-pkiCA                       OBJECT IDENTIFIER ::=              {id-oc 22}
id-oc-deltaCRL                    OBJECT IDENTIFIER ::=              {id-oc 23}
id-oc-cpCps                       OBJECT IDENTIFIER ::=              {id-oc 30}
id-oc-pkiCertPath                 OBJECT IDENTIFIER ::=              {id-oc 31}
```

--name forms--
```
id-nf-cRLDistPtNameForm   OBJECT IDENTIFIER          ::=        {id-nf 14}
```

--directory attributes--
```
id-at-userPassword                OBJECT IDENTIFIER      ::=      {id-at 35}
id-at-userCertificate             OBJECT IDENTIFIER      ::=      {id-at 36}
id-at-cAcertificate               OBJECT IDENTIFIER      ::=      {id-at 37}
id-at-authorityRevocationList     OBJECT IDENTIFIER      ::=      {id-at 38}
id-at-certificateRevocationList   OBJECT IDENTIFIER      ::=      {id-at 39}
id-at-crossCertificatePair        OBJECT IDENTIFIER      ::=      {id-at 40}
id-at-supportedAlgorithms         OBJECT IDENTIFIER      ::=      {id-at 52}
```

id-at-deltaRevocationList	*OBJECT IDENTIFIER*	*::=*	*{id-at 53}*
id-at-certificationPracticeStmt	*OBJECT IDENTIFIER*	*::=*	*{id-at 68}*
id-at-certificatePolicy	*OBJECT IDENTIFIER*	*::=*	*{id-at 69}*
id-at-pkiPath	*OBJECT IDENTIFIER*	*::=*	*{id-at 70}*

END

-- Certificate Extensions module

CertificateExtensions {joint-iso-itu-t ds(5) module(1) certificateExtensions(26) 4}
DEFINITIONS IMPLICIT TAGS ::=
BEGIN

-- EXPORTS ALL --

IMPORTS

>*id-at, id-ce, id-mr, informationFramework, authenticationFramework,*
>>*selectedAttributeTypes, upperBounds*
>>*FROM UsefulDefinitions {joint-iso-itu-t ds(5) module(1)*
>>*usefulDefinitions(0) 4}*

>*Name, RelativeDistinguishedName, ATTRIBUTE, Attribute, MATCHING-RULE*
>>*FROM InformationFramework informationFramework*

>*CertificateSerialNumber, CertificateList, AlgorithmIdentifier,*
>>*EXTENSION, Time, PolicyID*
>>*FROM AuthenticationFramework authenticationFramework*

>*DirectoryString*
>>*FROM SelectedAttributeTypes selectedAttributeTypes*

>*ub-name*
>>*FROM UpperBounds upperBounds*

>*ORAddress*
>>*FROM MTSAbstractService {joint-iso-itu-t mhs(6) mts(3)*
>>*modules(0) mts-abstract-service(1) version-1999 (1) } ;*

-- Unless explicitly noted otherwise, there is no significance to the ordering
-- of components of a SEQUENCE OF construct in this specification.

--public-key certificate and CRL extensions -

```
authorityKeyIdentifier EXTENSION ::= {
        SYNTAX                 AuthorityKeyIdentifier
        IDENTIFIED BY          id-ce-authorityKeyIdentifier }

AuthorityKeyIdentifier ::= SEQUENCE {
        keyIdentifier               [0] KeyIdentifier              OPTIONAL,
        authorityCertIssuer         [1] GeneralNames               OPTIONAL,
        authorityCertSerialNumber   [2] CertificateSerialNumber  OPTIONAL }
        ( WITH COMPONENTS           {..., authorityCertIssuer PRESENT,
                                    authorityCertSerialNumber PRESENT} /
        WITH COMPONENTS             {..., authorityCertIssuer ABSENT,
                                    authorityCertSerialNumber ABSENT} )

KeyIdentifier ::= OCTET STRING

subjectKeyIdentifier EXTENSION ::= {
        SYNTAX                 SubjectKeyIdentifier
        IDENTIFIED BY          id-ce-subjectKeyIdentifier }

SubjectKeyIdentifier ::= KeyIdentifier

keyUsage EXTENSION ::= {
        SYNTAX                 KeyUsage
        IDENTIFIED BY          id-ce-keyUsage }

KeyUsage ::= BIT STRING {
        digitalSignature            (0),
        nonRepudiation              (1),
        keyEncipherment             (2),
        dataEncipherment            (3),
        keyAgreement                (4),
        keyCertSign                 (5),
        cRLSign                     (6),
        encipherOnly                (7),
        decipherOnly                (8) }

extKeyUsage EXTENSION ::= {
        SYNTAX                 SEQUENCE SIZE (1..MAX) OF KeyPurposeId
        IDENTIFIED BY          id-ce-extKeyUsage }

KeyPurposeId ::= OBJECT IDENTIFIER

privateKeyUsagePeriod EXTENSION ::= {
        SYNTAX                 PrivateKeyUsagePeriod
        IDENTIFIED BY          id-ce-privateKeyUsagePeriod }
```

```
PrivateKeyUsagePeriod ::= SEQUENCE {
        notBefore   [0]        GeneralizedTime OPTIONAL,
        notAfter    [1]        GeneralizedTime OPTIONAL }
        ( WITH COMPONENTS {..., notBefore PRESENT} /
        WITH COMPONENTS {..., notAfter PRESENT} )



certificatePolicies EXTENSION ::= {
        SYNTAX               CertificatePoliciesSyntax
        IDENTIFIED BY        id-ce-certificatePolicies }

CertificatePoliciesSyntax ::= SEQUENCE SIZE (1..MAX) OF PolicyInformation

PolicyInformation ::= SEQUENCE {
        policyIdentifier   CertPolicyId,
        policyQualifiers   SEQUENCE SIZE (1..MAX) OF
                                PolicyQualifierInfo OPTIONAL }

CertPolicyId ::= OBJECT IDENTIFIER

PolicyQualifierInfo ::= SEQUENCE {
        policyQualifierId       CERT-POLICY-QUALIFIER.&id
                                ({SupportedPolicyQualifiers}),
        qualifier               CERT-POLICY-QUALIFIER.&Qualifier
                                ({SupportedPolicyQualifiers}{@policyQualifierId})
                                OPTIONAL }

SupportedPolicyQualifiers CERT-POLICY-QUALIFIER ::= { ... }

anyPolicy   OBJECT IDENTIFIER        ::=        { 2 5 29 32 0 }

CERT-POLICY-QUALIFIER ::= CLASS {
        &id          OBJECT IDENTIFIER UNIQUE,
        &Qualifier   OPTIONAL }

WITH SYNTAX {
        POLICY-QUALIFIER-ID          &id
        [QUALIFIER-TYPE     &Qualifier] }

policyMappings EXTENSION ::= {
        SYNTAX               PolicyMappingsSyntax
        IDENTIFIED BY        id-ce-policyMappings }

PolicyMappingsSyntax ::= SEQUENCE SIZE (1..MAX) OF SEQUENCE {
        issuerDomainPolicy   CertPolicyId,
        subjectDomainPolicy  CertPolicyId }
```

```
subjectAltName EXTENSION ::= {
        SYNTAX              GeneralNames
        IDENTIFIED BY       id-ce-subjectAltName }


GeneralNames ::= SEQUENCE SIZE (1..MAX) OF GeneralName


GeneralName ::= CHOICE {
        otherName                       [0]     INSTANCE OF OTHER-NAME,
        rfc822Name                      [1]     IA5String,
        dNSName                         [2]     IA5String,
        x400Address                     [3]     ORAddress,
        directoryName                   [4]     Name,
        ediPartyName                    [5]     EDIPartyName,
        uniformResourceIdentifier       [6]     IA5String,
        iPAddress                       [7]     OCTET STRING,
        registeredID                    [8]     OBJECT IDENTIFIER }


OTHER-NAME ::= TYPE-IDENTIFIER


EDIPartyName ::= SEQUENCE {
        nameAssigner        [0]     DirectoryString {ub-name} OPTIONAL,
        partyName           [1]     DirectoryString {ub-name} }



issuerAltName EXTENSION ::= {
        SYNTAX              GeneralNames
        IDENTIFIED BY       id-ce-issuerAltName }


subjectDirectoryAttributes EXTENSION ::= {
        SYNTAX              AttributesSyntax
        IDENTIFIED BY       id-ce-subjectDirectoryAttributes }


AttributesSyntax ::= SEQUENCE SIZE (1..MAX) OF Attribute




basicConstraints EXTENSION ::= {
        SYNTAX              BasicConstraintsSyntax
        IDENTIFIED BY       id-ce-basicConstraints }


BasicConstraintsSyntax ::= SEQUENCE {
        cA                  BOOLEAN DEFAULT FALSE,
        pathLenConstraint   INTEGER (0..MAX) OPTIONAL }


nameConstraints EXTENSION ::= {
        SYNTAX              NameConstraintsSyntax
        IDENTIFIED BY       id-ce-nameConstraints }
```

```
NameConstraintsSyntax ::= SEQUENCE {
        permittedSubtrees    [0]        GeneralSubtrees OPTIONAL,
        excludedSubtrees     [1]        GeneralSubtrees OPTIONAL }

GeneralSubtrees ::= SEQUENCE SIZE (1..MAX) OF GeneralSubtree


GeneralSubtree ::= SEQUENCE {
        base                            GeneralName,
        minimum              [0]        BaseDistance DEFAULT 0,
        maximum              [1]        BaseDistance OPTIONAL }

BaseDistance ::= INTEGER (0..MAX)



policyConstraints EXTENSION ::= {
        SYNTAX               PolicyConstraintsSyntax
        IDENTIFIED BY        id-ce-policyConstraints }

PolicyConstraintsSyntax ::= SEQUENCE {
        requireExplicitPolicy  [0] SkipCerts OPTIONAL,
        inhibitPolicyMapping [1] SkipCerts OPTIONAL }

SkipCerts ::= INTEGER (0..MAX)



cRLNumber EXTENSION ::= {
        SYNTAX               CRLNumber
        IDENTIFIED BY        id-ce-cRLNumber }

CRLNumber ::= INTEGER (0..MAX)

reasonCode EXTENSION ::= {
        SYNTAX               CRLReason
        IDENTIFIED BY        id-ce-reasonCode }

CRLReason ::= ENUMERATED {
        unspecified                     (0),
        keyCompromise                   (1),
        cACompromise                    (2),
        affiliationChanged              (3),
        superseded                      (4),
        cessationOfOperation            (5),
        certificateHold                 (6),
        removeFromCRL                   (8),
        privilegeWithdrawn              (9),
        aaCompromise                    (10) }
```

holdInstructionCode EXTENSION ::= {
    SYNTAX   *HoldInstruction*
    IDENTIFIED BY   *id-ce-instructionCode }*

HoldInstruction ::= OBJECT IDENTIFIER

invalidityDate EXTENSION ::= {
    SYNTAX   *GeneralizedTime*
    IDENTIFIED BY   *id-ce-invalidityDate }*

crlScope EXTENSION ::= {
    SYNTAX   *CRLScopeSyntax*
    IDENTIFIED BY   *id-ce-cRLScope }*

CRLScopeSyntax ::=   *SEQUENCE SIZE (1..MAX) OF PerAuthorityScope*

PerAuthorityScope ::= SEQUENCE {
    authorityName   *[0]*   *GeneralName OPTIONAL,*
    distributionPoint   *[1]*   *DistributionPointName OPTIONAL,*
    onlyContains   *[2]*   *OnlyCertificateTypes OPTIONAL,*
    onlySomeReasons   *[4]*   *ReasonFlags OPTIONAL,*
    serialNumberRange   *[5]*   *NumberRange OPTIONAL,*
    subjectKeyIdRange   *[6]*   *NumberRange OPTIONAL,*
    nameSubtrees   *[7]*   *GeneralNames OPTIONAL,*
    baseRevocationInfo   *[9]*   *BaseRevocationInfo OPTIONAL*
    }

OnlyCertificateTypes   *::= BIT STRING {*
    user   *(0),*
    authority   *(1),*
    attribute   *(2) }*

NumberRange ::= SEQUENCE {
    startingNumber   *[0]*   *INTEGER OPTIONAL,*
    endingNumber   *[1]*   *INTEGER OPTIONAL,*
    modulus   *INTEGER OPTIONAL }*

BaseRevocationInfo ::= SEQUENCE {
    cRLStreamIdentifier   *[0]*   *CRLStreamIdentifier*   *OPTIONAL,*
    cRLNumber   *[1]*   *CRLNumber,*
    baseThisUpdate   *[2]*   *GeneralizedTime }*

statusReferrals EXTENSION ::= {
    SYNTAX   *StatusReferrals*
    IDENTIFIED BY   *id-ce-statusReferrals }*

StatusReferrals ::= SEQUENCE SIZE (1..MAX) OF StatusReferral

StatusReferral ::= CHOICE {
    cRLReferral   [0]   CRLReferral,
    otherReferral   [1]   INSTANCE OF OTHER-REFERRAL}

CRLReferral ::= SEQUENCE {
    issuer   [0]   GeneralName OPTIONAL,
    location   [1]   GeneralName OPTIONAL,
    deltaRefInfo   [2]   DeltaRefInfo OPTIONAL,
    cRLScope   CRLScopeSyntax,
    lastUpdate   [3]   GeneralizedTime OPTIONAL,
    lastChangedCRL   [4]   GeneralizedTime OPTIONAL}

DeltaRefInfo ::= SEQUENCE {
    deltaLocation   GeneralName,
    lastDelta   GeneralizedTime OPTIONAL }

OTHER-REFERRAL ::= TYPE-IDENTIFIER

cRLStreamIdentifier EXTENSION   ::= {
    SYNTAX   CRLStreamIdentifier
    IDENTIFIED BY   id-ce-cRLStreamIdentifier }

CRLStreamIdentifier ::= INTEGER (0..MAX)

orderedList EXTENSION   ::= {
    SYNTAX   OrderedListSyntax
    IDENTIFIED BY   id-ce-orderedList }

OrderedListSyntax ::= ENUMERATED {
ascSerialNum   (0),
ascRevDate   (1) }

deltaInfo EXTENSION   ::=   {
    SYNTAX   DeltaInformation
    IDENTIFIED BY   id-ce-deltaInfo }

DeltaInformation ::=   SEQUENCE {
    deltaLocation   GeneralName,
    nextDelta   GeneralizedTime OPTIONAL }

cRLDistributionPoints EXTENSION ::= {
    SYNTAX   CRLDistPointsSyntax
    IDENTIFIED BY   id-ce-cRLDistributionPoints }

CRLDistPointsSyntax ::= SEQUENCE SIZE (1..MAX) OF DistributionPoint

DistributionPoint ::= SEQUENCE {
        distributionPoint   [0]   DistributionPointName OPTIONAL,
        reasons   [1]   ReasonFlags OPTIONAL,
        cRLIssuer   [2]   GeneralNames OPTIONAL }

DistributionPointName ::= CHOICE {
        fullName   [0]   GeneralNames,
        nameRelativeToCRLIssuer   [1]   RelativeDistinguishedName }

ReasonFlags ::= BIT STRING {
        unused   (0),
        keyCompromise   (1),
        cACompromise   (2),
        affiliationChanged   (3),
        superseded   (4),
        cessationOfOperation (5),
        certificateHold   (6),
        privilegeWithdrawn   (7),
        aACompromise   (8) }

issuingDistributionPoint EXTENSION ::= {
        SYNTAX   IssuingDistPointSyntax
        IDENTIFIED BY   id-ce-issuingDistributionPoint }

IssuingDistPointSyntax ::= SEQUENCE {
        distributionPoint   [0] DistributionPointName OPTIONAL,
        onlyContainsUserCerts   [1] BOOLEAN DEFAULT FALSE,
        onlyContainsAuthorityCerts [2] BOOLEAN DEFAULT FALSE,
        onlySomeReasons   [3] ReasonFlags OPTIONAL,
        indirectCRL   [4] BOOLEAN DEFAULT FALSE,
        onlyContainsAttributeCerts [5] BOOLEAN DEFAULT FALSE }

certificateIssuer EXTENSION ::= {
        SYNTAX   GeneralNames
        IDENTIFIED BY   id-ce-certificateIssuer }

deltaCRLIndicator EXTENSION ::= {
        SYNTAX   BaseCRLNumber
        IDENTIFIED BY   id-ce-deltaCRLIndicator }

BaseCRLNumber ::= CRLNumber

```
baseUpdateTime EXTENSION            ::= {
     SYNTAX               GeneralizedTime
     IDENTIFIED BY         id-ce-baseUpdateTime }



freshestCRL EXTENSION      ::= {
     SYNTAX     CRLDistPointsSyntax
     IDENTIFIED BY         id-ce-freshestCRL }

inhibitAnyPolicy   EXTENSION         ::= {
     SYNTAX SkipCerts
     IDENTIFIED BY         id-ce-inhibitAnyPolicy }
```

-- *PKI matching rules* --

```
certificateExactMatch MATCHING-RULE ::= {
     SYNTAX     CertificateExactAssertion
     ID              id-mr-certificateExactMatch }
CertificateExactAssertion ::= SEQUENCE {
     serialNumber          CertificateSerialNumber,
     issuer               Name }



certificateMatch MATCHING-RULE ::= {
     SYNTAX     CertificateAssertion
     ID              id-mr-certificateMatch }


CertificateAssertion ::= SEQUENCE {
     serialNumber              [0] CertificateSerialNumber      OPTIONAL,
     issuer                    [1] Name                         OPTIONAL,
     subjectKeyIdentifier      [2] SubjectKeyIdentifier         OPTIONAL,
     authorityKeyIdentifier    [3] AuthorityKeyIdentifier       OPTIONAL,
     certificateValid          [4] Time                         OPTIONAL,
     privateKeyValid           [5] GeneralizedTime              OPTIONAL,
     subjectPublicKeyAlgID     [6] OBJECT IDENTIFIER            OPTIONAL,
     keyUsage                  [7] KeyUsage                     OPTIONAL,
     subjectAltName            [8] AltNameType                  OPTIONAL,
     policy                    [9] CertPolicySet                OPTIONAL,
     pathToName                [10] Name                        OPTIONAL,
     subject                   [11] Name                        OPTIONAL,
     nameConstraints           [12] NameConstraintsSyntax       OPTIONAL }

AltNameType ::= CHOICE {
     builtinNameForm      ENUMERATED {
          rfc822Name                          (1),
          dNSName                             (2),
```

```
                x400Address                    (3),
                directoryName                  (4),
                ediPartyName                   (5),
                uniformResourceIdentifier      (6),
                iPAddress                      (7),
                registeredId                   (8) },
        otherNameForm      OBJECT IDENTIFIER }


CertPolicySet ::= SEQUENCE SIZE (1..MAX) OF CertPolicyId


certificatePairExactMatch MATCHING-RULE     ::=        {
        SYNTAX                CertificatePairExactAssertion
        ID          id-mr-certificatePairExactMatch }

CertificatePairExactAssertion ::= SEQUENCE {
        forwardAssertion      [0] CertificateExactAssertion OPTIONAL,
        reverseAssertion      [1] CertificateExactAssertion OPTIONAL }
        ( WITH COMPONENTS             {..., forwardAssertion PRESENT} /
          WITH COMPONENTS             {..., reverseAssertion PRESENT} )


certificatePairMatch MATCHING-RULE ::=        {
        SYNTAX CertificatePairAssertion
        ID          id-mr-certificatePairMatch }

CertificatePairAssertion ::= SEQUENCE {
        forwardAssertion      [0] CertificateAssertion OPTIONAL,
        reverseAssertion      [1] CertificateAssertion OPTIONAL }
        ( WITH COMPONENTS             {..., forwardAssertion PRESENT} /
          WITH COMPONENTS             {..., reverseAssertion PRESENT} )


certificateListExactMatch MATCHING-RULE     ::=        {
        SYNTAX      CertificateListExactAssertion
        ID          id-mr-certificateListExactMatch }


CertificateListExactAssertion ::= SEQUENCE {
        issuer                Name,
        thisUpdate            Time,
        distributionPoint     DistributionPointName OPTIONAL }

certificateListMatch MATCHING-RULE ::= {
        SYNTAX      CertificateListAssertion
        ID          id-mr-certificateListMatch }
```

```
CertificateListAssertion ::= SEQUENCE {
        issuer                              Name                        OPTIONAL,
        minCRLNumber           [0]          CRLNumber                   OPTIONAL,
        maxCRLNumber           [1]          CRLNumber                   OPTIONAL,
        reasonFlags                         ReasonFlags                 OPTIONAL,
        dateAndTime                         Time                        OPTIONAL,
        distributionPoint      [2]          DistributionPointName       OPTIONAL,
        authorityKeyIdentifier [3]          AuthorityKeyIdentifier      OPTIONAL }


algorithmIdentifierMatch MATCHING-RULE      ::=  {
        SYNTAX      AlgorithmIdentifier
        ID          id-mr-algorithmIdentifierMatch }

policyMatch MATCHING-RULE           ::= {
        SYNTAX      PolicyID
        ID          id-mr-policyMatch }

pkiPathMatch MATCHING-RULE  ::= {
SYNTAX      PkiPathMatchSyntax
ID          id-mr-pkiPathMatch }

PkiPathMatchSyntax          ::= SEQUENCE {
firstIssuer   Name,
lastSubject Name }
```

-- *Object identifier assignments* -

```
 id-ce-subjectDirectoryAttributes   OBJECT IDENTIFIER ::=      {id-ce 9}
id-ce-subjectKeyIdentifier          OBJECT IDENTIFIER ::=      {id-ce 14}
id-ce-keyUsage                      OBJECT IDENTIFIER ::=      {id-ce 15}
id-ce-privateKeyUsagePeriod         OBJECT IDENTIFIER ::=      {id-ce 16}
id-ce-subjectAltName                OBJECT IDENTIFIER ::=      {id-ce 17}
id-ce-issuerAltName                 OBJECT IDENTIFIER ::=      {id-ce 18}
id-ce-basicConstraints              OBJECT IDENTIFIER ::=      {id-ce 19}
id-ce-cRLNumber                     OBJECT IDENTIFIER ::=      {id-ce 20}
id-ce-reasonCode                    OBJECT IDENTIFIER ::=      {id-ce 21}
id-ce-instructionCode               OBJECT IDENTIFIER ::=      {id-ce 23}
id-ce-invalidityDate                OBJECT IDENTIFIER ::=      {id-ce 24}
id-ce-deltaCRLIndicator             OBJECT IDENTIFIER ::=      {id-ce 27}
id-ce-issuingDistributionPoint      OBJECT IDENTIFIER ::=      {id-ce 28}
id-ce-certificateIssuer             OBJECT IDENTIFIER ::=      {id-ce 29}
id-ce-nameConstraints               OBJECT IDENTIFIER ::=      {id-ce 30}
id-ce-cRLDistributionPoints         OBJECT IDENTIFIER ::=      {id-ce 31}
```

id-ce-certificatePolicies	*OBJECT IDENTIFIER ::=*	*{id-ce 32}*
id-ce-policyMappings	*OBJECT IDENTIFIER ::=*	*{id-ce 33}*
-- deprecated	*OBJECT IDENTIFIER ::=*	*{id-ce 34}*
id-ce-authorityKeyIdentifier	*OBJECT IDENTIFIER ::=*	*{id-ce 35}*
id-ce-policyConstraints	*OBJECT IDENTIFIER ::=*	*{id-ce 36}*
id-ce-extKeyUsage	*OBJECT IDENTIFIER ::=*	*{id-ce 37}*
id-ce-cRLStreamIdentifier	*OBJECT IDENTIFIER ::=*	*{id-ce 40}*
id-ce-cRLScope	*OBJECT IDENTIFIER ::=*	*{id-ce 44}*
id-ce-statusReferrals	*OBJECT IDENTIFIER ::=*	*{id-ce 45}*
id-ce-freshestCRL	*OBJECT IDENTIFIER ::=*	*{id-ce 46}*
id-ce-orderedList	*OBJECT IDENTIFIER ::=*	*{id-ce 47}*
id-ce-baseUpdateTime	*OBJECT IDENTIFIER ::=*	*{id-ce 51}*
id-ce-deltaInfo	*OBJECT IDENTIFIER ::=*	*{id-ce 53}*
id-ce-inhibitAnyPolicy	*OBJECT IDENTIFIER ::=*	*{id-ce 54}*

--matching rule OIDs--

id-mr-certificateExactMatch	*OBJECT IDENTIFIER ::=*	*{id-mr 34}*
id-mr-certificateMatch	*OBJECT IDENTIFIER ::=*	*{id-mr 35}*
id-mr-certificatePairExactMatch	*OBJECT IDENTIFIER ::=*	*{id-mr 36}*
id-mr-certificatePairMatch	*OBJECT IDENTIFIER ::=*	*{id-mr 37}*
id-mr-certificateListExactMatch	*OBJECT IDENTIFIER ::=*	*{id-mr 38}*
id-mr-certificateListMatch	*OBJECT IDENTIFIER ::=*	*{id-mr 39}*
id-mr-algorithmIdentifierMatch	*OBJECT IDENTIFIER ::=*	*{id-mr 40}*
id-mr-policyMatch	*OBJECT IDENTIFIER ::=*	*{id-mr 60}*
id-mr-pkiPathMatch	*OBJECT IDENTIFIER ::=*	*{id-mr 62}*

-- The following OBJECT IDENTIFIERS are not used by this specification:
-- {id-ce 2}, {id-ce 3}, {id-ce 4}, {id-ce 5}, {id-ce 6}, {id-ce 7},
-- {id-ce 8}, {id-ce 10}, {id-ce 11}, {id-ce 12}, {id-ce 13},
-- {id-ce 22}, {id-ce 25}, {id-ce 26}

END

-- Attribute Certificate Framework module
AttributeCertificateDefinitions {joint-iso-itu-t ds(5) module(1) attributeCertificateDefinitions(32) 4}
DEFINITIONS IMPLICIT TAGS ::=
BEGIN

-- EXPORTS ALL --

IMPORTS
        id-at, id-ce, id-mr, informationFramework, authenticationFramework,
                selectedAttributeTypes, upperBounds, id-oc, certificateExtensions
                FROM UsefulDefinitions {joint-iso-itu-t ds(5) module(1)
                usefulDefinitions(0) 4}

Name, RelativeDistinguishedName, ATTRIBUTE, Attribute,
    MATCHING-RULE, AttributeType, OBJECT-CLASS, top
    FROM InformationFramework informationFramework

CertificateSerialNumber, CertificateList, AlgorithmIdentifier,
    EXTENSION, SIGNED, InfoSyntax, PolicySyntax, Extensions, Certificate
    FROM AuthenticationFramework authenticationFramework

DirectoryString, TimeSpecification, UniqueIdentifier
    FROM SelectedAttributeTypes selectedAttributeTypes

GeneralName, GeneralNames, NameConstraintsSyntax, certificateListExactMatch
    FROM CertificateExtensions certificateExtensions

ub-name
    FROM UpperBounds upperBounds

UserNotice
    FROM PKIX1Implicit93 {iso(1) identified-organization(3) dod(6) internet(1)
    security(5) mechanisms(5) pkix(7) id-mod(0) id-pkix1-implicit-93(4)}

ORAddress
    FROM MTSAbstractService {joint-iso-itu-t mhs(6) mts(3)
    modules(0) mts-abstract-service(1) version-1999 (1) } ;

-- Unless explicitly noted otherwise, there is no significance to the ordering
-- of components of a SEQUENCE OF construct in this specification.

-- attribute certificate constructs --

AttributeCertificate ::= SIGNED {AttributeCertificateInfo}

AttributeCertificateInfo ::= SEQUENCE
    {
    version   AttCertVersion DEFAULT v1,
    holder   Holder,
    issuer   AttCertIssuer,
    signature   AlgorithmIdentifier,
    serialNumber   CertificateSerialNumber,
    attrCertValidityPeriod AttCertValidityPeriod,
    attributes   SEQUENCE OF Attribute,
    issuerUniqueID   UniqueIdentifier OPTIONAL,
    extensions   Extensions   OPTIONAL
    }

AttCertVersion ::= INTEGER {v1(0), v2(1) }

```
Holder        ::= SEQUENCE
              {
              baseCertificateID       [0] IssuerSerial          OPTIONAL,
                    -- the issuer and serial number of  the holder's Public Key Certificate
              entityName              [1] GeneralNames           OPTIONAL,
                    -- the name of the entity or role
              objectDigestInfo        [2] ObjectDigestInfo       OPTIONAL
                    -- if present, version must be v2
--at least one of baseCertificateID, entityName or objectDigestInfo must be present--}


ObjectDigestInfo   ::= SEQUENCE {
        digestedObjectType  ENUMERATED {
                publicKey               (0),
                publicKeyCert           (1),
                otherObjectTypes        (2) },
        otherObjectTypeID           OBJECT IDENTIFIER  OPTIONAL,
        digestAlgorithm                     AlgorithmIdentifier,
        objectDigest                BIT STRING }



AttCertIssuer ::= CHOICE {
    v1Form  GeneralNames, -- v1 or v2
    v2Form  [0] V2Form    -- v2 only
  }


V2Form ::= SEQUENCE {
    issuerName                      GeneralNames  OPTIONAL,
    baseCertificateID       [0]     IssuerSerial  OPTIONAL,
    objectDigestInfo        [1]     ObjectDigestInfo  OPTIONAL
  }
-- At least one component must be present
    ( WITH COMPONENTS { ..., issuerName  PRESENT } I
    WITH COMPONENTS { ..., baseCertificateID  PRESENT } I
    WITH COMPONENTS { ..., objectDigestInfo PRESENT } )



IssuerSerial ::= SEQUENCE {
        issuer      GeneralNames,
        serial      CertificateSerialNumber,
        issuerUID   UniqueIdentifier OPTIONAL }

AttCertValidityPeriod ::= SEQUENCE {
        notBeforeTime       GeneralizedTime,
        notAfterTime        GeneralizedTime }

AttributeCertificationPath ::= SEQUENCE {
        attributeCertificate            AttributeCertificate,
        acPath                          SEQUENCE OF ACPathData OPTIONAL }
```

```
ACPathData ::= SEQUENCE {
        certificate            [0] Certificate OPTIONAL,
        attributeCertificate   [1] AttributeCertificate OPTIONAL }
```

```
PrivilegePolicy::= OBJECT IDENTIFIER
```

--privilege attributes-

```
role   ATTRIBUTE ::= {
        WITH SYNTAX        RoleSyntax
        ID                 id-at-role }
```

```
RoleSyntax ::= SEQUENCE {
        roleAuthority      [0]      GeneralNames    OPTIONAL,
        roleName           [1]      GeneralName }
```

-- PMI object classes --

```
pmiUser OBJECT-CLASS ::= {
        SUBCLASS OF        {top}
        KIND               auxiliary
        MAY CONTAIN        {attributeCertificateAttribute}
        ID                 id-oc-pmiUser
        }
```

```
pmiAA OBJECT-CLASS ::= {
-- a PMI AA
        SUBCLASS OF        {top}
        KIND               auxiliary
        MAY CONTAIN        {aACertificate |
                           attributeCertificateRevocationList |
                           attributeAuthorityRevocationList}
        ID                 id-oc-pmiAA
        }
```

```
pmiSOA OBJECT-CLASS ::= {  -- a PMI Source of Authority
     SUBCLASS OF  {top}
     KIND         auxiliary
     MAY CONTAIN  {attributeCertificateRevocationList |
                  attributeAuthorityRevocationList |
                  attributeDescriptorCertificate}
        ID        id-oc-pmiSOA
        }
```

```
attCertCRLDistributionPt    OBJECT-CLASS ::= {
        SUBCLASS OF         {top}
        KIND                auxiliary
        MAY CONTAIN         { attributeCertificateRevocationList |
                            attributeAuthorityRevocationList }
        ID                  id-oc-attCertCRLDistributionPts
        }


pmiDelegationPath           OBJECT-CLASS   ::= {
        SUBCLASS OF         {top}
        KIND                auxiliary
        MAY CONTAIN         { delegationPath }
        ID                  id-oc-pmiDelegationPath }


privilegePolicy OBJECT-CLASS            ::= {
        SUBCLASS OF         {top}
        KIND                auxiliary
        MAY CONTAIN         {privPolicy }
        ID                  id-oc-privilegePolicy }
```

-- PMI directory attributes --

```
attributeCertificateAttribute ATTRIBUTE  ::= {
        WITH SYNTAX                 AttributeCertificate
        EQUALITY MATCHING RULE      attributeCertificateExactMatch
        ID                          id-at-attributeCertificate }


aACertificate       ATTRIBUTE           ::= {
        WITH SYNTAX                 AttributeCertificate
        EQUALITY MATCHING RULE      attributeCertificateExactMatch
        ID                          id-at-aACertificate }


attributeDescriptorCertificate  ATTRIBUTE ::= {
        WITH SYNTAX                 AttributeCertificate
        EQUALITY MATCHING RULE      attributeCertificateExactMatch
        ID                          id-at-attributeDescriptorCertificate }


attributeCertificateRevocationList          ATTRIBUTE ::= {
        WITH SYNTAX                 CertificateList
        EQUALITY MATCHING RULE      certificateListExactMatch
        ID                          id-at-attributeCertificateRevocationList}
```

attributeAuthorityRevocationList   *ATTRIBUTE*   *::= {*
        WITH SYNTAX   *CertificateList*
        EQUALITY MATCHING RULE   *certificateListExactMatch*
        ID   *id-at-attributeAuthorityRevocationList }*

delegationPath   *ATTRIBUTE*   *::= {*
        WITH SYNTAX   *AttCertPath*
        ID   *id-at-delegationPath }*

AttCertPath::= SEQUENCE OF AttributeCertificate

privPolicy   ATTRIBUTE   *::= {*
        WITH SYNTAX   *PolicySyntax*
        ID   *id-at-privPolicy }*

--Attribute certificate extensions and matching rules --

attributeCertificateExactMatch MATCHING-RULE ::= {
        SYNTAX   AttributeCertificateExactAssertion
        ID   id-mr-attributeCertificateExactMatch }

AttributeCertificateExactAssertion   ::=   SEQUENCE {
        serialNumber   CertificateSerialNumber OPTIONAL,
        issuer   IssuerSerial
        }

attributeCertificateMatch MATCHING-RULE ::= {
        SYNTAX AttributeCertificateAssertion
        ID   id-mr-attributeCertificateMatch }

AttributeCertificateAssertion ::= SEQUENCE {
        holder   [0]   CHOICE {
                baseCertificateID   [0] IssuerSerial,
                holderName   [1] GeneralNames} OPTIONAL,
        issuer   [1]   GeneralNames OPTIONAL,
        attCertValidity   [2]   GeneralizedTime OPTIONAL,
        attType   [3]   SET OF AttributeType OPTIONAL}
--At least one component of the sequence must be present

holderIssuerMatch MATCHING-RULE ::= {
        SYNTAX   HolderIssuerAssertion
        ID   id-mr-holderIssuerMatch }

```
HolderIssuerAssertion        ::=       SEQUENCE {
        holder      [0]      Holder    OPTIONAL,
        issuer      [1]      AttCertIssuer      OPTIONAL
        }


delegationPathMatch MATCHING-RULE ::= {
        SYNTAX DelMatchSyntax
        ID          id-mr-delegationPathMatch }


DelMatchSyntax    ::=  SEQUENCE {
        firstIssuer   AttCertIssuer,
        lastHolder    Holder }


sOAIdentifier EXTENSION ::= {
        SYNTAX               NULL
        IDENTIFIED BY        id-ce-sOAIdentifier }



authorityAttributeIdentifier EXTENSION  ::=
        {
        SYNTAX               AuthorityAttributeIdentifierSyntax
        IDENTIFIED BY        { id-ce-authorityAttributeIdentifier }
        }


AuthorityAttributeIdentifierSyntax      ::=       SEQUENCE SIZE (1..MAX) OF AuthAttId


AuthAttId    ::= IssuerSerial


authAttIdMatch MATCHING-RULE ::= {
        SYNTAX AuthorityAttributeIdentifierSyntax
        ID          id-mr-authAttIdMatch }



roleSpecCertIdentifier EXTENSION ::=
        {
        SYNTAX      RoleSpecCertIdentifierSyntax
        IDENTIFIED BY        { id-ce-roleSpecCertIdentifier }
}


RoleSpecCertIdentifierSyntax ::= SEQUENCE SIZE (1..MAX) OF RoleSpecCertIdentifier


RoleSpecCertIdentifier ::= SEQUENCE {
        roleName                       [0]      GeneralName,
        roleCertIssuer                 [1]      GeneralName,
        roleCertSerialNumber           [2]      CertificateSerialNumber      OPTIONAL,
        roleCertLocator                [3]      GeneralNames                 OPTIONAL
        }
```

```
roleSpecCertIdMatch MATCHING-RULE ::= {
    SYNTAX      RoleSpecCertIdentifierSyntax
    ID          id-mr-roleSpecCertIdMatch }


basicAttConstraints EXTENSION ::=
    {
        SYNTAX          BasicAttConstraintsSyntax
        IDENTIFIED BY  { id-ce-basicAttConstraints }
    }

BasicAttConstraintsSyntax ::= SEQUENCE
    {
        authority               BOOLEAN DEFAULT FALSE,
        pathLenConstraint       INTEGER (0..MAX) OPTIONAL
    }

basicAttConstraintsMatch MATCHING-RULE ::= {
    SYNTAX      BasicAttConstraintsSyntax
    ID          id-mr-basicAttConstraintsMatch }

delegatedNameConstraints EXTENSION ::= {
    SYNTAX              NameConstraintsSyntax
    IDENTIFIED BY       id-ce-delegatedNameConstraints }

delegatedNameConstraintsMatch MATCHING-RULE ::= {
    SYNTAX      NameConstraintsSyntax
    ID          id-mr-delegatedNameConstraintsMatch}

timeSpecification EXTENSION ::= {
    SYNTAX              TimeSpecification
    IDENTIFIED BY       id-ce-timeSpecification }


timeSpecificationMatch MATCHING-RULE ::= {
    SYNTAX      TimeSpecification
    ID          id-mr-timeSpecMatch }

acceptableCertPolicies EXTENSION ::= {
    SYNTAX              AcceptableCertPoliciesSyntax
    IDENTIFIED BY       id-ce-acceptableCertPolicies }

AcceptableCertPoliciesSyntax ::= SEQUENCE SIZE (1..MAX) OF CertPolicyId

CertPolicyId ::= OBJECT IDENTIFIER
```

```
acceptableCertPoliciesMatch MATCHING-RULE ::= {
        SYNTAX      AcceptableCertPoliciesSyntax
        ID          id-mr-acceptableCertPoliciesMatch }

attributeDescriptor EXTENSION ::= {
        SYNTAX          AttributeDescriptorSyntax
        IDENTIFIED BY   {id-ce-attributeDescriptor } }

AttributeDescriptorSyntax ::= SEQUENCE {
    identifier                  AttributeIdentifier,
    attributeSyntax             OCTET STRING (SIZE(1..MAX)),
    name                [0]     AttributeName  OPTIONAL,
    description         [1]     AttributeDescription   OPTIONAL,
    dominationRule              PrivilegePolicyIdentifier}

AttributeIdentifier ::= ATTRIBUTE.&id({AttributeIDs})

AttributeIDs ATTRIBUTE ::= {...}

AttributeName ::= UTF8String(SIZE(1..MAX))

AttributeDescription ::= UTF8String(SIZE(1..MAX))

PrivilegePolicyIdentifier      ::=     SEQUENCE {
    privilegePolicy             PrivilegePolicy,
    privPolSyntax               InfoSyntax }

attDescriptor MATCHING-RULE ::= {
        SYNTAX      AttributeDescriptorSyntax
        ID          id-mr-attDescriptorMatch }

userNotice  EXTENSION ::= {
        SYNTAX          SEQUENCE SIZE (1..MAX) OF UserNotice
        IDENTIFIED BY   id-ce-userNotice }

targetingInformation EXTENSION ::= {
        SYNTAX          SEQUENCE SIZE (1..MAX) OF Targets
        IDENTIFIED BY   id-ce-targetInformation }

Targets     ::= SEQUENCE SIZE (1..MAX) OF Target

Target::=   CHOICE {
        targetName      [0]     GeneralName,
        targetGroup     [1]     GeneralName,
        targetCert      [2]     TargetCert }
```

```
TargetCert  ::= SEQUENCE {
        targetCertificate    IssuerSerial,
        targetName           GeneralName OPTIONAL,
        certDigestInfo       ObjectDigestInfo OPTIONAL }


noRevAvail EXTENSION ::= {
        SYNTAX               NULL
        IDENTIFIED BY        id-ce-noRevAvail }


acceptablePrivilegePolicies EXTENSION ::= {
        SYNTAX               AcceptablePrivilegePoliciesSyntax
        IDENTIFIED BY        id-ce-acceptablePrivilegePolicies }

AcceptablePrivilegePoliciesSyntax    ::=        SEQUENCE SIZE (1..MAX) OF PrivilegePolicy
```

--object identifier assignments-

--object classes--

```
id-oc-pmiUser                        OBJECT IDENTIFIER ::=        {id-oc 24}
id-oc-pmiAA                          OBJECT IDENTIFIER ::=        {id-oc 25}
id-oc-pmiSOA                         OBJECT IDENTIFIER ::=        {id-oc 26}
id-oc-attCertCRLDistributionPts      OBJECT IDENTIFIER ::=        {id-oc 27}
id-oc-privilegePolicy                OBJECT IDENTIFIER ::=        {id-oc 32}
id-oc-pmiDelegationPath              OBJECT IDENTIFIER ::=        {id-oc 33}
```

--directory attributes--

```
id-at-attributeCertificate                   OBJECT IDENTIFIER ::=    {id-at 58}
id-at-attributeCertificateRevocationList     OBJECT IDENTIFIER ::=    {id-at 59}
id-at-aACertificate                          OBJECT IDENTIFIER ::=    {id-at 61}
id-at-attributeDescriptorCertificate         OBJECT IDENTIFIER ::=    {id-at 62}
id-at-attributeAuthorityRevocationList       OBJECT IDENTIFIER ::=    {id-at 63}
id-at-privPolicy                             OBJECT IDENTIFIER ::=    {id-at 71}
id-at-role                                   OBJECT IDENTIFIER ::=    {id-at 72}
id-at-delegationPath                         OBJECT IDENTIFIER ::=    {id-at 73}
```

--attribute certificate extensions-
```
id-ce-authorityAttributeIdentifier   OBJECT IDENTIFIER ::=    {id-ce 38}
id-ce-roleSpecCertIdentifier         OBJECT IDENTIFIER ::=    {id-ce 39}
id-ce-basicAttConstraints            OBJECT IDENTIFIER ::=    {id-ce 41}
```

id-ce-delegatedNameConstraints	*OBJECT IDENTIFIER ::=*	*{id-ce 42}*
id-ce-timeSpecification	*OBJECT IDENTIFIER ::=*	*{id-ce 43}*
id-ce-attributeDescriptor	*OBJECT IDENTIFIER ::=*	*{id-ce 48}*
id-ce-userNotice	*OBJECT IDENTIFIER ::=*	*{id-ce 49}*
id-ce-sOAIdentifier	*OBJECT IDENTIFIER ::=*	*{id-ce 50}*
id-ce-acceptableCertPolicies	*OBJECT IDENTIFIER ::=*	*{id-ce 52}*
id-ce-targetInformation	*OBJECT IDENTIFIER ::=*	*{id-ce 55}*
id-ce-noRevAvail	*OBJECT IDENTIFIER ::=*	*{id-ce 56}*
id-ce-acceptablePrivilegePolicies	*OBJECT IDENTIFIER ::=*	*{id-ce 57}*

--PMI matching rules--

id-mr-attributeCertificateMatch	*OBJECT IDENTIFIER ::=*	*{id-mr 42}*
id-mr-attributeCertificateExactMatch	*OBJECT IDENTIFIER ::=*	*{id-mr 45}*
id-mr-holderIssuerMatch	*OBJECT IDENTIFIER ::=*	*{id-mr 46}*
id-mr-authAttIdMatch	*OBJECT IDENTIFIER ::=*	*{id-mr 53}*
id-mr-roleSpecCertIdMatch	*OBJECT IDENTIFIER ::=*	*{id-mr 54}*
id-mr-basicAttConstraintsMatch	*OBJECT IDENTIFIER ::=*	*{id-mr 55}*
id-mr-delegatedNameConstraintsMatch	*OBJECT IDENTIFIER ::=*	*{id-mr 56}*
id-mr-timeSpecMatch	*OBJECT IDENTIFIER ::=*	*{id-mr 57}*
id-mr-attDescriptorMatch	*OBJECT IDENTIFIER ::=*	*{id-mr 58}*
id-mr-acceptableCertPoliciesMatch	*OBJECT IDENTIFIER ::=*	*{id-mr 59}*
id-mr-delegationPathMatch	*OBJECT IDENTIFIER ::=*	*{id-mr 61}*

END

Notes

1. Excerpts from ISO/IEC 9594-8 are reproduced with the permission of the International Organization for Standardization, ISO and the International Electrotechnical Commission, IEC. The complete standard can be obtained from any ISO or IEC member, or from the ISO or IEC Central Offices, Case postale, 1211 Geneva 20, Switzerland. Copyright remains with ISO and IEC. Excerpts from ITU-T Recommendation X.509 are made after prior authorization by ITU as the copyright holder; the choice of the excerpts is the authors' and therefore does not affect the responsibility of ITU in any way. The full text of ITU-T Recommendation X.509 may be obtained from the ITU Sales Section, Place des Nations, CH-1211 Geneva 20, Switzerland, Tel: +41 22 730 51 11, Fax: +41 22 730 5194.

United Nations Model Law on Electronic Commerce

T he following presents the full text of the United Nations Model Law on Electronic Commerce, an initiative completed in June 1996 by the United Nations Commission on International Trade Law (UNCITRAL). The Model Law is discussed in Chapter 8. The version presented here includes the addition of Article 5 *bis* as adopted by the Commission at its thirty-first session, in June 1998.[1]

United Nations Model Law on Electronic Commerce

PART ONE. ELECTRONIC COMMERCE IN GENERAL

Chapter I: General Provisions

Article 1. Sphere of application*

This Law** applies to any kind of information in the form of a data message used in the context*** of commercial**** activities.

* The Commission suggests the following text for States that might wish to limit the applicability of this Law to international data messages: This Law applies to a data message as defined in paragraph (1) of article 2 where the data message relates to international commerce.

** This Law does not override any rule of law intended for the protection of consumers.

*** The Commission suggests the following text for States that might wish to extend the applicability of this Law: This Law applies to any kind of information in the form of a data message, except in the following situations: [...].

**** The term "commercial" should be given a wide interpretation so as to cover matters arising from all relationships of a commercial nature, whether contractual or not. Relationships of a commercial nature include, but are not limited to, the following transactions: any trade transaction for the supply or exchange of goods or services; distribution agreement; commercial representation or agency; factoring; leasing; construction of works; consulting; engineering; licensing; investment; financing; banking; insurance; exploitation agreement or concession; joint venture and other forms of industrial or business cooperation; carriage of goods or passengers by air, sea, rail or road.

Article 2. Definitions

For the purposes of this Law:

(a) "Data message" means information generated, sent, received or stored by electronic, optical or similar means including, but not limited to, electronic data interchange (EDI), electronic mail, telegram, telex or telecopy;

(b) "Electronic data interchange (EDI)" means the electronic transfer from computer to computer of information using an agreed standard to structure the information;

(c) "Originator" of a data message means a person by whom, or on whose behalf, the data message purports to have been sent or generated prior to storage, if any, but it does not include a person acting as an intermediary with respect to that data message;

(d) "Addressee" of a data message means a person who is intended by the originator to receive the data message, but does not include a person acting as an intermediary with respect to that data message;

(e) "Intermediary", with respect to a particular data message, means a person who, on behalf of another person, sends, receives or stores that data message or provides other services with respect to that data message;

(f) "Information system" means a system for generating, sending, receiving, storing or otherwise processing data messages.

Article 3. Interpretation

(1) In the interpretation of this Law, regard is to be had to its international origin and to the need to promote uniformity in its application and the observance of good faith.

(2) Questions concerning matters governed by this Law which are not expressly settled in it are to be settled in conformity with the general principles on which this Law is based.

Article 4. Variation by agreement

(1) As between parties involved in generating, sending, receiving, storing or otherwise processing data messages, and except as otherwise provided, the provisions of chapter III may be varied by agreement.

(2) Paragraph (1) does not affect any right that may exist to modify by agreement any rule of law referred to in chapter II.

Chapter II : Application of Legal Requirements to Data Messages

Article 5. Legal recognition of data messages

Information shall not be denied legal effect, validity or enforceability solely on the grounds that it is in the form of a data message.

Article 5 bis. Incorporation by reference[2]

Information shall not be denied legal effect, validity or enforceability solely on the grounds that it is not contained in the data message purporting to give rise to such legal effect, but is merely referred to in that data message.

Article 6. Writing

(1) Where the law requires information to be in writing, that requirement is met by a data message if the information contained therein is accessible so as to be usable for subsequent reference.

(2) Paragraph (1) applies whether the requirement therein is in the form of an obligation or whether the law simply provides consequences for the information not being in writing.

(3) The provisions of this article do not apply to the following: [...].

Article 7. Signature

(1) Where the law requires a signature of a person, that requirement is met in relation to a data message if:

  (a) a method is used to identify that person and to indicate that person's approval of the information contained in the data message; and
  (b) that method is as reliable as was appropriate for the purpose for which the data message was generated or communicated, in the light of all the circumstances, including any relevant agreement.

(2) Paragraph (1) applies whether the requirement therein is in the form of an obligation or whether the law simply provides consequences for the absence of a signature.

(3) The provisions of this article do not apply to the following: [...].

Article 8. Original

(1) Where the law requires information to be presented or retained in its original form, that requirement is met by a data message if:

  (a) there exists a reliable assurance as to the integrity of the information from the time when it was first generated in its final form, as a data message or otherwise; and
  (b) where it is required that information be presented, that information is capable of being displayed to the person to whom it is to be presented.

(2) Paragraph (1) applies whether the requirement therein is in the form of an obligation or whether the law simply provides consequences for the information not being presented or retained in its original form.

(3) For the purposes of subparagraph (a) of paragraph (1):

  (a) the criteria for assessing integrity shall be whether the information has remained complete and unaltered, apart from the addition of any endorsement and any change which arises in the normal course of communication, storage and display; and
  (b) the standard of reliability required shall be assessed in the light of the purpose for which the information was generated and in the light of all the relevant circumstances.

(4) The provisions of this article do not apply to the following: [...].

Article 9. Admissibility and evidential weight of data messages

(1) In any legal proceedings, nothing in the application of the rules of evidence shall apply so as to deny the admissibility of a data message in evidence:

  (a) on the sole ground that it is a data message; or,
  (b) if it is the best evidence that the person adducing it could reasonably be expected to obtain, on the grounds that it is not in its original form.

(2) Information in the form of a data message shall be given due evidential weight. In assessing the evidential weight of a data message, regard shall be had to the reliability of the manner in which the data message was generated, stored or communicated, to the reliability of the manner in which the integrity of the information was maintained, to the manner in which its originator was identified, and to any other relevant factor.

Article 10. Retention of data messages

(1) Where the law requires that certain documents, records or information be retained, that requirement is met by retaining data messages, provided that the following conditions are satisfied:

(a) the information contained therein is accessible so as to be usable for subsequent reference; and

(b) the data message is retained in the format in which it was generated, sent or received, or in a format which can be demonstrated to represent accurately the information generated, sent or received; and

(c) such information, if any, is retained as enables the identification of the origin and destination of a data message and the date and time when it was sent or received.

(2) An obligation to retain documents, records or information in accordance with paragraph (1) does not extend to any information the sole purpose of which is to enable the message to be sent or received.

(3) A person may satisfy the requirement referred to in paragraph (1) by using the services of any other person, provided that the conditions set forth in subparagraphs (a), (b) and (c) of paragraph (1) are met.

Chapter III: Communication of Data Messages

Article 11. Formation and validity of contracts

(1) In the context of contract formation, unless otherwise agreed by the parties, an offer and the acceptance of an offer may be expressed by means of data messages. Where a data message is used in the formation of a contract, that contract shall not be denied validity or enforceability on the sole ground that a data message was used for that purpose.

(2) The provisions of this article do not apply to the following: [...].

Article 12. Recognition by parties of data messages

(1) As between the originator and the addressee of a data message, a declaration of will or other statement shall not be denied legal effect, validity or enforceability solely on the grounds that it is in the form of a data message.

(2) The provisions of this article do not apply to the following: [...].

Article 13. Attribution of data messages

(1) A data message is that of the originator if it was sent by the originator itself.

(2) As between the originator and the addressee, a data message is deemed to be that of the originator if it was sent:

(a) by a person who had the authority to act on behalf of the originator in respect of that data message; or

(b) by an information system programmed by or on behalf of the originator to operate automatically.

(3) As between the originator and the addressee, an addressee is entitled to regard a data message as being that of the originator, and to act on that assumption, if:

(a) in order to ascertain whether the data message was that of the originator, the addressee properly applied a procedure previously agreed to by the originator for that purpose; or

(b) the data message as received by the addressee resulted from the actions of a person whose relationship with the originator or with any agent of the originator enabled that person to gain access to a method used by the originator to identify data messages as its own.

(4) Paragraph (3) does not apply:

(a) as of the time when the addressee has both received notice from the originator that the data message is not that of the originator, and had reasonable time to act accordingly; or

(b) in a case within paragraph (3) (b), at any time when the addressee knew or should have known, had it exercised reasonable care or used any agreed procedure, that the data message was not that of the originator.

(5) Where a data message is that of the originator or is deemed to be that of the originator, or the addressee is entitled to act on that assumption, then, as between the originator and the addressee, the addressee is entitled to regard the data message as received as being what the originator intended to send, and to act on that assumption. The addressee is not so entitled when it knew or should have known, had it exercised reasonable care or used any agreed procedure, that the transmission resulted in any error in the data message as received.

(6) The addressee is entitled to regard each data message received as a separate data message and to act on that assumption, except to the extent that it duplicates another data message and the addressee knew or should have known, had it exercised reasonable care or used any agreed procedure, that the data message was a duplicate.

Article 14. Acknowledgement of receipt

(1) Paragraphs (2) to (4) of this article apply where, on or before sending a data message, or by means of that data message, the originator has requested or has agreed with the addressee that receipt of the data message be acknowledged.

(2) Where the originator has not agreed with the addressee that the acknowledgement be given in a particular form or by a particular method, an acknowledgement may be given by

(a) any communication by the addressee, automated or otherwise, or

(b) any conduct of the addressee, sufficient to indicate to the originator that the data message has been received.

(3) Where the originator has stated that the data message is conditional on receipt of the acknowledgement, the data message is treated as though it has never been sent, until the acknowledgement is received.

(4) Where the originator has not stated that the data message is conditional on receipt of the acknowledgement, and the acknowledgement has not been received by the originator within the time specified or agreed or, if no time has been specified or agreed, within a reasonable time the originator:

(a) may give notice to the addressee stating that no acknowledgement has been received and specifying a reasonable time by which the acknowledgement must be received; and

(b) if the acknowledgement is not received within the time specified in subparagraph (a), may, upon notice to the addressee, treat the data message as though it had never been sent, or exercise any other rights it may have.

(5) Where the originator receives the addressee's acknowledgement of receipt, it is presumed that the related data message was received by the addressee. That presumption does not imply that the data message corresponds to the message received.

(6) Where the received acknowledgement states that the related data message met technical requirements, either agreed upon or set forth in applicable standards, it is presumed that those requirements have been met.

(7) Except in so far as it relates to the sending or receipt of the data message, this article is not intended to deal with the legal consequences that may flow either from that data message or from the acknowledgement of its receipt.

Article 15. Time and place of dispatch and receipt of data messages

(1) Unless otherwise agreed between the originator and the addressee, the dispatch of a data message occurs when it enters an information system outside the control of the originator or of the person who sent the data message on behalf of the originator.

(2) Unless otherwise agreed between the originator and the addressee, the time of receipt of a data message is determined as follows:

(a) if the addressee has designated an information system for the purpose of receiving data messages, receipt occurs:

      (i) at the time when the data message enters the designated information system; or

     (ii) if the data message is sent to an information system of the addressee that is not the designated information system, at the time when the data message is retrieved by the addressee;

  (b) if the addressee has not designated an information system, receipt occurs when the data message enters an information system of the addressee.

(3) Paragraph (2) applies notwithstanding that the place where the information system is located may be different from the place where the data message is deemed to be received under paragraph (4).

(4) Unless otherwise agreed between the originator and the addressee, a data message is deemed to be dispatched at the place where the originator has its place of business, and is deemed to be received at the place where the addressee has its place of business. For the purposes of this paragraph:

  (a) if the originator or the addressee has more than one place of business, the place of business is that which has the closest relationship to the underlying transaction or, where there is no underlying transaction, the principal place of business;

  (b) if the originator or the addressee does not have a place of business, reference is to be made to its habitual residence.

(5) The provisions of this article do not apply to the following: [...].

PART TWO. ELECTRONIC COMMERCE IN SPECIFIC AREAS
Chapter I: Carriage of Goods

Article 16. Actions related to contracts of carriage of goods

Without derogating from the provisions of part I of this Law, this chapter applies to any action in connection with, or in pursuance of, a contract of carriage of goods, including but not limited to:

  (a) (i) furnishing the marks, number, quantity or weight of goods;
       (ii) stating or declaring the nature or value of goods;
       (iii) issuing a receipt for goods;
       (iv) confirming that goods have been loaded;
  (b) (i) notifying a person of terms and conditions of the contract;
       (ii) giving instructions to a carrier;
  (c) (i) claiming delivery of goods;
       (ii) authorizing release of goods;
       (iii) giving notice of loss of, or damage to, goods;
  (d) giving any other notice or statement in connection with the performance of the contract;

(e) undertaking to deliver goods to a named person or a person authorized to claim delivery;

(f) granting, acquiring, renouncing, surrendering, transferring or negotiating rights in goods;

(g) acquiring or transferring rights and obligations under the contract.

Article 17. Transport documents

(1) Subject to paragraph (3), where the law requires that any action referred to in article 16 be carried out in writing or by using a paper document, that requirement is met if the action is carried out by using one or more data messages.

(2) Paragraph (1) applies whether the requirement therein is in the form of an obligation or whether the law simply provides consequences for failing either to carry out the action in writing or to use a paper document.

(3) If a right is to be granted to, or an obligation is to be acquired by, one person and no other person, and if the law requires that, in order to effect this, the right or obligation must be conveyed to that person by the transfer, or use of, a paper document, that requirement is met if the right or obligation is conveyed by using one or more data messages, provided that a reliable method is used to render such data message or messages unique.

(4) For the purposes of paragraph (3), the standard of reliability required shall be assessed in the light of the purpose for which the right or obligation was conveyed and in the light of all the circumstances, including any relevant agreement.

(5) Where one or more data messages are used to effect any action in subparagraphs (f) and (g) of article 16, no paper document used to effect any such action is valid unless the use of data messages has been terminated and replaced by the use of paper documents. A paper document issued in these circumstances shall contain a statement of such termination. The replacement of data messages by paper documents shall not affect the rights or obligations of the parties involved.

(6) If a rule of law is compulsorily applicable to a contract of carriage of goods which is in, or is evidenced by, a paper document, that rule shall not be inapplicable to such a contract of carriage of goods which is evidenced by one or more data messages by reason of the fact that the contract is evidenced by such data message or messages instead of by a paper document.

The provisions of this article do not apply to the following: [...].

Notes

1. United Nations, UNCITRAL Model Law on Electronic Commerce with Guide to Enactment 1996 (1999).
2. As adopted by the Commission at its thirty-first session, in June 1998.

How to Obtain Referenced Documents

T he URLs noted along with many of the references in this book will, in general, yield information on how to obtain a copy of the referenced documents. Following are contact details, and other information, to assist in obtaining copies of various cited organizational publications that may otherwise be difficult to find.

F.1 American Bar Association (ABA) Publications

ABA publications can be obtained from:

American Bar Association
750 N. Lake Shore Drive
Chicago, IL 60611
Tel: +1 312 988 5522
<http://www.abanet.org/store/order.html>

F.2   American National Standards Institute (ANSI) Standards

ANSI standards can be obtained from:

> American National Standards Institute
> 11 West 42nd Street
> New York, NY 10036, U.S.A.
> Tel: +1 212 642 4900
> Fax: +1 212 302 1286
> <http://www.ansi.org>

ANSI X9 (financial services industry) standards can also be obtained from:

> American Bankers Association Customer Service Center
> 1120 Connecticut Ave., NW
> Washington, DC 20036, U.S.A.
> Tel: +1 800 338 0626 or +1 202 663 5087
> Fax: +1 202 663 7543
> e-mail: custserv@aba.com

F.3   Internet Publications

Internet documents in the *Request for Comments* (RFC) series can be downloaded free from the IETF Website at <http://www.ietf.org/rfc.html>. Internet Drafts can be similarly downloaded at <http://www.ietf.org/ID.html>.

Publications of the World Wide Consortium can be obtained at: <http://www.w3c.org>.

F.4   ISO and ISO/IEC Standards

In the references to international standards in this book, dates are not stated. All standards are revised regularly, and the reader is always referred to the latest version (as advised by ISO or its sales agents). Note that some standards are multi-part, e.g., a standard may comprise parts

ISO/IEC nnnn-1 and *ISO/IEC nnnn-2*. In this book, the convention *ISO/IEC nnnn* is used for a multi-part standard when referring to the collection of all parts, and *ISO/IEC nnnn-p* when referring to Part *p* only.

Published standards can be purchased from ISO sales agencies, most of which are national standards organizations. Agencies include:

Australia:	Standards Australia, Sydney
Belgium:	Institut belge de normalisation, Bruxelles
Canada:	Standards Council of Canada, Ottawa
Denmark:	Dansk Standardiseringsraad, Hellerup
France:	Association française de normalisation, Paris
Germany:	Deutsches Institut für Normung, Berlin
Italy:	Ente Nazionale Italiano di Unificazione, Milano
Japan:	Japanese Industrial Standards Committee, Tokyo
Netherlands:	Nederlands Normalisatie-instituut, Delft
New Zealand:	Standards Association of New Zealand, Wellington
Norway:	Norges Standardiseringsforbund, Oslo
Portugal:	Instituto Português de Qualidade, Lisboa
Spain:	Asociación Española de Normalización y Certificación, Madrid
Sweden:	Standardiseringskommissionen i Sverige, Stockholm
Switzerland:	Swiss Association for Standardization, Zurich
United Kingdom:	British Standards Institution, London
United States:	American National Standards Institute, New York

In other countries, contact your national standards organization, or:

ISO Central Secretariat,
Case postale 56
CH-1211 Geneva 20
Switzerland   Tel: +41 22 749 01 11

International standards are sometimes republished as national standards in some countries and become known under a national standard reference number. For details, contact your national standards organization, quoting the ISO or ISO/IEC standard number.

F.5   ITU Standards

ITU Recommendations published prior to April 1993 are called *CCITT Recommendations*; those published subsequently are called *ITU-T Recommendations*. For simplicity and forward compatibility, references in this book use the term *ITU-T Recommendation* for all of these standards.

ITU Recommendations are available both in hardcopy and online forms. For further information, contact:

> International Telecommunication Union
> General Secretariat—Sales Section
> Place des Nations, CH-1211
> Geneva 20, Switzerland
> Tel: +41 22 730 51 11 (general inquiries)
> +41 22 730 5554/5338 (online system inquiries)
> <http://www.itu.ch>

F.6   U.S. Federal Government Publications

U.S. Federal Information Processing Standards Publications (FIPS PUB) and most other NIST publications can be obtained from:

> National Technical Information Service,
> U.S. Department of Commerce,
> Springfield, VA 22161, U.S.A.
> Tel: +1 (703) 487 4650
> <http://www.ntis.gov>

Many government publications relating to computer security can be obtained online. For information, see <http://csrc.nist.gov>.

Legacy Application Security Standards

This appendix summarizes the main characteristics of the secure e-mail standards that preceded the adoption of S/MIME as the universal standard for e-mail security. The Web security protocol Secure HTTP (S/HTTP) is also described. Since none of these protocols is now in widespread use, this material is included mainly for historical purposes.

G.1   Privacy Enhanced Mail (PEM)

Privacy Enhanced Mail (PEM) was the result of work conducted by the IETF commencing in the late 1980s. This was the first serious effort to make Internet mail secure. The PEM work led to the publication in 1993 of a four-part series of Proposed Internet Standards.[1] The PEM specifications are very comprehensive. In particular, Part I (RFC 1421) defines a secure messaging protocol and Part II (RFC 1422) defines a supporting public-key infrastructure (the latter is discussed in Chapter 7).

The PEM secure messaging protocol was designed to support the basic message protection services identified in chapter 5. PEM operated by taking an unprotected message and folding its contents into a PEM message—PEM messages could then be transferred over the regular messaging backbone like other messages.

The PEM specification recognizes two alternative approaches to network-wide authentication and key management—a symmetric alternative and a public-key alternative.[2] Only the public-key alternative was ever implemented, however.

PEM constitutes an important landmark in the development of secure messaging protocols. However, PEM was never a recognized success in terms of commercial deployment, mainly because of its incompatibility with MIME—the Internet multi-media mail format that was developed around the same time.[3]

G.2 X.400 Security

X.400 is the family of internationally standardized electronic messaging protocols developed jointly by the International Telecommunication Union (ITU), International Organization for Standardization (ISO), and International Electrotechnical Commission (IEC).[4] The X.400 standards, which were first published in 1984, were used by various commercial e-mail service providers. While X.400 was not considered an Internet protocol, X.400 was frequently configured to interoperate with Internet messaging via mail gateways.

In the 1988 revision of the X.400 standards, a very comprehensive set of security features was added. These features included support not only for the basic message protection services, but also for confirmation services and several other enhanced security services. Any reader interested in learning about the full set of security services designed for electronic messaging is encouraged to study X.400 security.[5]

Unfortunately, the X.400 (1988) security features had one major shortcoming— rather than being designed as simply a set of message content formats, they were intricately linked with the X.400 submission, transfer, and delivery protocols. This meant that X.400-secured messages, unlike unprotected messages, could not be used through mail gateways and thus could not be conveyed over the Internet mail system.

G.3 Message Security Protocol (MSP)

In the late 1980s, the U.S. Government developed its own secure messaging protocol called the Message Security Protocol (MSP).[6] This protocol was adopted for use within the U.S. Department of Defense, in particular, for the Defense Messaging System (DMS) project. It was also considered a candidate protocol for use in other areas of the government and, possibly, the commercial arena.

MSP is a general message protection protocol, not unlike PKCS #7 or S/MIME, which encapsulates an unprotected message content to give a new, protected message content. It provides the basic message protection services plus some enhanced protection services—confirmation services (request and return of a signed message receipt) and services associated with conveying message labels for access control purposes. MSP was designed for conveyance over either X.400 or Internet messaging facilities.

An MSP message carries the original message contents (encrypted, if message confidentiality is requested) plus various security parameters required by recipients to decrypt and/or validate the message upon receipt. Also included are parameters that specify the algorithms used for encryption, integrity checking, and digital signature. The U.S. government implementations of MSP used the government cryptographic algorithms, such as DSA for digital signature. However, MSP was not itself algorithm-specific—for example, it was possible to use RSA technology in conjunction with MSP.

From a technical perspective, MSP is a more comprehensive security protocol than S/MIME or PEM. It was not accepted commercially, however, having been developed in isolation in the U.S. Department of Defense. MSP was influential, nevertheless, in causing the inclusion of certain features required by the Department of Defense in S/MIME Version 3.

G.4   Secure HTTP (S-HTTP)

Secure HTTP addresses a similar set of requirements as SSL/TLS, but comes from a different background and presents a different type of solution. S-HTTP was designed by Enterprise Integration Technologies[7] in response to requirements from CommerceNet, a consortium focused on promoting the establishment of technologies needed for Internet-based electronic commerce.[8]

S-HTTP was designed as a security extension to HTTP, which is essentially a request-response transaction protocol. This makes S-HTTP fundamentally different from SSL/TLS, which is a session protection protocol. The primary function of S-HTTP is to protect individual transaction request or response messages, in a somewhat similar fashion to how a secure messaging protocol protects e-mail messages. In fact, S-HTTP is largely built upon the base of secure messaging protocols discussed in the preceding subsections and chapter 5.

The security services provided by S-HTTP are the same as those provided by SSL, namely entity authentication, integrity (via an integrity check-value), and confidentiality (via encryption), with the addition of an option for digital signatures, which can provide a basis for the additional security service of non-repudiation.

S-HTTP provides a great deal of flexibility as to how messages are protected and how keys are managed. Specific message protection formats supported include PEM (RFC 1421) and PKCS #7. Key management, however, is not bound to the strict PEM infrastructure, nor to any strict set of rules. Encryption keys may be established through RSA key transport within the PEM or PKCS #7 envelope, may be pre-established via manual means, or may even be established from Kerberos tickets. Use of S-HTTP is indicated by a URL commencing with "shttp://"—note the risk of confusion with "https://" designating the use of SSL/TLS.

S-HTTP was used by some vendors for securing Web communications in the early days of Web deployment. However, it has now been almost entirely displaced by SSL/TLS, which was much more rapidly and broadly adopted.

Notes

1. J. Linn, *Privacy Enhancement for Internet Electronic Mail, Part I: Message Encryption and Authentication Procedures*, Request for Comments (RFC) 1421, Internet Activities Board, 1993 <ftp://ftp.isi.edu/in-notes/rfc1421.txt>; S. Kent, *Privacy Enhancement for Internet Electronic Mail, Part II: Certificate-Based Key Management*, Request for Comments (RFC) 1422, Internet Activities Board, 1993 <ftp://ftp.isi.edu/in-notes/rfc1422.txt>; D. Balenson, *Privacy Enhancement for Internet Electronic Mail, Part III: Algorithms, Modes, and Identifiers*, Request for Comments (RFC) 1423, Internet Activities Board, 1993 <ftp://ftp.isi.edu/in-notes/rfc1423.txt>; B. Kaliski, *Privacy Enhancement for Internet Electronic Mail, Part IV: Key Certification and Related Services*, Request for Comments (RFC) 1424, Internet Activities Board, 1993 <ftp://ftp.isi.edu/in-notes/rfc1424.txt>.

2. W. Ford, *Computer Communications Security: Principles, Standard Protocols and Techniques* (Upper Saddle River, NJ: Prentice Hall, Inc., 1994), Chap. 13 <http://www.prenhall.com/013/799452/79945-2.html>.

3. Another reason for the commercial failure of PEM was the excessive rigidity of the public-key infrastructure needed to support it.

4. ISO/IEC 10021, *Information Technology—Message Handling Systems*. Also published as ITU-T X.400 series Recommendations <http://www.itu.ch>.

5. Ford, *Computer Communications Security*, Chap. 13.

6. C. Dinkel (Ed.), *Secure Data Network System (SDNS) Network, Transport, and Message Security Protocols*, U.S. Department of Commerce, National Institute of Standards and Technology, Report NISTIR 90-4250, 1990.

7. A subsidiary of VeriFone, Inc. For more information on Secure HTTP, refer to: <http://www.verifone.com>.

8. For information on CommerceNet, see: <http://www.commerce.net>.

PKI Disclosure Statement

Certificate policies (CPs) and certification practice statements (CPSs) are generally very detailed documents containing complex legal and technical information. Although such detail and complex expression may be essential to assure proper operation and certainly, many PKI users, especially consumers, find these documents difficult to understand. Consequently, there is often a need for a supplemental and simplified instrument to assist PKI users in making informed trust decisions. In response, the International Chamber of Commerce (ICC), in informal cooperation with the Information Security Committee of the American Bar Association and other groups, developed a draft model *PKI Disclosure Statement* (PDS). A PDS is a supplementary instrument that provides a framework to disclose and emphasize critical information about the policies and practices of a certification authority or PKI that is normally addressed in much greater detail by an associated CP and CPS. A PDS is *not* intended to replace a CP or CPS. Also, the PDS provides a uniform method for easily accessing and comparing critical terms from relevant certification authorities or PKIs.

The model PDS provides structure and categories (and not substantive content) defining a harmonized set of statement types that would be contained in a deployed PDS. Each certification authority or PKI may draft specific substantive policy content to appear in its implementation of the PDS.

The following table presents the PDS, listing a section for each defined *statement type* (category) and a corresponding *descriptive statement* that may include hyperlinks or computer-based references to the relevant CP/CPS sections.

561

TABLE H.1

Statement Type	Statement Description
Certification authority, contact information	The name, location, and relevant contact information for the CA/PKI.
Certificate type, validation procedures, and usage	A description of each class or type of certificate issued by the certification authority, corresponding validation procedures, and any restrictions on certificate usage.
Reliance limits	The reliance limits, if any.
Obligations of subscribers	The description of, or reference to, the critical subscriber obligations.
Certificate status checking obligations of relying parties	The extent to which relying parties are obligated to check certificate status, and references to further explanation.
Limited warranty and disclaimer; Limitation of liability	Summary of the warranty, disclaimers, limitations of liability, and any applicable warranty or insurance programs.
Applicable agreements, Certification Practice Statement, Certificate Policy	Identification and references to applicable agreements CPS, CP, and other relevant documents.
Privacy policy	A description of and reference to the applicable privacy policy.
Refund policy	A description of and reference to the applicable refund policy.
Applicable law and dispute resolution	Statement of the choice of law and dispute resolution mechanisms (anticipated to often include an audit process and if applicable the reference to applicable dispute resolution services).
Certification authority and repository licenses, trust marks, and audit	Summary of any governmental licenses and/or seal programs; and a description of the audit firm.

Repudiation In Law

The legal concept of repudiation can be traced through various alternative meanings back to ancient times. Roman jurists and other ancient Western legal systems employed the term *repudiate* almost exclusively in the domain of family law. Repudiation generally signified an engaged man's "casting off or putting away of a woman betrothed." The term was also used, less frequently, in the contexts of divorce and paternity (to signify the casting off of a wife or son for various reasons).[1] Civil legal systems that are descendants of classical and revived Roman law still attach this meaning to the legal term *repudiate*.[2] Those who are familiar with canon law[3] might also associate *repudiation* with the refusal by a party to accept a benefice.

Under the common law, repudiation is most typically associated with contracts. Confusion in terminology has resulted from historical usage differences between English common law and equity, each originating in a different court. Moreover, lawyers tend to use *repudiation* to refer indiscriminately to both rightful and wrongful actions.[4] In one context, *repudiation* refers to the *legitimate* right of a party to deny the validity or enforceability of a contract on numerous grounds, including forgery[5], duress, illegality of the subject matter, and incapacity of one of the parties.[6] In another context, it refers to the *wrongful* refusal of a party to perform his or her obligations under a valid and enforceable contract.[7] Such a refusal constitutes a breach of contract and may give rise to rights and remedies in favor of the other party.[8] When this type of repudiation occurs before the time for performance has arrived, it is termed *anticipatory breach* or *anticipatory repudiation*, and the other party may be able to rescind the contract entirely or sue for damages immediately upon the repudiation.[9]

The term *non-repudiation* has surfaced in U.S. judicial opinions over the last fifteen years, but only to signify that a party has not repudiated, and does not intend to repudiate,[10] a contract or statement,[11] or that a party does not have the ability to void an agreement unilaterally.[12] To date, *non-repudiation* has not been used in any published U.S. judicial opinion in the information security sense—as a reference to the inherent ability of a specific communication medium and information security mechanism to prevent a party from denying that a particular message was sent or received. Nonetheless, over the past few years *non-repudiation* has appeared with increasing frequency in diverse legislation, regulation, private agreements, and guidelines regarding the subject of digital signatures.[13]

As discussed in Chapter 9, digital signature technology can provide a non-repudiation capability far more robust than traditional approaches and strategies for the hindrance of denial of obligations.[14] This new concept of digital non-repudiation takes the traditional meaning to another level of abstraction. Non-repudiation—in the digital communications sense—signifies that some attribute of the communication itself prevents or hinders the denial that the communication occurred, and further that it was conveyed without alteration and with authenticity.

Throughout history, lawmakers of both civil and commonlaw jurisdictions have sought rules that achieve the type and level of non-repudiation made possible by digital technology. Signatures, seals,[15] notaries, recording offices, and certified mail are all examples of traditional mechanisms employed in efforts to supply and bolster non-repudiation. Nonetheless, lawyers and commercial trading partners have not in the past consciously sought nor formally recognized non-repudiation as an express attribute of an authenticated document or communication. Explicit consciousness of this powerful issue has surfaced only very recently, as society has faced the challenge of first matching and then exceeding traditional legal protections in the emerging digital communications environment.

Notes

1. *Black's Law Dictionary* (West Publishing Co., 6th ed. 1990) ("repudiation").
   Although today we speak of engagement, marriage, and paternity as topics of
   family law, ancient and medieval lawyers conceived of these relationships as
   essentially contractual. Therefore, the connection between the legal concepts of
   repudiation in contract and domestic law is not as distant as it might appear.

2. Reinhard Zimmermann, *The Law of Obligations: Roman Foundations of the Civilian Tradition*, 815 n. 228 (1992) (tracing the concept of repudiation as a form of breach of contract that originated in Roman law and continued through German law).

3. The *canon law* is that body of ecclesiastical rules and jurisprudence developed by popes and cardinals of the Catholic faith, compiled by purists of the 12th, 13th, and 14th centuries, and adopted piecemeal into the laws of England and the continental European nations. Black's Law Dictionary (6th ed. 1990), "Canon—Canon law."

4. See P. S. Attiyah, An Introduction to the Law of Contract 294 (3d ed. 1981), quoted in *Black's Law Dictionary* (West Publishing Co., 7th ed. 1999) ("repudiation").

5. Repudiation based on misrepresentation of a signatory's identity is closely analogous to the type of repudiation this chapter addresses.

6. For a contract to be valid and binding, its parties must each have the legal capacity to enter into it. Mental incompetency, minority of years, and lack of authority might each give rise to a claim of incapacity. In times past, the marital status of women was also considered a basis for such a claim. Old law texts and treatises discussed incapacity under the heading "Infants, Lunatics and Married Women."

7. Such a refusal generally takes the form of a statement that the party does not intend to perform its obligations under the contract. Actions that imply the same may also constitute repudiation. U.S. *Restatement (Second) of Contracts* § 250 [hereinafter the Restatement].

8. See Section 3.4 regarding breach of contract.

9. Restatement §§ 250-57; Uniform Commercial Code § 2-610 [hereinafter UCC]. The leading case on point is the English case of *Hochster v. De la Tour*, 2 El. & Bl. 678, 118 Eng. Rep. 922 (Q.B. 1853). Some more recent examples include *Pitcher v. Lauritzen*, 423 P.2d 491 (Utah 1967); *Continental Casualty Co. v. Boerger*, 389 S.W.2d 566 (Tex. Civ. App. 1965); and *Robinson v. Raquet*, 36 P.2d 821 (Cal. App. 1934).

10. For example, the court in *Norris v. Wirtz*, slip opinion, No. 80 C 6836 (N.D. Ill. Dec. 3, 1985), stated that a party's "continued acknowledgment and performance of [its obligations] is regarded as a strong indication of non-repudiation."

See also: *Chicago District Council of Carpenters Pension Fund v. Dombrowski,* 545 F. Supp. 325, 328 (N.D. Ill. 1982) (explaining non-repudiation in circumstance of duress).

11. See, e.g., *Local 302, International Union of Operating Engineers v. West,* 882 F.2d 399, 401 (9th Cir. 1989); see also *United States ex rel. Johnson v. Lane,* 639 F.Supp. 260, 267 (N.D. Ill. 1986) (stating in the criminal procedure context that "non-repudiation can be critical to the weight given a confession").

12. This usage arises under a head of labor law termed the "*Deklewa* non-repudiation rule." See, e.g., *Mesa Verde Construction v. Northern California District Council of Laborers,* 861 F.2d 1124, 1129 (9th Cir. 1988). The National Labor Relations Board held in *Deklewa v. International Association of Bridge, Structural and Ornamental Ironworkers, Local 3,* 282 N.L.R.B. No. 184, 1986–87 NLRB Dec. (CCH) I 18,549 (Feb. 20, 1987), *enforced* 843 F.2d 770 (3d. Cir. 1988) (pre-hire agreements sanctioned under the National Labor Relations Act between employers and unions are not unilaterally voidable at will by either party).

13. See, e.g., The Electronic Signature Standard—§ 142.310 ("Digital signature, message integrity, non-repudiation, user authentication"). Notice of Proposed Rule Making for Security and Electronic Signature Standards (Public comment period ended October 13, 1998) <http://erm.aspe.hhs.gov/ora_web/plsql/ erm_rule.rule?user_id=&rule_id=62>. The code of the state of Washington recognizes non-repudiation as a critical feature of secure digital signatures. See Wash. Rev. Code § 19.34.010 (1994) ("provid[ing] a voluntary licensing mechanism for digital signature certification authorities by which [to] reasonably be assured as to the integrity, authenticity and non-repudiation of a digitally signed electronic communication."). On March 27, 1997, the OECD (Organisation for Economic Co-operation and Development) issued policy guidelines (defining non-repudiation as "a property achieved through cryptographic methods, which prevents an individual or entity from denying having performed a particular action related to data (such as mechanisms for non-rejection of authority (origin); for proof of obligation, intent, or commitment; or for proof of ownership)"). See OECD, *Guidelines for Cryptography Policy,* available at <http://www.oecd.org//dsti/sti/it/secur/prod/crypto2.htm>.

14. For a good summary of legal issues surrounding non-repudiation in a digital technology context, see Adrian McCullagh & William Caellin, "Non-Repudiation in

the Digital Environment," 5 First Monday (Aug. 7, 2000), available at
<http://firstmonday.org/issues/issue5_8/mccullagh/index.html>.

15. The technical evaluation of non-repudiation with digital signatures has a rough parallel to the evaluation of seals used for traditional paper-based documents. The use of seals in Europe began with the court of Frankish kings. At the time of the Norman conquest, only kings had seals. Seals entered the common law of England during Edward I's reign when it became required for an enforceable covenant to be sealed. By the end of the 13th c., most freemen had seals. *The History of English Law Before the Time of Edward I, Vol. II*, Frederick Pollack and Frederick William Maitland, pp. 221–2 (Boston: Little, Brown & Co., 1899). A sealed writing could be received as conclusive and irrebuttable evidence binding the person whose seal was attached. Later, when the doctrine of consideration became part of the English law of contract, a seal was interpreted as importing consideration. Spencer L. Kimball, *Historical Introduction to the Legal System*, pp. 143–47 (St. Paul, Minn.: West Publishing Co., 1966).

Public-Key Cryptosystems

$$T$$ his appendix provides a concise, high-level description of the underlying mathematics of some common public-key cryptosystems. For a more complete description of all mechanisms, see Schneier [1] or Menezes et al [2].

J.1 RSA Algorithm

For a full description of RSA mathematics, see the original paper by Rivest, Shamir, and Adleman [3]. A summary follows.

An RSA key pair is created thus: An integer e is chosen, to be the *public exponent*. Two large prime numbers, p and q, are randomly selected, satisfying the conditions that $(p - 1)$ and e have no common divisors, and $(q - 1)$ and e have no common divisors. A number n called the *public modulus* is then computed by multiplying p and q, i.e., $n = pq$. The values of n and e together form the public key. A *private exponent*, d, is then determined, such that $(de - 1)$ is divisible by both $(p - 1)$ and $(q - 1)$. The values of n and d (or p, q, and d) together constitute the private key.

The exponents have the important property that, using modular arithmetic, d functions as the inverse of e, that is, for any message M:

$$(M^e)^d \bmod n = M \bmod n$$

The encrypting process for message M involves calculating $M^e \bmod n$. This can be carried out by anyone who knows the public key, i.e., n and e. Decrypting of message M' involves calculating $M'^{\,d} \bmod n$. This requires knowledge of the private key.

J.2 The Digital Signature Algorithm (DSA)

The *Digital Signature Algorithm* (DSA) is specified in U.S. Federal Information Processing Standard 186-2 [4].

DSA employs an irreversible public-key system, based on the ElGamal approach [5], as extended by Schnorr [6]. Its security depends upon the difficulty of calculating discrete logarithms. Let:

$$y = g^x \bmod p$$

where p is a prime and g is an element of suitably large order [7] modulo p. It is simple to calculate y, given g, x, and p, but it is extremely difficult to calculate x, given y, g, and p. This gives a basis for a public-key system where x is a private key and y is a public key.

The system uses three integers, p, q, and g, which can be made public and common to a group of users. p is a prime modulus, of a size in the range of 512 to 1024 bits [8]. q is a 160-bit prime divisor of $p - 1$. g is chosen as follows:

$$g = j^{\,[(p-1)/q]} \bmod p,$$

where j is any random integer with $1 < j < p$ such that:

$$j^{\,[(p-1)/q]} \bmod p > 1$$

For a given originator, private key x is selected randomly, with $1 < x < q$. Public key y is calculated as indicated above.

The process of signing and verifying a message is illustrated in Figure J.1. The signer generates a digest of the message to be signed using a hash function. The digest is then processed by a DSA-signing operation which requires the private key x and which generates a signature comprising two 160-bit numbers, r and s. This signature accompa-

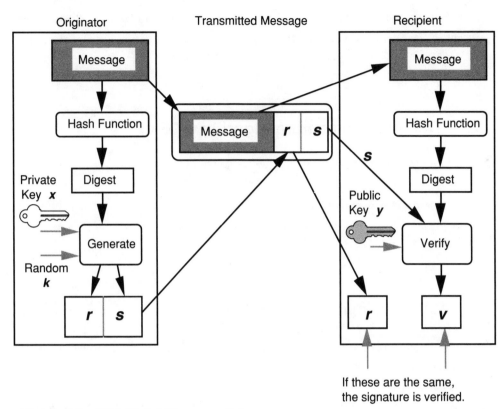

Figure J.1 DSA Digital Signature Scheme

nies the original message when it is communicated or stored. To sign a message that has digest h, the user chooses a random integer k (with $0 < k < q$) and computes:

$$r = (g^k \bmod p) \bmod q$$

$$s = (k^{-1}(h + xr)) \bmod q$$

where k^{-1} is the multiplicative inverse of $k \bmod q$, i.e., $(k^{-1} k) \bmod q = 1$ and $0 < k^{-1} < q$. The pair of values (r, s) constitutes the signature for the message.

To verify a received signature (say r', s') accompanying a message with digest h', the recipient first checks that $0 < r' < q$ and $0 < s' < q$. If either condition is violated, the signature is rejected. Otherwise, the recipient then computes from s' and h' a value v. For the signature to verify correctly, this value needs to be the same as the value r' sent in the signature. The calculation of v is as follows:

$$w = (s')^{-1} \bmod q$$

$$u1 = (h' \; w) \bmod q$$

$$u2 = (r' \; w) \bmod q$$

$$v = ((g^{u1} \; y^{u2}) \bmod p) \bmod q$$

For a mathematical proof of the validity of these formulae, and the infeasibility of generating a valid r, s pair without knowing the private key x, see the appendices to the DSA specification.

J.3   Diffie-Hellman Key Agreement

The Diffie-Hellman key agreement algorithm allows two communicating systems to agree upon a value for a secret symmetric encryption key [9]. It works as illustrated in Figure J.2.

Systems A and B agree, in advance, upon a prime number p and another number a known as a generator [10]. This agreement could be on the basis of published system wide constants, or it could result from previous communications. As the first step in deriving a key, system A generates a random number x, $1 < x < p - 1$. It then calculates $a^x \bmod p$ and sends this value to System B. System B generates a random number y, $1 < y < p - 1$, calculates a^y mod p, and sends this value to System A. Next, System A calculates $(a^y)^x \bmod p$ and System B calculates $(a^x)^y \bmod p$. Both systems now know a common key, $K = a^{xy} \bmod p$, which can be used as the key for a symmetric cryptosystem like DES to protect messages between them.

While the above exchange was occurring, an eavesdropper could have learned both a^x mod p and a^y mod p. However, because of the difficulty of computing discrete logarithms, it is not feasible for the eavesdropper to calculate x or y, hence it is not feasible to calculate K.

While the above description of Diffie-Hellman key derivation assumes that the two communicating systems can exchange messages in both directions online, there are several variations of the Diffie-Hellman technique, some of which can be employed to build self-contained protected messages as are needed for applications like e-mail. For example, if System A is a message originator and System B is the recipient, System B might select

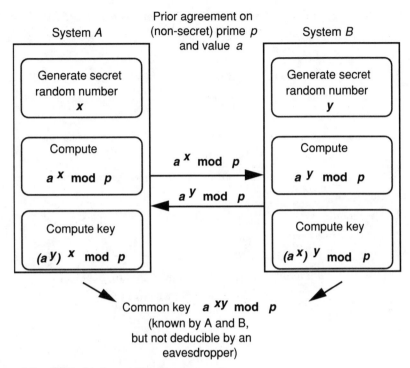

Figure J.2   Diffie-Hellman Key Agreement

one value of y for use over a period of time and publish the corresponding value a^y mod p for use by any other system, such as A, wishing to send encrypted messages to B. In this case, a^y mod p acts essentially as B's public key. Such a Diffie-Hellman variation can act as a substitute for the RSA key transport method used for e-mail protection.

Notes

1. B. Schneier, *Applied Cryptography*, 2nd Edition, (New York: Wiley, 1995).
2. A.J. Menezes, P.C. van Oorschot, and S.A. Vanstone, *Handbook of Applied Cryptography* (Boca Raton, FL: CRC Press, 1996).
3. R.L. Rivest, A. Shamir, and L. Adleman, "A Method for Obtaining Digital Signatures and Public-Key Cryptosystems," *Communications of the ACM*, vol. 21, no. 2 (February 1978), 120–126.

4. U.S. Department of Commerce, *Digital Signature Standard (DSS)*, Federal Information Processing Standards Publication 186–2, 2000 < http://csrc.nist.gov/fips/fips186–2.pdf>.

5. T. ElGamal, "A Public Key Cryptosystem and a Signature Scheme Based on Discrete Logarithms," *IEEE Transactions on Information Theory*, vol. IT-31, no. 4 (1985), 469–72.

6. C.P. Schnorr, "Efficient Signature Generation by Smart Cards," *Journal of Cryptology*, vol. 4, no. 3 (1991), 161–174.

7. This means that the smallest positive integer i, such that $g_i \bmod p = 1$, is sufficiently large.

8. The modulus size is an algorithm parameter, which can take values from 512 to 1024 bits in 64-bit increments.

9. W. Diffie and M. Hellman, "New Directions in Cryptography," *IEEE Transactions on Information Theory*, vol. IT-22, no. 6 (1976), 644–654.

10. The generator a is a primitive element in what is known as the Gallois field of p, or $GF(p)$.

European Signature Directive

DIRECTIVE 1999/   /EC OF THE EUROPEAN PARLIAMENT AND OF THE COUNCIL

of

....

on a Community framework for electronic signatures

(informal final version)

THE EUROPEAN PARLIAMENT AND THE COUNCIL OF THE EUROPEAN UNION,

Having regard to the Treaty establishing the European Community, and in particular Articles 47(2), 55 and 95 thereof,

Having regard to the proposal from the Commission [1],

Having regard to the Opinion of the Economic and Social Committee [2],

Having regard to the Opinion of the Committee of the Regions [3],

Acting in accordance with the procedure laid down in Article 251 of the Treaty [4],

Whereas:

(1)   On 16 April 1997 the Commission presented to the European Parliament, the Council, the Economic and Social Committee and the Committee of the Regions a Communication on an European Initiative in Electronic Commerce;

(2)   On 8 October 1997 the Commission presented to the European Parliament, the Council, the Economic and Social Committee and the Committee of the Regions a Communication on ensuring security and trust in electronic communication – Towards a European framework

---

[1]   OJ C 325, 23.10.1998, p. 5, and OJ C...
[2]   OJ C 40, 15. 2.1999, p. 29.
[3]   OJ C 93, 6. 4.1999, p. 33.
[4]   Opinion of the European Parliament of 13 January 1999 (OJ C 104, 14.4.1999, p. 49), Council Common Position of 28 June 1999 (OJ C 243, 27.8.1999, p. 33) and Decision of the European Parliament of 27 October 1999 (not yet published in the Official Journal).

for digital signatures and encryption;

(3)   On 1 December 1997 the Council invited the Commission to submit as soon as possible a proposal for a Directive of the European Parliament and of the Council on digital signatures;

(4)   Electronic communication and commerce necessitate "electronic signatures" and related services allowing data authentication; divergent rules with respect to legal recognition of electronic signatures and the accreditation of certification-service providers in the Member States may create a significant barrier to the use of electronic communications and electronic commerce; on the other hand, a clear Community framework regarding the conditions applying to electronic signatures will strengthen confidence in, and general acceptance of, the new technologies; legislation in the Member States should not hinder the free movement of goods and services in the internal market;

(5)   The interoperability of electronic-signature products should be promoted; in accordance with Article 14 of the Treaty, the internal market comprises an area without internal frontiers in which the free movement of goods is ensured; essential requirements specific to electronic-signature products must be met in order to ensure free movement within the internal market and to build trust in electronic signatures, without prejudice to Council Regulation (EC) No 3381/94 of 19 December 1994 setting up a Community regime for the control of exports of dual-use goods [1] and Council Decision 94/942/CFSP of 19 December 1994 on the joint action adopted by the Council concerning the control of exports of dual-use goods [2];

(6)   This Directive does not harmonise the provision of services with respect to the confidentiality of information where they are covered by national provisions concerned with public policy or public security;

(7)   The internal market ensures the free movement of persons, as a result of which citizens and residents of the European Union increasingly need to deal with authorities in Member

---

[1]   OJ L 367, 31.12.1994, p. 1. Regulation as amended by Regulation (EC) No 837/95 (OJ L 90, 21.4.1995, p. 1).

[2]   OJ L 367, 31.12.1994, p. 8. Decision as last amended by Decision 99/193/CFSP

States other than the one in which they reside; the availability of electronic communication could be of great service in this respect;

(8) Rapid technological development and the global character of the Internet necessitate an approach which is open to various technologies and services capable of authenticating data electronically;

(9) Electronic signatures will be used in a large variety of circumstances and applications, resulting in a wide range of new services and products related to or using electronic signatures; the definition of such products and services should not be limited to the issuance and management of certificates, but should also encompass any other service and product using, or ancillary to, electronic signatures, such as registration services, time-stamping services, directory services, computing services or consultancy services related to electronic signatures;

(10) The internal market enables certification-service-providers to develop their cross-border activities with a view to increasing their competitiveness, and thus to offer consumers and businesses new opportunities to exchange information and trade electronically in a secure way, regardless of frontiers; in order to stimulate the Community-wide provision of certification services over open networks, certification-service-providers should be free to provide their services without prior authorisation; prior authorisation means not only any permission whereby the certification-service-provider concerned has to obtain a decision by national authorities before being allowed to provide its certification services, but also any other measures having the same effect;

(11) Voluntary accreditation schemes aiming at an enhanced level of service-provision may offer certification-service-providers the appropriate framework for developing further their services towards the levels of trust, security and quality demanded by the evolving market; such schemes should encourage the development of best practice among certification-service-providers; certification-service-providers should be left free to adhere to and benefit from such accreditation schemes;

(12) Certification services can be offered either by a public entity or a legal or natural person,

(OJ L 73, 19.3.1999, p. 1).

when it is established in accordance with the national law; whereas Member States should not prohibit certification-service-providers from operating outside voluntary accreditation schemes; it should be ensured that such accreditation schemes do not reduce competition for certification services;

(13)   Member States may decide how they ensure the supervision of compliance with the provisions laid down in this Directive; this Directive does not preclude the establishment of private-sector-based supervision systems; this Directive does not oblige certification-service-providers to apply to be supervised under any applicable accreditation scheme;

(14)   It is important to strike a balance between consumer and business needs;

(15)   Annex III covers requirements for secure signature-creation devices to ensure the functionality of advanced electronic signatures; it does not cover the entire system environment in which such devices operate; the functioning of the internal market requires the Commission and the Member States to act swiftly to enable the bodies charged with the conformity assessment of secure signature devices with Annex III to be designated; in order to meet market needs conformity assessment must be timely and efficient;

(16)   This Directive contributes to the use and legal recognition of electronic signatures within the Community; a regulatory framework is not needed for electronic signatures exclusively used within systems, which are based on voluntary agreements under private law between a specified number of participants; the freedom of parties to agree among themselves the terms and conditions under which they accept electronically signed data should be respected to the extent allowed by national law; the legal effectiveness of electronic signatures used in such systems and their admissibility as evidence in legal proceedings should be recognised;

(17)   This Directive does not seek to harmonise national rules concerning contract law, particularly the formation and performance of contracts, or other formalities of a non-contractual nature concerning signatures; for this reason the provisions concerning the legal effect of electronic signatures should be without prejudice to requirements regarding form laid down in national law with regard to the conclusion of contracts or the rules determining where a contract is concluded;

(18)   The storage and copying of signature-creation data could cause a threat to the legal validity of electronic signatures;

(19)   Electronic signatures will be used in the public sector within national and Community administrations and in communications between such administrations and with citizens and economic operators, for example in the public procurement, taxation, social security, health and justice systems;

(20)   Harmonised criteria relating to the legal effects of electronic signatures will preserve a coherent legal framework across the Community; national law lays down different requirements for the legal validity of hand-written signatures; whereas certificates can be used to confirm the identity of a person signing electronically; advanced electronic signatures based on qualified certificates aim at a higher level of security; advanced electronic signatures which are based on a qualified certificate and which are created by a secure-signature-creation device can be regarded as legally equivalent to hand-written signatures only if the requirements for hand-written signatures are fulfilled;

(21)   In order to contribute to the general acceptance of electronic authentication methods it has to be ensured that electronic signatures can be used as evidence in legal proceedings in all Member States; the legal recognition of electronic signatures should be based upon objective criteria and not be linked to authorisation of the certification-service-provider involved; national law governs the legal spheres in which electronic documents and electronic signatures may be used; this Directive is without prejudice to the power of a national court to make a ruling regarding conformity with the requirements of this Directive and does not affect national rules regarding the unfettered judicial consideration of evidence;

(22)   Certification-service-providers providing certification-services to the public are subject to national rules regarding liability;

(23)   The development of international electronic commerce requires cross-border arrangements involving third countries; in order to ensure interoperability at a global level, agreements on multilateral rules with third countries on mutual recognition of certification services could be beneficial;

(24)   In order to increase user confidence in electronic communication and electronic commerce, certification-service-providers must observe data protection legislation and individual privacy;

(25)   Provisions on the use of pseudonyms in certificates should not prevent Member States from requiring identification of persons pursuant to Community or national law;

(26)   The measures necessary for the implementation of this Directive are to be adopted in accordance with Council Decision 1999/468/EC of 28 June 1999 laying down the procedures for the exercise of implementing powers conferred on the Commission [1];

(27)   Two years after its implementation the Commission will carry out a review of this Directive so as, inter alia, to ensure that the advance of technology or changes in the legal environment have not created barriers to achieving the aims stated in this Directive; it should examine the implications of associated technical areas and submit a report to the European Parliament and the Council on this subject;

(28)   In accordance with the principles of subsidiarity and proportionality as set out in Article 5 of the Treaty, the objective of creating a harmonised legal framework for the provision of electronic signatures and related services cannot be sufficiently achieved by the Member States and can therefore be better achieved by the Community; this Directive does not go beyond what is necessary to achieve that objective,

HAVE ADOPTED THIS DIRECTIVE:

Article 1

Scope

The purpose of this Directive is to facilitate the use of electronic signatures and to contribute to their legal recognition. It establishes a legal framework for electronic signatures and certain certification-services in order to ensure the proper functioning of the internal market.

It does not cover aspects related to the conclusion and validity of contracts or other legal obligations where there are requirements as regards form prescribed by national or Community law nor does it affect rules and limits, contained in national or Community law, governing the use of documents.

Article 2
Definitions

For the purpose of this Directive:

(1)   "electronic signature" means data in electronic form which are attached to or logically associated with other electronic data and which serve as a method of authentication;

(2)   "advanced electronic signature" means an electronic signature which meets the following requirements:

    (a)   it is uniquely linked to the signatory;

    (b)   it is capable of identifying the signatory;

    (c)   it is created using means that the signatory can maintain under his sole control; and

    (d)   it is linked to the data to which it relates in such a manner that any subsequent change of the data is detectable;

(3)   "signatory" means a person who holds a signature-creation device and acts either on his own behalf or on behalf of the natural or legal person or entity he represents;

(4)   "signature-creation data" means unique data, such as codes or private cryptographic keys, which are used by the signatory to create an electronic signature;

(5)   "signature-creation device" means configured software or hardware used to implement the signature-creation data;

(6)   "secure-signature-creation device" means a signature-creation device which meets the requirements laid down in Annex III;

(7)   "signature-verification-data" means data, such as codes or public cryptographic keys, which are used for the purpose of verifying an electronic signature;

---

[1]   OJ L 184, 17.7.1999, p. 23.

(8)   "signature-verification device" means configured software or hardware used to implement the signature-verification-data;

(9)   "certificate" means an electronic attestation which links signature-verification data to a person and confirms the identity of that person;

(10)   "qualified certificate" means a certificate which meets the requirements laid down in Annex I and is provided by a certification-service-provider who fulfils the requirements laid down in Annex II;

(11)   "certification-service-provider" means an entity or a legal or natural person who issues certificates or provides other services related to electronic signatures;

(12)   "electronic-signature-product" means hardware or software, or relevant components thereof, which are intended to be used by a certification-service-provider for the provision of electronic-signature services or are intended to be used for the creation or verification of electronic signatures;

(13)   "voluntary accreditation" means any permission, setting out rights and obligations specific to the provision of certification services, to be granted upon request by the certification-service-provider concerned, by the public or private body charged with the elaboration of, and supervision of compliance with, such rights and obligations, where the certification-service-provider is not entitled to exercise the rights stemming from the permission until it has received the decision by the body.

Article 3

Market access

1. Member States shall not make the provision of certification services subject to prior authorisation.

2. Without prejudice to the provisions of paragraph 1, Member States may introduce or maintain voluntary accreditation schemes aiming at enhanced levels of certification-service provision. All conditions related to such schemes must be objective, transparent, proportionate and

non-discriminatory. Member States may not limit the number of accredited certification-service-providers for reasons which fall within the scope of this Directive.

3. Each Member State shall ensure the establishment of an appropriate system that allows for supervision of certification-service-providers which are established on its territory and issue qualified certificates to the public.

4. The conformity of secure signature-creation-devices with the requirements laid down in Annex III shall be determined by appropriate public or private bodies designated by Member States. The Commission shall, pursuant to the procedure laid down in Article 9, establish criteria for Member States to determine whether a body should be designated.

A determination of conformity with the requirements laid down in Annex III made by the bodies referred to in the first subparagraph shall be recognised by all Member States.

5. The Commission may, in accordance with the procedure laid down in Article 9, establish and publish reference numbers of generally recognised standards for electronic-signature products in the Official Journal of the European Communities. Member States shall presume that there is compliance with the requirements laid down in Annex II, point (f), and Annex III when an electronic signature product meets those standards.

6. Member States and the Commission shall work together to promote the development and use of signature-verification devices in the light of the recommendations for secure signature-verification laid down in Annex IV and in the interests of the consumer.

7. Member States may make the use of electronic signatures in the public sector subject to possible additional requirements. Such requirements shall be objective, transparent, proportionate and non-discriminatory and shall relate only to the specific characteristics of the application concerned. Such requirements may not constitute an obstacle to cross-border services for citizens.

Article 4

Internal market principles

1. Each Member State shall apply the national provisions which it adopts pursuant to this Directive to certification-service-providers established on its territory and to the services which they provide.

Member States may not restrict the provision of certification-services originating in another Member State in the fields covered by this Directive.

2. Member States shall ensure that electronic-signature products which comply with this Directive are permitted to circulate freely in the internal market.

Article 5
Legal effects of electronic signatures

1. Member States shall ensure that advanced electronic signatures which are based on a qualified certificate and which are created by a secure-signature-creation device:

(a)   satisfy the legal requirements of a signature in relation to data in electronic form in the same manner as a handwritten signature satisfies those requirements in relation to paper-based data; and

(b)   are admissible as evidence in legal proceedings.

2. Member States shall ensure that an electronic signature is not denied legal effectiveness and admissibility as evidence in legal proceedings solely on the grounds that it is:

–   in electronic form, or

–   not based upon a qualified certificate, or

–   not based upon a qualified certificate issued by an accredited certification-service-provider, or

–   not created by a secure signature-creation device.

Article 6
Liability

1. As a minimum, Member States shall ensure that by issuing a certificate as a qualified certificate to the public or by guaranteeing such a certificate to the public a certification-service-provider is liable for damage caused to any entity or legal or natural person who reasonably relies on that certificate:

(a)   as regards the accuracy at the time of issuance of all information contained in the qualified certificate and as regards the fact that the certificate contains all the details prescribed for a qualified certificate;

(b)   for assurance that at the time of the issuance of the certificate, the signatory identified in the qualified certificate held the signature-creation data corresponding to the signature-verification data given or identified in the certificate;

(c)   for assurance that the signature-creation data and the signature-verification data can be used in a complementary manner in cases where the certification-service-provider generates them both;

unless the certification-service-provider proves that he has not acted negligently.

2. As a minimum Member States shall ensure that a certification-service-provider who has issued a certificate as a qualified certificate to the public is liable for damage caused to any entity or legal or natural person who reasonably relies on the certificate for failure to register revocation of the certificate unless the certification-service-provider proves that he has not acted negligently.

3. Member States shall ensure that a certification-service-provider may indicate in a qualified certificate limitations on the use of that certificate, provided that the limitations are recognisable to third parties. The certification-service-provider shall not be liable for damage arising from use of a qualified certificate which exceeds the limitations placed on it.

4. Member States shall ensure that a certification-service-provider may indicate in the qualified certificate a limit on the value of transactions for which the certificate can be used, provided that the limit is recognisable to third parties.

The certification-service-provider shall not be liable for damage resulting from this maximum limit being exceeded.

5. The provisions of paragraphs 1 to 4 shall be without prejudice to Council Directive 93/13/EEC of 5 April 1993 on unfair terms in consumer contracts [1].

Article 7

International aspects

1. Member States shall ensure that certificates which are issued as qualified certificates to the public by a certification-service-provider established in a third country are recognised as legally

equivalent to certificates issued by a certification-service-provider established within the Community if:

(a)   the certification-service-provider fulfils the requirements laid down in this Directive and has been accredited under a voluntary accreditation scheme established in a Member State; or

(b)   a certification-service-provider established within the Community which fulfils the requirements laid down in this Directive guarantees the certificate; or

(c)   the certificate or the certification-service-provider is recognised under a bilateral or multilateral agreement between the Community and third countries or international organisations.

2. In order to facilitate cross-border certification services with third countries and legal recognition of advanced electronic signatures originating in third countries, the Commission shall make proposals, where appropriate, to achieve the effective implementation of standards and international agreements applicable to certification services. In particular, and where necessary, it shall submit proposals to the Council for appropriate mandates for the negotiation of bilateral and multilateral agreements with third countries and international organisations. The Council shall decide by qualified majority.

3. Whenever the Commission is informed of any difficulties encountered by Community undertakings with respect to market access in third countries, it may, if necessary, submit proposals to the Council for an appropriate mandate for the negotiation of comparable rights for Community undertakings in these third countries. The Council shall decide by qualified majority.

Measures taken pursuant to this paragraph shall be without prejudice to the obligations of the Community and of the Member States under relevant international agreements.

Article 8

Data protection

1. Member States shall ensure that certification-service-providers and national bodies responsible for accreditation or supervision comply with the requirements laid down in Directive 95/46/EC of the European Parliament and of the Council of 24 October 1995 on the protection of individuals

---

[1]   OJ L 95, 21.4.1993, p. 29.

with regard to the processing of personal data and on the free movement of such data [1].

2. Member States shall ensure that a certification-service-provider which issues certificates to the public may collect personal data only directly from the data subject, or after the explicit consent of the data subject, and only insofar as it is necessary for the purposes of issuing and maintaining the certificate. The data may not be collected or processed for any other purposes without the explicit consent of the data subject.

3. Without prejudice to the legal effect given to pseudonyms under national law, Member States shall not prevent certification service providers from indicating in the certificate a pseudonym instead of the signatory's name.

Article 9

Committee

1. The Commission shall be assisted by an "Electronic-Signature Committee", hereinafter referred to as "the committee".

2. Where reference is made to this paragraph, Articles 4 and 7 of Decision 1999/468/EC shall apply, having regard to the provisions of Article 8 thereof.

The period laid down in Article 4(3) of Decision 1999/468/EC shall be set at three months.

3. The Committee shall adopt its own rules of procedure.

Article 10

Tasks of the committee

The committee shall clarify the requirements laid down in the Annexes to this Directive, the criteria referred to in Article 3(4) and the generally recognised standards for electronic signature products established and published pursuant to Article 3(5), in accordance with the procedure laid down in Article 9(2).

---

[1]   OJ L 281, 23.11.1995, p. 31.

Article 11

Notification

1. Member States shall notify to the Commission and the other Member States the following:

(a)   information on national voluntary accreditation schemes, including any additional
        requirements pursuant to Article 3(7);

(b)   the names and addresses of the national bodies responsible for accreditation and supervision
        as well as of the bodies referred to in Article 3(4);

(c)   the names and addresses of all accredited national certification service providers.

2. Any information supplied under paragraph 1 and changes in respect of that information shall be
notified by the Member States as soon as possible.

Article 12

Review

1. The Commission shall review the operation of this Directive and report thereon to the
European Parliament and to the Council by .... * at the latest.

2. The review shall inter alia assess whether the scope of this Directive should be modified, taking
account of technological, market and legal developments. The report shall in particular include an
assessment, on the basis of experience gained, of aspects of harmonisation. The report shall be
accompanied, where appropriate, by legislative proposals.

Article 13

Implementation

1. Member States shall bring into force the laws, regulations and administrative provisions
necessary to comply with this Directive before .... **. They shall forthwith inform the
Commission thereof.

When Member States adopt these measures, they shall contain a reference to this Directive or shall

---

*   Three years and six months after the date of entry into force of this Directive.
**   One year and six months after the date of entry into force of this Directive.

be accompanied by such a reference on the occasion of their official publication. The methods of making such reference shall be laid down by the Member States.

2. Member States shall communicate to the Commission the text of the main provisions of domestic law which they adopt in the field governed by this Directive.

<u>Article 14</u>

Entry into force

This Directive shall enter into force on the day of its publication in the Official Journal of the European Communities.

<u>Article 15</u>

Addressees

This Directive is addressed to the Member States.

Done at Brussels,

For the European Parliament   For the Council
        The President   The President

Requirements for qualified certificates

Qualified certificates must contain:

(a)   an indication that the certificate is issued as a qualified certificate;

(b)   the identification of the certification-service-provider and the State in which it is established;

(c)   the name of the signatory or a pseudonym, which shall be identified as such;

(d)   provision for a specific attribute of the signatory to be included if relevant, depending on the purpose for which the certificate is intended;

(e)   signature-verification data which correspond to signature-creation data under the control of the signatory;

(f)   an indication of the beginning and end of the period of validity of the certificate;

(g)   the identity code of the certificate;

(h)   the advanced electronic signature of the certification-service-provider issuing it;

(i)   limitations on the scope of use of the certificate, if applicable; and

(j)   limits on the value of transactions for which the certificate can be used, if applicable.

<u>**ANNEX II**</u>

<u>Requirements for certification-service-providers</u>
<u>issuing qualified certificates</u>

Certification-service-providers must:

(a)   demonstrate the reliability necessary for providing certification services;

(b)   ensure the operation of a prompt and secure directory and a secure and immediate revocation service;

(c)   ensure that the date and time when a certificate is issued or revoked can be determined precisely;

(d)   verify, by appropriate means in accordance with national law, the identity and, if applicable, any specific attributes of the person to which a qualified certificate is issued;

(e)   employ personnel who possess the expert knowledge, experience, and qualifications necessary for the services provided, in particular competence at managerial level, expertise in electronic signature technology and familiarity with proper security procedures; they must also apply administrative and management procedures which are adequate and correspond to recognised standards;

(f)   use trustworthy systems and products which are protected against modification and ensure the technical and cryptographic security of the processes supported by them;

(g)   take measures against forgery of certificates, and, in cases where the certification-service-provider generates signature-creation data, guarantee confidentiality during the process of generating such data;

(h)   maintain sufficient financial resources to operate in conformity with the requirements laid down in the Directive, in particular to bear the risk of liability for damages, for example, by obtaining appropriate insurance;

(i)   record all relevant information concerning a qualified certificate for an appropriate period of time, in particular for the purpose of providing evidence of certification for the purposes of legal proceedings. Such recording may be done electronically;

(j)   not store or copy signature-creation data of the person to whom the certification-service-provider provided key management services;

(k)   before entering into a contractual relationship with a person seeking a certificate to support his electronic signature, inform that person by a durable means of communication of the precise terms and conditions regarding the use of the certificate, including any limitations on its use, the existence of a voluntary accreditation scheme and procedures for complaints and dispute settlement. Such information, which may be transmitted electronically, must be in writing and in readily understandable language. Relevant parts of this information must also be made available on request to third-parties relying on the certificate;

(l)   use trustworthy systems to store certificates in a verifiable form so that:
- only authorised persons can make entries and changes,
- information can be checked for authenticity,
- certificates are publicly available for retrieval in only those cases for which the certificate-holder's consent has been obtained, and
- any technical changes compromising these security requirements are apparent to the operator.

Requirements for secure signature-creation devices

1. Secure-signature-creation devices must, by appropriate technical and procedural means, ensure at the least that:

   (a) the signature-creation-data used for signature generation can practically occur only once, and that their secrecy is reasonably assured;

   (b) the signature creation data used for signature generation cannot, with reasonable assurance, be derived and the signature is protected against forgery using currently available technology;

   (c) the signature-creation-data used for signature generation can be reliably protected by the legitimate signatory against the use of others.

2. Secure signature creation devices must not alter the data to be signed or prevent such data from being presented to the signatory prior to the signature process.

———

Recommendations for secure signature verification

During the signature-verification process it should be ensured with reasonable certainty that:

(a)   the data used for verifying the signature correspond to the data displayed to the verifier;

(b)   the signature is reliably verified and the result of that verification is correctly displayed;

(c)   the verifier can, as necessary, reliably establish the contents of the signed data;

(d)   the authenticity and validity of the certificate required at the time of signature verification are reliably verified;

(e)   the result of verification and the signatory's identity are correctly displayed;

(f)   the use of a pseudonym is clearly indicated; and

(g)   any security-relevant changes can be detected.

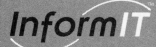